THE NEW INTERNATIONAL
GREEK TESTAMENT COMMENTARY

Editors
I. Howard Marshall
and
W. Ward Gasque

THE EPISTLE TO THE GALATIANS

The New International Greek Testament Commentary

THE EPISTLE TO THE
GALATIANS

A Commentary on the Greek Text

by

F. F. BRUCE

Emeritus Professor
University of Manchester

THE PATERNOSTER PRESS
EXETER
WILLIAM B. EERDMANS PUBLISHING COMPANY
GRAND RAPIDS, MICHIGAN

First published 1982 by The Paternoster Press,
3 Mount Radford Crescent, Exeter, UK EX2 4JW
This edition published jointly by Paternoster and
Wm. B. Eerdmans Publishing Co., 255 Jefferson Ave. SE,
Grand Rapids, MI 49503

Printed in the United States of America

Reprinted, June 1988

British Library Cataloguing in Publication Data
Bruce, F. F.
The Epistle of Paul to the Galatians: a
commentary on the Greek text.—(The New
international Greek Testament commentary; 2)
1. Bible. N.T. Galatians—Commentaries
I. Title II. Bible. N.T. Galatians. *Greek. 1982*
III. Series
227'.4'048   BS2685.3

Casebound ISBN 0-85364-299-0
Paperback ISBN 0-85364-300-8

Library of Congress Cataloging-in-Publication Data
Bruce, F. F. (Frederick Fyvie), 1910-
The Epistle to the Galatians.

(The New international Greek testament commentary)
Bibliography: p. 59.
Includes indexes.
1. Bible. N.T. Galatians—Commentaries. I. Title.
II. Series: New international Greek testament commentary
(Grand Rapids, Mich.)
BS2685.3.B75 1981   227'.407   81-17327
ISBN 0-8028-2387-4   AACR2

TO
CHARLES FRANCIS DIGBY MOULE

*in admiration, friendship
and gratitude*

CONTENTS

FOREWORD

While there have been many series of commentaries on the English text of the New Testament in recent years, it is a long time since any attempt has been made to cater particularly to the needs of students of the Greek text. It is true that at the present time there is something of a decline in the study of Greek in many traditional theological institutions, but there has been a welcome growth in the study of the New Testament in its original language in the newer evangelical schools, especially in North America and the Third World. It is hoped that *The New International Greek Testament Commentary* will demonstrate the value of studying the Greek New Testament and help towards the revival of such study.

The purpose of the series is to cater to the needs of students who want something less technical than a full-scale critical commentary. At the same time, the commentaries are intended to interact with modern scholarship and to make their own scholarly contribution to the study of the New Testament. There has been a wealth of detailed study of the New Testament in articles and monographs in recent years, and the series is meant to harvest the results of this research in a more easily accessible form. The commentaries will thus include adequate, but not exhaustive, bibliographies. They will attempt to treat all important problems of history and exegesis and interpretation which may arise.

One of the gains of recent scholarship has been the recognition of the primarily theological character of the books of the New Testament. This series will, therefore, attempt to provide a theological understanding of the text, based on historical-critical-linguistic exegesis. It will not, however, attempt to apply and expound the text for modern readers, although it is hoped that the exegesis will give some indication of the way in which the text should be expounded.

Within the limits set by the use of the English language, the series aims to be international in character; the contributors, however, have been chosen not primarily in order to achieve a spread between different countries but above all because of their specialized qualifications for their particular tasks. This publication is a joint venture of The Paternoster Press, Exeter, England, and Wm. B. Eerdmans Publishing Company, Grand Rapids, USA.

The supreme aim of this series is to serve those who are engaged in the ministry of the Word of God and thus to glorify his name. Our prayer is that it may be found helpful in this task.

I. Howard Marshall
W. Ward Gasque

PREFACE

Paul's letter to the churches of Galatia has been to me for many years a document of special interest and study. Accordingly, when I was invited to contribute to *The New International Greek Testament Commentary*, it was with alacrity that I undertook to write the volume on Galatians.

In general studies and lectures on Galatians, it is possible to pass rather lightly over certain minor cruces of interpretation. When one writes a commentary, however, it is necessary to examine them with care and reach some kind of conclusion about them, after considering all the reasonable options. Now that I have fulfilled my undertaking, I am indeed glad that I gave it. The writing of the commentary has been a richly rewarding experience.

I am, of course, greatly indebted to many earlier commentators and others who have written on Galatians. Joseph Barber Lightfoot and Ernest DeWitt Burton call for specially honourable mention here; so, among our contemporaries, does Hans Dieter Betz, whose *Hermeneia* volume appeared when my work was well on its way to completion; it has already established its right to stand among the really great commentaries on this epistle.

The substance of most of my Introduction was originally delivered in the form of public lectures in the John Rylands University Library, Manchester; these were subsequently published in the *Bulletin* of the Library between 1969 and 1973 as a series entitled 'Galatian Problems'. This material is reproduced here by kind permission.

The Greek text on which this commentary is based is that of the third edition of *The Greek New Testament* published by the United Bible Societies (1975); it is practically identical with that of the twenty-sixth edition of Nestle's *Novum Testamentum Graece*, edited by K. and B. Aland (1979).

F. F. B.

ABBREVIATIONS

1. *General*

AV	Authorized Version (King James Version)
Ep., Epp.	Epistle(s)
ETr	English Translation
frag.	fragment
FS	*Festschrift*
LXX	Septuagint
MT	Masoretic Text
NEB	New English Bible
NF	Neue Folge
NIV	New International Version
n.s.	new series
NT	New Testament
OT	Old Testament
phil.-hist. Kl.	philologisch-historische Klasse
RSV	Revised Standard Version
Vg.	Vulgate

2. *Books of the Old Testament*

Gn., Ex., Lv., Nu., Dt., Jos., Jdg., Ru., 1, 2 Sa., 1, 2 Ki., 1, 2 Ch., Ezr., Ne., Est., Jb., Ps(s)., Pr., Ec., Ct., Is., Je., La., Ezk., Dn., Ho., Joel, Am., Ob., Jon., Mi., Na., Hab., Zp., Hg., Zc., Mal.

3. *Books of the New Testament*

Mt., Mk., Lk., Jn., Acts, Rom., 1, 2 Cor., Gal., Eph., Phil., Col., 1, 2 Thes., 1, 2 Tim., Tit., Phm., Heb., Jas., 1, 2 Pet., 1, 2, 3 Jn., Jude, Rev.

4. *Old Testament Apocrypha and Pseudepigrapha*

Ad. Dan.	Additions to Daniel
Ad. Est.	Additions to Esther
Ass. Mos.	Assumption of Moses
1 Bar.	Baruch (Apocrypha) with The Letter of Jeremiah as ch. 6
2 Bar.	Syriac Apocalypse of Baruch
3 Bar.	Greek Apocalypse of Baruch
1 Enoch	Ethiopic Book of Enoch
2 Enoch	Slavonic Book of Enoch
3 Enoch	Hebrew Book of Enoch
1 Esd.	1 Esdras
2 Esd.	2 Esdras (4 Ezra; Apocalypse of Ezra)
Jub.	Jubilees
Jud.	Judith
1, 2, 3, 4 Macc.	1, 2, 3, 4 Maccabees
Man.	Prayer of Manasseh

Mart. Isa.	Martyrdom of Isaiah
Pss. Sol.	Psalms of Solomon
Sib.	Sibylline Oracles
Sir.	Wisdom of Ben Sira (Ecclesiasticus)
Test. Abr.	Testament of Abraham
Test. XII	Testaments of the Twelve Patriarchs
Test. Dan	Testament of Dan
Test. Jos.	Testament of Joseph
Tob.	Tobit
Wis.	Wisdom of Solomon

5. Dead Sea Scrolls and Related Texts

CD	Book of the Covenant of Damascus (Zadokite Work)
1QH	Hymns *(Hôḏāyôṯ)* from Qumran Cave 1
1QpHab	Commentary *(pesher)* on Habakkuk from Qumran Cave 1
1QS	Rule *(sereḵ)* of the Community from Qumran Cave 1
4QFlor	Florilegium from Qumran Cave 4
4QIs^d	Fourth copy of Isaiah from Qumran Cave 4
4QpNa	Commentary *(pesher)* on Nahum from Qumran Cave 4
11Q Temple	Temple Scroll from Qumran Cave 11

6. Rabbinical Literature

Ab.	(Pirqe) Abot (Mishnaic tractate)
Abot R. Nat.	*Abot de-Rabbi Nathan*
b.	Babylonian Talmud (before title of tractate)
Ber.	Berakot (tractate)
Gen. Rab.	*Genesis Rabbah* (midrash)
Ḥag.	Ḥagigah (tractate)
j.	Jerusalem (Palestinian) Talmud (before title of tractate)
m.	Mishnah (before title of tractate)
Meg.	Megillah (tractate)
Men.	Menaḥot (tractate)
Midr.	Midrash
Num. Rab.	*Numbers Rabbah* (midrash)
Orl.	Orlah (tractate)
Pesiq. R.	Pesiqta Rabbati
Qidd.	Qiddushin (tractate)
R.	Rabbi
Sanh.	Sanhedrin (tractate)
Shab.	Shabbat (tractate)
Ta'an.	Ta'anit (tractate)
Tg. Neof.	Targum Neofiti 1
Tg. Onq.	Targum of Onqelos
Tos.	Tosefta

7. Classical and Hellenistic Literature

Abr.	*De Abrahamo* (Philo)
Aet. Mund.	*De Aeternitate Mundi* (Philo)
Agric.	*De Agricultura* (Philo)
Aj.	*Ajax* (Sophocles)
Anab.	*Anabasis* (Xenophon; Arrian)
Ant.	*Antiquities* (Josephus)
Ap.	*Against Apion* (Josephus)
Apol.	*Apology of Socrates* (Plato)
Corp. Herm.	*Corpus Hermeticum*
Decal.	*De Decalogo* (Philo)
De Cor.	*De Corona* (Demosthenes)

Dem.	Demosthenes
De Or.	*De Oratore* (Cicero)
Diog. Laert.	Diogenes Laertius
Dio Cass.	Dio Cassius
Diss.	*Dissertationes* (Epictetus)
Div.	*De Divinatione* (Cicero)
Epict.	Epictetus
Eth. Nic.	*Nicomachean Ethics* (Aristotle)
Eur.	Euripides
Fug.	*De Fuga et Inventione* (Philo)
Geog.	*Geography* (Strabo)
Grg.	*Gorgias* (Plato)
Hist.	*History* (Thucydides; Polybius; Livy; Dio Cassius, etc.)
Hist. An.	*Historia Animalium* (Aristotle)
Inst.	*Institutio(nes)* (Gaius; Justinian; Quintilian)
Jos.	Josephus
LAB	*Liber Antiquitatum Biblicarum* (Pseudo-Philo)
Leg.	*Leges* (Plato)
Leg. All.	*Legum Allegoriae* (Philo)
Meid.	*Against Meidias* (Demosthenes)
Mem.	*Memorabilia* (Xenophon)
Migr. Abr.	*De Migratione Abrahami* (Philo)
Mor.	*Moralia* (Plutarch)
Mut. Nom.	*De Mutatione Nominum* (Philo)
Nat. Hist.	*Natural History* (Pliny)
O.T.	*Oedipus Tyrannus* (Sophocles)
Phdr.	*Phaedrus* (Plato)
Plut.	Plutarch
Post. C.	*De Posteritate Caini* (Philo)
Praem.	*De Praemiis et Poenis* (Philo)
Pyth.	*Pythian Odes* (Pindar)
Rep.	*Republic* (Plato)
Rer. Div. Her.	*Quis Rerum Divinarum Heres* (Philo)
Rhet.	*Rhetoric* (Aristotle)
Sob.	*De Sobrietate* (Philo)
Som.	*De Somniis* (Philo)
Soph.	Sophocles
Spec. Leg.	*De Specialibus Legibus* (Philo)
Vit. Cont.	*De Vita Contemplativa* (Philo)
Vit. Mos.	*De Vita Mosis* (Philo)
Vit. Phil.	*Vitae Philosophorum* (Diogenes Laertius)
Xen.	Xenophon

8. *Early Christian Literature*

Adv. Marc.	*Against Marcion* (Tertullian)
Apol.	*Apology* (Justin; Tertullian)
Barn.	Epistle of Barnabas
Clem. Alex.	Clement of Alexandria
Clem. Hom.	*Clementine Homilies*
Clem. Recog.	*Clementine Recognitions*
Comm. Act. Syn. Nic.	*Commentarius Actorum Synodi Nicaenae* (Gelasius Cyzicenus)
De Car.	*De Carnis Resurrectione* (Tertullian)
Dial.	*Dialogue with Trypho* (Justin)
Diog.	Diognetus
Ep. Diog.	*Epistle to Diognetus*
Epiph.	Epiphanius
Euseb.	Eusebius
Gos. Egy.	*Gospel of the Egyptians*

Gos. Heb.	Gospel according to the Hebrews
Haer.	Against Heresies (Irenaeus; Hippolytus; Epiphanius)
HE (Hist. Eccl.).	Ecclesiastical History (Eusebius)
Heges.	Hegesippus
Hyp.	Hypothetica (Clement of Alexandria)
Inst.	Divinae Institutiones (Lactantius)
Iren.	Irenaeus
Strom.	Stromata (Stromateis) (Clement of Alexandria)
Tert.	Tertullian

9. Periodicals, Collections, Series, Reference and Individual Works

AASOR	Annual of the American Schools of Oriental Research
ABR	Australian Biblical Review
AHAW	Abhandlungen der Heidelberger Akademie der Wissenschaften
AkGWG	Abhandlungen der königlichen Gesellschaft der Wissenschaften zu Göttingen
AS	Anatolian Studies
ATR	Anglican Theological Review
BAG	W. Bauer-W. F. Arndt-F. W. Gingrich, Greek-English Lexicon of the New Testament and Early Christian Literature (Chicago/Cambridge, 1957)
BC	The Beginnings of Christianity, ed. F. J. Foakes Jackson and K. Lake
BDF	F. Blass-A. Debrunner-R. W. Funk, Greek Grammar of the New Testament and Other Early Christian Literature (Chicago, 1961)
BFCT	Beiträge zur Förderung christlicher Theologie
Bib.	Biblica
BJRL	Bulletin of the John Rylands (University) Library (Manchester)
BNTC	Black's New Testament Commentaries
BR	Biblical Research
BU	Biblische Untersuchungen
BZ	Biblische Zeitschrift
BZAW	Beihefte zur Zeitschrift für die alttestamentliche Wissenschaft
BZNW	Beihefte zur Zeitschrift für die neutestamentliche Wissenschaft
CAH	Cambridge Ancient History
CBC	Cambridge Bible Commentaries on the New English Bible
CBQ	Catholic Biblical Quarterly
CD	Church Dogmatics (K. Barth)
CIG	Corpus Inscriptionum Graecarum
CIL	Corpus Inscriptionum Latinarum
CNT	Commentaire du Nouveau Testament
CR	Classical Review
CSEL	Corpus Scriptorum Ecclesiasticorum Latinorum
CSHB	Corpus Scriptorum Historiae Byzantinae
EEP	The Earlier Epistles of St. Paul (K. Lake)
EKKNT	Evangelisch-Katholischer Kommentar zum Neuen Testament
Enc Bib	Encyclopaedia Biblica
EQ	Evangelical Quarterly
Est Bib	Estudios Bíblicos
Exp Tim	Expository Times
FEUNTK	Forschungen zur Entstehung des Urchristentums des Neuen Testaments und der Kirche
HDB	Hastings' Dictonary of the Bible (I–V)
HJP	History of the Jewish People in the Age of Jesus, new English edition (E. Schürer)
HNT	Handbuch zum Neuen Testament (H. Lietzmann)
HTR	Harvard Theological Review
IB	Interpreter's Bible
ICC	International Critical Commentary
IEJ	Israel Exploration Journal
Inst.	Institutes of the Christian Religion (J. Calvin)

INT	*Introduction to the New Testament*
Int.	*Interpretation*
JBL	*Journal of Biblical Literature*
JBR	*Journal of Bible and Religion*
JJS	*Journal of Jewish Studies*
JR	*Journal of Religion*
JSNT	*Journal for the Study of the New Testament*
JTS	*Journal of Theological Studies*
KD	*Kerygma und Dogma*
KEK	Kritisch-Exegetischer Kommentar (Meyer Kommentar)
MAMA	*Monumenta Asiae Minoris Antiqua*
MHT	J. H. Moulton-W. F. Howard-N. Turner, *Grammar of New Testament Greek*, I–IV (Edinburgh, 1906–76)
MM	J. H. Moulton-G. Milligan, *Vocabulary of the Greek Testament* (Edinburgh, 1930)
MNTC	Moffatt New Testament Commentary
NBCR	*New Bible Commentary Revised* (London, 1970)
NCB	New Century Bible
Nestle-Aland[26]	*Novum Testamentum Graece,* ed. E. and E. Nestle; K. and B. Aland (Stuttgart, [26]1979)
NICNT	New International Commentary on the New Testament
NIDNTT	*New International Dictionary of New Testament Theology,* I–III (Exeter, 1975–78)
NovT	*Novum Testamentum*
NovTSup	Supplement(s) to *Novum Testamentum*
NPNF	Nicene and Post-Nicene Fathers (Grand Rapids)
NTAb	Neutestamentliche Abhandlungen
NTD	Das Neue Testament Deutsch
NTS	*New Testament Studies*
PG	*Patrologia Graeca* (ed. J.-P. Migne)
PL	*Patrologia Latina* (ed. J.-P. Migne)
P. Oxy.	Oxyrhynchus Papyri
P. Tebt.	Tebtunis Papyri
RB	*Revue Biblique*
RBén	*Revue Bénédictine*
RGG	*Religion in Geschichte und Gegenwart,* I–VII (Tübingen, [3]1956–65)
RSR	*Revue des Sciences Religieuses*
RTR	*Reformed Theological Review*
SAB	*Sitzungsberichte der königlichen preussischen Akademie der Wissenschaften zu Berlin*
SBT	Studies in Biblical Theology
SE	*Studia Evangelica*
SIG	*Sylloge Inscriptionum Graecarum* (W. Dittenberger)
SJT	*Scottish Journal of Theology*
SNTSM	Society for New Testament Studies Monograph
SPT	*St. Paul the Traveller and the Roman Citizen* (W. M. Ramsay)
SR	*Studies in Religion/Sciences Religieuses*
ST	*Studia Theologica*
TDNT	*Theological Dictionary of the New Testament,* I–X (Grand Rapids, 1964–76)
THK	Theologischer Handkommentar zum Neuen Testament
TKNT	Theologischer Kommentar zum Neuen Testament
TLZ	*Theologische Literaturzeitung*
TNTC	Tyndale New Testament Commentaries
TRu	*Theologische Rundschau*
TS	Texts and Studies (Cambridge)
TSK	*Theologische Studien und Kritiken*
TU	Texte und Untersuchungen (Berlin)

TZ	*Theologische Zeitschrift*
UBS³	*The Greek New Testament* (United Bible Societies, ³1975)
VD	*Verbum Domini*
VT	*Vetus Testamentum*
WA	Weimarer Ausgabe (Luther's works)
WH	B. F. Westcott-F. J. A. Hort, *The New Testament in Greek* (London, 1981)
WH App.	Ibid., Appendix
WMANT	Wissenschaftliche Monographien zum Alten und Neuen Testament
WTJ	*Westminster Theological Journal*
WUNT	*Wissenschaftliche Untersuchungen zum Neuen Testament*
ZAW	*Zeitschrift für die alttestamentliche Wissenschaft*
ZK	Zahn-Kommentar
ZNW	*Zeitschrift für die neutestamentliche Wissenschaft*
ZTK	*Zeitschrift für Theologie und Kirche*
ZWT	*Zeitschrift für wissenschaftliche Theologie*

Books denoted by author and short title may be readily identified by reference to the Select Bibliography (pp. 59–69).

Standard sigla are used in the textual notes.

INTRODUCTION

I
GALATIANS AMONG THE LETTERS OF PAUL

By common consent, Galatians is one of the four 'capital' epistles of Paul (the others being 1 and 2 Corinthians and Romans) and one of the best authenticated.[1] When the claims of other letters to Pauline authorship is under consideration, the standard of assessment is this fourfold group, and pre-eminently Galatians. Denial of the genuineness of Galatians, such as was made in the Dutch school of W. C. van Manen,[2] is recognized as a critical aberration in the history of NT study. From the first gathering together of the Pauline writings into a corpus, early in the second century AD, Galatians had a secure place among them.

The traditional criterion in the canonical arrangement of the Pauline letters, as far back as it can be traced, appears to have been descending order of length.[3] But Marcion, who about AD 140 was the first person (so far as is known) to compile a 'closed' canon of Christian writings, deviated from this principle of arrangement by taking Galatians out of its stichometric sequence and giving it pride of place at the head of his *Apostolikon*. Tertullian, our first witness for Marcion's order,[4] agrees with him to this extent, that he too holds Galatians to

---

1. Luther reckoned those NT documents which set forth the gospel plainly to be the right certain capital books—in particular, John and 1 John, Romans, Galatians, Ephesians and 1 Peter 'teach all that it is necessary and blessed for you to know, even if you never see or hear any other book or any other doctrine' (Preface to German NT, 1522, WA, *Die deutsche Bibel* 6.10). In the Tübingen tradition of F. C. Baur and his colleagues the designation 'capital epistles' *(Hauptbriefe)* is reserved for Galatians, 1 and 2 Corinthians and Romans, which 'bear so incontestably the character of Pauline originality, that there is no conceivable ground for the assertion of critical doubts in their case' (Baur, *Paul*, I, 246).

2. The English reader will find a convenient summary of van Manen's views in *Enc Bib s.v.* 'Paul', §§ 1–3, 33–51; cf. his apologia, 'A Wave of Hypercriticism', *Exp Tim* 9 (1897–98), 205–211, 257–259, 314–319.

3. In one form of early arrangement epistles with the same address were lumped together as one for this purpose; thus, in Marcion's canon, after Galatians (which was given programmatic primacy) 1 and 2 Corinthians together were placed first. Other principles of arrangement are discernible in early lists: in the Muratorian canon, for example, Romans comes last among Paul's letters to churches, perhaps because it was recognized as a *summa* of his teaching.

4. In *Adv. Marc.* 5.2–21 Tertullian undertakes to refute Marcion from his own *Apostolikon*, taking up the epistles one by one in Marcion's sequence. Cf. Epiph. *Haer.* 42.9.

be 'the primary epistle against Judaism' *(principalem aduersus iudaismum epistulam)*.[5] Marcion's placing of the epistle has not prevailed, but its primacy of importance among the writings of Paul has been widely, though not universally,[6] acknowledged from that day to this.

Among the writings of Paul it is with the letter to the Romans that Galatians has the closest affinity. 'The Epistle to the Galatians', wrote J. B. Lightfoot, 'stands in relation to the Roman letter, as the rough model to the finished statue; or rather, if I may press the metaphor without misapprehension, it is the first study of a single figure, which is worked into a group in the latter writing.'[7] Two dominant themes in Galatians which are given equal emphasis in Romans are the insistence on justification before God by faith, apart from legal works, and the presentation of the Spirit as the principle of the new life in Christ which believers enjoy as freeborn children of God. If there are features in Romans which have no parallel in Galatians, Galatians has features which are unparalleled in Romans, such as the autobiographical section in Gal. 1:11–2:14, with its defence of Paul's apostolic liberty. Romans must not be made the standard for interpreting Galatians: Galatians must be read and understood in its own right.[8]

There is little or nothing of the urgent note of polemic in Romans that pervades Galatians; for a repetition of that note we turn rather to 2 Cor. 10–13 or to Phil. 3. The people attacked in 2 Cor. 10–13 and Phil. 3 are not necessarily identical with the 'trouble-makers' against whom Paul polemicizes in Galatians, but he recognized their teaching and activity as similarly constituting a threat to the truth of the gospel, and used similar language in warning his converts against them.

---

5. *Adv. Marc.* 5.2.

6. Its importance has not been reckoned so great by those who consider the doctrine of justification by faith to be a 'subsidiary crater' within the rim of the main crater of the Pauline volcano—the main crater being 'the mystical doctrine of redemption through the being-in-Christ' (A. Schweitzer, *Mysticism*, 225); see pp. 50f.

7. Lightfoot, *Galatians*, 49. The relation between the two letters is not adequately presented when a sequence of parallel passages is drawn up, if attention is not paid to the features which are peculiar to each and unreproduced in the other. U. Wilckens in particular gives an unsatisfactory impression by simply presenting two parallel tables of chapter-and-verse references as evidence that Romans is, with respect to the doctrine of justification, 'a reproduction of the letter to the Galatians' (*Römer*, 48).

8. Cf. H. Hübner, *Das Gesetz bei Paulus* (Göttingen, 1978), 1ff. *et passim*.

II
THE GALATIAN CHURCHES

The Epistle to the Galatians is so called because it is explicitly addressed 'to the churches of Galatia' (1:2); moreover, the addressees are apostrophized in the course of the letter: 'O foolish Galatians!' (3:1). The question before us is: Where were these churches and who were these Galatians? Should we locate them in the territory of the former kingdom of Galatia or somewhere else in the more extensive Roman province of Galatia, which included the former kingdom and much additional territory? Were the recipients of the letter Galatians in the ethnic sense, or only in the political sense, as inhabitants of the Roman province of that name?

1. From kingdom to province

The Greek word Γαλάται is a variant form of Κέλται or Κέλτοι, 'Celts' (Latin *Galli*). When we first meet the Celts, they are resident in Central Europe, in the Danube basin. Some place-names in that area retain Celtic elements to the present day; Vienna (Latin *Vindobona*)[1] is a good example. From the Danube basin they migrated in a westerly direction into Switzerland, South Germany and North Italy, and then into Gaul and Britain; they also migrated in a south-easterly direction and settled in North-Central Asia Minor, giving their name to their new homeland as they also did to Gaul (Latin *Gallia*, Greek Γαλατία).[2]

Those Celts who migrated towards the south-east ravaged Thrace, Macedonia and Thessaly, and invaded Greece itself, but they got no further than Delphi, from which they were repulsed in 279 BC. The following year (278–277 BC), a large body of them crossed the Hellespont into Asia Minor at the invitation of Nicomedes, king of Bithynia, who thought he could use their services against his enemies. For a generation they menaced their neighbours in Asia Minor, until a series of defeats at the hands of Attalus I, king of Pergamum (*c.* 230

---

1. The first element is Celtic *windos*, 'white' (cf. Welsh *gwyn*, Gaelic *fionn*).

2. Livy (*Hist.* 38.12), Strabo (*Geog.* 12.5.1) and other writers give Galatia the alternative name *Gallograecia* (i.e. the land of the Greek-speaking Gauls).

BC), confined them within fixed limits, in territory which had formerly belonged to Phrygia. This territory, a broad strip of land stretching over 200 miles from south-west to north-east, between the longitudes of 31° and 35° E. and the latitudes of 39° and 40° 30′ N., was occupied by the three tribes of which the invading force consisted—the Tolistobogii in the west, with their centre at Pessinus,[3] the Trocmi in the east, with their centre at Tavium, and the Tectosages between them, around Ancyra, which in due course became the capital of the kingdom of Galatia (as today, under its modern name Ankara, it is the capital of the Turkish Republic).[4] Each tribe comprised four tetrarchies. The Galatians settled as overlords, with a subject population of Phrygians. As time went on they adopted the Phrygians' religion and culture, but not their language. The Phrygian language died out in Galatia, whereas it survived for some centuries in the neighbouring Phrygian territories. The Galatian speech also survived for several centuries, although the Galatians inevitably came to use Greek as the language of commerce and diplomacy.[5]

In 190 BC a body of Galatian mercenaries fought on the side of the Seleucid king Antiochus III against the Romans at the battle of Magnesia. Their presence attracted Roman reprisals against the Galatians, who were subdued the following year by the consul Manlius but were allowed to retain their independence under their own rulers on giving a pledge of good behaviour for the future.[6]

Henceforth Roman influence was paramount in Asia Minor, apart from the period (88–65 BC) during which Mithridates VI of Pontus dominated the peninsula. The Galatians quickly appreciated the wisdom of keeping on good terms with Rome. With Roman permission or connivance they augmented their territory during the second century BC. They suffered severely under Mithridates because of their friendship with Rome, but when he was finally defeated by Pompey in 64 BC their loyalty was rewarded by Galatia's receiving the status of a client kingdom, and so she remained for nearly forty years. When her last king, Amyntas, fell in battle against the warlike Homonades, who raided Galatia and other neighbouring states from their home base in the northern Taurus, Augustus reorganized the kingdom as an imperial province, governed by a *legatus pro praetore* (25 BC).[7]

By this time the kingdom of Galatia had expanded considerably beyond its original limits. In 36 BC, for example, Mark Antony presented Amyntas with Iconium, a city of Phrygia, together with part of Lycaonia and Pamphylia.[8] Some time after taking over Amyntas's kingdom, Augustus reduced its size by transferring Eastern Lycaonia and Cilicia Tracheia, which it had included, to the

---

3. Pessinus was not occupied by the Galatians until after 205 BC. When in that year the Romans, through the good offices of the Pergamene king Attalus I, sent to procure the image of the Magna Mater from Pessinus, it was still a Phrygian city (Livy, *Hist.* 29.11, 14).

4. Polybius, *Hist.* 5.77f., 111; Livy, *Hist.* 38.16; Strabo, *Geog.* 12.5.1–4.

5. Cf. W. M. Calder, *MAMA* VII (Manchester, 1956), xv.

6. Polybius, *Hist.* 22.16; Livy, *Hist.* 38.12ff.

7. Dio Cassius, *Hist.* 53.26.3.

8. Dio Cassius, *Hist.* 49.32. About 400 BC Xenophon calls Iconium 'the last city of Phrygia' (*Anab.* 1.2.19). Pliny the Elder (d. AD 79) assigns it to Lycaonia (*Nat. Hist.* 2.25), as do many writers from Cicero onwards. But *c*. AD 163 Hierax, one of Justin Martyr's co-defendants, describes himself as a slave 'torn away from Iconium in Phrygia' (*Acts of Justin* 3).

sovereignty of his ally Archelaus, king of Cappadocia. Even so, the province of Galatia comprised much territory to the south which had never been ethnically Galatian—Pisidia and the adjacent region which Strabo calls 'Phrygia towards Pisidia',[9] with Isaurica and Western Lycaonia. Rome inherited from Amyntas the task of crushing the Homonades, who were a constant menace to 'Phrygia towards Pisidia' in particular. They were ultimately subjugated by P. Sulpicius Quirinius, governor of Galatia, in the years following 12 BC.[10]

In 6 BC inland Paphlagonia, on the north, was added to the province of Galatia, as three or four years later were some areas to the north-east which had formerly belonged to Pontus. These latter areas were henceforth known as Pontus Galaticus.[11] By analogy with this it has been inferred that (for example) those parts of Phrygia and Lycaonia which were included in the province were known respectively as Phrygia Galatica and Lycaonia Galatica, to distinguish them from that part of Phrygia which lay within proconsular Asia (Phrygia Asiana) and from Eastern Lycaonia (Lycaonia Antiochiana)[12] which, from AD 37 to 40, and again from AD 41 onwards, belonged to Rome's ally Antiochus IV, king of Commagene. These terms are convenient enough, but without proper attestation we cannot assume confidently that they were part of the official Roman nomenclature.

In our period, then, Provincia Galatia stretched from Pontus on the Black Sea to Pamphylia on the Mediterranean.[13] Paul's 'churches of Galatia' might theoretically have been situated anywhere within these limits. The question is: Were they situated in the original Galatian territory ('North Galatia') or in Phrygia Galatica and Lycaonia Galatica ('South Galatia')? The latter alternative identifies them with the churches planted by Paul and Barnabas during their so-called first missionary journey (Acts 13:14–14:26)—in the Phrygian cities of Pisidian Antioch (modern Yalvaç) and Iconium (modern Konya) and in the Lycaonian cities of Lystra (modern Zostera, near Hatunsaray)[14] and Derbe (modern Kerti Hüyük, c. 15 miles NNE of Karaman, the ancient Laranda, or Devri Şehri, 2½ miles SSE of Kerti Hüyük). Derbe must have lain on the frontier between the Roman province of Galatia and the client kingdom of Commagene, if indeed it did not lie beyond the frontier (as Laranda did from AD 41 onwards).[15]

2. The 'North Galatian' hypothesis

The 'North Galatian' hypothesis held the field almost unchallenged until the eighteenth century. That it should have been taken for granted in the patristic

---

9. Strabo, *Geog.* 12.8.13: ἡ πρὸς Πισιδίαν [Φρυγία].

10. Ibid. 12.6.5; cf. R. Syme, 'Galatia and Pamphylia under Augustus', *Klio* 27 (1934), 122ff.

11. E.g. in *CIL* III.6818 Pontus Galaticus (distinguished from Pontus Polemonianus) is specified in a list of the regions over which the legate of Galatia exercised command.

12. *CIL* V.8660.

13. Cf. Pliny, *Nat. Hist.* 5.147: 'Galatia touches on Cabalia in Pamphylia.'

14. Cf. M. H. Ballance, *MAMA* VIII (Manchester, 1962), xiff.

15. Cf. M. H. Ballance, 'The Site of Derbe: A New Inscription', *AS* 7 (1957), 147–151, and 'Derbe and Faustinopolis', *AS* 14 (1964), 139f.; G. Ogg, 'Derbe', *NTS* 9 (1962–63), 367–370; B. Van Elderen, 'Some Archaeological Observations on Paul's First Missionary Journey', *Bruce FS*, 151–161, especially 156–161. That Derbe belonged to Galatia early in the first century AD is a natural inference from Strabo, *Geog.* 12.6.3.

age was natural.[16] In the second century (*c*. AD 137) Lycaonia Galatica was
detached and united with Cilicia and Isaurica to form an enlarged province of
Cilicia, and late in the third century (*c*. 297) the remainder of South Galatia
with some adjoining territories became a new province of Pisidia, with Pisidian
Antioch as its capital and Iconium as its second city.[17] The province of Galatia
was thus reduced to North Galatia, and when the church fathers, in their study
of our epistle, read of 'the churches of Galatia', they understood 'Galatia' without
more ado in the sense familiar in their day.

The Marcionite prologue to the Epistle to the Galatians[18] does indeed begin
with the surprising statement 'Galatians are Greeks'; but this may simply mean
that the recipients of the letter were Greek speaking—which could be inferred
from the fact that Paul wrote to them in Greek, not to mention the continuing
designation *Gallograecia*. Whether in actual fact the inhabitants of the reduced
province of Galatia in the Marcionite author's day spoke Greek or Celtic is
probably not a question in which he would have been greatly interested.

The linguistic question, however, did interest one Latin commentator on
Galatians. In the preface to the second book of his commentary on this epistle
Jerome tells how, in addition to Greek, the Galatians of his day (late fourth
century AD) spoke a vernacular which he recognized as similar to that which
he used to hear at Trier, where he had stayed for some time in his early twenties.[19]
Whether indeed the Celtic of North-Central Asia Minor and that spoken on the
banks of the Moselle were mutually intelligible in Jerome's time, when their
speakers had been so far separated for six and a half centuries or more, may be
doubted; Jerome may have recognized a resemblance between some words for
specific objects or actions.

In the same preface Jerome quotes the Christian writer Caecilius Firmianus
Lactantius as saying that the Galatians were so called because of the whiteness
of their skin, as though their name was derived from Greek γάλα ('milk').[20]
More has been made of his quotation from a poem by Hilary of Poitiers, of
Gallic origin himself, in which the Gauls were described as 'unteachable' (Latin
indociles); 'no wonder, then,' says Jerome, 'that the Galatians were called "foolish" and slow of understanding'.[21]

John Calvin in his commentary on Galatians (1548) followed his predecessors in holding the North Galatian view, but curiously combined it with the

---

16. Asterius, bishop of Amaseia in Pontus (d. AD 410), seems to understand 'the Galatic
region and Phrygia' of Acts 18:23 as meaning 'Lycaonia and the cities of Phrygia' (*Homilia VIII in
SS Petrum et Paulum*; Migne, *PG* 40.293D). W. M. Ramsay thought he represented a persisting
although scantily attested South Galatian tradition ('The "Galatia" of St. Paul and the "Galatic
Territory" of Acts', *Studia Biblica et Ecclesiastica* IV [Oxford, 1896], 16ff.). See p. 13 below.
17. Cf. W. M. Calder, 'A Hellenistic Survival at Eucarpia', *AS* 6 (1956), 49ff. In NT times
'Pisidian Antioch' (cf. Acts 13:14, Ἀντιόχειαν τὴν Πισιδίαν) was so called not because it was
in Pisidia but because it was, as Strabo calls it (*Geog*. 12.6.4), 'Antioch *near* Pisidia' (τὴν . . .
Ἀντιόχειαν . . . τὴν πρὸς τῇ Πισιδίᾳ). The later reading of Acts 13:14, 'Antioch of Pisidia'
(Ἀντιόχειαν τῆς Πισιδίας, interpreted by AV as 'Antioch in Pisidia'), reflects the fourth-century
situation.
18. See p. 20.
19. *In Gal. ii, praef.* (Migne, *PL* 26.382C).
20. Ibid. 379B-C.
21. Ibid. 380C.

view that the epistle was written before the Jerusalem council of Acts 15.[22] (He identified Paul and Barnabas's Jerusalem visit of Gal. 2:1ff. with the famine-relief visit of Acts 11:30.) One wonders when he supposed the evangelization of North Galatia to have taken place.

The first scholar known to us who held that the recipients of the Epistle to the Galatians at least included the churches planted by Paul and Barnabas on their first missionary journey appears to have been J. J. Schmidt[23] in 1748, followed in 1825 by J. P. Mynster, whose position might be described as 'Pan-Galatian' rather than either North or South Galatian.[24] In the nineteenth century (apart from its last decade) the South Galatian view was championed mainly by French scholars, such as Georges Perrot, who argued for it in *De Galatia Provincia Romana* (1867),[25] and Ernest Renan, who assumed it rather than argued for it in his *Saint Paul* (1869).[26] The majority of others continued to propound the North Galatian view, and among these others J. B. Lightfoot stands out with special distinction.[27]

Lightfoot's commentary on Galatians first appeared in 1865; it remains a standard work which no student of the letter can afford to overlook—and there are not many commentaries over a hundred years old of which this sort of thing can be said. He recognized the ambiguity in the phrase 'churches of Galatia', but rejected the view that they were the churches of Pisidian Antioch, Iconium, Lystra and Derbe in favour of locating them at Ancyra, Pessinus and perhaps Tavium (possibly also at Juliopolis, the ancient Gordion). His arguments against the South Galatian view are mainly to the effect that the churches planted during Paul and Barnabas's first missionary journey are not called Galatian churches in Acts—but Luke's usage is not necessarily Paul's.

His positive arguments for the North Galatian view include the consideration that the 'Galatic region' of Acts 16:6 and 18:23 is most probably ethnic Galatia, that Paul's two visits to the region mentioned in these passages coincide with his two visits to Galatia which he thought to be implied in Gal. 4:13, and especially that the temperament of the Galatian Christians reflected in the letter harmonizes (*a*) with the testimonies to the fickleness of the Gauls found in classical authors (especially Caesar)[28] and (*b*) with the fact that the Gauls were (Caesar again being witness) 'a superstitious people given over to ritual observances'[29] and that Deiotarus, king of Galatia in the mid-first century BC, was characterized by an 'extravagant devotion to augury'.[30]

The weight laid by a scholar of Lightfoot's calibre upon these alleged affinities between the recipients of Paul's letter and the Celts known to Caesar and

---

22. Calvin, *Galatians*, 24f.

23. Cf. W. G. Kümmel, *INT*, ETr (London, 1965), 192.

24. I.e. he propounded what Kümmel (loc. cit.) prefers to call the *Provinzhypothese* as against the *Landschaftshypothese (Kleine Theologische Schriften*; Copenhagen, 1825).

25. *De Galatia Provincia Romana* (Paris, 1867), 43f.

26. ETr, *Saint Paul* (London, 1890), 24ff., 63f., 169f., 173. See criticism of Renan in J. B. Lightfoot, *Colossians and Philemon*, 25f. n. 2.

27. Lightfoot, *Galatians*, 19ff.

28. Caesar, *De Bello Gallico* 2.1; 4.5.

29. *De Bello Gallico* 6.16.

30. Lightfoot, *Galatians*, p. 16, referring to Cicero, *Div*. 1.5; 2.36f.

his contemporaries is surprising. Caesar is not an entirely objective witness where the Gauls are concerned and, for the rest, the argument seems to reduce itself to a syllogism of this order:

> The Gauls were fickle and superstitious.
> Paul's Galatians were fickle and superstitious.
> Therefore: Paul's Galatians were Gauls.

The undistributed middle is not hard to recognize; the argument would be valid only if fickleness and superstition were not characteristic of other nations than the Gauls (and Galatians). We have to look no farther than the Galatians' Phrygian neighbours for another reputed example, while Luke's account of Paul's adventure at Lystra suggests that fickleness and superstition were not wanting among the Lycaonians.

3. The 'South Galatian' hypothesis

Nevertheless, Lightfoot's dismissal of the South Galatian view in favour of the traditional one was natural; when he wrote, the South Galatian view had not yet been placed on a sufficiently sound basis. The scholar by whom this was achieved was W. M. Ramsay (1851–1939), whose statement of the case in *The Church in the Roman Empire* (1893)[31] and *A Historical Commentary on St. Paul's Epistle to the Galatians* (1899) was founded on his systematic survey of Central Asia Minor on the spot, coupled with his comprehensive and detailed study of epigraphy and classical literature.

Ramsay's greatest work was accomplished in the 1880s and 1890s. It was his researches in those years that laid the archaeological foundation for the South Galatian hypothesis, and laid it so firmly that to many of his disciples it is no longer a mere hypothesis.[32] When he began his exploration of Asia Minor he accepted (mainly on Lightfoot's terms) the North Galatian view, as he also accepted F. C. Baur's reconstruction of the course of primitive Christian history. He abandoned the one view, as he abandoned the other, because of the compelling evidence of facts as he faced them *in situ*. The whole organization of Asia Minor in the first-century Roman Empire, he held—its administration and communications—pointed inexorably to the South Galatian destination of our epistle. In the preface to the fourth edition of *The Church in the Roman Empire* (1896) he tells his readers that they will find all the evidence for the South Galatian view in the first part of his *Cities and Bishoprics of Phrygia* (1895), although the view is neither mentioned nor discussed there. But the solid evidence for the South Galatian view is contained in such studies as his *Cities and Bishoprics of Phrygia* and his earlier *Historical Geography of Asia Minor* (1890)—studies conducted with no thought of the Epistle to the Galatians or of establishing or demolishing any theory about its destination.

In these earlier works Ramsay carefully avoided appealing to the usual

---

31. *The Church in the Roman Empire* (London, [5]1897), xiif., 8ff., 97ff.
32. Cf. J. A. Findlay, 'It is significant that all those who know the geography of Asia Minor well are "South Galatianists" to a man' (*Acts*, 166).

series of ambiguous arguments in favour of the South Galatian view.[33] Such arguments are:

(1) Paul habitually uses Roman imperial nomenclature—but then any inhabitants of the province of Galatia, including the ethnic Galatians, would have been 'Galatians' to him.

(2) Paul addresses his Galatians in Greek—but Greek would have been familiar in Ancyra and Pessinus at least.

(3) Paul mentions Barnabas (Gal. 2:1ff.), who was personally known to the South Galatians but not (so far as we can tell) to the North Galatians—but he mentions him also in 1 Cor. 9:6, and there is no evidence that he was personally known to the Corinthians.

(4) Paul's travel-companions in Acts 20:4, who presumably were carrying their churches' contributions to the Jerusalem fund, include South Galatians (Gaius of Derbe and Timothy of Lystra) but not North Galatians—but such an argument from silence is precarious (no Corinthian representative is named).

(5) The presence of Jewish emissaries is more probable in South Galatia than in North Galatia—but they might make it their business to visit any city where Paul had planted a church.

(6) Paul's Galatians received him 'as an angel of God' (Gal. 4:14), which is a remarkable coincidence with his identification with Hermes by the Lystrans (Acts 14:11ff.)—but the coincidence is somewhat spoiled by the Lystrans' later murderous attack on him (Acts 14:19).

He based his case rather on the facts of historical geography, coupled with his interpretation of Paul's policy as one of concentration on the main roads and centres of communication in the Roman provinces. The main line along which Christianity advanced in Asia Minor was the road from Syria through the Cilician Gates to Iconium and Ephesus, and so across the Aegean. There were two subsidiary lines: one following the land route by Philadelphia to Troas, and so across to Philippi and the Egnatian Way, and the other leading north from the Cilician Gates by Tyana and Cappadocian Caesarea to Amisos on the Black Sea. These are in fact the principal lines of penetration from the Cilician Gates into the peninsula, and none of them led through ethnic Galatia. The southern side of the Anatolian plateau was more important than the northern under the earlier Roman Empire; the full development of the northern side did not take place until Diocletian transferred the centre of imperial administration to Nicomedeia in AD 292. In Ramsay's view, the South Galatian hypothesis was the one which agreed best with the facts of the historical geography of Asia Minor.[34]

The North Galatian case, however, has never lacked defenders, especially in Germany, but few of these have dealt adequately with Ramsay's positive arguments. Among those who have dealt with them most seriously were P. W. Schmiedel, in the section which he contributed to the article 'Galatia' in the *Encyclopaedia Biblica* (1901),[35] and J. Moffatt, in his *Introduction to the Lit-*

---

33. He lists ten (including the six mentioned here) in *The Church in the Roman Empire*[5], 97ff.

34. *The Church in the Roman Empire*[5], 10f.; cf. *Historical Geography of Asia Minor* (London, 1890), 197ff.

35. §§ 8–13, following on W. J. Woodhouse's defence of the South Galatian view in §§ 5–7.

erature of the New Testament (1911).[36] Moffatt's arguments are about the weightiest ever presented for the North Galatian view after Ramsay's presentation of the evidence for South Galatia.[37] He appreciates the weakness of some traditional arguments for North Galatia—e.g. the appeal to the Galatians' alleged fickleness—and points out some weaknesses in Ramsay's case. Did Paul always follow the main roads and evangelize the principal centres of communication? Then what took him to Lystra and Derbe? In Ramsay's own words: 'How did the cosmopolitan Paul drift like a piece of timber borne by the current into this quiet backwater?'[38] On the other hand, Ancyra in North Galatia, the provincial seat of administration, was, on Ramsay's own showing, 'one of the greatest and most splendid cities of Asia Minor'.[39]

Even so, many of Moffatt's arguments, like Schmiedel's before him, and Lightfoot's still earlier, concern the interpretation of Acts and not of our epistle, like the argument that Luke's 'Galatic region' is ethnic Galatia, as against Ramsay's view that the 'Phrygian and Galatic region' of Acts 16:6 is Phrygia Galatica and the 'Galatic region' of Acts 18:23 Lycaonia Galatica. Moffatt admits that this is so: 'Luke's usage, it may be retorted, is not decisive for Paul. This is perfectly true, but Paul's use of Γαλατία corresponds to the inferences from Acts.'[40]

4. The evidence of Acts

The issue of the destination of the Epistle to the Galatians is strictly independent of the references to Galatian territory in Acts. Granted that Paul usually adopts Roman provincial nomenclature—as when, for example, he repeatedly refers to Achaia in the Roman sense, as including Corinth, and not in the traditional Greek sense, of a territory in the North-Western Peloponnese, to which Corinth did not belong—it might be argued that Luke prefers the more popular geographical terms and so would use Galatia in the ethnic sense.[41] But what are the facts?

---

36. J. Moffatt, *Introduction to the Literature of the New Testament*[3] (London, 1918), 90ff. Moffatt commends, in addition to Schmiedel's treatment, the defence of the North Galatian view in A. Steinmann's 'thoroughgoing essays' in *Die Abfassungszeit des Galaterbriefes* (Münster, 1906) and *Der Leserkreis des Galaterbriefes* (Münster, 1908).

37. One may justly take exception to Moffatt's remark that the identification of the Jerusalem visits of Acts 11:30 and Gal. 2:1ff. 'has found favour with several South Galatian advocates in their manipulation of the Lucan narratives' (*INT*, 102)—the word 'manipulation' conveys an unworthy innuendo.

38. Ramsay, *The Cities of St. Paul*, 408 (in reference to Lystra).

39. Moffatt, *INT*, 97; cf. Ramsay's words: 'Ancyra was quite a Romanized city, civilized and rich' (*HDB* II, *s.v.* 'Galatia', 84). But the earliest clear reference to Christianity at Ancyra is dated AD 192 (Eusebius, *Hist. Eccl.* 5.16.3), although it had no doubt been planted there a century earlier. Indeed, Ramsay himself, interpreting an entry in the early Syriac Martyrology with the aid of a Byzantine milestone inscription at Barata in Lycaonia, argued (somewhat precariously) for a large-scale martyrdom of Christians at Ancyra at the end of the first century AD or the beginning of the second ('Two Notes on Religious Antiquities in Asia Minor: I. Gaianus, Martyr at Ancyra of Galatia', *Exp Tim* 21 [1909–10], 64f.).

40. *INT*, 94.

41. Paul was not reverting to Homeric usage, in which all the Greeks are Achaians. Luke uses 'Achaia' in Acts 18:12 where he reproduces Gallio's official title, but 'Greece' in Acts 20:2.

There are two relevant passages in Acts. The first is in Acts 16:6, where Paul and Silas, having journeyed on their westward way from Syria and the Cilician Gates through Derbe and Lystra and co-opted Timothy as their travelling companion at the latter place, 'went through the Phrygian and Galatic region (τὴν Φρυγίαν καὶ Γαλατικὴν χώραν),⁴² having been forbidden by the Holy Spirit to speak the word in Asia.' Accordingly, instead of proceeding west to Ephesus, 'they came opposite Mysia (κατὰ τὴν Μυσίαν)⁴³ and attempted to go into Bithynia, but the Spirit of Jesus did not allow them, so, passing by Mysia, they came down to Troas'—and from there crossed over to Macedonia. Where, having regard to this fairly detailed itinerary, should we locate the 'Phrygian and Galatic region' through which the missionary party passed after receiving the prohibition to evangelize Asia? Ramsay, as we have seen, identified it with Phrygia Galatica—the part of Phrygia included within the province of Galatia, Strabo's 'Phrygia towards Pisidia'. Lightfoot's suggestion was that it denoted ethnic Galatia, because that area had once been Phrygian (before the second half of the third century BC) but had subsequently become Galatian.⁴⁴ But such an antiquarianism is uncharacteristic of Luke. Kirsopp Lake, who in his *Earlier Epistles of St. Paul* (1911) had followed Ramsay's interpretation,⁴⁵ reviewed the evidence afresh for his note on 'Paul's route in Asia Minor' in Volume V of *The Beginnings of Christianity*, Part I (1933), and concluded that the most probable explanation was that Paul, instead of going west from Iconium along the Lycus and Maeander valleys,

went north through Phrygia and territory where Galatians were numerous. If this view be accepted 'Phrygian and Galatian country' means territory in which sometimes Phrygian and sometimes Gaelic⁴⁶ was the language of the villagers. His route may have been through Laodicea, Amorion, and Orkistos (surely a Gaelic place)⁴⁷ to Nakoleia and perhaps to Dorylaeum. Either Nakoleia or Dorylaeum might be said to be κατὰ τὴν Μυσίαν. He was also on the direct road to Nicaea, and certainly from Nakoleia and probably from Dorylaeum there was a straight road to Troas, 'skirting' Mysia—if that be the meaning of παρελθών. In one or the other of these places he was once more prevented

---

42. The non-repetition of the article before Γαλατικὴν χώραν (except in the Byzantine text) suggests that this, and not 'Phrygia and the Galatic region', is the proper translation. Φρύγιος appears as an adjective of both two and three terminations but predominantly of three, even in later Greek; Φρυγίαν is therefore most probably an adjective here, and not a noun, as (e.g.) E. Haenchen asserts (*Acts*, 483). For the present construction cf. Lk. 3:1, τῆς Ἰτουραίας καὶ Τραχωνίτιδος χώρας ('the Ituraean and Trachonitid region'). See C. J. Hemer, 'The Adjective "Phrygia" ', *JTS* n.s. 27 (1976), 122–126; 'Phrygia: A Further Note', *JTS* n.s. 28 (1977), 99–101; 'Luke the Historian', *BJRL* 60 (1977–78), 45f.

43. 'When they had reached such a point that a line drawn across the country at right angles to the general line of their route would touch Mysia' (Ramsay, *Church in the Roman Empire⁵*, 75 n.); W. M. Calder suggests 'in the latitude of Mysia' (letter dated 18 February 1953).

44. *Galatians*, 22; he recognized that Φρυγίαν and Γαλατικήν were both adjectives qualifying χώραν (cf. his *Colossians*, 23).

45. *The Earlier Epistles of St. Paul* (London, ²1914), 255ff.

46. He means Gallic or Galatian; Gaelic is a Q-Celtic language, whereas Gallic was P-Celtic.

47. Presumably taking it as cognate with Latin *porcus*, with normal Celtic loss of Indo-European **p* (?cf. *Orcades*, 'Orkneys'). But Orkistos, in the province of Asia, was Phrygian speaking (cf. Calder in *MAMA* VII, x).

by revelation from working as he had intended—this time in Bithynia—and so he turned to the left and went through Mysia to Troas.[48]

This route, as Lake remarks, does not differ substantially from that postulated by Ramsay, apart from the interpretation of the 'Phrygian and Galatic region'. But the aspect in which it does differ from Ramsay's comes to grief on the hard facts. The frontier between Galatic Phrygia and ethnic Galatia has been delimited much more precisely than it was in Ramsay's day;[49] it ran due west from a point near the northernmost part of Lake Tatta (Tuz Gölü) to Orkistos (where the Sangarius divided the province of Asia from the province of Galatia)—say from 32° 50′ E. and rather north of 39° N. Since Paul's plan, according to Acts 15:36, was to visit all the cities which he and Barnabas had evangelized in South Galatia a year or two earlier, he and his companions probably intended to travel west from Lystra through Iconium and Pisidian Antioch. The prohibition against preaching in Asia was probably communicated at Lystra:[50] the Pastoral Epistles contain reminiscences of prophetic utterances given on the occasion when Timothy joined the apostolic company.[51] Now they had to follow some other road than that which led to Ephesus, but it was necessary to go on to Iconium in any case. If by this time they thought of Bithynia they could cut out Pisidian Antioch and take the road to Phrygia Paroreios (the territory lying north and south of the range of Sultan Dağ), or they could go on to Pisidian Antioch and reach Phrygia Paroreios from there by crossing Sultan Dağ. In either case they would arrive at Philomelium. Leaving Philomelium by either of two possible routes for the north-west, they passed at once into Phrygia Asiana: they would not touch ethnic Galatia or pass through any village where the Celtic language would be heard.

The 'Phrygian and Galatic region' cannot be understood in the sense suggested by Lake: it can only mean the territory through which Paul and his friends passed after leaving Lystra, the territory in which Iconium and Pisidian Antioch were situated. Even if they by-passed both these cities and made straight for Mysia after receiving the divine monition at Lystra, they would still have crossed from Lycaonia Galatica into Phrygia Galatica and continued in the latter region until they reached the frontier of the province of Asia. To reach a road which would take them through territory where the Phrygian and Celtic tongues would both be heard, they would have had to go straight north from Lystra until they reached the latitude of 39° N. (without hearing a word of Celtic) and then turn west through a series of villages, remote from any contact with city life. There indeed they would have heard Phrygian on their left and Celtic on their right. But why should Paul make a detour to visit such a district 'unless he had a prophetic vision of what Lake was going to say in the fulness of time, and some interest in proving him right?'[52]

---

48. *BC*, I. 5, 236.
49. Cf. W. M. Calder, 'The Boundary of Galatic Phrygia', *MAMA* VII, ixff.
50. Ramsay unnecessarily followed J. B. Lightfoot (*Biblical Essays* [London, 1893], 237) in adopting the inferior Byzantine reading διελθόντες instead of διῆλθον, thus making the prohibition come after their passing through Derbe and Lystra (*SPT*, 195f.). The prohibition was given in good time to enable the missionaries to change their plans without inconvenience.
51. 1 Tim. 1:18; 4:14 (cf. 2 Tim. 1:6).
52. W. M. Calder, letter, 18 February 1953.

The narrative of Acts 15:41–16:8 is certainly more intelligible if the 'Phrygian and Galatic region' is that part of Phrygia included in the province of Galatia. Although there were naturally lines of communication linking the various regions of the province, the cities of North Galatia were not readily accessible from the road leading from the Cilician Gates through Lystra. Any one proposing to evangelize North Galatia would have been better advised to set out from some other place than Lystra.

The second passage in Acts which is relevant to our subject is 18:23, where Paul, having paid a hasty visit to Palestine after his Corinthian ministry (probably in the summer of AD 52), returned to the west to begin his evangelization of Ephesus and 'went from place to place through the Galatic region and Phrygia (τὴν Γαλατικὴν χώραν καὶ Φρυγίαν), strengthening all the disciples'. It may be that by this geographical phrase Luke means much the same as the 'Phrygian and Galatic region' of Acts 16:6. Ramsay thought the 'Galatic region' of Acts 18:23 was Galatic Lycaonia, in distinction from that part of Lycaonia which belonged to the kingdom of Commagene (Lycaonia Antiochiana),[53] but this is uncertain. The 'Galatic region' might be Galatic Lycaonia and Galatic Phrygia while 'Phrygia' on this occasion could include Asian Phrygia. The reference to Paul's 'strengthening all the disciples' indicates that he was not pioneering but retracing his former footsteps. If the expression in Acts 16:6 could cover ethnic Galatia, so could the expression in Acts 18:23; if ethnic Galatia is excluded from the former passage, it is excluded here too. It is simplest to understand Acts 18:23 in the sense of Paul's passing once more through Derbe, Lystra, Iconium and Pisidian Antioch. In Acts 19:1 he is said to have passed through 'the upper country' (τὰ ἀνωτερικὰ μέρη) on his way to Ephesus. More or less any part of inland Asia Minor could have been called 'the upper country' in relation to Ephesus: here the reference may be to the road leading due west from Pisidian Antioch, reaching Ephesus by the north side of Mount Messogis, instead of the main road farther south following the Lycus and Maeander valleys.[54]

5. Other references

Other NT references to Galatia or the Galatians can be disposed of quickly. The 'churches of Galatia' which, according to 1 Corinthians 16:1, had received Paul's instructions about the collection for Jerusalem, are no doubt identical with the 'churches of Galatia' addressed in Gal. 1:2. If Paul's companions on his last journey to Jerusalem (Acts 20:4) were the delegates of the contributing churches, it may be relevant that they include two South Galatians, Gaius of Derbe[55] and

---

53. *Church in the Roman Empire*[5], pp. 90ff.
54. See further C. J. Hemer, 'Acts and Galatians reconsidered', *Themelios* 2 (1977), 81–88.
55. The Western text has 'Gaius of Doberus' (in Macedonia), perhaps by way of harmonization with 'Gaius and Aristarchus, Macedonians who were Paul's companions in travel' (Acts 19:29, where Μακεδόνας immediately followed by συνεκδήμους may be a dittography for Μακεδόνα, which would then refer only to Aristarchus, called in Acts 27:2 'a Macedonian from Thessalonica').

Timothy (of Lystra), but no North Galatians; as has been said above, however, the list of companions may not be exhaustive.[56]

The 'Galatia' to which Crescens went (2 Tim. 4:10) is not easily identified; its significance is the more complicated because of the variant (but improbable) reading 'Gaul' (Γαλλίαν for Γαλατίαν).[57]

As for 'Galatia' in 1 Pet. 1:1, that seems to denote the province in general, as it is named along with other Anatolian provinces—Pontus, Cappadocia, Asia and Bithynia—as an area in which 'exiles of the dispersion' (i.e. Christians) lived.[58]

6. The present state of the question

The debate on the location of Paul's Galatians does not appear to be carried on today as seriously as it once was. R. M. Grant holds that in general 'Acts does not assist us in locating these churches' but suggests that the Spirit's prohibition in Acts 16:6 'may well be a theological expression of one aspect of Paul's illness'[59] which, according to Gal. 4:13, occasioned Paul's first visit to Galatia. We have been accustomed to hearing the argument pressed against the South Galatian view that there is no hint in Acts 13:13ff. that Paul was ill when he first visited Pisidian Antioch and the other cities of Galatic Phrygia and Lycaonia, and the answer readily presented itself that equally there is no hint of illness in the record of his passing through the Phrygian and Galatic region of Acts 16:6. But the force of this answer (negative as it was) is now threatened. Even so, Grant's interpretation of the Spirit's prohibition is no more probable than Ramsay's suggestion that Paul went up from the Pamphylian coast to the highlands of Pisidian Antioch (3,600 feet above sea level) because of an attack of malaria (which he identified with the 'splinter in the flesh' of 2 Cor. 12:7).[60] Grant's understanding of the Spirit's prohibition in the light of Gal. 4:13, along with the unlikelihood that Paul would address as 'Galatians' (Gal. 3:1) people who spoke Lycaonian (Acts 14:11),[61] leads him to conclude 'that the letter was addressed to a group of communities near Ancyra'[62]—a conclusion which is sustained with difficulty when the journey of Acts 15:41–16:8 is plotted on the map.

It is disquieting to see how superficially the North Galatian hypothesis is defended by many of its champions nowadays, when we think of the careful arguments adduced by scholars of two and three generations ago—especially disquieting to see how little attention is paid to the relevant data of historical geography. Thus in Willi Marxsen's *Introduction to the New Testament* we read:

---

56. Cf. p. 9. See W.-H. Ollrog, *Paulus und seine Mitarbeiter* (Neukirchen/Vluyn, 1979), 52–58.

57. So Codd. ℵ C and a few other authorities; cf. Eusebius, *Hist. Eccl.* 3.4.8.

58. Lightfoot, *Galatians*, 19 n. 5; cf. Ramsay, *Church in the Roman Empire*[5], 110f.; F. J. A. Hort, *First Peter*, 157ff.; C. J. Hemer, 'The Address of 1 Peter', *Exp Tim* 89 (1977–78), 239–243.

59. *A Historical Introduction to the NT* (London, 1963), 185. See p. 208 below.

60. *Church in the Roman Empire*[5], 62ff.; *SPT*, 92ff.

61. But the point is that (on the South Galatian view) Paul's addressees included people who were not Lycaonians linguistically, but who were 'Galatians' politically (see p. 16 below).

62. *Historical Introduction*, 185.

'If Paul meant by "Galatia" the Roman province, he could have been in the southern part of the province even on the first missionary journey—although not in the "region of Galatia", as Acts always calls it.'[63] This implies that the Γαλατικὴ χώρα—an expression which occurs but *twice* in Acts (16:6; 18:23)—can refer only to ethnic Galatia; in fact the adjective Γαλατικός (Latin *Galaticus*) is well attested for those regions of the province which were not ethnically Galatian,[64] and also for the province as a whole,[65] but not at this period for ethnic Galatia.[66]

Marxsen continues: 'The South Galatian hypothesis, however, is extremely improbable.' In support of this statement three arguments are adduced:

1. 'The assertion that is often made, that Paul always uses the names of the Roman provinces, is incorrect.'[67]

If anyone said that Paul *always* uses the names of the Roman provinces, he would be imprudent; the fact is that Paul *normally* uses them. There may be deviations from this norm, but they will be recognizable deviations, and the burden of proof lies on those who understand Γαλατία and Γαλάται in his writings in another than the provincial sense.

2. 'Besides, Paul would hardly have been able to say in 1:21, "Then I came into the regions of Syria and Cilicia", for this is the Pauline parallel to the first missionary journey in Acts. According to the South Galatian hypothesis he must have founded the Galatian churches at that time but there is no mention of this.'

This argument seems to imply that Paul might have included the churches of Pisidian Antioch, Iconium, Lystra and Derbe in 'the regions of Syria and Cilicia'[68] (if Acts 13–14 rightly makes him evangelize these cities at this stage), but not those which he calls 'the churches of Galatia'; the latter would therefore be different from the four churches of Acts and be located in North Galatia. That Paul would have included the South Galatian churches in 'the regions of Syria and Cilicia' is incredible; Gal. 1:21 is parallel, not to the 'first missionary journey' of Acts 13–14 but to the interval between Acts 9:31 and 11:30, when

---

63. *INT*, ETr (Oxford, 1968), 46.

64. E.g. Pontus Galaticus (cf. p. 5 n. 11).

65. E.g. in *CIG* 3991, where an official entrusted with the delimitation of boundaries *c*. AD 54 is called 'procurator of the Galatic province' (Γαλατικῆς ἐπαρχείας).

66. About AD 150 Arrian (*Anab.* 2.4.1) can describe Alexander the Great as setting out 'for Galatic Ancyra', or 'for Ancyra of the Galatic territory' (ἐπ᾽ Ἀγκύρας τῆς Γαλατικῆς), meaning the land which was to become 'Galatic' in the century after Alexander; by Arrian's time the province of Galatia had begun to shrink back to its ethnic limits. (There is a variant reading, preferred by the Loeb edition: τῆς Γαλατίας, 'of Galatia'.)

67. He refers to E. Haenchen's note on Acts 16:6 to the effect that 'the assertion that Paul always uses the Roman names for the provinces has, without foundation, wellnigh become a dogma' (Haenchen, *Acts*, 483 n. 2). If this were so, it were a grievous fault in a situation which calls for evidence, not dogma. Haenchen is right in pointing out that a number of terms occurring in Paul could be used either in the technical Roman sense or more generally and traditionally (e.g. Macedonia, Asia), but this argues neither for nor against the technical Roman sense in other instances.

68. Marxsen may mean, like H. H. Wendt, *Die Apostelgeschichte* (Göttingen, ⁹1913), 242f. (an earlier edition of which is cited by Ramsay, *Church in the Roman Empire*[5], 106ff.), that Paul was inaccurate in Gal. 1:21, but that the North Galatians would not have noticed this, whereas the South Galatians would have done so since it concerned them. Even if Paul was inaccurate, does a man perpetrate inaccuracies only when he knows that his readers or hearers will not notice them?

Paul was active first in Tarsus and then in Antioch—the two leading cities of the united province of Syria-Cilicia.[69]

3. 'Finally it seems unlikely that Paul would address the inhabitants of Pisidia and Lycaonia as "Galatians" (3:1: "O foolish Galatians"). This can only be a racial term and cannot refer to the inhabitants of a Roman administrative district.'

This argument, which is sometimes reinforced by the consideration that to address Christians who were not ethnic Galatians as 'Galatians' would be psychologically disastrous,[70] will hardly stand up to investigation. What comprehensive term could have been used (other than 'Galatians') to address Pisidians (or rather Phrygians) and Lycaonians together? We may reflect that the one comprehensive term which is acceptable when Englishmen, Welsh, Cornish and Scots are referred to or addressed together is 'British', which 'ethnically' is appropriate only to the Welsh and Cornish (and the Bretons, who are part of another political unit). The name Britain, or Great Britain, to denote the whole island, is a political expedient; yet Highland and Lowland Scots would much rather be called British (which they are not 'ethnically') than English (which is applicable to them only linguistically, and even so is unacceptable).[71]

If Paul's readers found anything objectionable in being called 'foolish Galatians', the objection arose from the adjective 'foolish' rather than from the substantive 'Galatians'. If they were South Galatians, some of them lived in Phrygia and some in Lycaonia, and in addition to Phrygians and Lycaonians they included Jews, Greeks and perhaps Romans (since Pisidian Antioch was a Roman colony). The one political feature which they shared in common was their residence within the frontiers of the province of Galatia; the only political term that could be applied to them all was Galatians. Ramsay's judgment may be quite soundly based: 'I can entertain no doubt that about AD 50 the address by which an orator would most please the Iconians, in situations where the term "Iconians" was unsuitable, was ἄνδρες Γαλάται, "gentlemen of the Galatic province." '[72] Even 'Phrygians' might not have been very acceptable to the Iconians, because of its currency in a sense practically synonymous with 'slaves' or 'cowards'[73] (and it would have been in every way inapplicable to the people of Lystra and Derbe). As for the people of Pisidian Antioch, they might well have preferred the designation 'Galatians' to either 'Phrygians' or 'Pisidians', for if 'Phrygians' was tantamount to 'slaves' or 'cowards', 'Pisidians' (which the people of Antioch were not in any case) would have been little better than 'barbarians'.

W. G. Kümmel's *Introduction to the New Testament*, in which the North Galatian destination is upheld, similarly lays weight on the reference to 'the

---

69. Syria and Cilicia were united to form one province in 27 BC; cf. J. G. C. Anderson, 'Provincia Cappadocia,' *CR* 45 (1931), 189ff., and in *CAH* X (1934), 279. See pp. 102f. below.

70. Cf. Lightfoot, *Galatians*, 19.

71. In an inscription of AD 57 a man of Apollonia in Phrygia Galatica thanks Zeus for bringing him back safely, 'to my home in the land of the Galatians' (Γαλατῶν γαίης ἤγαγες ἐς πατρίδα). See *MAMA* IV (Manchester, 1933), §140, for the text of the inscription.

72. *Church in the Roman Empire*[5], 43; cf. *HDB* II, 92 (*s.v.* 'Galatia').

73. Cf. Aristophanes, *Wasps* 433, where a slave in Athens bears the name Φρύξ ('Phrygian'), and the proverb 'more timid than a Phrygian hare' quoted by Strabo, *Geog.* 1.2.30.

regions of Syria and Cilicia' in Gal. 1:21 and the address 'O foolish Galatians' in Gal. 3:1;[74] but the defence of the North Galatian hypothesis deserves weightier arguments than these.

In fact, more recent statements of the North Galatian case represent no advance on Lightfoot and fall short of the statements of Schmiedel and Moffatt. This may be due in some measure to the fashion of paying more attention to the style of Luke's narrative than to the narrative itself;[75] besides, if the narrative is regarded as a partly fictitious and in any case idealized construction by a writer of a later generation, detailed study of its historical geography is not of the first relevance. Against this fashion it must be recognized that Luke's narrative is true to its dramatic date,[76] and in this regard the study of its historical geography is of the utmost importance.

In recent years especially there has tended to be a correlation between acceptance of the South Galatian view and a high estimate of the historical reliability of Acts, on the one hand, and between acceptance of the North Galatian view and a more sceptical assessment of Acts on the other. This correlation may be little more than coincidental: it is neither necessary nor deliberate. An exception is provided by R. H. Fuller's *Critical Introduction to the New Testament* in the Duckworth series. There, as in the identically entitled volume by A. S. Peake which Fuller's work has replaced,[77] the South Galatian view is adopted but (in contrast to Peake's treatment) there is a lower estimate of the historical value of Acts. 'The motive, conscious or unconscious, behind the North Galatian theory', says Fuller, 'seems to be the desire to avoid making Gal. the earliest Pauline letter'.[78] This is doubtful, because by no means all South Galatianists make Galatians the earliest Pauline letter: those who infer from the reference to the 'former' or 'first' visit (τὸ πρότερον) in Gal. 4:13 that Paul had visited the South Galatian churches twice before he wrote to them must date his letter after Acts 16:6. Fuller undertakes to satisfy the North Galatianists' difficulty by taking the first missionary journey of Acts as a duplicate of the second, so that Paul's visit to South Galatia in Acts 16:1–6 was really his first (after the Council of Jerusalem), and the visit of Acts 18:23 was his second. Galatians is then dated during Paul's Ephesian ministry. But this dating of the epistle is independent of Fuller's view of the structure of Acts: it was held, for example, by T. W. Manson, who accepted Luke's narrative of the first and second missionary journeys as it stands and favoured the 'South Galatian' theory.[79]

The question of the North or South Galatian destination of our epistle is not one in which it is proper to take up partisan attitudes or indulge in dogmatic

---

74. W. G. Kümmel, *INT*, ETr, 193.

75. Cf. M. Dibelius, *Studies in the Acts of the Apostles*, ETr (London, 1956), 1ff.

76. Cf. H. J. Cadbury, *The Book of Acts in History* (New York, 1955); A. N. Sherwin-White, *Roman Society and Roman Law in the New Testament* (Oxford, 1963), 48ff., 144ff., 189; M. Hengel, *Acts and the History of Earliest Christianity*, ETr (London, 1979).

77. A. S. Peake, *A Critical Introduction to the New Testament* (London, 1909), 17ff.

78. R. H. Fuller, *A Critical Introduction to the New Testament* (London, 1966), 25.

79. 'The Problem of the Epistle to the Galatians', *BJRL* 24 (1940), 59–80, reprinted in *Studies in the Gospels and Epistles* (Manchester, 1962), 168–189. Before Manson, E. D. Burton held that the balance of probability favoured the South Galatian view of the epistle's destination and a date for it during Paul's Ephesian ministry (*Galatians*, xliv, xlix); a similar position is preferred by J. A. T. Robinson, *Redating the NT* (London, 1976), 55–57.

assertions; and it ill becomes champions of either view to disparage the rival view or those who maintain it. The fact that so many competent scholars can be cited in support of either position suggests that the evidence for neither is absolutely conclusive. But the weight of the evidence, it seems to me, favours the South Galatian view. If the Epistle to the Galatians was indeed addressed to the churches of Pisidian Antioch, Iconium, Lystra and Derbe, then we have important historical, geographical, literary and epigraphic data which will provide material for its better understanding.

III
THE GALATIAN PROBLEM

1. The occasion of the letter

The occasion of the letter was Paul's receiving news of people who had visited his Galatian mission-field and were persuading his converts there to accept a different form of teaching from that which he had given them. He refers to these people as 'trouble-makers' (ταράσσοντες, 1:7; 5:10) or 'agitators' (ἀναστατοῦντες, 5:12). According to the information reaching Paul, they were trying to impose on the Galatian Christians some requirements of the Jewish law, preeminently circumcision; there is also some word of the observance of special days, presumably those of the Jewish sacred calendar (4:10). It might have been expected that Jewish food-restrictions would also have figured in the new teaching; if so, Paul makes no reference to their doing so, although insistence on those food-restrictions by some Christians is implied in his account of Peter's withdrawal from table-fellowship with Gentiles at Antioch (2:11–14).

The new teaching is denounced by Paul as a perversion of the true gospel of Christ (1:7), and the Galatian Christians who pay heed to it are warned that to submit to it is to turn away from God (1:6), to be severed from Christ, to fall from grace (5:4). The trouble-makers are incurring a curse because they substitute a spurious message for gospel truth (1:8f.); they are exposing themselves to the certainty of divine judgment (5:10). Even if they demand only a token measure of law-keeping from the Galatians, any such demand involves acceptance of the principle of justification by works of the law. This principle is clean contrary to the gospel of justification by faith—even if it were practicable, which it is not (3:11). Persuasive as the new teaching may be, it does not come from God (5:8), as did the original message which brought salvation to the members of the Galatian churches (1:6); the two are incompatible.

It is clearly implied, moreover, that the 'trouble-makers' tried to gain credence for their teaching among Paul's converts by disparaging him and casting doubt on his apostolic credentials. In consequence, the Galatians who lent a ready ear to this teaching had a sense of estrangement from Paul, not to speak of hostility to him (4:16)—the fruit of an uneasy conscience.

Paul therefore judges it necessary in his letter to dwell at some length on the divine authority of his gospel and of his commission to preach it: he embarks on an autobiographical sketch of the first fourteen or seventeen years of his apostleship with the aim of establishing his independence in particular of the leaders of the Jerusalem church (1:11–2:10).

We do not know how precisely Paul learned of the trouble-makers' activity in Galatia—whether by letter, or by first-hand information brought by a visitor or visitors from there, or at second hand. Our only source of knowledge about their teaching is Paul's letter; if (as some have supposed, without any positive warrant) Paul himself was inadequately informed about it, we have no means of correcting or supplementing his information.[1]

What then can be said about this 'other gospel' which the Galatian Christians were disposed to embrace, or about the identity and motives of those who pressed it on them? These questions constitute what has been called 'the singular problem of the Epistle to the Galatians'.[2]

2. The early consensus

Why speak of a 'singular problem'? To many readers of the letter, from the second century onwards, the nature of the 'other gospel' has been self-evident, and the character of its proponents not greatly in doubt. The second-century Marcionite prologues to the letters of Paul[3] began with the prologue to Galatians, which runs thus:

The Galatians are Greeks.[4] They at first received the word of truth from the apostle, but after his departure they were tempted by false apostles to turn to the law and circumcision. The apostle calls them back to the true faith,[5] writing to them from Ephesus.

In this prologue the 'law' to which the Galatians were being tempted to turn was the Jewish law; this is indicated by its collocation with 'circumcision', as well as by the plain meaning of the repeated references to law in the letter itself.

The same understanding of the argument of Galatians recurs throughout the patristic literature. For example, Marius Victorinus, the earliest Latin commentator on the letter, puts it thus:

---

1. See p. 25.
2. See p. 24.
3. The original Greek text of the Marcionite prologues has been lost, but Latin translations survive in most Vulgate manuscripts (their heretical source having been forgotten). In order to be understood, they have to be read in the sequence in which Marcion arranged the Pauline letters. See D. de Bruyne, 'Prologues Bibliques d'Origine Marcionite', *RBén* 24 (1907), 1–16; A. von Harnack, 'Der marcionitische Ursprung der ältesten Vulgata-Prologe zu den Paulusbriefen', *ZNW* 24 (1925), 204–218; A. Souter, *Text and Canon of the NT* (London, ²1954), 188–191. A serious challenge to de Bruyne's thesis was presented by J. Regul, *Die antimarcionitischen Evangelienprologe* (Freiburg, 1949). But the Marcionite origin of seven of the Pauline prologues was upheld by K. T. Schäfer, 'Marius Victorinus und die marcionitischen Prologe zu den Paulusbriefen', *RBén* 80 (1970), 7–16. See further N. A. Dahl, 'The Origin of the Earliest Prologues to the Pauline Letters', *Semeia* 12 (1978), 233–277.
4. See p. 6.
5. Or 'to belief in the truth'.

The sum of the letter is as follows: the Galatians are going astray because they are adding Judaism to the gospel of faith in Christ, observing in a material sense the sabbath and circumcision, together with the other works which they received in accordance with the law. Disturbed by these tendencies Paul writes this letter, wishing to put them right and call them back from Judaism, in order that they may preserve faith in Christ alone, and receive from Christ the hope of salvation and of his promises, because no one is saved by the works of the law. So, in order to show that what they are adding is wrong, he wishes to confirm [the truth of] his gospel.[6]

In the Reformation period we find no significant change, except that the Reformers pressed an analogy between the situation with which Paul dealt and that of their own day. Luther begins his preface to the epistle thus:

The Galatians had been brought by St. Paul to right Christian belief, from the law to the gospel. But after his departure there came the false apostles, who were disciples of the true apostles, and turned the Galatians back again to believe that they must attain blessedness through the work of the law, and that they were sinning if they did not hold the work of the law, as according to Acts 15 certain highly-placed people in Jerusalem insisted.[7]

This is expanded as follows in his commentary on the epistle:

St. Paul goeth about to establish the doctrine of faith, grace, forgiveness of sins, or Christian righteousness, to the end that we may have a perfect knowledge and difference between Christian righteousness and all other kinds of righteousness. . . . For if the article of justification be lost, then is all true Christian doctrine lost. . . .

Christ [says Paul] hath mercifully called you in grace, that ye should be freemen under Christ, and not bondmen under Moses, whose disciples ye are now become again by the means of your false apostles, who by the law of Moses called you not unto grace, but unto wrath, to the hating of God, to sin and death. . . .

Hereby it may easily be gathered, that these false apostles had condemned the Gospel of Paul among the Galatians, saying: Paul indeed hath begun well, but to have begun well is not enough, for there remain yet many higher matters; like as they say in the fifteenth chapter of the Acts: It is not enough for you to believe in Christ, or to be baptized, but it behoveth also that ye be circumcised; 'for except ye be circumcised after the manner of Moses, ye cannot be saved'. This is as much to say, as that Christ is a good workman, which hath indeed begun a building, but he hath not finished it; for this must Moses do.[8]

Luther goes on to draw a parallel with the 'fantastical spirits, Anabaptists and others' of his day as well as with the 'Papists'.[9]

According to John Calvin (1548), Paul

had faithfully instructed them [the Galatians] in the pure gospel, but false apostles had entered in his absence and corrupted the true seed by false and corrupt dogmas. For they taught that the observance of ceremonies was still necessary. This might seem trivial; but Paul fights for it as a fundamental article of the Christian faith. And rightly so, for it is

---

6. C. Marius Victorinus Afer, *In Galatas*, introd. (ed. A. Locher, 1).

7. *Luthers Werke*, WA: *Die deutsche Bibel*, 7, 172f.

8. M. Luther, *A Commentary on St. Paul's Epistle to the Galatians*. A revised and completed translation [by P. S. Watson] based on the 'Middleton' edition of the English version of 1575 (London, 1953), 21, 26, 62, 63.

9. Ibid., 63ff.

no light evil to quench the brightness of the gospel, lay a snare for consciences and remove the distinction between the old and new covenants. He saw that these errors were also related to an ungodly and destructive opinion on the deserving of righteousness. . . .

The false apostles, who had deceived the Galatians to advance their own claims, pretended that they had received a commission from the apostles. Their method of infiltration was to get it believed that they represented the apostles and delivered a message from them. But they took away from Paul the name and authority of apostle. . . . In attacking Paul they were really attacking the truth of the gospel.[10]

In other words, the Galatian converts were being urged to observe ceremonies of the OT law as integral to the gospel and to accept a doctrine of justification by personal merit. Since Paul's preaching excluded all this, it must be undermined by an attempt to diminish his status in the eyes of his converts.

This understanding of the situation prevailed into the nineteenth century, when it was taken up by the Tübingen school of F. C. Baur and his associates, who integrated it into their account of primitive Christian history. 'What led the Apostle to write this Epistle to the Galatian Churches', wrote Baur, 'we learn very clearly from the Epistle itself'. The Galatians' falling away from the gospel as Paul preached it

was due to the influence of strange teachers who . . . represented to them that, as a first step to the Christian salvation, they must submit to circumcision (v. 2, 11). Here we first meet with those Judaising opponents with whom the Apostle had to maintain so severe a struggle in the churches which he founded, and they appear here quite in the harsh and uncompromising Judaistic character which marks them as opponents of Pauline Christianity. . . . In one word, they were Jews or Jewish Christians of the genuine old stamp, who could so little understand the more liberal atmosphere of Pauline Christianity that they would have thought the very ground of their existence was cut from under them if Judaism were no longer to have its absolute power and importance.[11]

In principle, according to Baur, the declared opponents of Pauline Christianity were in agreement with the leaders of the Jerusalem church; indeed, those leaders 'are themselves the opponents against whom the Apostle contends in refuting these principles'.[12] But their reluctant recognition, at the Jerusalem conference, that Paul and Barnabas had been entrusted with the gospel for the Gentiles, tied their hands and compelled them to take the position of non-belligerents. Other members of the Jerusalem church, however, were not so bound, and they were the infiltrators or trouble-makers who endeavoured to subvert Paul's teaching and apostolic authority among his Gentile converts, including the churches of Galatia.

Bishop Lightfoot sums the matter up concisely:

The Epistle to the Galatians is especially distinguished among St. Paul's letters by its unity of purpose. The Galatian apostasy in its double aspect, as a denial of his own authority and a repudiation of the doctrine of grace, is never lost sight of from beginning to end.[13]

---

10. J. Calvin, *Galatians*, ETr, 4f.
11. F. C. Baur, *Paul: his Life and Works*, ETr, I (London, 1876), 251–253; cf. his *Church History of the First Three Centuries*, ETr, I (London, 1878), 49–60.
12. Baur, *Paul*, I, 121.
13. J. B. Lightfoot, *Galatians*, 63.

This 'apostasy', as he calls it,

was a Judaism of the sharp Pharisaic type, unclouded or unrelieved by any haze of Essene mysticism, such as prevailed a few years later in the neighbouring Colossian Church.[14] The necessity of circumcision was strongly insisted upon. Great stress was laid on the observance of 'days and months and seasons and years'. In short, nothing less than submission to the whole ceremonial law seems to have been contemplated by the innovators. At all events, this was the logical consequence of the adoption of the initiatory rite.[15]

But far from accepting the Tübingen interpretation, Lightfoot regards the Epistle to the Galatians as refuting it most conclusively, 'for it shows the true relations existing between St. Paul and the Twelve'.[16] Far from agreeing in principle with the judaizing propagandists, the Jerusalem leaders agreed in principle with Paul; if Paul at Antioch charged Peter with 'play-acting'[17] when he withdrew from table-fellowship with Gentile Christians, it was precisely because Peter on this occasion was acting in a manner at variance with his real principles.

Lightfoot's account of the situation in the Galatian churches calls, in my judgment, for very little modification. But during the present century variant accounts of the situation have been put forward by highly reputable scholars, and these accounts merit serious assessment.

3. Other explanations

In 1919 Wilhelm Lütgert published a monograph with the title *Law and Spirit*[18] in which he argued that in the Galatian situation Paul had to wage war on two fronts simultaneously. Not only had he to deal with the attempt to impose on his converts circumcision and other obligations of the Jewish law; he had also to deal with radicals of the opposite stripe to the Judaizers, with those who wished to sever the gospel from its OT roots and who held that the new life in the Spirit gave them the entrée into a realm of knowledge which dismissed the 'things of the flesh' as irrelevant and had little regard for those ethical distinctions on which Paul—inconsistently, to their way of thinking—insisted. It was against these people, said Lütgert, and not against the Judaizers, that Paul had to defend his claim to apostolic authority in independence of Jerusalem. By their standards, any one who was dependent on Jerusalem was insufficiently emancipated from the old order of Judaism; hence Paul's emphatic assertion that he had received his commission and his message from no human source—least of all from the Jerusalem 'pillars'—but by direct revelation from the exalted Lord. These were the people, too, who needed the warning not to turn their Christian freedom into licence (5:13); the Judaizers, on the contrary, had to be warned not to exchange their freedom for the 'yoke of slavery' (5:1).

---

14. Cf. J. B. Lightfoot, *Colossians and Philemon*, 73ff., 349ff.
15. Lightfoot, *Galatians*, 27.
16. Ibid., 68.
17. Gal. 2:13.
18. W. Lütgert, *Gesetz und Geist: eine Untersuchung zur Vorgeschichte des Galaterbriefes* (Gütersloh, 1919).

Lütgert's thesis was elaborated (with modifications) ten years later by James Hardy Ropes, in his monograph entitled *The Singular Problem of the Epistle to the Galatians*.[19] Ropes attempted, by means of a short commentary on Galatians included in his monograph, to show that this thesis illuminated each successive section of the epistle. In Gal. 3:6–29, for example, the radicals who wished to forget the OT antecedents of the gospel had to be reminded that, Gentiles as they were, they were children of Abraham by faith in Christ—children of Abraham in the sense that mattered most.

Ropes also argued that the Galatian Judaizers need not have been influenced by intruding visitors from Judaea; 'all that we need suppose is that certain gentile Christians had proved susceptible to the efforts of local synagogue Jews, and had tried to persuade the churches as a whole to accept Jewish rites, including circumcision'.[20]

In an article published in 1945 F. R. Crownfield undertook to do justice both to the arguments of Lütgert and Ropes and to those pointing to the traditional identification of the trouble-makers as straightforward Judaizers by representing the trouble-makers as syncretistic Jews, for whom legalism was a means to the end of higher enlightenment.[21]

Johannes Munck, Professor of New Testament in Aarhus, Denmark, propounded a novel line in the interpretation of our epistle when in 1954 he maintained that the Judaizers in the churches of Galatia were not Jewish Christians, not visitors from Judaea, not local synagogue Jews, but Gentile Christians, Paul's own converts.[22] All that they knew about Jewish Christianity and the Jerusalem church they knew from Paul. 'His words about Jerusalem and the Judaean churches were full of sympathy and understanding'.[23] Knowing that the Jerusalem Christians were circumcised and kept many of the ordinances observed by the Jews among whom they lived, some of Paul's converts concluded that he had only half-evangelized them and that they should conform to Jerusalem practice. Moreover, Paul taught his converts to use the Greek version of the Hebrew scriptures as their Bible.[24] While he was with them he showed them how those scriptures spoke of the salvation of the Gentiles, but when he had left them they read in those same scriptures much that spoke of Abraham and his posterity as the recipients of God's blessing, much that spoke of the glory of Israel and the subjection of the Gentiles, much that spoke of the keeping of the law as a condition of enjoying divine approval. Was it strange, then, that they should draw those practical conclusions which so horrified Paul when he heard of them?

But there are several indications throughout the letter that the trouble-makers in the Galatian churches were incomers, not some of Paul's Gentile converts. He refers to them throughout in the third person, while he addresses his converts

---

19. J. H. Ropes, *The Singular Problem of the Epistle to the Galatians*. Harvard Theological Studies, 14 (Cambridge, Mass., 1929).

20. *Singular Problem*, 45.

21. F. R. Crownfield, 'The Singular Problem of the Dual Galatians', *JBL* 64 (1945), 491–500.

22. J. Munck, *Paulus und die Heilsgeschichte* (Copenhagen, 1954), 79ff.; ETr, *Paul and the Salvation of Mankind* (London, 1959), 87ff.

23. Munck, *Paul and the Salvation of Mankind*, 131.

24. Ibid., 132.

in the second person. In his letters to the Corinthians offenders within the church of Corinth are rebuked in the second person, while interlopers from elsewhere are denounced in the third person. So we may conclude that it is outsiders whom Paul has in view when he says to the Galatian Christians. 'The persons I have referred to are paying court to you, but not with honest intentions: what they really want is to bar the door to you so that you may pay court to them' (4:17, NEB margin).

Walter Schmithals, in an article published in 1956,[25] put forward a simpler account than that of Lütgert and Ropes: Paul was not waging a war on two fronts; the sole target of his attack was a body of Jewish Christian Gnostics such as Schmithals had already identified with the target of Paul's attack in the Corinthian correspondence.[26] But Gnosticism has really to be read into the teaching of these people as reflected in Paul's attack on them before it can be read out of it.[27] And it is begging the question to argue, as Willi Marxsen does, that this is due to Paul's own failure to understand properly what they were teaching[28] (he heard that they were teaching circumcision and assumed too hastily that they were straightforward Judaizers, whereas they were in fact 'introducing something new—a Christian-Jewish-Gnostic syncretism'):[29] if we cannot determine the nature of their teaching from Paul's refutation of it, we have no other evidence to guide us.

There is nothing improbable *per se* in Paul's having to defend the gospel on two fronts at once; he certainly had to do so at Corinth.[30] But there is no substantial evidence of his having to do so in the churches of Galatia. No doubt he realized the necessity of warning his converts there, as elsewhere, against misinterpreting his message of liberty in an antinomian sense: they must not turn their freedom into licence to indulge in the 'works of the flesh', but rather live in mutual love, the first 'fruit of the Spirit' (5:13f., 22). But while he reminds them that those who manifest the works of the flesh 'will never inherit the kingdom of God' (5:21), this is not the main thrust of his letter. The 'work of the flesh' which posed the most deadly threat in the churches of Galatia appears to have been a quarrelsome spirit; hence Paul's warning in 5:15: 'But if you go on fighting one another tooth and nail, all you can expect is mutual annihilation'. The course which he recommends to them is a larger measure of that faith which is 'active in love' and in that love to 'be servants to one another' (5:6, 13).

4. Against whom does Paul defend himself?

Paul's insistence on his independence of Jerusalem is quite intelligible as part of his argument against Judaizers whose main appeal was to the Jerusalem

---

25. W. Schmithals, 'Die Häretiker in Galatien', *ZNW* 47 (1956), 25–67, reprinted (in revised form) in his *Paulus und die Gnostiker* (Hamburg-Bergstedt, 1965), 9–46; ETr, *Paul and the Gnostics* (Nashville/New York, 1972), 13–64.

26. Schmithals, *Die Gnosis in Korinth* (Göttingen, 1956, ²1965); ETr, *Gnosticism in Corinth* (Nashville/New York, 1917).

27. Cf. R. McL. Wilson, 'Gnostics—in Galatia?', *SE* 4 = TU 102 (Berlin, 1968), 358ff.

28. W. Marxsen, *INT*, 55, 58.

29. Ibid., 56.

30. Cf. H. Chadwick, 'All Things to all Men", *NTS* 1 (1954–55), 261–275.

leaders. These Judaizers argued: 'The Jerusalem leaders are the only persons with authority to say what the true gospel is, and this authority they received direct from Christ. Paul has no comparable authority: any commission he exercises was derived by him from the Jerusalem leaders, and if he differs from them on the content or implications of the gospel, he is acting and teaching quite arbitrarily. In fact', they may have added, 'Paul went up to Jerusalem shortly after his conversion and spent some time with the apostles there. They instructed him in the first principles of the gospel and, seeing that he was a man of uncommon intellect, magnanimously wiped out from their minds his record as a persecutor and authorized him to preach to others the gospel which he had learned from them. But when he left Jerusalem for Syria and Cilicia he began to adapt the gospel to make it palatable to Gentiles. The Jerusalem leaders practised circumcision and observed the law and the customs, but Paul struck out on a line of his own, omitting circumcision and other ancient observances from the message he preached, and thus he betrayed his ancestral heritage. This law-free gospel has no authority but his own; he certainly did not receive it from the apostles, who disapproved of his course of action. Their disapproval was publicly shown on one occasion at Antioch, when there was a direct confrontation between Peter and him on the necessity of maintaining the Jewish food-laws.'

To this Paul replies: 'At no time did I derive any commission from the Jerusalem leaders. My call to apostleship and the gospel I proclaim were alike received by me "through a revelation of Jesus Christ" (1:12). My apostleship was to be discharged among the Gentiles; the gospel which I received by revelation was to be preached among the Gentiles, and the Jerusalem leaders recognized this when they "acknowledged that I had been entrusted with the gospel for Gentiles as surely as Peter had been entrusted with the gospel for Jews; for God, whose action made Peter an apostle to the Jews, also made me an apostle to the Gentiles" (2:7f.). If it is a question of defining the content or the implications of the gospel so far as it affects Gentiles, I speak with authority—not I indeed, but the Lord, who called and commissioned me. As for the confrontation with Cephas (Peter) at Antioch, that came about because Peter, under pressure from visitors from Judaea, went back on his established practice of eating at the same table as uncircumcised Gentile Christians. This action of his was a virtual denial of the gospel which both he and I preached—the gospel which made no distinction between believers in Christ, whether they were Jews or Gentiles' (2:11–14).

Paul, indeed, did not differ from the Jerusalem leaders with regard to the essential content of the gospel: it was based on the facts of Christ's death, burial and resurrection, and these were proclaimed equally by both sides (cf. 1 Cor. 15:11). But there might well be differences of opinion with regard to the practical implications of the gospel in the lives of Gentile believers, and in this sphere Paul, commissioned by Christ to be the Gentiles' apostle, would brook no interference from those whose apostolate was to the Jews, and still less from people who claimed to speak in their name.

But what of his words in Gal. 5:11: 'And I, my friends, if I am still advocating circumcision, why is it I am still persecuted'? What was the point of charging Paul with advocating circumcision, and what was meant by this charge? The point of the charge was probably this: 'Don't listen to Paul when he says you must not be circumcised; he preaches circumcision himself'. This was contrary to the Galatians' experience of Paul's preaching, but if (as was suggested) Paul was a trimmer, adapting his preaching to his environment, then plainly he need not be taken too seriously. That this sort of thing was actually suggested may be implied in Paul's indignant words in 1:10: 'Does my language now sound as if I were canvassing for men's support? . . . Do you think I am currying favour with men? If I still sought men's favour, I should be no servant of Christ'.[31]

But what was meant by the charge that Paul himself advocated circumcision? Was there anything in his teaching or action that lent it colour? We can well imagine how readily such an action as his circumcision of Timothy[32] could be appealed to in this way; but perhaps all that was meant was that, true to his policy of living like a Jew among Jews, he did not discountenance the practice of circumcision among *Jewish* Christians. There is a relevant passage in Acts 21:21, where Paul, on his last visit to Jerusalem, is told by the elders of the mother-church that rumours have reached Jerusalem 'that you teach all the Jews in the gentile world to turn their backs on Moses, telling them to give up circumcising their children and following our way of life'. The elders make it plain that they know these rumours to be unfounded, and the narrative goes on to represent Paul as acquiescing in their suggestion that he should give a public demonstration that they were unfounded. There is no need to regard this as an example of Luke's policy of making the gulf between Paul and the Jerusalem church less unbridgeable than, according to the Tübingen tradition, it actually was; there is nothing in Paul's letters which contradicts the picture given of him in Acts 21. Even in Galatians, his most uncompromising deliverance on this subject, his concern is solely with the imposing of circumcision on Gentile Christians; whether Jewish Christians continued to circumcise their children or not was probably a matter of small importance in his eyes, on a par with their continued observance or non-observance of the sabbath and the levitical food-laws, so long as it was not made a ground of justification before God.

5. The circumcision question

The most certain feature of the false gospel was its insistence on circumcision. In itself circumcision was neither here nor there so far as Paul was concerned: he says so twice in this very letter (5:6; 6:15). What disturbed him was the enforcement or acceptance of circumcision as a legal obligation, as though it were essential to salvation or to membership in the community of the people of God. There is nothing inconsistent with Paul's principles in his circumcision of Timothy, as a matter of expediency, according to the record of

---

31. Cf. H. Chadwick, 'All Things to all Men', 261f.
32. Or of Titus, if this is indeed implied in Gal. 2:3—but see pp. 111ff.

Acts 16:3[33]—although it is easy to appreciate how this action could have been misrepresented or misunderstood. But in the situation which obtained in the churches of Galatia it was a very different matter: 'Mark my words: I, Paul, say to you that if you receive circumcision Christ will do you no good at all. Once again, you can take it from me that every man who receives circumcision is under obligation to keep the entire law' (Gal. 5:2f.). If circumcision was accepted because it was required by the law of Israel, it was impossible to stop there: every part of that law was of equal obligation. But none of those who were disposed to accept circumcision as a legal obligation, nor any of those who pressed them to do so, contemplated keeping the *whole* law: as for the latter, says Paul, 'they only want you to be circumcised in order to boast of your having submitted to that outward rite' (6:13). Any one who admitted the principle of salvation by keeping the law and did not take seriously the consequent obligation to keep it in its entirety would incur the doom invoked by the law itself: 'A curse is on all who do not persevere in doing everything that is written in the book of the law' (3:10, quoting Dt. 27:26). When that curse had been incurred, the only way to be delivered from it was through the redemptive death of Christ: 'Christ bought us freedom from the curse of the law by becoming for our sake an accursed thing; for Scripture says, "A curse is on everyone who is hanged on a gibbet". And the purpose of it all was that the blessing of Abraham should in Christ Jesus be extended to the Gentiles, so that we might receive the promised Spirit through faith' (3:13f., quoting Dt. 21:23). It was preposterous for those who had experienced this deliverance to expose themselves to the sanctions of the law all over again by acknowledging a token obligation to keep it—just as preposterous as it would be for people set free from the yoke of slavery to place their necks voluntarily and deliberately under that yoke anew. The gospel of salvation by grace and the doctrine of salvation by law-keeping were mutually exclusive: to accept the latter was to renounce the former. 'When you seek to be justified by way of law, your relation with Christ is completely severed: you have fallen out of the dominion of God's grace' (5:4).

It is not certain that in all schools of Jewish thought at this time circumcision was insisted on as a *sine qua non* for admission into the commonwealth of Israel. Philo seems to know of those who argued that, provided the spiritual significance of circumcision was maintained, it was permissible to dispense with the external rite; and he opposes them: 'let us not abolish the law of circumcision on the ground that circumcision signifies the cutting away of pleasure and passions of every sort and the destruction of ungodly conceit'.[34] About AD 40 Ananias, the Jewish instructor of King Izates of Adiabene, assured him that he could worship God according to the Jewish law without being circumcised; but later, when Izates was persuaded by another Jew, Eleazar by name, that he could not hope

---

33. Timothy's circumcision is recorded quite incidentally; there is no further reference to it, and it betrays no 'tendency' on Luke's part. As the son of a Jewish mother, who had been brought up by her in the Jewish faith, he was a Jew in everything but circumcision, which had not been performed because his (late) father was a Greek, as the local Jews knew. Presumably Paul judged it advisable to make him a thorough-going Jewish Christian, but the precise point of the phrase 'out of consideration for the Jews who lived in those parts' is somewhat obscure. See A. E. Harvey, *The New English Bible: Companion to the New Testament* (Oxford and Cambridge, 1970), 459.

34. Philo, *Migr. Abr.* 92.

to be a true proselyte and win divine approval without circumcision, he submitted to the rite.[35] In debates with the school of Shammai, some members of the school of Hillel maintained that, for Gentiles to become proselytes of Judaism, the initiatory baptism was sufficient apart from circumcision[36]—but this is more likely to have been a position defended in debate than a matter of practice. Those Gentiles who went all the way in the direction of Judaism but stopped short of circumcision were treated as God-fearers, still outside the Jewish fellowship, and not admitted as proselytes to membership within it.[37]

Paul's line was not that of those Hillelites who argued that circumcision was not essential to a Gentile's becoming a Jew, if he underwent proselyte baptism. He was not concerned to make Gentiles into Jews, but to introduce Jews and Gentiles alike into a new community through faith in Jesus as Lord. In this new community circumcision was irrelevant, and any attempt to treat it as essential was inadmissible. Circumcision, with many other features of the law of Israel—food-restrictions, sacred seasons, and the like—had traditionally kept Jews and Gentiles apart; such things had no place in the 'new creation' (6:15) where there was 'no such thing as Jew and Greek' (3:28). Any attempt to impose them was to put the clock back to the time before the coming of Christ.

6. The 'elements' of the world

Together with circumcision, the Galatians were observing special 'days and months and seasons and years' (4:10). And what was wrong with that? In itself, nothing. To Paul, the observance or non-observance of a sacred calendar was religiously indifferent, just as circumcision was. 'This man regards one day more highly than another, while that man regards all days alike. On such a point everyone should have reached conviction in his own mind' (Rom. 14:5). According to the record of Acts, Paul regulated his own movements in some measure according to the Jewish calendar, especially in arranging his visits to Jerusalem,[38] and this was in complete accord with his settled policy, as set out in 1 Cor. 9:19ff., to conform to Jewish ways in Jewish company and to Gentile ways in Gentile company, so as to commend the gospel to Jews and Gentiles alike. But to observe sacred occasions as a matter of religious obligation, as though this were of the essence of gospel faith and church membership, was a retrograde step, back from liberty to bondage; it was, in fact, a token of submission to the 'elements (or elemental forces) of the world' (Gal. 4:3, 9).

Whatever dictated Paul's choice of the word 'elements' ($\sigma\tau\omega\iota\chi\epsilon\tilde{\iota}\alpha$) in this context (see pp. 193f.), it is plain that the observance of the Jewish law is here interpreted as submission to them (pp. 203ff.). 'During our minority', says Paul, 'we were slaves to the *stoicheia* of the universe' (4:3). If the Galatians accept

---

35. Josephus, *Ant*. 20.34ff.

36. b. Yᵉḇāmôṯ 46a *(baraita)*.

37. Like Cornelius of Caesarea, who, despite his piety (Acts 10:2ff., 22), was still classed as an uncircumcised Gentile, with whom no observant Jew could have table-fellowship (Acts 10:28; 11:3).

38. Cf. Acts 18:21 (Western text); 20:16 (cf. 27:9); also 1 Cor. 16:8.

the Jewish law as a religious obligation, they will be subject to this slavery, but curiously, although the Galatians are Gentiles, Paul says they will *revert* to this slavery. 'Formerly, when you did not acknowledge God, you were the slaves of beings which in their nature are no gods'.[39] But now that you do acknowledge God—or rather, now that he has acknowledged you—how can you turn back to the mean and beggarly *stoicheia*? Why do you propose to enter their service all over again?' (4:8f.). Is Paul equating his own former Judaism and their former paganism as both alike consisting in the service of the *stoicheia*? Plainly he is.

It is immediately after these words that he reproaches them for keeping special 'days and months and seasons and years'. Three of these four terms appear in the Greek version of Gn. 1:14, where it is recorded that the heavenly luminaries were appointed 'for signs and for seasons and for days and years'.

Among the objects of pagan worship the deities who shared their names with the planets were particularly prominent. In the faith of Israel such deities were included among the $b^e n\hat{e}$ $^{'e}l\bar{o}h\hat{i}m$, members of the heavenly court of God Most High.[40] The Jews did not worship those beings as the Gentiles did. If, in the age before Christ, they regulated their religious life by ordinances imposed through the agency of these beings, that was in keeping with the stage of spiritual infancy through which they were then passing. But for believers who had been emancipated by Christ and attained their spiritual majority through faith in him to revert to such ordinances was little short of apostasy and scarcely to be distinguished from relapsing into pagan worship.

It was in the light of the gospel that these *stoicheia* were 'mean and beggarly': Christ had exposed their bankruptcy. For those who did not live in the good of Christian freedom the *stoicheia* were 'principalities and powers', keeping the souls of men in bondage.[41] Their overthrow by Christ on the cross is depicted in the Epistle to the Colossians, the only other writing in the Pauline corpus where the *stoicheia* figure—and figure in much the same way as they do in Galatians (although the 'heresy' which Paul combats in Colossians is apparently a more complex form of syncretism than the 'other' gospel which he denounces in Galatians).[42]

According to Paul, pagan worship was always culpable because it involved idolatry and the vices which followed from idolatry;[43] Jewish worship in the pre-Christian stage of God's dealings with men was far from being culpable—it was divinely instituted—but it had the character of infancy and immaturity as compared with the coming of age into which men were introduced by faith in Christ. Just as a minor required the direction of tutors, guardians or slave-attendants, so the people of God in the days of their minority were under the control of the *stoicheia*. But for believers in Christ to put themselves under the control of these *stoicheia* afresh was not just reverting to infancy; it was tantamount to a declaration that the death of Jesus had no redemptive power: 'I will not nullify the

---

39. An echo of Dt. 32:17 (cf. 1 Cor. 10:20).
40. Cf. Dt. 32:8 (reading 'sons of God' rather than MT 'sons of Israel').
41. Cf. G. B. Caird, *Principalities and Powers* (Oxford, 1956); H. Schlier, *Principalities and Powers in the New Testament*, ETr (Freiburg, 1961).
42. Col. 2:15.
43. Cf. Rom. 1:18ff.

grace of God; if righteousness comes by law, then Christ died for nothing' (Gal. 2:21). Paul could hardly have expressed himself with greater urgency or severity had his converts been on the point of relapsing into paganism. We may compare the attitude of the writer to the Hebrews towards another group that was in danger of giving up its distinctive Christian standing and merging in its former Jewish environment: this, he warns, would be downright apostasy, desertion from the living God (Heb. 3:12).

7. The preferred solution

The simplest interpretation of Galatians, on the basis of its internal evidence, agrees remarkably with the statement in Acts 15:1 that, some time after the extension of the gospel to Asia Minor, 'fierce dissension and controversy' arose in the church of Syrian Antioch because 'certain persons who had come down from Judaea began to teach the brotherhood that those who were not circumcised in accordance with Mosaic practice could not be saved'. If such persons also visited Antioch's daughter-churches in Galatia with this same teaching, and found some acceptance for it there, the stage would be set for the Epistle to the Galatians—whether such a visit was paid about the same time or later.

While the 'trouble-makers' were no doubt moved by religious zeal, there are hints of another kind of motivation. Paul charges them with the aim of avoiding persecution 'for the cross of Christ' (6:12). Moreover, he implies that if he himself preached circumcision (as some alleged he still did), he would not be persecuted as he was. So far as Paul was concerned, his public proclamation of the law-free gospel must have given offence to Jewish communities wherever he went; but necessity was laid upon him—he had no option but to preach the gospel, the law-free gospel (1 Cor. 9:16). But why should the trouble-makers be so anxious to avoid persecution? Could they not have avoided it by staying at home and minding their own business?

An illuminating suggestion was made by Robert Jewett in an article published in 1971.[44] There was a resurgence of 'zealot' activity in Judaea under the governors Tiberius Julius Alexander (c. AD 46–48), who crucified two insurgent leaders, sons of Judas the Galilaean (Jos., Ant. 20.102), and his successor Ventidius Cumanus (c. 48–52), during whose period of office disorders increased (Ant. 20.105–136; War 2.223–246). Zealot vengeance was liable to be visited on Jews who fraternized with Gentiles, and Jewish Christians who shared table-fellowship with their Gentile brethren were exposed to such reprisals. If Gentile Christians could be persuaded to accept circumcision, this (it was hoped) would protect Jewish Christians against zealot vengeance. The persuasion would be more effective if Gentile believers were assured that circumcision was a condition required by God from all men who wished to be accepted by him.[45]

This, then, could have been a further motive for those people who visited

---

44. R. Jewett, 'The Agitators and the Galatian Congregation', NTS 17 (1970–71), 198–212.
45. Cf. M. Hengel, Die Zeloten (Leiden, 1961), 201–204.

the churches of Galatia and tried to persuade Paul's Gentile converts there that unless they received circumcision and other customs of Jewish religion they could not hope to win recognition from the church of Jerusalem and other fellow-believers of Jewish birth—that in their eyes they would have at most the status which Gentile God-fearers had in the eyes of the synagogue. The 'full' gospel included circumcision as an indispensable requirement; the gospel which they had received from Paul was a truncated gospel. To which Paul replied that such a 'full' gospel, denying as it did the all-sufficiency of Christ, was no gospel at all, and in so far as it involved a reversion to legal bondage it undercut the message of justification by faith, disallowed the claim that Jesus by his death and resurrection had inaugurated the messianic age which superseded the age of law and thus in effect disallowed his title to be the Messiah. Far from being a gospel in any sense, such teaching was plain apostasy from Christ. Hence, no matter who its propagator might be, *anathema estō*.

IV
THE TRUTH
OF THE GOSPEL

1. Galatians and the primitive message

The letter includes in its opening salutation words which are commonly recognized as drawn from an early Christian confession of faith, which Paul did not formulate although he subscribed to it. The Pauline greeting, 'Grace to you and peace from God our Father and the Lord Jesus Christ', is followed by a construction with article and participle (equivalent to an adjective clause) in which Christ is described as the one 'who gave himself for our sins, that he might deliver us from the present evil age, according to the will of our God and Father, to whom be the glory for ever and ever. Amen' (Gal. 1:4f.). Two pieces of common and primitive Christian belief find expression here: (a) that Christ 'gave himself for our sins'—with which we may compare 1 Cor. 15:3, 'Christ died for our sins', or Rom. 4:25, 'who was delivered up for our trespasses'—and (b) that the purpose of his so doing was our deliverance 'from the present evil age'. This presents the Christian reinterpretation of the current Jewish doctrine of the two ages, the transition between the present age (the epoch of wickedness, as it is called in the Qumran texts) and the age to come (the age of new life and righteousness) being marked by the Christ-event—historically in his death and resurrection and existentially in the experience of his people when by faith they enter into union with him.[1] To these two items should be added one that appears earlier in the salutation, where 'God the Father' is qualified by the participial phrase 'who raised him [i.e. Jesus] from the dead' (Gal. 1:1), a phrase recurring throughout the NT epistles, as in Rom. 4:24; 8:11; 10:9; 2 Cor. 4:14; 1 Pet. 1:21.

Further extracts from the common stock of primitive Christianity appear in Gal. 4:4, 'When the time had fully come, God sent forth his Son, born of woman'—possibly with the further phrase 'born under law', but the following words, 'to redeem those that were under law, that we might receive adoption as sons' (Gal. 4:5), are characteristically Pauline. Yet when Paul goes on to link

---

1. Cf. 2 Cor. 5:17.

this adoption of believers into the family of God with their receiving from God 'the Spirit of his Son', he adduces as a demonstration of this their invocation of God as 'Abba! Father!' (Gal. 4:6). From the earliest times, it appears, Greek-speaking Christians took over from the Aramaic-speaking church the word *Abba* which Jesus had used in addressing God or speaking about him (cf. Mk. 14:36), adding to it the Greek equivalent ὁ πατήρ (cf. Rom. 8:15).[2] Thus Paul weaves his distinctive teaching around a core of primitive usage.

The same is true of the death of Christ, which evidently played a central part in the message first brought to the Galatians, 'before whose eyes Jesus Christ was publicly portrayed as crucified' (Gal. 3:1). Paul's elaboration of the doctrine of Christ's passion is seen in his argument in Gal. 3:10–14 that, by enduring the form of death upon which the divine curse had been pronounced in the law (Dt. 21:23), Christ had redeemed his people from the curse which the law pronounced on those who failed to keep it perfectly (Dt. 27:26).[3] A further Pauline insight into the significance of the cross of Christ appears in Gal. 6:14 where, playing on a double meaning of the verb σταυρόω, he says that it constitutes a fence separating him from the *kosmos*.

Baptism was the common sign of initiation into the Christian fellowship; in addition to its primitive association with repentance, cleansing and the remission of sins, Paul views it as the token of incorporation into Christ: 'as many of you as were baptized into Christ have put on Christ' (Gal. 3:27).[4] Through membership in Christ, who is Abraham's offspring, they too—even Gentiles—become Abraham's offspring and heirs of the promises made to the patriarch by God (Gal. 3:29).

The reception of the Spirit in the Galatian churches, as elsewhere in the early apostolic age,[5] was attended by mighty works (Gal. 3:5), but Paul elaborates the doctrine of the Spirit along lines of his own, contrasting life under the Spirit's leadership with life under law in terms of freedom as opposed to bondage (Gal. 5:1, 18).

Most of the OT *testimonia* quoted in Galatians are characteristically Pauline, and some are peculiar to this letter. We shall be cautious, therefore, in assigning them to the common stock of primitive Christian *testimonia*. C. H. Dodd suggests that two of them may be so assigned: *(a)* the conflation of Gn. 12:3 and 22:18 in Gal. 3:8, 'in you shall all the nations be blessed' (cf. Acts 3:25 for a different conflation of the same two texts),[6] and *(b)* the statement of Hab. 2:4, quoted in Gal. 3:11 (as in Rom. 1:17) in the sense, 'he who is righteous (justified) by faith will come to life', which (in the light of its different usage in

---

2. Cf. A. M. Hunter, *Paul and his Predecessors* (London, [2]1961), 50, where Paul's acquaintance with the Lord's Prayer is suggested; see also J. A. T. Robinson's comments on Christian baptism, adoption and the reception of the Spirit as reflecting 'the association at the baptism of Jesus of the gift of the Spirit with the declaration of Sonship' ('The One Baptism as a Category of New Testament Soteriology', *SJT* 6 [1953], 262).

3. See pp. 157ff.

4. Cf. Rom. 6:3ff.

5. Cf. Acts 2:43 *et passim*; Heb. 2:4.

6. C. H. Dodd, *According to the Scriptures* (London, 1952), 43f.

Heb. 10:38) he thinks may have been a *testimonium* to the coming of Christ even before Galatians was written.[7] I should mention two more.

In Gal. 3:13 Paul, as we have seen,[8] quotes Dt. 21:23 (LXX), 'cursed is everyone who is hanged on a tree' (κρεμάμενος ἐπὶ ξύλου) and expounds it along with Dt. 27:26 by means of the rabbinical device of *gezerah shawah*.[9] But it appears that Dt. 21:23 had already been applied to the crucifixion of Christ, if we consider the use of the phrase 'hanging him on a tree' (κρεμάσαντες ἐπὶ ξύλου) in two speeches in Acts (5:30; 10:39) which there is no reason to regard as free Lukan compositions, since each is a summary of primitive kerygmatic motifs.[10] Quite early Jesus' followers came to terms with the fact that their Master died the death on which the law pronounced a curse, although Paul, *more suo*, relates the fact to Jesus' satisfaction and abrogation of the Torah.

Again, the application of Is. 54:1 in Gal. 4:27, where the 'barren one' is interpreted of the Gentile church by contrast with the married woman, here understood as 'the present Jerusalem', might well be regarded as original to Paul.[11] But at least it is taken from one of the most fertile fields of *testimonia*, Is. 40–66, which appears to have been given an extensive Christian interpretation at an early date. If Is. 54:1 had already received a Christian interpretation, Paul certainly adapts it to his current argument; one may wonder if this text suggested to him his allegorical exegesis of the Genesis story of Hagar and Sarah, with their respective sons, rather than *vice versa*.

Be that as it may. If we try to summarize the primitive Christian message, proclaimed by Paul and his predecessors alike, as it is presupposed in the letter to the Galatians, the result might be somewhat as follows:

Jesus our Lord, the Son of God, was sent into the world by his Father when the due time came. He was born into the family of Abraham[12] and lived under the Jewish law. He was crucified by his enemies, but in his death he gave himself for his people's sins. God raised him from the dead, to be the Saviour of all who believe in him; he has sent his Spirit into their hearts, enabling them to call God 'Father' as Jesus did, to exhibit his love in their lives and to look forward confidently to the realization of their hope.

2. The standard of judgment

When Paul charges his Galatian converts with turning away so quickly to follow 'a different gospel' which could not properly be called a gospel at all, and anathematizes all who preach any other gospel than that which those converts had received from him (Gal. 1:6–9), was there (we may ask) any objective

---

7. *According to the Scriptures*, 50f.

8. See p. 34.

9. See p. 165 below.

10. Cf. Acts 13:29; 1 Pet. 2:24.

11. The attempt by V. Burch in J. R. Harris, *Testimonies*, II (Cambridge, 1920), 32ff., to ascribe this use of Is. 54:1 to a pre-Pauline 'testimony' collection, is based on too ready an assumption of the primitiveness of the Cyprianic *Testimonia aduersus Iudaeos*; Cyprian's citation of Is. 54:1 in *Testimonia* 1.20 is much more likely to be dependent on Gal. 4:27. See pp. 222f. below.

12. The primitive message also proclaimed him as Son of David but, although Paul was aware of this (cf. Rom. 1:3; 15:12), it naturally played no significant part in his Gentile mission.

standard by which judgment could be pronounced between his gospel and the 'different gospel'? Can we be as sure as he was that his version was genuine and the other spurious? Certainly, with the benefit of hindsight we can agree that, if Christianity was to become a universal faith, a version like Paul's was more likely to achieve this end than that of his opponents; but how did the situation look when the letter to the Galatians was written? Was there any general consensus regarding the 'authentic' gospel in reference to which other self-styled 'gospels' might be exposed as false?

We can appreciate how slender Paul's case for the gospel he preached must have appeared if he was the only one who preached it. Paul was a latecomer to the Christian faith, as every one knew. He had not been a companion of Jesus on earth as the original apostles had been; and when he first made contact with the followers of Jesus it was as a persecutor, not as a champion. What reason was there to accept such a man's interpretation of the message of Jesus in preference to that of others?

Paul finds it necessary to answer this question, and the necessity of doing so places him in a delicate situation. He wants to maintain that the leaders of the Jerusalem church recognize the authenticity of the gospel which he preaches; he wants (perhaps even more) to maintain his personal independence of the authority of the Jerusalem leaders. Accordingly, he asserts his independence of their authority before he (after a fashion) appeals to their authority. 'In my early zeal for the ancestral traditions of Judaism', he says (if his words may be summarized), 'I devastated[13] the church, until God (who had designated me from birth for my apostolic service) revealed his Son in me so that I might be his herald among the Gentiles.[14] I embarked on this ministry at once, without consulting either the Jerusalem apostles or anyone else. Not until three years had elapsed did I go to Jerusalem to visit Cephas; the only other apostle I met was James, the Lord's brother. That was all the contact I had with Jerusalem in my early Christian days; after two weeks there I went off into Syria and Cilicia to preach the faith I had once endeavoured to overthrow. Not until fourteen years had elapsed did I go up to Jerusalem again' (Gal. 1:13–2:1a). This narrative is designed to support his claim that he derived the gospel which he preached from no human intermediary but by the revelation of Jesus Christ granted him at Damascus.

Then comes the account of the conference held in Jerusalem between Paul and Barnabas on the one hand and the Jerusalem leaders on the other (Gal. 2:1–10).[15] Paul is still careful to maintain his independence—'those men of repute', he says, 'added nothing to me (Gal. 2:6), whether in relation to the content of the gospel or the authority to preach it; but they acknowledged the genuineness of the gospel which I was already preaching.' This acknowledgement on their part is implied in his statement that he 'laid before them' the gospel which he preached among the Gentiles (2:2). Far from criticizing it or finding it defective, they agreed that, as they themselves had been commissioned to carry the gospel to the Jews, Paul and Barnabas had been commissioned to carry

---

13. See pp. 90f.
14. See p. 92.
15. See pp. 106ff. below.

it to the Gentiles.[16] Two separate constituencies are distinguished, but there is no suggestion that there were two distinct versions of the gospel for the respective constituencies. In the light of Paul's solemn imprecations in Gal. 1:8f., it is evident that he would have dismissed the possibility of such a thing as preposterous.[17] No doubt the approach and emphasis would differ: a considerable body of background knowledge could be assumed in Jewish audiences which pagan audiences lacked. Without prejudging the nature of the sermons in Acts, we can see that Luke takes this for granted: Paul's address in the synagogue of Pisidian Antioch (Acts 13:16–41) presupposes familiarity with a long stretch of sacred history which would have been unintelligible had it been introduced into his Areopagitica at Athens (17:22–31). Again, the circumcision issue did not arise in the mission to Jews, who were circumcised already. It is conceivable that, when Paul and Barnabas shook hands with the Jerusalem leaders on the demarcation of their respective spheres of activity, too much was taken for granted on both sides, and trouble arose when those unventilated questions came into the open. Paul assumed that Cephas saw eye to eye with him on the status of Gentiles in the church, and indeed his assumption was not unfounded if Cephas, on his first coming to Antioch, practised table-fellowship with Gentiles as Paul assures us he did. All the greater was Paul's sense of disillusionment when Cephas withdrew from this table-fellowship at the instance of one or more who 'came from James' (Gal. 2:12) and when subsequent attempts were made by people claiming authorization from Jerusalem to intervene in Paul's mission-field. But worse still in his eyes was the urging of circumcision on his Gentile converts as a religious obligation apart from which they could not become genuine children of Abraham and be admitted into the true covenant-community.

Those who urged circumcision on the churches of Galatia no doubt felt quite sincerely that if this practice went by default, even for Gentile believers, the continuity of the history of salvation was interrupted. If the Jerusalem leaders were disposed to waive the circumcision requirement, that simply stamped them as compromisers. As for Paul, who refused to have his Gentile converts circumcised, it was he who was the heretic and they themselves who were orthodox, for they remained faithful to the terms of the unchangeable covenant, which Paul repudiated. One may say, with Otto Kuss, that 'faithfulness in matters of factual detail need not amount to faithfulness in regard to the genuine content of the message'; but this simply brings us back to the question of how the genuine content of the message was to be ascertained.[18]

That salvation was to be found in Jesus Christ was a proposition to which

---

16. Cf. Acts 13:47, where Paul and Barnabas base their commission on Yahweh's words to his Servant in Is. 49:6.

17. Cf. Rom. 3:30, 'God is one; and he will justify the circumcised on the ground of their faith and the uncircumcised through their faith.'

18. *Auslegung und Verkündigung*, I (Regensburg, 1963), 30. Kuss adds immediately that it is from the standpoint of faith that the genuine content of the message is to be certainly determined. It is from such a standpoint that his pupil, J. Eckert, says at the end of his monograph *Die urchristliche Verkündigung im Streit zwischen Paulus und seinen Gegnern nach dem Galaterbrief* (Regensburg, 1971): 'As highly as the apostle's striving for unity with the Jerusalem church and its "men of repute" is to be valued, . . . so little must his fight against the "other gospel" in Galatia—a fight which, in the last analysis, was concerned with the proclamation of the salvation to be found in Jesus Christ alone—lose its exemplary significance' (238).

Paul and his judaizing opponents would equally have subscribed. They might even have agreed that salvation was to be found in him alone. But on what conditions was the salvation found in Christ alone to be secured? This was the crucial question. No doubt Jesus did sit very loose to the traditions of the elders,[19] but when it was a question of the admission of Gentiles to the fellowship of his disciples, could Paul or any one else adduce a single utterance of his which suggested that circumcision could be dispensed with? (Indeed, when we consider the important part played by the circumcision question in the development of the early church, we may be impressed by the absence from our gospel tradition of any attempt to find a dominical ruling to which one side or the other could have appealed.) Paul might have appealed to the spirit of Jesus' teaching, or (as he did) to the logical implication of the gospel,[20] but people like his opponents would be satisfied with nothing less than verbatim chapter-and-verse authority; and this was not forthcoming.

3. Paul's gospel and the teaching of Jesus

From the perspective of nineteen centuries' distance, despite our ignorance of many elements in the situation that were well known to the protagonists, we can probably present an objective argument in defence of Paul's claim that the message he preached was the authentic gospel of Christ. It is this: two things on which Paul pre-eminently insisted—that salvation was provided by God's grace and that faith was the means by which men appropriated it—are repeatedly emphasized in the ministry of Jesus, and especially in his parables, regardless of the strata of gospel tradition to which appeal may be made. When we reflect on the complete lack of evidence in Paul's letters that he knew the parables of Jesus, we may wonder how Paul managed to discern so unerringly the heart of his Master's message. We may suspect that this discernment was implicit in the 'revelation of Jesus Christ' which, according to him, was the essence of his conversion experience.

The response of faith regularly won the approval of Jesus, sometimes his surprised approval, as when it came from a Gentile,[21] and was a sure means of securing his help and blessing; in face of unbelief, on the other hand, he was inhibited from performing works of mercy and power.[22] 'Faith as a grain of mustard seed'[23] was what he desired to see, but too often looked for in vain, even in his own disciples.

As regards the teaching of the parables, the point we are making can be illustrated from two, belonging to two quite distinct lines of tradition—Luke's special material and Matthew's special material.

In the Lukan parable of the Prodigal Son (Lk. 15:11–32), the father might very well have adopted other means for the rehabilitation of his younger son

---

19. Cf. Mk. 7:1–23.
20. Cf. Gal. 3:2–5; 4:4–7, etc.
21. Cf. Mt. 8:10//Lk. 7:9.
22. Cf. Mk. 6:5//Mt. 13:58.
23. Cf. Mt. 17:20//Lk. 17:6.

than those described (with approval) by Jesus. When the black sheep of the family came home in disgrace, the father, having a father's heart, might well have consented to give him a second chance. Listening to his carefully rehearsed speech, he might have said, 'That's all very well, young man; we have heard fine phrases before. If you really mean what you say, you can buckle to and work as you have never worked before, and if you do so, we may let you work your passage. But first you must prove yourself; we can't let by-gones be by-gones as though nothing had happened.' Even that would have been generous; it might have done the young man a world of good, and even the elder brother might have been content to let him be put on probation. But for Jesus, and for Paul, divine grace does not operate like that. God does not put repentant sinners on probation to see how they will turn out; he gives them an unrestrained welcome and invests them as his true-born sons. For Jesus, and for Paul, the initiative always rests with the grace of God. He bestows the reconciliation or redemption; men receive it. 'Treat me as one of your hired servants', says the prodigal to his father; but the father speaks of him as 'this my son'. So, says Paul, 'through God you are no longer a slave but a son, and if a son then an heir' (Gal. 4:7).

In the Matthaean parable of the Labourers in the Vineyard (Mt. 20:1–16), the last-hired workmen did not bargain with their employer about their pay. If a denarius was the fair rate for a day's work, those who worked for the last hour only might have expected a small fraction of that, but they accepted his undertaking to give them 'whatever is right' and in the event they received a denarius like the others who had worked all day. The grace of God is not to be parcelled out and adjusted to the varieties of individual merit. There was, as T. W. Manson pointed out, a coin worth one-twelfth of a denarius. 'It was called a *pondion*. But there is no such thing as a twelfth part of the love of God.'[24]

This is completely in line with Paul's understanding of the gospel. If law is the basis of men's acceptance with God, then the details of personal merit and demerit are of the utmost relevance. But the great blessings of the gospel had come to the Galatian Christians, as they knew very well, not by the works of the law but by the response of faith—the faith which works by love.[25] And when we speak in terms of love, we are on a plane where law is not at home.

During the ministry, Jesus' action and attitude supplied the parables with a living commentary sufficient to convey their meaning to those who responded in faith; later, the church felt it necessary to supply its own verbal commentary. The eschatological note which sounds in the parables is heard in Paul's teaching about justification by faith.[26] 'The law was our custodian until Christ came', says Paul, 'that we might be justified by faith. But now that faith has come, we are

---

24. T. W. Manson, *The Sayings of Jesus* (London, [2]1949), 220. It should not be overlooked that a very different emphasis is found in some other parts of the material peculiar to Matthew, which indeed have lent themselves to a directly anti-Pauline interpretation, such as the criticism in Mt. 5:19 of the man who 'relaxes one of the least of these commandments and teaches men so' (on this also see T. W. Manson, *The Sayings of Jesus*, 25, 154).

25. Gal. 3:2, 5; 5:6.

26. For the thesis that Jesus' proclamation of the kingdom of God and Paul's teaching on justification by faith are but different ways of setting forth one and the same message see E. Jüngel, *Paulus und Jesus* (Tübingen, 1962).

no longer under a custodian; for in Christ Jesus you are all sons of God, through faith' (Gal. 3:24–26). In other words, as he says to the Romans, 'Christ is the end of the law, that every one who has faith may be justified' (Rom. 10:4).[27] Already, with the coming of Christ and the completion of his redemptive work, the age of law had come to an end for the people of God. They had not reached the absolute end (the end of 1 Cor. 15:24), but they had reached its threshold—that period 'between the times' during which the presence of the Spirit in their lives confirmed to them their status and heritage as sons and daughters of God (Gal. 4:6): 'through the Spirit, by faith, we wait for the hope of righteousness' (Gal. 5:5).

When Paul calls Christ 'the end of the law' he is expressing a theological insight. But this insight was based on sound historical fact: many of Paul's fellow-Pharisees who engaged in debate with Jesus during his ministry must have felt that, on a practical level, his conduct and teaching involved 'the end of the law'—not only because of his rejection of their oral traditions but because of the sovereignty with which he treated such elements of the written law as the sabbath institution and food regulations. True, as we have seen, he does not appear to have made any pronouncement on the circumcision question. But when we consider how he related the law as a whole to the basic requirements of love to God and love to one's neighbour, and insisted on the paramountcy of heart-devotion, 'truth in the inward parts', righteousness, mercy and faith,[28] the conclusion is inescapable that he would not have included circumcision among the weightier matters of the law. If no word of his on the subject has survived (apart from the incidental *ad hominem* argument in the course of a sabbath debate in Jn. 7:22f.), it is simply because the issue did not arise in the situation of his ministry. When, later, it did arise in the situation of the Gentile mission, it is difficult to deny that Paul's position was in keeping with Jesus' general attitude to the externalities of religion.

Paul, like Jesus, shocked the guardians of Israel's law by his insistence on treating the law as a means to an end and not as an end in itself, by his refusal to let pious people seek security before God in their own piety, by his breaking down of barriers in the name of the God who 'justifies the ungodly' (Rom. 4:5) and by his proclamation of a message of good news for the outsider. In all this Paul saw more clearly than most of his Christian contemporaries into the inwardness of Jesus' teaching.

4. The law of Christ

After the relegation of law to the status of an outmoded order in the main body of the letter, it might strike one as something of a paradox towards the end of the letter when Paul speaks of 'the law of Christ'. 'If you are led by the Spirit', he has said, 'you are not under law' (Gal. 5:18), but now: 'Bear one another's burdens, and so you will fulfil the law of Christ' (Gal. 6:2). Yet we

---

27. On this see C. E. B. Cranfield, *Romans*, 515–520; E. Käsemann, *Romans*, 279–283 (two diametrically opposed interpretations).
28. Mt. 23:23; cf. Lk. 11:42.

have been prepared for this: the law in the form in which Paul served it in his pre-Christian days has been replaced by something better, but the law as interpreted in the teaching and example of Christ is still in force. The difference for Paul was that the law as he previously knew it was a yoke of bondage, whereas the law of Christ was the way of freedom. 'You were called to freedom, my brothers', he writes; 'only do not use your freedom as an opportunity for the flesh, but through love be servants one of another. For the whole law is fulfilled in one word: "You shall love your neighbour as yourself" ' (Gal. 5:13f.).[29] On the law as summarized in this 'one word' from Lv. 19:18, together with its twin commandment of love to God in Dt. 6:5, Jesus said the whole law and the prophets depended (Mt. 22:40).[30] But the nature of law is radically transformed when it is interpreted in terms of love; and it is this transformation which is involved when, in Paul's language, legal bondage gives way to the freedom of the Spirit.

Paul might have heard in the school of Gamaliel something to the effect that the whole law was comprehended in the commandment of love to one's neighbour—in an earlier generation Hillel had summarized it in the injunction, 'Do not to another what is hateful to yourself'[31]—but since he speaks of 'the law of Christ' it is a reasonable inference that he knew of the use which Christ had made of Lv. 19:18. 'Bear one another's burdens' seems to be a generalizing expansion of the particular instance mentioned in Paul's preceding exhortation: 'if a man is overtaken in any trespass, you who are spiritual should restore him in a spirit of gentleness' (Gal. 6:1). This is strangely reminiscent of a dominical injunction preserved only in Matthew's special material:[32] 'If your brother sins,[33] go and tell him his fault, between you and him alone. If he listens to you, you have gained your brother' (Mt. 18:15).

It is not so clear in Galatians as it is in some of the other letters of Paul that he fills out the details of 'the law of Christ' by drawing on a body of ethical catechesis widely used throughout the churches of his day. It has been pointed out that the recurring triad 'faith, hope, love', which seems to have been included in this catechesis, appears in Gal. 5:5f.: 'For through the Spirit, by *faith*, we wait for the *hope* of righteousness. For in Christ Jesus neither circumcision nor uncircumcision is of any avail, but faith working through *love*.'[34] But the three members of the triad are so independently integrated into the context here that it is doubtful if the triad would be, or was intended to be, recognized as such. We may observe, however, that this passage contains the only reference to the parousia in Galatians (for 'the hope of righteousness'[35] is the hope to which the justification of believers points them forward) and the only reference to the rôle of the Spirit as the guarantee of this hope.[36]

As for 'faith working through love', Paul held that the faith by which men

---

29. Cf. Rom. 13:9. See pp. 241f. below.
30. Cf. Mk. 12:29ff.; Lk. 10:27.
31. b. Shab. 31a; cf. *Abot R. Nat.* 2.26.
32. Cf. C. H. Dodd, 'Matthew and Paul', *NT Studies* (Manchester, 1953), 58f.
33. The added words 'against you' (D W Θ fam.13 etc.) are probably an early gloss, restricting the original intention.
34. Cf. A. M. Hunter, *Paul and his Predecessors*, 33ff.
35. Elsewhere called 'the hope of salvation' (1 Thes. 5:8) and 'the hope of glory' (Col. 1:27).
36. Expounded fully in Rom. 8:9–25.

and women are justified before God finds practical expression in lives which exhibit the law of love. The law of love cannot be enforced by penal sanctions; the fruit of the Spirit, as Paul enumerates its ninefold variety—love, joy, peace, patience, kindness, goodness, faithfulness, gentleness, self-control[37]—is not produced by legal enactments but simply because it is the nature of a life controlled by the Spirit to produce such fruit. As Paul says, curiously echoing an Aristotelian remark,[38] 'There is no law dealing with such things as these' (Gal. 5:23). 'The Spirit's law of life in Christ Jesus', as he calls it elsewhere (Rom. 8:2), has little more than the term 'law' in common with that from which the gospel has liberated him and (he trusts) his Galatian converts.[39]

Galatians is the most 'Pauline' of all the Pauline letters—so much so, indeed, that those who derive their understanding of Paulinism exclusively, or even mainly, from this letter are apt to present a lop-sided construction of the apostle's teaching—to become 'more Pauline than Paul',[40] like Marcion in the second century. Against the danger of such a lop-sided construction Paul himself provides the necessary safeguards in other letters. But even in this most Pauline letter the careful student may discern how much of the essential gospel Paul had in common with those who were apostles before him and, above all, how much he had in common with Jesus himself.

---

37. Gal. 5:22f.
38. See pp. 255f.
39. The law belongs to the former αἰών, from which the gospel has delivered believers (Gal. 1:4).
40. H. Küng, ' "Early Catholicism" in the NT as a Problem in Controversial Theology', *The Living Church*, ETr (London, 1963), 268f.

V
DATE AND
RELATED QUESTIONS

It is strange that, while Galatians is the most indubitably authentic of all the Pauline letters, it should be so difficult to attain certainty on the identity of the addressees and the time at which it was written. It is the most difficult of Paul's 'capital letters' to date precisely—more difficult even than 2 Cor. 10–13.

Where and when, in the course of Paul's apostolic career, was this letter written? One traditional way of handling this question is to ask at what point in the record of Acts it should be placed. The better way, however, is to try to establish where it stands, chronologically and otherwise, in relation to his other letters.

1. Galatians and the record of Acts

The former approach is not to be dismissed as irrelevant. One's estimate of its relevance, indeed, will depend on the estimate made of the historical accuracy of the record of Acts. If it is a historical romance, or if the author so misunderstood his sources as to envisage two missionary journeys in Central Asia Minor (those of Acts 13:13–14:23 and 16:1–6) when there was only one, then it is pointless to try to locate Galatians with reference to its narrative. But the position adopted here is that the author of Acts wrote with a historical intention, and that his evidence deserves to be treated seriously and used critically.

The dating of the letter in the context of Acts will depend partly on whether the addressees are regarded as 'South Galatians' or 'North Galatians'. If they were South Galatians, then the letter could conceivably have been written any time after the end of the missionary expedition related in Acts 13:4–14:26; if, on the other hand, they were North Galatians, it must have been written after the journey summarized in Acts 16:6, when Paul 'went through the Phrygian and Galatic region' (i.e. between the Jerusalem Council and the evangelization of Macedonia) and probably after the journey summarized in Acts 18:23, when he traversed 'the Galatic region and Phrygia' (i.e. between the end of his eighteen

months in Corinth and the beginning of his lengthy stay in Ephesus)—that is to
say, not earlier than Paul's Ephesian ministry, and probably during that ministry.[1]

One remark in the letter which could have a bearing on this problem is
Paul's incidental reminder to his readers that 'it was because of a bodily ailment
that I preached the gospel to you at first' (Gal. 4:13). The phrase 'at first' (τὸ
πρότερον) possibly, though not necessarily, implies that by the time he wrote
he had paid them at least two visits. Not necessarily, I say, because the words
may simply mean 'it was bodily illness that originally led to my bringing you
the Gospel'. That is how the NEB text has it, although a footnote offers in place
of 'originally' the alternative renderings 'formerly' or 'on the first of my two
visits'. If Paul's words imply two visits, when were they paid? Proponents of
the North Galatian view can point to the two occasions mentioned by Luke when
Paul passed through Galatia (Acts 16:6; 18:23).[2] On the South Galatian view
Paul's first visit was that of Acts 13:14ff., and the implied second one could be
his visit to Derbe, Lystra, Iconium and the 'Phrygian and Galatic region' (Phrygia Galatica?) recorded in Acts 16:1–6,[3] but it could also be taken to refer to
Paul and Barnabas's retracing of their steps from Derbe through Lystra and
Iconium to Pisidian Antioch at the end of the former visit (Acts 14:21–23).[4] In
that case it might be possible to date Galatians before the Jerusalem Council of
Acts 15:6ff.—i.e. soon after the last event mentioned in the autobiographical
outline of Gal. 1:13–2:14. One advantage in this dating is that it would explain
why Paul in Galatians does not cut the ground entirely from under the Judaizers'
feet by appealing to the Council's ruling that circumcision and all that went with
it should not be imposed on Gentile converts.

It is difficult to decide what weight can be given to the phrase 'so quickly'
(οὕτως ταχέως) in Gal. 1:6: 'I am astonished that you are so quickly deserting
him who called you in the grace of Christ and turning to a different gospel.' The
point of reference is the Galatians' conversion, and the implication is that no
very long time had elapsed since it took place. Naturally those who date Galatians rather early among the epistles of Paul feel that they are doing due justice
to the phrase 'so quickly'—if the addressees were the South Galatians evangelized by Paul and Barnabas (Acts 13:14ff.) and the letter was written on the eve
of the Council of Jerusalem (Acts 15), then a bare year had elapsed. But if they
were North Galatians a date (preferably early) in Paul's Ephesian residence is
indicated, and in any case those who maintain a later date point out quite rightly
that 'so quickly' is a relative expression. 'I cannot think it strange', wrote Bishop
Lightfoot, 'that the Apostle, speaking of truths destined to outlive the life of
kingdoms and of nations, should complain that his converts had *so soon* deserted

---

1. This is the majority opinion on the date of Galatians, whether or not the addressees are
identified with 'North Galatians'. A careful presentation of the case for an Ephesian provenance will
be found in E. D. Burton, *Galatians*, xlvii–lii.

2. Cf. J. B. Lightfoot, *Galatians*, 24f., 41, 174f.

3. This was W. M. Ramsay's earlier view; cf. his *SPT* (London, 1895), 182ff., and *Galatians*
(London, 1899), 405ff. He thought then that it was sent from Antioch (cf. Acts 18:22f.). On this
dating Gal. 5:11 can be illuminated by Paul's circumcision of Timothy, which took place during the
visit of Acts 16:1–6.

4. This was Ramsay's later view; cf. *The Teaching of Paul in Terms of the Present Day* (London,
1913), 391; *SPT* (London, [14]1920), xxxf.

from the faith, even though a whole decade of years might have passed since they were first brought to the knowledge of Christ'—although he adds that 'so long a period . . . is not required on any probable hypothesis as to the date of the epistle'.[5] Plainly we cannot use 'so quickly' as one of our foundation-stones.

2. Galatians and other Pauline letters: Lightfoot's argument

But we must turn now to consider the place of Galatians among the letters of Paul.

Since Galatians goes traditionally along with 1 and 2 Corinthians and Romans as one of Paul's four 'capital' epistles, it is natural that it should have been grouped rather closely with them in date. F. C. Baur, for example, thought that the appearance of these four, in the sequence Galatians, 1 and 2 Corinthians, Romans, at the beginning of Marcion's *Apostolikon*, was inexplicable unless a chronological order was being followed,[6] and he himself accepted this as the chronological order of the four.[7]

Lightfoot acknowledged that in his day this chronological order was 'the generally received opinion',[8] but gave his reasons for departing from it so as to place Galatians after 2 Corinthians and immediately before Romans. This had the advantage of placing Galatians next in date to the two epistles with which he believed it to exhibit the greatest degree of affinity.

The close relationship between Galatians and Romans[9] has led many scholars, like Lightfoot, to prefer a date for Galatians not far removed from that of Romans, which can be fixed fairly precisely during the winter preceding Paul's last visit to Jerusalem (cf. Rom. 15:25ff.; Acts 20:2ff.). The insistence on justification by faith, not by legal works, with the citation of Hab. 2:4 in the sense 'He who through faith is righteous shall live' (Gal. 3:11; Rom. 1:17) and the appeal to the precedent of Abraham, who 'believed God, and it was reckoned to him for righteousness' (Gn. 15:6, quoted in Gal. 3:6; Rom. 4:3), figures prominently in the argument of both letters. So does the interpretation of the promise made to Abraham as fulfilled in the Gentile mission, although the *testimonia* adduced are different in the two letters—in Gal. 3:8, 'In you shall all the nations be blessed' (Gn. 12:3; 18:18); in Rom. 4:17, 'I have made you the father of many nations' (Gn. 17:5). The statement in Gal. 5:17, that 'the desires of the flesh are against the Spirit, and the desires of the Spirit are against the flesh; for these are opposed to each other, to prevent you from doing what you would', has been thought to be amplified in the picture of inner tension drawn in Rom. 7:14–25,[10] while the admonition 'Walk by the Spirit, and you will not gratify the desires of the flesh' (Gal. 5:16) might serve as a summary

---

5. Lightfoot, *Galatians*, 42.
6. The position of Galatians at the head of Marcion's *Apostolikon* is due to considerations not so much of chronology (in which Marcion had little interest) as of theological fitness; see p. 1 above.
7. F. C. Baur, *Paul*, I, 247f.
8. Lightfoot, *Galatians*, 40.
9. Cf. Lightfoot, *Galatians*, 49, quoted on p. 2 above.
10. But see pp. 244f.

of Rom. 8:1–17. Both letters bring out the close relation between the Christian's freedom from slavery to sin or from legal bondage and his being led by the Spirit (Gal. 5:18; Rom. 8:14), at whose prompting he acknowledges his new status as a son of God and joint-heir with Christ in the invocation 'Abba, Father'[11] (Gal. 4:6; Rom. 8:15f.). In both letters the law of God is summed up in the single commandment: 'Thou shalt love thy neighbour as thyself'[12] (Gal. 5:14; Rom. 13:9).

All this comes to expression in Galatians in a situation of anxiety, indignation and conflict; in Romans it is expounded more dispassionately and in a more logical sequence. Yet we need not suppose that the understanding and presentation of the gospel which we find in Galatians first took shape in Paul's mind under the exigencies of the judaizing controversy which called forth that letter. It is true that in certain areas of Paul's thinking a progression can be traced as we move from his earlier letters to his later ones.[13] But on such a fundamental matter as the way of salvation it would be surprising to find a progression sufficiently marked to affect the centre of his thinking. If the evidence clearly demanded this, we should accept it, but the evidence makes no such demand.[14]

But at present we must bear in mind the relatively brief interval of time between Paul's earliest letters and those of the Roman captivity—not much, if at all, more than twelve years. (If some or all of the letters traditionally assigned to his Roman captivity were written during an earlier captivity, then the interval is further reduced.) If we leave the letters of the Roman captivity out of our reckoning, and think only of the 'capital letters' and the Thessalonian correspondence, they were written within nine years at the outside. Most of the letters would have been written when Paul was in his fifties. He had experienced his revolutionary conversion in (probably) his early thirties; from then on the main features of his belief were sufficiently stable to make it no surprising thing to find him repeating them at an interval of several years when an appropriate occasion arose.

Johannes Weiss is probably right in pointing to Paul's 'hidden years', before he joined Barnabas at Antioch, as the most formative in the development of his Christian thought, whereas 'in the letters we have to do with the fully matured man'. He is too sweeping in his judgment when he goes on to say that 'the "development" which some think they can discern in the period of his letters— ten years, at the most—is not worth considering at all';[15] but his words provide a salutary corrective to excessive speculation about Paul's inner development. A mind like Paul's does not stop growing at the mid-century point, but it tends to advance along lines whose general direction has been determined during the preceding years. Paul may equally well have reproduced in Romans some of the distinctive positions of Galatians whether Galatians was written one year or ten years before.

---

11. See pp. 199f.
12. See p. 241.
13. E.g. on resurrection, or on the body of Christ.
14. See p. 50.
15. J. Weiss, *Earliest Christianity*, ETr, I (New York, 1959), 206. Even during the 'hidden years' the development of Paul's Christian thought was the working out of what was implied in the Damascus-road revelation. Cf. S. Kim, *The Origin of Paul's Gospel* (Tübingen, 1981).

The affinity between Galatians and 2 Corinthians, Lightfoot held, was of a different order; it consisted 'not so much in words and arguments as in tone and feeling'.[16] He quoted Benjamin Jowett to this effect: in both Galatians and 2 Corinthians, said Jowett, 'there is a greater display of his own feelings than in any other portion of his writings, a deeper contrast of inward exaltation and outward suffering, more of personal entreaty, a greater readiness to impart himself'.[17] This is indeed true, although I think the resemblance thus described is due to the fact that Paul's emotions were deeply stirred on both occasions rather than to the chronological contiguity of the two letters.

Lightfoot himself, however, added further considerations: e.g. the parallel between Christ's being 'made a curse for us' in Gal. 3:13 and his being 'made sin for us' in 2 Cor. 5:21; the repetition of the sowing-and-reaping sequence as an ethical figure in Gal. 6:7 and 2 Cor. 9:6; such common phrases as 'a different gospel' (Gal. 1:6; 2 Cor. 11:4), 'a new creation' (Gal. 6:15; 2 Cor. 5:17), to be 'zealously concerned for' people (Gal. 4:17; 2 Cor. 11:2), to 'persuade men' (Gal. 1:10; 2 Cor. 5:11). In the lists of vices in 2 Cor. 12:20f., Gal. 5:19–21 and Rom. 1:29f. and 13:13 he was disposed to find the middle term in the Galatians passage.[18] More important, however, in his eyes was the progression which he traced from the Corinthian correspondence through Galatians to Romans in respect of Paul's personal history (the 'marks of Jesus' in Gal. 6:17 being perhaps the result of the experiences of 1 Cor. 15:30–32; 2 Cor. 1:8–10),[19] the development of the Judaic opposition and the increasingly full exposition of the truth of the gospel. The admonition with regard to the restoration of offenders in Gal. 6:1 might have as its background the restoration of the Corinthian offender in 2 Cor. 2:5–11 (cf. 7:11f.); the warning that 'God is not mocked' coupled with the admonition to persevere in well-doing (Gal. 6:7–10) might reflect the Galatian churches' slowness in contributing to the Jerusalem fund regarding which they had received instructions from Paul before he wrote 1 Cor. 16:1. Lightfoot's argument is cumulative, but when its several parts are allowed to make their combined impression, then, he says, if the Corinthian correspondence is interposed between Galatians and Romans, 'the dislocation is felt at once'.[20]

To Lightfoot, 2 Corinthians formed one continuous letter, whereas the majority opinion today is that it is composite—in particular, that chapters 1–9 and 10–13 did not originally belong to the same letter. In adducing evidence from 2 Corinthians suggesting that it was written before Galatians, he adduces it from both parts of the letter as we have it, but especially from chapters 10–13. And the resemblance in tone between 2 Cor. 10–13 and the whole of Galatians is sufficiently obvious to call for no elaboration.

---

16. Lightfoot, *Galatians*, 44. Theodore of Mopsuestia observed a resemblance between these two epistles (*In Ep. ad Galatas, Argumentum*).

17. B. Jowett, *The Epistles of St. Paul to the Thessalonians, Galatians, Romans*, I (London, [2]1859), 120.

18. Lightfoot, *Galatians*, 45 n. 3.

19. They were much more probably the result of his being stoned at Lystra (Acts 14:19; cf. 2 Cor. 11:25), as some at least of his readers had good reason to know.

20. Lightfoot, *Galatians*, 50.

3. Galatians and other Pauline letters: C. H. Buck's argument

A fresh investigation of the relation borne by Galatians to 2 Corinthians on
the one hand and to Romans on the other was published in 1951 by C. H. Buck,
Jr. in an important article contributed to the *Journal of Biblical Literature*.[21]
Ignoring the last four chapters of 2 Corinthians because of uncertainty regarding
their date, Buck concentrated on chapters 1–9. He presented a synoptic arrangement of 2 Cor. 3:17; 4:10–5:5 with Gal. 4:1–7; 5:13–25 and Rom. 8:2–25 so
as to show that the last passage 'reproduces with remarkable fidelity the logical
outlines of arguments which also occur in II Corinthians 1–9 and Galatians',[22]
drawing words and arguments from the two earlier letters, conflating ideas which
originally were formally separate in such a way as to reveal that they shared the
same underlying thought and application. For example, when Paul speaks in
Rom. 8:23 of believers 'who have the first fruits of the Spirit', groaning inwardly
as they wait for 'adoption as sons, the redemption of our bodies', he combines
the idea of 'adoption as sons' (υἱοθεσία), which is treated at some length in
Galatians, with that of 'the redemption of our bodies', which is the subject of
2 Cor. 4:16–5:10. (It may be observed, in passing, that the treatment in Romans
reflects a further development: in Romans what believers have received here and
now is 'the spirit of adoption *or* sonship', enabling them to anticipate the full
'adoption as sons' which will be manifested at the parousia, whereas in Galatians
they have received their adoption as sons already, thanks to God's sending his
Son to redeem them, and because they are sons, God has sent the Spirit of his
Son into their hearts.)

This, however, would simply confirm that Romans was later than both
2 Cor. 1–9 and Galatians; Buck believes it possible to go further in the confirmation of Lightfoot's thesis and show that Galatians, while earlier than Romans,
was later than 2 Cor. 1–9. He points out that the antithesis Spirit–flesh occurs
in 2 Cor. 1–9, Galatians and Romans whereas the antithesis faith–works, which
is intimately associated with the former antithesis in Galatians, is absent from
2 Corinthians, even in a 'discussion of the identical problem'—the question of
Christian freedom. 'If Paul had already written Galatians', he asks, 'is it conceivable that he could, at some later time, have written II Corinthians 1–9, with
its vehement anti-legal position, without once employing the antithesis, faith–
works?'[23] The only way to give an affirmative answer to this question, he concludes, would be to assume that, having used the faith–works antithesis in Galatians, Paul 'then decided to abandon this line of argument and therefore
consciously avoided it in II Corinthians 1–9' and 'that shortly after the writing
of II Corinthians 1–9 Paul again changed his mind and in Romans revived the
abandoned argument'. The improbability of this twofold assumption forces him
'to the conclusion that Galatians was written not only before Romans but also

---

21. C. H. Buck, Jr., 'The Date of Galatians', *JBL* 70 (1951), 113–122.
22. Ibid., 116.
23. Ibid., 120.

after II Corinthians 1–9',[24] and this conclusion, in the light of his arguments, has commended itself to others as inescapable.[25]

But 2 Cor. 1–9 is not concerned with the 'identical problem' tackled in Galatians, nor does it take up such a 'vehement anti-legal position' as Galatians does. In 2 Cor. 1–9 Paul displays for the most part a relaxed, almost euphoric, frame of mind, in his relief at the good news brought to him by Titus from Corinth; there is none of the intense agitation which marks Galatians. The only passage in 2 Cor. 1–9 which could properly be called 'anti-legal' is chapter 3, and there Paul is not, as in Galatians, warning his readers against seeking salvation in works of the law but emphasizing the glory of the new covenant, to the ministry of which he has been called, by contrasting it with the evanescent glory of the old covenant. And the antithesis which he employs in this connection is Spirit–letter (vv 6, 7), not Spirit–flesh; the substantive 'flesh' (σάρξ) does not appear in this chapter, and when the adjective 'fleshy' (σάρκινος) is used, it relates to the new covenant, not to the old: the terms of the new covenant are inscribed not (like those of the old) 'on stone tablets' but 'on fleshy tablets, i.e. on hearts' (ἐν πλαξὶν καρδίαις σαρκίναις). This, of course, is the literal usage of the word, not Paul's distinctive theological usage, but the theological usage occurs in 2 Cor. 1–9 only in the phrase 'after the flesh' (κατὰ σάρκα, 1:17; 5:16 bis), and if 'after the flesh' is in antithesis to 'after the Spirit' (κατὰ πνεῦμα), the antithesis is implied, not expressed. The antithesis Spirit–letter of 2 Cor. 3:6f. is taken up again in Romans (2:29; 7:6), although it is absent from Galatians. One could imagine Buck's rhetorical question being reworded thus: 'If Paul had already written 2 Corinthians 1–9, is it conceivable that he could, at some later time, have written Galatians, with its vehement anti-legal position, without once employing the antithesis, Spirit–letter?' If Buck is right, it must be conceivable, because this is what he believes to have happened; but if that is conceivable, it is equally conceivable that Paul, having used the faith–works antithesis in Galatians, because it was so apposite to the Galatian crisis, did not use it in 2 Cor. 1–9, because it was not apposite to the Corinthian situation, but used it again in Romans, together with the antitheses Spirit–flesh (as in Galatians) and Spirit–letter (as in 2 Corinthians), because in Romans he was concerned to give a more comprehensive and systematic exposition of the gospel. Conclusions about relative dating based on considerations like these are not so compelling as Buck suggests.

Much the same might be said about the arguments of C. E. Faw who, writing ten years later,[26] dotted the i's and crossed the t's of the case made by Lightfoot and Buck for dating Galatians between 2 Corinthians and Romans, and added some emphases of his own regarding the development of Paul's acceptance of death, his employment of death and resurrection in a symbolic sense and his special use of "crucifixion" to denote symbolic death.[27]

---

24. Ibid., 120f.
25. Cf. J. C. O'Neill, *The Theology of Acts in its Historical Setting* (London, 1961), 96f., where Buck's argument is described as 'objectively convincing'.
26. C. E. Faw, 'The Anomaly of Galatians', *BR* 4 (1960), 25–38.
27. Cf. C. E. Faw, 'Death and Resurrection in Paul's Letters', *JBR* 27 (1959), 291ff.

4. Justification by faith and the date of Galatians

Buck combines his dating of Galatians between 2 Cor. 1–9 and Romans with the view, alluded to above, that the doctrine of justification by faith, 'while not necessarily incompatible with Paul's earlier doctrine, was actually formulated and expressed by him for the first time when he found it necessary to answer the arguments of the Judaizers in Galatia'.[28] This view, which is not essential to Buck's dating of Galatians, was in some degree anticipated by William Wrede, according to whom justification by faith is Paul's *'polemical doctrine'* and 'is only made intelligible by the struggle of his life, his controversy with Judaism and Jewish Christianity, and is only intended for this'.[29] Buck's statement of this view is indeed much more moderate than Wrede's. For Wrede, 'the whole Pauline religion can be expounded without a word being said about this doctrine'[30]—an odd assertion, when we reflect that in Paul's own exposition of his gospel, the letter to the Romans, written in a non-polemical situation, he gives justification by faith a cardinal place.[31]

It is true that several of Paul's positions took the form they did in response to lines of argument and teaching which he found it necessary to oppose.[32] But the essence of justification by faith was more probably implicit in the logic of his conversion. If the former Pharisee no longer hoped for acceptance with God on the ground of his devotion to the Torah, on what ground did his assurance of such acceptance thenceforth rest? It may have been late in his career that Paul wrote of his ambition to 'gain Christ and be found in him, not having a righteousness of my own, based on law, but that which is through faith in Christ, the righteousness from God that depends on faith' (Phil. 3:8f.); but there was never a time, from his conversion onward, when he could not have used the same words. When, in Gal. 2:20, he says that 'the life which I now live in the flesh[33] I live by faith[34] in the Son of God', there is no hint that he is using a new form of words which had just taken shape under the exigency of confuting the Judaizers in Galatia. And the argument of Gal. 3:10–14, where Christ, by dying

---

28. C. H. Buck, 'The Date of Galatians', 121f.

29. W. Wrede, *Paul*, ETr (London, 1907), 123.

30. Ibid. Cf. W. Heitmüller, *Luthers Stellung in der Religionsgeschichte des Christentums* (Marburg, 1917), 19f., and the discussion in K. Holl, *Gesammelte Aufsätze*, II (Tübingen, 1928), 18f.

31. It is the presupposition also of Paul's language in 1 Cor. 1:30 ('Christ Jesus, whom God made . . . our righteousness') and 2 Cor. 5:21 ('that in him we might become the righteousness of God'). One might argue that in Gal. 2:15ff. Paul assumes that Peter agrees with him 'that a man is not justified by works of the law but through faith in Jesus Christ' (cf. Acts 15:7–11), but for the difficulty of deciding where Paul's rebuke to Peter ends and his general reflections on the principle involved begin. Cf. C. von Weizsäcker, *The Apostolic Age*, ETr, I (London, 1907), 74f.

32. His exposition of the cosmic significance of the work of Christ in reaction against the Colossian 'heresy' is a good example.

33. Gk. ἐν σαρκί, an instance of the non-theological use of 'flesh' (= mortal body) even in Galatians.

34. The saving or justifying principle of faith, insisted on in Galatians and Romans, is present in the Corinthian letters even more frequently than πίστις in the sense of a special spiritual gift (as in 1 Cor. 12:9; Rom. 12:6); cf. 1 Cor. 2:5; 15:14, 17; 2 Cor. 1:24 (πίστις); 1 Cor. 1:21; 3:5; 14:22; 15:2, 11 (πιστεύω).

the death which incurred the divine curse, transferred to himself the curse which his people had incurred by breaking the law,[35] must have commended itself to Paul sooner rather than later in his Christian career as the solution to the intolerably scandalous problem which he had previously found in the Christian claim— that the Messiah, upon whom, practically by definition, the blessing of God rested uniquely, should nevertheless have suffered the death upon which, according to the law, the curse of God rested explicitly.

The centrality of Paul's doctrine of justification to his whole conception of the gospel, not only in polemical situations, is given proper emphasis by some contemporary German theologians. For example, Günther Bornkamm, in his monograph on *Paul*, shows that 'Paul's doctrine of justification is to be regarded not as theological theorizing on the primitive gospel, but as its proper development and exposition'.[36] Paul's soteriology is the interpretation of his Christology: 'to set out the gospel concerning Christ *as* a gospel of justification, and vice versa, is a decisive concern of his whole theology.'[37] And Ernst Käsemann, in his *Perspectives on Paul*, affirms that 'the Pauline doctrine of justification is entirely and solely Christology, a Christology, indeed, won from Jesus' cross and hence an offensive Christology'.[38] It is a polemical or 'fighting doctrine'[39] indeed, but not on that account a subordinate element in Paul's gospel, for the attitudes and presuppositions against which it fights are not simply those of first-century Judaism but attitudes and presuppositions which equally require to be opposed in the twentieth century and cannot be effectively opposed except by this 'fighting doctrine', which alone is 'the break-through to the new creation'.[40] Käsemann is no mean fighter himself, and speaks from personal experience as well as from exegetical insight.

5. Other arguments

Some reference should be made to C. H. Dodd's correlation of what he regarded as the probable sequence of Paul's letters with the evidence of development in Paul's thought.[41] He believed that the 'affliction in Asia' mentioned in 2 Cor. 1:8–10 marked a psychological watershed, if not 'a sort of second conversion', in Paul's experience, after which 'the traces of fanaticism and intolerance [found in some of his earlier letters] disappear, almost if not quite completely, along with all that insistence on his own dignity'.[42] In Dodd's view, such letters as Galatians and 2 Cor. 10–13, in which these features are discernible, were written before this psychological watershed, whereas 2 Cor. 1–9, from which they have practically disappeared, should (at least for the most

---

35. See pp. 157f.
36. G. Bornkamm, *Paul*, ETr (London, 1971), 116.
37. Ibid., 117.
38. E. Käsemann, *Perspectives on Paul*, ETr (London, 1971), 73.
39. Ibid., 70.
40. Ibid., 73.
41. C. H. Dodd, 'The Mind of Paul', *BJRL* 17 (1933), 91ff.; 18 (1934), 69ff., reprinted in *NT Studies* (Manchester, 1953), 67–128.
42. *NT Studies*, 81.

part)[43] self-evidently be dated after it. There is much to be said for Dodd's exposition of 'the mind of Paul', but I cannot go all the way with him, for, while I too recognize in 2 Cor. 10–13 a separate letter from chapters 1–9, I am disposed to date it later, not earlier, than chapters 1–9.[44] I am unable therefore to appeal to Dodd's thesis in support of a date for Galatians earlier than that of 2 Cor. 1–9 since, if 2 Cor. 10–13 could have been written after 2 Cor. 1–9, so (theoretically) could Galatians.

T. W. Manson dated Galatians to Paul's Ephesian period (although to him the recipients were the South Galatians).[45] Pointing out that Paul devotes two-fifths of the letter to defending his apostolic status against a violent attack, and a further two-fifths to a counter-attack against the position of the circumcision party, he observed that 'the only time when Paul appears to have had to face an attack of this kind and of this gravity is in the Ephesian period; and the situation revealed in the Philippian and Corinthian letters is, I think, substantially that presupposed by Galatians'.[46] I am not so sure, however, that Paul's apostolic status was seriously called in question during one phase only of his apostolic career; those who challenged it were liable to do so whenever an opportunity arose. And the judaizing propaganda of the Corinthian correspondence seems to me to belong to a later stage than that of Galatians. In the Galatian crisis pressure was put upon Paul's Gentile converts to accept circumcision in particular (with other features of Judaism like the sacred calendar); in the Corinthian crisis circumcision does not appear to have figured (it is mentioned incidentally and uncontroversially in 1 Cor. 7:18f.). The reason, I believe, is that after the publication of the apostolic decree of Acts 15:20, 29, it would have been difficult for judaizing preachers invoking the authority of the leaders of the Jerusalem church to impose circumcision on Gentile Christians.[47] What they did try to impose on the Corinthian church was the literal force of the food-regulations annexed to the decree, regarding which Paul took a more liberal and enlightened line.[48] (The syncretism at Colossae, in which circumcision played a part, was a local Phrygian development, not something imposed by Judaean emissaries, and it is not clear whether the 'mutilation party' against which the Philippians are put on their guard comprised Jews or judaizing Christians.)[49]

An attractive account of the relation of Galatians to the three other 'capital

---

43. 2 Cor. 6:14–7:1, frequently considered to be an interpolation, might be an exception.

44. Cf. C. K. Barrett, *Second Corinthians*, 5–21. Again, if Phil. 3:2 should be dated after 2 Corinthians, as Dodd held, its fierce invective would be another exception to his rule. Cf. T. W. Manson: 'if Philippians is to be dated after the spiritual crisis, Chapter iii can only be regarded as either a relapse or a misplaced survival from an earlier stage in Paul's career' (*Studies in the Gospels and Epistles*, 164).

45. T. W. Manson, 'The Problem of the Epistle to the Galatians', *BJRL* 24 (1940), 59–80, reprinted in *Studies in the Gospels and Epistles*, 168–189.

46. T. W. Manson, *Studies*, 169.

47. But see *Studies*, 186 n. 1, where Manson points out 'that circumcision is not even mentioned in the Apostolic letter'. Perhaps its omission was more eloquent than any specific statement ruling that Gentile converts were exempt from it.

48. Cf. C. K. Barrett, 'Things Offered to Idols', *NTS* 11 (1964–65), 138–153.

49. That they were Jews has been held, *inter alios*, by J. G. Machen, *The Origin of Paul's Religion* (London, 1921), 104, and F. W. Beare, *Philippians*, 104. For the view that they were Judaizers, cf. T. W. Manson, *Studies*, 163.

epistles' has been put forward by John Drane.[50] The strong libertarian emphasis of Galatians (necessary in dealing with Christians who were being drawn into legalism) was apt to be misapplied by some converts from paganism. This is shown by the enthusiasts in the Corinthian church who (without necessarily having read Galatians) turned the liberty with which Christ had set them free into a gnosticizing type of antinomianism (the very thing against which Paul issues a warning in Gal. 5:13) and adopted the slogan 'Everything is permissible' (1 Cor. 6:12; 10:23). In 1 Corinthians Paul counteracts this tendency by laying down limits and guiding-lines which some of his converts might have had difficulty in distinguishing from a new code of rules and regulations. In 2 Corinthians and Romans it is possible to recognize a synthesis of the extremes which find expression in the two earlier letters.

It might be thought that Drane has imposed a Hegelian pattern on the Pauline correspondence, but that is not so: the pattern emerged from his study of the documents. And it was not in the interests of this pattern that he dated Galatians earliest of the four letters; he had accepted that dating on independent grounds before embarking on this particular study.

When the epistles are read in the light of this thesis, several of their features appear in a fresh light. For example, the emphasis on the gospel as 'tradition' in 1 Corinthians could be understood as balancing the emphasis on the gospel as 'revelation' in Galatians. The rather detailed ethical directives and caveats given in 1 Corinthians ('Everything is permissible, *but* . . .') could be regarded as correctives to false inferences drawn from Paul's insistence on Christian freedom. Even the exhortations to women in 1 Corinthians about public decorum in dress and utterance could be regarded as correctives to an irresponsible exploitation of his principle that in Christ there is 'no male and female' (Gal. 3:28), although this is more doubtful.[51] Even if Drane's thesis–antithesis–synthesis pattern be accepted, it could not be used as an argument for the early date of Galatians, since it presupposes the early date.

6. Galatians and Thessalonians

Thus far nothing has been said about the relation of Galatians to 1 and 2 Thessalonians, but the earlier Galatians is dated, the more necessary it becomes to consider this relation. Above all, if Galatians is to be dated before the promulgation of the Jerusalem decree of Acts 15:28f., then it is earlier than 1 and 2 Thessalonians. But both in evangelism and in eschatology the Thessalonian letters give the impression of being less developed than Galatians.

So far as evangelism is concerned, the words of 1 Thes. 1:9, 'you turned to God from idols, to serve a living and true God', might have been applied to Jewish proselytes from paganism. But such proselytes would have been told that the next stage was an undertaking to keep the law of Moses; this would, among

---

50. J. W. Drane, *Paul: Libertine or Legalist?* (London, 1975).

51. For the possibility that 1 Cor. 14:34f. is an interpolation cf. G. Zuntz, *The Text of the Epistles* (London, 1953), 17.

other things, safeguard them on the day of final judgment. The Thessalonian Christians were told, on the other hand, that the corollary to serving the living and true God was waiting for his Son from heaven, Jesus, whom he had raised from the dead; *he* would safeguard them on the day of final judgment, delivering them from 'the wrath to come' (1 Thes. 1:10). So far as turning to God from idols is concerned, the Galatians are reminded that they have done just that (Gal. 4:8f.) and are urged not to act in a manner inconsistent with their having done so. But in Galatians, as in the other capital epistles, the content of Christian salvation is expressed in richer terms—of being justified before God through faith in Christ and entering into the enjoyment of all the blessings which flow from justification. There is little enough about this in the Thessalonian correspondence.

So far as eschatology is concerned, Paul's teaching is as clear, though not as detailed, in Galatians as anywhere else in his letters. The coming of Christ has inaugurated a new phase in the history of God's dealings with his people: with his appearance the 'fulness of the time' has come (Gal. 4:4); the age of law has been superseded by the age of the Spirit. Believers in Christ have been delivered by his death from 'the present evil age' (1:4)—which implies that they have become heirs of the new, resurrection age, whose blessings they enjoy by anticipation through the Spirit. It is through the Spirit that, by faith, they 'wait for the hope of righteousness' (Gal. 5:5)—the glory into which they will enter at the consummation. This is the nearest Paul comes in Galatians to speaking of the parousia.[52] The contrast between this reticence and the apocalyptic note in 1 and 2 Thessalonians cannot be overlooked.[53]

Is it likely that the apostle, whose expectation of an early parousia finds such repeated and vivid expression in 1 and 2 Thessalonians, should refer to the subject so briefly and allusively in a letter written earlier than either of these? If Paul's thought be pictured as maturing from a more apocalyptic to a less apocalyptic conception of things to come, from the outlook of 1 and 2 Thessalonians to that of 2 Corinthians and Romans, then Galatians belongs to the later stage, not to the earlier. Against this it might be argued that it is hazardous to plot the development of Paul's thought on the basis of occasional letters each of which dealt with a situation as it arose, that the apocalyptic note of 1 and 2 Thessalonians represents Paul's reaction to the eschatological excitement in the church of Thessalonica, just as the quite different note of Galatians represents his reaction to the legalism which was infiltrating the churches of Galatia. If the main emphases of Galatians are given at best a secondary place in the Thessalonian correspondence, it might be asked, why should it be surprising that the main emphases of 1 and 2 Thessalonians receive barely secondary attention in Galatians?

It is apposite to recall F. C. Burkitt's treatment of this problem, as it is for any one who (like him) dates Galatians before the Jerusalem decree. He argued that 1 and 2 Thessalonians, 'while full of genuinely Pauline ideas and expressions', should be taken to be, 'as they profess to be, the Letters of Paul and

---

52. Cf. U. Wilckens, *Römer*, 30–33.
53. The authenticity of 2 Thessalonians is here accepted.

Silvanus and Timothy, and that this means that whoever was the scribe they were drafted by Silvanus'.[54] Silvanus, then, might be responsible for those aspects of the Thessalonian letters which present such a contrast to the tone of Galatians— and this, with modification, remains an acceptable thesis.[55]

7. Conclusion

A comparative study of Galatians alongside those Pauline letters which can be more certainly dated is not decisive for the dating of this letter. But nothing in such a comparative study prohibits our giving Galatians a place quite early among the Pauline letters, if an early place appears probable on other grounds. When, as we are told in Acts 15:1, Judaean visitors came to Syrian Antioch and started to teach the Christians there that those who were not circumcised in accordance with the law of Moses could not be saved, it is antecedently probable that others who wished to press the same line visited the recently formed daughter-churches of Antioch, not only in Syria and Cilicia, as the apostolic letter indicates (Acts 15:23), but also in South Galatia. If so, then the letter to the Galatians was written as soon as Paul got news of what was afoot, on the eve of the Jerusalem meeting described in Acts 15:6ff. This, it is suggested, would yield the most satisfactory correlation of the data of Galatians and Acts and the most satisfactory dating of Galatians. It must be conceded that, if this is so, Galatians is the earliest among the extant letters of Paul.[56] I know of no evidence to make this conclusion impossible, or even improbable. Even on this early dating, Paul had been a Christian for at least fifteen years, and the main outlines of his understanding of the gospel, which took shape from his Damascus-road

---

54. F. C. Burkitt, *Christian Beginnings* (London, 1924), 116–118 (on Galatians), 128–133 (on Thessalonians).

55. See F. F. Bruce, *Thessalonians*, Word Biblical Commentary (Waco, forthcoming).

56. Among those who have maintained this dating are J. Calvin, *Commentary on Galatians* (Geneva, 1548); ETr by T. H. L. Parker (Edinburgh, 1965), 24; V. Weber, *Die Abfassung des Galaterbriefs vor dem Apostelkonzil* (Ravensburg, 1900); D. Round, *The Date of St. Paul's Epistle to the Galatians* (Cambridge, 1906); K. Lake, *The Earlier Epistles of Paul* (London, 1911), 297ff. (he later abandoned this view for one which involved an identification of the Jerusalem visits of Acts 11:30 and 15:2); C. W. Emmet, *St. Paul's Epistle to the Galatians*, Reader's Commentary (London, 1912), xivff., and *The Beginnings of Christianity*, ed. F. J. Foakes Jackson and K. Lake, I, 2 (London, 1922), 269ff.; W. M. Ramsay, *The Teaching of Paul*, 372ff., and *SPT*[14], xxii, xxxi; D. Plooij, *De chronologie van het leven van Paulus* (Leiden, 1918), 111ff.; A. W. F. Blunt, *The Acts of the Apostles*, Clarendon Bible (Oxford, 1922), 182ff., and *The Epistle to the Galatians*, Clarendon Bible (Oxford, 1925), 22ff.; F. C. Burkitt, *Christian Beginnings* (London, 1924), 116ff.; H. N. Bate, *A Guide to the Epistles of St. Paul* (London, 1926), 45ff.; G. S. Duncan, *The Epistle to the Galatians*, Moffatt Commentary (London, 1934), xxiiff.; F. Amiot, *S. Paul: Épître aux Galates* (Paris, 1946), 32; W. L. Knox, *The Acts of the Apostles* (Cambridge, 1948), 40ff.; R. Heard, *Introduction to the NT* (London, 1950), 183; H. F. D. Sparks, *The Formation of the NT* (London, 1952), 60f.; C. S. C. Williams, *The Acts of the Apostles*, BNTC (London, 1957), 30 (tentatively); F. R. Coad, in *A Bible Commentary for Today*, ed. G. C. D. Howley (London, 1979), 1490. It is difficult to know what significance to attach to the frequent observation that most of the proponents of this dating are British. For judicious summings up cf. J. G. Machen, *The Origin of Paul's Religion*, 80ff.; G. B. Caird, *The Apostolic Age* (London, 1955), 200ff.; D. Guthrie, *NT Introduction: The Pauline Epistles* (London, 1961), 79ff.

experience, would have been as well defined by then as they were ever likely to be. Galatians, whatever its date, is a most important document of primitive Christianity, but if it is the earliest extant Christian document, its importance is enhanced.

VI
STRUCTURE

I. SALUTATION (1:1–5)
II. NO OTHER GOSPEL (1:6–10)
    (a) Paul's indignant astonishment (1:6–9)
    (b) Paul is no men-pleaser (1:10)
III. AUTOBIOGRAPHICAL SKETCH: PAUL'S INDEPENDENT GOSPEL (1:11–2:14)
    (a) Paul's gospel received by revelation (1:11–12)
    (b) Paul's earlier career (1:13–14)
    (c) Paul becomes an apostle (1:15–17)
    (d) Paul meets the Jerusalem church leaders (1:18–20)
    (e) Paul in Syria and Cilicia (1:21–24)
    (f) Conference in Jerusalem (2:1–10)
    (g) Conflict at Antioch (2:11–14)
IV. FAITH RECEIVES THE PROMISE (2:15–5:1)
    (a) Both Jews and Gentiles are justified by faith (2:15–21)
    (b) The primacy of faith over law (3:1–6)
    (c) The blessing of Abraham (3:7–9)
    (d) The curse of the law (3:10–14)
    (e) The priority and permanence of the promise (3:15–18)
    (f) The purpose of the law (3:19–22)
    (g) Liberation from the law (3:23–25)
    (h) Jews and Gentiles one in Christ (3:26–29)
    (i) From slavery to sonship (4:1–7)
    (j) No turning back! (4:8–11)
    (k) Personal appeal (4:12–20)
    (l) A lesson from scripture (4:21–5:1)
V. CHRISTIAN FREEDOM (5:2–12)
    (a) The law demands total commitment (5:2–6)
    (b) Stern words for the trouble-makers (5:7–12)
VI. FLESH AND SPIRIT (5:13–26)
    (a) The way of love (5:13–15)
    (b) Walking by the Spirit (5:16–18)
    (c) The works of the flesh (5:19–21)

(d) The fruit of the Spirit (5:22–26)

VII. MUTUAL HELP AND SERVICE (6:1–10)

VIII. CONCLUDING COMMENTS AND FINAL GREETING (6:11–18)

    (a) The true ground of boasting (6:11–16)

    (b) The marks of Jesus (6:17)

    (c) Final greeting (6:18)

This analysis, on which the following commentary is based, may help the reader, as it has helped the commentator, to appreciate the flow of Paul's argument; it is not claimed that it corresponds to Paul's conscious strategy in constructing his argument.

Among suggestions about the structure of the epistle, special mention must be made of the case persuasively presented by Hans Dieter Betz, who recognizes in it an example of the 'apologetic letter' genre, constructed according to contemporary rhetorical principles with the following main divisions: (i) epistolary prescript (1:1–5); (ii) exordium (1:6–11); (iii) narratio (1:12–2:14); (iv) propositio (2:15–21); (v) probatio (3:1–4:31); (vi) exhortatio (5:1–6:10); (vii) epistolary postscript or conclusio (6:11–18).[1] Betz's analysis corresponds well enough to the development of Paul's argument; one may wonder, however, if in the excitement and urgency of the crisis with which he was suddenly confronted Paul would have been consciously careful to construct his letter according to the canons of the rhetorical schools.

---

1. H. D. Betz, *Galatians*, 14–25; 'The Literary Composition and Function of Paul's Letter to the Galatians', *NTS* 21 (1974–75), 353–379; 'Galatians, Letter to the', *IDBSup*.

VII
SELECT BIBLIOGRAPHY

1. COMMENTARIES AND MONOGRAPHS ON GALATIANS

(a) Early Church

Syriac

Ephrem: S. *Ephraemi Syri commentarii in epistolas D. Pauli*, nunc primum ex Armenio in Latinum sermonem a patribus Mekhitaristis translati (Venice, 1893).

Greek

Chrysostom: S. *Joannis Chrysostomi interpretatio omnium epistolarum paulina-rum per homilias facta*, ed. F. Field (Oxford, 1852), ETr in NPNF, series 1. 13, 1–48.

Theodore of Mopsuestia: *Theodori episcopi Mopsuesteni in epistolas B. Pauli commentarii* I–II, ed. H. B. Swete (Cambridge, 1880–1882): I, 1–111.

Theodoret of Cyrus: *B. Theodoreti episcopi Cyrensis interpretatio epistolae ad Galatas* (*PG* 82.459–504).

See also: Staab, K., *Pauluskommentare aus der griechischen Kirche aus Kate-nenhandschriften gesammelt und herausgegeben*, NTAb 15 (Münster, 1933).

Latin

C. Marius Victorinus: *Marii Victorini Afri commentarii in epistulas Pauli*, ed. A. Locher, Bibliotheca Teubneriana (Leipzig, 1972): *Ad Galatas*.

Ambrosiaster: *Ambrosiastri qui dicitur commentarius in epistulas paulinas*, ed. H. J. Vogels, CSEL 81, I–III (Vienna, 1966–69): *Ad Galatas*, III.3–68.

Jerome: S. *Eusebii Hieronymi . . . commentariorum in epistolam ad Galatas libri tres* (*PL* 26.331–468).

Augustine: S. *Aurelii Augustini Hipponensis episcopi epistulae ad Galatas ex-positionis liber unus* (*PL* 35.2105–2148).

Pelagius: *Pelagius's exposition of thirteen epistles of St. Paul*, ed. A. Souter, I–III, TS 9 (Cambridge, 1922–31): *Ad Galatas*, II.306–343.

See also: Souter, A., *The Earliest Latin Commentaries on the Epistles of St. Paul* (Oxford, 1927).

(b) Reformation Period

Luther, M., *Luthers Vorlesung über den Galaterbrief, 1516/17*, ed. H. von Schubert, *AHAW,* phil.-hist. Kl. (Heidelberg, 1918).

Luther, M., *In epistolam Pauli ad Galatas M. Lutheri commentarius, 1518/19.* WA 2, 443–618.

Luther, M., *In epistolam S. Pauli ad Galatas commentarius ex praelectione D. Martini Lutheri collectus, 1531/35.* WA 40/1–2.

Luther, M., ETr: *Lectures on Galatians*, ed. J. Pelikan, *Luther's Works*, American edition, 26–27 (St. Louis, 1963–64)

Luther, M., ETr: *A Commentary on St. Paul's Epistle to the Galatians*. A revised and completed translation based on the 'Middleton' edition of the English version of 1575, ed. P. S. Watson (London, 1953).

Calvin, J., *Commentarius in Epistolam ad Galatas* (Geneva, 1548).

Calvin, J., ETr: *The Epistles of Paul the Apostle to the Galatians, Ephesians, Philippians and Colossians*, trans. T. H. L. Parker (Edinburgh, 1965), 3–119.

(c) Modern Period

Alford, H., *The Greek Testament*, I–IV (London and Cambridge, 1874–80): III, 1–67.

Allan, J. A., *The Epistle of Paul the Apostle to the Galatians*, Torch Commentaries (London, 1951).

Amiot, F., *Saint Paul: Epître aux Galates* (Paris, 1946).

Askwith, E. H., *The Epistle to the Galatians: An Essay on its Destination and Date* (London, 1902).

Bentley, R., *Critica Sacra*, ed. A. A. Ellis (Cambridge, 1862): *Epistola Beati Pauli Apostoli ad Galatas*, 93–117.

Betz, H. D., *Galatians: A Commentary on Paul's Letter to the Churches in Galatia*, Hermeneia (Philadelphia, 1979).

Beyer, H. W., *Der Brief an die Galater*. Neu bearbeitet von P. Althaus, NTD (Göttingen, [8]1962).

Bligh, J., *Galatians: A Discussion of St. Paul's Epistle* (London, 1969).

Bligh, J., *Galatians in Greek* (Detroit, 1966).

Blunt, A. W. F., *The Epistle to the Galatians*, Clarendon Bible (Oxford, 1925).

Bonnard, P., *L'Épître de Saint Paul aux Galates*, CNT (Neuchâtel & Paris, [2]1972).

Bousset, W., 'Der Brief an die Galater', *Die Schriften des Neuen Testaments*, II (Göttingen, [3]1917), 28–72.

Bring, R., *Commentary on Galatians*, ETr (Philadelphia, 1961).

Bruggen, J. van, *'Na Veertien Jaren': De datering van het in Galaten 2 genoemde overleg te Jerusalem* (Kampen, 1973).

Burton, E. DeWitt, *The Epistle to the Galatians*, ICC (Edinburgh, 1921).

Cole, R. A., *The Epistle of Paul to the Galatians*, TNTC (London, 1965).

Duncan, G. S., *The Epistle of Paul to the Galatians*, MNTC (London, 1934).

Eckert, J., *Die urchristliche Verkündigung im Streit zwischen Paulus und seinen Gegnern nach dem Galaterbrief*, BU 6 (Regensburg, 1971).

Emmet, C. W., *St. Paul's Epistle to the Galatians*, Readers' Commentary (London, 1912).

Findlay, G. G., *The Epistle to the Galatians*, Expositor's Bible (London, 1888).

Grayston, K., *The Epistles to the Galatians and to the Philippians*, Epworth Commentaries (London, 1957).

Guthrie, D., *Galatians*, NCB (London, 1969).

Harvey, A. E., *The New English Bible: Companion to the New Testament* (Oxford/Cambridge, 1970), 598–616.

Hendriksen, W., *Exposition of Galatians*, New Testament Commentary (Grand Rapids, 1968).

Hogg, C. F., and Vine, W. E., *The Epistle to the Galatians* (London/Glasgow, 1922).

Howard, G., *Paul: Crisis in Galatia*, SNTSM 35 (Cambridge, 1979).

Huxtable, E., *The Epistle to the Galatians*, Pulpit Commentary (London, 1880).

Kelly, W., *Lectures on the Epistle of Paul the Apostle to the Galatians* (London, 1865).

Lagrange, M.-J., *Saint Paul, Épître aux Galates* (Paris, ²1925).

Lietzmann, H., *An die Galater*, HNT (Tübingen, ²1923).

Lightfoot, J. B., *Saint Paul's Epistle to the Galatians* (London, 1865).

Loisy, A., *L'Épître aux Galates* (Paris, 1916).

Lührmann, D., *Der Brief an die Galater*, Zürcher Bibelkommentare (Zürich, 1978).

Lütgert, W., *Gesetz und Geist: eine Untersuchung zur Vorgeschichte des Galaterbriefes*, BFCT 22/6 (Gütersloh, 1919).

Machen, J. G., *Notes on Galatians*, ed. J. H. Skilton (Philadelphia, 1972).

Mussner, F., *Der Galaterbrief*, Herders TKNT (Freiburg, ³1977).

Neil, W., *The Letter of Paul to the Galatians*, CBC (Cambridge, 1967).

Oepke, A., *Der Brief des Paulus an die Galater*, THK (Berlin, ²1957).

O'Neill, J. C., *The Recovery of Paul's Letter to the Galatians* (London, 1972).

Quesnell, Q., *The Gospel of Christian Freedom* (New York, 1969).

Ramos, F. P., *La Libertad en la Carta a los Gálatas* (Madrid, 1977).

Ramsay, W. M., *A Historical Commentary on St. Paul's Epistle to the Galatians* (London, 1899).

Rendall, F., 'The Epistle of Paul to the Galatians,' *Expositor's Greek Testament* III (London, 1903), 121–200.

Ridderbos, H. N., *The Epistle of Paul to the Churches of Galatia*, NICNT (Grand Rapids, 1953).

Ropes, J. H., *The Singular Problem of the Epistle to the Galatians*, Harvard Theological Studies 14 (Cambridge, Mass., 1929).

Round, D., *The Date of St. Paul's Epistle to the Galatians* (Cambridge, 1906).

Schlier, H., *Der Brief an die Galater*, KEK (Göttingen, ⁵1971).

Sieffert, F., *Der Brief an die Galater*, KEK (Göttingen, ⁴1899).

Stamm, R. T., 'The Epistle to the Galatians', *IB* X (Nashville, 1953), 427–593.

Steinmann, A., *Die Abfassungszeit des Galaterbriefes* (Münster, 1906).

Steinmann, A., *Der Leserkreis des Galaterbriefes* (Münster, 1908).

Tenney, M. C., *Galatians: The Charter of Christian Liberty* (Grand Rapids, 1950).

Weber, V., *Die Abfassung des Galaterbriefes vor dem Apostelkonzil* (Ravensburg, 1900).

Weber, V., *Die Adressaten des Galaterbriefes: Beweis der rein südgalatischen Theorie* (Ravensburg, 1900).
Zahn, T., *Der Brief des Paulus an die Galater*, ZK (Leipzig, [3]1922).

2. COMMENTARIES AND MONOGRAPHS ON OTHER NEW TESTAMENT BOOKS

Acts

Blunt, A. W. F., *The Acts of the Apostles*, Clarendon Bible (Oxford, 1922).
Cadbury, H. J., *The Book of Acts in History* (New York, 1955).
Dibelius, M., *Studies in the Acts of the Apostles*, ETr (London, 1956).
Ehrhardt, A., *The Acts of the Apostles: Ten Lectures* (Manchester, 1969).
Findlay, J. A., *The Acts of the Apostles* (London, 1934).
Haenchen, E., *The Acts of the Apostles*, ETr (Oxford, 1971).
Harnack, A., *The Acts of the Apostles*, ETr (London, 1909).
Hengel, M., *Acts and the History of Earliest Christianity*, ETr (London, 1979).
Jackson, F. J. F., and Lake, K. (ed.), *The Beginnings of Christianity* I.1–5 (London, 1920–33).
Knox, W. L., *The Acts of the Apostles* (Cambridge, 1948).
Marshall, I. H. *The Acts of the Apostles*, TNTC (Leicester, 1980).
O'Neill, J. C., *The Theology of Acts in its Historical Setting* (London, [2]1970).
Wendt, H. H., *Die Apostelgeschichte*, KEK (Göttingen, [5]1913).
Williams, C. S. C., *A Commentary on the Acts of the Apostles*, BNTC (London, 1957).

Romans

Barrett, C. K., *A Commentary on the Epistle to the Romans*, BNTC (London, 1957).
Barth, K., *The Epistle to the Romans*, ETr (Oxford, 1933).
Bruce, F. F., *The Epistle of Paul to the Romans*, TNTC (London, 1963).
Cranfield, C. E. B., *The Epistle to the Romans*, ICC, I–II (Edinburgh, 1975–79).
Käsemann, E., *Commentary on Romans*, ETr (Grand Rapids, 1980).
Kuss, O., *Der Römerbrief*, I–III (Regensburg, 1957–78), unfinished.
Murray, J., *The Epistle to the Romans*, NICNT, I–II (Grand Rapids, 1959–65).
Wilckens, U., *Der Brief an die Römer*, EKKNT, I– (Köln/Neukirchen-Vluyn, 1978–).

1 and 2 Corinthians

Barrett, C. K., *A Commentary on the First Epistle to the Corinthians*, BNTC (London, 1968).
Barrett, C. K., *A Commentary on the Second Epistle to the Corinthians*, BNTC (London, 1973).
Schmithals, W., *Gnosticism in Corinth*, ETr (Nashville/New York, 1971).

Ephesians

Kirby, J. C. *Ephesians, Baptism and Pentecost* (London, 1968).
Robinson, J. A., *St. Paul's Epistle to the Ephesians* (London, [2]1904).

Philippians

Beare, F. W., *A Commentary on the Epistle to the Philippians*, BNTC (London, 1959).

Lightfoot, J. B., *Saint Paul's Epistle to the Philippians* (London, ⁶1881).

Colossians

Lightfoot, J. B., *Saint Paul's Epistles to the Colossians and to Philemon* (London, 1879).

Percy, E., *Die Probleme der Kolosser- und Epheserbriefe* (Lund, 1964).

1 and 2 Thessalonians

Best, E., *A Commentary on the First and Second Epistles to the Thessalonians*, BNTC (London, 1972).

1 Peter

Hort, F. J. A., *The First Epistle of St. Peter, I.1–II.17* (London, 1898).

3. NEW TESTAMENT INTRODUCTIONS (abbreviated *INT*)

Fuller, R. H., *A Critical Introduction to the New Testament* (London, 1966).

Grant, R. M., *A Historical Introduction to the New Testament* (London, 1963).

Guthrie, D., *New Testament Introduction* (London, ³1970).

Heard, R., *An Introduction to the New Testament* (London, 1950).

Kümmel, W. G., *Introduction to the New Testament*, ETr (London, 1966).

Marxsen, W., *Introduction to the New Testament*, ETr (Oxford, 1968).

Moffatt, J., *An Introduction to the Literature of the New Testament* (Edinburgh, ³1918).

Peake, A. S., *A Critical Introduction to the New Testament* (London, 1909).

Sparks, H. F. D., *The Formation of the New Testament* (London, 1952).

4. FESTSCHRIFTEN AND DENKSCHRIFTEN (abbreviated *FS*)

Black FS (1): *Neotestamentica et Semitica: Studies in honour of Matthew Black*, ed. E. E. Ellis and M. Wilcox (Edinburgh, 1969).

Black FS (2): *Text and Interpretation: Studies in the New Testament presented to Matthew Black*, ed. E. Best and R. McL. Wilson (Cambridge, 1979).

Bruce FS: Apostolic History and the Gospel: Biblical and Historical Essays presented to F. F. Bruce, ed. W. W. Gasque and R. P. Martin (Exeter, 1970).

Bultmann FS: *Neutestamentliche Studien für Rudolf Bultmann*, ed. W. Eltester, BZNW 21 (Berlin, 1954).

Cullmann FS (1): *Neotestamentica et Patristica: eine Freundesgabe . . . Oscar Cullmann . . . überreicht*, ed. W. C. van Unnik, NovTSup 6 (Leiden, 1962).

Cullmann FS (2): *Neues Testament und Geschichte: historisches Geschehen und Deutung im Neuen Testament . . .*, ed. H. Baltensweiler and B. Reicke (Zürich, 1972).

Daube FS: Donum Gentilicium: New Testament Studies in Honour of David Daube, ed. C. K. Barrett, E. Bammel, W. D. Davies (Oxford, 1978).

Deissmann FS: Festgabe für Adolf Deissmann zum 60. Geburtstag (Tübingen, 1927).

Grant FS: Early Christian Literature and the Classical Intellectual Tradition. In

Honorem Robert M. Grant, ed. W. R. Schoedel and R. L. Wilken, *Théologie Historique* 53 (Paris, 1979).

Grosheide FS: Arcana Revelata . . . aangeboden an F. W. Grosheide, ed. N. J. Hommes *et al*. (Kampen, 1951).

Käsemann FS: Rechtfertigung: Festschrift für Ernst Käsemann, ed. J. Friedrich, W. Pöhlmann, P. Stuhlmacher (Tübingen/Göttingen, 1976).

Knox FS: Christian History and Interpretation: Studies presented to John Knox, ed. W. R. Farmer, C. F. D. Moule, R. R. Niebuhr (Cambridge, 1967).

Manson FS: New Testament Essays: Studies in Memory of Thomas Walter Manson, ed. A. J. B. Higgins (Manchester, 1959).

Morris FS: Reconciliation and Hope: New Testament Essays on Atonement and Eschatology presented to L. L. Morris, ed. R. Banks (Exeter, 1974).

Moule FS: Christ and Spirit in the New Testament: Studies in honour of Charles Francis Digby Moule, ed. B. Lindars and S. S. Smalley (Cambridge, 1973).

Oudersluys FS: Saved by Hope: Essays in Honor of Richard C. Oudersluys, ed. J. I. Cook (Grand Rapids, 1978).

Rigaux FS: Mélanges Bibliques en hommage au R. P. Béda Rigaux, ed. A. Descamps and A. de Halleux (Gembloux, 1970).

Rost FS: Das Ferne und Nahe Wort: Festschrift Leonhard Rost zur Vollendung seines 70. Lebensjahres, ed. F. Maass, BZAW 105 (Berlin, 1967).

Schnackenburg FS: Neues Testament und Kirche: Festschrift für Rudolf Schnackenburg, ed. J. Gnilka (Freiburg/Vienna, 1974).

Simon FS: Mélanges offerts à Marcel Simon: Paganisme, Judaïsme, Christianisme, ed. A. Benoit, M. Philonenko, C. Vogel (Paris, 1978).

Stählin FS: Verborum Veritas: Festschrift für Gustav Stählin zum 70. Geburtstag, ed. O. Böcher and K. Haacker (Wuppertal, 1970).

Tenney FS: Current Issues in Biblical and Patristic Interpretation: Studies in Honor of Merrill C. Tenney, ed. G. F. Hawthorne (Grand Rapids, 1975).

De Zwaan FS: Studia Paulina in honorem Johannis de Zwaan septuagenarii, ed. J. N. Sevenster and W. C. van Unnik (Haarlem, 1953).

5. OTHER WORKS

Bandstra, A. J., *The Law and the Elements of the World* (Kampen, 1964).

Barclay, W., *Flesh and Spirit* (London, 1962).

Barnikol, E., *Der nichtpaulinische Ursprung des Parallelismus der Apostel Paulus und Petrus, Gal. 2,7-8*, FEUNTK 5 (Kiel, 1931).

Barnikol, E., *Die vorchristliche und frühchristliche Zeit des Paulus nach seinen geschichtlichen und geographischen Selbstzeugnissen im Galaterbrief*, FEUNTK 1 (Kiel, 1929).

Barr, J., *The Semantics of Biblical Language* (Oxford, 1961).

Barrett, C. K., *The Signs of an Apostle* (London, 1970).

Bate, H. N., *A Guide to the Epistles of St. Paul* (London, 1926).

Baur, F. C., *Paul: his Life and Works*, ETr, I-II (London, ²1876, 1875).

Baur, F. C., *Church History of the First Three Centuries*, ETr, I–II (London, 1878–79).

Bornkamm, G., *Paul*, ETr (New York, 1971).

Brown, R. E., and others (ed.), *Peter in the New Testament* (New York, 1973).

Brown, R. E., and others (ed.), *Mary in the New Testament* (London, 1978).

Bruce, F. F., *Paul: Apostle of the Free Spirit* (Exeter, ²1980).

Bruce, F. F., *Men and Movements in the Primitive Church* (Exeter, 1979).

Bruner, F. D., *A Theology of the Holy Spirit* (Grand Rapids, 1970).

Bruns, K. G., and Sachau, E. (ed.), *Syrisch-römisches Rechtsbuch aus dem fünften Jahrhundert* (Leipzig, 1880).

Buchanan, J., *The Doctrine of Justification* (Edinburgh, 1867).

Bultmann, R., *Exegetica* (Tübingen, 1967).

Bultmann, R., *Existence and Faith*, ETr (London, 1964).

Bultmann, R., *Theology of the New Testament*, ETr, I–II (London, 1952–55).

Burkitt, F. C., *Christian Beginnings* (London, 1924).

Caird, G. B., *The Apostolic Age* (London, 1955).

Caird, G. B., *Principalities and Powers* (Oxford, 1956).

Clark, S. B., *Man and Woman in Christ* (Ann Arbor, 1980).

Cullmann, O., *The Christology of the New Testament*, ETr (London, 1959).

Cullmann, O., *Peter: Disciple—Apostle—Martyr*, ETr (London, ²1962).

Cullmann, O., *Salvation in History*, ETr (London, 1967).

Daube, D., *The New Testament and Rabbinic Judaism* (London, 1956).

Davies, W. D., *Paul and Rabbinic Judaism* (London, ³1980).

Davies, W. D., *Torah in the Messianic Age and/or the Age to Come* (Philadelphia, 1952).

DeBoer, W. P., *The Imitation of Paul* (Kampen, 1962).

Deissmann, A., *Light from the Ancient East*, ETr (London, ²1927).

Deissmann, A., *Paul: A Study in Social and Religious History*, ETr (London, 1926).

Denney, J., *The Death of Christ* (London, ⁶1907).

Dix, G., *Jew and Greek* (London, 1953).

Dodd, C. H., *According to the Scriptures* (London, 1952).

Dodd, C. H., *The Bible and the Greeks* (London, 1935).

Dodd, C. H., *Gospel and Law* (Cambridge, 1951).

Dodd, C. H., *New Testament Studies* (Manchester, 1953).

Dodd, C. H., *More New Testament Studies* (Manchester, 1968).

Drane, J. W., *Paul: Libertine or Legalist?* (London, 1975).

Dülmen, A. van, *Die Theologie des Gesetzes bei Paulus* (Stuttgart, 1968).

Dungan, D. L., *The Sayings of Jesus in the Churches of Paul* (Oxford, 1971).

Dunn, J. D. G., *Baptism in the Holy Spirit*, SBT n.s. 15 (London, 1970).

Dunn, J. D. G., *Jesus and the Spirit* (London, 1975).

Dunn, J. D. G., *Unity and Diversity in the New Testament* (London, 1977).

Ellis, E. E., *Prophecy and Hermeneutic in Early Christianity* (Tübingen/Grand Rapids, 1978).

Féret, H. M., *Pierre et Paul à Antioche et à Jérusalem* (Paris, 1955).

Field, F., *Notes on the Translation of the New Testament* (Cambridge, 1899).

Fridrichsen, A., *The Apostle and his Message* (Uppsala, 1947).

Fuller, R. H., *The Formation of the Resurrection Narratives* (London, 1972).

Furnish, V. P., *The Love Command in the New Testament* (Nashville, 1972).

Gaechter, P., *Petrus und seine Zeit* (Vienna/Munich, 1958).

Gerhardsson, B., *Memory and Manuscript* (Lund/Copenhagen, 1961).

Gore, C., *The Reconstruction of Belief* (London, 1925).

Güttgemanns, E., *Der leidende Apostel und sein Herr* (Göttingen, 1966).

Hahn, F., *Mission in the New Testament*, ETr, SBT 47 (London, 1965).

Halmel, A., *Über römisches Recht im Galaterbrief: eine Untersuchung zur Geschichte des Paulinismus* (Essen, 1895).

Hanson, A. T., *Studies in Paul's Technique and Theology* (London, 1974).

Harnack, A., *Marcion: Das Evangelium vom fremden Gott* (Leipzig, [2]1924).

Harris, J. R., *Testimonies*, I–II (Cambridge, 1916–20).

Haussleiter, J., *Der Glaube Jesu Christi und der christliche Glaube* (Leipzig, 1891).

Heitmüller, W., *Luthers Stellung in der Religionsgeschichte des Christentums* (Marburg, 1917).

Hengel, M., *Crucifixion*, ETr (London, 1977).

Hengel, M., *The Son of God*, ETr (London, 1976).

Hengel, M., *Die Zeloten* (Leiden, 1961).

Heussi, K., *Die römische Petrustradition in kritischer Sicht* (Tübingen, 1955).

Hill, D., *Greek Words and Hebrew Meanings* (Cambridge, 1967).

Holl, K., *Gesammelte Aufsätze zur Kirchengeschichte*, II: *Der Osten* (Tübingen, 1928).

Hübner, H., *Das Gesetz bei Paulus* (Göttingen, 1978).

Hunter, A. M., *Paul and his Predecessors* (London, [2]1961).

Jackson, F. J. F., and Lake, K. (ed.), *The Beginnings of Christianity*, Part 1, I–V (London, 1920–33).

Jeremias, J., *Abba: Studien zur neutestamentlichen Theologie und Zeitgeschichte* (Göttingen, 1966).

Jeremias, J., *The Central Message of the New Testament* (London, 1965).

Jeremias, J., *The Prayers of Jesus*, ETr (London, 1967).

Jewett, P. K., *Man as Male and Female* (Grand Rapids, 1975).

Jewett, R., *Dating Paul's Life* (London, 1979).

Jewett, R., *Paul's Anthropological Terms* (Leiden, 1971).

Jüngel, E., *Paulus und Jesus* (Tübingen, 1962).

Käsemann, E., *New Testament Questions of Today*, ETr (London, 1961).

Käsemann, E., *Perspectives on Paul*, ETr (London, 1971).

Kim, S., *The Origin of Paul's Gospel*, WUNT 2/4 (Tübingen, 1981).

Klausner, J., *From Jesus to Paul*, ETr (London, 1944).

Klein, G., *Studien über Paulus* (Stockholm, 1918).

Klein, G., *Rekonstruktion und Interpretation* (Munich, 1969).

Klein, G., *Die zwölf Apostel* (Göttingen, 1961).

Knox, J., *Chapters in a Life of Paul* (London, 1954).

Kramer, W., *Christ, Lord, Son of God*, ETr, SBT 50 (London, 1966).

Kümmel, W. G., *The Theology of the New Testament*, ETr (London, 1974).

Küng, H., *Justification*, ETr (Edinburgh, 1961).

Küng, H., *The Living Church*, ETr (London, 1963).

Kuss, O., *Auslegung und Verkündigung*, I–III (Regensburg, 1963–71).

Lake, K., *The Earlier Epistles of St. Paul* (London, 1911).

Lampe, G. W. H., *The Seal of the Spirit* (London, 1951).

Leipoldt, J., *Die Frau in der antiken Welt und im Urchristentum* (Leipzig, [2]1962).

Lightfoot, J. B., *Biblical Essays* (London, 1893).

Lindars, B., *New Testament Apologetic* (London, 1961).

Lindemann, A. *Paulus im ältesten Christentum* (Tübingen, 1977).

Lohmeyer, E., *Galiläa und Jerusalem* (Göttingen, 1936).

Longenecker, R. N., *Biblical Exegesis in the Apostolic Period* (Grand Rapids, 1975).

Longenecker, R. N., *Paul, Apostle of Liberty* (Grand Rapids, 1964).

Lorenzi, L. de (ed.), *Paul de Tarse* (Rome, 1979).

Lorenzi, L. de (ed.), *Paolo a una chiesa divisa* (Rome, 1980).

Lüdemann, G., *Paulus der Heidenapostel, I: Studien zur Chronologie* (Göttingen, 1980).

Luz, U., *Das Geschichtsverständnis bei Paulus* (Munich, 1968).

Machen, J. G., *The Origin of Paul's Religion* (New York, 1921).

Manson, T. W., *The Sayings of Jesus* (London, ²1949).

Manson, T. W., *Studies in the Gospels and Epistles* (Manchester, 1962).

Marshall, I. H., *The Origins of New Testament Christology* (Leicester, 1977).

Mitteis, L., *Reichsrecht und Volksrecht in den östlichen Provinzen des römischen Kaiserreichs* (Leipzig, 1891).

Moffatt, J., *Grace in the New Testament* (London, 1931).

Moffatt, J., *Love in the New Testament* (London, 1929).

Moule, C. F. D., *The Birth of the New Testament* (London, 1962).

Moule, C. F. D., *An Idiom-Book of New Testament Greek* (Cambridge, 1953).

Moule, C. F. D., *The Origin of Christology* (Cambridge, 1977).

Moule, C. F. D., *The Phenomenon of the New Testament* (London, ³1981).

Munck, J., *Paul and the Salvation of Mankind*, ETr (London, 1959).

Neusner, J., *The Rabbinic Traditions about the Pharisees before 70*, I–III (Leiden, 1971).

Nickle, K. F., *The Collection: A Study in Paul's Strategy*, SBT 49 (London, 1966).

Nock, A. D., *Essays on Religion and the Ancient World*, I–II (Oxford, 1972). 1972).

Nock, A. D., *St. Paul* (London, 1938).

O'Brien, P. T., *Introductory Thanksgivings in the Letters of Paul*, NovTSup 49 (Leiden, 1977).

Ogg, G., *The Chronology of the Life of Paul* (London, 1968).

Ollrog, W.-H., *Paulus und seine Mitarbeiter: Untersuchungen zu Theorie und Praxis der paulinischen Mission*, WMANT 50 (Neukirchen/Vluyn, 1979).

Perrot, G., *De Galatia Provincia Romana* (Paris, 1867).

Plooij, D., *De Chronologie van het Leven van Paulus* (Leiden, 1918).

Ramsay, W. M., *The Church in the Roman Empire before A.D. 170* (London, ⁵1897).

Ramsay, W. M., *Cities and Bishoprics of Phrygia*, I–II (Oxford, 1895–97).

Ramsay, W. M., *The Cities of St. Paul* (London, 1907).

Ramsay, W. M., *Historical Geography of Asia Minor* (London, 1890).

Ramsay, W. M., *St. Paul the Traveller and the Roman Citizen* (London, ¹⁴1920).

Ramsay, W. M., *The Teaching of Paul in Terms of the Present Day* (London, 1913).

Regul, J., *Die antimarcionitischen Evangelienprologe* (Freiburg, 1969).

Renan, E., *St. Paul*, ETr (London, 1887).

Richardson, P., *Israel in the Apostolic Church*, SNTSM 10 (Cambridge, 1969).

Richardson, P., *Paul's Ethic of Freedom* (Philadelphia, 1979).

Ridderbos, H. N., *Paul: An Outline of his Theology*, ETr (Grand Rapids, 1975).

Ridderbos, H. N., *When the Time Had Fully Come* (Grand Rapids, 1957).

Robinson, J. A. T., *Redating the New Testament* (London, 1976).

Sanders, E. P., *Paul and Palestinian Judaism* (London, 1977).

Schlier, H., *Principalities and Powers in the New Testament*, ETr (Freiburg, 1961).

Schmithals, W., *The Office of Apostle in the Early Church*, ETr (London, 1971).

Schmithals, W., *Paul and the Gnostics*, ETr (Nashville/New York, 1972).

Schmithals, W., *Paul and James*, ETr, SBT 46 (London, 1965).

Schmitz, O., *Die Christusgemeinschaft des Paulus im Lichte seines Genetivgebrauchs* (Gütersloh, 1924).

Schnackenburg, R., *Baptism in the Thought of St. Paul*, ETr (Oxford, 1964).

Schniewind, H., *Euangelion*, I–II (Gütersloh, 1927–31).

Schoeps, H.-J., *Aus frühchristlicher Zeit* (Tübingen, 1950).

Schoeps, H.-J., *Paul: The Theology of the Apostle in the Light of Jewish Religious History*, ETr (London, 1961).

Schoeps, H.-J., *Theologie und Geschichte des Judenchristentums* (Tübingen, 1949).

Schubert, P., *Form and Function of the Pauline Thanksgivings*, BZNW 20 (Berlin, 1939).

Schürer, E., *The History of the Jewish People in the Age of Jesus Christ*, ETr, I–III (Edinburgh, 1973–).

Schütz, J. H., *Paul and the Anatomy of Apostolic Authority*, SNTSM 26 (Cambridge, 1975).

Schweitzer, A., *The Mysticism of Paul the Apostle*, ETr (London, 1931).

Schweizer, E., *Beiträge zur Theologie des Neuen Testaments* (Zürich, 1970).

Scougal, H., *The Life of God in the Soul of Man* (*c.* 1672/3, reprinted London, 1961).

Sherwin-White, A. N., *Roman Society and Roman Law in the New Testament* (Oxford, 1963).

Spicq, C., *Agape in the New Testament*, ETr, I–II (St. Louis, 1963–66).

Stuhlmacher, P., *Das paulinische Evangelium*, I– (Göttingen, 1968–).

Swete, H. B., *The Holy Spirit in the New Testament* (London, 1909).

Tannehill, R. C., *Dying and Rising with Christ*, BZNW 32 (Berlin, 1967).

Trench, R. C., *Synonyms of the New Testament* (Dublin, [8]1876, reprinted London, 1961).

Vögtle, A., *Die Tugend- und Lasterkataloge im Neuen Testament* (Münster, 1936).

Vos, G., *The Pauline Eschatology* (Grand Rapids, [2]1952).

Wagner, G., *Pauline Baptism and the Pagan Mysteries*, ETr (Edinburgh/London, 1967).

Walker, D., 'The Legal Terminology in the Epistle to the Galatians', *The Gift of Tongues* (Edinburgh, 1906), 81–175.

Weiss, J., *Earliest Christianity*, ETr, I–II (New York, 1959).

Weizsäcker, C. von, *The Apostolic Age*, ETr, I–II (London, 1907–12).

White, J. L., *The Body of the Greek Letter* (Missoula, 1972).

Whiteley, D. E. H., *The Theology of St. Paul* (Oxford, 1964).

Wibbing, S., *Die Tugend- und Lasterkataloge im Neuen Testament und ihre Traditionsgeschichte*, BZNW 25 (Berlin, 1959).

Wikenhauser, A., *Pauline Mysticism*, ETr (Edinburgh/London, 1960).

Wiles, G. P., *Paul's Intercessory Prayers*, SNTSM 24 (Cambridge, 1974).

Williams, N. P., *The Grace of God* (London, 1930).

Wilson, S. G., *The Gentiles and the Gentile Mission in Luke-Acts*, SNTSM 23 (Cambridge, 19).

Wissmann, E., *Das Verhältnis von* ΠΙΣΤΙΣ *und Christusfrömmigkeit bei Paulus* (Göttingen, 1926).

Wrede, W., *Paul*, ETr (London, 1907).

Ziesler, J. A., *The Meaning of Righteousness in Paul*, SNTSM 20 (Cambridge, 1972).

Zuntz, G., *The Text of the Epistles* (London, 1953).

COMMENTARY

I
SALUTATION
(1:1–5)

Paul greets the churches of Galatia, emphasizing the divine source of his apostolic commission.

Paul, an apostle (commissioned) neither by men nor through man, but through Jesus Christ and God the Father who raised him from the dead, and all the brothers who are with me, to the churches of Galatia: grace and peace be yours from God our Father and the Lord Jesus Christ, who gave himself for our sins in order to deliver us from the present evil age according to the will of our God and Father, to whom be the glory for ever and ever. Amen.

TEXTUAL NOTES

v 1 καὶ θεου πατρος *om* Mcion (& αὐτον *pro* αὐτον?)
v 3 ημων και κυριου ℵ A 33 81 *al* / και κυριου ημων P⁴⁶, ⁵¹ᵛⁱᵈ B D G H byz lat syr
    cop^{sa} / και κυριου 1877 Pelag Chrys Aug / ημων και κυριου ημων cop^{bo} eth
v 4 υπερ P⁵¹ B H 33 *pm* TR / περι P⁴⁶ᵛⁱᵈ ℵ* A D G Ψ byz

Letters in Near Eastern antiquity were regularly introduced by the formula: 'X to Y: greetings'. Cf. *'artaḥšast' melek̠ mal^e k̠ayyā' l^e'ezrā' k̠ah^a nā' sāpar dāṯā' dî-'^e lāh š^e mayyā' g^e mîr*, 'Artaxerxes, king of kings, to Ezra the priest, scribe of the law of the God of heaven, greetings' (Ezr. 7:12); Θέων Θέωνι τῷ πατρὶ χαίρειν, 'Theon to Theon his father, greetings' (P. Oxy. 119.1); *M. Cicero Q. fratri s[alutem]*, 'Marcus Cicero to Quintus his brother, health' (Cicero, *Ep. ad Q. fratrem*, i.2). The introductions to the various NT letters exhibit the same pattern, including the letters of Paul, one or more of the three elements (the author, the addressee, the greetings) being variously amplified as may be appropriate to the occasion.

The three elements are readily recognizable in the introduction to this letter: (*a*) 'Paul . . . and all the brothers who are with me' (1:1, 2a), (*b*) 'to the churches of Galatia' (1:2b), (*c*) 'grace and peace . . .' (1:3). The first and third elements are considerably amplified.

1:1 Παῦλος ἀπόστολος. More often than not Paul introduces himself as an apostle. In Rom. 1:1 he calls himself 'a slave (δοῦλος) of Christ Jesus' but adds κλητὸς ἀπόστολος in the next phrase (cf. 1 Cor. 1:1); in Phil. 1:1 he describes himself and Timothy as 'slaves of Christ Jesus'; in Phm. 1 he designates himself 'a prisoner (δέσμιος) of Christ Jesus'.

An ἀπόστολος is, in general, 'one who is sent' (the word is so used in Jn. 13:16), but regularly in the NT he is one who has received a special commission from Christ. When Paul uses the term of himself, he claims a status not inferior to those who, as he says, 'were apostles before me' (v 17): if they had been commissioned by Christ (which he does not dispute), so had he. Paul knew of other apostles who were commissioned by men, like the ἀπόστολοι ἐκκλησιῶν to whom he refers in 2 Cor. 8:23—men whose commission was entirely valid, but took its character from those by whom they were commissioned. If the NT ἀπόστολος bears some relation to Heb. šālûaḥ or šālîaḥ (which seems probable), then of the one as of the other it was true that šᵉlûḥô šel 'āḏām kᵉmôṯô, 'a man's delegate is like himself' (m. Ber. 5.5), i.e. the authority of the person commissioned is that of the person who commissions him. So, when Paul speaks or acts as an apostle of Christ, he does so with Christ's authority (cf. 2 Cor. 10:8).

There is a voluminous bibliography on apostles and apostleship. See *inter alia* K. H. Rengstorf, *TDNT* I, 407–447 (*s.v.* ἀπόστολος); H. Riesenfeld, *RGG*³ I, 497–499 (*s.v.* 'Apostel'); D. Müller and C. Brown, *NIDNTT* I, 126–137 (*s.v.* 'Apostle'); E. Käsemann, 'Die Legitimität des Apostels', *ZNW* 41 (1942), 33–71; A. Fridrichsen, *The Apostle and his Message* (Uppsala, 1947); H. von Campenhausen, 'Der urchristliche Apostelbegriff', *ST* 1 (1948–49), 96–130; J. Munck, 'Paul, the Apostles and the Twelve', *ST* 3 (1950–51), 96–110; E. Lohse, 'Ursprung und Prägung des christlichen Apostolats', *TZ* 9 (1953), 259–275; G. Klein, *Die zwölf Apostel* (Göttingen, 1961); R. Schnackenburg, 'Apostles before and during Paul's Time', *Bruce FS*, 287–303; C. K. Barrett, *The Signs of an Apostle* (London, 1970), and '*Shaliaḥ* and Apostle', *Daube FS*, 88–102; W. Schmithals, *The Office of Apostle in the Early Church*, ETr (London, 1971); J. H. Schütz, *Paul and the Anatomy of Apostolic Authority* (Cambridge, 1975).

Unlike that of the ἀπόστολοι ἐκκλησιῶν, Paul's apostolic commission was not derived 'from men' (οὐκ ἀπ' ἀνθρώπων). It was not even derived through a human intermediary (οὐδὲ δι' ἀνθρώπου); it was received immediately 'through Jesus Christ'. We should probably be right in inferring from Paul's emphatic language that his Galatian converts had been given a different account of his apostleship—an account which maintained that he had no commission apart from what he had received from men who had been Christian leaders before him, whether the apostles and elders of the Jerusalem church or the Christian leaders of Damascus or Antioch: even if his commission could be traced back ultimately to Christ, it was transmitted through these leaders. Paul denies this: his commission was received directly, without mediation, from the risen Christ. The occasion of his receiving it was his Damascus-road experience in which, as he says below in vv 15f., 'God . . . saw fit to reveal his Son in me'.

It is strange, then, to find the preposition διά, used to indicate mediation in the phrase οὐδὲ δι' ἀνθρώπου, repeated before 'Ιησοῦ Χριστοῦ. Paul hardly means that Jesus Christ was the intermediary through whom he received his apostleship. One could indeed conceive his meaning to be that he received it from God the Father through Jesus Christ, but that is excluded in the present context because θεοῦ πατρός stands under the regimen of διά as much as does Ἰησοῦ Χριστοῦ (διὰ Ἰησοῦ Χριστοῦ καὶ θεοῦ πατρός). Moreover, when Paul enlarges on the subject in the course of this letter or elsewhere, he makes it plain that he is the commissioned apostle of the risen Lord, to whom he is accountable for the discharge of his commission (cf. v 10; 6:17; 1 Cor. 4:1–4; 9:1f., 14–27; Rom. 15:15–21). It may be concluded, then, that while διά before ἀνθρώπου means 'through' in the sense of mediation, it is used in the more general sense of agency when it precedes Ἰησοῦ Χριστοῦ καὶ θεοῦ πατρός. Cf. δι᾽ οὗ ἐκλήθητε, said of God (1 Cor. 1:9); δι᾽ οὗ τὰ πάντα, also said of God (Heb. 2:10); see BDF 223 (2).

Paul enlarges on the unmediated character of his dominical commission in the narrative of vv 15ff.

In distinguishing 'Jesus Christ and God the Father' from human authority or agency Paul sets Christ in a category apart from ordinary men (see note on v 12). Now that he is risen and exalted, Christ is naturally thought of and mentioned alongside God the Father, at whose right hand he is enthroned, according to the common primitive-Christian application of Ps. 110:1 (cf. Rom. 8:34). The unselfconscious way in which Paul repeatedly couples God and Christ together bears eloquent witness to his understanding of the person and status of Christ.

τοῦ ἐγείραντος αὐτὸν ἐκ νεκρῶν. God the Father is further defined as he who raised Christ from the dead. Like other Jews who believed in the resurrection, Paul had been brought up to acclaim God as 'the raiser of the dead' (mᵉhayyeh hammēṯîm, as he is called in the second of the Eighteen Benedictions; cf. Rom. 4:17, θεοῦ τοῦ ζῳοποιοῦντος τοὺς νεκρούς, and 2 Cor. 1:9, τῷ θεῷ τῷ ἐγείροντι τοὺς νεκρούς). But now he had learned that the first stage in the expected resurrection had already come with the raising of Christ. The raising of Christ, moreover, was specially relevant to Paul's commissioning, for it was his Damascus-road experience that simultaneously confronted him with the risen Christ, thereby convincing him that God had indeed raised Christ from the dead, and brought home to him the call of the risen Christ to be his apostle to the Gentile world. The call was Christ's, but it was also God's, for it was God who revealed his Son to Paul in that confrontation (vv 15f.).

1:2 καὶ οἱ σὺν ἐμοὶ ἀδελφοί. In the initial salutation of several of his letters Paul associates with himself by name one or more of his companions who are with him at the time of writing (cf. 1 Cor. 1:1; 2 Cor. 1:1; Phil. 1:1; Col. 1:1; 1 Thes. 1:1; 2 Thes. 1:1; Phm. 1). Here he mentions no one by name, but associates with himself 'all the brothers who are with me'. Our conclusions about the probable identity of those brothers will depend on our view of the provenance and date of the letter. If it was sent from Syrian Antioch, not long after Paul and Barnabas returned from their evangelization of the cities of South Galatia (cf. Acts 14:26ff.), we should think of the leaders of the Antiochene church, including pre-eminently Barnabas (cf. Acts 13:1). In that case it might be asked why Barnabas is not singled out by name, since he was Paul's senior colleague in the evangelization of South Galatia. R. J. Bauckham ('Barnabas in Galatians', *JSNT*, Issue 2 [1979], 65) suggests that Paul's generalizing phrase 'covers his embarrassment in not being able to ask his partner to endorse the letter' after the painful incident narrated below in 2:11–13. On the other hand, Paul may wish to indicate to the Galatians that he is expressing no merely individual viewpoint, but one shared by his colleagues. The phrase οἱ σὺν ἐμοὶ ἀδελφοί occurs in the final greetings of Phil. 4:21, where the reference (less general than πάντες οἱ ἅγιοι in the following verse) seems to be to his missionary associates.

ταῖς ἐκκλησίαις τῆς Γαλατίας. The addressees are specified with the utmost brevity. 'The churches of Galatia' are mentioned again in 1 Cor. 16:1. It has been argued above (pp. 5–18) that the churches addressed here are those of South Galatia, whose founding by Paul and Barnabas is recorded in Acts 13:14–14:23.

It was evidently a circular letter, designed to be taken by a messenger to one of the Galatian churches, then to the next on his itinerary, and so on until each church had heard its contents. If some of the churches wished to make and retain a copy, that could no doubt be done. But Paul apparently did not send several copies, one for each church; his words in 6:11 imply that each church would see the one copy that he sent and take note of the 'large letters' that characterized his own handwriting.

1:3 χάρις ὑμῖν καὶ εἰρήνη. The normal word of salutation at the beginning of a Greek letter was χαίρειν ('rejoice'); the normal word of salutation at the beginning of a Jewish letter was šālôm, εἰρήνη ('peace'). The amplified form 'mercy and peace' (cf. 6:16) seems to have been current in some Jewish circles (cf. 2 Bar. 78:2). The form χάρις καὶ εἰρήνη is characteristically Pauline; both ' grace' and 'peace' have their full Christian force. Grace is God's unconditioned good will towards mankind which is decisively expressed in the saving work of Christ (cf. v 6; 2:21); peace is the state of life—peace with God (Rom. 5:1) and peace with one another (Eph. 2:14–18)—enjoyed by those who have effectively experienced the divine grace (cf. 5:22; 6:16).

See E. Lohmeyer, 'Probleme paulinischer Theologie, I. Briefliche Grussüberschriften', *ZNW* 26 (1927), 158–173 (where it is argued that the formula was primarily liturgical and only secondarily epistolary); A. Pujol, 'De salutatione apostolica "gratia vobis et pax" ', *VD* 12 (1932), 38–40, 76–82; C. E. B. Cranfield, *Romans*, 71f.; E. Käsemann, *Romans*, 16.

The Christian force of the grace and peace is emphasized by the added words ἀπὸ θεοῦ πατρὸς ἡμῶν καὶ κυρίου Ἰησοῦ Χριστοῦ. These added words appear, with minor variations, in most of Paul's opening salutations (they are missing in 1 Thes. 1:1; καὶ κυρίου Ἰησοῦ Χριστοῦ is missing in Col. 1:2). As in v 2 'Jesus Christ' and 'God the Father' are brought together under the common regimen of διά, so here 'God our Father' and 'the Lord Jesus Christ' are brought together under the common regimen of ἀπό. Such language bespeaks the exalted place which the risen Christ occupies in Paul's thinking. In resurrection he wears a heavenly humanity, as 'a life-giving spirit' (1 Cor. 15:45–49), and has been invested by God with the designation κύριος, 'Lord'— 'the name which is above every name' (Phil. 2:9). God and Christ are completely at one in the bestowal of salvation: the grace which lies behind this salvation is indiscriminately called 'the grace of God' (2:21) and 'the grace of Christ' (1:6), and the peace which this salvation produces is indiscriminately called 'the peace of God' (Phil. 4:7) and 'the peace of Christ' (Col. 3:15).

1:4 τοῦ δόντος ἑαυτόν κτλ. Exceptionally, the third element in the salutation ('grace and peace . . .') is further amplified here with what appears to be part of an early confession of faith or kerygmatic summary, which is reflected in several NT contexts. δοῦναι ἑαυτόν is identical with δοῦναι τὴν ψυχὴν αὐτοῦ in Mk. 10:45, except that the latter preserves the Semitic idiom (Aram. *leméhēḇ napšēh*, where *nepeš* with pronominal suffix does duty for the reflexive pronoun). Cf. 2:20, τοῦ . . . παραδόντος ἑαυτὸν ὑπὲρ ἐμοῦ. Paul more often uses παραδίδωμι than the simple δίδωμι in this connexion, but cf. 1 Tim. 2:6, ὁ δοὺς ἑαυτὸν ἀντίλυτρον ὑπὲρ πάντων, and Tit. 2:14, ὃς ἔδωκεν ἑαυτὸν ὑπὲρ ἡμῶν (in a later development of the present formula).

ὑπὲρ τῶν ἁμαρτιῶν ἡμῶν. ὑπέρ is better attested here than the variant περί. Cf. 1 Cor. 15:3, Χριστὸς ἀπέθανεν ὑπὲρ τῶν ἁμαρτιῶν ἡμῶν (also in a traditional kerygmatic summary). 'For our sins' means 'for the forgiveness or expiation of our sins' (for the sense cf. Mk. 10:45, δοῦναι τὴν ψυχὴν αὐτοῦ λύτρον ἀντὶ πολλῶν); the wording possibly owes something to the fourth Isaianic servant song (cf. Is. 53:5, 12 LXX, ἐτραυματίσθη διὰ τὰς ἁμαρτίας ἡμῶν . . . διὰ τὰς ἀνομίας αὐτῶν παρεδόθη); cf. Rom. 4:25, ὃς παρεδόθη διὰ τὰ παραπτώματα ἡμῶν. The use of ὑπέρ with the genitive here rather than διά with the accusative may be influenced by ὑπὲρ ἡμῶν in a similar context (cf. 3:13; Rom. 5:8; 8:32; 2 Cor. 5:21; 1 Thes. 5:10; Tit. 2:14; also ὑπὲρ ἐμοῦ in Gal. 2:20); but one may compare the use of ὑπέρ in 3 Ki. (MT 1 Ki.) 16:18f., ἀπέθανεν ὑπὲρ τῶν ἁμαρτιῶν αὐτοῦ, where ὑπέρ must mean 'because of': Zimri died as a penalty for his sins (hardly by way of an atonement for them). Cf. Polycarp 1:2, ὃς ὑπέμεινεν ὑπὲρ τῶν ἁμαρτιῶν ἡμῶν ἕως θανάτου καταντῆσαι ('who suffered for our sins even to the point of death').

ὅπως ἐξέληται ἡμᾶς. Christ's self-oblation not only procures for his people the forgiveness of their past sins; it delivers them from the realm in which sin is irresistible into the realm where he himself is Lord. Cf. Rom. 14:9, 'to this end Christ died and came to life, that he might be Lord both of the dead and of the living.'

This is the only occurrence of ἐξαιρέομαι in Paul: he prefers σῴζω, ῥύομαι, ἐλευθερόω or (ἐξ)αγοράζω to express the saving act of God in Christ. It is common in the LXX in this sense, however (especially to translate the hiph'il of *nāṣal*), and the LXX usage is followed in Acts—not only in OT allusions and quotations (7:10, 34) but elsewhere (12:11; 23:27; 26:17). Paul's use of ἐξαιρέομαι here adds weight to the opinion that he is quoting a form of words well known to his readers, which summed up the gospel which they had received and from which, he feared, they were now departing. See F. Bovon, 'Une formule prépaulinienne dans l'Épître aux Galates', in *Simon FS*, 91–107, especially 97–105.

The pattern of this form of words, in which the statement about Christ's self-giving is followed by a clause of purpose, is followed closely in Tit. 2:14, 'who gave himself for us, that he might redeem us (ἵνα λυτρώσηται ἡμᾶς) from all iniquity and purify for himself a people of his own (λαὸν περιούσιον), zealous for good works'.

For deliverance from 'this present evil age' (ἐκ τοῦ αἰῶνος τοῦ ἐνεστῶτος πονηροῦ) cf. Sir. 51:11, ἐξείλου με ἐκ καιροῦ πονηροῦ. But there καιρὸς πονηρός is 'an evil plight', some deadly peril from which Ben Sira was delivered (so the Hebrew text, *wayᵉmallᵉṭēnî bᵉyôm ṣārāh*, 'and he rescued me in the day of trouble'), whereas Paul's αἰὼν πονηρός is an age dominated by an ethically evil power—one which, far from being 'according to the will of our God and Father', is totally opposed to it.

Those who accept the gospel are thereby delivered from the godless *Zeitgeist*: for the missionary setting of such language cf. E. Haenchen (*Acts*, 184 n. 8) on Acts 2:40, 'Save yourselves from this perverse generation' (an echo of the description of the wilderness generation in Dt. 1:35; 32:5). But the designation of the present age (ὁ αἰὼν ὁ ἐνεστώς, Heb. *hā'ôlām hazzeh*) as 'evil', by contrast with the age to come (ὁ αἰὼν ὁ ἐρχόμενος, Heb. *hā'ôlām habbā'*), belonged to Paul's background: the gospel sharpened this awareness of the ethical distinction between the two ages. A parallel is provided in Qumran literature, where the current age is the 'epoch of wickedness' (*qēṣ hāriš'āh*, e.g. 1QpHab 5:7f.) during which Belial, the power opposed to the will of God, is let loose. Another sectarian Jewish outlook is expressed in 4 Ezr. 7:12f.: 'The entrances of this world (Lat. *huius saeculi*) are narrow and painful and toilsome; they are few and evil, full of dangers and beset by great hardship' (as distinct from the broad and safe entrances to 'the greater world', which lead to immortality)— where, however, the ethical emphasis is played down. Yet another parallel is provided by the 'Freer logion', where the disciples say, 'This age (ὁ αἰὼν οὗτος) of lawlessness and unbelief is subject to Satan' (Mk. 16:14 W).

The deliverance of which Paul speaks is not out of the material world but from the evil which dominates it (cf. Jn. 17:15 where κόσμος has much the same sense as Paul's αἰών). Similarly in Rom. 12:2 Paul urges the Roman Christians not to be conformed to this age (τῷ αἰῶνι τούτῳ) but to be transformed by inward renewal so as to prove by experience how good (by contrast) the will of God is. So here, κατὰ τὸ θέλημα τοῦ θεοῦ καὶ πατρὸς ἡμῶν may imply not only that believers' deliverance from 'the present evil age' is in accordance with God's will but that such deliverance enables them to live in conformity with God's will.

Here, then, is Paul's 'realized eschatology'. Temporally, the age to come, the resurrection age, still lies in the future; spiritually, believers in Christ have here and now been made partakers of it, because they share the risen life of Christ (cf. 2:19f.), who has already entered the resurrection age. They have thus been delivered from the control of the powers which dominate the present age. As 1 Cor. 7:31 puts it, 'the form of this world (τὸ σχῆμα τοῦ κόσμου τούτου) is passing away', and therefore believers in Christ should manifest a spirit of detachment from it. The indwelling Spirit not only helps them to look forward in confidence to the life of the age to come (cf. 5:5); he enables them to enjoy it even while in mortal body they live in the present age. Thanks to the work of the Spirit, applying to believers the redemption and victory won by Christ, the 'not yet' has become for them the 'already'.

It is particularly relevant to the argument of this letter that the law, to which the Galatian Christians were being urged to submit, belongs to this present age: it is associated with 'the elemental powers of the world' (τὰ στοιχεῖα τοῦ κόσμου) under which they were enslaved before they came to faith in Christ (4:3, 9).

On αἰών in Paul see E. D. Burton, *Galatians*, 426–433. It has much the same force as the Johannine κόσμος in the sense of the 'godless world' (cf. 1 Jn. 2:15–17); indeed, Paul occasionally uses κόσμος as a synonym for αἰών (cf. 1 Cor. 1:20; 2:12; 3:19; also 7:31, quoted above), denoting not only the current era of world history but the way of life that characterizes it.

The appended phrase, 'according to the will of our God and Father', may have a further significance. It is Christ who 'gave himself for our sins that he might deliver us . . .'; the appended phrase reminds us afresh that in this self-giving and deliverance Christ and God are at one, that 'God has reconciled us to himself through Christ'—that, in fact, 'God was in Christ reconciling the world to himself' (2 Cor. 5:18f.).

This is probably the earliest written statement in the NT about the significance of the death of Christ. It relates his death to the supersession of the old age by the new. His people accordingly (as other places in the Pauline corpus affirm) are those 'upon whom the ends of the ages have come' (1 Cor. 10:11; cf. similar phraseology in Heb. 1:2; 9:26; 1 Pet. 1:20); they have been delivered by God 'from the dominion of darkness and transferred . . . to the kingdom of his beloved Son' (Col. 1:13). Moreover, it relates his death to the forgiveness of his people's sins. This is not an insight peculiar to Paul; he uses language to the same effect in other passages where there is reason to recognize pre-Pauline summaries of the Christian faith and message. To the Corinthians as early as AD 50 he 'delivered', as part of the gospel which he had 'received' and which he shared with the leaders of the Jerusalem church, 'that Christ died for our sins in accordance with the scriptures' (1 Cor. 15:3); to the Romans (not as telling them something new but using words with which he could presume their acquaintance and agreement) he describes the risen Lord as the one 'who was delivered up for our trespasses' (Rom. 4:25). (See R. Bultmann, *Theology of the NT*, ETr, I [London, 1952], 46f.) But if this interpretation of the death of Christ was widely held among his followers within twenty years after the event, it is antecedently probable that he himself gave the impetus to it. The earliest evangelist represents him as accepting his death in this spirit: speaking of himself as giving his life as 'a ransom for many' (Mk. 10:45), speaking of his 'covenant blood' as 'poured out for many' (Mk. 14:24; the epexegetic εἰς ἄφεσιν ἁμαρτιῶν in Mt. 26:28 makes explicit what is implicit in Mark's account).

1:5 ᾧ ἡ δόξα εἰς τοὺς αἰῶνας τῶν αἰώνων. This addition of a doxology to the end of the introductory salutation is unparalleled in Paul's letters (there is a NT parallel in Rev. 1:5b, 6). But the doxology may be prompted here by the gospel summary of v 4 (cf. the doxology of 1 Tim. 1:17 following the amplified 'faithful saying' of vv 15f.). There is the further possibility that the doxology here takes the place of the missing thanksgiving (see note on v 6).

The antecedent to the relative ᾧ is probably the immediately preceding 'our God and Father' (cf. Phil. 4:20). The 'glory' (Heb. *kāḇôḏ*) of the God of Israel in the OT is primarily the radiance of his presence; when 'glory' is ascribed to him it denotes the transcendent praise and worship of which he is worthy (cf. Pss. 29:2; 96:8, 'Ascribe to Yahweh the glory due to his name'). εἰς τοὺς αἰῶνας τῶν αἰώνων is a more emphatic variant (cf. Ps. 84:5 [LXX 83:4]) of the commoner Septuagintalism εἰς τὸν αἰῶνα τοῦ αἰῶνος, meaning 'for all eternity' in the most unlimited sense. Like the doxologies appended to the first four books of the OT psalter (Pss. 41:13; 72:19; 89:52; 106:48), the NT doxologies regularly end with 'Amen'. As this letter was read in the churches of Galatia, the hearers would add their 'Amen' to Paul's at the end of the doxology, thus endorsing the ascription of glory to God (cf. 2 Cor. 1:20).

II
NO OTHER GOSPEL
(1:6–10)

Paul expresses his astonishment that the Galatian Christians are turning so quickly from the gospel they received from him and accepting a different form of teaching which is no gospel at all. He invokes a solemn curse on any one who brings a counterfeit gospel, and insists that his concern is to please God, and not to trim his message to suit his audience.

(a) Paul's indignant astonishment (1:6–9)

I am astonished that you are removing yourselves so quickly from him who called you by [Christ's] grace to another 'gospel' —which is not really 'another gospel'; only, there are some people who are confusing you and wish to pervert the gospel of Christ. But even if we, or an angel from heaven, preach a gospel [to you] other than the one which we preached to you, let him be accursed. As we have said before, so now I say again: if any one brings you a gospel other than the one which you received, let him be accursed.

TEXTUAL NOTES

v 6 ουτως *om* G 1 *al*

Χριστου P^{51} א A B Ψ byz lat$^{f\,vg}$ syr^{pesh} cop^{bo} / Ιησου Χριστου D 326 syr^{hcl} / θεου 7 327 Orig^{lat} /*om* P^{46vid} G H^{vid} lat$^{a\,b\,vg.cod}$ Mcion Tert Cypr Ambst Pelag Ephr

v 9 προειρηκαμεν / προειρηκα א* *pc* lat^a syr^{pesh}

1:6 θαυμάζω κτλ. In most of Paul's letters the introductory salutation is followed by words of thanksgiving to God for some feature of the recipients' life or faith, usually with εὐχαριστέω— 'I (we) thank God . . .' (Rom. 1:4; 1 Cor. 1:4; Phil. 1:3; Col. 1:3; 1 Thes. 1:2; 2 Thes. 1:3, 'we are bound to thank God'; Phm. 4; cf. 2 Tim. 1:3)—and twice with the verbal adjective εὐλογητός, 'Blessed be God . . .' (2 Cor. 1:3; Eph. 1:3). Galatians is the solitary exception; it plunges at once into words of remonstrance.

See P. Schubert, *Form and Function of the Pauline Thanksgivings* (Berlin, 1939); P. T. O'Brien, *Introductory Thanksgivings in the Letters of Paul* (Leiden, 1977); also G. P. Wiles, *Paul's Intercessory Prayers* (Cambridge, 1974).

If Galatians is indeed Paul's first extant letter, it might be said that it was written before he had established his practice of following his salutation with an expression of thanks to God. But the thanksgiving formula after the salutation was common form in Greek letter-writing, although Paul developed it in his own distinctive way. The most probable account of the omission of any thanksgiving here is that Paul was impelled by a sense of overmastering urgency to come straight to the point. Evidently he had just received the news of his Galatian converts' abandonment of the gospel of free grace which he had preached to them, and he reacts to that news on the spot. The replacement of words of gratitude or joy by an expression of astonishment or indignation at news just received (or at the addressee's failure to send news), often introduced by θαυμάζω, is amply paralleled in the papyri (cf. J. L. White, *The Body of the Greek Letter* [Missoula, 1972], 18f., 49f.). Paul wishes he were present with his Galatian friends, to have the matter out with them face to face (4:20), but as this cannot be, he sends them this letter.

P. T. O'Brien points out that, just as no thanksgiving period in the other Pauline letters omits a reference to the gospel, so in Gal. 1:6–9 the theme of the gospel is raised in the expression of astonishment which here replaces the normal thanksgiving. 'Because the Galatians have departed from the gospel of Christ there can be no thanksgiving; instead, a curse is pronounced on anyone who brings another message' (*Introductory Thanksgivings*, 141 n. 1).

οὕτως ταχέως. This expression does not afford any precise indication of the interval between the Galatians' conversion and Paul's reception of the disquieting news about them; he is emphasizing his astonishment, but the shorter the interval, the more pointed would his 'so soon' be.

μετατίθεσθε. The passive of μετατίθημι is used (*inter alia*) of a change of position—either geographically, as in the removal of the patriarchs' bones from Egypt to Shechem (Acts 7:16) or Enoch's translation from earth (Heb. 11:5), or in religious belief and practice, as here (cf. 2 Macc. 7:24, μεταθέμενον ἀπὸ τῶν πατρίων, 'turning from the ways of one's fathers').

ἀπὸ τοῦ καλέσαντος ὑμᾶς, i.e. from God (cf. 5:8). The verb καλέω is part of Paul's vocabulary for emphasizing the divine initiative in salvation (cf. 5:13; Rom. 8:30; 9:11; 1 Cor. 1:9). What he says of the Galatian believers here he says of himself in v 15, where καλέσας is followed by διὰ τῆς χάριτος αὐτοῦ as τοῦ καλέσαντος ὑμᾶς is followed by ἐν χάριτι [Χριστοῦ] here. In v 15 the grace is God's, and so it may be here (the textual evidence is rather evenly divided between the addition or absence of the genitive Χριστοῦ).

Whatever the reading may be, the grace of which Paul speaks is not simply a benevolent attitude on the part of God or Christ (see on v 3); it is demonstrated in God's saving act in the death of Christ, by which the undeserving, the 'ungodly' (Rom. 5:6), are redeemed, justified and reconciled. Grace and law are mutually exclusive as means of justification (cf. 5:4): 'if it is by grace, it is no longer on the basis of [legal] works; otherwise grace would no longer be grace' (Rom. 11:6). Cf. J. Moffatt, *Grace in the NT* (London, 1931).

1:6f. εἰς ἕτερον εὐαγγέλιον, ὃ οὐκ ἔστιν ἄλλο. Here the conventional distinction between ἕτερος (of a different kind) and ἄλλος (another of the same kind) may be recognized; see R. C. Trench, *Synonyms of the NT* (London, [⁸1876] 1961), § xiv, 334–337; E. D. Burton, *Galatians*, 420–422. On the other hand, BDF 306 (4) sees no essential distinction: 'ἄλλο is used pleonastically to a certain extent in order to introduce εἰ μὴ . . . (cf. *nihil aliud nisi*) "not that there is any other, except that . . ." .'

The message which the Galatian Christians are disposed to accept in place of that which they received from Paul is so different from Paul's message that it constitutes ἕτερον εὐαγγέλιον, 'a different "gospel" '—and therefore, in fact, no gospel at all, since there can be no 'other gospel' (ἄλλο εὐαγγέλιον) in the proper sense of the word 'gospel' than the proclamation of justification by faith, apart from works of the law.

Probably Paul did not maintain a rigid distinction between ἕτερος and ἄλλος: in 2 Cor. 11:4 he speaks of interlopers in the Corinthian church who proclaim ἄλλον Ἰησοῦν . . . πνεῦμα ἕτερον . . . εὐαγγέλιον ἕτερον, where ἄλλον seems to be used synonymously with ἕτερον, perhaps because it is used with Ἰησοῦν, for in the nature of things no 'other Jesus' can be proclaimed as Saviour than the Jesus who died for his people's sins and was raised from the dead: any ἄλλος Ἰησοῦς must inevitably be ἕτερος Ἰησοῦς.

•In the NT the εὐαγγέλιον is (*a*) the proclamation by Jesus that the kingdom of God has drawn near; (*b*) the proclamation by the disciples that in Jesus the kingdom of God is fully manifested, that he by his humiliation and exaltation is set forth as Messiah, Lord, Son of God. The second phase of the εὐαγγέλιον arises necessarily out of the first: the passion and triumph of Jesus, which formed the basis of the apostolic preaching, crowned his ministry and embodied and confirmed all that he had taught about the kingdom of God. O. A. Piper has distinguished 'two patterns in which the good news is presented, namely the Kingdom type and the Resurrection type'. The difference between them lies 'in perspective rather than in substance' ('Change of Perspective', *Int*. 16 [1962], 402–417, especially 416f.).

The background of the substantive εὐαγγέλιον and its related verb εὐαγγελίζομαι, as used in the NT, must be sought here and there in Is. 40–66. The good news of Zion's liberation and restoration, celebrated in Is. 40:9, ὁ εὐαγγελιζόμενος Σειών, 'O thou that tellest good tidings to Zion' (cf. Is. 60:6 LXX, τὸ σωτήριον κυρίου εὐαγγελιοῦνται), is interpreted in the NT as adumbrating the good news of a greater liberation and restoration—the salvation procured by Christ. The words of Is. 52:7, ὡς πόδες εὐαγγελιζομένου ἀκοὴν εἰρήνης, ὡς εὐαγγελιζόμενος ἀγαθά, are applied by Paul in Rom. 10:15 to preachers of the Christian gospel. In Is. 40–66 it is Yahweh himself who is ultimately proclaimed in the good news: the herald is told to 'say to the cities of Judah, "Behold your God!" ' (Is. 40:9). So in the NT the bearers of the gospel summarize their commission in words such as these: 'what we preach is not ourselves, but Jesus Christ as Lord' (2 Cor. 4:5). This comes close to the Hellenistic usage of the word-group, which has to do with 'the God-Emperor who is venerated in the cult and the εὐαγγέλιον which proclaims him' (J. Schniewind, *Euangelion*, II [Gütersloh, 1931], 183).

Most important of all texts in Is. 40–66 for the NT usage is Is. 61:1, where an unnamed speaker introduces himself by saying, 'The Spirit of the Lord

Yahweh is upon me, because Yahweh has anointed me to bring good tidings to the poor' (LXX εὐαγγελίσασθαι πτωχοῖς). In Lk. 4:17–19 Jesus is depicted as reading this scripture in the Nazareth synagogue and applying it to himself— newly anointed, 'made Messiah', for the proclamation of this gospel. Not only so, but in the earlier 'Q' incident of Jesus' reply to John the Baptist's message from prison (Lk. 7:22; Mt. 11:5) the fact that 'the poor have good news preached to them' (πτωχοὶ εὐαγγελίζονται) is emphasized as the conclusive proof that Jesus is indeed the 'coming one' to whom John had pointed forward.

1:7 εἰ μή here has the sense of πλὴν ὅτι (cf. Acts 20:23), 'except that'. No one would think of calling this substitute message a 'gospel', Paul implies, except with the intention of confusing the minds of believers. Gospel it is not; it is a message of bondage, not of freedom. It is a form of the doctrine of salvation by law-keeping from which Paul himself had been liberated by the true gospel which he received on the Damascus road 'by revelation of Jesus Christ' (v 12). That was the gospel which he preached to others, including the Galatians, and there could be no other. It might be expressed in a variety of ways: its presentation to Jews no doubt differed from its presentation to Gentiles (cf. 2:7), but its touchstone was the proclamation of salvation and life through the grace of God, to be appropriated by 'the hearing of faith' (cf. 3:2, 5).

The preachers of this substitute message are called οἱ ταράσσοντες, 'the disturbers' of the peace which the true gospel had brought to the Galatians. Far from bearing any positive relation to the true gospel, their message is a coun- terfeit, calculated 'to pervert (μεταστρέψαι) the gospel of Christ.' With ταράσσοντες here may be compared the even stronger participle ἀναστατοῦντες in 5:12. The nature of their ταραχή or ἀναστάτωσις appears more clearly in the sequel: among other things, they were pressing the necessity of circumcision on the male converts in the Galatian churches: circumcision, they maintained, was an indispensable condition for justification before God. The identity of these trouble-makers is not immediately apparent: since Paul always refers to them in the third person, while he addresses his Galatian converts in the second person, it is unlikely that they emerged within the Galatian churches (as was argued by J. Munck, *Paul and the Salvation of Mankind*, ETr [London, 1959], 87ff.). They themselves may have been subject to pressures which can only be guessed at; Paul says nothing about this. What is clear is that he understood their insistence on circumcision—a rite which in itself, he held, was of no moment (5:6; 6:15)— to involve a retrogression from justification by grace to justification by law- keeping, a retrogression from the liberty of the Spirit to religious slavery. Such an insistence undermined the authentic gospel, substituting a false foundation for that which God had laid (cf. 1 Cor. 3:11).

Paul himself had for long sought justification before God by his observance of the Jewish law, until his Damascus-road experience taught him the fruitless- ness of such a quest and the bankruptcy of the way of law-keeping as a means of getting right with God. The assurance of ultimate acceptance by God, which could never be his while he lived under law, he received on the spot when he yielded submission to the risen Christ. On the spot, too, he realized that the law, to which he had devoted all his gifts and resources, had not been able to prevent him from pursuing the sinful course (as he now knew it to be) of persecuting the church of God (cf. v 13); the law had not even been able to show him that the course was sinful. The law, he says later, 'was added because of transgressions' (3:19), i.e. to bring transgressions into the open and even to stimulate their commission; and in his personal experience this was true in a special sense: it was his devotion to the law that led him into the sin of sins—persecuting the followers of Christ. He himself knew the joyful sense of release from legal bondage when he placed his faith in Christ, and he desired the same release for his fellow-Jews; but that Gentiles, who had come to faith in Christ and experienced his saving grace without ever having lived under Jewish law, should now wish to assume the yoke of that law was a perversion of all reasonable order.

1:8 ἀλλὰ καὶ ἐὰν ἡμεῖς κτλ. It is the message, not the messenger, that ultimately matters. The gospel preached by Paul is not the true gospel because it is Paul who preaches it; it is the true gospel because the risen Christ gave it to Paul to preach. If Paul himself, or any other apostle, or even an angel were to bring a different message from that which had proved its saving power to the Galatians when they heard and believed it, both the messenger and his counterfeit message should be rejected. The authority and character of the preacher are important, no doubt, but their importance is secondary: more important is the content of what is preached. Luther expressed the idea in his own paradoxical style: 'That which does not teach Christ is not apostolic, even if Peter and Paul be the teachers. On the other hand, that which does teach Christ is apostolic, even if Judas, Annas, Pilate or Herod should propound it' (Preface to Epistle of James, WA, *Die deutsche Bibel*, 7.384f.). By 'teaching Christ' Luther meant nothing other than preaching the gospel of justification by faith alone.

παρ' ὃ (also in v 9), 'beyond that which', 'other than' (cf. 1 Cor. 3:11, παρὰ τὸν κείμενον, 'other than that which has been laid down').

ἀνάθεμα ἔστω (also in v 9). This is a more solemn formula than the imprecation of Rev. 22:18f. (echoing Dt. 4:2; 29:19f.) on amplifying or diminishing the text of the Apocalypse. ἀνάθεμα is the regular LXX rendering of Heb. *ḥērem*, 'ban'. In a holy war the *ḥērem* involved in practice the destruction of everyone and everything that fell under it. In theory whatever was under the *ḥērem* was completely devoted to Yahweh—that is why it was sacrilege for Achan to take for himself some of the spoils of Jericho (Jos. 7:1, 20f.). But while that was the original sense of *ḥērem* and of ἀνάθεμα (a derivative of ἀνατίθημι, 'dedicate'), it is not the sense here. The sense here is, 'May the divine curse rest on him' (cf. Rom. 9:3, where Paul says he could pray to be himself ἀνάθεμα . . . ἀπὸ τοῦ Χριστοῦ, 'accursed from Christ', if his Jewish kinsfolk could be saved thereby).

But why should he express himself so vehemently against those who preached a different message from his own? Partly because he held the preaching of salvation by law-keeping to be a snare and a delusion, which put the souls of men and women in jeopardy; partly, also, because of its adverse implications for the authenticity of Christ. In Paul's eyes, the acknowledgement of Jesus as Messiah logically implied the abrogation of the law (see note on 3:19 below). If Christ displaced the law as the activating centre of Paul's own life, he equally displaced the law in the economy of God, in the ordering of salvation-history. Therefore, if the law was still in force as the way of salvation and life, the messianic age had not yet dawned, and Jesus accordingly was not the Messiah. In that case Jesus had been rightly convicted and sentenced because his messianic claims were false. Any teaching which logically led to such a conclusion was, for Paul, self-evidently perverse: any one who implied by such teaching that Jesus was anathema (cf. 1 Cor. 12:3) was himself anathema.

1:9 So seriously does Paul mean this that, after the rather rhetorical language of v 8, he repeats it more soberly (εἴ τις . . .) but none the less emphatically.

ὡς προειρήκαμεν probably refers to his having said so in v 8. He repeats it in order to impress it the more forcibly on his readers' minds. It is less likely that he had found it necessary to give them this warning by word of mouth when he was with them (so W. Schmithals, *Paul and the Gnostics*, ETr [Nashville/New York, 1972], 18f.); the issue of legalism had not arisen then. With πάλιν λέγω cf. 5:3, μαρτύρομαι δὲ πάλιν.

παρελάβετε, 'you received'. In this kind of context παραλαμβάνω (like Heb. *qibbēl*) is the correlative of παραδίδωμι (like Heb. *māsar*), 'deliver'; the two words are used of the receiving and handing on of tradition. The Galatians 'received' from Paul the gospel which he in turn had received directly 'by revelation of Jesus Christ', as he claims in v 12 (see note *ad loc.*).

(b) Paul is no men-pleaser (1:10)

Is it human beings or God that I am trying to persuade now? Or am I seeking to please human beings? If I were still pleasing human beings, I should not be Christ's bondslave.

1:10 Ἄρτι . . . ἔτι . . .; it appears from the content of these two questions, especially from the force of the temporal adverbs ἄρτι ('now') and ἔτι ('still'), that Paul's consistency had been called in question. Whatever he might do or teach now, it was suggested, he had acted and taught differently at one time. He was suspected, in fact, of adapting his practice and preaching to please his changing company from one time or place to another.

One can well understand how Paul, whose settled policy it was to 'become all things to all men' (1 Cor. 9:22), was charged with vacillation. It was easier for some people to take note of his changing conduct—exercising his liberty at one time and voluntarily restricting it at another—without appreciating his overriding consistency: 'I do it all for the sake of the gospel' (1 Cor. 9:23). (See H. Chadwick, 'All Things to All Men', *NTS* 1 [1954–55], 261–275; D. Daube, *The NT and Rabbinic Judaism* [London, 1956], 336–361.)

Persuading men and women was Paul's constant business, according to the only other occurrence of the transitive πείθω in his writings: ἀνθρώπους πείθομεν (2 Cor. 5:11). The content of this persuasion is summed up in the same context: 'Be reconciled to God' (2 Cor. 5:20)—an appeal entrusted to Paul in his role as ambassador for Christ. *Pleasing* men and women was not what he was called to do. He was called to serve Christ: he could not make that his business, and aim to please his hearers at the same time. Thus in 1 Cor. 4:3f. he is not concerned about other people's assessment of him: 'it is the Lord who judges me', he says, so he makes it his business to please the Lord. 'Men-pleasers' (ἀνθρωπάρεσκοι) were opportunists, rendering 'eye-service' (Col.

3:22; Eph. 6:6). As for his own apostolic duty, 'we speak', he said, 'not to please men, but to please God, who tests our hearts. For', he adds, 'we never used words of flattery . . .' (1 Thes. 2:4f.)—which men-pleasers would naturally do. (If, in 1 Cor. 10:33, he speaks of his endeavour 'to please all men in everything I do', the context makes it plain that it is a question of subordinating his own interests to the interests of others, with a view to their salvation. Similarly in Rom. 15:1–3 he insists, with an appeal to the example of Christ, that it is the duty of each Christian, and especially of one who is 'strong', to 'please his neighbour for his good, to edify him', instead of pleasing oneself.)

The implied answer to the question, 'Is it human beings or God that I am trying to persuade now?' seems therefore to be 'Human beings'. Persuading God was a concept entirely foreign to Paul's mind: it was the kind of thing that religious charlatans and practitioners of magic thought they could do. It was a common superstition, denounced by Hebrew prophets and by the higher paganism alike, that the deity could be persuaded by gifts: δῶρα θεοὺς πείθει (Hesiod, quoted in Plato, *Rep*. 3.390E); πείθειν δῶρα καὶ θεοὺς λόγος (Eur. *Medea* 964). The present relevance of 'persuading God' may lie in the anathema which Paul has just pronounced: it was all very well for him to anathematize the trouble-makers, but his anathema would be ineffective, it was implied, unless he could persuade God to endorse it.

W. Schmithals (*Paul and the Gnostics*, 56–58) takes the emphasis in the former question to lie on πείθω—'Am I *persuading* men?' Paul's opponents, he suggests, charged him with making converts by the use of rhetorical devices, such as would be appropriate to teaching which was κατὰ ἄνθρωπον but not to the communication of spiritual truth (cf. 1 Cor. 2:1–13). But according to Schmithals, Paul's repudiation of the charge that he used such persuasion implies that he understood it (wrongly) in the sense of dishonest methods, whereas later he understood it better and countered it with the claim that he used the persuasion of sober reasoning (2 Cor. 5:11–15). There is no good reason to suppose that Paul misunderstood the charge: he was frequently obliged to rebut the insinuation that he used underhand methods (2 Cor. 2:17; 4:1–3; 1 Thes. 2:9–12). Schmithals further suggests that Paul's alleged misunderstanding is responsible for the addition of ἢ τὸν θεόν—which, says W. Bousset, 'one would prefer to dispense with entirely' (*Galater*, 34)—Paul, by this account, replies to the charge by saying that he uses persuasion on no one at all, neither men nor God. It is much more satisfactory to take him to mean that he persuades men, not God, and pleases God, not men; indeed, he pleases God by persuading men. Cf. R. Bultmann's second thoughts in *TDNT* VI, 2 (*s.v.* πείθω): 'hence ἀνθρώποις ἀρέσκειν is materially identical with τὸν θεὸν (πείθειν)'—the implied charge being that, by preaching a law-free gospel, Paul was pleasing men by making the way of salvation easier for them and trying to persuade God to accept them on less arduous terms than those laid down in the law.

The question of pleasing men might have more specific reference to his care to preserve good relations with the Jerusalem church leaders on the one hand while asserting his independence of them on the other, or to his countenancing circumcision on some occasions (cf. 5:11) and prohibiting it on others (cf. 5:2). C. H. Talbert sees the indirect occasion of the letter in Acts 16:1–4, which presents two instances of Paul's so-called 'men-pleasing'—his circumcision of Timothy and his delivery of the Jerusalem decree to the recently planted churches of South Galatia ('Again: Paul's Visits to Jerusalem', *NovT* 9 [1967], 26–40). These incidents do at least illustrate what some of Paul's friends saw as his disconcerting adaptability. See also J. Jeremias, *Abba* (Göttingen, 1966), 285f.; H. Schlier, *Galater*, 41f.; P. Richardson, 'Pauline Inconsistency', *NTS* 26 (1979–80), 347–362, especially 358–360.

There may be an echo of the charge of men-pleasing in *Clem. Hom.* 18.10, where Peter accuses Simon Magus (often a Clementine disguise for Paul) of speaking ἀρεσκόντως τοῖς παροῦσιν ὄχλοις, 'so as to please the multitudes who are present'.

εἰ ἔτι . . . οὐκ ἂν ἤμην, a good example of the classical unfulfilled condition, referring to the present. Paul repeatedly calls himself a 'slave' (δοῦλος) of Christ (Rom. 1:1, etc.), implying that he was unreservedly at Christ's disposal; for Christ's sake he is also the slave of others (2 Cor. 4:5), implying that he is unreservedly at *their* disposal in the service of Christ. But a slave cannot afford to aim at pleasing any one other than his master. (For εἰ ἔτι . . . cf. 5:11, εἰ περιτομὴν ἔτι κηρύσσω, which would indeed be an example of 'pleasing men'.)

III
AUTOBIOGRAPHICAL SKETCH:
PAUL'S INDEPENDENT GOSPEL
(1:11–2:14)

Emphasizing afresh that he received his gospel when Christ was revealed to him on the Damascus road, Paul reviews his early training in Judaism, his persecution of the church, the radical change wrought in him by the revelation of the Son of God, and his immediate obedience to the commission then laid on him to preach Christ in the Gentile world. He insists that he had begun this work before ever he met the leaders of the Jerusalem church, and that on the two occasions when he did meet them, separated by many years, they conferred no authority on him but acknowledged the validity of the commission which he was already discharging. They agreed that this commission was to Gentiles, as theirs was to Jews, and the only charge they gave him was a plea to remember the poor of the Jerusalem church.

When, not long afterwards, there was a confrontation at Antioch between Cephas (Peter) and himself, it was because a temporizing course of action on the part of Cephas threatened to compromise the gospel principle that justification before God, for Jews and Gentiles alike, comes only through faith in Christ.

(a) Paul's gospel received by revelation (1:11–12)

Let me assure you, brothers, that the gospel which was preached by me is no gospel according to man. It was from no human being that I received it, or learned it; it was by a revelation of Jesus Christ.

TEXTUAL NOTES
v 11 γαρ B D* G *pc* lat cop^{sa} / δε P^{46} ℵ* A byz syr cop^{bo}
v 12 ουτε (before εδιδαχθην) P^{46} B byz / ουδε ℵ A D* G Ψ 33 81 *al*

Paul here begins an autobiographical summary which continues to 2:14; it occupies nearly one-fifth of the whole letter. It therefore constitutes a substantial part of his argument, and should help the modern reader to reconstruct at least one element in the situation to which Paul addresses himself. That element took the form of a denial of Paul's independent standing as an apostle. He is at pains, therefore, to rebut that denial, and to emphasize, with all the solemnity of which he is capable, that the gospel which he preaches, together with his commission to preach it, was received by him directly from the risen Christ, without any intermediary.

1:11 What Paul calls here τὸ εὐαγγέλιον τὸ εὐαγγελισθὲν ὑπ' ἐμοῦ (cf. τὸ εὐαγγέλιόν μου, Rom. 2:16) is elsewhere called 'the gospel of God' (1 Thes. 2:8f.; 2 Cor. 11:7), because God is its author; 'the gospel of Christ' (1 Thes. 3:2; 2 Cor. 2:12; Rom. 15:9), because Christ is its subject-matter; or, more comprehensively, 'the gospel of God concerning his Son' (Rom. 1:1–3). Other words or phrases used as the object of εὐαγγελίζομαι, or of its near-synonyms κηρύσσω and καταγγέλλω (Paul usually treats εὐαγγελίζομαι as intransitive except with its cognate accusative εὐαγγέλιον), indicate the content or substance of the gospel: 'Christ' (cf. αὐτόν, v 16), 'Christ crucified' (1 Cor. 1:23), 'Christ Jesus our Lord' (2 Cor. 4:5), 'the faith', i.e. the message of salvation by faith (v 23), 'peace' (Eph. 2:17), 'the unsearchable riches of Christ' (Eph. 3:8).

But the gospel preached by Paul was the law-free gospel, the gospel to which anything like the obligation to be circumcised was completely alien. And this law-free gospel, he insists, is the gospel which he received by divine revelation on the Damascus road and which he was commissioned to make known among the Gentiles. It was no gospel κατὰ ἄνθρωπον, for no earthly authority had imparted it to him, neither was it the product of his own reasoning.

1:12 οὐδὲ γὰρ ἐγὼ παρὰ ἀνθρώπου παρέλαβον αὐτό. There may seem to be a formal contradiction between this assertion and other statements in which Paul uses παραλαμβάνω and παραδίδωμι of himself according to the usual terminology of transmission—receiving (from predecessors) and delivering (to successors), as in 1 Cor. 11:23 (with regard to the actions and words of Jesus at the Last Supper) and 15:3 (with regard to the saving events of Christ's death, burial, resurrection and subsequent appearances). But there is no material contradiction. Paul was indebted for his gospel to no human being—not even to those who were 'in Christ' before him. His language (cf. v 1) should not be pressed to imply that he denied ἀνθρωπότης to the risen Christ; his readers knew quite well what he meant in denying all human origin or basis to his gospel. Paul's gospel—Jesus Christ is the Son of God; Jesus Christ is the risen Lord—was revealed to him on the Damascus road. No doubt he had heard such claims made for Jesus in the days of his persecuting zeal, but it was not the witness of the persecuted disciples that convinced him. He rejected their witness as blasphemous until he learned the truth by unmediated disclosure from heaven. On the other hand, facts about the life and teaching of Jesus, about his death, burial and resurrection appearances, were imparted to him after his conversion by those who had prior knowledge of them (see on vv 18f.).

J. D. G. Dunn suggests convincingly that 'Paul regarded the kerygmatic tradition' which he received from the Jerusalem leaders 'as *confirming* his own convictions about Jesus which stemmed immediately from his conversion and commissioning on the Damascus road, and also as providing an invaluable way of expressing what was his gospel anyway, because it was a widely accepted formulation and not just his own idiosyncratic mode of expression' (*Unity*, 66).

W. Schmithals infers from Paul's language that his opponents claimed immediate divine revelation as the authority for their version of the gospel; he takes Paul to mean: 'If they did not receive their gospel from man, as they claim, but by revelation, then neither did I receive mine from-man, but by revelation of Jesus Christ' (*Paul and the Gnostics*, 20, 103f.). But they more probably claimed to have received the gospel in its purity from those who themselves received it directly from the Lord.

οὔτε ἐδιδάχθην, sc. παρὰ ἀνθρώπου. There is little difference here between παρέλαβον and ἐδιδάχθην (cf. Phil 4:9, ἃ καὶ ἐμάθετε καὶ παρελάβετε . . .). Paul himself taught the Christian way to others (cf. 1 Cor. 4:17), but his only teacher was the Lord by the Spirit.

ἀλλὰ δι' ἀποκαλύψεως ᾽Ιησοῦ Χριστοῦ. That ᾽Ιησοῦ Χριστοῦ here is an objective genitive is rendered most probable by the wording of vv 15f.: God 'was pleased to *reveal his Son* (ἀποκαλύψαι τὸν υἱὸν αὐτοῦ) in me'. That is to say, God the Father was the revealer; it was Jesus Christ who was revealed, and in that revelation Paul received his gospel, together with the command to make it known in the Gentile world. The gospel and the risen Christ were inseparable; both were revealed to Paul in the same moment. To preach the gospel (v 11) was to preach Christ (v 16).

It is plain throughout Paul's letters (cf. Phil. 3:7–10) that what happened on the Damascus road was no isolated mystical experience, no mere 'flash of insight or intellectual conviction, but a personal encounter, the beginning of a personal relationship which became the dominating passion of his life. . . . Religious experience for Paul is basically experience of union with Christ' (J. D. G. Dunn, *Unity*, 190, 195).

See P. H. Menoud, 'Revelation and Tradition: The Influence of Paul's Conversion on his Theology', *Int.* 7 (1953), 131–141; J. Dupont, 'The Conversion of Paul and its Influence on his Understanding of Salvation by Faith', *Bruce FS*, 176–194; G. Bornkamm, 'The Revelation of Christ to Paul on the Damascus Road and Paul's Doctrine of Justification and Reconciliation', *Morris FS*, 90–103; S. Kim, *The Origin of Paul's Gospel* (Tübingen, 1981).

It has been suggested that the criticisms of Paul's gospel, to which he makes reference in vv 11–12, have controlled the structure of most of the letter. In v 11 his gospel is accused of being κατὰ ἄνθρωπου, while in v 12 it is said to be derived παρὰ ἀνθρώπον. Both these criticisms, it is suggested, are now to receive detailed rebuttal, but in reverse order: in 1:13–2:21 Paul shows that his gospel was not derived παρὰ ἀνθρώπου, and in 3:1–6:10 he argues that it is not κατὰ ἄνθρωπον. The bulk of the letter could then be viewed as an elaborate chiasmus (see BDF 477 [2] summarizing J. Jeremias, 'Chiasmus in den Paulusbriefen', *ZNW* 49 [1958], 145–156, especially 152f.).

(b) Paul's earlier career (1:13–14)

You have heard about my former course of life in Judaism, how beyond all measure I persecuted the church of God and laid it waste. I forged ahead in

Judaism beyond many contemporaries in my nation, being more exceedingly zealous for my ancestral traditions.

1:13 Ἠκούσατε. Paul's converts might have heard something about his former career as a persecutor from his own lips, but it is plain from the sequel that others were circulating reports about him—reports which he regards as deliberately disparaging and which he rebuts from his own first-hand testimony. While he himself might speak of his persecuting career in order to magnify the grace of God which rescued him from it, others might draw attention to it in order to insinuate that Paul was a doubtful character who could not be fully trusted. See v 20.

ἀναστροφή, conduct, course of life, occurs in this sense elsewhere in the Pauline corpus in Eph. 4:22 and 1 Tim. 4:12 (there are six occurrences in 1 Peter). The verb ἀναστρέφομαι (middle) is similarly used ('behave', 'conduct oneself') in 2 Cor. 1:12; Eph. 2:3; 1 Tim. 3:15.

᾽Ιουδαϊσμός occurs in the NT only here and in v 14. The verb ἰουδαΐζω, of which it is a derivative, is found in 2:14, but there it is used of Gentiles 'judaizing', living like Jews (ἰουδαϊκῶς ζῆν), as in Est. 8:17 LXX; Josephus, *War* 2.454, 463. Here ᾽Ιουδαϊσμός means simply 'Judaism', Jewish faith and life (as in 2 Macc. 2:21; 8:1; 14:38; 4 Macc. 4:26). καθ᾽ ὑπερβολήν, 'excessively', 'beyond all measure'. Paul is the only NT writer to use this (quite classical) phrase (cf. Rom. 7:13; 1 Cor. 12:31; 2 Cor. 1:8; 4:17).

ἐδίωκον τὴν ἐκκλησίαν τοῦ θεοῦ. Paul refers to his persecuting activity in much the same language in Phil. 3:6 where, as here, it is the outstanding token of his one-time zeal for the law (κατὰ ζῆλος διώκων τὴν ἐκκλησίαν); 1 Cor. 15:9, where it should have disqualified him, even after his conversion, from being an apostle, but for the divine grace which nevertheless commissioned him (cf. 1 Tim. 1:13). He does not explicitly say that he carried on his persecuting activity in Jerusalem, but where else would he have found 'the church of God' at that early date? To be sure, he 'persecuted them even to foreign cities' (Acts 26:11), but Jerusalem was the disciples' main centre; it would have been pointless to persecute them elsewhere and leave their headquarters unscathed (see note on v 22). In this respect the evidence of Acts (8:3; 26:10) is in no way contrary to that of Paul's letters. Reading between the lines of Acts one may conclude that, among the disciples, the Hellenists were the principal targets for his attack, but Paul makes no distinction between 'Hebrews' and 'Hellenists' when he speaks of 'persecuting the church'. Even so, if the Hellenists who were associated with Stephen not only maintained that Jesus was the Messiah but also proclaimed the abrogation of the customs delivered by Moses (Acts 6:14), they might well have incurred Paul's double detestation.

Luke expressly represents the apostles as remaining in Jerusalem during the persecution, from which, because of the popular good will they enjoyed, they may well have been exempt (πλὴν τῶν ἀποστόλων, Acts 8:1), by contrast with the later persecution under Herod Agrippa I, after Peter had begun to fraternize with Gentiles; then the attack was directed particularly against the apostles (Acts 12:1-4). Perhaps in the earlier persecution 'local Hebrew Christians still loyal to temple and law would be relatively secure' (Dunn, *Unity*, 274). Paul adds ἐπόρθουν as a stronger synonym of ἐδίωκον. The verb πορθέω, used of the sacking of cities (cf. v 23), was an apt one to use in the light of Luke's fuller description in Acts 8:3.

1:14 The verb προκόπτω ('advance', 'increase') is used of Jesus' 'advancing' in wisdom, stature and grace in Luke 2:52. Josephus (*Life*, 8) describes how as a boy he 'made great progress in education' (εἰς μεγάλην παιδείας προὔκοπτον ἐπίδοσιν); this is a common Hellenistic use of the word (cf. G. Stählin, *TDNT* VI, 705f., 709ff., *s.v.* προκόπτω).

συνηλικιώτας, a Hellenistic term for a member of the same age-group (ἡλικία, 'age').

ἐν τῷ γένει μου. For γένος ('class', 'race', 'family') in reference to the Jewish nation cf. 2 Cor. 11:26; Phil. 3:5 (also Acts 7:19; 13:26).

περισσοτέρως, 'more exceedingly', 'more abundantly' (cf. 2 Cor. 1:12; 7:13, 15; 12:15), used by Paul in the sense of ὑπερβαλλόντως (2 Cor. 11:23).

It is best to give ζηλωτής the general sense of 'zealous' here. The word appears in a specialized sense of the party of the Zealots who emerge by that name in AD 66, perpetuating the ideals of Judas the Galilaean and his 'fourth philosophy' (Jos., *War* 2.441, 651; 4.160f.). This may be the force of the so-briquet of Simon the Zealot (Lk. 6:15; Acts 1:13; cf. 'Cananaean', from Aram. *qan'anā'*, in Mk. 3:18; Mt. 10:4), but we do not know enough to be certain about this. Elsewhere in the NT the word has the more general force, as when James and his fellow-elders speak of the thousands of 'zealots for the law' in the Jerusalem church (Acts 21:20; cf. Acts 22:3; 1 Cor. 14:12; Tit. 2:14; 1 Pet. 3:13). Paul's 'zeal' was shown pre-eminently in his attempt to exterminate the church: to use language which he employs in another connexion in Rom. 10:2, it was a religious zeal (ζῆλος θεοῦ) but an uninstructed zeal (οὐ κατ' ἐπίγνωσιν). There is an ambivalence about ζῆλος—it may be good or bad, not only in respect of its object but also in respect of the spirit in which it is cherished (see on 5:20, where it is listed as a 'work of the flesh'). The Corinthians' zeal for the Jerusalem relief fund is praised in 2 Cor. 9:2, but in 2 Cor. 12:20 ζῆλος (the same word) stands in a list of vices against which they are warned.

The 'ancestral traditions' (πατρικαὶ παραδόσεις; cf. the compound adjective πατροπαράδοτος used of the former idolatrous practices of Gentile converts in 1 Pet. 1:18) comprise the ancestral tenets and customs to which Paul had been brought up in his father's house and in the school which he attended—according to Acts 22:3, the school of Gamaliel I in Jerusalem, where he was trained according to the exactitude of 'the ancestral law' (τοῦ πατρῴου νόμου), 'being a zealot for God' (ζηλωτὴς ὑπάρχων τοῦ θεοῦ). His claim is amplified in Phil. 3:5f., where he describes himself as 'a Hebrew born of Hebrews, as to the law a Pharisee, . . . as to righteousness under the law blameless' (cf. Acts 23:6; 26:5). The 'traditions' would be more particularly those enshrined in the oral law (*tôrāh še-be'al peh*) or *halakhah* handed down in Pharisaic schools.

(c) Paul becomes an apostle (1:15–17)

But when he who set me apart while I was as yet unborn and called me by his grace saw fit to reveal his Son in me, that I should make his good news known among the Gentiles, immediately—without conferring with any human being, or going up to Jerusalem to those who were apostles before me—I set out for Arabia, and came back again to Damascus.

TEXTUAL NOTES

v 15 ευδοκησεν P⁴⁶ B G 629 *pc* lat syrᵖᵉˢʰ Irenˡᵃᵗ Euseb / *add* ο θεος ℵ A D Ψ byz syrʰᶜˡ** cop

και καλεσας δια της χαριτος αυτου *om* P⁴⁶ 6 1739 1881 *pc*

v 17 ανηλθον / απηλθον P⁵¹ B D G *pc* / ηλθον P⁴⁶

1:15 'God' [ὁ θεός] was probably added to the text for the sake of explicitness: 'he who set me apart . . . and called me by his grace' is, of course, God, the implied subject of εὐδόκησεν ('was well pleased', 'resolved', 'saw fit').

ἀφορίσας, in the same sense as in Rom. 1:1, where Paul speaks of himself as 'set apart (ἀφωρισμένος) for the gospel of God'. It is just conceivable that Paul has at the back of his mind the basic sense of 'Pharisee' (Heb. *pārûš*, Aram. *pᵉrîš*, 'separated'): now he is, so to speak, a 'separated person' in quite a different sense from formerly. But such a play on words, even if it was present to Paul's own mind, would not have been appreciated by his readers. ἐκ κοιλίας μητρός μου, a Septuagintalism (Heb. *mibbeṭen 'immî*), lit. 'from my mother's womb' (cf. Jdg. 13:5; Ps. 22 [LXX 21]:10; 58 [LXX 57]:3; 71 [LXX 70]:6); it may mean either 'since my birth' or 'since before my birth' (here the latter would be apposite). Before ever he was born, Paul means, God had his eye on him and set him apart for his apostolic ministry.

This language is strongly reminiscent of that in which some of the OT prophets relate their calls. Cf. Je. 1:5, 'Before I formed you in the womb (ἐν κοιλίᾳ) I knew you, and before you were born I consecrated you; I appointed you a prophet to the nations (εἰς ἔθνη)'; Is. 49:1–6, where the Servant says, 'Yahweh called me from the womb (ἐκ κοιλίας μητρός μου ἐκάλεσε), from the body of my mother he named my name', not only to minister to Israel but to be 'a light to the nations (φῶς ἐθνῶν), that my salvation may reach to the end of the earth.' It is not by chance that in Acts 13:47 these last words are quoted by Paul and Barnabas in the synagogue of Pisidian Antioch as their authority for taking the gospel to the Gentiles. In Paul's view, it was for others to take up the Servant's mission to Israel, but he knew himself called to fulfil that part of the Servant's vocation which involved the spreading of God's saving light among the Gentiles, near and far, as he indicates in the words which follow.

See J. Munck, *Paul*, 24ff.

καὶ καλέσας διὰ τῆς χάριτος αὐτοῦ. Cf. v 5, where God is the one 'who called you in grace'. There the general call of God to all his people is in view; here that is included, but it involves also the special call of God to Paul for his personal life-work. For 'grace' in this connexion cf. Rom. 1:5.

1:16 ἀποκαλύψαι τὸν υἱὸν αὐτοῦ ἐν ἐμοί. This is the ἀποκάλυψις Ἰησοῦ Χριστοῦ mentioned above in v 12. The reference is to Paul's Damascus-road experience in which, as he puts it elsewhere, 'I have seen Jesus our Lord' (1 Cor. 9:1), 'last of all he appeared [in resurrection] also to me' (1 Cor. 15:8),

'I was apprehended by Christ Jesus' (Phil. 3:12). The prepositional phrase ἐν ἐμοί could be a substitute for the simple dative (cf. φανερόν ἐστιν ἐν αὐτοῖς, Rom. 1:19; ἐν τοῖς ἀπολλυμένοις ἐστὶν κεκαλυμμένον, 2 Cor. 4:3), but here it probably points to the inwardness of the experience. For Paul the outward vision and the inward illumination coincided: Jesus, whom he persecuted, was revealed as the Son of God, and the revelation was the act of God himself.

See BDF 220 (1); A. Fridrichsen, *Apostle*, 12, 22 n. 23.

When Paul speaks in 2 Cor. 4:4 of 'seeing the light of the gospel of the glory of Christ, who is the image of God', and goes on to say that God 'has shone in our hearts to give the light of the knowledge of the glory of God in the face of Christ' (2 Cor. 4:6), his choice of language is most probably based on his Damascus-road vision. If so, he saw 'Jesus our Lord' then in a form which identified him not only as the Son of God but also as the image of God, the reflexion of the divine glory.

We may compare the experience of Isaiah, who was both cleansed and commissioned in the course of his vision of the glory of God (Is. 6:1–9a), or of Ezekiel, whose call came in the course of a similar vision (Ezk. 1:4–3:11). For Ezekiel the divine glory was perceptible in 'a likeness as it were of a human form' (Ezk. 1:26); for Paul the human form manifested the lineaments of a particular person: 'the face of Christ'. The appearance of the risen Christ to him was an objective experience, in which Christ took the initiative: the repeated ὤφθη of 1 Cor. 15:5–8 ('he let himself be seen') means that the appearance of the risen Christ to him was as real as his earlier appearances to Peter, James and others, not that their experiences were as 'visionary' as Paul's.

Attempts which have been made, since C. Holsten, 'Die Christus-Vision des Paulus und die Genesis des paulinischen Evangeliums', *ZWT* 4 (1861), 223–284, to present a psychological analysis of Paul's experience have failed to account for all the data.

Perhaps Paul's making τὸν υἱὸν αὐτοῦ the object of ἀποκαλύψαι implies that it was specifically as the Son of God that the risen Christ appeared to him. Luke may preserve a reminiscence of this when he summarizes Paul's first preaching of Christ in the words: 'He is the Son of God' (Acts 9:20).

See S. Kim, *The Origin of Paul's Gospel*, 100–233. On 'the Son of God' see O. Cullmann, *Christology*, 270–305; W. Kramer, *Christ, Lord, Son of God*, 108–128, 183–194; G. Bornkamm, *Paul*, 249; M. Hengel, *The Son of God*; C. F. D. Moule, *Christology*, 22–31; I. H. Marshall, *Christology*, 111–123; W. G. Kümmel, *Theology*, 151–154, 160–165.

ἵνα εὐαγγελίζωμαι αὐτὸν ἐν τοῖς ἔθνεσιν. The purpose of the revelation, that Paul should proclaim the gospel of Christ among the Gentiles, was part of the revelation itself: conversion and commission came together. It was then that he received from the risen Lord 'grace and apostleship [perhaps a hendiadys for 'grace of apostleship'], to bring about the obedience of faith for the sake of his name among all the nations' (Rom. 1:5). Indeed, the logic of 'the gospel according to Paul' was implicit in his Damascus-road experience. Paul grasped this in essence there and then, although the fuller implications of the experience became plain to him more gradually. But the bankruptcy of the law and the all-sufficiency of Christ came home to him at once. Knowledge of the law was the prerogative of Jews, but if salvation was bestowed by grace (as it was now bestowed on Paul) and not on the ground of law-keeping, then it was accessible to Gentiles equally with Jews. There is no good reason to hold with A. Fridrichsen (*Apostle*, 13, 23 n. 26) that this element in the revelation was first imparted to Paul in a subsequent vision (cf. Acts 22:21, together with O. Betz, 'Die Vision des Paulus im Tempel von Jerusalem', *Stählin FS*, 113–123). See further on Gal. 2:7.

Neither can it necessarily be inferred from Paul's language here that before his conversion he was engaged in a proselytizing mission among the Gentiles, however probable this may be on other grounds (see further on 5:11).

The adverb εὐθέως modifies not so much the two immediately following negative clauses (οὐ προσανεθέμην . . . οὐδὲ ἀνῆλθον . . .) as the affirmative clause to which they lead up (ἀλλ' ἀπῆλθον . . .).

οὐ προσαναθέμην, 'I did not consult'. In 2:16 the same verb has the sense 'contribute', 'confer'; see also ἀνεθέμην, 'I laid before', in 2:2.

σαρκὶ καὶ αἵματι, 'flesh and blood', i.e. mortal humanity; cf. Mt. 16:17, 'flesh and blood has not revealed (ἀπεκάλυψεν) this to you', i.e. 'no human being has told you this'; 1 Cor. 15:50, 'flesh and blood [i.e. the mortal body] cannot inherit the kingdom of God'. For the reverse order αἷμα καὶ σάρξ cf. Eph. 6:12; Heb. 2:14. Similar phrases occur in Euripides, frag. 687.1f.; Polyaenus, *Strategica* 3.11.1 (αἷμα καὶ σάρκας); Wis. 12:5 (σαρκῶν . . . καὶ αἵματος); Sir. 14:18 (σαρκὸς καὶ αἵματος, rendering Heb. *bāśār wādām*); 17:31. Heb. *bāśār wādām* occurs *passim* in rabbinical literature.

1:17 οὐδὲ ἀνῆλθον εἰς Ἱεροσόλυμα. In the NT one regularly 'goes up' to Jerusalem, more or less as in England one 'goes up to town' (i.e. to London). The verb used is commonly ἀναβαίνω (almost a technical term for going up to Jerusalem; see J. Schneider, *TDNT* I, 519, *s.v.* βαίνω), as in 2:1 (cf. Mk. 10:32f.; Lk. 2:42; Jn. 2:13; 5:1; Acts 21:15; also 2 Sa. [LXX 2 Ki.] 8:7; 1 Esd. 2:5; Ezr. 1:3; 7:7; 1 Macc. 4:36f.; 3 Macc. 3:16). Here and in v 18 Paul uses ἀνῆλθον, which is synonymous with ἀνέβην (2:1); it should not be rendered 'I went back', 'I returned' (for which the appropriate compound would be ἐπανῆλθον; cf. Lk. 10:35; 19:15). Cf. Jn. 6:3, ἀνῆλθεν εἰς τὸ ὄρος ('he went up into the hill country').

Only in vv 17f. and 2:1 does Paul use the hellenized neuter plural Ἱεροσόλυμα for Jerusalem; in the seven other places where he refers to the city by name (including Gal. 4:25f.; see p. 220) he uses the Septuagintal Ἱερουσαλήμ.

πρὸς τοὺς πρὸ ἐμοῦ ἀποστόλους, among whom (*pace* Schmithals) he includes not only Peter and, presumably, the eleven, but also (most probably) James the Lord's brother (cf. v 19) and possibly others. Apostleship for Paul is mission, with the implication of direct commissioning. πρὸ ἐμοῦ is temporal; it does not denote precedence in status.

In 1 Cor. 9:1 Paul's claim to be an apostle is closely bound up with his claim to have 'seen Jesus our Lord'—i.e. in resurrection. It seems to follow that others to whom the risen Lord appeared should similarly be recognized as apostles—the twelve as a whole (including Cephas/Peter) as well as James and 'all the apostles' (1 Cor. 15:5, 7). It may well have been to their seeing the risen Lord that James and 'all the apostles' of 1 Cor. 15:7 owed their apostolic title.

If the five hundred of 1 Cor. 15:6 should be included, then the apostles were a numerous body indeed. Probably, however, there is the additional implication of special commissioning by the risen Lord. This might cover such ἀπόστολοι as Andronicus and Junia(s) (Rom. 16:7).

W. Schmithals (*Office of Apostle*, 1971) introduced a new hypothesis into the long debate about apostleship. The NT use of the term, he argued, is gnostic in origin. Evidence for gnostic ἀπόστολοι at a later date is provided, perhaps, by Rev. 2:2 (ἀποστόλους . . . ψευδεῖς) and more certainly by Tert. *De praesc.* 30.13 (*probent se nouos apostolos esse*); cf. Heges. ap. Euseb. *HE* 4.22.6 (ψευδ-απόστολοι), Dion. Cor. ap. Euseb. *HE* 4.23.12 (οἱ τοῦ διαβόλου ἀπόστολοι); but their existence in Paul's day is not proven (the ψευδαπόστολοι of 2 Cor. 11:13, μετασχηματιζόμενοι εἰς ἀποστόλους Χριστοῦ, are not obviously gnostics). According to Schmithals the twelve (a post-Easter conception read back into the pre-Easter situation) were not originally apostles; it is Luke who makes this equation and indeed confines the apostolate to the twelve. Paul, he holds, does not refer to the twelve as apostles; even Peter is not counted an apostle in 1 Cor. 9:5; 15:5, although the designation is conceded to him in Gal. 1:18f. (by implication) and 2:8 (εἰς ἀποστολὴν τῆς περιτομῆς).

But whatever be the textual status of the clause οὓς καὶ ἀποστόλους ὠνόμασεν referring to the twelve in Mk. 3:14, they are the objects of Christ's ἀποστέλλειν (cf. Mk. 6:7); and it is from their first being sent out δύο δύο in the course of the Galilaean ministry that they were originally called ἀπόστολοι, even if they had to be re-established and re-commissioned by their Lord after he rose again. The twelve must have been pre-eminent among those in Jerusalem who were 'apostles' already at the time of Paul's conversion.

In emphasizing his independence of the Jerusalem leaders, Paul has regard to the demands of his present *apologia*. As appears in 2:2, he was well aware of the importance of maintaining fellowship with those leaders if his own apostolic ministry was to be effective. Elsewhere he insists that his gospel was based on the same saving events as theirs, since the risen Lord who appeared to him had already appeared to them: 'whether therefore it was I or they, so we preach, and so you believed' (1 Cor. 15:11). But here he is rebutting the account which had evidently won wide circulation, that the Jerusalem leaders instructed him soon after his conversion in the principles of the gospel (including, it may have been said, the continuing requirement of circumcision), but that he broke loose from their tutelage and pursued a line of his own with his circumcision-free gospel—a line which lacked any recognizable authority. Paul has already denied this account of the matter in v 12; now he says in effect: 'That is impossible, for I had begun to preach the gospel in response to the Lord's Damascus-road commission before ever I met the leaders of the Jerusalem church; and when at last I did meet them, it was for too short a time for them to impart much in the way of instruction. Many more years elapsed, in fact, before I had an opportunity of setting my law-free gospel before them, and when I did so they acknowledged it to be the valid gospel for the Gentiles, to whom I had been manifestly sent to preach it.'

ἀπῆλθον εἰς Ἀραβίαν—a reference, probably, to the Nabataean kingdom, founded in the 2nd century BC with its capital at Petra; at this time it stretched from the neighbourhood of Damascus south into the Hijaz. The Nabataean king at the time of Paul's conversion was Aretas IV (9 BC – AD 40), at present embroiled with his western neighbour Herod Antipas, tetrarch of Galilee and Peraea (4 BC – AD 39), because of the insult offered to his family some years earlier when Antipas divorced Aretas's daughter so as to be free to marry Herodias (Jos., *Ant.* 18.109–115).

It is possible that in 'Arabia' Paul communed with God in the wilderness where Moses and Elijah had communed with him centuries before; but in the present context the primary purpose of his Arabian visit appears to have been the immediate fulfilment of his commission to preach the Son of God 'among the Gentiles'. There were Gentiles in abundance in the Nabataean realm, both settled population and Bedouin. Nothing is said of the planting of any church, but a beginning in preaching the gospel is indicated. Paul's argument at this point is: 'As soon as I was converted, I began my apostolic service, and had been thus engaged for three years before ever I saw the leaders of the Jerusalem church.' That his visit to 'Arabia' was not undertaken solely for the purpose of a contemplative retreat in the desert is confirmed by the incident which he recalls in 2 Cor. 11:32f.: 'In Damascus the ethnarch of King Aretas was guarding the city of the Damascenes to arrest me, and I was let down through a window in a basket and escaped his hands.' He had evidently done something to attract the hostile attention of the Nabataean authorities if the Nabataean king's representative in Damascus attempted to kidnap him as he left the city. His attempt, and Paul's escape, presumably took place after Paul 'returned to Damascus', as he says here.

The mention of his return to Damascus (καὶ πάλιν ὑπέστρεψα εἰς Δαμασκόν) confirms the record of Acts (9:3; 22:6; 26:12f.) that it was at or near Damascus that he was confronted by the risen Christ.

Damascus, one of the oldest continuously-inhabited cities in the world (cf. Gn. 14:5; 15:2), was an Amorite centre in patriarchal times, but later became the capital of an Aramaean kingdom. It was captured and annexed by the Assyrians in 732 BC and was thereafter controlled by the successive empires which dominated that part of the Near East. In 66 BC it fell into the hands of the Romans, in whose power it thereafter remained (apart from a brief occupation by the Parthians in 40–39 BC) as one of the cities of the Decapolis, under the general supervision of the imperial legate of Syria. Under the Seleucids Damascus had become hellenized and rebuilt on the grid pattern, with the various installations characteristic of a Hellenistic city. Arguments that it was controlled by the Nabataean kings from AD 37 to 61 (based on the absence of Roman coins from its coin record between those years) are not conclusive (see Schürer, *HJP*, I, 581f.). R. Jewett, *Dating Paul's Life* (London, 1979), 30–33, suggests that the principate of Gaius (AD 37–41), who re-established a system of client-kings in that part of the world, provides a setting in which Aretas could have acquired control of Damascus; this is possible, but a change of government in Damascus need not be postulated on the basis of 2 Cor. 11:32f. alone. However, the Nabataean territory certainly adjoined the environs of Damascus closely on the southeast, and there was doubtless a considerable Nabataean community in the city, whose interests were looked after by the king's ethnarch. The Jewish community in Damascus was also large, even if its numbers did not come up to Josephus's estimate of 10,500 (*War* 2.561) or 18,000 (*War* 7.368).

We cannot be sure if the disciples of Jesus within the Jewish community of Damascus had any links with the 'covenanters' of Damascus attested in the *Zadokite Work* (if indeed we are right in putting a literal interpretation on 'Damascus' in that work). Nor is there any cogency in E. Lohmeyer's theory that members of the family of Jesus had settled in Damascus because they expected to witness the parousia there (*Galiläa*, 54ff.; cf. H.-J. Schoeps, *Judenchristentum*, 270ff.). In any case, while it was with the disciples in Damascus that Paul first enjoyed Christian fellowship, it was not from them that he derived his gospel (see Bruce, *Paul*, 76–82).

(d) Paul meets the Jerusalem church leaders (1:18–20)

Next, after three years I went up to Jerusalem to get to know Cephas, and stayed with him for fifteen days. But I saw none of the other apostles, except James, the Lord's brother. Look: in what I am writing to you, as God is my witness, I am telling no lie.

TEXTUAL NOTES

v 18 Κηφαν $P^{46, \ 51*}$ $\aleph^*$ A B *pc* syr$^{pesh \ hcl.mg}$ cop / Πετρον $\aleph^2$ D G Ψ byz lat syr^{hcl}

1:18 Ἔπειτα, 'then', 'next'. This is the first of three successive occurrences of ἔπειτα (cf. v 21; 2:1). The force of Paul's argument here depends on his giving a consecutive account of his career since his conversion, with special reference to his visits to Jerusalem. His case would be weakened if his readers were given reason to suspect that he had omitted any material detail—it would be particularly suspicious if he omitted a visit to Jerusalem.

μετὰ τρία ἔτη, perhaps by inclusive reckoning; if so, we should say 'in the third year' (cf. the explanation of μετὰ τρεῖς ἡμέρας in Mk. 8:31; 10:34 as τῇ τρίτῃ ἡμέρᾳ or τῇ ἡμέρᾳ τῇ τρίτῃ in the parallel passages Lk. 9:22; 18:33). But Paul emphasizes the interval which elapsed between his conversion and his first subsequent visit to Jerusalem, implying that in this interval he had already begun his apostolic ministry without any authorization or even recognition on the part of the Jerusalem leaders.

ἀνῆλθον εἰς Ἱεροσόλυμα. Cf. v 17, with notes *ad loc*. Despite disparities between the two accounts (see note on v 20), this must be the visit of Acts 9:26–30 (*pace* P. Parker, 'Once More, Acts and Galatians', *JBL* 86 [1967], 175ff., who denies that the visit of Acts 9:26–30 took place and equates this visit with that of Acts 11:30).

ἱστορῆσαι Κηφᾶν. Κηφᾶς is Aram. *kēpā'* ('rock', 'stone') supplied with a Greek case-ending. By this form Paul regularly designates the apostle who is more commonly called Peter (Πέτρος), the Greek rendering of the Aramaic term. Outside Paul's letters, Κηφᾶς occurs (with the explanation ὃ ἑρμηνεύεται Πέτρος) only in Jn. 1:42, where Jesus hails Simon, Andrew's brother, thus. Paul uses the Greek form Πέτρος only in Gal. 2:7f. (see note *ad loc.* for a possible explanation).

Aram. *kēpā'* should no doubt be discerned behind both Πέτρος and πέτρα in Mt. 16:18 where Jesus says, 'You are Peter (Πέτρος), and on this rock (πέτρα) I will build my church.' Like Heb. *kēp* (Jb. 30:6; Je. 4:29), the Aramaic word means 'rock'. In 11QtgJob it is used twice (Jb. 39:1, 28) as the rendering of Heb. *sela'* ('crag'), and it seems to have the same sense in several places in 4QEn^{aram} (e.g. 1 Enoch 4; 89:29, 32). It appears once as a personal name in the Elephantine papyri of the 5th century BC; cf. E. G. Kraeling, *The Brooklyn Museum Aramaic Papyri* (New Haven, 1953), 227 (text 8, line 10). See J. A. Fitzmyer, 'Aramaic *Kepha'* and Peter's Name in the NT', *Black FS* (2), 121-132.

If ἱστορῆσαι is used here with its classical force, it means that Paul went up to Jerusalem to interview Cephas, to make inquiry of him. We may be sure in any case that this is what Paul did. But there is substantial evidence in Hellenistic usage for ἱστορέω in the sense of 'making someone's acquaintance' (cf. Jos., *War* 6.81; Plut., *Theseus* 30, *Pompey* 40, *Lucullus* 2, *De curiositate* 2; Epict., *Diss.* 2.14.28; 3.7.1), and this may be the sense in which Paul uses it here. (The verb occurs three times in the LXX—in 1 Esd. 1:33 bis, 42—but with the sense 'record', 'report', which is irrelevant to the present instance.) It was important for Paul to get to know the leader of the original apostles, who was also at this time the unchallenged leader of the Jerusalem church. That Cephas could at the same time give him information which it was important for him to know—first-hand information about Jesus' life and teaching, death and resurrection-appearances—should go without saying, were it not that it has seemed to some scholars to be ruled out of court by Paul's disclaimer in v 12 and his expressed resolution in 2 Cor. 5:16 not 'to know Christ after the flesh' (cf. R. Bultmann, 'The Significance of the Historical Jesus for the Theology of Paul' [1929], ETr in *Faith and Understanding*, I [London, 1966], 241; H.-J. Schoeps, *Paul*, 52, 72, 79). But to know Christ 'after the flesh' (κατὰ σάρκα) is to make a worldly and negative assessment of him, by contrast with that acquaintance with him through the Spirit which began for Paul on the Damascus road; it does not exclude an interest in the 'historical' Jesus—in what Jesus did and said during his Palestinian ministry.

One piece of information which he most probably received during this visit was that Jesus, having been raised from death on the third day, 'appeared to Cephas' (1 Cor. 15:5). That Jesus in resurrection appeared personally to Simon Peter is attested independently in Lk. 24:34 and may be implied elsewhere in the resurrection narratives of the Gospels (cf. R. H. Fuller, *The Formation of the Resurrection Narratives* [London, 1972], 34f.). It may also have been from Cephas that Paul learned how, after his appearance to Cephas, Jesus appeared 'then to the twelve, then . . . to more than five hundred brethren at one time' (the further statement, at the end of 1 Cor. 15:6, that most of these brethren were still alive is Paul's addition, twenty years after he originally received the information).

καὶ ἐπέμεινα πρὸς αὐτὸν ἡμέρας δεκάπεντε. Fifteen days would give Paul ample opportunity to learn as much of the story of Jesus as Cephas could tell him. The preposition πρός in the sense of 'with' (as in Mk. 6:3) is probably a colloquial Hellenistic usage (in Jn. 1:1f. it is taken up and applied to the relation of the Logos with God; cf. 1 Jn. 1:2). But whatever took place between Paul and Cephas during these two weeks, nothing took place which could modify the absoluteness of Paul's affirmation that he received his gospel direct from the risen Christ, through no intermediary. That affirmation (v 12) is the major premise of the argument implicit in the whole autobiographical outline which follows it. 'A late catechumenate and a crash course in missionary work with Peter are thus ruled out' (G. Bornkamm, *Paul*, 28).

1:19 ἕτερον δὲ τῶν ἀποστόλων οὐκ εἶδον. Precisely whom Paul reckoned among the apostles at that time (cf. v 17) may be uncertain, but W. Schmithal's argument, noted above, that they did not include the 'twelve' (apart from Cephas, so far as our present context is concerned) is quite unacceptable. If Paul's language here leaves open the possibility that he did see others of the 'twelve' in addition to Cephas—if, in fact, 'it is hardly believable that during a fourteen-day stay in Jerusalem Paul could remain unknown to the restricted number of the "Twelve" ' (Schmithals, *Paul and the Gnostics*, 22 n. 26)—those against whom he is arguing would have seized on what they recognized as a damaging admission, inadequately camouflaged by his failure to make explicit mention of the rest of the 'twelve'.

εἰ μὴ Ἰάκωβον τὸν ἀδελφὸν τοῦ κυρίου. Paul was anxious both then and throughout his apostolic career to establish and maintain bonds of fellowship with the Jerusalem church and its leaders. There was another of those leaders in Jerusalem at this time whom he made a point of meeting—James, the Lord's brother. He should in all probability be identified with the James who is named as the first of four brothers of Jesus in Mk. 6:3 (cf. Mt. 13:55) in a context which suggests that they, with an unspecified number of unnamed sisters, were, like Jesus himself, children of Mary. The Lord's 'brothers' are mentioned by Paul in 1 Cor. 9:5 as well-known Christian figures in the mid-fifties.

There is disagreement among early Christian writers about the exact relation which those 'brothers' bore to Jesus. Tertullian (*Adv. Marc.* 4.19; *De Car.* 7) appears to have regarded them as uterine brothers, the sons of Joseph and Mary; others, like the author of the *Protevangelium* of James (9:2), took them to be sons of Joseph by a previous marriage. This latter view was defended by Epiphanius in a letter subsequently incorporated in *Haer.* 78. The view that they were uterine brothers was explicitly affirmed about AD 380 by Helvidius of Rome, who disapproved of the prevalent tendency to exalt virginity above marriage and child-rearing. Helvidius was answered in 383 by Jerome (*Adversus Helvidium de perpetua virginitate beatae Mariae*), who propounded a third view—that the Lord's ἀδελφοί were actually his first cousins, the sons of Alphaeus by 'Mary of Clopas', whom he inferred from Jn. 19:25 to be the Virgin's sister (cf. Mk. 15:40). This view, as Jerome claimed, safeguarded the perpetual virginity not only of Mary but also of Joseph. It is plain that the controversy was occasioned rather by considerations of theological propriety than by a concern for historical fact. J. B. Lightfoot conveniently distinguishes the three principal views just listed as the Epiphanian, the Helvidian and the Hieronymian ('The Brethren of the Lord', *Galatians*, 252–291). See also R. E. Brown, K. P. Donfried, J. A. Fitzmyer, J. Reumann (ed.), *Mary in the NT* (London, 1978), 65–72, 270–278.

James was perhaps already the leader of one group in the Jerusalem church. About nine years later 'James and the brethren' seem to form a distinct group from those associated with Peter (Acts 12:17). James's influence was destined to increase rapidly until he became the acknowledged leader of the Jerusalem church as a whole, taking precedence even over Cephas/Peter (see 2:9, 12 below, with notes *ad loc.*). This is the more remarkable because the references to Jesus' family in the gospel tradition (both Markan and Johannine) imply that they were far from being followers of his during his ministry. 'Even his brothers', says the fourth Evangelist, 'did not believe in him' (Jn. 7:5), and we should gather as much from Mk. 3:21, 31–35. But according to Paul (1 Cor. 9:5) and Luke (Acts 1:14) they had a distinct place among his followers from the early post-resurrection period onwards. If it be asked how this change in their attitude came about, at a time when Jesus' shameful death might well have confirmed in their minds the misgivings which they had felt about him all along, Paul's statement in 1 Cor. 15:7, that Christ in resurrection 'appeared to James', points to the answer.

A. Harnack, 'Die Verklärungsgeschichte Jesu, der Bericht des Paulus (I Kor 15, 3ff.) und die beiden Christusvisionen des Petrus' (*SAB*, phil.-hist. Kl., 1922, 62–80), argued that the accounts of the resurrection appearances to Cephas and James were originally rival accounts, derived from two separate groups—the Petrine and the Jacobean. The Petrine ('he appeared to Cephas, then to the twelve, then . . . to more than five hundred brethren at one time') was the earlier, but was displaced by a later one in which the first appearance was granted to James ('he appeared to James, then to all the apostles'). Paul in that case would have put the two rival accounts together in sequence, with his repeated ἔπειτα or εἶτα, giving priority to the Petrine one, so that both accounts led up to the later appearance granted to himself.

On the other hand, Paul is our only near-contemporary authority for the appearance to James, and he explicitly dates it later (ἔπειτα) than the appearance to Cephas. Moreover, here in Gal. 1:18f. he provides evidence of an occasion, early in his Christian career, when he had an opportunity to hear both accounts direct from the principals themselves, and presumably to conclude which of the two saw the risen Christ first. That is to say, if it was during Paul's present visit to Jerusalem that he learned of the risen Lord's appearance to Cephas, it was no doubt during the same visit that he learned of his subsequent (ἔπειτα) appearance to James, while he himself would be able to add his personal testimony: 'Last of all . . . he appeared also to me' (1 Cor. 15:8). The appearance of the risen Christ evidently produced in James a revolutionary effect comparable to that which it later produced in Paul.

There is no other canonical mention of the appearance to James (as there is of the appearance to Cephas); an imaginatively embellished account from *Gos. Heb.* is quoted by Jerome, *De viris illustribus* 2: 'Now when the Lord had given his linen garment to the priest's servant, he went to James and appeared to him. For James had sworn that he would eat no bread from that hour when he had drunk the cup of the Lord until he saw him rising from the dead. [And again, a little later:] "Bring a table and bread", said the Lord; [and immediately it continues:] He took bread and gave thanks and broke it, and thereafter he gave it to James the Just and said to him, "My brother, eat your bread, because the Son of Man has risen from those who sleep".'

The most natural way to understand Paul's construction ἕτερον . . . οὐκ εἶδον εἰ μὴ . . . is: 'The only other apostle I saw [apart from Cephas] was James the Lord's brother.' It is less natural to take it to mean 'I saw none of the other apostles, but I did see James the Lord's brother' (cf. J. G. Machen, *Galatians*, 76–80). It would be difficult to improve on J. B. Lightfoot's observation that εἰ μή has (as always) exceptive force, the question here being 'whether the exception refers to the whole clause or to the verb alone'. In the present construction 'the sense of ἕτερον naturally links it with εἰ μή, from which it cannot be separated without harshness, and ἕτερον carries τῶν ἀποστόλων with it' (*Galatians*, 84f.). L. P. Trudinger, *'Heteron de tōn apostolōn ouk eidon, ei mē Iakōbon . . .*: A Note on Galatians i.19', *NovT* 17 (1975), 200–202, argues for the rendering: 'Apart from the apostles I saw no one but James, the Lord's brother'. But, as was pointed out in a reply to him by G. Howard, 'Was James an Apostle? A Reflection on a New Proposal for Gal i 19', *NovT* 19 (1977), 63f., if Paul had wished to say this, he would have expressed himself differently, saying perhaps ἕτερον δὲ ἢ τοὺς ἀποστόλους . . . (or παρὰ τοὺς ἀποστόλους . . . or ἐκτὸς τῶν ἀποστόλων . . .). Trudinger's rendering provides a closer harmonization with Acts 9:27, where Barnabas is said to have used his good offices and brought Paul πρὸς τοὺς ἀποστόλους ('to the apostles'). But it is best to take τοὺς ἀποστόλους in Acts 9:27 as an instance of the generalizing plural.

A good parallel to the present construction, with the pronoun in the negative clause qualified by a genitive, is 1 Cor. 1:14, οὐδένα ὑμῶν ἐβάπτισα εἰ μή Κρίσπον καὶ Γάϊον, 'I baptized none of you but Crispus and Gaius' (where Crispus and Gaius are included in ὑμῶν). Where the exception relates to the negatived verb only, this is made plain by the context, as in 2:16, οὐ δικαιοῦται ἄνθρωπος ἐξ ἔργων νόμου εἰ μὴ διὰ πίστεως . . . , 'one is not justified by legal works but [one *is* justified] through faith'. There is nothing in the present context to suggest that here the exception relates to οὐκ εἶδον only.

Probably few would have questioned the rendering here preferred but for misgivings about the designation of James as an apostle. But there is nothing anomalous in the designation, so far as Paul's usage of ἀπόστολος is concerned. He clearly did not restrict the designation to the twelve. If, in the summary of resurrection appearances in 1 Cor. 15:5–7 he links the appearance to Cephas with a following appearance to 'the twelve' (to whose number Cephas belonged), his linking of the appearance to James with a following appearance to 'all the apostles' suggests that he included James among 'all the apostles'.

According to C. Marius Victorinus Afer, *In epistulam Pauli ad Galatas* . . . (on 1:19), the Symmachians (Ebionites) regarded this James as the twelfth apostle (ed. A. Locher [Leipzig, 1972], 14).

At any rate, during that first post-conversion visit to Jerusalem, Paul had only a limited opportunity of conferring with 'flesh and blood'; should any one suppose that he met the whole apostolic college at that time, he would be mistaken, as Paul asserts most solemnly.

1:20 ἰδοὺ ἐνώπιον τοῦ θεοῦ ὅτι οὐ ψεύδομαι. Paul's oath that he is telling the truth may be based on (Roman) judicial procedure. He is defending himself against the charge that he proclaims a man-made, second-hand gospel and that his commission to proclaim it was derived from men. There may be the further implied charge that he has not been faithful even to that human commission—that he has abridged or adulterated the message which was delivered to him by others.

To this compound accusation Paul replies with a twofold line of defence:

(i) his gospel was not derived from mortal man but from God; it was part and parcel of that 'revelation of Jesus Christ' which God imparted to him; (ii) even if this claim of his were (*per impossibile*) disproved, then, wherever his gospel came from, it could not have come from Jerusalem. J. P. Sampley, ' "Before God, I do not lie" (Gal. 1.20: Paul's Self-Defence in the Light of Roman Legal Praxis', *NTS* 23 (1976-77), 477-482, points out that the proffering of oaths in court was generally discouraged, 'unless it is absolutely necessary' (Quintilian, *Institutio oratoria* 9.2.98). Paul did consider it absolutely necessary at this point, where the independence of his gospel and of his apostleship was at stake. His readers might find it unlikely that he met only two men of apostolic standing during the two weeks of this Jerusalem visit, and these two, perhaps, the leaders of distinct groups in the mother-church. It might have been expected that more of the apostles would have been present in Jerusalem; possibly Paul himself had expected to meet more of them, but in the event he could congratulate himself (for the sake of his present defence) that he had met so few.

The vehement solemnity with which Paul calls God to witness that he is not lying implies that another account of the matter was current and might have reached his Galatian converts—an account which represented him as having gone to Jerusalem to receive from those who were apostles before him the authority to exercise his own ministry.

O. Linton, 'The Third Aspect: A Neglected Point of View', *ST* 3 (1949), 79-95, has argued that this variant account is the one on which Luke drew for the narrative of Acts 9:1-30. But although Luke has Paul meeting more church leaders and engaging in more public activity on this first visit to Jerusalem than Paul's present account allows, he does not imply Paul's indebtedness to the Jerusalem apostles for his gospel or his commission to preach it: on the contrary, according to Luke, 'immediately' upon Paul's baptism (three days after his conversion) he was proclaiming Jesus in Damascus as 'the Son of God', with no commission save that of the risen Lord (Acts 9:20). (The risen Lord may have used Ananias of Damascus as his mouthpiece, as reported in Acts 22:12-16, but Ananias had self-evidently no commissioning authority in his own right.)

(e) Paul in Syria and Cilicia (1:21-24)

Then I came into the territories of Syria and Cilicia. I remained unknown by face to the churches of Judaea which are in Christ; they only kept on hearing, 'Our former persecutor is now preaching the faith which he once laid waste', and they glorified God on my account.

1:21 ἔπειτα ἦλθον εἰς τὰ κλίματα τῆς Συρίας καὶ τῆς Κιλικίας. Paul continues, by means of a further ἔπειτα, to assure his readers that no suspicious gaps are left in his narrative. Between the two Jerusalem visits of 1:18f. and 2:1-10 he had no opportunity for contact with the mother-church and its leaders, for after the former visit he set off at once for Syria and Cilicia, and remained in those parts for several years.

κλίματα, sometimes used by geographers in the sense of 'latitudes', has no technical sense here. W. M. Ramsay, in a discussion of its present context (*Galatians*, 278–280), deprecates the rendering 'regions', preferring to keep 'region' as the rendering of χώρα when it is used with the precise force of Lat. *regio*, the administrative subdivision of a province (as in Acts 16:6; 18:23). Paul uses the word again in 2 Cor. 11:10 (ἐν τοῖς κλίμασιν τῆς 'Αχαΐας) and Rom. 15:23 (ἐν τοῖς κλίμασι τούτοις), in the same general sense as here ('territories', 'districts').

At this time Syria and Eastern Cilicia (Cilicia Pedias) constituted one Roman province. Both areas had been reduced to provincial status under Pompey— Cilicia after his victory over the pirates in 67 BC and Syria after his victory over Mithridates in 64 BC. From *c*. 25 BC Eastern Cilicia (including Tarsus) was united administratively with Syria to form one imperial province (Syria-Cilicia), governed by a *legatus pro praetore* with his headquarters in Syrian Antioch. This arrangement lasted until AD 72, when Eastern Cilicia was detached from Syria and united with Western Cilicia (Cilicia Tracheia) to form the province of Cilicia.

Paul's brief statement here is in agreement with the narrative of Acts 9:30; 11:25f., according to which his Jerusalem friends took him down to Caesarea and put him on board a ship bound for Tarsus, from which he was fetched by Barnabas some years later to join him in caring for the church in Antioch. It is probably implied that Paul's apostolic work during this period in Syria and Cilicia was more fruitful than his witness in Nabataean Arabia had been; at any rate enough was happening for news of Paul's activity to get back to Judaea.

1:22 ἤμην δὲ ἀγνοούμενος. This periphrastic construction of the imperfect tense of εἰμί with the present participle emphasizes the continuity of the state or action indicated by the main verb; cf. ἀκούοντες ἦσαν, v 23. See G. Björck, HN ΔΙΔΑΣΚΩΝ: *Die periphrastischen Konstruktionen im Griechischen* (Uppsala, 1940).

ταῖς ἐκκλησίαις τῆς 'Ιουδαίας ταῖς ἐν Χριστῷ. The 'churches of Judaea' comprised groups of believers who had been forced to leave Jerusalem in the persecution that followed Stephen's death, together with others which had been formed through the evangelistic outreach of Jerusalem disciples even before that. If, as the record of Acts implies, the 'disciples at Damascus' at the time of Paul's conversion included Damascene residents as well as refugees from the persecution in Judaea (τοὺς ἐκεῖσε ὄντας, Acts 22:5), the same situation could have been found in Palestine itself.

These churches are here described in terms remarkably similar to those of 1 Thes. 2:14, where 'the churches of God which are in Judaea in Christ Jesus' are said to have suffered persecution at the hands of their fellow-countrymen. At the time when both epistles were written, the Roman province of Judaea included Galilee as well as Judaea (in the narrower sense) and Samaria (as it had done since the death of Herod Agrippa I in AD 44); 'Judaea' may then denote here the whole of Palestine. If so, 'the churches of Judaea which are in Christ' would be identical with 'the church throughout all Judaea and Galilee and Samaria' (Acts 9:31). Paul regularly speaks of the 'church' (singular) in a city but the 'churches' (plural) in a province or more extensive area. When he recalls his persecution of 'the church of God' (v 13) he means, in the first instance, the church in Jerusalem; thanks to the scattering of its members in the persecution, that church had now become 'the churches of Judaea'. Neither here nor in 1 Thes. 2:14 can the Judaean churches be exclusive of the Jerusalem church. That is to say, Paul does not mean: 'I was known, of course, by face to the church of Jerusalem but not to the Judaean churches outside Jerusalem' (as is maintained in A. Ehrhardt, *Acts*, 63). The whole thrust of his present argument emphasizes the fewness of his contacts with the Jerusalem church in particular, and only then with the Judaean churches in general. There would have been little value in his insisting that he remained unknown by face to the churches of Judaea if his readers had been free to infer that he *was* known to the Jerusalem church at large: that was the very impression which he was concerned to remove.

It may be, indeed, that at the time of Paul's first post-conversion visit to Jerusalem most of the believers had left the city because of the recent persecution and had not yet begun to return. Luke says that in the first intensity of the persecution 'they were all scattered throughout the region of Judaea and Samaria, except the apostles' (Acts 8:1), no distinction being made between 'Hebrews' and Hellenists. It took some time for the dispersed church to reconstitute itself in Jerusalem. After some years it had done so, in greater numbers than before, but when Paul visited the city about AD 35 even the apostles appear to have been absent for the most part—at least Paul saw none but Cephas and James.

But if 'the churches of Judaea' consisted in large degree of refugees from Jerusalem, driven from the city by a persecution in which Paul played a leading part, is it likely that he was 'unknown by face' to so many of them? Does not this statement of his support the argument that Jerusalem was not the centre of his persecuting activity? (Cf., e.g., E. Haenchen, *Acts*, 297ff., for the view that the persecution was carried on in and around Damascus.) It is possible that, as a leader, he had underlings to do the day-to-day and house-to-house harrying of believers for him, so that he had no direct dealings with the rank and file. But here he is speaking of himself as a Christian: in this new role he remained 'unknown by face', or 'unknown personally' (τῷ προσώπῳ) to the churches of Judaea, who nevertheless knew of him as their 'former persecutor' (v 23).

The phrase ἐν Χριστῷ, by which the churches of Judaea are qualified (cf. ἐν Χριστῷ ᾽Ιησοῦ, 1 Thes. 2:14; also Phil. 1:1), is an 'incorporative' locution, characteristically Pauline, denoting the people of Christ as members of his 'body', sharers in his risen life. Its full incorporative force is apparent in 3:26–28 (see notes *ad loc*.), but sometimes it is used more generally, much as we use the adjective 'Christian' (Gk. Χριστιανός is used in the NT only by non-Christians, directly or by implication; cf. its three occurrences: Acts 11:26; 26:28; 1 Pet. 4:16). Thus the NEB renders the present instance 'Christ's congregations in Judaea', whereas ἐν Χριστῷ ᾽Ιησοῦ in 2:4 is rendered 'in the fellowship of Christ Jesus'. C. F. D. Moule includes our text among a few passages where 'Christ (or the Lord) seems to be the "place", the *locus*, where believers are found' (*Christology*, 56).

1:23 μόνον δὲ ἀκούοντες ἦσαν, 'Only they kept on hearing'—as in v 22 the periphrastic construction emphasizes the continuous (or repeated) character of the action. The participle refers back to ταῖς ἐκκλησίαις (v 22); the masculine ἀκούοντες (instead of the feminine ἀκούουσαι) is a construction *ad sensum*, implying that it was the members of those churches that heard the reports.

ὅτι is *recitativum*; the words which it introduces do not convey the direct speech of those from whom the reports ultimately emanated, but the direct speech of those in Judaea who received and disseminated the reports. It was not the new converts in Syria and Cilicia that referred to Paul as '*our* former persecutor'; it was the Judaean churches. As some of the members of those churches received the news, they would pass it on to others: 'Have you heard? Our former persecutor (ὁ διώκων ἡμᾶς ποτε) is preaching the gospel which he once tried to destroy.'

νῦν εὐαγγελίζεται τὴν πίστιν. πίστις is here practically synonymous with εὐαγγέλιον (the gospel of salvation by faith). 'It is striking proof of the large space occupied by "faith" in the mind of the infant Church, that it should so soon have passed into a synonym for the Gospel. . . . Here its meaning seems to hover between the Gospel and the Church' (J. B. Lightfoot, *Galatians*, 86). On 'faith' see further on 2:16; 3:6–9, 23–26. For constructions with εὐαγγελίζομαι see note on v 11.

ἥν ποτε ἐπόρθει, the same verb as was used in v 13. There the object was 'the church of God'; here it is the faith which the church professed and the message in which that faith was proclaimed.

No account is made of any difference in emphasis or content between the gospel as Paul was proclaiming it and the gospel as the Judaeans understood it. They probably knew nothing of any such difference: what they knew was that Paul was now proclaiming the same faith in Christ as they themselves had embraced—the faith for which they had once been persecuted by him.

1:24 καὶ ἐδόξαζον ἐν ἐμοὶ τὸν θεόν, 'they glorified God on my account'—every time they heard such news (imperfect tense)—because of the transforming grace that had been manifested 'in me'. J. B. Lightfoot compares Is. 49:3 LXX: ἐν σοὶ ἐνδοξασθήσομαι (*Galatians*, 86).

E. Bammel, 'Galater 1, 23', *ZNW* 59 (1968), 108–112, sees features of a martyr aretalogy in vv 23, 24. But whereas such aretalogies frequently portray the miserable end of the persecutor (e.g. Antiochus IV in 2 Macc. 9:5–12, 28; Galerius in Euseb., *HE* 8.16.3–5; cf. Lactantius, *De mortibus persecutorum*), here it is the conversion and apostolic witness of the persecutor that brings glory and praise to God. The agitators may have denounced Paul to the Galatian churches as one who (whether they knew it or not) formerly persecuted the saints; the reply to such denunciations is to tell how the persecuted saints came to glorify God for what he had wrought in and through the former persecutor.

Thus, during the years which followed Paul's brief visit to Jerusalem, as in the shorter interval which preceded it, he was actively engaged in preaching the gospel, without requiring or receiving any authorization to do so from the leaders of the mother-church.

(f) Conference in Jerusalem (2:1–10)

Then, after the lapse of fourteen years, I went up to Jerusalem again, together with Barnabas, and I took Titus along too. I went up in accordance with reve-lation, and I set before them the gospel which I preach among the Gentiles — privately, I mean, before the 'men of repute', lest perchance I should prove to be running, or to have run, in vain. (But not even Titus, who was with me, was compelled to be circumcised, Greek though he was. It was because of the false brethren who had been smuggled in [that this question later arose]. They infiltrated into our company to spy out the freedom which we have in Christ Jesus, in order to bring us into bondage. But to them we made no submission, not even for an hour: our purpose was that the truth of the gospel should remain unimpaired with you.) But as for the 'men of some repute'—it makes no difference to me what sort of people they once were, for God has no favourites—those 'men of repute', I say, conferred no additional authority on me. On the contrary, they saw that I had been entrusted with the gospel for the uncircumcision, just as Peter had been entrusted with it for the circumcision—for the same Lord who had empowered Peter for his apostleship among the circumcised had also empowered me for my apostleship to the Gentiles. So then, James, Cephas and John, the men of repute as 'pillars' among them, recognized the grace that had been bestowed on me, and they shook hands with Barnabas and me as a token of fellowship, agreeing that we should [go] to the Gentiles and they themselves to the circumcision. 'Only', they said, 'continue to remember the "poor" '—and in fact I had taken the initiative in attending to this very matter.

TEXTUAL NOTES

v 1 παλιν ανεβην / ανεβην παλιν D G / ανεβην lat^c cop^{bo} Mcion Iren^{lat} Tert Ambst Chr / παλιν ανηλθον C

v 4 δε / *om* lat^f Mcion
ινα *add* μη G
καταδουλωσουσιν ℵ A B* C D E *pl* / καταδουλωσωσιν B² G / καταδουλωσωνται TR

v 5 οις ουδε P^{46} ℵ B D^c G byz vg / ουδε Mcion Ephr Graeci ap. Ambst / *om* D* Iren^{lat} Tert Ambst Pelag
τη υποταγη *om* P^{46}

v 6 ο P^{46} ℵ *al* / *om* B C D G byz

v 9 Ιακωβος και Κηφας / *om* και Κηφας A / Ιακωβος και Πετρος P^{46} lat^r / Πετρος και Ιακωβος D G lat$^{ab\,vg.codd}$ Mcion Ambst

2:1 Ἔπειτα, 'then', 'next', as in 1:18, 21, implies that Paul is omitting nothing material to his argument—in particular, that he is omitting no visit to Jerusalem or other contact with the church there or its leaders. Had he been suspected of leaving out (however innocently) any such visit or contact, the question would have been asked: 'But what happened on that occasion which you have suppressed?' The conference which he is about to describe was his first meeting with the Jerusalem leaders after the end of the fifteen days of 1:18f. Many interesting and important events had no doubt taken place during that interval, but nothing relevant to his present argument.

διὰ δεκατεσσάρων ἐτῶν. For this temporal use of διά with the genitive cf. Mk. 2:1 (δι' ἡμερῶν, 'in the course of some days'); Acts 24:17 (δι' ἐτῶν . . . πλειόνων, 'after the lapse of several years'); 27:5 *v.l.* (δι' ἡμερῶν δεκάπεντε, 'in the course of fifteen days'). The variation of preposition here from 1:18 (μετὰ ἔτη τρία) may be purely stylistic; it cannot in itself decide the question whether the fourteen years are to be reckoned from the preceding Jerusalem visit or (like that visit) from Paul's conversion. For the latter interpretation see G. Ogg, *Chronology*, 56f.; for the former, R. Jewett, *Dating*, 52–54.

The relation between the time-note here and 2 Cor. 12:2 ('fourteen years ago') is fortuitous. J. Knox, 'Fourteen Years Later', *JR* 16 (1936), 341–349; 'The Pauline Chronology', *JBL* 58 (1939), 15–30, argued that the two notes referred to the same interval, and that the experience of 2 Cor. 12:1ff. was coincident with Paul's conversion, but later, in view of 'objections from many critics' and 'after no little vacillation', he abandoned this view (*Chapters*, 78 n. 3). There is this to be said about the two notes: the experience which took place fourteen years before Paul wrote 2 Cor. 12:1ff. probably took place within the fourteen years of Gal. 2:1, during his ministry in Syria and Cilicia.

πάλιν ἀνέβην εἰς Ἰεροσόλυμα. Here πάλιν, if it is part of the original text (H. Lietzmann, *An die Galater*, 9, thought not), means 'a second time', whereas in 1:17 (πάλιν ὑπέστρεψα εἰς Δαμασκόν) it means 'back'. Paul does not name the starting-point of this second journey to Jerusalem, but it was evidently from 'the territories of Syria and Cilicia' (1:21) and most probably from Antioch. On ἀναβαίνω see note on 1:17.

μετὰ Βαρναβᾶ. Barnabas, according to Acts 11:25f., was Paul's senior colleague in the leadership of the church of Antioch, from which they both visited Jerusalem together on the occasions mentioned in Acts 11:27–30 (cf. 12:25) and 15:1–5. Paul mentions Barnabas in Gal. 2:1–13 and again in 1 Cor. 9:6 in terms which mark the two men out as close associates. The references to Barnabas in Acts and in the Pauline letters supplement and confirm each other.

According to Luke, Barnabas was a Levite from Cyprus whose personal name was Joseph. He was an associate of the twelve in the early days of the Jerusalem church, and it was they who gave him the sobriquet Barnabas, explained as meaning 'son of encouragement' (υἱὸς παρακλήσεως, Acts 4:36). When Paul paid his first post-conversion visit to Jerusalem, it was Barnabas, says Luke, who first introduced him to 'the apostles' (described on p. 101 above as a generalizing plural) and presumably vouched for his *bona fides* (Acts 9:27). Later, when Gentile evangelization began in Antioch, it was Barnabas who was sent there by the church of Jerusalem to supervise and direct the work; he fetched Paul from Tarsus to join him in this ministry, and he and Paul were sent to Jerusalem by the Antiochene Christians a year or two later with financial aid for the mother-church (Acts 11:22–30).

See R. J. Bauckham, 'Barnabas in Galatians', *JSNT*, Issue 2 (1979), 61–70.

συμπαραλαβὼν καὶ Τίτον. Titus, a Gentile Christian (v 3), evidently from Antioch, had already manifested qualities which prompted Paul to take him along with him and give him some experience in responsible negotiations. These qualities later commended him to Paul as a reliable and acceptable representative in his delicate dealings with the Corinthian church, both in the matter of Paul's personal relationship with that church (2 Cor. 2:12f.; 7:5–16) and in that of the Jerusalem relief fund (2 Cor. 8:6–24; 9:3–5; 12:18). Titus later appears as addressee of one of the Pastoral Letters; it is doubtless on the basis of Tit. 1:5 that he is traditionally claimed as the first bishop of the Cretan church.

The singular participle συμπαραλαβών (for this verb cf. Acts 15:37f.) may imply that Paul took the initiative in bringing Titus along. Luther suggested that Paul regarded Titus as a test case: 'he took him along then, in order to prove that grace was equally sufficient for Gentiles and Jews, whether in circumcision or without circumcision' (*Vorlesung*, *ad loc.*, quoted by H. Schlier, *Galater*, 65 n. 5).

The absence of Titus's name from Acts is a problem with no certain solution. It was suggested by W. M. Ramsay that he was Luke's brother, and that the absence of his name is on a par with the absence of Luke's (Luke being identified with the author of Acts); cf. *SPT*, 390; A. Souter, 'A Suggested Relationship between Titus and Luke', *Exp Tim* 18 (1906–7), 285; 'The Relationship between Titus and Luke', ibid., 335f. See also T. Zahn, *Urausgabe der Apostelgeschichte des Lucas* (Leipzig, 1916), 146, for the text of an African compendium of biblical prophecy (early 4th century) which includes in the names of Acts 13:1 *Lucius Cirenensis, qui manet usque adhuc, et Ticius conlactaneus—* were the compilers thinking of Luke the physician and Titus? (Zahn found this work helpful for his reconstruction of the Western text of Acts.) C. K. Barrett points out that, in view of the very guarded allusion to the Jerusalem relief fund in Acts (cf. Acts 24:17), Titus's close association with that fund could be considered as a reason for the omission of his name from Acts ('Titus', *Black FS* [1], 2).

2:2 ἀνέβην δὲ κατὰ ἀποκάλυψιν. We may have no other reference to this 'revelation'. Some have related it to the prophecy of Agabus (Acts 11:27–30), in pursuance of which the Christians of Antioch contributed a sum of money to help their Jerusalem brethren in time of famine, and sent it to them by the hand of Barnabas and Paul: so W. M. Ramsay, *SPT*, 57; C. W. Emmet, *Galatians*, 13, and *BC*, I.2, 279; cf. also S. G. Wilson, *Gentiles*, 183. But Paul's language suggests rather a revelation received by himself, from which he gathered that he should visit Jerusalem. Perhaps Barnabas was going there in any case, and the revelation persuaded Paul that he should go with him. T. W. Manson was disposed to identify the 'revelation' with the Spirit's command to the five leading teachers of the Antiochene church (one of whom was Paul) that Barnabas and Paul should be released for missionary service farther afield (Acts 13:1f.); a visit to Jerusalem on the eve of such a 'big new missionary enterprise' he judged to be eminently suitable, even if it is not recorded in Acts (*Studies*, 177). (Cf. W. Schmithals, *Paul and James*, 52.) If the famine-relief visit of Acts 11:30 took place before this, as Manson accepted, we are faced with the difficulty that Paul omitted one Jerusalem visit from his present narrative of events.

Is this visit identical with one of Paul's Jerusalem visits mentioned in Acts or is it (as Manson suggested) a visit passed over in silence by Luke? Two visits to Jerusalem by Barnabas and Paul together are recorded by Luke—the famine-relief visit of Acts 11:30 (12:25) and the visit to the Council of Jerusalem in Acts 15:2ff. It has been held that these two were originally variant accounts, drawn from two separate sources, of one and the same visit, of which Gal. 2:1–10 presents a first-hand account: so J. Wellhausen, 'Noten zur Apostelgeschichte', *Nachrichten von der königlichen Gesellschaft der Wissenschaften zu Göttingen*, phil.-hist. Kl. (1907), 1ff.; E. Schwartz, 'Zur Chronologie des Paulus', ibid., 263ff.; K. Lake, *BC*, I.5, 199ff. Otherwise the majority view is that the visit of Gal. 2:1–10 is identical with that of Acts 15:2ff. The view taken here is that it is to be identified with the visit of Acts 11:30, in the fourteenth year after Paul's conversion. Yet others (e.g. J. Knox, *Chapters*, 68f.; J. van Bruggen, *'Na Veertien Jaren'* [Kampen, 1973], 40–43, 223–225) have identified it with Paul's Jerusalem visit briefly mentioned in Acts 18:22.

καὶ ἀνεθέμην αὐτοῖς. The only other NT occurrence of ἀνατίθημι, also in the 2nd aorist middle, is in Acts 25:14, where Festus 'communicated' (ἀνέθετο) to the younger Agrippa the facts of Paul's case; cf. 2 Macc. 3:9, where Heliodorus 'communicated' (ἀνέθετο) to the high priest the information he had received about the wealth stored in the temple treasury; also Mi. 7:5 LXX: 'beware of communicating (ἀναθέσθαι) anything to your wife.' This meaning, though not classical, is well attested in Hellenistic Greek. MM (38) cite a papyrus of AD 233 for the sense 'communicate with a view to consultation'. It is most unlikely that Paul would have modified his gospel had the Jerusalem leaders *not* approved of it—he had higher authority than theirs for maintaining it unchanged, and 'no one is likely to want the *independence* of his gospel to be confirmed' (W. Schmithals, *Paul and James*, 43). But the approval of those leaders made his task less difficult and (as here) could serve his apologetic purpose. At the beginning of his apostolic career Paul did not communicate or submit his gospel to any one (οὐ προσανεθέμην) before proceeding to preach it forthwith (1:16); now the time had come to share it with the Jerusalem leaders, and indeed direction to do so may have been the substance of the revelation in accordance with which he paid his present visit.

τὸ εὐαγγέλιον ὃ κηρύσσω ἐν τοῖς ἔθνεσιν has already been mentioned in 1:11f., 16. The burden of this gospel is Christ crucified and risen, presented to Gentiles (as well as to Jews) as the object of their faith (cf. v 16).

κατ᾿ ἰδίαν δὲ τοῖς δοκοῦσιν. Those to whom (αὐτοῖς) Paul communicated the terms of his Gentile kerygma are more specifically defined as τοῖς δοκοῦσιν, 'the men of repute'. Later in the paragraph the expression is amplified: τῶν δοκούντων εἶναί τι (v 6a), οἱ δοκοῦντες στῦλοι εἶναι (v 9). Their identity is stated in v 9: James, Cephas and John. But whether οἱ δοκοῦντες is amplified or stands alone (as here and in v 6b), it carries no insinuation of sarcasm or irony, as though they only *seemed* to be leaders but were not really so. Josephus uses οἱ προὔχειν δοκοῦντες (literally, 'those who seemed to excel') of the men highly (and properly) esteemed in a community (cf. *War* 3.453; 4.141, 159).

If Paul meant that he submitted his gospel to these leaders for their authorization, he would be going far to undermine his preceding argument, with its claim that he was independent of Jerusalem. He set it before them: 'this', he said, 'is what I preach among the Gentiles' (the present tense of κηρύσσω implies that he was still preaching it at the time he sent this letter). In the light of v 7 we may conclude that he gave them an account of his gospel ministry to date (cf. Acts 15:12). The Jerusalem leaders could see that it was basically the same gospel as they themselves preached among the Jews—the gospel summarized in 1 Cor. 15:3–7, of which Paul could say a few years later, 'Whether then it was I or they [Cephas, James, etc.], so we preach and so you believed' (1 Cor. 15:11). The circumcision-free emphasis in Paul's proclamation of it to the Gentiles had naturally no counterpart in its proclamation to Jews, who were already circumcised.

Paul mentions that he communicated his gospel not to the Jerusalem church

as a whole but privately (κατ' ἰδίαν) to its leaders. Against the view that this
was a private session convened to reach an agreement which could then be set
before a larger body (the πλῆθος of Acts 15:12) W. L. Knox's remark is apposite: 'We have no reason for supposing that the Church had by this date
reached that stage of democracy in which the public meeting registers its assent
to a decision reached in advance by its leading members' (*The Acts of the Apostles*
[Cambridge, 1948], 42).

A. S. Geyser suggests that the meeting was held in private because the
leaders were in hiding on account of the persecution under Herod Agrippa I
('Paul, the Apostolic Decree and the Liberals in Corinth', *De Zwaan FS*, 131).
But on any dating of this visit, Agrippa's death (AD 44) must have taken place
some time before it, and the implication of Acts 12:17 is that James the Lord's
brother was not affected by the persecution (he had not forfeited public good
will by fraternizing with Gentiles, as Peter had done).

It is more likely that Paul and Barnabas met the Jerusalem leaders privately
in the first instance because they might hope to get a more sympathetic hearing
from them, away from the pressure of the rank and file, than they might have
received had they communicated the law-free gospel to a general meeting of the
mother-church.

Had Paul not communicated his gospel to Cephas and James on his previous
visit? 'Can it be assumed that during Paul's first visit to Jerusalem (Gal. 1:18ff.)
the question of the relation of the Pauline mission to the Jews and the Jewish
Christians had remained unanswered or had actually not been discussed? Impossible!' (W. Schmithals, *Paul and James*, 50). The impossibility is not so great
as Schmithals supposes. It may well be, indeed, that the subject was ventilated
on that earlier occasion. But whereas now the main purpose of Paul's visit
appears to have been to communicate his gospel to the Jerusalem leaders, then
the main purpose of his visit had been to get to know Cephas. Now, with
fourteen years' experience of Gentile evangelization, he could adduce solid evidence to the effectiveness of his preaching.

G. Howard (*Crisis*, 21ff.) argues that this second visit was absolutely the
first occasion on which Paul told the Jerusalem leaders of the uniqueness of his
apostolic call and law-free message. In his view, the 'revelation' in accordance
with which Paul now went up to Jerusalem was his inaugural Damascus-road
'revelation of Jesus Christ' (cf. κατὰ ἀποκάλυψιν in Rom. 16:25; Eph. 3:3).
The delay between the revelation and the visit could be explained by Paul's
resolve to wait until 'his apostolic position and his Gentile mission had grown
strong enough to convince them of his divine approval' (ibid., 39).

μή πως εἰς κενὸν τρέχω ἢ ἔδραμον, 'lest I should run (present subjunctive), or should [prove to] have run (aorist indicative), in vain'. For the construction cf. 4:11 below and 1 Thes. 3:5, μή πως ἐπείρασεν ὑμᾶς ὁ σατανᾶς καὶ
εἰς κενὸν γένηται ὁ κόπος ἡμῶν, 'lest Satan should [prove to] have tempted
(aorist indicative) you and our labour should become (aorist subjunctive) fruitless'. For the sense cf. Phil. 2:16, where Paul will rejoice on 'the day of Christ'
if his converts maintain their faithful testimony, for then he will have the evidence
that he has not 'run in vain or laboured in vain' (ὅτι οὐκ εἰς κενὸν ἔδραμον
οὐδὲ εἰς κενὸν κεκοπίακα). The last clause in Phil. 2:16 recalls Is. 49:4,

where the Servant says, 'I have laboured in vain (κενῶς ἐκοπίασα), I have spent my strength for nothing and vanity'—and the same LXX passage may underlie Paul's thought here and elsewhere. Athletic imagery came readily to Paul's mind.

But his language gives one pause. On the face of it, the meaning seems to be that, in default of a recognition by the Jerusalem leaders that his message was the authentic gospel, his apostolic service would have been, and would continue to be, fruitless. The substance of his gospel, indeed, was not to be changed out of deference to any earthly authority, not even the authority of those who were apostles before him. What Paul was concerned about was not the validity of his gospel (of which he had divine assurance) but its practicability. His commission was not derived from Jerusalem, but it could not be executed effectively except in fellowship with Jerusalem. A cleavage between his Gentile mission and the mother-church would be disastrous: Christ would be divided, and all the energy which Paul had devoted, and hoped to devote, to the evangelizing of the Gentile world would be frustrated.

On Paul's attitude to the Jerusalem church see B. Gerhardsson, *Memory and Manuscript* (Lund, 1961), 274–280.

2:3 ἀλλ' οὐδὲ Τίτος ὁ σὺν ἐμοί, Ἕλλην ὤν, ἠναγκάσθη περιτμηθῆναι. The account of Paul's laying his gospel before the men of repute is taken up again in v 6; vv 3–5 form a digression in his narrative; see BDF 448 (6), where ἀλλ' οὐδὲ Τίτος κτλ is said to be 'probably an afterthought'. The reference to Titus reminds Paul of something to which, perhaps, no importance was attached at the time but which provided a helpful precedent in the light of later events. Ἕλλην in the NT always means a Greek of Gentile origin—it can indeed be used over against Ἰουδαῖος in the sense of 'Gentile' (cf. Rom. 1:16; 2:9f.)— whereas Ἑλληνιστής usually means a Greek-speaking Jew. The antithesis Jew/Greek for a hellenized Jew like Paul corresponded to the antithesis Jew/Aramaean in Mishnaic Hebrew and Jewish Aramaic. In the Old Syriac Gospels, in Christian Palestinian Syriac and in the Peshitta (as here) Ἕλλην in this sense is rendered *'ᵃramî*, 'Aramaean'.

E. H. Askwith, *Galatians*, 117, takes Ἕλλην ὤν closely with ὁ σὺν ἐμοί, 'not even Titus, who was accompanying me as a Greek, was compelled to be circumcised.' This would imply that Paul deliberately took this Gentile Christian along with him (cf. the quotation from Luther on p. 108 above). Titus was a Gentile Christian, not only one of Paul's converts but his chosen and trusted 'partner and fellow-worker' (2 Cor. 8:23). If any one was disposed to argue that Gentile converts should be circumcised, Titus was a test case. Probably Paul did not take him along to be a test case—the circumcision of Gentile converts had not become an issue at that time, we gather—but in retrospect Titus could be cited as a test case.

To us, Paul's statement that 'not even Titus was compelled to be circumcised' is formally ambiguous. It was presumably not ambiguous to the Galatians, who would have been informed already if Titus had actually been circumcised; but Paul could presuppose knowledge on their part which his modern readers do not share. The meaning of the statement might be:

(i) Far from their requiring the circumcision of Gentile believers, not even Titus was compelled to be circumcised; *or*

(ii) Not even Titus was *compelled* to be circumcised; he was circumcised indeed, but on his own initiative (or on Paul's).

As the sentence stands, the placing of 'not even' (οὐδέ) before 'Titus' imports an emphasis which is more appropriate to the former than to the latter alternative. But the sentence is to be taken closely with the following words of vv 4 and 5, and a decision about its meaning cannot be reached except in relation to them—although their text, construction and significance are themselves so ambiguous that complete certainty is unattainable.

2:4 διὰ δὲ τοὺς παρεισάκτους ψευδαδέλφους. One important question is whether these 'false brothers' intruded into the conference which Paul has begun to describe or into some Gentile Christian circle at a later date. The definite article τούς suggests that the Galatians knew of them. These ψευδάδελφοι, as in 2 Cor. 11:26, 'were at least persons who passed as Christians' (C. K. Barrett, 'ΨΕΥΔΑΠΟΣΤΟΛΟΙ [2 Cor. 11.13]', *Rigaux FS*, 379), and in the eyes of some, perhaps most, Jewish Christians they were genuine believers. Paul, however, does not acknowledge them as genuine believers; in his eyes they are counterfeits, for whom true gospel liberty means nothing. Their purpose is to bring believers—more particularly, preachers and converts of the Gentile mission—'into bondage', and in the context of this letter 'into bondage' means 'under law'. Whoever they were, their outlook and aims were the same as those of the people who were now trying to impose a legal yoke on the churches of Galatia.

The verb παρεισάγω, with transitive force, appears in 2 Pet. 2:1 in reference to 'false teachers (ψευδοδιδάσκαλοι) who will secretly bring in (παρεισάξουσιν) destructive heresies'. As with παρεισῆλθον in the following clause and several other compounds of παρεισ-, there is a sense of furtive or at least intrusive action. The passive force of the verbal adjective παρείσακτος should not be pressed to the point where it could be said (as by T. Zahn, *Galater*, 85) that more blame attaches to those who smuggled these intruders in than to the intruders themselves. Paul does not encourage us to ask who smuggled them in; his language suggests that the initiative and the responsibility were their own, when he goes on to say that 'they infiltrated (παρεισῆλθον) into our company to spy out the freedom (ἐλευθερία) which we have in Christ Jesus'. This freedom characterizes the life which springs from the gospel of free grace; in this atmosphere of freedom a Gentile believer can associate with Jewish believers, even in Jerusalem, without any one's raising the question of circumcision: Jewish and Gentile believers can enjoy table-fellowship together without any mention of restrictive food-laws. The freedom which we have 'in Christ Jesus'—'in the fellowship of Christ Jesus' (NEB); see notes on 3:26–28—is the freedom with which 'Christ has set us free' (5:1).

With παρεισῆλθον we may compare Rom. 5:19, 'law intruded' (παρεισῆλθεν), i.e. came on to the main highway of salvation-history by a side road. See note on 3:19 below.

The 'spying' (κατασκοπῆσαι) of the false brothers had no friendly purpose, in Paul's judgment: they wished to put an end to this freedom, to make those who enjoyed it exchange it for bondage. More particularly, those who now lived in a fellowship where 'neither circumcision counts for anything, nor uncircumcision' (6:15; cf. 5:6) were to be compelled to accept circumcision. It may be that the ψευδάδελφοι claimed the right to exercise 'supervision' (ἐπισκοπή), but Paul defines their activity not as authorized ἐπισκοπή but as unauthorized κατασκοπή, 'spying' (see E. Fuchs, *s.v.* κατασκοπέω, *TDNT* VII, 417 with n. 1).

We have to consider the relation, if any, between the ψευδάδελφοι mentioned here and certain other groups who are met elsewhere in the NT. It is possible that these people were associated, if not identical, with the visitors from Jerusalem who, according to Acts 15:1, taught the 'disciples' (i.e. the Gentile Christians) at Antioch that they could not be saved unless they were circumcised. 'The opponents of Paul whom we meet in Gal. 2, II Cor. 10–13 and Acts 21 are in the end of the day not easy to differentiate from the later Ebionites' (J. D. G. Dunn, *Unity*, 263). The Ebionites probably did perpetuate in later generations the attitudes of the more legally minded Jewish Christians whom we come across here and there in the apostolic writings. The Ebionites opposed the sacrificial cultus, but there is no evidence that the 'Judaizers' of the apostolic age were at all attached to it. (The discharge of a Nazirite vow, of the kind mentioned in Acts 21:23f., was not part of the regular cultus.) The Ebionites' attitude, however, was probably a development (aided perhaps by Essene influence) after the fall of the temple in AD 70 had come to be recognized as God's judgment on the building and everything associated with it. See H.-J. Schoeps, *Judenchristentum*, *passim*.

ἵνα ἡμᾶς καταδουλώσουσιν. As the gospel of grace liberates (cf. 4:26; 5:1a), so legalism (see note on v 16) enslaves (cf. 4:24f.; 5:1b, 3). The textual variation between καταδουλώσουσιν (future indicative) and καταδουλώσωσιν (aorist subjunctive) makes no difference to the meaning. The weaker variant καταδουλώσωνται (aorist subjunctive middle, a classicism) suggests that the false brothers wished to bring them into bondage *to themselves*.

The clause beginning διὰ δὲ τοὺς παρεισάκτους ψευδαδέλφους is not completed by a principal verb (unless we adopt the Western reading of v 5); it may be easier to supply one when the significance of v 5 has been considered.

2:5 οἷς οὐδὲ πρὸς ὥραν εἴξαμεν τῇ ὑποταγῇ, 'to whom we did not yield in submission even for an hour.' The Western text omits οἷς οὐδέ, and thus presents the opposite sense: 'but because of the false brethren who had been smuggled in, . . . we yielded in submission for an hour' (i.e. for a short time). The Western omission of the negative οὐδέ might be accidental, but more probably it reflects the understanding of v 3 according to which Titus *was* circumcised—not by compulsion but on his own initiative (cf. A. D. Nock, *St. Paul* [London, 1938], 109) or else as a concession on Paul's part (on the principle, presumably, of *reculer pour mieux sauter*). But it is difficult to see a logical connexion between this reading of the situation and the following statement of purpose: 'in order that the truth of the gospel might remain [unimpaired] with you'. How the circumcision of a Gentile Christian could have been supposed by any one, especially by Paul, to help to maintain the gospel of free grace for Gentile Christians in general, passes understanding. F. C. Burkitt might ask, 'who can doubt that it was the knife which really did circumcise Titus that has cut the syntax of Galatians ii.3-5 to pieces?' (*Christian Beginnings* [London,

1924], 118); but there are many who can and do doubt it, and with good reason. 'If he was circumcised, the fact would be well advertised in Galatia by Paul's opponents, and the involved and stumbling verbiage of these verses would be worse than useless as a camouflage for that nasty fact' (T. W. Manson, *Studies*, 175f.).

The Western reading, with its omission of the negative, is attested and accepted by Irenaeus (*Haer.* 3.13.3) and Tertullian (*Adv. Marc.* 5.3.3). Tertullian indeed knows and quotes the negative form, but cannot approve of it, and charges Marcion with this 'falsification of scripture'. (Marcion, of course, could not have tolerated the idea that Paul submitted to any kind of Jewish-Christian authority, 'even for an hour'.) Paul and his associates, says Tertullian, 'did yield because there were people on whose behalf it was expedient to yield', and he adduces as examples of such yielding not the circumcision of Titus (he takes Paul to mean that Titus was not circumcised) but Paul's circumcision of Timothy (Acts 16:3) and his later association with Nazirites in the temple (Acts 21:23ff.). These Tertullian takes to be instances of Paul's policy of accommodating himself 'to those under law . . . as one under law' (1 Cor. 9:20). Marius Victorinus (*In Gal.*, *ad loc.*) endeavours to reconcile the two readings—the negative reading indicating Paul's regular policy, as when he refused to have Titus circumcised, the Western reading indicating those occasions when he compromised from expediency, as in the circumcision of Timothy. Ambrosiaster (*In Gal.*, *ad loc.*) takes a similar line to Tertullian: Paul denies that Titus was circumcised; 'but lest it should be cast up to him that he himself had circumcised Timothy, he sets forth his reasons for doing what he said should not be done: "It was because of the false brethren who had been smuggled in that we yielded in submission for an hour".'

It may be interpolated here that there may have been good cause, in Paul's eyes, why Titus, a Gentile (Ἕλλην ὤν), should not be circumcised, whereas Timothy, the son of a Jewish mother (to this day a primary criterion of Jewishness), should be circumcised (cf. H. D. Betz, *Galatians*, 89). The study of the contrast between διὰ τοὺς Ἰουδαίους τοὺς ὄντας ἐν τοῖς τόποις ἐκείνοις (Acts 16:3) and διὰ . . . τοὺς παρεισάκτους ψευδαδέλφους (in our present context) would be illuminating, but belongs more to the exegesis of Acts than to that of Galatians.

Jerome knows both readings (the Vulgate renders οἷς οὐδέ by *quibus neque*): '*Either*', he says, 'we should read, according to the Greek codices, "to whom we did not yield in submission even for an hour", in order that the following clause, "that the truth of the gospel might remain with you", can be understood; *or*, if we are to trust a certain Latin copy, we should accept the sense to be that the yielding in submission was not the circumcising of Titus but the going to Jerusalem' (*In Gal.*, *ad loc.*). But there is too great a distance between ἀνέβην εἰς Ἱεροσόλυμα (v 1) and εἴξαμεν (v 5) for this exegesis of the Western reading to be at all credible.

If the omission of οἷς took place independently of the omission of οὐδέ, it was probably an attempt to improve the style by producing a coherent sentence: διὰ δὲ τοὺς παρεισάκτους ψευδαδέλφους . . . [οὐδὲ] πρὸς ὥραν εἴξαμεν. . . . But on the principle *praestat lectio ardua* the relative οἷς should be retained, and the verb to be understood with διὰ δὲ τοὺς παρεισάκτους ψευδαδέλφους should be inferred from the context. Let the discussion of the textual problem be concluded with the reminder that the negative reading (οἷς οὐδὲ . . .) is attested by all Greek witnesses except the first hand in D.

ἵνα ἡ ἀλήθεια τοῦ εὐαγγελίου διαμείνῃ πρὸς ὑμᾶς. Had Paul and his colleagues given way on this issue, even temporarily, the 'truth' or integrity of the gospel would have been compromised. The true gospel proclaimed that justification and the reception of the Spirit were gifts of God's grace, bestowed on all who believed in Jesus, Jews and Gentiles alike, regardless of legal requirements. To have yielded an inch to those who were demanding the circumcision of Gentile converts would have denied the law-free character of the gospel. Paul was determined then to preserve the law-free gospel for his Gentile converts, to resist those who in effect were requiring that they should become Jews in order to become Christians; and he was determined now that the law-free gospel should remain unimpaired for his Gentile converts in Galatia (πρὸς ὑμᾶς).

The phrase, 'the truth of the gospel', is repeated below in v 14, where those who, in Paul's judgment, were compromising on a similar matter of principle at a somewhat later date are charged with not 'pursuing a straight course in accordance with the truth of the gospel'. D. W. B. Robinson, 'The Circumcision of Titus, and Paul's "Liberty" ', *ABR* 12 (1964), 24–42, points out the relation of 'the truth of the gospel' and the verb ἀναγκάζω in both contexts: in the former the truth of the gospel would have been subverted if Titus had been compelled to be circumcised; in the latter it was being subverted because of those who were 'compelling Gentiles to live like Jews'. (Robinson, however, holds that Paul did circumcise Titus—not under compulsion but in the exercise of his Christian liberty.)

We may now survey vv 3–5 and ask when the infiltration of the 'false brethren' took place. The majority view is that it took place during the Jerusalem visit that is described in vv 1–10. That is to say, while Paul and Barnabas were engaged in discussions with the 'men of repute' in the Jerusalem church, those intruders wormed their way into the discussions and demanded that Gentile converts—in particular Titus, who was present—should be circumcised.

But this infiltration, 'to spy out the freedom which we have in Christ Jesus', may have taken place elsewhere, and on another occasion. Paul's language suggests that the 'false brethren' intruded into the headquarters of the Gentile mission—and where else but in Antioch? If it was indeed to Antioch that they came, we are bound to think of the arrival in Antioch of men from Judaea who, according to Luke, insisted on the circumcision of Gentile converts, but without any mandate from the leaders of the Jerusalem church (Acts 15:1, 24). The identification of the ψευδάδελφοι with those Judaeans who came down to Antioch has been supported by J. Weiss, *Earliest Christianity*, I, 263ff.; H. Lietzmann, *An die Galater*, 11; H. Schlier, *Galater*, 39; A. Oepke, *Galaterbrief*, 47; F. Hahn, *Mission in the NT* (London, 1963), 78. These scholars, identifying the present conference in Jerusalem with that of Acts 15:2ff., supposed that Paul was referring to an infiltration that had taken place (at Antioch) before he and Barnabas paid this visit to Jerusalem.

But if this visit to Jerusalem took place some time before that of Acts

15:2ff., then it may have preceded the infiltration. In that case Paul implies that the question of requiring the circumcision of Gentile converts was not even raised during the Jerusalem conference which he is here describing. Had any one been disposed to raise it, there was an obvious opportunity of doing so: Titus was with them. Yet, so far from any pressure being brought to bear for the circumcision of Titus, that issue did not arise until later, when the 'false brethren' (of whom the Galatians had apparently heard) wormed their way into the church of Antioch. And did they receive any countenance from Paul and his colleagues? Not for a moment!

This understanding of the passage involves taking vv 4 and 5 as a parenthesis within the digression vv 3–5. For the parenthetic nature of vv 4 and 5 cf. T. W. Manson, *Studies*, 175f.; also A. S. Geyser, 'Paul, the Apostolic Decree and the Liberals in Corinth', *De Zwaan FS*, 132, who suggests that by means of this parenthesis 'Paul for a moment breaks the account of the proceedings at Jerusalem during the famine visit, to cast a glance at the proceedings in the churches of Galatia at the time of writing his letter to the Galatians'. But the proceedings at which Paul casts a glance in vv 4 and 5 were past when Paul wrote to the Galatians and took place outside Galatia: Paul appears to have been absent when the Galatian churches were invaded by the 'agitators'; hence he had to write to the churches instead of dealing with the trouble on the spot.

Special attention has been paid to vv 3–5 in a series of papers by B. Orchard. He recognizes the three verses as a parenthesis (vv 4 and 5 constituting a secondary parenthesis within the larger one). Paul, he says, mentions the non-circumcision of Titus parenthetically because, while he was dictating the letter, 'it suddenly struck him as a forcible argument with which to refute the Judaizers of Galatia that the fact that the Apostles did nothing about the Gentile Titus . . . on that occasion showed that they agreed with him in recognizing "the freedom of the Gentiles" from the burden of the Mosaic Law. And so, forsaking all of a sudden the train of thought he has pursued in verses 1 and 2, he breaks in with this new debating point against his Judaizing opponents, for all the world as if he were afraid he would forget it if he did not set it down there and then' ('A New Solution of the Galatians Problem', *BJRL* 28 [1944], 154–174, especially 165–167); cf. also his 'A Note on the Meaning of Galatians ii.3-5', *JTS* 43 (1942), 173–177; 'The Ellipsis between Galatians 2,3 and 2,4', *Bib* 54 (1973), 469–481, with 'reaction' by A. C. M. Blommerde, 'Is there an Ellipsis between Galatians 2,3 and 2,4?' *Bib* 56 (1975), 100–102, and reply by B. Orchard, 'Once again the Ellipsis between Gal. 2,3 and 2,4', *Bib* 57 (1976), 254f.; 'Ellipsis and Parenthesis in Ga 2:1–10 and 2 Th 2:1–12', *Paul de Tarse: Apôtre de notre Temps*, ed. L. de Lorenzi (Rome, 1979), 249–258. His proposed filling of the ellipsis at the end of v 3 is: 'because of false brethren . . . *the liberty of the Gentiles is now in danger*' ('A New Solution . . .', 167) or '*this question has now arisen*' ('Ellipsis and Parenthesis . . .', 251). This account of the matter seems most satisfactory, except that (on the assumption that it was into the Antiochene church that the 'false brethren' first intruded) I should prefer to fill the ellipsis with '*the question of circumcising Gentile converts was first raised*'.

The suggested course of events, then, would be as follows. When Paul and Barnabas visited Jerusalem on the occasion referred to in v 1, nothing was said about requiring Gentile converts to be circumcised, although Titus was with them and would have constituted a test case had any one been minded to raise the question. The question was not raised until later, when certain 'false brethren' infiltrated the church of Antioch, the headquarters of Gentile Christianity, and tried to insist on circumcision. Paul and his colleagues made no concession to those men—whatever rumours to the contrary may have been spread abroad— for a concession on this issue would have jeopardized the integrity of the gospel. And the position which Paul and his colleagues took then is the position which Paul takes now towards the crisis in the churches of Galatia.

2:6 ἀπὸ δὲ τῶν δοκούντων εἶναί τι. Paul now resumes the main thread of his narrative from the point where he broke off at the end of v 2. He had set his gospel before the men of repute at Jerusalem, but (as he now says) from those 'men of some repute' he received no supplement to his gospel, nothing that could have given him greater authority to preach it than he already possessed.

Does the addition of εἶναί τι after τῶν δοκούντων (cf. Plato, *Grg.* 472A, δοκούντων εἶναί τι, 'people of repute') convey some difference of nuance from the simpler τοῖς δοκοῦσιν of v 2? A nuance of disparagement might be inferred from the similar wording of 6:3, εἰ γὰρ δοκεῖ τις εἶναί τι μηδὲν ὤν, φρεναπατᾷ ἑαυτόν. But in 6:3 it is the man himself who thinks he is some- thing, and he is self-deceived, for what he thinks himself to be is at odds with the fact of the matter: he is a mere nonentity (μηδὲν ὤν). The Jerusalem leaders are held in repute by their fellow-Christians, not by themselves; and there is no hint that their repute lacks foundation: they are far from being nonentities.

If, however, a certain 'dismissive' tone can be detected in Paul's wording here and in v 9 (cf. J. D. G. Dunn, *Unity*, 408 n. 49), we may compare the similarly dismissive references to the ὑπέρλιαν ἀπόστολοι (probably the same men) in 2 Cor. 11:5; 12:11. Paul does not question the Jerusalem leaders' per- sonal status and prestige; what he does object to is the appeal made in some quarters to their status and prestige to diminish his own—in particular, the argument that their authority is so much superior to his that, if he acts or teaches in independence of them, his action and teaching lack all validity. That an appeal was indeed being made to their superior authority to the detriment of Paul's apostolic liberty is implied still more clearly in the following parenthesis: ὁποῖ- οί ποτε ἦσαν οὐδέν μοι διαφέρει· πρόσωπον [ὁ] θεὸς ἀνθρώπου οὐ λαμβάνει.

We must decide whether the enclitic ποτε simply adds indefiniteness to the pronoun ὁποῖοι (like the English suffix '-ever' in 'whatever', etc.; cf. BDF 303) or has temporal force, 'formerly', 'once upon a time' (as in 1:13, 23; cf. *ali- quando* in the Latin versions). If it has temporal force, it must be further decided whether the time referred to is that of the conference, on which Paul, at the date of writing, looks back (so F. Sieffert, *Galater*, 119; T. Zahn, *Galater*, 98; A. Oepke, *Galaterbrief*, 48), or an earlier period. If it had reference to the time of the conference, one might have expected Paul to say τότε, 'then', since he is writing about the conference at this point in his narrative. Much more probably ποτε refers to an earlier period. If the superiority of the Jerusalem leaders was being emphasized in such a way as to diminish Paul's, the argument would lean heavily on the admitted fact that two of those leaders (Cephas and John) had been close associates of Jesus during his ministry, members of the 'twelve', that the other (James) was a member of the holy family, and that all three of them were foundation-members of the original church, whereas Paul was a relative latecomer. So when Paul says, 'whatever they once were makes no difference to me', he most probably has in mind their connexion with the historical Jesus and their role in the foundation of the church. Whatever advantages those experiences gave them, they did not give them superior authority to his, for his authority was derived by direct commission from the exalted Lord, and there could be no higher authorization than that. See C. K. Barrett as quoted on p. 123.

One unusual interpretation of ὁποῖοί ποτε ἦσαν is that put forward confidently, but implausibly, by K. Heussi, 'Galater 2 und der Lebensausgang der jerusalemischen Urapostel', *TLZ* 77 (1952), 67–72, and *Die römische Petrustradition in kritischer Sicht* (Tübingen, 1955), 3f., etc., that Paul refers to the 'men of repute' in the past tense because by the time this letter was written all three of them had died: James (not the Lord's brother but the son of Zebedee!) and his brother John in the persecution under Herod Agrippa I (Acts 12:1f.) and Cephas/Peter in the brief interval between 1 Corinthians (1:12; 3:22; 9:5) and Galatians, which he dated after 1 Corinthians. So far as Paul's language goes, it implies that all three leaders were alive at the time of writing: if any of them had died since the conference, it would probably have been indicated, as it certainly is not by ὁποῖοί ποτε ἦσαν. See K. Aland, 'Wann starb Petrus?', *NTS* 2 (1955–56), 267–275.

The expression πρόσωπον λαμβάνω is a literal rendering of Heb. *nāśā' pānîm*, 'lift the face' (e.g. of a suppliant) and thus 'show favour'. While the Hebrew phrase is ethically neutral—e.g. on the one hand God says to Lot in Gn. 19:21 *nāśā'tî pānékā* (LXX ἐθαύμασά σου τὸ πρόσωπον), 'I grant you (*this*) favour', but on the other hand he is described in Dt. 10:17 as one who *lō' yiśśā' pānîm* (LXX οὐ θαυμάζει πρόσωπον), 'is not partial'—Gk. πρόσωπον λαμβάνω is regularly used *in malam partem*, of showing not favour but favouritism. This phrase (cf. Lk. 20:21) or a compound, such as προσωπολήμπτης (Acts 10:34), προσωπολημψία (Rom. 2:11; Eph. 6:9; Col. 3:25; Jas. 2:1) or ἀπροσωπολήμπτως (1 Pet. 1:17), appears repeatedly in the NT to convey the consistent biblical insight that God shows no partiality. Here it means that God does not favour companions or relatives of the historical Jesus over someone, like Paul, who received his apostolic commission later—although, in a different context (1 Cor. 15:9), Paul can speak of himself as 'the least of the apostles, unfit to be an apostle', by contrast, presumably, with other apostles and witnesses who, unlike him, had not 'persecuted the church of God'.

ἐμοὶ γὰρ οἱ δοκοῦντες οὐδὲν προσανέθεντο, 'to me (I say) the men of repute contributed nothing.' Had Paul completed the clause beginning ἀπὸ δὲ τῶν δοκούντων, he would have said something like οὐδὲν παρέλαβον or οὐδὲν ἐδιδάχθην (cf. 1:12). But he breaks off with a parenthesis, after which he changes the construction by making οἱ δοκοῦντες the subject. This is one of his 'numerous and flagrant' anacolutha; he has 'either forgotten the opening clause, or deemed it convenient to replace it with a new form' (BDF 467). It would not be too fanciful to see in the anacolutha of vv 3–10 evidence of the emotional stress under which Paul laboured as he rebutted attacks on his apostolic liberty. After this anacoluthon Paul returns (by means of the resumptive γάϱ) and completes the sense, if not the construction, of the clause which was broken off.

The pronoun ἐμοί comes in an emphatic position: others might derive some form of authorization from the Jerusalem leaders (as, according to Acts 11:22, Barnabas did on an earlier occasion), but Paul derived none. They contributed (προσανέθεντο, 'communicated in addition') nothing to him. They found nothing defective in the gospel which he communicated (ἀνεθέμην) to them (v 2). It is not necessary to take προσανατίθεμαι here in the sense which it bears in 1:16; it may be material to observe that in 1:16 the aorist middle is used intransitively whereas here it has an object (οὐδέν). No question was raised, apparently, about the comparative contents of Paul's gospel and theirs, any more than the question was raised about Paul's authority to preach his gospel. His gospel was unexceptionable; his commission was undisputed: the agenda, we gather, concentrated on the demarcation of the respective spheres of service of the parties to the discussion.

2:7–8 ἀλλὰ τοὐναντίον, 'But on the contrary'—far from adding anything to my gospel, the 'men of repute' acknowledged it as the gospel for the uncircumcised (τῆς ἀκροβυστίας) with which I had been entrusted as surely as Peter had been entrusted with the gospel for the circumcised (τῆς περιτομῆς). Paul here uses ἀκροβυστία (used in the LXX, e.g. Gn. 34:16, etc., as the equivalent of Heb. 'orlāh, and probably a disguised form of the etymologically transparent ἀκροποσθία, attested in Hippocrates, *Aphorisms* 6.19, and Aristotle, *Hist. An.* 493.a.29) and περιτομή as collective nouns for 'Gentiles' and 'Jews' respectively (cf. Rom. 2:26f.; 3:30; Eph. 2:11). For πιστεύομαι in the sense 'be entrusted' (with the gospel) cf. 1 Cor. 9:17; 1 Thes. 2:4; 1 Tim. 1:11; Tit. 1:3. Paul was initially entrusted with the gospel for the Gentiles at his conversion (1:15), and since then he had been continuously engaged in discharging that trust. This was now recognized by the 'men of repute' not only on the basis of distant hearsay (1:23) but on the basis of Paul's own communication (v 2): as they received a first-hand account of his activity thus far, they could not deny that God had worked effectively in him (ἐνήργησεν καὶ ἐμοί) as he fulfilled his Gentile mission.

But a remarkable parallel is drawn between Paul's divinely empowered mission to the Gentiles and Peter's to the Jews—a parallel discerned not only by Paul himself but also (it appears) by the 'men of repute'. That Peter had already evangelized his own people very effectively, not only in Jerusalem but elsewhere in Judaea, is attested in Luke's record (e.g. Acts 2:14ff.; 3:12ff.; 9:32ff.). To be sure, Luke records one occasion when he evangelized Gentiles— in the house of Cornelius at Caesarea (Acts 10:1–11:18; 15:7–9)—but that occasion, epoch-making as it was, was exceptional. Similarly, Luke gives Paul a limited mission to Jews (Acts 9:15; 26:20), but makes it plain that his distinctive mission was to Gentiles (Acts 22:21). In Paul's account, however, the demarcation of the Jewish and Gentile mission-fields was based on the recognition that his own Gentile mission and Peter's Jewish mission were equally attended by signs of divine power which set the seal of divine approval on the one as on the other.

Peter's mission is described as his ἀποστολὴ τῆς περιτομῆς just as Paul's own mission is an ἀποστολή (Rom. 1:5; 1 Cor. 9:2). Even if James is referred to as an apostle in 1:19, it appears that, where ἀποστολή in the sense of mission was concerned, Peter retained the primacy among the original apostles and other church leaders (cf. 1 Cor. 9:5). It may be that there was an official, Jerusalem-based element in Peter's apostolate that was absent from Paul's own unfettered pioneer ministry (Rom. 15:20). See C. K. Barrett, 'Shaliaḥ and Apostle', Daube FS, 100f. Nevertheless the two ministries are practically placed on a level here, and it is indicated that this situation was accepted by both sides.

Peter's gospel for the Jews may have had different emphases and nuances from Paul's gospel for the Gentiles, but plainly these did not make it in Paul's eyes a 'different gospel' in the sense of 1:6–9. It was based on the same recital of saving events as Paul's and, like Paul's, it proclaimed the grace of God brought near in Christ for men and women's acceptance by faith (1 Cor. 15:11).

The agitators in the Galatian churches might well have said that they too believed the gospel which Peter and Paul preached in common, but that they disagreed with Paul's particular interpretation of it—in particular, with his insistence that it abrogated the requirement of circumcision for membership in the people of God. Paul's interpretation was completely controlled by his Damascus-road experience, although he would have called it not 'interpretation' but 'revelation' (1:12, 16). We have no comparable first-hand account from Peter, but we may be sure that the εὐαγγέλιον . . . τῆς περιτομῆς with which he was entrusted was a gospel for the 'circumcision' (i.e. for the Jews) but not in any sense a gospel of circumcision. There was, of course, no reason why circumcision should figure at all in the preaching of the gospel to Jews. But the message to which the Galatian Christians were disposed to submit could indeed be called a 'gospel of circumcision' and therefore in Paul's sight a perversion of the true gospel and completely inadmissible, whereas the gospel preached by Peter was acceptable.

A further point that calls for comment in vv 7f. is the twofold use of the name Πέτρος for the apostle whom Paul normally calls Κηφᾶς. The Western reading Πέτρος for Κηφᾶς in 1:18; 2:9, 11, 14 is secondary, and there is no textual basis for the view—propounded by A. Merx, Das Evangelium des Matthäus (Berlin, 1902), 161ff., and K. Holl, 'Der Kirchenbegriff des Paulus in seinem Verhältnis zu dem der Urgemeinde' (1921), Gesammelte Aufsätze zur Kirchengeschichte, II (Tübingen, 1928), 45 n. 3—that Κηφᾶς originally stood in vv 7f.

It may indeed be that Paul 'used "Cephas" and "Peter" indifferently, and on no fixed principle' (K. Lake, EEP, 116), but the exceptional use of 'Peter' in vv 7f. may be related to the fact that the substance of these two verses is recapitulated at the beginning of v 9. In view of this, one favoured explanation of the change of name is that put forward by E. Dinkler, 'Der Brief an die Galater', Verkündigung und Forschung, 1–3 (1953–55), 182f. (cf. his 'Die Petrus-Rom Frage', TRu NF 25 [1959], 198; O. Cullmann, Peter: Disciple-Apostle-Martyr, ETr [London, 1953], 18, and TDNT VI, 100 n. 6, s.v. Πέτρος; G. Klein, Rekonstruktion, 106), that the clauses containing Πέτρος are extracted from a more or less official record of the conference, the reference to Paul being changed to the pronoun of the first person singular so as to integrate the extract into the construction of its autobiographical context. Dinkler tentatively reconstructed the original minute: . . . ὅτι Παῦλος πιστεύεται [why not πεπίστευται?]

τὸ εὐαγγέλιον τῆς ἀκροβυστίας καθὼς Πέτρος τῆς περιτομῆς· ὁ γὰρ ἐνεργήσας Πέτρῳ εἰς ἀποστολὴν τῆς περιτομῆς ἐνήργησεν καὶ Παύλῳ εἰς τὰ ἔθνη. This proposal has the *relative* merit of being less improbable than most of the rival explanations, including that of J. Munck (*Paul*, 62 n. 2), according to which v 9 is the citation and vv 7f. Paul's reconstruction (which leaves the exceptional use of Πέτρος unaccounted for). It would be wisest to follow H. D. Betz (*Galatians*, 97), who finds Dinkler's proposal unacceptable as a whole, since v 7 is in the main Paul's construction, but agrees that 'the non-Pauline notions of the "gospel of circumcision" and "of uncircumcision" as well as the name "Peter" may very well come from an underlying official statement'.

Other, less convincing, suggestions are that Πέτρος was the personal name and Κηφᾶς the official name (P. Gaechter, *Petrus und seine Zeit* [Wien/ München, 1958], 385) or that Πέτρος was the title (not yet a personal name) which Cephas bore 'in his capacity as God's apostolic mandatory for the world of Israel' (P. Stuhlmacher, *Das paulinische Evangelium*, I. *Vorgeschichte* [Göttingen, 1968], 94).

More radical are the solutions proffered by E. Barnikol, who cut the knot by treating vv 7f. as a later gloss (*Der nichtpaulinische Ursprung des Parallelismus der Apostel Paulus und Petrus = Forschungen zur Entstehung des Urchristentums, des Neuen Testaments und der Kirche*, 5 [Kiel, 1931]), or by D. Warner, who argues that the whole section, vv 3–8, was interpolated by a Greek Christian 'of Paul's way of thought, though even more critical of the position of Peter and the other Apostles'—possibly by Titus, acting as Paul's amanuensis and inserting this section in his master's name and in the hope of furthering his cause ('Galatians ii.3–8: As an Interpolation', *Exp Tim* 62 [1950–51], 380).

See also T. Zahn, *Galater*, 68 n. 77, on the textual evidence for Κηφᾶς/Πέτρος in vv 7f. and elsewhere.

2:9 καὶ γνόντες τὴν χάριν τὴν δοθεῖσάν μοι, 'and having recognized the grace given to me'. V 9 repeats the substance of vv 7 and 8, with significant additions. The participle γνόντες catches up the ἰδόντες of v 7. The 'grace' given to Paul is his apostleship to the Gentiles; cf. 1:16 above (also Rom. 1:5; 12:3; 15:15; 1 Cor. 3:10; Eph. 3:8; Phil. 1:7).

Ἰάκωβος καὶ Κηφᾶς καὶ Ἰωάννης. Here for the first time the 'men of repute' are named. The identity of the sequence of names with the traditional order of the catholic epistles of James, Peter and John in the NT canon may be nothing more than a coincidence. The primacy given to James is noteworthy. This James is, of course, the Lord's brother (as in 1:19; 2:12) and not the Zebedaean, despite K. Heussi's theory mentioned in the notes on v 6. Apart from the fact that James the Zebedaean is excluded by the present context, he is chronologically excluded. It is uncertain whether Herod Agrippa I died before or after Passovertide in AD 44 (see K. Lake, *BC*, I.5, 446–452), so it is uncertain whether the execution of James should be dated in the spring of AD 43 or 44 (cf. Acts 12:1–3); either way, it would be difficult to fit the chronological data of Gal. 1:18 and 2:1, even on the shortest reckoning, into the interval between Paul's conversion and James's execution.

On Paul's earlier visit to Jerusalem Cephas was the most important man in the church; Paul went up specifically to meet him, and adds that he also saw James. But all our evidence (scanty as it is) indicates that James became increasingly influential in the Jerusalem church. An opportunity to increase his influence at the expense of Cephas/Peter came with the latter's departure from Jerusalem after his escape from Herod Agrippa's prison (Acts 12:17). By the time of the present conference Cephas/Peter had returned to Jerusalem, but not for long. From about mid-century onwards he and the remaining survivors of the eleven appear to have embarked on a wider ministry in the eastern Mediterranean world; James was left to guide the mother-church with a council of elders among whom he was *primus inter pares*. It is clear from v 12 that even Cephas took James's directives seriously.

G. Klein (*Rekonstruktion*, 107–115) takes the view that at the time of the conference Peter was still the dominant figure, and therefore he is mentioned alone in vv. 7–8, but that by the time this letter was written James had moved into the position of supremacy, hence the order of precedence in v 9. Against this see W. Schmithals, *Paul and James*, 49 n. 31.

The 'John' who is named as one of the three is most probably John the son of Zebedee; this is the only place where he (or any other John) is mentioned in Paul's writings. John appears in the earlier chapters of Acts as an associate of Peter on a couple of important occasions (Acts 3:1–4:22; 8:14–25), although he plays a silent part alongside his vocal colleague. The idea that John was executed at the same time as his brother James (cf. E. Schwartz, 'Über den Tod der Söhne Zebedaei', *AkGWG* 7.5 [1907], 266ff., and 'Noch einmal der Tod der Söhne Zebedaei', *ZNW* 11 [1910], 89–104; J. Moffatt, *INT*, 603–613) is a 'critical myth' based on such flimsy evidence that it 'would have provoked derision if it had been adduced in favour of a conservative conclusion' (A. S. Peake, *Holborn Review* 19 [1928], 394; cf. J. H. Bernard, *Studia Sacra* [London, 1917], 260ff.).

It would be difficult not to identify οἱ δοϰοῦντες στῦλοι εἶναί τι with οἱ δοϰοῦντες of vv 2 and 6. In saying that the three men just named are 'reputed to be pillars' Paul does not deny this assessment of their importance but does not commit himself to acceptance of it. The word στῦλοι, 'pillars', used in this figurative sense, implies that those so described provide support and defence for their fellows, like A. E. Housman's 'army of mercenaries':

> Their shoulders held the sky suspended;
> They stood, and earth's foundations stay.

In some such sense Abraham and Moses are referred to in later rabbinical literature as 'pillars of the world' (*Ex. Rab.* 2:13 on Ex. 3:4). Similar language is used of the mother and her seven sons who were martyred under Antiochus IV (4 Macc. 17:3), of Peter and Paul who 'contended unto death' (1 Clem. 5:2; cf. K. Beyschlag, *Clemens Romanus und der Frühkatholizismus* [Tübingen, 1966], 334), of Alexandrian confessors under persecution (Dionysius of Alexandria apud Euseb. *HE* 6.41.14). But the present meaning is more likely to be in line with that of the apocalyptic letter to the church of Philadelphia: 'He who conquers, I will make him a pillar (στῦλος) in the sanctuary (ναός) of my God' (Rev. 3:12). The thought of the believing community as God's sanctuary (ναός) is found in Paul's letters (e.g. 1 Cor. 3:16f.; 2 Cor. 6:16; Eph. 2:21), and elsewhere in the NT οἶϰος is used similarly (e.g. Heb. 3:6; 10:21; 1 Pet. 2:5). The 'pillars' of this sanctuary would be its leaders, and possibly its foundation-members, like the 'twelve men and three priests' with whom the council of the Qumran community was well and truly founded as 'a holy house for Israel and a most holy council (*sōḏ*) for Aaron' (1QS 8:1–6). C. K. Barrett ('Paul and the "Pillar" Apostles', *De Zwaan FS*, 15ff.) suggests that originally the term στῦλοι as applied to James, Cephas and John was 'strictly eschatological' in meaning, marking them out as 'the basis of the new people' of God. Out of this eschatological assessment, he thinks, there soon developed 'an institutional view of their position'—a development of which Paul may have disapproved. It is in this light that Barrett understands Paul's remark in v 6: 'What they once were makes no difference to me now; God has no special favour for them as men'—in other words, 'They have their special place in the last days, but this gives them no exclusive rights in the Church' (19).

In the gospel tradition, from the twelve men who were to be rulers of Israel in the new age (Mt. 19:28; Lk. 22:29f.) three appear to have been selected by Jesus to enjoy special access to the purpose of his ministry—Peter and the two sons of Zebedee, James and John (cf. Mk. 5:37; 9:2; 14:33; in Mk. 13:3 Peter's brother Andrew makes a fourth with them). Of these three, James the son of Zebedee had by now been executed by Herod Agrippa I. It is conceivable that these three were at first regarded as the 'pillars' and that, on the death of one James, his namesake was co-opted to take his place as a 'pillar' (not, of course, to take his place as member of the twelve). It is possible on the other hand, though perhaps less likely, that James the Lord's brother had been co-opted earlier, so that before the death of James the Zebedaean there were four pillars.

As the ministry to the Jews, entrusted to Peter in vv 7 and 8, is allotted to all three 'pillars' in v 9, so the ministry to the Gentiles, entrusted to Paul in vv 7 and 8, is allotted to Paul and Barnabas together in v 9. This is an argument against G. Klein's thesis that a diminution in Peter's status may be discerned between vv 7f. and 9. No parallel diminution of Paul's status in favour of Barnabas is implied in the transition from vv 7f. to 9: what was said of Paul in vv 7f., it appears from v 9, applied also to Barnabas, and correspondingly what was said of Peter in vv 7f. applied also to James and John. Now the three men on the one side exchange 'right hands of fellowship' with the two men on the other side, in token of their agreement about the two spheres of ministry.

Until the phrase ἐμοὶ καὶ Βαρναβᾷ here there has been no mention of Barnabas since v 1; the reader might be pardoned for forgetting that he was a participant in the conference. But the failure to mention him in the main account of the conference is easily explained: it was Paul's commission, not Barnabas's, that was being questioned in the churches of Galatia, so Paul concentrates on his own relations with the Jerusalem leaders. Barnabas's commission, in any case, was on a different footing from Paul's. It is nowhere suggested that Barnabas claimed to have been directly called by the risen Christ; there is nothing in Paul's references to him inconsistent with Luke's statement that Barnabas's first contact with the Gentile mission was when he was sent by the Jerusalem church to supervise the gospel outreach in Syrian Antioch (Acts 11:22). In Antioch, if not earlier, Barnabas quickly realized his vocation to Gentile evangelization, and he and Paul seem to have shared certain distinctive features of missionary policy, such as maintaining themselves and declining to live at their converts' expense (1 Cor. 9:6).

But Barnabas is so closely associated here with Paul's ἀποστολή that it would probably be wrong to deny him the designation ἀπόστολος in the wider Pauline sense. It is a matter of interest, though not directly relevant to Pauline usage, that in the two places where Luke calls Paul an 'apostle' he uses the noun in the plural, speaking of Paul and Barnabas as οἱ ἀπόστολοι (Acts 14:4, 14)—but this may refer to them as 'sent out' (ἐκπεμφθέντες) by the Holy Spirit from Antioch (Acts 13:4).

ἵνα ἡμεῖς εἰς τὰ ἔθνη, αὐτοὶ δὲ εἰς τὴν περιτομήν. For the ellipsis of the verb cf. the second clause of 5:13. Here some such verb as πορευθῶμεν . . . πορευθῶσιν ('go') or εὐαγγελιζώμεθα . . . εὐαγγελίζωνται ('preach the gospel') may be understood (for εὐαγγελίζομαι construed with εἰς cf. 2 Cor. 10:16). The conjunction ἵνα here fulfils the function of classical ἐφ' ᾧτε ('on condition that', 'on the understanding that'). In classical Greek ἡμεῖς would have been followed by μέν, balancing the δέ after αὐτοί.

Was the pillars' agreement to confine their apostolic ministry henceforth to the Jews a limitation of an original wider commission? There is another strand of early Christian tradition in which Peter and his colleagues had a mission to the nations conferred on them by the risen Christ. In Mt. 28:19 the eleven are charged by him to 'go and make disciples of all the nations'; in Acts 1:8 they are to be his witnesses 'to the end of the earth' (cf. Lk. 24:47f.); in Jn. 17:18 (cf. 20:21) they are sent into 'the world'; in 1 Pet. 1:1ff. Peter's constituency is envisaged as comprising Gentile Christians in Asia Minor; the *Didache* is so called because it presents 'the Lord's teaching to the Gentiles through the twelve apostles' (the apostle to the Gentiles *par excellence* being rather pointedly left out of the picture). None of this impairs the trustworthiness of Paul's account of the Jerusalem agreement, but plainly other interpretations of the role of the twelve and their associates were current.

No understanding of the agreement is probable which implies that Paul, provided his liberty to preach a circumcision-free gospel to Gentiles was safe-guarded, would have been quite happy for a circumcision-bound gospel to be preached to Jews by the Jerusalem authorities. In Paul's eyes the compelling logic of the Christ-event pointed to the supersession of the age of law by the age of the Spirit (3:13f.); it was because there was now but one way of justification for Jews and Gentiles alike—justification by faith (cf. Rom. 3:29f.)—that 'in Christ Jesus' there was 'neither Jew nor Greek' (Gal. 3:28). Indeed, the following narrative of Paul's dispute with Cephas at Antioch makes it evident that for Paul (and, in principle, for Cephas too) those who were born Jews could find justification only 'by faith in Christ and not by works of law' as much as 'sinners of the Gentiles' (vv 15f.).

As it was, the conference appeared to have a happy and friendly outcome. The demarcation of the two mission-fields was agreed upon by both parties. But the agreement may have concealed some ambiguities, which came to light later and led to tension between Paul and church leaders in Judaea. If only the Jerusalem leaders' record of the conference and the agreement had been preserved to us, we should know if their interpretation of the issues was identical with Paul's.

For example, was the demarcation to be interpreted in territorial or in communal terms? In territorial terms, says E. D. Burton (*Galatians*, 96–99); in communal terms, says W. Schmithals (*Paul and James*, 45): 'it is hard to understand the attempt to explain the distinction between τὰ ἔθνη and ἡ περιτομή otherwise than ethnographically.' But perhaps the issue was not defined so precisely; in either case, it must have been difficult to define the boundaries of the two mission-fields. There were Jewish colonies in most of the great cities of the eastern Mediterranean world: were the Jerusalem leaders debarred from evangelizing the Jews of Ephesus, Corinth or Rome? Almost certainly not. But since the churches founded in those cities comprised both Jewish and Gentile converts, some overlapping of the two spheres was inevitable. Again, was Paul debarred from visiting synagogues in Gentile cities, if only to evangelize the Gentile God-fearers who attended the services? (That he did so as a matter of regular policy is explicitly stated in Acts.) With Rom. 11:13f. in mind, E. Best asks, 'did Paul preach to Jews at all after his agreement with the Jerusalem pillars?' (*Thessalonians*, 6). W. Schmithals had answered this question in advance with an unhesitating No: 'If Paul had preached to the Jews in his world-wide mission area a gospel free from the control of the Law, and had incorporated them into his churches which disregarded the Law in their daily life, he would have made the position of the Christian churches in Judea untenable—assuming the unity of Christendom' (*Paul and James*, 48). But the diversity of Christendom has to be recognized as well as its unity, and whatever may be concluded today about the logic of the first-century situation, those who were involved in the situation saw it differently. God-fearing Gentiles, who provided the nucleus of the church in many cities, were more conveniently found in synagogues, but Paul could not preach to them there without preaching to Jews at the same time.

Where there was full mutual confidence (as there was, apparently, between Paul and Apollos), charges of building on another's foundation (1 Cor. 3:10ff.; Rom. 15:20) or invading someone else's κανών or 'field' (2 Cor. 10:13–16) would not arise. But in the absence of such confidence—and the confidence between the parties to the Jerusalem agreement was to be shaken very soon afterwards—misunderstandings, not to say recriminations, were bound to develop.

On receiving Paul's account of the conference and agreement, some might have said to him, 'So you did receive the recognition of the Jerusalem leaders!' To this, his reply would probably have been: 'I did not receive their recognition as though my commission had been defective without it; they recognized that I had already been called to this ministry, but they did not in any sense bestow on me the right to exercise it.' The nature of the recognition which Paul received could easily have been misunderstood or misrepresented. Perhaps the Jerusalem leaders would not have given exactly the same account of the matter as Paul does. According to E. Haenchen, what they said to him was: 'You may waive circumcision in the mission to the Gentiles'—but if Paul had reproduced their decision in these terms, it 'would have made Jerusalem appear still the superior authority, which had simply thought fit to make a gracious concession' (*Acts*, 467). In our more sophisticated days we are familiar with the device of calculated ambiguity in ecclesiastical as in other agreements; but such ambiguity as inhered in this agreement was not deliberate but inadvertent. Nevertheless, a study of Paul's Corinthian correspondence illustrates the difficulties to which it led.

2:10 μόνον τῶν πτωχῶν ἵνα μνημονεύωμεν, 'Only, we were to remember the poor': a good example of the imperatival use of ἵνα (cf. Mk. 5:23; 2 Cor. 8:7; Eph. 5:33); see C. F. D. Moule, *Idiom-Book*, 144f., with other literature cited there. In direct speech, the 'pillars' said something like 'Please remember . . .' or, if we give full force to the present tense of the verb, 'Please go on remembering . . .'. By μόνον Paul implies that the 'pillars' imposed no conditions, made no stipulations, apart from the request for Christian aid (which could in no way be construed as an 'addition' to Paul's gospel). With that exception they 'laid upon them no further burden'. These last words are taken from the apostolic letter of Acts 15:23–29, but it is not suggested that Paul had that letter in mind, or even knew of it at this stage. It is not as though he imagined someone saying, 'But did they not require you to observe the "necessary things" laid down in the Jerusalem decree?' and answered, 'No, they did not; they "only" asked us to remember the poor.' The social decree of Acts 15:28f. had probably not been promulgated even when Paul sent his letter to the Galatians, let alone when the conference of vv 1–10 took place. (Had it been already promulgated, some reference might have been made to it in the ensuing dispute between Paul and Cephas at Antioch.)

The πτωχοί are primarily the poorer members of the Jerusalem church; cf. Rom. 15:26 where, some years later, the churches of Macedonia and Achaia are said to have agreed 'to make some contribution for the poor (εἰς τοὺς πτωχούς) among the saints at Jerusalem'. There is some evidence, however, that the Jerusalem church referred to its membership collectively as 'the poor'; hence the later designation of an important Jewish-Christian community as 'Ebionites' (Heb. *hā'ebyônîm*, 'the poor').

Marcion omitted vv 6–9a from his apostolic text, and omitted καὶ Βαρναβᾷ and κοινωνίας from v 9b, so that the 'we' in μνημονεύωμεν refers to Paul on the one side and to the Jerusalem leaders on the other: he was to remember the poor among the Gentiles and they were to remember the poor among the Jews. Cf. Tert., *Adv. Marc.* 5.3; A. Harnack, *Marcion: Das Evangelium vom fremden Gott*[2] = TU 45 (Leipzig, 1924), 45.

ὃ καὶ ἐσπούδασα αὐτὸ τοῦτο ποιῆσαι, 'indeed, I showed eagerness to do this very thing'. 'Since αὐτό in this sense ("very") cannot be joined to the relative' it 'must be supported by τοῦτο' (BDF 297).

The energy with which, in the following years, Paul organized a relief fund in his Gentile churches for their brethren in Jerusalem (1 Cor. 16:1–4; 2 Cor. 8:1–9:15; Rom. 15:25–28) is an eloquent commentary on this statement. But the aorist ἐσπούδασα is noteworthy: it does not refer only, or even chiefly, to that relief fund. Paul means not only that he henceforth adopted this policy, but that he had already done so—he thinks of the famine relief which he and Barnabas brought to Jerusalem from Antioch, according to Acts 11:30. 'The aorist ἐσπούδασα fits in well with the fact that Paul had actually just brought alms to Jerusalem: it is almost a pluperfect' (C. W. Emmet, *BC*, I.2, 279).

Paul's language not only indicates his spontaneous consent to the Jerusalem leaders' request; it emphasizes that this was a matter in which he had taken the initiative—it was not to be supposed that he was a mere agent or emissary of the Jerusalem authorities for the collecting of funds for the mother-church, a *šᵉlîaḥ ṣiyyôn* ('messenger of Zion'), as J. Klausner suggested (*From Jesus to Paul*, ETr [London, 1944], 364f.; cf. H.-J. Schoeps, *Paul*, 69). See D. R. Hall,

'St. Paul and Famine Relief: A Study in Galatians 2[10]', *Exp Tim* 82 (1970–71), 309–311. Similarly Paul emphasizes in Rom. 15:26f. that the donations to the later relief fund are made spontaneously by the contributing Gentile churches— 'not as an exaction but as a willing gift', as he puts it in 2 Cor. 9:5. But we are not told if the Jerusalem leaders regarded the donations in this way. It might be argued that their present stipulation about remembering the poor was not a request but a command. K. Holl ('Der Kirchenbegriff', 44–67) argued that they looked on the Gentile churches' contributions as a legally required tribute. This cannot be proved. Still less can it be proved that (as Holl further suggested) Paul's reference to 'the poor among the saints at Jerusalem' (Rom. 15:26) conceals his embarrassment over the fact that the collection was destined for the church of Jerusalem as a whole; he often enough speaks of the collection (or ministry) 'for the saints' (1 Cor. 16:1; 2 Cor. 8:4; 9:1; Rom. 15:26) with no hint of embarrassment. On the present occasion the Jerusalem leaders, being sensible men, no doubt knew that monetary gifts are more likely to be made generously if one says 'Please' when asking for them.

But how did the churches of Galatia view the matter? Paul has, throughout this autobiographical sketch, emphasized his independence of the Jerusalem authorities; now, he says, they did ask him (and Barnabas) to 'remember the poor', and he consented to do so. He points out, indeed, that he had already taken some initiative along this line: he did not raise money for the Jerusalem church simply because the 'pillars' had asked him to do so, but as an important element in his own apostolic policy. If the Galatians chose not to accept his assurance on this point, or to prefer another interpretation of the facts than his, there was little he could do about it.

When this letter was sent, Paul had not yet launched the great Jerusalem relief fund to which he refers in his Corinthian and Roman correspondence. The instructions given to the churches of Galatia which were substantially repeated in 1 Cor. 16:1–4 were certainly not given in this letter. The general admonitions of Gal. 6:2, 6–10 (see notes *ad loc*.) could cover such a fund, but they include no practical directions about its collection and administration.

After 1 Cor. 16:1 Paul's references to the Jerusalem relief fund make no mention of Galatian participation. Macedonia and Achaia alone figure in 2 Cor. 8:1–9:15 and Rom. 15:25–28. It would be precarious to infer from this that the churches of Galatia withdrew from the enterprise: members of these churches were among Paul's companions on his last journey to Jerusalem (Acts 20:7)— Gaius of Derbe and Timothy (of Lystra). (To this it may be replied that Timothy was there as Paul's aide-de-camp, not as representing the church in Lystra, which is not named by Luke in this context; and that the Western text brings Gaius from Doberus, identifying him with the Macedonian Gaius of Acts 19:29; but see p. 13 n. 55.) L. W. Hurtado, 'The Jerusalem Collection and the Book of Galatians', *JSNT*, Issue 5 (Oct. 1979), 46–62, suggests that questions had been raised in the Galatian churches about the Jerusalem fund, and Paul had to make it plain that the fund was his own responsibility, not something imposed on him as a duty by higher authority in Jerusalem. (If he uses the language of authority when dealing with it in 2 Cor. 8:1–9:15, that authority derives from his own apostolic vocation, not from Jerusalem; but even his own apostolic authority must be combined with the Gentile churches' spontaneous generosity if the fund is to accomplish its purpose.) This reading of the text, however, implies a later date for Galatians than that accepted as probable in this commentary.

(g) Conflict at Antioch (2:11–14)

But when Cephas came to Antioch, I opposed him to his face, because he was in the wrong. Before certain people came from James, he ate along with the Gentiles, but when those people came, he proceeded to draw back and separate himself, through fear of the circumcision party. The rest of the Jews also joined him in his play-acting, to the point where even Barnabas was carried away with them in their play-acting. But when I saw that they were not following the right road in accordance with the truth of the gospel, I said to Cephas in front of them all, 'If you, Jew as you are, live like a Gentile and not like a Jew, how can you compel the Gentiles to live like Jews?'

TEXTUAL NOTES

v 11 Κηφας ℵ A B Ψ *al* lat^{vg} syr$^{pesh\ hcl.mg}$ / Πετρος D G byz lat^r syr^{hcl} Mcion Ambst

v 12 τινας / τινα P^{46} lat$^{d\ e\ g^c\ r*}$

συνησθιεν / συνησθιον P^{46} lat$^{vg(F)}$

ηλθον A C D² H Ψ byz lat / ηλθεν P^{46} ℵ B D* G *al* Or

v 13 και οι λοιποι / οι λοιποι P^{46} B 1739 lat^{vg} Or

v 14 Κηφα ℵ A B C H Ψ *pc* lat$^{c\ vg}$ syr$^{pesh\ hcl.mg}$ cop / Πετρω D G byz syr^{hcl} Ambst

και ουχι (ουκ) Ιουδαικως / *om* P^{46} 917 1881 lat$^{abde\ vg.cod}$ Ambst

2:11 Peter's coming to Antioch is not introduced by ἔπειτα as are the preceding stages in this autobiographical sketch: there was not the same apologetic need to emphasize the consecutive flow of events on this occasion. But it is most natural to take this as an incident that followed the conference of vv 1–10. There has indeed been a sequence of commentators and others, from Augustine (*Ep.* 82.11) onwards, who have placed this incident before the conference; cf. T. Zahn, *Galater*, 110; J. Munck, *Paul*, 100–103; H. M. Féret, *Pierre et Paul à Antioche et à Jérusalem* (Paris, 1955), with reply by J. Dupont, 'Pierre et Paul à Antioche et à Jérusalem', *RSR* 45 (1957), 225–239. The case for regarding the order of narration as the chronological order (vv 11–14 relating to a later occasion than vv 1–10) is presented cogently by G. Ogg (*Chronology*, 89–98). But, whereas most commentators identify the conference of vv 1–10 with the council described in Acts 15:6–29, the view taken in this commentary is that the conference of vv 1–10 was earlier than the council at which the apostolic decree of Acts 15:28f. was promulgated, and that the confrontation between the two apostles at Antioch took place between these two meetings. Indeed, the purpose of the decree was in large measure to solve the social problem which arose during Cephas's visit to Antioch.

The incident of vv 11–14 should probably be dated in the period following Barnabas and Paul's return to Antioch after their mission in Cyprus and South Galatia (Acts 14:26–28). If the demarcation of the two spheres of evangelism in vv 8f. had been envisaged as hard and fast, whether territorially or communally, one would have to ask what Cephas was doing in Antioch, the headquarters of Gentile Christianity. He was not confining himself to missionary work among the Jews of the city; he was enjoying table-fellowship with Gentiles—Gentile Christians, presumably. The Jerusalem agreement was flexible enough to accommodate such friendly fellowship as this. It was Cephas's *volte-face* that made Paul speak out so bluntly, 'because he was in the wrong'—literally 'condemned' (κατεγνωσμένος), not by any external authority but (as Paul saw it) by the inconsistency of his own conduct. For this use of κατεγνωσμένος cf. Josephus, *War* 2.135, where the Essenes (like the Friends of today) avoid oaths because 'he who is not believed unless he invokes God is condemned already' (ἤδη . . . κατεγνῶσθαι). See F. W. Mozley, 'Two Words in Galatians', *Expositor*, series 8, 4 (1912), 143–146. U. Wilckens takes the sense to be 'condemned in the sight of God' (*TDNT* VIII, 568 n. 51, *s.v.* ὑποκρίνομαι).

There may be a late echo of this confrontation in *Clem. Hom.* 17.19, where Peter debates with Simon Magus (a thin disguise for Paul), denying that Christ had appeared to the latter, as he claims (κἂν ὅτι ὤφθη σοι; cf. 1 Cor. 15:8), and protesting, 'You have opposed (ἀνθέστηκας) me . . . , as though I stood condemned' (κατεγνωσμένος).

2:12 This picture of Cephas enjoying unreserved table-fellowship (which included participation in the memorial breaking of bread) with the Gentile members of the Antiochene church is in complete accord with the picture given of him in Acts, where, after learning on Simon the tanner's roof-top in Joppa not to call any one unclean whom God had cleansed, he is happy to visit Cornelius in Caesarea and eat with him and his family (Acts 10:28; 11:3). 'The figure of a Judaizing St. Peter is a figment of the Tübingen critics with no basis in history' (K. Lake, *EEP*, 116).

This free and easy fellowship with Gentiles, then, was practised by Cephas at Antioch as a matter of course (συνήσθιεν, imperfect) until some people (τινας) came from James. For τινας a few witnesses have the singular τινα, a reading which probably originated in an attempt to harmonize with the singular ἦλθεν exhibited by several normally reliable witnesses in the next clause. It would make little material difference whether one messenger or several came from James (T. W. Manson, *Studies*, 178, prefers the two singular readings). But D. W. B. Robinson ('The Circumcision of Titus, and Paul's Liberty', 40f.), accepting τινα, treats it as the neuter plural ('certain things') referring to the κρίματα or δόγματα promulgated by the Council of Jerusalem at James's instance (Acts 15:19; 16:4); when these were brought to Antioch, he suggests, Cephas felt himself obliged by them 'to eat, from now on, only with the ritually "clean" '. Apart from the unlikelihood that Paul would have referred to the Jerusalem resolutions so vaguely, if any credence is to be given to the record of Acts 15 (as Robinson's interpretation requires) Cephas/Peter was one of the 'apostles' by whose authority the letter embodying the resolutions was sent to the church of Antioch and her daughter churches. D. R. Catchpole, 'Paul, James and the Apostolic Decree', *NTS* 23 (1976–77), 428–444, similarly argues that Cephas at Antioch tried to impose the Jerusalem decree on Gentile Christians. But the decree appears to have been promulgated in order to facilitate social fellowship between Jewish and Gentile Christians. The present confrontation at

Antioch underlined the importance of drafting some policy for the acceptable regulation of such fellowship. It was resolved at the ensuing council, against some opposition, that circumcision must not be required of Gentile Christians (this question does not appear to have arisen at the earlier conference of vv 1–10, described above), but that they should undertake to conform to the most important Jewish food-restrictions (in particular, the avoidance of the flesh of pagan sacrifices and of flesh from which the blood had not been drained) and the Jewish code of relations between the sexes (any breach of this code being 'fornication', πορνεία, in the sense of Acts 15:20, 29). If Paul makes no mention of this decree in Galatians, the reason may be that it had not yet been promulgated; his failure to mention it in 1 Corinthians, where relations between the sexes and the eating of the flesh of pagan sacrifices are specifically discussed, is to be explained otherwise; cf. C. K. Barrett, 'Things Sacrificed to Idols', *NTS* 11 (1964–65), 138–153, especially 149f.

It would be unwise to identify the 'certain people' who came from James with the 'certain people' (τινες) of Acts 15:1 who came down to Antioch from Judaea and insisted that circumcision was necessary for salvation. These men are disowned by the authors of the apostolic letter (Acts 15:24); it is more likely that they were connected with the 'false brethren' of v 4. The τινας mentioned here were simply messengers from James.

What was their message? It may have been something like this: 'news is reaching us in Jerusalem that you are habitually practising table-fellowship with Gentiles. This is causing grave scandal to our more conservative brethren here. Not only so: it is becoming common knowledge outside the church, so that our attempts to evangelize our fellow-Jews are being seriously hampered' (cf. T. W. Manson, *Studies*, 178–181).

It may have had even graver import. The mid-forties witnessed a revival of militancy among Jewish freedom fighters, adherents of the 'fourth philosophy', as Josephus calls it (*War* 2.118; *Ant*. 18.23). Repressive action was taken against them by Tiberius Julius Alexander, procurator of Judaea (*c*. AD 46–48), who crucified two of their leaders, Jacob and Simon, sons of that Judas the Galilaean who led the revolt against the provincial census of AD 6 (Jos. *Ant*. 20.102). B. Reicke ('Der geschichtliche Hintergrund des Apostelkonzils und der Antiochia-Episode, Gal 2,1–14', *De Zwaan FS*, 172–187) thinks rather of the period beginning AD 52, when the insurgency was intensified, and dates this 'Antioch episode' during Paul's visit to Antioch mentioned in Acts 18:22f. In the eyes of such militants, Jews who fraternized with Gentiles and adopted Gentile ways were traitors, and the leaders of the Jerusalem church may have felt themselves endangered by their colleague's free-and-easy conduct at Antioch (see on 6:12).

In spite of the impressive attestation of the singular ἦλθεν, the plural is probably to be preferred (ὅτε δὲ ἦλθον, 'but when they came'). The singular may have been influenced by the occurrence of ὅτε δὲ ἦλθεν, 'but when (Cephas) came', at the beginning of v 11. It would indeed be just possible to retain ὅτε δὲ ἦλθεν here and translate 'and when he (Cephas) came' (in the same sense as at the beginning of v 11, recapitulating the earlier occurrence of the three words), but this would be intolerably awkward; the verb here rather catches up the preceding ἐλθεῖν.

ὑπέστελλεν καὶ ἀφώριζεν ἑαυτόν, 'he drew back and separated himself':

the double imperfect suggests that he did not make an abrupt break with his former practice, but proceeded to change it gradually. ὑπέστελλεν is probably intransitive; it might be construed as transitive, with ἑαυτόν as its object as well as object to ἀφώριζεν. If it is intransitive, we might render 'he retreated' (as though for shelter); if transitive, 'he drew himself back'. K. H. Rengstorf takes this action as the antithesis to ὀρθοποδεῖν πρὸς τὴν ἀλήθειαν τοῦ εὐαγγελίου in v 14 (TDNT VII, 598, s.v. ὑποστέλλω).

φοβούμενος τοὺς ἐκ περιτομῆς, 'fearing those of the circumcision'. οἱ ἐκ περιτομῆς may have various meanings according to the context: 'the circumcision party', i.e. Judaizers within the church (Acts 11:2; Tit. 1:10); the circumcised members of the church, i.e. Jewish Christians in a non-partisan sense (Acts 10:45; Col. 4:11); circumcised people, i.e. Jews (Rom. 4:12b). Of whom was Peter afraid on this occasion? Not of his fellow-Jewish Christians in Antioch; they with him had been sharing table-fellowship with their Gentile brethren (cf. v 13, οἱ λοιποὶ ᾽Ιουδαῖοι); not even of James's messengers (there is no reason for equating τοὺς ἐκ περιτομῆς with τινας ἀπὸ ᾽Ιακώβου) nor of James himself—he may have respected James's authority, but why should he be afraid of him? The people who inspired fear were the Jewish militants to whom James's message possibly referred. See for various views G. Dix, Jew and Greek (London, 1953), 43ff.; J. Munck, Paul, 106–109 (he thinks that οἱ ἐκ περιτομῆς were Gentile Christians); W. Schmithals, Paul and James, 66–68. Schmithals points out that 'Paul utters no word of criticism against either James's messengers or James himself' (68), although his interpretation of this fact is open to doubt.

C. K. Barrett (᾽ΨΕΥΔΑΠΟΣΤΟΛΟΙ', 387) regards τοὺς ἐκ περιτομῆς as the Jewish Christian party in Jerusalem, who frightened Cephas 'presumably by threats of breaking off fellowship'—although more forceful measures may be implied in Paul's reference to 'dangers from false brethren' in 2 Cor. 11:26.

See also E. E. Ellis, 'The Circumcision Party and the Early Christian Mission', TU 102 (1968), 390–399, reprinted in Prophecy and Hermeneutic in Early Christianity (Tübingen/Grand Rapids, 1978), 116–128.

2:13 καὶ συνυπεκρίθησαν αὐτῷ [καὶ] οἱ λοιποὶ ᾽Ιουδαῖοι, 'the other Jews [also] joined in his play-acting'. The 'other Jews' here are the Jewish Christians of Antioch— 'Jews by birth' (φύσει ᾽Ιουδαῖοι), to borrow a phrase from v 15. If they were normally happy to share social fellowship with their fellow-Christians of Gentile birth, they may have felt on this occasion that courtesy dictated some conformity to the stricter practice of the visitors from Jerusalem, so they followed the example of Cephas. Paul calls their action ὑπόκρισις, 'play-acting', because it did not spring from inner conviction (ὑποκρίνομαι was used distinctively in classical Greek of the role of the actor on the Attic stage). He would not have approved of Jewish Christians who abstained on principle from eating with Gentile Christians, but he would not have stigmatized their abstention as ὑπόκρισις. He applied the term to Cephas's abstention because it sprang from expediency, not principle: hitherto Cephas had eaten in Gentile company with a good conscience.

But that Barnabas— 'even Barnabas'—should have been 'led away' with the others (συναπήχθη) to join this charade of separate tables was for Paul the last straw. He probably felt Barnabas's action more keenly than any one else's, because he and Barnabas had enjoyed mutual confidence as colleagues for so long. If it is to the churches of South Galatia that this letter is addressed, then the readers knew Barnabas: their churches came into being as a result of the preaching of Barnabas and Paul together. R. J. Bauckham ('Barnabas in Galatians') ascribes Paul's reticence about Barnabas in Galatians to his feeling of desertion and isolation over what he regarded as Barnabas's defection, which had taken place very shortly before this letter was written. Barnabas was the last man of whom such action would have been expected. This was effectively the end of their close association: the personal dispute over John Mark which Luke records in Acts 15:36–39 would not have caused a parting of their ways had it not been for this more serious difference. Yet in this context it is Cephas's action on which Paul concentrates, not only because the initiative was his but also because it was Paul's relation to Cephas that was being made an issue in the Galatian churches. The Galatians had no doubt heard of Barnabas's part in the Antioch episode, but Cephas's authority was greater than Barnabas's, and Cephas's authority, as they heard the story, had been exercised against Paul's policy: Paul, it appeared, had been put in his place by the prince of the apostles. What had Paul to say to this?

2:14 ἀλλ' ὅτε εἶδον ὅτι οὐκ ὀρθοποδοῦσιν πρὸς τὴν ἀλήθειαν τοῦ εὐαγγελίου, 'But when I saw that they were not on the right road towards the truth of the gospel': so G. D. Kilpatrick, 'Gal 2, 14 ὀρθοποδεῖν', *Studien für Bultmann*, 269–274. He mentions two other possible meanings of the verb: (i) 'walk straight or upright' (as opposed to limping), (ii) 'make straight for the goal'—but considers that 'be on the right road' is most appropriate in the present context. In Paul's eyes, they were taking the wrong road, which was leading them astray from gospel truth. We might take πρός to mean 'according to' rather than 'towards'. On ὀρθοποδέω cf. also J. G. Winter, 'Another instance of ὀρθοποδεῖν', *HTR* 34 (1941), 161f.; C. H. Roberts, 'A Note on Galatians 2:14', *JTS* 40 (1939), 55f.

The phrase 'the truth of the gospel' has occurred in v 5; see note there on the parallels between the two contexts.

εἶπον τῷ Κηφᾷ ἔμπροσθεν πάντων. The rebuke was thus public as well as personal ('to his face'). It has been asked why Paul did not follow the injunction of Mt. 18:15, 'If your brother sins, go and tell him his fault, between you and him alone' (where εἰς σέ after ἁμαρτήσῃ may be an addition to the original text). Paul may or may not have known this injunction in its Matthaean form, but he certainly knew the spirit of it, for he reproduces it in 6:1 below. For aught we know, he may have remonstrated with Cephas privately before rebuking him publicly. But perhaps he would have said that, since the offence was public, the rebuke had also to be public. Even Augustine confessed, in another connexion, that he had difficulty at times in deciding whether to follow Mt. 18:15 or 1 Tim. 5:20, 'Those who sin (or who persist in sinning, τοὺς ἁμαρτάνοντας) rebuke in the presence of all, that the rest may stand in fear' (*Ep.* 95.3).

Εἰ σὺ Ἰουδαῖος ὑπάρχων ἐθνικῶς καὶ οὐχὶ Ἰουδαϊκῶς ζῇς, πῶς τὰ ἔθνη ἀναγκάζεις Ἰουδαΐζειν; 'If you, Jew as you are (by birth and upbringing), live in the Gentile and not in the Jewish way (as Cephas had been doing habitually in Antioch, and presumably in other Gentile communities in which he found himself from time to time), how do you compel the Gentiles to live like Jews?' Ἰουδαΐζειν and Ἰουδαϊκῶς ζῆν are here synonymous (see note on Ἰουδαϊσμός, 1:13); if a single verb were used as a synonym for ἐθνικῶς ζῆν, it might well be ἑλληνίζειν. Having been happy to live like a Gentile among Gentiles, Cephas had now turned around and begun to practise Jewish-style social separation. This in effect amounted to saying to Gentile Christians, 'Unless you conform to the Jewish way of life we cannot have social relations with you.' This was practically compelling them to 'judaize'. Some Jewish Christians might have complained that they were being compelled to 'hellenize' (against their most poignant ancestral traditions) in order to maintain table-fellowship with Gentile Christians. Cephas, however, could not make this complaint: he 'hellenized' voluntarily, until the messengers from James came. Paul's mature policy, where there were conflicting convictions of this kind, was that one side should consider the other, and especially that the stronger should consider the weaker, in a spirit of Christian charity (Rom. 14:1ff.), but anything that smacked of compulsion was abhorrent to him.

We find ourselves wishing, as with the agreement reached at the recent Jerusalem conference, that we had more than one account of this confrontation—Cephas's, for instance, or, perhaps better still, Barnabas's (since we already have Paul's). But in fact it is not difficult to imagine how Cephas would have defended his action. He would have claimed that he acted out of consideration for weaker brethren—the weaker brethren on this occasion being those back home in Jerusalem. Tertullian (*Adv. Marc.* 1.20) read his motives thus, and put Paul's critical reaction down to his immaturity: later on, he points out, Paul 'was to become in practice all things to all men—to those under law, as under law' (1 Cor. 9:20). The trouble was, however, that Cephas's concern for the weaker brethren in Jerusalem conflicted with Paul's concern for the Gentile brethren in Antioch, who were being made to feel like second-class citizens.

Again, Tertullian suggests that, 'since Paul himself became "all things to all men in order to win them all"', Peter too may well have had this policy in mind in acting differently from what he was accustomed to teach' (*Adv. Marc.* 4.3). That Cephas had some reason on his side was acknowledged by Barnabas, who followed his example. But for Paul the liberty of the Gentiles was endangered by their action as surely as it was by the intrusion of the false brethren mentioned in v 4. If Gentile Christians were not fit company for Jewish Christians, it must be because their Christianity was defective: faith in Christ and baptism into his name were insufficient and must be supplemented by something else. And that 'something else' could only be a measure of conformity to Jewish law or custom: they must, in other words, 'judaize'.

This controversy between the two apostles was so painfully unedifying to some later fathers of the church that they tried to remove the offence which it presented. Clem. Alex., *Hyp.* (*apud* Euseb. *HE* 1.12), distinguished the Cephas of this episode from the apostle. Towards the end of the fourth century there was an interesting exchange of correspondence between Jerome and Augustine on the subject. Jerome, in his commentary on Galatians, said that Paul actually believed that Peter's action was justified, but opposed it at Antioch 'in order to soothe the minds of trouble-makers' (*ut quasi animos tumultuantium deliniret*); Augustine took him to task for this, and gave his own more reasonable account of the matter. Jerome claimed the authority of others, especially Origen, for his interpretation. (See Augustine, *Epp*. 28.3; 40.3f.; 82.4ff.; Jerome, *Ep*. 112.4ff.) Had Jerome been right, Paul would have been at least as guilty of 'play-acting' as those whom he criticizes on this score.

If the dispute had been amicably resolved by the time Paul sent this letter, we might have expected him to say so. We might also have expected him to say whether the church of Antioch as a whole supported him or Cephas, but he does not. Perhaps it goes without saying that a Gentile church would follow the apostle who asserted the liberty of the Gentiles—but when the course currently being pursued by the Gentile churches of Galatia is considered, one cannot be sure. Certainly Antioch ceased shortly after this to be Paul's missionary base, but as he carried the gospel farther west other bases, nearer the scene of apostolic activity, would in any case have proved more suitable than Antioch. (His stay there in AD 52, mentioned in Acts 18:22f., does not imply that Antioch was still his base.)

Whatever loss of mutual confidence may have been occasioned by the dispute between the two apostles, it did not lead to a breach between the Gentile mission and Jerusalem: Paul continued to 'remember the poor' as the 'pillars' had asked him to do.

G. Howard (*Crisis*, 42–45) suggests that Peter had so recently been introduced to the full freedom of the gospel as Paul understood it that he 'took some time to work out its practical implications'; however, he 'soon incorporated it into his own preaching and allowed himself to become a foundation for unity in the church'. Similarly J. D. G. Dunn concludes that Peter broadened his own outlook 'as Christianity broadened its outreach and character . . . , at the cost to be sure of losing his leading role in Jerusalem, but with the result that he became the most hopeful symbol of unity for that growing Christianity which more and more came to think of itself as the Church Catholic'—the bridge-man (*pontifex*) '*who did more than any other to hold together the diversity of first-century Christianity*' (*Unity*, 385f.).

IV
FAITH RECEIVES THE PROMISE
(2:15–5:1)

Mention of the incident at Antioch leads Paul on to assert plainly that Jews and Gentiles alike are justified by faith in Christ and not by legal works. It is preposterous, he adds, for those who by faith have received the Spirit to go back to reliance on keeping the law.

The gospel proclaims the fulfilment of the promise made by God to Abraham. All the nations were to be blessed with him, and since it was by faith that he received the blessing, so it is with them. The law, far from conveying a blessing, pronounces a curse on the law-breaker. From this curse Christ has redeemed his people by absorbing it in himself through his death by crucifixion. Thus they receive the blessing promised to Abraham—that is, they receive the Spirit through faith.

The superiority of the gospel over the law is shown also in the fact that Abraham received the promise centuries before the law was given. A testamentary disposition, once validated, cannot be invalidated by any subsequent provision; so the promise, confirmed by God, cannot be set aside by the law. The law was given not to impart life but to increase the sum-total of sin; the promise, with the righteousness and life which it secures, is obtained not through keeping the law but through faith in Christ.

The law, in fact, is like a slave-attendant placed in charge of a freeborn child until he attains his majority. The people of God have attained their majority through faith in Christ; in him they have entered a new order of existence, in which distinctions of the old order become irrelevant. Until the child comes of age, although he is potentially heir to a rich estate, he is not given his liberty but is treated like a slave. So we remained under the control of the law until the coming of Christ. He has redeemed us from legal bondage and given us a new status as mature and responsible sons and daughters of God. It is sons and daughters, not slaves, who receive the Spirit and are enabled by him to call God 'Abba, Father', as Jesus himself did. How can any one who has come of age desire to be restricted all over again by the leading-strings of infancy?

Paul then appeals to the Galatians to give him the same confidence and affection as they did when first he came to them. They are indeed his dear children, but they have been misled by trouble-makers who simply wish to swell the number of their personal followers.

He next recalls the Genesis story of the expulsion of Hagar and Ishmael in favour of Sarah and Isaac, to show that it is those who enjoy the freedom of the Spirit, not those who are enslaved to the law, that are the trueborn children of God. The Galatians have been set free by Christ: let them not turn back the clock and submit to bondage again.

(a) Both Jews and Gentiles are justified by faith (2:15–21)

As for us who are Jews by birth and not 'sinners of the Gentiles', knowing that it is not by legal works that any human being is justified but only by faith in Jesus Christ, we also have believed in Christ Jesus in order to be justified through faith in Christ and not by legal works, because by legal works 'no living person will be justified'. But if, seeking to be justified in Christ, we ourselves also have been found to be sinners, is Christ then a minister of sin? Far from it! For if I build again the things which I broke down I make myself a transgressor. Through the law I died in relation to law in order to live in relation to God. I have·been crucified with Christ, and it is no longer I who live, but Christ lives in me. The life I now live in mortal body I live by faith in the Son of God, who loved me and gave himself up for me. I do not make the grace of God null and void, for if it is through law that righteousness comes, then Christ died to no purpose.

TEXTUAL NOTES

v 16　δε *om* P^{46} A D^2 Ψ byz syr^{hcl} cop

　　εκ πιστεως Χριστου / εκ πιστεως G Tyc Pelag

v 20　υιου του θεου א A C D^2 Ψ byz lat^f ^{vg} syr$^{pesh\ hcl}$ cop Clem Ambst Chrys Hier Aug / θεου του υιου 1985 / θεου και Χριστου P^{46} B D^* G lat$^{d\ e\ g}$ M.Vict Pelag / του θεου 330

　　αγαπησαντος / αγορασαντος Mcion Pelag (cf. 3:13)

2:15 It is difficult to decide at what point Paul's quotation of his rebuke to Peter comes to an end and passes into his general exposition of the principle at stake. He probably summarizes his rebuke to Peter and then develops its implications, thus passing smoothly from the personal occasion to the universal principle, from *Individualgeschichte* to *Weltgeschichte*, as used in the titles of papers by G. Klein, 'Individualgeschichte und Weltgeschichte bei Paulus' (1963), republished (with *Nachtrag*) in *Rekonstruktion*, 180–224, and by W. G. Kümmel (largely a reply to Klein), ' "Individualgeschichte" und "Weltgeschichte" in Gal. 2:15–21', *Moule FS*, 157–173. Klein, following R. Bultmann, 'Zur Auslegung von Gal. 2, 15–18' (1952), *Exegetica* (Tübingen, 1967), 394–399, treats v 15 as an independent sentence (relating to the old order), set over against v 16 (relating to the new order), and denies a place to salvation history in Paul's exposition. Kümmel, doing more justice to what Paul says, takes vv 15 and 16 together as one sentence, introducing the presentation of justification by faith as the fulfilment of the promise to Abraham and thus as the climax of salvation history (cf. 2 Cor. 6:2, 'now is the day of salvation').

ἡμεῖς φύσει Ἰουδαῖοι καὶ οὐκ ἐθνῶν ἁμαρτωλοί, 'we (who are) Jews by birth and not "sinners of the Gentiles" ': these words form the subject of the sentence which is continued in v 16 and are caught up again in καὶ ἡμεῖς (v 16). 'We' is emphatic—'we' as distinct from 'them' (the Gentiles). The status of believers of Jewish birth (like Paul, Peter and Barnabas) is different now from what it was when they lived under the law. At that time the law constituted a barrier between them and the Gentiles. They themselves were 'righteous', being within the covenant; the Gentiles, being outside the covenant, were ἄνομοι (Rom. 2:12–16; 1 Cor. 9:21) and *ipso facto* ἁμαρτωλοί (compare Lk. 24:7 with Acts 2:23)—a judgment which was confirmed in Jewish eyes by the general level of pagan morality (cf. Rom. 1:18–32; Eph. 4:17–19; 5:11f.). See E. P. Sanders, 'On the Question of Fulfilling the Law in Paul and Rabbinic Judaism', *Daube FS*, 103–126. 'Sinners of the Gentiles' may be a quotation from the vocabulary of law-abiding Jews. But now that Paul, Peter, Barnabas and other 'Jews by birth' have embraced the way of faith in Christ, the barrier is down and there is no distinction between Jew and Gentile either in respect of sin (Rom. 3:22) or in respect of access to God's justifying grace (Rom. 10:12).

2:16 εἰδότες [δὲ] ὅτι οὐ δικαιοῦται ἄνθρωπος ἐξ ἔργων νόμου, 'knowing that it is not by legal works that any human being is justified': these words anticipate the amplified quotation of Ps. 143 (LXX 142):2 at the end of this verse. The ἔργα νόμου are the actions prescribed by the law. They are not deprecated in themselves, for the law of God is 'holy and just and good' (Rom. 7:12)—even if Paul's attitude to the law is more radical in Galatians than in Romans, this statement is as valid for Galatians as for Romans (cf. Gal. 5:14). What is deprecated is the performing of them in a spirit of legalism, or with the idea that their performance will win acceptance before God; cf. 3:2, 5, 10; also Rom. 3:20, 28. (The noun ἔργα by itself has much the same sense in Rom. 4:2, 6; 9:11, 32; 11:6; Eph. 2:9; cf. Tit. 3:5, οὐκ ἐξ ἔργων τῶν ἐν δικαιοσύνῃ ἃ ἐποιήσαμεν ἡμεῖς.) The antithesis to ἐξ ἔργων νόμου is ἐκ πίστεως (see note on 3:7).

The threefold occurrence of ἐξ ἔργων νόμου in this sentence is striking. C. E. B. Cranfield, 'St. Paul and the Law', *SJT* 17 (1964), 43–68, especially 55 (cf. his *Romans*, 845–862, especially 853), points out that Paul had no ready word or phrase in Greek to express what we mean by 'legalism', and therefore had to use 'law' (as in Gal. 3:11, ἐν νόμῳ) or a phrase containing 'law' (such as ἐξ ἔργων νόμου) to express it. In fact, as C. F. D. Moule points out ('Obligation in the Ethic of Paul', *Knox FS*, 392), Paul had no distinctive word or phrase for other particular aspects of law; hence the necessity of deducing from the context the nuance which he has in mind. Moule distinguishes in particular what he calls the 'revelatory' and 'legalistic' senses of νόμος, and by means of this distinction is able to give a satisfactory answer to the question whether, in Paul's view, Christ has abrogated the law or not (cf. Rom. 10:4). 'Paul saw Christ as the *fulfilment* of law, when law means God's revelation of himself and of his character and purpose, but as the *condemnation* and *termination* of any attempt to use law to justify oneself. And it is this latter use of law which may conveniently be called (for short) "legalism".' If 'law means the upward striving of human religion and morality, and therefore colours all human activity with sin, for it represents man's attempt to scale God's throne' (C. K. Barrett, *Romans*, 129), it is Moule's latter use of law that is presumably implied.

In making this affirmation, Paul was in a strong position: if any one could base a claim on 'works of law', it was he. His pre-Christian record, 'as to righteousness by law', was 'blameless' (Phil. 3:6). But he learned that even this record did not justify him before God; now his hope was founded on 'not having a righteousness of my own, based on law, but that which is through faith in Christ' (Phil. 3:9).

The verb δικαιόω means 'make δίκαιος', 'put in the right' or 'in the clear' (to use a modernism). In this kind of context those are δίκαιοι who have been set right with God, pardoned and accepted by him; cf. 3:11 for Paul's understanding of the adjective as used in Hab. 2:4b (LXX). The words in the δικαιο-group may have either a 'relational' or a 'behavioural' sense. For example, the noun δικαιοσύνη means not only personal or corporate justice or righteousness of character but also, and distinctively, the state of being right with God, as in v 21. The old question of Jb. 9:1, 'How can a man be just (LXX δίκαιος) before God?' is not quoted by Paul, but that is the question with which he is concerned. He considers one answer ('By works of law')—the answer which he himself would previously have given—and dismisses it; he offers a new answer ('By faith in Christ').

See J. Buchanan, *The Doctrine of Justification* (Edinburgh, 1867); H. Küng, *Justification*, ETr (London, 1966); D. Hill, *Greek Words and Hebrew Meanings* (Cambridge, 1967), 82–162; E. Käsemann, ' "The Righteousness of God" in Paul', *NT Questions of Today*, ETr (London, 1969), 168–182, and 'Justification and Salvation History in the Epistle to the Romans', *Perspectives on Paul*, ETr (London, 1971), 60–78; J. A. Ziesler, *The Meaning of Righteousness in Paul* (Cambridge, 1972); H. Seebass and C. Brown, 'Righteousness, Justification', *NIDNTT* III, 352–377, with ample bibliography.

As in Rom. 3:28, ἄνθρωπος may be more than the equivalent of the indefinite pronoun τις. The Jew or the Gentile now stands before God as a human being, neither privileged (as Jew) nor underprivileged (as Gentile), to be given a status before him not by legal works, in which the Jew would have an (at least theoretical) advantage, but on a basis (faith in Christ) equally open to Jew and Gentile (cf. Rom. 3:28–30).

ἐὰν μὴ διὰ πίστεως Ἰησοῦ Χριστοῦ. Here ἐὰν μή means 'but', the previous option, ἐξ ἔργων νόμου, being excluded. διὰ πίστεως Ἰησοῦ Χριστοῦ, 'through faith in Jesus Christ'. The genitive Ἰησοῦ Χριστοῦ could be objective (so we take it) or subjective, as though the phrase meant 'through Jesus Christ's faith(fulness)'. This latter construction has been defended by J. Haussleiter, *Der Glaube Jesu Christi und der christliche Glaube* (Leipzig, 1891); G. Kittel, 'πίστις Ἰησοῦ Χριστοῦ bei Paulus', *TSK* 79 (1906), 419–436; K. Barth, *The Epistle to the Romans*, ETr (Oxford, 1933), 41, 96; A. G. Hebert, ' "Faithfulness" and Faith', *Theology* 58 (1955), 373–379; T. F. Torrance, 'One Aspect of the Biblical Conception of Faith', *Exp Tim* 68 (1956–57), 111f. (with reply by C. F. D. Moule, ibid., 157); E. R. Goodenough with A. T. Kraabel, 'Paul and the Hellenization of Christianity', *Religions in Antiquity: Essays in Memory of E. R. Goodenough*, ed. J. Neusner = *Suppl. Numen* 15 (Leiden,

1967), 35–80; G. Howard, 'On the "Faith of Christ" ', *HTR* 61 (1967), 459–465, 'Romans 3:21–31 and the Inclusion of the Gentiles', *HTR* 64 (1970), especially 228–231, 'The "Faith of Christ" ', *Exp Tim* 85 (1973–74), 212–214, and *Crisis*, 57f.; D. W. B. Robinson, ' "Faith of Jesus Christ"—A NT Debate', *RTR* 29 (1970), 71–81.

When the genitive is taken as subjective, the phrase is variously interpreted as meaning 'Christ's faith' (in God), or 'Christ's faithfulness' (to God), or God's faithfulness revealed in Christ (so Barth, Hebert).

In defence of the objective genitive see, in addition to C. F. D. Moule (cited above), J. Murray, *Romans*, 363–374; J. Barr, *The Semantics of Biblical Language* (Oxford, 1961), 161–205. C. E. B. Cranfield (*Romans*, 203 n. 2) briefly dismisses the subjective interpretation as 'altogether unconvincing'.

The principal and, indeed, conclusive argument for taking the genitive to be objective here is that, when Paul expresses himself by the verb πιστεύω and not by the noun πίστις, Christ is the undoubted object of the faith, as in the clause immediately following: καὶ ἡμεῖς εἰς Χριστὸν Ἰησοῦν ἐπιστεύσαμεν ('even we have believed in Christ Jesus'). This determines the sense of the preceding διὰ πίστεως Ἰησοῦ Χριστοῦ and of ἐκ πίστεως Χριστοῦ in the next clause. See C. H. Dodd, *The Bible and the Greeks* (London, 1935), 65–70.

R. Bultmann (*TDNT* VI, 203, *s.v.* πίστις) points out that πίστις Χριστοῦ Ἰησοῦ is tantamount to believing 'that Jesus died and rose' (1 Thes. 5:14). 'Paul never defines faith. The nature of faith is given in the object to which faith is directed. . . . Faith always means faith in . . . or faith that . . .' (G. Bornkamm, *Paul*, 141). 'Faith in . . .', one should say, *as well as* 'faith that . . .': it is the personal faith that unites one to Christ along with all fellow-members of the new covenant community—all those who, in Paul's idiom, are 'in Christ'.

καὶ ἡμεῖς εἰς Χριστὸν Ἰησοῦν ἐπιστεύσαμεν, 'even we (or we also) have believed in Christ Jesus'. The attempt to press a distinction between the form 'Christ Jesus' (commoner in Paul) and 'Jesus Christ' (as in the preceding clause) is precarious. 'Christ Jesus' might mean 'the now exalted Christ who is identical with the earthly Jesus', but one cannot suppose that Paul intended to convey all this every time he used this form. By καὶ ἡμεῖς he means 'even we who are Jews by birth' (catching up the words of v 15)—even we (or we also) find our justification by faith in Christ and not by legal works, as truly as 'sinners of the Gentiles' do. Whether or not this is part of what Paul said to Peter at Antioch, it is implied in what he said, and Peter's endorsement of it is taken for granted. The argument of vv 15–21 would have been pointless unless the premises on which it is based (stated in vv 15f.) were shared by both sides. Peter's assent, which is here assumed, finds substantial expression in the words with which he is credited in Acts 15:9, 11 (although the specific language of justification is not there used): 'God . . . made no distinction between us [Jewish believers] and them [Gentile believers], but cleansed their hearts by *faith*. . . . Through the grace of the Lord Jesus, we *believe* so as to be saved, just as they do.'

ἵνα δικαιωθῶμεν ἐκ πίστεως Χριστοῦ. No material difference can be discerned between the single form 'Christ' here and the double forms 'Jesus Christ' and 'Christ Jesus' in the preceding clauses. Nor can any material difference be discerned between ἐκ πίστεως here and διὰ πίστεως above; the variation is purely stylistic (cf. ἐκ πίστεως . . . διὰ τῆς πίστεως in Rom. 3:30). We have a further variant ἐν πίστει in v 20 below.

It is perhaps for emphasis that Paul repeats οὐκ ἐξ ἔργων νόμου. It might go without saying that if 'we' have believed in Christ in order to be justified by faith in him, then justification cannot be based on legal works; but there was no harm in spelling it out again. Besides, the repetition of the words leads on naturally to Paul's introduction to his quotation from Ps. 143 (LXX 142):2: ὅτι ἐξ ἔργων νόμου οὐ δικαιωθήσεται πᾶσα σάρξ. Here, as later in Rom. 3:20, Paul substitutes πᾶσα σάρξ for πᾶς ζῶν of the LXX (ὅτι οὐ δικαιωθήσεται ἐνώπιόν σου πᾶς ζῶν, which follows Heb. *kol ḥāy*) and inserts ἐξ ἔργων νόμου before οὐ δικαιωθήσεται. It may be inferred that for him at least this paraphrase of Ps. 143 (LXX 142):2 had become a habitual proof-text for the doctrine of justification by faith apart from works of law. (In the context of the psalm it is emphasized that no one can hope to win a case at law against God.) Here πᾶσα σάρξ means 'all mankind', as frequently in the OT (e.g. Ps. 65 [LXX 64]:2; Je. 12:12; Joel 2:28); cf. 1 Cor. 1:29.

As Paul uses justification by faith to refute legalism in the Galatian churches, he finds it equally effective as a weapon against 'gnosticizing' tendencies at Corinth (cf. 1 Cor. 1:30; 6:11).

Paul's application of Ps. 143:2, according to H.-J. Schoeps, 'considered from the standpoint of the rabbinic understanding of the law, stems from a partial aspect of the law wrongly isolated from the saving significance of the law as a whole' (*Paul*, 196). There is indeed a contradiction between the Pauline and the rabbinic understanding: Paul denied any saving significance to the law. On the other hand, there is at least a formal analogy between his insistence on justification by divine grace and sentiments expressed in some of the hymns of the Qumran community: 'I know that there is no righteousness in man and no perfection of way in a son of man; to God Most High belong all the works of righteousness . . .' (1QH 4.30f.); 'I will call God my righteousness and the Most High the establisher of my goodness' (1QS 10.11f.); 'As for me, my judgment belongs to God and in his hand is my perfection of way' (1QS 11.2); 'In his compassion he has brought me near and in his loving kindness comes my judgment; in the righteousness of his truth he has judged me and in the riches of his goodness he makes atonement for all my sins' (1QS 11.13f.).

See S. Schulz, 'Zur Rechtfertigung aus Gnaden in Qumran und bei Paulus', *ZTK* 56 (1959), 155–185; E. P. Sanders, *PPJ*, 305–312; O. Betz, 'Rechtfertigung in Qumran', *Käsemann FS*, 17–36; E. Käsemann, *Romans*, 25–32.

2:17 εἰ δὲ ζητοῦντες δικαιωθῆναι ἐν Χριστῷ εὑρέθημεν καὶ αὐτοὶ ἁμαρτωλοί. The interpretation of vv 15–21 is beset by problems because Paul appears to be answering various charges which were circulating against him. To understand the point and relevance of his answers adequately it would be necessary to identify those charges, but as it is they can be inferred only from his answers.

Here he may simply mean that when law-abiding Jews like Peter and himself cease to look to the law as the basis of their justification before God and find that justification in Christ instead, they put themselves effectively on a level with 'sinners of the Gentiles': they have, in that sense, 'been found sinners'—they themselves (καὶ αὐτοί) as much as lesser breeds without the law. But this applies to all Jewish Christians, even to those who have not appreciated the law-free character of the gospel: by yielding faith to Christ they have in logic, if not in consciousness, abandoned faith in the law, and have had to take their place as sinners, utterly in need of God's justifying grace. If Paul has something more specific in mind, such as a charge against himself arising, perhaps, out of the recent episode at Antioch, it is impossible to identify it.

ἆρα Χριστὸς ἁμαρτίας διάκονος; 'Is Christ a servant of sin?' The interrogative particle ἆρα, accented with a circumflex as in UBS³, Nestle-Aland²⁶ and other editions, occurs nowhere else in Paul, whereas the inferential particle ἄρα (accented as paroxytone) is quite frequent (cf. v 21; 3:7, 29; 5:11; 6:10). If ἄρα be read here, it yields excellent sense: 'Is Christ then (in that case) a servant of sin?' See J. Lambrecht, 'The Line of Thought in Gal. 2.14b–21', *NTS* 24 (1977–78), 489f., with bibliographical references in footnotes. C. F. D. Moule, *Idiom-Book*, 196, and 'A Note on Galatians ii.17, 18', *Exp Tim* 56 (1944–45), 223, agrees with the accentuation ἄρα but treats the clause not as a question but as a statement of the necessary implication of Peter's behaviour, which Peter answers with a μὴ γένοιτο. Paul then replies, 'You may repudiate the position with a μὴ γένοιτο, but that is the position in which you logically place yourself by your action, *for* if I build again. . . .' But every other Pauline instance of μὴ γένοιτο, used thus as an independent sentence, follows a question (in *diatribe* style); there is thus a presumption that it does so here, and the evidence is not sufficiently strong to mark out the present μὴ γένοιτο as Peter's imagined reply to Paul's shocking statement of the conclusion to which Peter's action points.

In what sense, then, would it follow that Christ is 'a servant of sin'? Not because Peter's action implied that Christ's justifying work was unable to remove sin (although this interpretation was preferred by R. Bultmann, 'Zur Auslegung . . .', *Exegetica*, 395f.), but because, in the argument of Paul's opponents, if law-abiding Jews had now to be reckoned as 'sinners', just like those who lived without the law, then the number of sinners in the world was substantially increased, and so (as they understood Paul's position) Christ was made a servant or agent of sin. But the law-free gospel of justification by faith did not make them sinners for the first time; it revealed that they were already sinners, that they were included among the 'all' who, as Paul puts it in Rom. 3:23, 'have sinned and fall short of the glory of God'. The gospel did not increase the sumtotal of sinners—it was, in fact, the law that did that, according to 3:19—and therefore Christ was in no sense an agent of sin.

μὴ γένοιτο, 'Far from it!' or 'Perish the thought!' This is Paul's characteristic way of repudiating the implication of some question, real or imagined, which is posed by way of an objection to his argument. The idea expressed in the objection is ethically or theologically monstrous; μὴ γένοιτο (in form the negative of γένοιτο, sometimes used in the LXX to render 'Amen', as in Ps. 72 [LXX 71]:19, γένοιτο, γένοιτο) is equivalent to Heb. *has wᵉšālôm*. Paul regularly follows up μὴ γένοιτο with a reasoned rebuttal, as here. He is particularly prone to say μὴ γένοιτο when it is suggested that freedom from law will encourage people to sin (cf. Rom. 6:1f., 15); if that were so, then Christ (as presented by Paul) would indeed be an agent of sin.

2:18 εἰ γὰρ ἃ κατέλυσα ταῦτα πάλιν οἰκοδομῶ, παραβάτην ἐμαυτὸν συνιστάνω. One way or another, someone who builds up what he formerly demolished acknowledges his fault, explicitly in his former demolition or implicitly in his present rebuilding. If the one activity was right, the other must be wrong.

Paul's language could be taken to refer to one of several specific situations. (i) It could refer to Peter's attempt to rebuild the social partition between Jews and Gentiles which he had earlier broken down. (ii) It could refer to Paul's now preaching the gospel which he had once tried to eradicate, in the sense of 1:23. (iii) It could refer to a rumour that Paul was, in practice, modifying his assertion of the completely law-free character of the gospel, e.g. the report that he was still preaching circumcision (5:11). We have to be guided by the sense which his language most naturally bears in the context of his present argument, paying special attention to the particle γάρ.

Probably Paul is not referring to one specific situation. The use of γάρ suggests that he is explaining why the charge that his gospel makes Christ a minister of sin is inadmissible. The 'I' in v 18 is not primarily personal; Paul uses it to refer to any one who behaves in the manner indicated. The clause παραβάτην ἐμαυτὸν συνιστάνω at the end of v 18 is almost equivalent to εὑρέθην ἁμαρτωλός (so Bultmann, 'Zur Auslegung . . .', 399). If law-abiding Jews take the position of sinners and turn to Christ for justification, that does not make him a minister of sin, *for* the fact is this: any one who, having received justification through faith in Christ, thereafter reinstates law in place of Christ makes himself a sinner all over again—and Christ cannot be held responsible for that. If the law was still in force, as the Galatians were being urged to believe, then those who sought salvation elsewhere were transgressors by its standard; if it was no longer in force—if Christ occupied the place which was now rightly his in salvation history—then those who sought their justification before God anywhere but in Christ remained unjustified, that is to say, they were still in their sins. It is the latter contingency that Paul has in mind as he writes to the Galatians: if they sought their justification in the law by submitting to circumcision, Christ would be of no advantage to them (5:2).

For other understandings of παραβάτην ἐμαυτὸν συνιστάνω, see H. Schlier, *Galater*, 96; J. Schneider, *TDNT* V, 741 n. 4, *s.v.* παραβάτης; R. C. Tannehill, *Dying and Rising*, 56.

2:19 ἐγὼ γὰρ διὰ νόμου νόμῳ ἀπέθανον. A proper understanding of γάρ would throw light not only on the following words of v 19 but also on the meaning of what precedes in v 18. Certainty is unattainable, but the sense could well be: 'The question of transgressing the law does not arise for one who has died in relation to the law.' Transgression implies a law to be transgressed, as Paul notes in Rom. 4:15b; 5:13; it is in the presence of law that sin shows itself in the form of transgression. But the possibility that 'I constitute myself a transgressor' before the law is now excluded, *for* 'I have died in relation to the law'. Death in relation to the law is more relevant to Jewish Christians who once lived under law: if it is preposterous for them, after dying to the law, to put themselves under law again, it is even more preposterous for Gentile Christians like the Galatians to assume the yoke of a law to which they had no ancestral commitment.

All believers in Christ have 'died in relation to sin' (Rom. 6:2, 11), but the

point stressed here is that, at the same time, they have 'died in relation to law'—
Jewish believers specifically and consciously so. Paul—for he puts the case in
the first person singular—no longer lives under the power of the law; he has
been released from its dominion and has entered into new life. 'With death
obligations towards the law have ceased' (H.-J. Schoeps, *Paul*, 193). It is fundamental to Paul's understanding of the law that he can define one and the same
experience as death to law (cf. Rom. 7:4–6) and death to sin (Rom. 6:2). To be
under law is to be exposed to the power of sin, for 'the power of sin is the law'
(1 Cor. 15:56); it is the law that provides sin with a vantage-point from which
to invade Mansoul (cf. Rom. 7:7–11). But to those who have entered into new
life in Christ the assurance is given: '*sin* will have no more dominion over you,
since you are not *under law* but under grace' (Rom. 6:14). Cf. P. Benoit, 'La
loi et la croix d'après Saint Paul (Rom VII,7–VIII,4)', *RB* 47 (1938), 488–509
(especially 502 n. 3).

C. F. D. Moule, 'Death "to sin", "to law", and "to the world": A Note
on Certain Datives', *Rigaux FS*, 367–375, suggests that the construction of
ἀποθανεῖν with the dative was created by analogy with ζῆν followed by the
dative in a relational sense (e.g. ζῆν τῷ θεῷ, as in 4 Macc. 7:19; 16:25; Lk.
20:38).

Paul, then, 'died to the law' in order to 'live to God' (revealed in Christ).
But how was it διὰ νόμου that he died νόμῳ? According to T. Zahn (*Galater*,
133), the law showed him his need of redemption and referred him to faith.
More adequately, R. C. Tannehill (*Dying and Rising*, 59) understands Paul's
wording in the light of the law's relation to Christ. As appears below in 3:13,
Christ bore the curse of the law and exhausted its penalty on his people's behalf:
in this sense Christ died διὰ νόμου, and 'the believer's death to the law is also
"through law" because he died in Christ's death'—as Paul goes on immediately
to affirm: Χριστῷ συνεσταύρωμαι. The law has no further claim on him who
in death satisfied its last demand, and the believer who has 'died with Christ' is
similarly 'discharged from the law' (Rom. 7:6).

But there may also be a note of personal experience in ἐγὼ . . . διὰ νόμου.
. . . Paul continues to use the first person singular as he speaks for Jewish
Christians in general, but the emphatic ἐγώ (while it perhaps anticipates the ἐγώ
of v 20) suggests that he knew in a special way what it meant to die to law
'through law'. It was Paul's zeal for the law that made him so ardent a persecutor
of the church (cf. Phil. 3:6). After his conversion, his persecuting activity was
seen by him to have been unspeakably sinful (cf. 1 Cor. 15:9); but the law, to
which he had been so utterly dedicated, had proved incapable of showing him
the sinfulness of his course or preventing him from pursuing it. Rather, in this
respect the law had led him into sin. In the revelation of Jesus Christ on the
Damascus road the moral bankruptcy of the law was disclosed: for Paul, therefore, this involved the end of his old life 'under law' and the beginning of his
new life 'in Christ'. In this sense it was διὰ νόμου that he died νόμῳ . . . ἵνα
θεῷ ζήσω. The nature of this 'life to God' is made plain in v 20. 'I live in
relation to God', Paul implies, 'because Christ lives in me.' The death that Christ
died, 'he died in relation to sin, once for all; but the life that he lives, he lives
in relation to God' (Rom. 6:10). By faith-union with him, therefore, his people
must consider themselves 'dead in relation to sin and alive in relation to God in

Christ Jesus' (Rom. 6:11), (Christ's death in relation to sin has to do with his finished work as his people's sin-bearer [cf. 2 Cor. 5:21, ὑπὲρ ἡμῶν ἁμαρτίαν ἐποίησεν]; *their* death in relation to sin has reference to their former existence as sinners.) Paul expresses something which is true of all believers, but it may be that his continued use of 'I' to express it reflects his awareness that his personal preaching and conduct have been called in question.

A change of lordship, from law to Christ, has taken place, but that is not all, says Paul: 'I have been crucified with Christ'. Those who place their faith in Christ are united with him by that faith—united so closely that his experience now becomes theirs: they share his death to the old order ('under law'; cf. 4:4) and his resurrection to new life. This, for Paul, is what is signified in baptism (cf. 3:27)—although he himself did not wait for his baptism to experience it; it came true in him at a stroke on the Damascus road. As Christ's death was death by crucifixion, the believer is said not only to have died with him but to have been 'crucified with him' (Χριστῷ συνεσταύρωμαι). In the passion narrative συσταυρόω is used literally of the two robbers who were 'crucified with' Jesus (Mt. 27:44; Mk. 15:43; Jn. 19:32); here it is used figuratively, as also in Rom. 6:6, 'the person we formerly were was crucified with him' (ὁ παλαιὸς ἡμῶν ἄνθρωπος συνεσταυρώθη). The figure is deliberately bold, designed to emphasize the finality of the death which has put an end to the old order and interposed a barrier between it and the new life in Christ (cf. 5:24; 6:14). The perfect tense συνεσταύρωμαι emphasizes that participation in the crucified Christ has become the believer's settled way of life. 'Union with Christ is nothing if it is not union with Christ in his death' (J. D. G. Dunn, *Unity*, 195).

An extension of this thought is Paul's insistence on sharing the sufferings of Christ (cf. 6:17 with Rom. 8:17; 2 Cor. 1:5; 4:10f.; Phil. 3:10; Col. 1:24).

2:20 ζῶ δὲ οὐκέτι ἐγώ, 'and it is no longer *I* who live'. '*I* died (in relation to law)', Paul has just said; we might expect him to follow this up with 'now I live (in Christ)'. The repetition of ἐγώ is not accidental. But so completely is self dethroned in the new order that in this context Paul will not say ἐγὼ ζῶ but 'it is no longer *I* who live; it is Christ who lives in me' (ζῇ δὲ ἐν ἐμοὶ Χριστός). Cf. Phil. 1:21, ἐμοὶ γὰρ τὸ ζῆν Χριστός.

Having died with Christ in his death, the believer now lives with Christ in his life—i.e. his resurrection life. In fact, this new life in Christ is nothing less than the risen Christ living his life in the believer. The risen Christ is the operative power in the new order, as sin was in the old (cf. Rom. 7:17, 20); Ἰησοῦς Χριστὸς ἐν ὑμῖν (2 Cor. 13:5). In Paul's general teaching, it is by the Spirit that the risen life of Christ is communicated to his people and maintained within them. It makes little practical difference whether he speaks of Christ living in them or the Spirit dwelling in them (cf. Rom. 8:10a, 11a), although the latter expression is commoner (contrariwise, although it makes little practical difference whether he speaks of them as being 'in Christ' or 'in the Spirit', it is the former expression that is commoner). Cf. 3:26–29; 4:6; 5:16–25 with notes.

ὃ δὲ νῦν ζῶ ἐν σαρκί. For the construction cf. Rom. 6:10, ὃ δὲ ζῇ, 'the life that he lives'. Even the believer's present life in mortal body, says Paul, is lived in faith-union with Christ, the Son of God (the textual variants are interesting but make no difference to the sense). Cf. Eph. 3:17, 'that Christ may dwell in your hearts by faith' (διὰ τῆς πίστεως). This is not simply the exercise of faith in contrast to sight, as in 2 Cor. 5:7 where, so long as we are in mortal body, 'we walk by faith (διὰ πίστεως), not by sight', but faith as the bond of union with the risen Christ. To live by faith in this sense is tantamount to 'living by the Spirit' (5:25) which, as in Rom. 8:9–11, enables the believer even now to anticipate the life to come. This aspect of Paul's teaching is characterized by E. P. Sanders as 'participationist eschatology' (*PPJ*, 549). See further E. Wissmann, *Das Verhältnis von* ΠΙΣΤΙΣ *und Christusfrömmigkeit bei Paulus* (Göttingen, 1926), 112.

The phrase ἐν σαρκί here is non-theological: as in 2 Cor. 10:3 (where it is contrasted with κατὰ σάρκα in the special Pauline sense of σάρξ), it means 'in mortal body'; cf. the fuller expression ἐν τῇ θνητῇ σαρκὶ ἡμῶν of 2 Cor. 4:11 (and the θνητὸν σῶμα of Rom. 6:12; 8:11). When σάρξ is used by Paul with the meaning that he distinctively gives it, to live ἐν σαρκί is to lead an unregenerate life: 'those who are ἐν σαρκί cannot please God', but those in whom the Spirit of God dwells are not ἐν σαρκί (Rom. 8:8f.). This distinctive use of σάρξ occurs below in 3:3; 4:23, 29; 5:13, 16f., 19, 24; 6:8. There is, nevertheless, an umistakable tension set up by the coexistence of life in mortal body and life in Christ—by the fact that the life of the age to come ἐν Χριστῷ has 'already' begun while mortal life ἐν σαρκί has 'not yet' come to an end.

τοῦ υἱοῦ τοῦ θεοῦ. ' "Son" describes the close bond of love between God and Jesus and thus emphasises the greatness of the sacrifice. . . . The Son of God title has for him [Paul] the function of describing the greatness of the saving act of God who offered up the One closest to Him' (E. Schweizer, *TDNT* VIII, 384, *s.v.* υἱός). Here, however, it is the active role of the Son of God that is emphasized: τοῦ ἀγαπήσαντός με καὶ παραδόντος ἑαυτὸν ὑπὲρ ἐμοῦ.

When Paul speaks of divine love to mankind, either God or Christ may be the subject. Compare 1 Thes. 1:4, ἀδελφοὶ ἠγαπημένοι ὑπὸ τοῦ θεοῦ, with 2 Thes. 2:13, ἀδελφοὶ ἠγαπημένοι ὑπὸ κυρίου (where κυρίου in the context is certainly equivalent to Χριστοῦ). In 2 Thes. 2:16 the participial phrase ὁ ἀγαπήσας ἡμᾶς may be attached in grammatical strictness to the nearer nominative [ὁ] θεὸς ὁ πατὴρ ἡμῶν, but in sense it goes with the double nominative ὁ κύριος ἡμῶν Ἰησοῦς Χριστὸς καὶ [ὁ] θεὸς ὁ πατὴρ ἡμῶν. In Rom. 8:37, ὑπερνικῶμεν διὰ τοῦ ἀγαπήσαντος ἡμᾶς, 'the one who has loved us' is not explicitly named, but the preposition διά points to Christ (cf. for similar sense 1 Cor. 15:57, τῷ διδόντι ἡμῖν τὸ νῖκος διὰ τοῦ κυρίου ἡμῶν Ἰησοῦ Χριστοῦ). In Eph. 2:4 God is the subject, in Eph. 5:2, 25 Christ is the subject and in these last two passages we may well discern an echo of the present passage, for ἠγάπησεν is followed by παρέδωκεν ἑαυτόν, with Christ as the subject of both verbs. So ἡ ἀγάπη τοῦ θεοῦ (2 Cor. 13:14) and ἡ ἀγάπη τοῦ Χριστοῦ (Rom. 8:35; 2 Cor. 5:14) can be expressed comprehensively as 'the love of God which is in Christ Jesus our Lord' (Rom. 8:39).

When the death of Christ is described by Paul as his being 'given up' (in accordance with what seems to have been a traditional use of παραδίδωμι in a kerygmatic formula), God may be the subject—whether expressly, as in Rom. 8:32 (ὑπὲρ ἡμῶν πάντων παρέδωκεν αὐτόν), or by implication, as in the passive construction of Rom. 4:25 (ὃς παρεδόθη διὰ τὰ παραπτώματα ἡμῶν)—or, as here, Christ is the subject and the action is reflexive (cf. 1:4 above, with the simple verb: τοῦ δόντος ἑαυτὸν ὑπὲρ τῶν ἁμαρτιῶν ἡμῶν). This use of παραδίδωμι may be based on a Christian interpretation of Is.

52:13–53:12 LXX, where it is said of the Servant that κύριος παρέδωκεν αὐτὸν ταῖς ἁμαρτίαις ἡμῶν (Is. 53:6) and παρεδόθη εἰς θάνατον ἡ ψυχὴ αὐτοῦ (Is. 53:12). It is a point of interest that in the prayer of consecration in the Greek liturgy the verb παρεδίδοτο in the quotation from 1 Cor. 11:23 is amplified by the addition of the reflexive μᾶλλον δὲ ἑαυτὸν παρεδίδου ('in the night in which he was given up, or rather gave himself up . . .').

M. D. Hooker points out that (over against God the Father's initiative in vindicating his Son by raising him from the dead) 'when Paul explores the theme of redemption . . . and the way in which God has dealt with the plight of mankind, . . . Jesus' own role is understood as less passive and more active: he is not only "given up" by God on our behalf (Rom. viii.32) but "gives himself up" for our sakes' ('Interchange and Atonement', *BJRL* 60 [1977–78], 480).

Both in the love and in the 'giving up' which manifested it God and Christ are one: 'God in Christ was reconciling the world to himself' (2 Cor. 5:19); 'God in Christ has forgiven you' (Eph. 4:32).

While Paul is still using the pronoun 'I' / 'me' representatively, it is difficult not to recognize the intense personal feeling in his words: it was a source of unending wonder to him 'that I, even I, have mercy found'. For a comparable expression of personal devotion to Christ cf. Phil. 3:7–14. Charles Wesley tells of the part these words played in his own conversion experience: as he studied Luther's commentary on Galatians, he says, he found special blessing in 'his conclusion of the second chapter. I laboured, waited, and prayed to feel "who loved *me* and gave himself for *me*" ' (*Journal*, I [London, 1849], 90).

'Man is not free in his inner being; when he withdraws from the world and knows that he is placed in the presence of God, he discovers that what he wills is not matched by his ability to do it, and that there is a schism of his personality into two "I's", so that he can experience freedom only as freedom from himself. He achieves it in the surrender of his old "I", and in letting himself be crucified with Christ. Now he lives with Christ, yet no longer as "I", but in such a way that Christ is a new "I" in him' (R. Bultmann, 'Points of Contact and Conflict' [1946], ETr in *Essays Philosophical and Theological* [London, 1955], 141). Or more concisely, with J. Denney: 'The whole of Christian life is a response to the love exhibited in the death of the Son of God for men' (*The Death of Christ* [London, ⁶1907], 151).

2:21 οὐκ ἀθετῶ τὴν χάριν τοῦ θεοῦ, but that is what the Judaizers were doing. Yet Paul is not primarily contrasting himself with them; otherwise he would have said ἐγώ before ἀθετῶ for emphasis. 'Whoever after the coming of Christ pleads the validity of the law, denies the saving significance of the death of Jesus Christ and nullifies God's grace' (H.-J. Schoeps, *Paul*, 193). Perhaps Paul is replying to a charge that his law-free gospel led to a misuse of the grace of God. For there are two ways of nullifying God's grace, or receiving it 'in vain' (εἰς κενόν, 2 Cor. 6:1): one, by receiving it and then going on as though it made no difference by continuing to live 'under law' (cf. 5:4), and the other, by receiving it and then going on as though it made no difference, by continuing to sin 'that grace may abound' (Rom. 6:1). In neither way does Paul nullify the grace of God: he refuses to return to legal bondage but at the same time he repudiates the suggestion that freedom from law means freedom to sin— μὴ γένοιτο (Rom. 6:15)!

εἰ γὰρ διὰ νόμου δικαιοσύνη, ἄρα Χριστὸς δωρεὰν ἀπέθανεν. The death of Christ, according to Paul, was endured to secure his people's justification before God (cf. 3:10–14; Rom. 3:21–26); had the works of the law been sufficient to achieve this end, the death of Christ was superfluous. Paul's argument is based on his firm conviction that Christ did not die in vain; therefore righteousness (here, the righteous status that God bestows on believers) is not attained through law. Paul's negative estimate of the efficacy of law was reached not so much through his experience of living under law as because of the positive 'revelation of Jesus Christ' on the Damascus road (1:12, 16) which unfolded to him the significance of the total Christ-event, especially the death and resurrection (cf. 1:1b, 4).

A similar construction to the present one occurs in 3:21: 'if a law had been given that was able to impart life, then righteousness would indeed be based on law'. For the inferential ἄρα introducing an apodosis after εἰ, cf. v 17 (with note *ad loc.*); 3:29.

Χριστὸς . . . ἀπέθανεν is a foundation fact of the gospel; but whereas the true gospel proclaims the efficacy of Christ's death ὑπὲρ τῶν ἁμαρτιῶν ἡμῶν (cf. 1 Cor. 15:3), this spurious 'gospel' denies that efficacy: if it is accepted, then 'Christ died' not savingly but 'in vain'.

Having thus stated the universal principle in vv 15–21, Paul proceeds in 3:1ff. to apply it to his readers' situation.

(b) The primacy of faith over law (3:1–6)

You foolish Galatians! Who has hypnotized you, after 'Jesus Christ crucified' was placarded before your very eyes? This is all I want you to tell me: was it by legal works that you received the Spirit, or by the message of faith? How can you be so foolish? You began with the Spirit; are you now trying to attain completion by the flesh? Have all your sufferings been to no purpose?—if indeed they are to no purpose. Well then, God supplies you with the Spirit and performs mighty works among you: does he do so by legal works or by the message of faith? (By faith, of course,) just as (in the words of scripture,) 'Abraham believed God, and it was reckoned to him as righteousness.'

TEXTUAL NOTES

v 1 εβασκανεν ℵ A B D* G *pc* lat^{vg} syr^{pesh} / *add* τη αληθεια μη πειθεσθαι (under influence of 5:7) C D² K L P Ψ byz lat$^{vg(cl)}$ syr^{hcl}
προεγραφη / *add* εν υμιν D G byz lat$^{vg(cl)}$ syr^{hcl}

3:1 ὦ ἀνόητοι Γαλάται. For the vocative cf. 2 Cor. 6:11 (Κορίνθιοι); Phil. 4:15 (Φιλιππήσιοι). In these two places the readers are addressed as residents in specific cities; in this letter, which is being sent to churches in several cities, the readers are addressed as residents in a specific province (see p. 16 on the appropriateness or otherwise of calling them Γαλάται). The prefixed ὦ (absent from 2 Cor. 6:11 and Phil. 4:15) expresses emotion (unlike the vocative ὦ in Attic which was quite unemotional); some would therefore accent it ὤ (cf. BDF 146.2).

For the vocative ἀνόητοι cf. Lk. 24:25, where it is applied by the risen Lord to the two disciples on the Emmaus road and coupled with βραδεῖς τῇ καρδίᾳ, 'slow of heart' (i.e. of understanding). In Rom. 1:14 ἀνόητος is the antithesis of σοφός. Paul uses the adjective here and in v 3 to emphasize the illogicality of the Galatians' retrogression.

τίς ὑμᾶς ἐβάσκανεν; βασκαίνω (here only in the NT) means 'fascinate' (from the cognate Lat. *fascino*) or 'bewitch' (originally by means of the evil eye). The other meaning, 'envy' (cf. Dt. 28:56 LXX), is not relevant here. Translate: 'who has hypnotized you?' Their new behaviour was so strange, so completely at odds with the liberating message which they had previously accepted, that it appeared as if someone had put a spell on them. Cf. R. Haughton, *The Liberated Heart* (London, 1975), 100f.

The added clause in AV/KJV, 'that ye should not obey the truth', has intruded into the text here under the influence of 5:7. Jerome remarks (*ad loc*.): 'In certain manuscripts (*in quibusdam codicibus*) it reads: "Who has bewitched you that you should not obey the truth?" But because this is not present in the Greek copies of Adamantius [i.e. Origen], we have omitted it.'

οἷς κατ᾽ ὀφθαλμοὺς ᾽Ιησοῦς Χριστὸς προεγράφη ἐσταυρωμένος. Elsewhere in the NT προγράφω has its ordinary sense 'write in advance'—e.g. in OT prophecy (Rom. 15:4; Jude 4) or in a previous letter or earlier in the same letter (Eph. 3:3). But here the prefix προ- is locative, not temporal: 'display before (one's audience)', as on a public placard—a thoroughly classical usage. Luther ('welchen Jesus Christus vor die Augen gemalt war') and others have thought that the idea is of a verbal picture painted before the hearers' eyes (κατ᾽ ὀφθαλμούς), a vivid description of the crucifixion of Christ; G. Bornkamm (with greater probability) prefers the idea of a notice or proclamation publicly set up, 'a decree promulgated by authority' (*Paul*, 159). Marius Victorinus (*ad loc*.) curiously understands προγράφω in the sense of Lat. *proscribo* ('proscribe'): 'Christ was proscribed, i.e. his property was divided into lots and sold— the property (namely) which he had in us, and which has been put up to auction, sold and dissipated by the persuasive influence of Judaism.'

Evidently in the cities of Galatia, as later in Corinth, Paul was resolved to know nothing 'except Jesus Christ and him crucified' (1 Cor. 2:2). The cross of Christ, with all that it involved, was central to his gospel. Cf. 1 Cor. 1:18, where he calls the gospel 'the word of the cross' (ὁ λόγος τοῦ σταυροῦ), and 15:3, where Christ's death 'for our sins' occupies the primary place in the kerygma which was common to Paul and the Jerusalem apostles. The gospel of Christ crucified, as Paul saw it, so completely ruled out the law as a means of getting right with God that it was scarcely credible that people who had once embraced such a gospel should ever turn to the law for salvation. (One might almost say, 'should ever turn *back* to the law', except that these Gentiles had never been under the law; yet see 4:9, ἐπιστρέφετε πάλιν.)

3:2 τοῦτο μόνον θέλω μαθεῖν ἀφ᾽ ὑμῶν, 'This is the only thing I want to learn from you'. If they conceded this point—and in the light of their experience they could do no other—they had conceded Paul's case: the ground was taken away from the judaizing argument. The question is a feature of Paul's *diatribe* style.

ἐξ ἔργων νόμου τὸ πνεῦμα ἐλάβετε ἢ ἐξ ἀκοῆς πίστεως; 'Was it by works of law or by hearing with faith that you received the Spirit?' Paul assumes that they had received the Spirit—his presence and power were manifested among them by the δυνάμεις of v 5—and that they knew that they had received him when they heard and believed the law-free gospel. Cf. 3:14b, ἵνα τὴν ἐπαγγελίαν τοῦ πνεύματος λάβωμεν διὰ τῆς πίστεως. The statement that Paul does not bring possession of the Spirit into connexion with righteousness by faith (A. Schweitzer, *Mysticism*, 220f.) is unfounded. Justification (2:16) and the gift of the Spirit are alike received not ἐξ ἔργων νόμου but διὰ πίστεως— through one and the same act of faith. The ἀκοὴ πίστεως is hearing the gospel and believing it, or (by metonymy) the gospel itself, which is presented to be heard and believed. Paul's use of this expression for the gospel may be influenced by Is. 53:1 (LXX), τίς ἐπίστευσε τῇ ἀκοῇ ἡμῶν; ('who has believed our message?'), which he quotes in Rom. 10:16 as referring to the gospel and treats as a premise leading to the conclusion: 'So faith comes from what is heard (ἄρα ἡ πίστις ἐξ ἀκοῆς), and what is heard comes by the preaching of Christ' (ἡ δὲ ἀκοὴ διὰ ῥήματος Χριστοῦ).' Cf. 1 Thes. 2:13, παραλαβόντες λόγον ἀκοῆς παρ' ἡμῶν τοῦ θεοῦ, 'when you received the word which you heard (lit. the word of hearing) from us—the word of God.' (See E. P. Sanders, *PPJ*, 482f.)

The use of ἀκοή to denote the content of what is heard, as well as the faculty, organ or act of hearing, is attested in classical and later Greek from Thucydides (*Hist.* 1.20.1) onwards.

It is implied that there could be no higher privilege for mortal men and women than the gift of the Spirit. Since this gift was received through believing the gospel and not through obedience to the law, the superiority and sufficiency of the gospel called for no further demonstration. The Spirit is the guarantee of final salvation; the Spirit is received by faith. Does it not follow that final salvation depends on faith? 'The gift of the Spirit and justification are two sides of the one coin. The blessing of Abraham is equated with the latter in vv. 8f., and with the former in v. 14. Both times the means given is faith' (J. D. G. Dunn, *Baptism in the Holy Spirit* [London, 1970], 108).

3:3 οὕτως ἀνόητοί ἐστε; The question Paul has just asked (v 2), with the conclusion to which it plainly points, justifies the unflattering adjective which he has already applied to his readers: their action is a return from maturity to immaturity.

ἐναρξάμενοι πνεύματι νῦν σαρκὶ ἐπιτελεῖσθε; If they had been asked, like the twelve disciples of Ephesus, 'Did you receive the Holy Spirit when you believed?' (Acts 19:2), their intelligent answer would have been 'Yes!' They began their Christian career in (or with) the Spirit; can they now find it conceivable that the perfection of that career is to be sought on the lower plane of 'flesh'? 'Flesh' here is not simply the body, in which circumcision is carried out, but human nature in its unregenerate weakness, relying on such inadequate resources as were available before the coming of faith, having no access as yet to the power of the Spirit. In Paul's experience as well as in his theology, legal works were a feature of life according to the 'flesh', not according to the Spirit.

The two verbs ἐνάρχομαι and ἐπιτελέω are similarly used of the beginning and completion of the Christian way in Phil. 1:6, 'he who has begun (ἐναρξάμενος) a good work in you will bring it to completion (ἐπιτελέσει) against the day of Jesus Christ.' There, however, the completion is achieved on the same plane as the inception.

The Spirit in Pauline teaching belongs to the foundation of the gospel; his reception does not mark a second and higher stage than justification. Both in John (7:39; 16:7; 20:22) and in Acts (1:8; 2:38) the gift of the Spirit is similarly the sequel and confirmation of Christ's redemptive work.

It is disputed whether the datives πνεύματι . . . σαρκὶ should be taken to indicate manner in which or instrument by which (see discussions in H. Schlier, *Galater*, 123; BDF 198.5). The distinction is more grammatical than substantial.

3:4 τοσαῦτα ἐπάθετε εἰκῆ; When πάσχω is used thus without further definition it may mean more generally 'experience' or more particularly 'suffer'. If the former is meant here, the sense will be, 'Have you experienced such great things (the gift of the Spirit, the ensuing mighty works) to no purpose?' Cf. BAG 639 (*s.v.* πάσχω, 1). If the latter is meant, the sense will be, 'Have you suffered so many things (or, have you endured such great sufferings) to no purpose?' A parallel to the latter sense comes in Acts 9:16, ὅσα δεῖ αὐτὸν ὑπὲρ τοῦ ὀνόματός μου παθεῖν, 'how many things he must suffer (or, how great sufferings he must endure) for my name'.

W. Michaelis (*TDNT* V, 905, *s.v.* πάσχω) argues that πάσχω, when used absolutely, always implies unpleasant suffering, except where the context shows that it is used *sensu bono*. In taking issue with A. Oepke (*Galater*, 68), who argues that it is used here *sensu bono*, Michaelis points out that Oepke's appeal to Josephus, *Ant*. 3.312, is inadmissible, since the context there makes it clear that ὅσα παθόντες ἐξ αὐτοῦ is used *in bonam partem*, of all the benefits which the Israelites had received from God.

What the Galatians had actually suffered is uncertain. There is no reference to their being positively persecuted for the faith, as the Thessalonian Christians were (1 Thes. 2:14; 2 Thes. 1:4f.). But sufferings of any kind endured for the gospel's sake would indeed be pointless (εἰκῆ) if, after all, salvation could be attained by law-keeping. If circumcision and the like could procure justification before God, then persecution for the cross of Christ and the σκάνδαλον attached to it could be by-passed (cf. 4:29; 5:11; 6:12).

Paul's added words, εἴ γε καὶ εἰκῆ ('if indeed it has been to no purpose'), express some hope that the situation is not yet irretrievable; they may yet be regained for the truth of the gospel. Cf. 4:11, φοβοῦμαι ὑμᾶς μή πως εἰκῆ κεκοπίακα εἰς ὑμᾶς ('I am afraid that I have toiled over you to no purpose'); 1 Cor. 15:2, ἐκτὸς εἰ μὴ εἰκῆ ἐπιστεύσατε ('unless indeed you believed to no purpose'), where Paul is rather more sanguine than he is in writing to the Galatians.

3:5 ὁ οὖν ἐπιχορηγῶν ὑμῖν τὸ πνεῦμα καὶ ἐνεργῶν δυνάμεις ἐν ὑμῖν, 'he who supplies the Spirit to you and performs mighty works among you', i.e. God. ἐπιχορηγέω is a Hellenistic compound of χορηγέω, having the general sense of 'supply'; if it is God who here supplies the Spirit, it is equally God who in 2 Cor. 9:10 'supplies (ἐπιχορηγῶν) seed for the sower and bread for food'. In Col. 2:19 the verb is used of the supply of nourishment by Christ as head to his body the church (cf. ἐπιχορηγία in Eph. 4:16). With the present wording cf. Phil. 1:19, διὰ . . . ἐπιχορηγίας τοῦ πνεύματος Ἰησοῦ Χριστοῦ ('through the supply of the Spirit of Jesus Christ'), where, however, τοῦ πνεύματος may not be objective (corresponding to the object τὸ πνεῦμα here) but subjective: 'the help supplied by the Spirit of Jesus Christ'. Jesus' own mighty works during his ministry were performed in the power of the Spirit (cf. Mt. 12:28; Lk. 4:14).

The present participles ἐπιχορηγῶν and ἐνεργῶν probably imply that this divine activity still continues: Paul is not simply referring to something which the Galatians had witnessed once for all when first they believed the gospel. In Galatia, as later in Corinth, 'the signs of an apostle were performed . . . in all patience, with signs and wonders and mighty works (δυνάμεσιν)' (2 Cor. 12:12). Paul would not have appealed to mighty works accomplished by the power of the Spirit and experienced by the Galatians if in fact they had experienced nothing of the kind. That the introduction of the gospel to new territories was regularly accompanied by miraculous healings and other 'signs and wonders' is attested throughout the NT not only in Paul's writings but in Hebrews (2:4) and in Acts (2:43 et passim). Paul knows well enough that miracles in themselves prove nothing (in 2 Thes. 2:9 they are satanically energized phenomena attending the appearance of the 'man of lawlessness', and even in Rom. 15:19, where he describes his own apostolic record, their evidential value is secondary); when he expounds the doctrine of the Spirit along his chosen lines it is the ethical 'fruit of the Spirit' that he emphasizes (cf. 5:22f.). But here he makes an ad hominem appeal to the Galatians' experience: their acceptance of the gospel as Paul preached it was in fact followed by miraculous signs, whereas presumably nothing of that sort accompanied the activity of the agitators.

Here δυνάμεις is used comprehensively of the manifestations of the Spirit's power; in 1 Cor. 12:10, 28f., it is used of one group of such manifestations: some believers receive ἐνεργήματα δυνάμεων while others receive χαρίσματα ἰαμάτων and a variety of other gifts. Even when δυνάμεις constitute one group of manifestations alongside others, they should not be too rigidly demarcated from those others; healings, for example, although separately mentioned, were one form of mighty work. But when the word is used comprehensively, as it is here, it no doubt includes several of the manifestations separately listed in 1 Cor. 12. Even in this wider sense, probably not all the Galatian Christians had been empowered to perform mighty works, but their performance was a feature of their life together, and marked out their churches as communities of the Spirit.

The verb ἐνεργέω, here used of God's performing mighty works among them, was used in 2:8 of his enabling Peter and Paul to discharge their respective apostleships; it is used in 1 Cor. 12:6, 11 (as here) of the divine authorship of spiritual manifestations.

ἐξ ἔργων νόμου ἢ ἐξ ἀκοῆς πίστεως; as in v 2, but here we have to supply ἐπιχορηγεῖ τὸ πνεῦμα καὶ ἐνεργεῖ δυνάμεις (as implied by the participles earlier in the sentence).

For Paul, the antithesis between law and Spirit was as absolute as the antithesis between works and faith; cf. 2 Cor. 3:6b, τὸ γὰρ γράμμα ἀποκτέννει, τὸ δὲ πνεῦμα ζῳοποιεῖ. The presence of the Spirit in power is an unmistakable sign that the new age has dawned (cf. Joel 2:28ff.); its mighty works are δυνάμεις . . . μέλλοντος αἰῶνος (Heb. 6:5); it displaces the law and rules out of court every attempt to achieve righteousness by works which the law prescribes.

It is a natural inference from Paul's rhetorical questions that the 'other gospel' which was being presented to the Galatian Christians took no account of the Spirit. If that is so, it cannot be regarded as a form of gnosticism. Elsewhere (as at Corinth) Paul had to deal with his opponents' claim to be men of the Spirit, a claim which was backed up by appeals to visions, revelations and mighty works (cf. 2 Cor. 11:4; 12:1ff.). But there is no hint that the agitators in Galatia made any such claim. It was as the sequel to Paul's preaching that the Galatian Christians received the Spirit, and Paul's knowledge of this forms the background of his reference to 'those who are spiritual' (οἱ πνευματικοί) in 6:1 and his ethical exhortation: 'If we live by the Spirit, let us also walk by the Spirit' (5:25). Nevertheless, W. Schmithals, in line with his thesis that the agitators (like Paul's opponents elsewhere) were Gnostics, holds that as part of their programme they stressed ecstatic experiences and other spiritual manifestations, but that (in the light of Gal. 3:2) Paul may not have been aware of this (*Paul and the Gnostics*, 46–51, especially 47 n. 98). It is difficult to treat this suggestion seriously. How much Paul did or did not know about the agitators' teaching is debatable, but all that *we* know about it must be derived from this letter, and if there were any gaps in his information, we have no means of filling them in or even of recognizing their existence.

On the other hand, it has been suggested that Paul's own unqualified statements about the primacy of the Spirit over law, taken by themselves as they stand in Galatians, 'can with a great deal of justification be called blatantly Gnostic' (cf. J. W. Drane, *Paul: Libertine or Legalist?*, 112). But a much more apt description than 'blatantly Gnostic'—which, apart from anything else, could be dismissed as anachronistic—would be 'essentially charismatic'. It is Paul above all others who introduced the term χάρισμα to the Christian vocabulary in relation to the ministry of the Spirit, and although it does not occur in Galatians the reality which it conveys is implicit in this verse. That 'charismatic' is far preferable to 'gnostic' as a description of Paul's teaching is evident from the emphasis with which he gives 'knowledge' (γνῶσις) quite an inferior place to 'love' (ἀγάπη), the primary 'fruit of the Spirit' (cf. 5:13f., 22; also 1 Cor. 8:1; 13:8–13).

3:6 καθὼς Ἀβραὰμ ἐπίστευσεν τῷ θεῷ, καὶ ἐλογίσθη αὐτῷ εἰς δικαιοσύνην. Just as God supplies the Spirit and works miracles among them 'by the hearing of faith', so it was by faith that he justified Abraham. The connexion implied in καθὼς would be lost unless there were the closest possible link between receiving the Spirit and being justified. True, Abraham could not be said to have received the Spirit through faith, for he lived in the age of promise, not of fulfilment (see note on v 14). The Galatians, who lived in the age of fulfilment, had received the Spirit as well as a righteous standing before God—alike by faith. Similarly, it was 'by the hearing of faith' and not by legal works that Abraham received a righteous standing before God. When he heard the promise of God, he believed, 'and it was reckoned to him as righteousness'.

Abraham, according to the Genesis narrative, was called by God to leave his homeland in Mesopotamia and journey by divine direction to another land where he and his descendants would receive unsurpassed blessings. In obedience to the call he travelled to Canaan, where he led a nomadic existence for the rest of his life. Shortly after his arrival there, when as yet he was childless, God promised him that his offspring would be more numerous than the stars he could see in the night sky. Nothing could have seemed less likely, yet Abraham believed this incredible promise because of the trustworthiness of him who made it: 'he believed in Yahweh, and he [Yahweh] reckoned it to him as righteousness' (Gn. 15:6).

This is one of Paul's two key-texts for his teaching about justification by faith (cf. Rom. 4:3), the other being Hab. 2:4b (quoted in v 11 below; cf. Rom. 1:17).

In itself, the statement of Gn. 15:6 could mean that Abraham's faith was reckoned as meritorious by God and entered to his credit account, as it is said of Phinehas's act of zeal in Ps. 106 (LXX 105):30f. (cf. Nu. 25:10–12): 'that has been reckoned to him as righteousness (LXX καὶ ἐλογίσθη αὐτῷ εἰς δι-καιοσύνην) from generation to generation for ever.' Cf. W. R. Farmer, 'The Patriarch Phineas', *ATR* 34 (1952), 26–30. (A similar instance is Mattathias's act of zeal in 1 Macc. 2:52.) Philo interprets Abraham's faith as meritorious (*Rer. Div. Her.* 90–95; cf. *Leg. All.* 3.228). It is not certain that Jas. 2:23 does so (cf. B. Lindars, *NT Apologetic*, 225; J. D. G. Dunn, *Unity*, 96, 251). But Paul interprets the text so as to exclude merit, thus showing 'a more careful regard for the context' (B. Lindars, *NT Apologetic*, 225). Cf. Rom. 4:4f., where he says that the reckoning is not κατὰ ὀφείλημα but κατὰ χάριν. See H. W. Heidland, *TDNT* IV, 289–292, *s.v.* λογίζομαι.

(c) The blessing of Abraham (3:7–9)

You must recognize, then, that it is the people of faith who are Abraham's sons. And Scripture, foreseeing that God was to justify the Gentiles on the ground of faith, preached the gospel to Abraham in advance: 'In you all the Gentiles will be blessed.' So then, it is the people of faith who are blessed along with Abraham, the man of faith.

3:7 With his reference to Abraham in v 6, Paul introduces his distinctive understanding of salvation-history. V 6 both concludes one section of his argument and begins a new one: it is connected with what goes before it by καθώς and with what follows by the ἄρα of v 7.

The history of salvation for Paul begins with Abraham, to whom the gospel was preached in advance (v 8), and reaches its climax in Christ. The promise made to Abraham finds its fulfilment in Christ, to whom indeed it primarily referred. But between the promise and the fulfilment there intervened the age of law, introduced parenthetically for the purpose which is stated below in v 19, but lacking any direct or effective relevance to the saving work of God.

There is in some quarters uneasiness over the idea that Paul held and expounded a doctrine of salvation-history. Marcion in the second century felt more than uneasiness over the idea; he totally rejected it. He did not use the terminology of salvation-history, but it was his conviction that the OT (not only the law, but even Abraham) could have nothing to do with the gospel of Jesus that made him expunge vv 6–9 from his text of Gal. 3. A modern expression of uneasiness comes from E. Fuchs, *Studies of the Historical Jesus*, ETr (London, 1964), 175. He cannot agree that in this passage Paul is thinking unequivocally in terms of salvation-history. The new relation 'between Abraham's promise and the largely Gentile heirs of this promise . . . breaks the salvation-history scheme of promise-fulfilment which had previously applied to Israel. For Paul everything now depends not on Israel's history but solely on faith, and this is true not only of the heirs, but even of Abraham himself.' But this is simply to say that Paul no longer held such a doctrine of salvation-history as he might have held in his pre-Christian days. What Paul is expounding here is true salvation-history, but Christian salvation-history, in which the principle of faith is of paramount importance, for Abraham and for his spiritual heirs. The inclusion of these heirs, believing Gentiles, in the promise made to Abraham is essential to salvation-history as Paul understands it.

A more judicious account is given by E. Käsemann, *Perspectives on Paul*, ETr (London, 1971), 60–78: he distinguishes Paul's salvation-history from that spurious outlook sometimes bearing the same designation—that so-called salvation-history with which 'one is always on the safe side' (62)—but insists on the centrality of the factor of faith. Salvation-history 'forms the horizon of Pauline theology' (66), but the horizon must be defined in reference to the centre. Salvation-history is the 'sphere' of justification, but 'justification remains the centre, the beginning and the end of salvation history' (76). See also O. Cullmann, *Salvation in History*, ETr (London, 1967), 45–47, 248–268. See further on 2:15.

In Paul's exposition of salvation-history the Gentiles occupy a special place, as they did in God's promise to Abraham. The promise that in (or rather *with*) Abraham and his offspring all the nations of the earth—i.e. all the Gentiles (πάντα τὰ ἔθνη)—would be blessed was fulfilled in Christ, Abraham's offspring *par excellence*. But for the fulfilment of the promise to be brought home to its Gentile beneficiaries, the Gentile mission was necessary. Here Paul's own role acquires eschatological significance. Paul, as apostle to the Gentiles, has his distinctive place, if not in the fulfilment of God's promise to Abraham, then certainly in the confirmation of that promise to its stated beneficiaries.

When Paul here sets forth the significance of Abraham's faith being reckoned to him as righteousness, he does not use the argument which he develops in Rom. 4:10–12, that Abraham's faith was so reckoned to him while he was as yet uncircumcised. This is not because he had not at this stage thought of the argument of Rom. 4:10–12 (it lies on the surface of the Genesis narrative) but perhaps because it was not likely to have the desired effect on the Gentile Christians of Galatia. They might well have answered that that they were justified by faith while they were uncircumcised, as Abraham was; that they proposed to accept circumcision after being justified by faith, as Abraham did; and that for them, as for Abraham, circumcision would be a seal of the justification by faith which they had received in their uncircumcised state.

The Galatian Christians had apparently been told by the agitators how necessary it was for them to be true sons of Abraham, and therefore to be circumcised, as Abraham was. Circumcision was given by God to Abraham as the sign of his covenant with Abraham and his descendants, who were accordingly to receive this sign: 'Every male among you shall be circumcised. . . . So shall my covenant be in your flesh an everlasting covenant' (Gn. 17:10–13).

Although circumcision was thus instituted, according to the pentateuchal record, many generations before the law was given, it was reaffirmed in the law (Lv. 12:3) and Paul treats it as part of the law. Moreover, it was a seal 'in the flesh' (ἐπὶ τῆς σαρκὸς ὑμῶν) and thus for Paul belonged to the wrong side of the antithesis flesh/spirit (cf. v 1). (Although modern students of Paul's terminology distinguish between his distinctive use of σάρξ and the ordinary use of the term to denote the substance of the body, Paul did not keep them in strictly separate compartments; cf. v 3.) In Paul's eyes, for those who had been justified by faith to be subsequently circumcised would be a perverse attempt to seek perfection in the flesh after 'having begun with the Spirit' (v 3), and his Galatian converts should recognize this. The initial γινώσκετε of v 7 may be either indicative or imperative, but is more probably imperative: since Abraham's faith was reckoned to him as righteousness, let them learn that it is men and women of faith who are Abraham's true children.

It is not circumcision that makes a man a son of Abraham in the sense that matters most, but faith. The antithesis between ἐκ πίστεως (ἐξ ἀκοῆς πίστεως) and ἐξ ἔργων νόμου which is explicit in vv 2, 5, 11, is implied here; and circumcision is an ἔργον νόμου. The Galatians were being urged to become children of Abraham by adoption (since they were not his children by natural birth), and this, they were told, involved circumcision, just as it did for proselytes from paganism to Judaism. Paul maintains that, having believed the gospel and received God's gift of righteousness, they are Abraham's children already, in the only sense that matters in God's sight. Abraham's heritage is the heritage of faith, and those who share this heritage are thereby manifested as sons of Abraham. It is pointless to try to interpret this in terms of the law of inheritance, whether Greek or Roman, as W. M. Ramsay did (*Galatians*, 343); υἱοὶ Ἀβραάμ is an instance of the idiomatic Hebrew use of 'sons' (*bᵉnê*) with a following genitive to denote character.

If Paul uses the masculine υἱοὶ Ἀβραάμ rather than τέκνα Ἀβραάμ (for which cf. 4:28; Rom. 9:7), this is not simply due to the fact that males only were circumcised; rather, υἱοί includes θυγατέρες, as in v 26, where it is obvious from the context that υἱοὶ θεοῦ embraces both men and women.

For οἱ ἐκ πίστεως (those who are characterized by such faith as Abraham showed when he believed God) cf. v 9; also ὁ ἐκ πίστεως Ἀβραάμ, 'he who is characterized by Abraham's faith' (Rom. 4:9). Contrast ὅσοι . . . ἐξ ἔργων νόμου εἰσίν (v 10); οἱ ἐκ νόμου (Rom. 4:14; cf. Rom. 4:16; οἱ ἐκ περιτομῆς (2:12).

3:8 προϊδοῦσα δὲ ἡ γραφὴ κτλ. ἡ γραφή is here practically equivalent to ὁ θεός, as in Rom. 9:17 (cf. B. B. Warfield, *The Inspiration and*

Authority of the Bible [Philadelphia, 1948], 299–348). Scripture records the promise of God, which conveyed to Abraham the good news (προευηγγελίσατο) that all nations would be blessed in his offspring. Paul might well have said προϊδὼν δὲ ὁ θεὸς κτλ and omitted ὁ θεός from the ὅτι clause, but he uses 'the scripture' here more or less as an extension of the divine personality. The written text (γραφή) of Gn. 12:3 or 18:18 is, of course, centuries later than the lifetime of Abraham. But the scripture embodies and perpetuates the promise, so that the good news which was 'preached beforehand' to Abraham is still preached by the scripture to those who read it or hear it read, especially to those living in the age when the promise has been fulfilled. If the promise was good news for Abraham, it is good news also for the nations (Gentiles) who are to be blessed in (or with) him.

ἐκ πίστεως, 'on the ground of [their] faith'—the kind of faith with which Abraham responded to the promise of God. G. Howard (*Crisis*, 57) sees rather a reference to God keeping faith with his promise, which is certainly a factor in Paul's argument, but not primarily in view in ἐκ πίστεως (cf. note on 2:16).

δικαιοῖ τὰ ἔθνη, present tense, because it is God's abiding policy.

Ἐνευλογηθήσονται ἐν σοὶ πάντα τὰ ἔθνη. The quotation conflates Gn. 12:3, where God says to Abraham, εὐλογηθήσονται ἐν σοὶ πᾶσαι αἱ φυλαὶ (Heb. *mišpᵉḥōṯ*) τῆς γῆς, and 18:18, where God says of him, ἐνευλογηθήσονται ἐν αὐτῷ πάντα τὰ ἔθνη (Heb. *gôyê*) τῆς γῆς. The form with ἔθνη (cf. also Gn. 22:18, cited below in v 16) naturally lent itself better than that with φυλαί, 'tribes' (cf. πατριαί, 'families', in the quotation in Acts 3:25), to Paul's present argument: he is concerned with the extension to Gentiles of the principle of righteousness by faith which is attested for Abraham. (For other Pauline conflations of OT texts cf. Rom. 9:33; 11:8, 26f.; 2 Cor. 6:16–18.)

The argument which begins with v 8 may be regarded as a midrashic interpretation of Gn. 12:3 and 18:18 comparable to the interpretation of Gn. 15:6 in Rom. 4:3–25 or that of Ex. 34:29–35 in 2 Cor. 3:7–18 (cf. J. D. G. Dunn, *Unity*, 88). The essence of the midrash is the reinterpretation of the text or texts in the light of the Christ-event. The same may be said of the typological application of the narrative of Isaac and Ishmael in 4:21–31 below.

The Greek passive ἐνευλογηθήσονται is unambiguous: in (with) Abraham all the nations *will be blessed*. But in Gn. 12:3 and 18:18 (cf. 28:14) the LXX passive renders the Heb. niph'al *(nibrᵉḵû)*, which may have reflexive force (so Gn. 18:18 RSV: 'all the nations of the earth shall bless themselves by him'), like the hithpael *(hiṯbārᵉḵû)* of Gn. 22:18 and 26:4b. The reflexive interpretation means that Abraham will become proverbial for divine blessing and prosperity, so that in days to come men and women everywhere, wishing to call down the greatest prosperity on themselves, will say, 'May I be as blessed as Abraham was!' But the use of the niph'al *nibrᵉḵû* 'is usually taken in a passive sense. J. Schreiner, "Segen für die Völker in der Verheissung an die Väter", *BZ* 6 (1962), p. 7, endeavours to bring out the distinctive sense of the niph'al by translating "acquire blessing for themselves" ' ['(für) sich Segen erwerben, sich Segen verschaffen'] (R. E. Clements, *Abraham and David* [London, 1967], 15 n. 3).

Even so, that others will receive divine blessing through Abraham is expressly stated in Gn. 12:3a, 'I will bless those who bless you' (cf. Nu. 24:9); and with the reference to all the tribes or nations of the earth 'something like the note of universalism is already struck in these words' (C. R. North, *The OT Interpretation of History* [London, 1946], 26). The LXX translators understood the verbal form (and even that in Gn. 22:18 and 26:4b; cf. note on v 16 below) to have passive force, and accordingly used the passive voice in their Greek rendering; it is the sense which they gave it that Paul sees fulfilled in his Gentile mission.

3:9 ὥστε οἱ ἐκ πίστεως εὐλογοῦνται σὺν τῷ πιστῷ ᾿Αβραάμ, 'so it is they who are marked by belief [in God] that are blessed with believing Abraham'. οἱ ἐκ πίστεως is used as in v 7. Men and women of faith are not only sons and daughters of Abraham but have a share in the blessing promised to him. In using the preposition σύν, Paul conveys the precise force of Heb. *bᵉ*, translated ἐν in the LXX in Gn. 12:3 and 18:18, 'Not "in thee . . ." but "with thee" (or "by means of thee") "shall all families of the earth bless themselves" is the correct translation' (C. G. Montefiore, *The OT and After* [London, 1923], 85). The Gentiles who are to be blessed with Abraham, says Paul, are those who like him believe God; the blessing they receive is the blessing he received—in the first instance, justification. In the present context the adjective πιστός applied to Abraham means not 'faithful' (AV, RV) or 'trustworthy' (as in Sir. 44:20, ἐν πειρασμῷ εὑρέθη πιστός, rendering Heb. *ûḇᵉnissûy nimṣā' ne'ᵉmān*, 'and in testing he was found faithful'), but 'believing' (cf. RSV: 'Abraham who had faith').

(d) The curse of the law (3:10–14)

All those who are (seeking justification) by legal works are under a curse, for it is written: 'Cursed is every one who does not persevere in all the things that are written in the book of the law, to do them.' Clearly no one is justified in God's sight by law because (as scripture says) 'it is the one who is righteous by faith *that will find life.' But the law is not (based) on faith; rather (as scripture says again), 'he who has* done *them will find life therein.' Christ has redeemed us from the curse of the law by becoming a curse on our behalf—because it is written: 'Cursed is every one who is hanged on a gibbet'—in order that the blessing of Abraham might come to the Gentiles in Christ Jesus, in order that we might receive the promise of the Spirit through faith.*

TEXTUAL NOTES

v 14 επαγγελιαν ℵ A B C D² Ψ byz lat^{pl} syr cop arm Orig Ambst Hier Aug / ευλογιαν P⁴⁶ D* G *pc* lat^b Mcion Ambst Eph Vig

3:10 ὅσοι γὰρ ἐξ ἔργων νόμου εἰσίν. The threefold occurrence of ἐξ ἔργων νόμου in 2:16 implies that the reference here is to those who rely on the law, or on their performance of the law, for their acceptance with God. Cf. C. E. B. Cranfield's expansion: 'as many as are legalists, refusing to accept the righteous status God has made available in Christ and insisting on thinking that they can earn their own righteous status by their fulfilment of the law's demands' (*Romans*, 848).

R. Bring (*Galatians*, 120–125) understands by ἔργα νόμου here the Jewish misinterpretation of the law, as though Paul meant, 'Cursed is every one who transgresses the law by trying to keep it legalistically, for Dt. 27:26 says . . .'. But this puts an improbable strain on Paul's language. An even greater strain is involved in D. P. Fuller's interpretation: the person who strives to attain a righteous status by legal works is in effect trying to bribe God and so contravening the spirit of Dt. 10:17 and 27:25 (where bribery is forbidden)—thereby incurring the curse pronounced on the law-breaker ('Paul and the Works of the Law', *WTJ* 38 [1975–76], 28–42, especially 32).

ὑπὸ κατάραν εἰσίν· γέγραπται γὰρ κτλ. The following quotation comes from Dt. 27:26, which concludes the 'Shechemite dodecalogue'—the twelve curses pronounced by Levites standing on Mount Ebal, to each of which the people responded with 'Amen'. The LXX adds emphasis to the MT by inserting πᾶς after ἐπικατάρατος and πᾶσιν after ὃς οὐκ ἐμμένει. It may be that the curses (with the corresponding blessings recited on Mount Gerizim, Dt. 28:1–6) were not pronounced once and for all, but were repeated periodically as part of a covenant-renewal ceremony. An elaborated form was repeated on solemn occasions by the covenant-community of Qumran (1QS 2:1–18).

The whole dodecalogue, A. Alt points out, 'is concerned with crimes committed in secret, in the hope that they would never appear before a human court' ('The Origins of Israelite Law' [1934], ETr in *Essays on OT History and Religion* [Oxford, 1966], 115). Therefore no specific penalty is prescribed for each offence mentioned, but Yahweh is called upon in effect to execute his curse on the wrongdoer. By their 'Amen' the people as a whole dissociate themselves from such evil actions and those who practise them; the curse thus involves exclusion from the covenant-community (cf. Ex. 12:15, 19; 30:33, etc., for those ritual offences whose perpetrator will be 'cut off from Israel' or 'from his people').

While the first eleven curses of the dodecalogue invoke a ban on specific acts of religious or social misdemeanour, the twelfth is more comprehensive, and (especially in its more emphatic LXX wording) lends itself readily to Paul's argument. But in addition to taking over the twofold 'all' added by the LXX, Paul replaces πᾶσιν τοῖς λόγοις τοῦ νόμου τούτου (LXX) by the equally deuteronomic πᾶσιν τοῖς γεγραμμένοις ἐν τῷ βιβλίῳ τοῦ νόμου. In the LXX, as in the MT, the curse is pronounced on the person who 'does not confirm (Heb. *yāqîm*, 'uphold') the words of *this law* by doing them'. But in Paul's version of the text the denunciation is generalized: it is not 'this law' (the dodecalogue) that he has in mind, but the written Torah (cf. Dt. 31:26; Jos. 1:8) in all its details.

M. Noth observes that the context of the dodecalogue speaks of blessing for the law-keeper as well as cursing for the law-breaker, but argues that Paul does not misrepresent the original intention of the passage. On the basis of the Deuteronomic (Dt. 12–26) and Holiness (Lv. 17–26) codes alike, 'there is no place for the idea of good, meritorious works and a reward which may be earned thereby; the blessing is not earned, but freely promised. On the basis of this law there is only one possibility for man of having his own independent activity: that is transgression, defection, followed by curse and judgment. And so, indeed, "all those who rely on the works of the law are under a curse" ' (*The Laws in the Pentateuch and Other Studies*, ETr [Edinburgh, 1966], 131).

Philo (*Praem*. 79–126, 127–172) allegorizes both the blessings and the curses. At a later date, the rabbis of the Amoraic period emphasize the verb *yāqîm* ('confirm', 'uphold') in Dt. 27:26 as requiring that one should maintain the divine authority of the law and protest against transgressions of it, not that one should achieve perfection (cf. E. P. Sanders, *PPJ*, 137). Paul himself may have the same verb in mind in Rom. 3:31, where he says that by receiving justification by faith we do not nullify the law but 'uphold' it (νόμον ἱστάνομεν).

Here, however, he is concerned to stress the unfulfillable character of the law: by the standard of the law every one is 'under a curse' because no one is able to keep it in its entirety.

But one may inquire more particularly: why is the curse incurred by all who rely on legal works for justification? Is it simply (i) because no one keeps *everything* prescribed by the law, so that, by reason of however limited a failure to attain full marks, every one becomes liable to the curse (cf. 5:3)? Or is it (ii) because the curse falls on every one who seeks justification by the law, even if he does attain full marks?

(i) In the former case, Paul may be saying that a failure to keep one point of the law is a failure to keep the law *as such* (cf. Jas. 2:10), and therefore incurs the curse invoked on the law-breaker. This is a view popularly ascribed to the school of Shammai, which is said to have reckoned a 99 percent achievement as a failure whereas the school of Hillel in effect treated 51 percent as a pass-mark, carrying entitlement to enter the world to come; cf. C. G. Montefiore and H. Loewe, *A Rabbinic Anthology* (London, 1938), 594–597, 664 n. 33.

If indeed Paul expresses a Shammaite interpretation here, that would put in question the common assumption that he was, like his teacher Gamaliel, a Hillelite. It is true that later tradition makes Gamaliel the successor (either immediately, or at one remove) to Hillel as head of his school, if not indeed Hillel's son or grandson. But the earlier traditions which reflect some direct memory of Gamaliel and his teaching do not associate him with the school of Hillel (cf. J. Neusner, *The Rabbinic Traditions about the Pharisees before 70*, I [Leiden, 1971], 341–376).

Paul's Hillelite affinities (maintained by J. Jeremias, 'Paulus als Hillelit', *Black FS* [1], 88–94) have been denied by K. Haacker ('War Paulus Hillelit?', *Das Institutum Judaicum der Universität Tübingen* [1971–72], 106–120; 'Die Berufung des Verfolgers und die Rechtfertigung des Gottlosen', *Theologische Beiträge* 6 [1975], 1–19) and H. Hübner ('Gal 3, 10 und die Herkunft des Paulus', *KD* 19 [1973], 215–231; *Das Gesetz bei Paulus*, 16–43 and especially 135f. n. 16).

E. P. Sanders, on the other hand, does not believe that Paul provides enough evidence to show whether before his conversion he had been a Shammaite or a Hillelite, if either; he maintains, moreover, that neither the statements insisting on total law-keeping nor those which hold out hope if the merits outweigh the demerits amount to a 'systematic soteriology' (*PPJ*, 138 n. 61; 'Fulfilling the Law in Paul and Rabbinic Judaism', *Daube FS*, 126 addendum). The whole 'weighing' interpretation of rabbinic theology, according to Sanders, is misguided, no matter to which school it is ascribed. The rabbis of our period assumed that all who were within the covenant would attain salvation—have a portion in the world to come—except those whose impenitent wickedness or apostasy put them effectively outside the covenant. Within the covenant repentance could always atone for breaches of the law. This 'covenant nomism', as Sanders calls it, was common ground to the rival rabbinic schools and did not constitute a matter for disagreement; hence it is more often presupposed than asserted in their debates (*PPJ, passim*; cf. also his 'Patterns of Religion in Paul and Rabbinic Judaism: A Holistic Method of Comparison', *HTR* 66 [1973], 455–478).

The limited part that repentance plays in Paul's soteriology suggests that he approached the whole question with different presuppositions from those of the rabbis. Cf. M. E. Andrews, 'Paul and Repentance', *JBL* 54 (1935), 125: 'When he [Paul] made possession of the Spirit the *sine qua non* of salvation as well as of a worthy ethical life, repentance was excluded by the simple expedient of being replaced by something more effective.' See also J. Knox, *Chapters*, 142–145.

(ii) But does Paul mean that even for one who does persevere in doing all things written in the book of the law justification is not thereby assured? It appears that he does. Here pre-eminently, as in his other deviations from the pattern of rabbinic theology, Paul's thinking is dominated by the logic of his conversion experience. In the attempt to establish his own righteousness (Rom. 10:3) Paul's achievement was greater than that of many: 'as regards the righteousness which rests in the law', he says, 'I was blameless' (Phil. 3:6). Yet it was not on this ground that he was justified before God, but because of the righteousness which is granted 'through faith in Christ, the righteousness from God on the ground of faith' (Phil. 3:9).

It might well seem to follow from the language of Dt. 27:26 that every one who does persevere in doing all that the law prescribes is immune from the curse pronounced on the law-breaker. This indeed is implied in Lv. 18:5 ('the one who does them will find life thereby'), which Paul quotes below in v 12. But he quotes it only to set it aside in favour of the principle of faith (as contrasted with works) laid down in Hab. 2:4b, 'it is the one who is righteous by faith (not the one who perseveres in doing the whole law) that will find life.' 'Having argued in 3:10 that one who seeks justification by works of law will be cursed, obviously because he cannot keep the law perfectly, Paul then argues (3:11, 12) that one cannot in any case be justified by works of law. It is by definition impossible' (E. P. Sanders, 'Fulfilling the Law . . .', 106).

Paul's confrontation with the risen Christ on the Damascus road after his grounding in Judaism, and the new understanding of salvation-history which sprang from that confrontation, compelled him to see the legal path to salvation closed by a barrier (which he would not have refused to identify with the cross) which carried a notice reading: 'No road this way.'

There was, indeed, provision made in the law itself for those who failed to keep it—for those, at any rate, whose failure was inadvertent and not deliberate. Why does Paul make no reference to the sin-offering, or to the day of atonement?

One reason may be that the sacrificial ritual had not been mentioned by the agitators. Even they knew that this part of the law at least had been rendered obsolete by the death of Christ. 'Those who looked upon this death as a sacrifice soon ceased to offer to God any blood-sacrifice at all' (A. Harnack, *What is Christianity?* ETr [London, 1904], 159). Long before the writer to the Hebrews spelt out the rationale of this in detail, the principle was accepted by the disciples of Jesus as a matter of course. The Galatians evidently had no thought of meeting Paul's argument here with the objection that the law made sacrificial provision for the removal of the curse. And if they had done so, Paul would have replied that, if the law as such was ineffectual for setting men and women right with God, the sacrificial ritual was *ipso facto* ineffectual. It had, in any case, been superseded by a provision which was supremely effectual. Christ had been set forth by God as a *hilastērion*, to be received by faith; he had been sent 'in the likeness of sinful flesh and as an offering for sin', so that the ethical fruit which the law could not produce might be manifested in the lives of those 'who walk not according to the flesh but according to the Spirit' (Rom. 3:25; 8:3f.).

3:11 ὅτι δὲ ἐν νόμῳ οὐδεὶς δικαιοῦται παρὰ τῷ θεῷ δῆλον. Cf. 2:16 for a repeated affirmation of the same principle, supported by the quotation of Ps. 143 (LXX 142):2. To the fuller phrase ἐξ ἔργων νόμου there the more concise ἐν νόμῳ corresponds here: after ἐξ ἔργων νόμου in v 10 ἐν νόμῳ suffices to express the same idea (cf. Phil. 3:6, δικαιοσύνην τὴν ἐν νόμῳ); see D. P. Fuller, 'Paul and "the Works of the Law" ', 40.

How is one justified in the sight of God? Paul has answered this question by pointing to the experience of Abraham (v 6). It might be argued, however, that Abraham's was a special case; hence Paul cites the statement of justification by faith as a permanent principle in Hab. 2:4b, which in the present context (cf. Rom. 1:17) must be given the sense: 'It is the one that is righteous (justified) by faith [not by law] that will live (find life).' If life is assured to those who are justified by faith, then it is not assured to those who seek justification by law-keeping, whether they succeed in keeping the law or not.

In the original setting of this oracle, Habakkuk cries on God to intervene and punish the oppression that he sees around him. The tyranny of the native rulers of Judah has been checked by the Babylonian invaders, the executors of divine judgment, but the invaders have proved more oppressive by far. Are they 'to keep on . . . mercilessly slaying nations for ever?' (Hab. 1:17). The prophet waits patiently for a response to his complaint, and at last it comes. 'The mills of God grind slowly, but they grind exceeding small': the vindication for which he longs will indeed be realized, 'it will surely come, it will not delay' (Hab. 2:3). Let the righteous man wait in faith for this consummation; by his faith he will preserve his life (Heb. *ṣaddîq be'emûnāṯô yiḥyeh*); cf. Jesus' words to his disciples in Lk. 21:18 for very much the same assurance: 'By your endurance you will gain your lives.'

In the LXX it is not simply for the fulfilment of his vision and the vindication of divine justice that the prophet waits but for the coming of God: 'he will surely come, he will not delay' (ἐρχόμενος ἥξει καὶ οὐ μὴ χρονίσῃ). Heb. *'emûnāṯô*, 'his faith(fulness)', has been read with a different pronominal suffix: *'emûnāṯî*, 'my faith(fulness)': 'the righteous one will live by my faithfulness' (or 'by faith in me'), ὁ δὲ δίκαιος ἐκ πίστεώς μου ζήσεται (B). The 'C' group of LXX witnesses has μου before (not after) ἐκ πίστεως, which might yield the same sense (with somewhat greater emphasis on the pronoun) or (if μου be construed with ὁ δίκαιος) might mean 'my righteous one will live by faith(fulness)'. This latter form is quoted in Heb. 10:38a as an encouragement to persevere in believing hope and not lose heart because the parousia is delayed: 'The coming one (ὁ ἐρχόμενος, instead of the anarthrous LXX ἐρχόμενος) will come and will not delay' (Heb. 10:37, quoting Hab. 2:3b).

It may be that Hab. 2:3f. was current in primitive Christian times as a *testimonium* to the certainty of Christ's coming, and that this primitive currency is reflected independently in Paul and in Heb. 10:37f. C. H. Dodd (*According to the Scriptures* [London, 1952], 50f.) thought it likely that the currency of the *testimonium* antedated Paul's writing to the Galatians, because Paul's argument here is very much *ad hominem*, and would be the more effective if it was already common ground between him and his opponents that, when the coming one came, the righteous would live by faith.

In the Qumran literature the Hebrew text of Hab. 2:4b is applied to 'all the doers of the law in the house of Judah, whom God will save from the place of judgment because of their toil (*'āmāl*) and their faith in (or 'loyalty to') the Teacher of Righteousness' (1QpHab 8:1–3). The Teacher of Righteousness was not only a spiritual leader but a figure of eschatological significance. Acceptance of his teaching, or loyally keeping to the path which he marked out for his followers, was the way to eternal life.

Paul omits the possessive pronoun from his quotation altogether, although it would have made little difference to his argument had he included it: ἐκ πίστεώς μου (or μου ἐκ πίστεως) would have meant 'by faith in me (God)', while ἐκ πίστεως αὐτοῦ (had he translated *be'emûnāṭô* literally) would have meant 'by his faith (in me)'. The faith by which one becomes righteous in God's sight is faith in God, believing acceptance of his promise, such as Abraham showed.

Righteousness by faith is for Paul so closely bound up with true life that the two terms—'righteousness' and 'life'—can in practice be used interchangeably (cf. v 21b).

3:12 If Ps. 143 (LXX 142):2 (especially as glossed by Paul) shows how one is *not* justified before God (by law), Hab. 2:4b shows how one *is* justified (by faith). Law and faith, for Paul, are unrelated: the gospel calls for faith, but law requires works. 'The law is not based on faith' (ὁ δὲ νόμος οὐκ ἔστιν ἐκ πίστεως); any blessing associated with it lies in obedience to its precepts, as is plain from Lv. 18:5, quoted by Paul in the form ὁ ποιήσας αὐτὰ ζήσεται ἐν αὐτοῖς (cf. the LXX: ἃ ποιήσας ἄνθρωπος ζήσεται ἐν αὐτοῖς). Paul's αὐτά, like the LXX ἅ, refers to προστάγματα . . . καὶ . . . κρίματα ('ordinances and judgments') of the preceding clause in Lv. 18:5, but for readers of this letter it would rather recall τοῦ ποιῆσαι αὐτά ('to do them', i.e. 'all things written in the book of the law') at the end of v 10 above. (Cf. Ezk. 20:13, ἃ ποιήσει αὐτὰ ἄνθρωπος καὶ ζήσεται ἐν αὐτοῖς, quoting Lv. 18:5.) Since the law is not ἐκ πίστεως, whereas justification is only ἐκ πίστεως (v 11), therefore justification cannot come by the law.

G. Howard, taking πίστις in the sense of 'faithfulness' (see note on 2:16), interprets the first clause of v 12 to mean that the law, which required perfect fulfilment by mankind, could never be the means of fulfilling God's promise to

Abraham; the promise could be fulfilled only by God's faithfulness in extending his blessing to the Gentiles (*Crisis*, 63f.).

There are two other NT references to Lv. 18:5. In Lk. 10:28 Jesus replies to the lawyer who had correctly recited the two great commandments with the words, 'You have answered right; do this, and you will live (τοῦτο ποίει καὶ ζήσῃ)'—the lawyer's immediate attempt to justify himself shows that he realized that this was not so easy as it sounded. More relevantly to our present passage, in Rom. 10:5 Paul sets out the way of justification by the law in terms of Lv. 18:5 (Μωϋσῆς γὰρ γράφει τὴν δικαιοσύνην τὴν ἐκ [τοῦ] νόμου ὅτι ὁ ποιήσας αὐτὰ ἄνθρωπος ζήσεται ἐν αὐτοῖς). He then proceeds (Rom. 10:6–10) to set out the way of justification by faith in terms of a *pesher* on Dt. 30:12–14, carefully omitting αὐτὸ ποιεῖν from the end of his quotation (cf. Bruce, *Romans*, 203f.).

K. Barth has maintained (*CD* II/2, ETr [Edinburgh, 1957], 245) that in Rom. 10:5 ὁ ποιήσας ἄνθρωπος (Lv. 18:5) is Jesus. He is followed in this by C. E. B. Cranfield, who takes the reference to be to 'the one Man who has done the righteousness of the Law in His life and, above all, in His death, in the sense of fulfilling the law's requirements perfectly and so earning as His right a righteous status before God' (*Romans*, 521). Cranfield admits that Gal. 3:12 'might, at first sight, seem to tell against this interpretation', but holds (again with Barth) that here too Paul has Christ's perfect obedience in mind in quoting Lv. 18:5, 'for otherwise a step in the argument is missing'—Christ's becoming accursed for us would have no redemptive power apart from his perfect obedience (*Romans*, 522 n. 2).

This understanding of the personal righteousness of Christ and its relation to the righteousness which he has procured for believers is perfectly in keeping with Paul's thought, but it cannot, strictly speaking, be regarded as the straight exegesis of Gal. 3:12, nor even of Rom. 10:5.

D. P. Fuller ('Paul and "The Works of the Law" ', 41) sees a distinction between the use of Lv. 18:5 here and its use in Rom. 10:5, because in Rom. 10:5 Paul cites Moses as authority for the law, whereas 'the meaning which he intends these words to convey in Galatians 3:12 is not the meaning that Moses himself intended'. Granted that Paul interprets Lv. 18:5 here in the sense of justification by legal works, it is difficult to see that he interprets it at all otherwise in Rom. 10:5. True, in the context of Lv. 18:5 the promise of life to those who do what God commands is a genuine promise, but in Rom. 10:5 as well as in Gal. 3:12 Paul indicates that, with the coming of the gospel, that way to life has now been closed, even if once it was open—and it is doubtful if he would concede even that (his Damascus-road experience had shown him the incompetence of the way of law-keeping and the power of the way of faith). Vv 10–12 'provide a crushing refutation of the Galatians who wanted to accept circumcision. Not only would they obligate themselves to obey a law which they could not fulfil, thus falling under its curse, but following that law is in any case a way that cannot lead to salvation' (E. P. Sanders, 'Fulfilling the Law . . .', 106).

In his quotation of Lv. 18:5, as in his quotation of Hab. 2:4b, Paul understands 'life' practically in the sense of 'justification'.

3:13 Χριστὸς ἡμᾶς ἐξηγόρασεν ἐκ τῆς κατάρας τοῦ νόμου. The 'curse of the law' is the curse pronounced on the law-breaker in Dt. 27:26, quoted in v 10 above. From this curse Christ has redeemed his people, says Paul, by becoming a curse on their behalf (γενόμενος ὑπὲρ ἡμῶν κατάρα). But how? To be born under law, as he was (4:4), involves no curse, if one keeps the law. And this Christ did, according to Paul (cf. 2 Cor. 5:21, τὸν μὴ γνόντα ἁμαρτίαν). By his lifelong obedience (cf. Rom. 5:19) he remained immune from the curse of the law, yet the circumstances of his death brought him unavoidably under that curse. The text which Paul quotes to this effect had reference originally to the exposure of the corpse of an executed criminal: 'if a man has committed a crime punishable by death, and you hang him on a tree [pole], his body shall not remain all night upon the tree [pole], but you shall bury him the same day, for a hanged man is accursed by God; you shall not defile your land which Yahweh your God gives you for an inheritance' (Dt. 21:22f.).

The exposure of a criminal's corpse on a tree or pole, then, was not to be prolonged beyond sundown: such continued exposure was an affront not only to human decency but to God himself (Heb. qilᵉlaṭ 'ᵉlōhîm could mean 'affront to God' rather than 'accursed by God', although the LXX chooses the latter rendering). An early instance of this is recorded in Jos. 10:26f.: when Joshua captured the Canaanite kings who were defeated in the battle of Beth-horon, he 'put them to death, and he hung them on five trees. And they hung upon the trees until evening; but at the time of the going down of the sun, Joshua commanded, and they took them down from the trees, and threw them into the cave where they had hidden themselves, and they set great stones against the mouth of the cave' (cf. the treatment of the king of Ai in Jos. 8:29). So, in the Johannine passion narrative, the bodies of Jesus and the two robbers who were crucified with him were removed from their crosses before sundown, at the instance of the Jewish authorities, who were specially concerned that the sanctity of the ensuing sabbath should not be violated (Jn. 19:31; cf. Mk. 15:42f.).

Another OT instance of the hanging up of the corpses of criminals may be relevant for Paul's argument. In the apostasy of Baal-peor the wrath of Yahweh, manifested in the outbreak of plague, was averted from Israel when the chiefs of the people were hanged (παραδειγματίζω) 'in the sun' before him (Nu. 25:4). The LXX verb implies not only public exposure but also the making of a public example, to effect atonement for covenant-violation. Cf. 2 Sa. (LXX 2 Ki.) 21:6, where seven sons of Saul were similarly hanged up (LXX ἐξηλιάζω) before Yahweh (whose displeasure on this occasion had been manifested by a famine). The curse of Dt. 27:26 was pronounced at the end of a covenant-renewal ceremony and had special reference therefore to the covenant-breaker. Christ accordingly underwent the penalty prescribed for the covenant-breaker.

It is a matter of coincidence, no doubt, that in Heb. 6:6 the verb παραδειγματίζω is used of the crucifying (or re-crucifying, ἀνασταυροῦντας) of Christ, but the collocation of the two ideas there provides sufficient evidence that crucifixion ranked as one form of παραδειγματίζειν. The Palestinian Targum on Nu. 25:4f. links that passage with Dt. 21:23 by inserting an explicit reference to the 'wood' on which the chiefs of the people were hanged and by stipulating that their bodies should be taken down and buried 'at the departure of the sun' (cf. A. T. Hanson, Studies, 6).

When Philo (Spec. Leg. 3.152) discusses Dt. 21:22f., he replaces κρεμάννυμι by ἀνασκολοπίζω, 'impale', 'crucify'. Elsewhere (*Post. C.* 61; *Som.* 2.213) he associates ἀνασκολοπίζω with 'nailing up' (προσηλόω), indicating that he has crucifixion in mind rather than impalement. Crucifixion is manifestly implied in Gal. 3:13 and the places in Acts (5:30; 10:39) where Jesus is spoken of as κρεμάμενος ἐπὶ ξύλου (cf. προσπήξαντες, Acts 2:23), since the reference is to the historical crucifixion of Jesus.

The hanging (impalement, crucifixion) of *living* men was not a traditional Jewish mode of execution, though it was common among the surrounding nations (cf. Ezr. 6:11; Est. 5:14; 7:10; 1 Macc. 1:61). When the Nahum commentary from Qumran refers to Alexander Jannaeus's crucifixion of his captured enemies, it expresses abhorrence at his 'hanging them alive, which was never done in Israel' (4QpNa 1:7f.). But whether it was a corpse or a living person that was hanged, the principle of Dt. 21:22f. was equally applicable in Jewish law. This is spelt out in 11Q Temple Scroll 64:6–13, where regulations are formulated for hanging a man 'on a tree, that he may die', as well as for hanging an executed man 'on a tree', and both forms of hanging are related to Dt. 21:22f. (where *qilᵉlaṭ 'ᵉlōhîm*, 'a curse of God', is expanded to *mᵉqulᵉlê 'ᵉlōhîm wa'ᵃnāšîm*, 'accursed by God and men'). One type of criminal who is to be hanged 'on a tree, that he may die', is he who has wronged his people by informing against them and delivering them up to a foreign power; another is he who 'has cursed (*qālal*) his people and the children of Israel'.

See the discussions by Y. Yadin, 'Pesher Nahum (4QpNahum) Reconsidered', *IEJ* 21 (1971), 1–12; J. A. Fitzmyer, 'Crucifixion in Ancient Palestine, Qumran Literature, and the NT', *CBQ* 40 (1978), 493–513 (especially 498–507, 510–512).

As Paul quotes Dt. 21:23, it shares a common term with Dt. 27:26 (quoted in v 10), and thus provides an instance of the exegetical principle known to the rabbis as *gezerah shawah* ('equal category'). Where two texts share a common term in this way, each may throw light on the other (cf. the common term ζήσεται in Hab. 2:4b and Lv. 18:5, quoted in vv 11f.). Paul's present use of *gezerah shawah* is based on the Greek version; there is no term common to the two texts in Hebrew. Whereas Dt. 21:23 MT says that a hanged man is *qilᵉlaṭ 'ᵉlōhîm* (lit. 'a curse of God'), Dt. 27:26 MT calls the law-breaker *'ārûr* ('cursed'). The LXX, however, uses a form of the verb (ἐπι)καταράομαι in both places—the perfect participle passive κεκατηραμένος in Dt. 21:23 and the verbal adjective ἐπικατάρατος in Dt. 27:26. (Yet Paul shows that he knew the Hebrew text of Dt. 21:23, for in his exposition he uses the noun κατάρα, corresponding to Heb. *qᵉlālāh*.)

Paul probably uses ἐπικατάρατος (in preference to the LXX κεκατηραμένος) when quoting Dt. 21:23 here by way of assimilation to his quotation of Dt. 27:26 in v 10 (cf. M. Wilcox, ' "Upon the Tree"—Deut. 21:22–23 in the NT', *JBL* 96 [1977], 85–99, especially 87). He omits 'by God' after ἐπικατάρατος in v 13 (contrast the LXX κεκατηραμένος ὑπὸ θεοῦ—probably not (as has been suggested) to avoid an unseemly collocation of the divine name with the idea of cursing but to avoid the implication that Christ in his death was cursed *by God*. This implication would conflict with Paul's conviction that Christ's enduring the cross was his supreme act of obedience to God (cf. Rom. 5:19) and that 'in Christ God was reconciling the world to himself' (2 Cor. 5:19). Paul leaves the question, 'By whom was Christ cursed?' unanswered; what he does make plain is that the curse which Christ 'became' was his people's curse, as the death which he died was their death. Death 'is the experience in which the final repulsion of evil by God is decisively expressed; and Christ died. In His death everything was made His that sin had made ours—everything in sin except its sinfulness' (J. Denney, *The Death of Christ*, 160). So in 2 Cor. 5:21 Paul speaks of Christ as having been 'made sin for us'—'that is, he came to stand in that relation with God which normally is the result of sin, estranged from God and the object of his wrath' (C. K. Barrett, *2 Corinthians*, 180).

Whereas in Dt. 21:23 the MT leaves *tālûy* ('hanged') unqualified, the LXX (followed by Paul) adds ἐπὶ ξύλου (reproduced from Dt. 21:22); cf. the quotation in 11Q Temple Scroll 64:12, *tālûy 'al hā'ēṣ* ('hanged on the tree').

According to H.-J. Schoeps (*Paul*, 179f.), following G. Klein, *Studien über Paulus* (Stockholm, 1918), 62–67, Paul resolves the problem presented by Christ's crucifixion by playing on the double meaning of the Hebrew participle *tālûy*—on the one hand, 'hanged', on the other hand, 'lifted up', 'exalted' (cf. the ambivalence of ὑψόω in John, also the double sense of 'lift up your head' in Gn. 40:13, 19)—and thus showing how the curse was transformed into a blessing. There is nothing in the context to warrant this interpretation; it would, indeed, involve the absurd sense: 'An exalted one is accursed by God.'

It is not improbable that the argument of vv 10–13 was worked out in Paul's mind at the beginning of his Christian career. The root of his hostility to the followers of Jesus is not easy to uncover: their general position appeared to him to be a threat to the law of God, but especially, perhaps, their insistence that the crucified one was the Messiah of Israel. Since the Messiah, almost by definition, enjoyed the unique blessing of God, whereas a crucified person, according to the law, died under the curse of God, the identification of the crucified Jesus with the Messiah was a blasphemous contradiction in terms. This was so even if his death on the cross was undeserved, not to speak of the interpretation of Dt. 21:23 attested later in the Mishnah (*Sanh*. 6:4) which inferred from *qilᵉlaṭ 'ᵉlōhîm* that the hanged man had blasphemed the Name. When Paul was compelled to recognize that the crucified Jesus, risen from the dead, was Messiah and Son of God, he was faced with the problem how and why he nevertheless had died under the divine curse. The solution set forth here in vv 10–13 probably came to him sooner rather than later: Christ had endured the curse on his people's behalf (by being 'hanged on a tree') in order to redeem them from the curse pronounced on those who failed to keep the law. This argument would have been all of a piece with his swift and radical reappraisal of the place of the law in God's ways with mankind.

The verb ἐξαγοράζω is used of the redemptive work of Christ here and in 4:5. The simple verb ἀγοράζω is used in 1 Cor. 6:20; 7:23, 'you were bought with a price', where the readers are expected to know what the 'price' (τιμή) was (cf. Rev. 5:9, ἠγόρασας . . . ἐν τῷ αἵματί σου). It is not implied, however, that the price was paid to some person or entity entitled to exact it.

In saying that 'Christ has redeemed *us*', whom does Paul mean by 'us'? It might be argued that only Jews were 'under law' (cf. 4:5) and therefore liable to the curse incurred by the law-breaker; Gentiles—ἔθνη τὰ μὴ νόμον ἔχοντα, as they are called in Rom. 2:14—had not incurred the curse as law-breaking

Jews had done. But Paul's argument excludes the possibility of his meaning that only Jewish believers were redeemed from the curse of the law. The 'Gentiles who have not the law' nevertheless 'show that what the law requires is written on their hearts' (Rom. 2:14f.); they have an innate sense of right and wrong, as is attested by the accusing or excusing activity of their conscience; and if they are law-breakers in this sense, they too are in principle liable to 'the curse of the law'. This indeed might be implied in Paul's inclusion of the emphatic LXX insertions πᾶς and πᾶσιν in his quotation of Dt. 27:26 (v 10): 'every one', whether Jew or Gentile, is subject to the curse who does not persevere in 'everything', whether specifically 'written in the book of the law' or more generally 'written on their hearts'. That Gentiles as well as Jews are in view is confirmed by the emphasis on εἰς τὰ ἔθνη in the continuation of the present sentence (v 14); cf. τὰ πάντα in v 22 (συνέκλεισεν ἡ γραφὴ τὰ πάντα ὑπὸ ἁμαρτίαν) and the inclusive language and argument of vv 23–27; 4:4–6. (Cf. G. Howard, *Crisis*, 59.)

3:14 ἵνα εἰς τὰ ἔθνη ἡ εὐλογία τοῦ Ἀβραὰμ γένηται ἐν Χριστῷ Ἰησοῦ. The two ἵνα clauses of v 14 are co-ordinate: both express the purpose of Christ's redemptive death—the one in more general terms, the other in a more specific interpretation. The 'blessing of Abraham' (i.e. the blessing promised to Abraham) which is granted to faith replaces the 'curse' incurred under the law; this reinforces the effectiveness of Gn. 15:6 (quoted in v 6) as a solvent to the apparent contradiction between Hab. 2:4b and Lv. 18:5 (cf. H.-J. Schoeps, *Paul*, 177f.).

The law makes a distinction between the people of Israel, to whom it was given, and the Gentiles, to whom it was not given. But the promise to Abraham explicitly embraced the Gentiles (πάντα τὰ ἔθνη) within its scope; they were to have a share in the blessing promised to him. Their share in his blessing was confirmed to them 'in Christ Jesus', not only because he was the one who redeemed his people from the curse of the law but also (as is declared in v 16) because he was the offspring (σπέρμα) of Abraham in whom, according to a further elaboration of the promise, all the Gentiles were to be blessed.

The repetition of the promise to Abraham, after the offering up of Isaac, in the form ἐνευλογηθήσονται ἐν τῷ σπέρματί σου πάντα τὰ ἔθνη (Gn. 22:18) has suggested to some commentators that Paul has the narrative of the binding of Isaac ('*ᵃqēḏaṭ yiṣḥāq*) in mind here. Cf. N. A. Dahl: 'Apart from Ro 8:32 the clearest Pauline allusion to Gn 22 is found in Gal 3:13–14' ('The Atonement—An Adequate Reward for Akedah?' in *Black FS* [1], 23). Dahl indeed sees a possible link between 'a man hanging on a tree' and 'a ram caught in a thicket' (Gn. 22:13); this, however, is far-fetched. M. Wilcox (' "Upon the Tree" . . .', 97) prefers to link the ξύλον of Gal. 3:13 with the ξύλα laid on Isaac in Gn. 22:6a, 7b, 9; cf. *Gen. Rab.* 56:4 (on Gn. 22:6), where Isaac carries the wood 'like one who carries his cross (*ṣᵉlûḇô*) on his shoulder'. C. H. Cosgrove ('The Mosaic Law Preaches Faith: A Study in Galatians 3', *WTJ* 41 [1978–79], 146–171) goes so far as to find an 'implicit Isaac-Christ typology' throughout vv 13–29. But Isaac personally does not figure in the present argument: indeed, both in Gn. 22:18 and here Abraham's 'offspring' belongs to future generations, although Isaac is the indispensable link between Abraham and that more distant offspring. See further on 4:22ff.

But in what form does the 'blessing of Abraham' now come on believing Gentiles? The answer to this question is supplied in the second ἵνα clause: ἵνα τὴν ἐπαγγελίαν τοῦ πνεύματος λάβωμεν διὰ τῆς πίστεως. (The article τῆς before πίστεως probably points back to ἐκ πίστεως in vv 7, 9, 11f.) The substance of the 'promise' is the gift of the Spirit or (according to the variant reading εὐλογίαν, which is probably an inadvertent assimilation to the preceding clause and not a deliberate Marcionism) the promised 'blessing' is the gift of the Spirit. The Galatians have already been reminded in v 2 that it was by the message of faith that they received the Spirit.

According to N. A. Dahl ('The Atonement . . .'), this second ἵνα clause is Paul's interpretative comment on 'a fragment of pre-Pauline tradition' preserved in 3:13, 14a, by which he 'identifies the blessing of Abraham with the Spirit, given as a down-payment even to Gentile believers' (23). Whereas the pre-Pauline tradition makes Christ liberate his people from the curse incurred by transgression of the law, Paul sees him as liberating his people from the law itself. But the distinction here envisaged by Dahl probably did not exist in Paul's mind: as Paul saw it, the curse was incurred by all who are ἐξ ἔργων νόμου, transgressors or not (v 10).

Our receiving the blessing because Christ endured the curse is a notable example of the gospel principle of 'interchange', as expounded by M. D. Hooker: 'Paul does not explain how one who is made a curse becomes a source of blessing; but since it is "in Christ" that the blessing comes, and since it is by being identified with the one true descendant of Abraham that Jews and Gentiles receive the promise, it is clear that the curse has been annulled—transformed into blessing. This can only be through the resurrection: the judgement of the Law—that Christ was under a curse—has been withdrawn; God himself has vindicated his Son as righteous, and those who have faith in him are reckoned righteous and live' ('Interchange and Atonement', *BJRL* 60 [1977–78], 470f.; cf. also her 'Interchange in Christ', *JTS* n.s. 22 [1971], 356f.).

So, Abraham by faith received justification and the promise of blessing; now that Christ has accomplished his redemptive work, Abraham's children (cf. v 7), likewise by faith, receive justification and the promised blessing—the gift of the Spirit. They receive this blessing, moreover, 'in Christ Jesus', the Son of Abraham—as it is written, 'In your offspring all the nations of the earth shall be blessed.'

(e) The priority and permanence of the promise (3:15–18)

My brothers, I use a human analogy. Even when it is a human being's testament that is involved, no one (else) annuls it or adds a codicil to it once it has been validated. Now it was to Abraham and to his 'offspring' that the promises were spoken. It does not say, 'And to (your) offsprings', as though referring to many individuals, but 'And to your offspring', with reference to one person, namely Christ. What I mean is this: the testament or covenant, which was validated in advance by God, cannot be invalidated by the law (which was given four hundred and thirty years later), as though the effect of the law were to make the promise null and void. For if the inheritance were based on law, it would no longer be based on promise. But it is by a promise that God has granted it to Abraham.

TEXTUAL NOTES

v 16 ὅς / ὁ D* 81 Iren^[lat] Tert / οὗ G
v 17 θεου P^46 ℵ A B Ψ *pc* lat^[r vg] / θεου εις Χριστον D G I byz lat^[vet] syr

3:15 Ἀδελφοί, κατὰ ἄνθρωπον λέγω. Paul speaks κατὰ ἄνθρωπον when he draws an analogy from human life, as here (cf. 1 Cor. 9:8), uses a figure of speech (cf. 1 Cor. 15:32) or quotes a current argument which he repudiates so vigorously that he apologizes for referring to it (cf. Rom. 3:5).

The present analogy is drawn from judicial practice: if his readers, despite all that has been said above, persist in appealing to the law, let them consider that the divine promise was embodied in a settlement which was made long before the giving of the law and which therefore cannot be annulled or even modified by the law. Among studies of Paul's references to judicial practice in this epistle see A. Halmel, *Über römisches Recht im Galaterbrief: Eine Untersuchung zur Geschichte des Paulinismus* (Essen, 1895); D. Walker, 'The Legal Terminology in the Epistle to the Galatians', *The Gift of Tongues and Other Essays* (Edinburgh, 1906), 81–175. (Walker, following Halmel, finds Paul's legal terminology here to be Roman, as against Ramsay, *Galatians*, 349–375, who argues that it is basically Greek.)

ὅμως, 'nevertheless', comes strangely in its present position (but cf. 1 Cor. 14:7). It might be explained as being displaced: 'though it be but a man's testament, *nevertheless* no one annuls it once it is proved.' On the other hand, it might be accented ὁμῶς and translated 'likewise': '(As with God's covenant), so likewise a human testament is not annulled . . .' (cf. BDF 450.2). This is not so probable here as it is in 1 Cor. 14:7.

ἀνθρώπου κεκυρωμένην διαθήκην. Since it is a human analogy that Paul is using, διαθήκη in the immediate context is likely to have its current secular sense of 'will', 'testamentary disposition', rather than its distinctively biblical sense of 'covenant'. The distinctively biblical sense arises from the LXX employment of διαθήκη as the equivalent of Heb. *berît*, 'covenant'.

Yet it was the biblical use that suggested to Paul his discussion of the διαθήκη at this point. The promise to Abraham was confirmed by a covenant, in which God undertook to give the holy land to his descendants in perpetuity (Gn. 15:18–21; 17:2–14). One clause in the covenant promise of Gn. 17:4, 'you shall be the father of a multitude of nations' (πολλῶν ἐθνῶν), was to be exploited by Paul in Rom. 4:17 to show that Abraham was the father of Gentile believers (which he maintains here on a more general basis; cf. v 7 above).

The διαθήκη (*berît*) made with Abraham had this in common with an ordinary testament, that it was largely concerned with inheritance (κληρονομία, v 18)—the inheritance to be received by Abraham's descendants being, according to Paul, the twofold blessing of justification by faith and the gift of the Spirit.

Throughout the OT, the *bᵉrît* made by God with his people is regularly a 'covenant of grant', a settlement graciously bestowed by the superior party on an inferior. It has been widely argued that the OT 'covenant' formulary is modelled on the 'vassal treaty' current in the ancient Near East, in which an imperial suzerain brought a lesser power into treaty relationship with himself, promising protection and help in return for such services as the lesser power was in a position to render; cf. G. E. Mendenhall, *Law and Covenant in Israel and the Ancient Near East* (Pittsburgh, 1955); K. Baltzer, *The Covenant Formulary*, ETr (Oxford, 1971). This was on a different footing from a 'parity covenant', a treaty between equals or near-equals such as the Israelites were forbidden to make with the Canaanites (Ex. 23:32)—because it would infringe the covenant which their divine suzerain had established with them—or that which successive kings of Damascus made with successive kings of Judah (1 Ki. 15:19). The 'statutes' (*dᵉbārîm*) of the OT law-codes—'Thou shalt (not) . . .'—are patterned rather on the vassal treaty formulations than on the ancient Near Eastern law-codes with their casuistic ('If a man...') form (cf. the Heb. *mišpāṭîm* of, e.g., Ex. 21:2–22:17).

Outstanding OT covenants are those made by God with Noah (Gn. 9:9–17), with Abraham and his family (Gn. 15:18–21; 17:2–14), with Israel in the days of Moses (Ex. 19:5f.; 24:3–8; 34:10; Dt. 29:1), and with David and his house (2 Sa. 23:5; Is. 55:3). It is by contrast with the covenant of Moses' day that the new covenant foretold by Jeremiah is to be established in perpetuity (Je. 31:31–34; cf. 2 Cor. 3:2–14; Heb. 8:6–9:22).

All this, however, has little to do with Paul's present argument. He is concerned not with the treaty-form of covenant but with a will or testament, which was one form of a unilateral διαθήκη, a disposition or settlement.

οὐδεὶς ἀθετεῖ, 'no one annuls'. When a deed of settlement is properly signed, sealed and delivered and the property legally conveyed, not even the original owner can revoke it or alter its terms. As for a testamentary disposition, Roman law and most other systems permitted the testator to cancel or modify it (by codicils or otherwise) at any point during his lifetime, but only with his death could it be validated (κυροῦσθαι). By that time he was no longer in a position to change it, and no one else was allowed to do so. Paul does not say in so many words, as the writer to the Hebrews says, that a will becomes effective only when the testator's death is registered (Heb. 9:16f.); he assumes it as something that is universally known, whereas it is an essential link in the argument of Heb. 9:15–22.

W. M. Ramsay (*Galatians*, 353) argued that the judicial references in this epistle were not to Roman law but to Greek law modified by local usage. He drew (especially with regard to the law affecting inheritance) on K. G. Bruns and E. Sachau (ed.), *Syrisch-römisches Rechtsbuch aus dem fünften Jahrhundert* (Leipzig, 1880), although he preferred to call the work the 'Graeco-Syrian' law-book. According to Ramsay, the validation of a will, in many cities throughout the Greek world, depended on its being duly registered and deposited (either in original or in a certified copy) in the public record office. Once this was done, not even the testator was permitted to alter it, unless such permission had been expressly written into it. This irrevocable character attached to a will especially where the inheritance of sons was concerned—above all (and this is particularly important in reference to the υἱοθεσία of 4:5) where the inheritance of *adopted* sons was concerned. L. Mitteis, *Reichsrecht und Volksrecht in den östlichen Provinzen des römischen Kaiserreichs* (Leipzig, 1891), 213ff., quotes a relevant passage from Lucian, *The Disinherited*, 12, which shows how in the Greek world the rights of an adopted son were even more secure than those of a son by birth.

The evidence adduced by Ramsay is important, but it can support nothing like the weight which he placed on it; in particular, it has no real bearing (as he supposed it to have) on the validity of the South Galatian hypothesis of the destination of the letter. His arguments were subjected at the time to meticulous scrutiny by P. W. Schmiedel ('Galatia', *Enc Bib*, 1608–1611) and shown to be far less conclusive than Ramsay maintained.

ἢ ἐπιδιατάσσεται, 'or adds a codicil to it'. The compound verb (cf. v 19 for the simpler διατάσσω) has been found thus far in Christian writings only; this is its earliest extant literary attestation. The testator in Roman law could add a codicil at any time that he chose, but after his death (or before it, for that matter) nobody else might do so. Ramsay maintained that in the Greek procedure which he thought to be in view here it was permissible to execute an ἐπιδιαθήκη or supplementary will (e.g. making provision for a second son and heir by adoption), but even that could not revoke the terms of the first will. An example of an ἐπιδιαθήκη is Papyrus 21 (126 BC) in B. P. Grenfell (ed.), *An Alexandrian Erotic Fragment and Other Greek Papyri* (Oxford, 1896), 44–48. (The noun ἐπιδιαθήκη is used in the plural by Josephus, *Ant*. 17.226, of the last codicil to Herod's will, in which Archelaus was nominated king in place of Antipas. As Herod and his sons were Roman citizens, his will was drawn up and executed in accordance with Roman law.)

E. Bammel, 'Gottes διαθήκη (Gal. iii.15–17) und das jüdische Rechtsdenken', *NTS* 6 (1959–60), 313–319, argues that Paul has neither Greek nor Roman analogies in mind, but the Jewish institution of the *mattᵉnat bārî'* , the irrevocable 'gift of a healthy person', in contrast to the last will and testament of someone at the point of death.

3:16 τῷ δὲ Ἀβραὰμ ἐρρέθησαν αἱ ἐπαγγελίαι καὶ τῷ σπέρματι αὐτοῦ. The promise embraces not only Abraham but his posterity. If in Gn. 18:18 it is in (or with) Abraham that all the nations of the earth will be blessed, in Gn. 22:18 the promise runs: 'In your offspring (σπέρμα) all the nations of the earth will be blessed' (cf. Gn. 26:4b; 28:14). In Gn. 22:18 (and 26:4b) the Hebrew conjugation is the reflexive Hithpael (*hiṯbārᵉ ḵû*), not Niphal, but even so it is represented by the passive in the LXX. In Sir. 44:21 (ἐνευλογηθῆναι ἔθνη ἐν τῷ σπέρματι αὐτοῦ) the Hebrew text as well as the Greek translation seems to indicate that the nations would be the objects of the blessing, if *lbrk bzr'w gwym* be vocalized *lᵉḇārēḵ* [infinitive Piel, rather than Niphal *libbārēḵ* for *lᵉhibbārēḵ*] *bᵉzar'ô gôyim* ('to bless the nations in his offspring').

In the Genesis narrative the patriarchal promises relate in part to the land (Gn. 12:7; 13:15, 17; 26:4; 28:13) and in part to other aspects of the heritage (especially the universal blessing). But where the promises are given *to* Abraham's offspring (τῷ σπέρματι αὐτοῦ, as Paul says here), and not to others *in* or *with* Abraham's offspring, the reference is to the land ('To your offspring I will give this land', Gn. 12:7; cf. 13:15; 15:18; 17:8; 24:7, etc.). The reference to the land, however, plays no part in the argument of Galatians; in Rom. 4:13 it appears as 'the promise to Abraham and his offspring, that he should inherit the world' (τὸ κληρονόμον αὐτὸν εἶναι κόσμου)—a promise fulfilled (like the twin-promise that in Abraham and his offspring all nations would be blessed) in the worldwide expansion of the gospel through the Gentile mission. (The writer to the Hebrews, for his part, interprets the promise of the land in terms of 'a better country, that is, a heavenly one' [Heb. 11:16]). For Paul's present argument the promise to Abraham's offspring, as to Abraham himself, is the promise that in the one, as in the other, all the nations will be blessed.

On the patriarchal promises see J. Hoftijzer, *Die Verheissungen an die drei Erzväter* (Leiden, 1956); D. J. A. Clines, *The Theme of the Pentateuch* (Sheffield, 1978), 26f., 29, 31–43, 81–96, 111–118; C. Westermann, *The Promises to the Fathers: Studies on the Patriarchal Narratives*, ETr (Philadelphia, 1980).

οὐ λέγει, Καὶ τοῖς σπέρμασιν, ὡς ἐπὶ πολλῶν, ἀλλ' ὡς ἐφ' ἑνός, Καὶ τῷ σπέρματί σου, ὅς ἐστιν Χριστός. The subject of λέγει is either ὁ θεός or (as in v 8) ἡ γραφή. The repeated ὡς, indicating the subjective motivation or intention of the subject, may be construed with the understood participle λέγων or (if the implied subject be ἡ γραφή) λέγουσα. The relative ὅς, instead of agreeing in gender with its antecedent σπέρματι, is attracted in gender to the following Χριστός (unless we are dealing with a sense construction, as in 4:19).

There is no need to make heavy weather of Paul's insistence that the biblical text has σπέρματι (singular) and not σπέρμασιν (plural). The essence of his argument can be expressed quite acceptably if it is pointed out that the biblical text uses a collective singular ('offspring') which could refer either to a single descendant or to many descendants. In the first instance the reference is to a single descendant, Christ, through whom the promised blessing was to come to all the Gentiles. In the second instance the reference is to all who receive this blessing; in v 29 all who belong to Christ are thereby included in Abraham's offspring. Paul was well aware that the collective noun could indicate a plurality of descendants as well as a single descendant. So, in Rom. 4:18, he identifies Abraham's offspring of Gn. 15:5 with the many nations of Gn. 17:5, interpreting the latter as Gentile believers.

The plural σπέρματα does occur in the LXX (as in Lv. 26:16), but with the sense 'varieties of seed', which is irrelevant where human offspring is in view.

A. Halmel (*Über römisches Recht . . .*), who regarded all Paul's judicial analogies in this epistle as framed on Roman procedure, argued that the singular σπέρμα, with reference to a particular individual, conformed to Roman practice, in which a bequest could not be made to an undefined plurality but to a *certa persona* (cf. summary in D. Walker, 'Legal Terminology', 105–107). But Paul is now concerned with biblical exegesis, not with judicial analogies, and parallels to his exegetical argument are more readily found in Jewish than in Roman sources. Arguments based on the singular or plural of Heb. *zera'* ('seed') occur in m. Shab. 9:2 and b. Shab. 84b (on Is. 61:11), as on the singular or plural of *dām* ('blood') in *Gen. Rab.* 22:9 (on Gn. 4:10; 2 Ki. 9:26; 2 Ch. 24:25). Cf.

Philo, *Mut. Nom*. 145, where much is made of the fact that in Gn. 17:16 LXX Abraham is promised not πολλὰ τέκνα ('many children') by Sarah but τέκνον ('a child'), 'because excellence cannot be estimated by number but rather by value'. This kind of argument might have weighed more with some of Paul's opponents than any number of analogies from Greek or Roman law.

In Jewish exegesis it is recognized that *zera'* usually refers to a plurality of descendants. Thus the various Targums generally render Heb. *zar'ᵉkā* ('your seed') in the promise to Abraham by Aram. *bᵉnayk* ('your children'). There are places, however, where it is recognized that the biblical context points to an individual: thus in Gn. 4:25 'another seed' (*zera' 'aḥēr*, LXX σπέρμα ἕτερον) is Seth, in Gn. 21:12, 13 Abraham's 'seed' is respectively Isaac and Ishmael, in 2 Sa. 7:12–15 David's 'seed' is primarily Solomon. In the NT, as Solomon in Nathan's oracle is swallowed up in the coming Messiah (cf. the application of 2 Sa. 7:14 to Christ in Heb. 1:5b, a form of exegesis anticipated in 4QFlor. 1:10f.), so Isaac, as Abraham's 'seed', is swallowed up in Christ, in whom the promise to Abraham (καὶ τῷ σπέρματι αὐτοῦ) reached its fruition. M. Wilcox ('The Promise of the "Seed" in the NT and the Targumim', *JSNT*, Issue 5 [October 1979], 2–20) draws attention to the paraphrase of the promise to Abraham in Jub. 16:17f. ('from the sons of Isaac one should become a holy seed, and should not be reckoned among the Gentiles; for he should become the portion of the Most High, and all his seed . . . should be unto the Lord a people for [his] possession above all nations and . . . a kingdom of priests and a holy nation') and Ps.-Philo, *LAB* 8:3, ' "unto thy seed will I give this land; and thy name shall be called Abraham, and Sarai thy wife shall be called Sarah. And I will give thee of her an eternal seed and make my covenant with thee." And Abraham knew Sarah his wife, and she conceived and bore Isaac' (who is thus apparently equated with the 'eternal seed'). These late texts seem to envisage one pre-eminent descendant of Abraham through whom the promise made regarding his 'seed' would be fulfilled.

See further D. Daube, 'The Interpretation of a Generic Singular', *The NT and Rabbinic Judaism* (London, 1956), 438–444.

3:17 τοῦτο δὲ λέγω, 'What I mean is this': the promise to Abraham was complete in itself, and had all the confirmation it required from the authority of God who made it (cf. Heb. 6:13–18). The prefix προ- in προκεκυρωμένην indicates that it was validated at the time it was given, long before the law. Nothing of later date, therefore, can invalidate the promise or in any way make it less secure than it was when Abraham first received it. The law was given in Moses' day, much later than the promise to Abraham—430 years later, according to the LXX reading of Ex. 12:40, which includes in that figure the patriarchs' sojourning in Canaan as well as their descendants' residence in Egypt. (In the MT the interval between the promise and the law was more like 645 years; in *Seder 'Olam* 3 the 430 years are reckoned from the covenant of Gn. 15 to the exodus.) The law therefore cannot annul or weaken the promise; and the gospel, with its corollaries of justification and the gift of the Spirit, is the fulfilment of the *promise*.

R. E. Clements (*Abraham and David*, 57f.) finds an OT antecedent to Paul's contrast between the covenant of law made at Sinai and the covenant of promise made to Abraham in the contrast between the Deuteronomic emphasis on the covenant of Horeb-Sinai and the Priestly interpretation which gave primacy to the Abrahamic covenant, with its permanent validity. 'The Abrahamic covenant stood as a witness to the primacy of grace in all God's dealings with his people Israel, and testified to the belief that election was an act of God, and not a state to which men could attain by their obedience to a law.'

H.-J. Schoeps compares Paul's appeal from the law back to the Abrahamic promise with Jesus' appeal from the law back to the creation ordinances—in relation, e.g., to the sabbath (Mk. 2:27) and to marriage (Mk. 10:5–9)—and finds a common principle in both ('Restitutio principii als kritisches Prinzip der nova lex Jesu', *Aus frühchristlicher Zeit* [Tübingen, 1950], 271). Cf. also D. Daube, 'Evangelisten und Rabbinen', *ZNW* 48 (1957), 119–126, especially 125f.

3:18 εἰ γὰρ ἐκ νόμου ἡ κληρονομία, οὐκέτι ἐξ ἐπαγγελίας, 'for if the inheritance were based on law, it would no longer be based on promise'. The inheritance has been implied in vv 15–17: promises made with regard to a man's descendants involve the principle of inheritance. If the inheritance of Abraham's descendants were based on law—more specifically, the Mosaic law—then it would belong to the people of the law (cf. v 10, ὅσοι . . . ἐξ ἔργων νόμου εἰσίν), i.e. the Jewish nation. But if it is based on the promise made to Abraham, generations before the giving of the law, then the law cannot affect it. It belongs to the people of faith (cf. v 7, οἱ ἐκ πίστεως) who, whether of Gentile or Jewish birth, are the true children of Abraham. And it is certainly on promise that the inheritance is based: τῷ δὲ Ἀβραὰμ δι' ἐπαγγελίας κεχάρισται ὁ θεός—by promise, and therefore by faith, for it was on account of his faith in the promise of God that Abraham was justified (v 6). The perfect κεχάρισται implies that God not only granted the inheritance to Abraham in the past but continues to make it good to his descendants. The promise to Abraham was entirely a covenant of grant (cf. K. M. Campbell, 'Covenant or Testament?' *EQ* 44 [1972], 107–111, especially 108).

A. Halmel (*Über römisches Recht* . . .) argued that Paul treats the law as a codicil to the promise, in accordance with the clear direction in Roman law that a codicil cannot affect inheritance (cf. Gaius, *Inst.* 2.273, 'codicillis heres non instituitur'; Justinian, *Inst.* 2.25.2, 'codicillis hereditas neque dari neque adimi potest'). 'Thus the legal inferiority of a codicil as compared with a will illustrates the inferiority and transitoriness of the Law as compared with the Promise' (D. Walker, 'Legal Terminology', 111, summarizing Halmel). But it is as certain as anything can be that Paul did not regard the law as a codicil to the promise. It was a completely different instrument, quite unrelated to the promise, introduced for a distinct purpose, as Paul now goes on to say.

(f) The purpose of the law (3:19–22)

What was the purpose of the law, then? It was added for the sake of transgressions, until the coming of the offspring to whom the promise had been made. It was administered through angels, by the agency of a mediator. Now a mediator is not for one party (only), but God is one. Is the law then contrary to the promises [of God]? Far from it! If a law had been given that was able to impart life, then righteousness would indeed have been based on law. But scripture has confined all under (the power of) sin in order that the promise might be given to believers on the basis of faith in Jesus Christ.

TEXTUAL NOTES

v 19 νομος; των παραβασεων χαριν προσετεθη / νομος; των παραδοσεων χαριν ετεθη D* / νομος; των πραξεων χαριν ετεθη lat^{dm} / νομος των πραξεων; P^{46} / νομος των πραξεων; ετεθη G Iren^{lat} Ambst

v 21 του θεου ℵ A C D G (*om* του) Ψ byz lat syr cop arm Ambst Chrys Hier Aug / του Χριστου 104 / *om* P^{46} B lat^{d e} Ambst M.Vict

εκ νομου αν ην A C *al* / αν εκ νομου ην K L P byz / εκ νομου ην αν ℵ *al* / εκ νομου ην D *al* / εκ νομου G / εν νομω ην αν P^{46} / εν νομω αν ην B

3:19 τί οὖν ὁ νόμος; To the question 'Why then the law?' (here the ellipsis of the verb is as natural in English as in Greek) two answers are given: (i) to multiply (and even to stimulate) transgressions; (ii) to confine all in the prison-house of sin, from which there is no exit but the way of faith.

τῶν παραβάσεων χάριν, 'that is, in order that there might be transgressions, the conscious disobeying of definite commandments' (C. E. B. Cranfield, 'St. Paul and the Law', *SJT* 17 [1964], 46). χάριν expresses purpose, not antecedent cause. The law was brought into the situation as an additional factor, in order to produce transgressions. Compare the argument of Rom. 4:15; 5:12–21: 'where there is no law, there is no transgression' (παράβασις), but 'law came in by a side road (παρεισῆλθεν) to increase the trespass (παράπτωμα)'. That the promulgation of specific enactments creates a corresponding category of specific violations, with opportunity (and perhaps temptation) to commit these violations, is a fact of human experience. But Paul's statement goes beyond this: the *purpose* of the law was to increase the sum-total of transgression.

Cranfield adds that the law 'also *increases sin in the sense that it makes men sin more*', especially because it tempts sinful men 'to try to use it as a means to the establishment of a claim upon God', which he regards as the essence of legalism ('St. Paul and the Law', 46f.). Cf. 1 Cor. 15:56, 'the power of sin is the law'.

H. Hübner asks *whose* purpose it was that the law should produce transgressions, and finds the answer to his question in the following reference to angels. It was the angels who planned by means of the law to incite human beings to commit acts of transgression. Such angels are to be regarded as demonic beings who, unlike God, desired men's downfall, not their welfare (*Das Gesetz bei Paulus*, 28f.). 'It is evident', he adds (33), 'that Paul's whole course of argument here concerning the purpose of the law has a blasphemous sound in Jewish ears; it must shock Jews as such and not merely the Pharisaic section.' But even if he is right in discerning the angels' hostile intention, their intention is viewed as overruled, if not directed, by God for the accomplishment of *his* purpose. Even in Galatians the law is ultimately *God's* law (if only by implication). E. P. Sanders (*PPJ*, 550) concedes that Paul makes an extreme statement here 'in the heat of the argument', but finds evidence of 'soberer reflection' in Rom. 2:13; 10:2; Phil. 3:6.

There is, indeed, not much difference between this statement and that of Rom. 5:20a, except that there is no word of angels there. When Paul says that the law 'was added' (προσετέθη), he does not mean that it was added to the promise as a kind of supplement to it; he means that it was added to the human situation for a special purpose—a purpose totally different from that of the promise. The use of the verb παρεισέρχομαι (cf. its sinister nuance in 2:4 above) in Rom. 5:20a ('the law came in by a side road') provides an apt comment on the sense of προσετέθη here.

Several Western witnesses to the text exhibit the simple verb ἐτέθη ('was laid down') in place of προσετέθη, but this variant is usually combined with an alteration of παραβάσεων designed to remove what a scribe or editor felt to be the scandalous statement that the purpose of the law was the production of transgressions. The alteration of παραβάσεων to παραδόσεων made the purpose of the law the creation of traditions (presumably in the sense of 1:14); its replacement by πράξεων yielded a reference to the 'law of works'.

ἄχρις οὗ ἔλθῃ τὸ σπέρμα ᾧ ἐπήγγελται, 'until the coming of (Abraham's) offspring to whom the promise had been made', i.e. Christ (cf. v 16). The perfect ἐπήγγελται either has pluperfect force or, like the perfect καχάρισται in v 18, it emphasizes the abiding validity of the promise.

The law, then, was to remain in force until the coming of Christ; this is repeated in greater detail in vv 23–25. The suggestion has been made that Paul's Jewish education had taught him that the law would be abrogated with the advent of the messianic age, so that, when he was persuaded that Jesus was the Messiah, he drew the logical conclusion. There was an early Jewish doctrine of three epochs in world-history—the age of chaos, the age of law, and the messianic age—each lasting for 2,000 years, after which the eternal sabbath rest would be enjoyed (b. Sanh. 97a; m. Tamid 7:4). This doctrine was said to emanate from 'the school of Elijah'—a phrase which denotes the same kind of antiquity for *haggadah* as 'a commandment of Moses from Sinai' denotes for *halakhah* (W. Bacher, *Tradition und Tradenten* [Frankfurt, 1914], 25ff., 233f.). For one brought up in this doctrine it followed that, 'if the "Days of the Messiah" have commenced, those of the Torah came to their close. On the other hand, if the Law, the Torah, still retained its validity, it was proclaimed thereby that the Messiah had not yet arrived' (L. Baeck, 'The Faith of Paul', *JJS* 3 [1952], 106; cf. H.-J. Schoeps, *Paul*, 171ff.). For a comprehensive discussion see W. D. Davies, *Torah in the Messianic Age and/or the Age to Come* (Philadelphia, 1952).

But the question of Paul's earlier instruction on this subject is of minor importance: the logic which impelled him to the conviction that Christ had displaced the Torah was the logic of his Damascus-road conversion. See note on 1:8f. above.

διαταγεὶς δι' ἀγγέλων, 'administered through angels'; cf. Stephen in Acts 7:53 (εἰς διαταγὰς ἀγγέλων), also Heb. 2:2, where the law is 'the word spoken through angels' (ὁ δι' ἀγγέλων λαληθεὶς λόγος).

The angelic administration of the law finds no place in the OT. The nearest thing to it is the description of the theophany in Dt. 33:2, 'Yahweh came from Sinai, . . . he came from his holy myriads; from his right hand came a fiery law for them.' The phrase 'a fiery law' (Heb. '*ēš dāṭ*) is of uncertain meaning; the LXX renders the clause ἐκ δεξιῶν αὐτοῦ ἄγγελοι μετ' αὐτοῦ ('at his right hand were angels with him'). 'It is probable', wrote John Calvin, 'that both Paul and Stephen derived from this passage their statement that the law was "ordained by angels in the hand of a mediator", for its authority was greatly confirmed by its having so many witnesses' (*Harmony of the Last Four Books of the Pentateuch*, ETr, IV [Edinburgh, 1855], 381).

Paul, like Stephen, refers to the angelic administration of the law as something well known. But it is difficult to find any extant reference to it before the date of this epistle. In *Jub.* 1:29ff. the angel of the presence takes the tablets 'of the law and of the testimony of the weeks' and dictates their contents to Moses; but this cannot be equated with the administration of the law by angels. Philo (*Som.* 1.141–143), discussing the angels seen by Jacob in his dream at Bethel, describes them as 'mediators' (μεσῖται) and says that it was to one of these mediators that the people said at Sinai, 'You speak to us, . . . but let not God speak to us, lest we die' (Ex. 20:19)—although it was actually to Moses that this request was addressed. No more than the author of Jubilees does Philo speak of the angelic *administration* of the law. Comparison is also made with Test. Dan. 6:2, ἐγγίζετε τῷ θεῷ καὶ τῷ ἀγγέλῳ τῷ παραιτουμένῳ ὑμᾶς ('draw near to God and to the angel who intercedes for you'), but this angel is 'the mediator (μεσίτης) of God and man for the peace of Israel' and champions Israel (like Michael in Dn. 12:1) against 'the kingdom of the enemy'.

What may be the earliest non-biblical reference comes in a speech which Josephus (*Ant.* 15.136) puts into the mouth of Herod, of all people: 'we have learned the noblest of our doctrines and the holiest of our laws through angels sent from God' (δι᾽ ἀγγέλων παρὰ τοῦ θεοῦ)—although it has been held that the ἄγγελοι here are human messengers, prophets (or priests); cf. R. Marcus in the Loeb edition of Josephus, VIII (London, 1963), 66f.; also W. D. Davies, 'A Note on Josephus, Antiquities 15:136', *HTR* 47 (1954), 135–140, who is disposed to agree with Marcus that ἄγγελοι may be prophets but concludes that, even if they are angels, this in no way implies a limited duration for the law which, for Josephus, ἀθάνατος διαμένει (*Ap.* 2.277).

The tannaitic midrashim—*Mek.* on Ex. 20:18, *Sipre Nu.* 102 on Nu. 12:5 (cf. *Pesiq. R.* 21, 103a)—state, on the basis of Ps. 68:17, that God was attended at the law-giving on Sinai by myriads of angels but this, again, does not amount to their being the administrators of the law.

As for the NT references, Stephen's point is that the people showed their impiety by disregarding the law even though it was administered by beings as high and holy as angels, while the writer to the Hebrews argues that if 'the word spoken through angels' was safeguarded by the severest sanctions, much more terrible must be the penalty for rejecting the saving message brought not by angels but by the Lord himself. Paul, for the polemic purposes of his present argument, uses the angelic administration as evidence of the inferiority of the law to the promise, which was given directly by God.

It has been asked if these administrators of the law should be thought of as good angels or bad angels. If they are the ministering angels who attended God when he appeared at Sinai, then they are *ex hypothesi* good angels, but some of the rabbis (e.g. Raba in b. Ber. 25b; RR. Joshua b. Levi and Judah b. Simon in *Pesiq. R.* 21, 97a; 25, 128a) suggested that they were not greatly pleased that God should give his law to human beings. According to

A. Marmorstein, 'Jews and Judaism in the Earliest Christian Apologies', *Expositor*, series 8, 17 (1919), 100–116 (especially 113), these suggestions 'can only be understood as the denial of the often repeated idea that Moses received the Torah from the angels'.

ἐν χειρὶ μεσίτου. The mediator has commonly been identified with Moses; cf. the repeated phrase ἐν χειρὶ Μωϋσέως in the LXX (Lv. 26:46; Nu. 4:37, etc.). Moses certainly was the Israelites' mediator with God throughout the wilderness wanderings; see Philo, *Vit. Mos.* 2.166 (μεσίτης καὶ διαλλάκτης); also the certainly pre-Pauline Ass. Mos. 1:14, where Moses calls himself τῆς διαθήκης μεσίτης (Greek as quoted by Gelasius Cyzicenus, *Comm. Act. Syn. Nic.* 2.18). It is plain in the Pentateuch that Moses served as go-between, receiving the law from God to give to the people (as in Dt. 5:5, 'I stood between [ἀνὰ μέσον] Yahweh and you') and presenting their pleas to God (as in Dt. 5:22–31). A. Oepke (*TDNT* IV, 615, 618, *s.v.* μεσίτης) compares the application of the term *sarsôr* ('agent', 'commissioner') to Moses in rabbinical literature, e.g. by R. Samuel b. Isaac (*c.* AD 300) in j. Meg. 4.74d: 'the Torah was given by the hand(s) of a *sarsôr*' (a close equivalent to Paul's ἐν χειρὶ μεσίτου).

To some the Mosaic identification of the mediator here is obvious: 'The reference is of course to the part played by Moses' (C. E. B. Cranfield, *Romans*, 858; similarly H. D. Betz, *Galatians*, 170). But to others the identification is not so clear: 'The question of the identity of the "mediator" is even more fraught with problems' than the function of the angels (C. H. Cosgrove, 'The Mosaic Law Preaches Faith', 158). In their view the 'mediator' here is so closely associated with the angels that one might think more readily of the angels' mediator than of the Israelites' mediator. H.-J. Schoeps indeed holds that Paul viewed Moses as mediating between the angels and the people. Paul, however, has a further remark to make about the mediator.

3:20 ὁ δὲ μεσίτης ἑνὸς οὐκ ἔστιν, ὁ δὲ θεὸς εἷς ἐστιν. The negative in the former clause goes logically with ἑνός, but is attracted to the verb.

The two statements in v 20 are completely intelligible if each is taken by itself. It goes without saying that a mediator requires at least two parties between which he is to mediate; he cannot mediate on behalf of one party only. That God is one is the theological basis of Judaism and Christianity alike: εἷς ὁ θεός (Rom. 3:30); ἡμῖν εἷς θεὸς ὁ πατήρ (1 Cor. 8:6). See E. Peterson, ΕΙΣ ΘΕΟΣ (Göttingen, 1926).

It is the relation between the two clauses that constitutes the interpretative problem. In what way does the affirmation that God is one form an antithesis to what is said about the mediator? The number of solutions offered to the problem has been reckoned to exceed 300—one might wonder, indeed, if this is Robert Browning's 'great text in Galatians' with its 'twenty-nine distinct damnations' for the unwary exegete.

It is natural to suppose that Paul has in mind the fact that, in making his promise to Abraham, God acted unilaterally, in sovereign grace. In giving the law, he employed mediation; in bestowing the promise, he acted on his own, as one (εἷς). No angelic intervention, no human mediation, was involved: God promised, and Abraham believed. But 'God is one' would be a strange way of saying this.

A. Oepke (*TDNT* IV, 619, *s.v.* μεσίτης) takes Paul to mean: A mediator usually negotiates between two pluralities (here, the angels on the one side and the Israelites on the other). But God, being one and not a plurality, requires no mediator. To this it may be replied that a mediator may intervene as effectively between two individuals (cf. the *môkiah*, LXX μεσίτης, of Jb. 9:33) as between one individual and a plurality (cf. 1 Tim. 2:5) or between two pluralities.

We can scarcely hope to grasp Paul's meaning unless we posit a logical relation between ἑνός in the former clause and εἷς in the latter. If a mediator is not 'of one', whereas God is 'one', it follows that the mediator to whom Paul refers here is not God's mediator.

Whose mediator is he, then? H. Lietzmann (*An die Galater*, 21f.) argues that, since he is not the mediator of one but of many, he must (in this case) be the representative not of God (who is one) but of the angels (who are many). G. Klein agrees and, taking Moses to be the mediator in question, concludes that Moses is here the 'functionary' of the angels—the functionary, indeed, of powers opposed to God ('Individualgeschichte und Weltgeschichte bei Paulus', *Rekonstruktion*, 210).

But there is nothing in the context to warrant this view. Moses was in no way qualified to be the representative of angels; he was in every way qualified to be his people's representative, and indeed he served them effectively in this way on many occasions. Yet v 19 brings the μεσίτης so closely into association with the angels that a μεσίτης of the angels may well be implied. If the angels' μεσίτης was not Moses, who was he? A. Vanhoye ('Un médiateur des anges en Ga 3, 19–20', *Bib*. 59 [1978], 403–411) thinks of the angel of the presence who was with Moses in the wilderness and 'who spoke to him at Mount Sinai', as Stephen says in the same sentence which states that Moses 'received living oracles to give to us' (Acts 7:38; cf. Ex. 23:20f.; 32:34; 33:14). This angel, he suggests, was the μεσίτης of the angels as Moses was the μεσίτης of the Israelites; he compares the roles of the two *'anšê benayim* in the valley of Elah, where Goliath represented the Philistines and David the Israelites, except that in the valley of Elah the two representatives clashed in conflict whereas at Sinai they met for communication (cf. 1 Sa. [LXX 1 Ki.] 17:4, 23; in v 23 LXX^A renders *'îš benayim* by ἀνὴρ ὁ ἀμεσσαῖος, presumably a corruption of ἀνὴρ ὁ μεσαῖος, 'the middleman'). On the whole, Vanhoye's interpretation commends itself as the best solution of the problem.

Perhaps the point about the law is that it 'was negotiated not directly between the principals but through deputies' (W. H. Isaacs, 'Galatians iii.20', *Exp Tim* 35 [1923–24], 567). And a point to note about ὁ μεσίτης is that the article here is not generic: whatever be true of mediators in general, 'the mediator' in this situation (the law-giving) is a representative not of one, but of many.

The one God is God of Jews and Gentiles alike (cf. Rom. 3:29f.). The law divided them; the gospel brings them together. And since the God of Jews and Gentiles is one, it is fitting that he should provide one way of salvation for both—the way of faith (cf. U. Mauser, 'Galater iii.20: Die Universalität des Heils', *NTS* 13 [1966–67], 258–270).

As for the law, it is shown to have been intrusive, temporary, secondary and preparatory. That is, says C. E. B. Cranfield (*Romans*, 858f.), the law apart from Christ—*nuda lex*, as Calvin styles it (*Inst.* 2.7.2). See notes below on 5:14 ('the whole law') and 6:2 ('the law of Christ').

3:21 ὁ οὖν νόμος κατὰ τῶν ἐπαγγελιῶν; 'Is the law then contrary to the promises?' The direction of the argument thus might prepare us for an affirmative answer, rather than for Paul's emphatic μὴ γένοιτο. This is not the only place in his writings where Paul repudiates an inference which might be drawn from his argument (cf., for a good parallel to this instance, Rom. 7:7). If the promises are God's promises, the law (even in Galatians) is God's law; they cannot therefore be opposed in principle to each other. Now, after interposing his μὴ γένοιτο, he goes on, characteristically, to state his reason. True, he says (in a near-parenthesis), if a law had been given which could impart life, then righteousness (justification) would certainly be based on law. (This is another of the rare Pauline instances of an unfulfilled condition; cf. 1:10b.) But the law as a means of justification and life, in terms of Lv. 18:5 (cf. v 12 above), has been superseded by faith, in terms of Hab. 2:4b (cf. v 11 above); the conclusion is that, despite what is said in Lv. 18:5 (and in Rom. 7:10, ἡ ἐντολὴ ἡ εἰς ζωήν), the law in fact proved unable to give life. Could it have given life, then indeed 'Christ died in vain' (2:21). It proved, on the contrary, to lead to death: 'the written code kills' (2 Cor. 3:6). The establishment of righteousness by faith as the way to life implies the inability and displacement of the law. Once again, ζωοποιέω is practically synonymous with δικαιόω. To be justified (by faith) is to receive life (by faith); 'dikaiosynē, which often means the righteousness which leads to life, can become simply the equivalent of "life" ' (E. P. Sanders, *PPJ*, 503).

3:22 ἀλλὰ συνέκλεισεν κτλ. Paul goes on to show why the law, despite its purpose of producing transgressions, is not contrary to the promises. Since it is God's law, it serves as God's instrument to accomplish his purpose. It cannot of itself impart life, but (ἀλλά) by showing the bankruptcy of human effort it shuts men and women up to the grace of God as their only hope.

The law does indeed produce transgressions, and by that very fact it demonstrates its inability to lead to justification and life. Those who use it as a way to justification and life are in fact misusing it; it is this misuse that nullifies the promise. What the law does is to bring to light the universal human plight: all are 'under sin'. If, realizing this, men and women look round for a way of deliverance from their plight, they find it in the promise. Believing the promise, and the one who has made it, they are justified—justified by faith in Jesus Christ, in whom the promise and its fulfilment are embodied. Far from being against the promises, then, the law drives men and women to flee from its condemnation and seek refuge in the promises.

ἡ γραφή, here tantamount to 'the written law', concentrated in such an uncompromising form as Dt. 27:26 (quoted in v 10 above). It might indeed be held that, as in v 8, ἡ γραφή is practically equivalent to 'God', who speaks in scripture (the more so since the verb συνκλείω is used similarly in Rom. 11:32, where God is the subject: 'God has consigned them all to disobedience, that he may have mercy upon all'). But here the figure of speech is more vivid than in v 8: the written law is the official who locks the law-breaker up in the prison-house of which sin is the jailor. Unlike τοὺς πάντας in Rom. 11:32, the more general τὰ πάντα here is neuter plural; it embraces the whole human situation—man and all his works—in the aeon which the gospel age has displaced. Those who come to their senses in the prison-house and recognize the

hopelessness of their predicament will be the readier to embrace the promise of
liberty and life: the law thus serves the interests of the promise—and of the
beneficiaries of the promise.

ὑπὸ ἁμαρτίαν, cf. Rom. 3:9, πάντας ὑφ' ἁμαρτίαν εἶναι, 'that all are
under (the dominion of) sin'; 7:14, πεπραμένος ὑπὸ τὴν ἁμαρτίαν, 'sold
under sin', 'sold into the ownership of sin'. This is the first of a series of
ὑπό phrases; cf. ὑπὸ νόμον (v 23; 4:4f.), ὑπὸ παιδαγωγόν (v 25), ὑπὸ
ἐπιτρόπους καὶ οἰκονόμους (4:2), ὑπὸ τὰ στοιχεῖα τοῦ κόσμου (4:3).

ἐκ πίστεως Ἰησοῦ Χριστοῦ. For the objective genitive see note on 2:16.
The faith by which the true children of Abraham (v 6) inherit the promises made
to Abraham and his posterity (v 16) is specifically identified as 'faith in Jesus
Christ', the σπέρμα τοῦ Ἀβραάμ par excellence. G. Howard (Crisis, 58, 65)
takes the phrase to mean (as in 2:16) 'through the faithful act of Christ'; but the
following τοῖς πιστεύουσιν points in the other direction: 'that the promise
based on faith in Jesus Christ might be given to those exercising such faith'.

(g) Liberation from the law (3:23–25)

*Before faith came we were guarded and confined under law, until the reve-
lation of the faith that was to come. So the law has been our custodian until (the
coming of) Christ, in order that we might be justified by faith. But now that faith
has come, we are no longer under a custodian.*

TEXTUAL NOTE
v 24   γεγονεν / εγενετο P⁴⁶ B Clem.Alexᵖᵃʳᵗⁱᵐ

3:23 The sense of v 22 is here repeated in different terms. The 'coming of
faith'—the 'faith in Jesus Christ' just mentioned (in other words, the gospel)—
may be understood both on the plane of salvation-history and in the personal
experience of believers. On the plane of salvation-history the coming of faith
coincides with the appearance of Christ, in whom the parenthetic age of law was
displaced by the age of faith (cf. 4:4), which fulfils the promise made to Abraham. In the personal experience of believers it coincides with their abandonment
of the attempt to establish a righteous standing of their own, based on legal
works, and their acceptance of the righteousness which comes by faith in Christ
(cf. Rom. 10:3f.; Phil. 3:9).

ὑπὸ νόμον ἐφρουρούμεθα συγκλειόμενοι is remarkably parallel to the
confinement of v 22, but here, instead of sin as the jailor, law is the warden or
custodian—a distinction without much of a difference, so that the reader might
be disposed to ask, like the imaginary interlocutor of Rom. 7:7, 'Is the law sin?'
To be ὑπὸ νόμον in the sense of v 23 is another way of expressing the experience
of being ὑπὸ ἁμαρτίαν in the sense of v 22. To be 'under law' is in practice
to be 'under sin'—not because law and sin are identical, but because law, while

forbidding sin, stimulates the very thing that it forbids. Cf. Rom. 6:14, where it is because 'you are no longer under law, but under grace', that 'sin shall not have dominion over you'—the implication being that sin has dominion over men and women so long as they are 'under law'. As will be seen in 4:4, one purpose of the coming of Christ is the redemption of his people from their bondage 'under law'.

As Gentiles and Jews alike are 'confined under sin' in v 22, so Gentiles and Jews alike are 'confined under law' here. For the sense in which Gentiles could be regarded as being 'under law' see note on v 13 above. G. Howard (*Crisis*, 60–64) maintains that the law is the law of Moses, whether Gentiles or Jews are said to be under it—not in the sense that all are subject to its specific demands, but in the sense that 'the law is a suppressor and a restrainer of mankind'; men and women are suppressed under its tyranny, but are released from that tyranny by Christ. The law kept the Gentiles out of the privileges of the people of God and kept Israel apart from the rest of mankind; this divisive force has been overcome by the unifying effect of Christ's redemptive act.

εἰς τὴν μέλλουσαν πίστιν ἀποκαλυφθῆναι. For the construction cf. Rom. 8:18, πρὸς τὴν μέλλουσαν δόξαν ἀποκαλυφθῆναι εἰς ἡμᾶς (for the more classical construction cf. 1 Pet. 5:1, τῆς μελλούσης ἀποκαλυφθῆναι δόξης). The revelation of glory marks the consummation of Christ's saving work; the revelation of faith marks its inception.

3:24 ὥστε ὁ νόμος παιδαγωγὸς ἡμῶν γέγονεν εἰς Χριστόν. The παιδαγωγός was the personal slave-attendant who accompanied the free-born boy wherever he went, from the time he left his nurse's care. It was his duty to teach the boy good manners (with the use of the birch, if necessary), take him to school (carrying his satchel and other effects), wait for him there, in the waiting room or in the παιδαγωγεῖον, a place reserved specifically for παιδαγωγοί (Dem. *De Cor*. 258), or even in the classroom itself (cf. the Duris cup [early 5th century BC] in E. Pottier, *Douris et les peintres de vases grecs* [Paris, 1905], 112, fig. 22), then take him home and test his memory by making him recite the lesson he had learned. During the boy's minority the παιδαγωγός imposed a necessary restraint on his liberty until, with his coming of age, he could be trusted to use his liberty responsibly.

The παιδαγωγός, who, for all his disciplinary function, might establish a bond of close affection with his charge, was not an instructor, not a 'pedagogue' in the modern sense. Paul does not ascribe an educative role to the law, unlike Plato, who regards the law as imparting παιδεία (cf. *Leg*. 7.809a, [τὸν νομοφύλακα] πῶς ἂν ἡμῖν ὁ νόμος αὐτὸς παιδεύσειεν ἱκανῶς; 'How would the law itself give an adequate education [to our guardian of the law]?'). The παιδεία provided by wisdom in Proverbs is generally related by the rabbis to the instructive role of the Torah (see m. Ab. 3.18 for Aqiba's interpretation in this sense of Pr. 4:2, 'I [Wisdom] give you good doctrine [a reference to 'instruction' in the preceding verse, LXX παιδεία]; forsake not my law'). Nor does Paul suppose that the presence of this παιδαγωγός will protect his charge from doing wrong, unlike Philo (*Mut. Nom*. 217), who assumes that this will be the effect of the presence of a παιδαγωγός (παιδαγωγοῦ μὲν παρόντος οὐκ ἂν ἁμάρτοι ὁ ἀγόμενος, 'when the παιδαγωγός is present his charge will not go astray').

A. Oepke (*Galater*, 86–88) mentions various kinds of παιδαγωγός. Ancient authors disagree about their qualities. No doubt some were good and some were bad. A modern analogy is suggested by J. D. G. Dunn's use of the term 'baby-sitter'.

In the phrase εἰς Χριστόν the preposition εἰς has temporal force: 'until Christ' (contrast NIV, 'to lead us to Christ'). As the slave-attendant kept the boy under his control until he came of age, so the law kept the people of God in leading-strings until, with the coming of faith, they attained their spiritual majority in Christ. Cf. v 19, ἄχρις οὗ ἔλθῃ τὸ σπέρμα ᾧ ἐπήγγελται.

ἵνα ἐκ πίστεως δικαιωθῶμεν. This clause amplifies the temporal phrase εἰς Χριστόν. The appearance of Christ gave effect to the purpose of God— 'that we (Jews and Gentiles without distinction) should be justified by faith', in accordance with the promise to Abraham. The justifying act of God in Christ obliterates the partition which the law erected between the two communities.

3:25 ἐλθούσης δὲ τῆς πίστεως οὐκέτι ὑπὸ παιδαγωγόν ἐσμεν, because with the coming of faith believers have come of age and no longer require to be under the control of a slave-attendant: ὑπὸ παιδαγωγόν has the same sense as ὑπὸ νόμον in v 23.

To the figure of a prison warden, then, Paul adds that of a slave-attendant to describe the function of the law before the gospel age. Another, but related, figure is employed in 4:1f., but first he pauses to make one of his greatest affirmations about the new order of liberated existence 'in Christ'.

(h) Jews and Gentiles one in Christ (3:26–29)

For through faith you are all sons of God in Christ Jesus. All of you who were baptized into Christ have put on Christ. (In him) there is neither Jew nor Greek, there is neither slave nor freeman, there is no 'male and female'; for in Christ Jesus you are all one. And if you belong to Christ, then you are Abraham's offspring, heirs according to promise.

TEXTUAL NOTES

v 26   της *om* P⁴⁶ P Clem.Alex Cyr
    εν Χριστω / Χριστου P⁴⁶ 1739 *pc*
v 28   ουκ ενι . . . ουκ ενι . . . ουκ ενι / ουκετι . . . ουκετι *(vid)* . . . *(lacuna)* P⁴⁶
    ουδε ελευθερος / η ελευθερος D*
    και θηλυ / η θηλυ Chr
    εἷς / ἕν G 33 lat
    εἷς εστε εν Χριστω / εστε Χριστου P⁴⁶ ℵ* A

3:26 πάντες γὰρ υἱοὶ θεοῦ ἐστε. Those addressed as 'you' in v 26 are identical with those indicated by the inclusive 'we' in vv 23–25: Gentile and Jewish believers are together in view. In v 7 those who are ἐκ πίστεως are 'sons of Abraham'; here an even higher status is accorded them, for διὰ τῆς πίστεως ('through the faith' mentioned repeatedly in the foregoing verses) they are 'sons of God'—'sons of God in Christ Jesus', who is himself the Son of God *par excellence* (cf. 1:16; 2:20; 4:4). If it is 'through faith' that they have entered into this relationship, then it is not by legal works (cf. 2:16, etc.). The phrase ἐν Χριστῷ ᾿Ιησοῦ is probably not governed by πίστεως, as though the meaning were 'faith in Christ Jesus'—this idea is usually expressed by Paul with the objective genitive, which indeed is exhibited here in P⁴⁶, by assimilation with (e.g.) v 22. (For πίστις followed by ἐν cf. Eph. 1:15; Col. 1:4; 1 Tim. 3:13; 2 Tim. 1:13; followed by εἰς, Col. 2:5.) Believers in Christ are united with him, participate in him, are incorporated into him, and as he is God's Son inherently, so in him they become God's sons and daughters by adoption, anticipating now by the Spirit what is to be fully manifested in the coming glory (for further exposition of υἱοθεσία see notes on 4:4–7 below).

The distinctively Pauline expressions 'in Christ', 'in Christ Jesus', 'in the Lord', are by no means mere *theologoumena*; they express an early and wide-spread Christian experience: 'the religious experience of the Christian is not merely experience like that of Jesus, it is experience which at all characteristic and distinctive points is derived from Jesus the Lord, and which only makes sense when this derivative and dependent character is recognized' (J. D. G. Dunn, *Jesus and the Spirit* [London, 1975], 342). It is not peculiar to Paul; it is closely akin to, if not identical with, the Johannine insistence on mutual 'abiding', illustrated by the parable of the vine and the branches (Jn. 15:4–10). The concept is that which in 1 Cor. 6:15–17; 12:12–27 (cf. Rom. 12:4f.) Paul expresses in terms of the body of Christ, that body of which the people of Christ are members. It is difficult to find an adequate precedent for this idea of an 'inclusive' Christ: it is different, for example, from the alleged Hebrew concept of 'corporate personality'. The idea is sometimes spoken of as an instance of 'Pauline mysticism' (cf. A. Schweitzer, *Mysticism*, 116ff., 270ff.), though 'mysticism' is not the aptest term to apply to it. Even less apt is the attempt to depict the idea by means of geometrical diagrams, as in A. Deissmann, *Paul: A Study in Social and Religious History*, ETr (London, 1926), 293–299. One of the most satisfying treatments of the subject is the chapter 'The Corporate Christ' in C. F. D. Moule, *Christology*, 47–96; cf. a chapter with the same title in his *The Phenomenon of the NT* (London, 1967), 21–42.

The body of Christ (the believing community as a whole), together with its members one by one, is vitalized by the life of the risen Christ and energized by his Spirit. Incorporation into this body is effected by personal faith in Christ and sacramentally sealed in baptism (cf. v 27). Membership in the body of Christ has a far-reaching effect on each one who is so incorporated as well as on the community as such. Thus Paul knew himself to be 'a man in Christ' (2 Cor. 12:2); he had been 'crucified with Christ' and henceforth lived as one united by faith to the risen Son of God (2:20 above). His personal appropriation of the love manifested to mankind in the self-giving of Christ was as real as his awareness of faith-union with Christ as the source of his new life. For him in a special way this involved sharing the sufferings of Christ in the course of his apostolic service (see 6:17 below with notes). But each individual believer was a man or woman 'in Christ', in whom Christ lived, and this inclusive relationship with Christ was to be shown forth in the ordinary life of each.

The relation of life 'in Christ' to justification by faith is repeatedly debated. Thus, arguing that 'righteousness by faith and participation in Christ ultimately amount to the same thing', E. P. Sanders speaks of Gal. 3:24–27 'as reflecting better the way Paul thought and Rom. 5:1 as being an unusually schematic presentation which he does not systematically maintain' (*PPJ*, 506 with n. 68). He contrasts this position of his with that of D. O. Via ('Justification and Deliverance: Existential Dialectic', *SR* 1 [1971], 204–212), which views Rom. 5:1 as Paul's exact thought and Gal. 3:24–27 as an instance in which Paul 'uses language inexactly and juxtaposes the two'—justification (in the sense of acquittal) and deliverance (freedom from the power of sin)—'in an unclear way', whereas Paul's 'dominant tendency' was to distinguish the two. In fact, we shall understand both justification and participation (or incorporation) better if we maintain a distinction between them in our thinking. Paul was justified by faith and incorporated into Christ simultaneously and instantaneously on the Damascus road, but he did not confuse the two realities. In Phil. 3:8–11, for example, it is because he no longer had 'a righteousness of my own, based on law, but that which is through faith in Christ', that he could make it his settled purpose in life to advance in the knowledge of Christ, 'and the power of his resurrection, and the fellowship of his sufferings'.

3:27 ὅσοι γὰρ εἰς Χριστὸν ἐβαπτίσθητε, Χριστὸν ἐνεδύσασθε. To be 'baptized into Christ' is to be incorporated into him by baptism, and hence to be 'in Christ'. A fuller statement is given in Rom. 6:3–11, although there the theme of 'baptism into Christ Jesus' is developed as a disincentive to continuing in sin, which is not Paul's point in this immediate context.

This is the only reference to baptism in Galatians, and it is difficult to suppose that the readers would not have understood it as a statement about their initiatory baptism in water 'into the name of the Lord Jesus' (that Paul's converts were so baptized is a reasonable inference from 1 Cor. 1:13: 'was it into *Paul's* name that you were baptized?'). J. D. G. Dunn, however, expresses the opinion that 'βαπτίζεσθαι εἰς Χριστόν is simply a metaphor drawn from the rite of baptism to describe the entry of the believer into Christian experience—or, more precisely, the entry of the believer into the spiritual relationship of the Christian with Christ, which takes place in conversion-initiation' (*Baptism in the Holy Spirit* [London, 1970], 109).

Christian baptism took over from the baptism of John its connexion with repentance and remission of sins and its significance as a pointer to the new age. But it was now administered specifically in Jesus' name and was the outward and visible sign of admission to the new community: 'in one Spirit', says Paul to the Corinthians, 'we were all baptized into one body' (1 Cor. 12:13).

The question arises here: if Paul makes baptism the gateway to 'being-in-Christ', is he not attaching soteriological efficacy to a rite which in itself is as external or 'material' as circumcision? With reference to the 'creative act of justification', E. P. Sanders says that its *Sitz im Leben* 'is baptism, and the gift of the Spirit the means. For Paul, baptism, justification of the sinner, and [new] creation are inseparable' (*PPJ*, 533n.). This may be true, but Paul, who had learned so clearly the religious inadequacy of the old circumcision, was not the man to ascribe *ex opere operato* efficacy to another external rite. If he were asked where and when he received justification by faith, he would have pointed to the Damascus road at the moment when the Lord appeared to him; his baptism, which took place some days later, could have been no more than a seal of what had happened there and then. (Even in Acts 9:17f. it is implied that his baptism followed his filling with the Spirit.) If it is remembered that repentance and faith, with baptism in water and reception of the Spirit, followed by first communion, constituted one complex experience of Christian initiation, then what is true of the experience as a whole can in practice be predicated of any element in it. The creative agency, however, is the Spirit. Baptism in water *per se* is no guarantee of salvation (cf. 1 Cor. 10:1–12) as the indwelling presence of the Spirit is (cf. 4:6 below; Rom. 8:9).

On baptism in Paul see also O. Cullmann, *Baptism in the NT*, ETr (London, 1950), 23ff.; G. W. H. Lampe, *The Seal of the Spirit* (London, 1951), 3ff.; G. R. Beasley-Murray, *Baptism in the NT* (London, 1962), 127ff.; D. E. H. Whiteley, *The Theology of St. Paul* (Oxford, 1964), 166ff.; R. Schnackenburg, *Baptism in the Thought of St. Paul*, ETr (Oxford, 1964); G. Wagner, *Pauline Baptism and the Pagan Mysteries*, ETr (Edinburgh, 1967); K. Barth, *CD* IV/4, ETr (Edinburgh, 1969), 32ff. (on the relation and distinction between water baptism and Spirit baptism); H. Ridderbos, *Paul: An Outline of his Theology*, ETr (Grand Rapids, 1975), 396ff.; J. D. G. Dunn, *Unity*, 158ff.

To 'put on Christ' is for Paul another way of expressing incorporation into him. The closest parallel to Χριστὸν ἐνεδύσασθε here is Rom. 13:14, ἐνδύσασθε τὸν κύριον ᾿Ιησοῦν Χριστόν, but there believers are exhorted to do what they are here said to have done already. This indicative/imperative oscillation is not unparalleled in Paul. 'Be what you are', he says in effect, meaning 'Be in ordinary practice what God's grace has made you.' So in Rom. 6:11f. those who are said to have 'died to sin' in Rom. 6:2 are urged to consider themselves 'dead to sin'; as regards the use of the 'putting on' figure, believers are said in Col. 3:9f. to 'have put off the old man' [the one they formerly were in their unregenerate state] . . . and put on the new man', whereas in Eph. 4:22ff. (if ἀποθέσθαι and ἐνδύσασθαι are infinitives in an indirect command) they are exhorted to 'put off the old man . . . and put on the new man'. But in Col. 3:10 and Eph. 4:24 putting on the new man implies the assumption of a new way of life (which indeed is the point of the exhortation to 'put on the Lord Jesus Christ' in Rom. 13:14), whereas in Gal. 3:27 the ethical aspect is not primarily in view (it is introduced in due course, in 5:13ff.). Here it is the new status, the new order of existence 'in Christ Jesus', that is emphasized.

The metaphorical sense of 'putting on' *may* have been suggested by the converts' divesting themselves of their clothes before baptism and being reclothed afterwards (cf. C. F. D. Moule, *Worship in the NT* [London, 1961], 52f.). Certainly ' "to put on Christ" is simply a figurative usage to describe more expressively the spiritual transformation which makes one a Christian' (J. D. G. Dunn, *Baptism in the Holy Spirit*, 110; cf. his *Unity*, 159); but this still leaves open the question of the origin of this particular figurative usage. S. J. Mikolaski, saying that 'we strip off the clothes of the old life to be clothed with the garments of Christ's righteousness through faith-baptism', points to OT precedents in Ps. 132:9; Is. 61:10; 64:6; Zc. 3:3 (*NBCR*, 1099). The OT background is much more convincing than the attempt to find a pagan background. In some forms of religious initiation known in the Graeco-Roman world the donning of a new garment appears to have symbolized the conferment of immortality or even participation in the divine nature (cf. J. Leipoldt, *Die urchristliche Taufe im Licht der Religionsgeschichte* [Leipzig, 1928], 60; H.-J. Schoeps, *Paul*, 112f.; cf. G. Wagner, *Pauline Baptism and the Pagan Mysteries*, 29 n. 102 *et passim*, for a critique of theories accounting for Pauline baptismal imagery in such terms). While Paul was not influenced by such ideas or practices, they could certainly have influenced some of his Gentile converts in their understanding of his teaching. (For gnostic usage see H. D. Betz, *Galatians,* 188 n. 61.)

3:28 οὐκ ἔνι. In origin, ἔνι is a strengthened form of the preposition ἐν, but in classical usage it became a variant of ἔνεστι(ν) (cf. 1 Cor. 6:5). Here, however (as in Col. 3:11; Jas. 1:17, where also it is negatived by οὐκ), it is an emphatic equivalent of ἐστίν.

We have parallels to such open religious fellowship elsewhere in antiquity; for example, in *SIG*³ III.985 there is an account of a private cult-group in Philadelphia, founded in the first or second century BC by one Dionysius in pursuance of directions received from Zeus in a dream, which was explicitly open to 'men and women, free persons and household slaves', and in which ethical probity was insisted on.

The first stipulation here, however, is that in Christ there is neither Jew nor Greek (for Ἕλλην in the sense of 'Gentile' see on 2:3); the breaking down of the middle wall of partition between these two was fundamental to Paul's gospel (Eph. 2:14f.). By similarly excluding the religious distinction between slaves and the freeborn, and between male and female, Paul makes a threefold affirmation which corresponds to a number of Jewish formulas in which the threefold distinction is maintained, as in the morning prayer in which the male Jew thanks God that he was not made a Gentile, a slave or a woman (S. Singer, *The Authorised Daily Prayer Book* [London, 1939], 5f.). This threefold thanksgiving can be traced back as far as R. Judah b. Elai, *c*. AD 150 (t. Ber. 7.18), or his contemporary R. Me'ir (b. Men. 43b)—both with 'brutish man' [*bôr*] instead of 'slave'. The reason for the threefold thanksgiving was not any positive disparagement of Gentiles, slaves or women as persons but the fact that they were disqualified from several religious privileges which were open to free Jewish males.

The formula may be even earlier, for it seems to have been modelled on a Greek formula going back as far as Thales (6th century BC), who is reported by Hermippus to have said that there were three things for which he was grateful to fortune: that he was born a human being and not a beast, a man and not a woman, a Greek and not a barbarian (Diog. Laert., *Vit. Phil.* 1.33). Substantially the same saying is attributed to Socrates (Diog. Laert., ibid.) and Plato (Plut., *Marius* 46.1; Lactantius, *Inst.* 3.19.17). A comparable saying from a Zoroastrian source is mentioned by H. D. Betz, *Galatians*, 185 n. 26 (quoting J. Darmesteter, *Une prière judéo-persane* [Paris, 1891]).

It is not unlikely that Paul himself had been brought up to thank God that he was born a Jew and not a Gentile, a freeman and not a slave, a man and not a woman. If so, he takes up each of these three distinctions which had considerable importance in Judaism and affirms that in Christ they are all irrelevant. He may here express an insight of his own, arising out of his sure grasp of what was involved in the attitude and achievement of Jesus. Another view is that he is quoting 'what is almost surely a fragment of an early baptismal formula' (R. Scroggs, *IDBSup* 966, *s.v.* 'Woman in the NT'; he cites the parallel structures of 1 Cor. 12:12f. and Col. 3:9–11); if so, it may be asked if the formula was not based on Paul's own teaching and practice.

Paul makes some reference to these three dual categories in 1 Cor. 7 where he exhorts the circumcised and uncircumcised to remain as they were in this regard at the time of their conversion (vv 18f.), the slave and the free person to be content with their respective stations in life and not try to change them (vv 21–23), and married and unmarried persons to continue so, in the one way or the other: 'in whatever state each was called, there let him/her remain with God' (v 24). Either way, it can make no difference to one's status in Christ.

οὐκ ἔνι 'Ιουδαῖος οὐδὲ "Ελλην. The cleavage between Jew and Gentile was for Judaism the most radical within the human race. It was indeed possible for a Gentile to become a Jewish proselyte; some Jewish teachers indeed thought that the greatest kindness they could show to Gentiles was to win them: 'love your fellow-creatures', said Hillel, 'and bring them near to the Torah' (m. Ab. 1.12). But a Gentile who became a proselyte crossed over to the Jewish side of the gulf; the gulf remained. It is clear both from Paul's letters and from the record of Acts that the gospel principle of complete equality of Jew and Gentile before God was not accepted in the early church without a struggle. There were influential voices in the church which maintained that Gentiles could be admitted into its membership on a similar footing to the admission of proselytes into the Jewish community: they must be circumcised (if males) and conform in some degree to Jewish law and custom. Some who took this line probably regarded the indiscriminate evangelization of Gentiles as unwise; they could well have taken up and appropriated the *logion*: 'Let the children first be fed, for it is not right to take the children's bread and throw it to the dogs' (Mk. 7:27).

This attitude seems to have hardened in the interval between the Jerusalem conference of Gal. 2:1–10 and the development of the crisis which called forth the present letter: on the former occasion, no voice was apparently raised to demand that the Gentile Titus should be circumcised, but now (in part, perhaps, because of external pressure) circumcision was being urged upon the Gentile members of the Galatian churches.

Paul's position was clear-cut: had the law shown itself able to impart life, this would have given the Jews an overwhelming advantage; but since the law's inability to do any such thing had been demonstrated, there was now no distinction between Jews and Gentiles before God in respect either of their moral bankruptcy or of their need to receive his pardoning grace. The law-free gospel put both communities on one and the same level before God, so that 'in Christ' there was 'neither Jew nor Greek' (cf. also Rom. 1:16; 3:22f.; 10:12; 15:8f.; 1 Cor. 1:24; Eph. 2:13–22; 3:6; Col. 3:11).

οὐκ ἔνι δοῦλος οὐδὲ ἐλεύθερος. The social inferiority of slaves was marked enough in Jewish society, but still more so in Mediterranean society generally and most of all in Roman law.

Paul's general attitude to the status of Christian slaves is shown in 1 Cor. 7:22, 'he who was called in the Lord as a slave is the Lord's freedman (ἀπελεύθερος); likewise he who was free when called is Christ's slave'. Christian slaves should not chafe at their underprivileged status in the world; 'in Christ'—and on the practical level that meant in the church—they were entitled to enjoy equal rank with their free brothers and sisters. This could mean, for example, that someone who was a slave in the outside world might be entrusted with spiritual leadership in the church, and if the owner of the slave was a member of the same church, he would submit to that spiritual leadership. There is sufficient evidence that this was not merely a theoretical possibility.

When Paul sent Onesimus back to his master Philemon, 'no longer as a slave but better than a slave, as a beloved brother' (Phm. 16), we do not know if Philemon responded to the apostle's hint and sent Onesimus back to continue serving him or retained Onesimus in much the same kind of household service as formerly. But Onesimus was now a fellow-member with Philemon in the church of Colossae (Col. 4:9). The church provided a setting in which the master-slave relationship (or, if Philemon emancipated Onesimus, the patron-freedman relationship) was irrelevant. If it could be established that Philemon's slave was the Onesimus who was bishop of Ephesus half-a-century later (Ign. *Eph*. 1:3; cf. J. Knox, *Philemon among the Letters of Paul* [London, ²1960], 88–92), this would provide sufficient evidence that former servile status was no bar to church leadership. Callixtus, bishop of Rome early in the 3rd century (AD 217–222), was an ex-slave, if Hippolytus is to be believed (*Haer*. 9.11f.), and Pius I, an earlier occupant of the same see, was, if not a slave himself, at least the brother of a slave (Hermas, author of the *Shepherd*), according to the compiler of the Muratorian canon (lines 73–77).

On the general subject see M. I. Finley (ed.), *Slavery in Classical Antiquity* (New York, ²1968), and in relation to Christianity, S. S. Bartchy, ΜΑΛΛΟΝ ΧΡΗΣΑΙ: *First-Century Slavery and 1 Corinthians 7:21* (Missoula, 1973).

οὐκ ἔνι ἄρσεν καὶ θῆλυ. There is a slight change of construction here (with no substantial change in meaning): Paul does not say, following the precedent of the two companion clauses, οὐκ ἔνι ἄρσεν οὐδὲ θῆλυ. The reason for the change is probably the influence of Gn. 1:27, ἄρσεν καὶ θῆλυ ἐποίησεν αὐτούς, 'he made them male and female' (cf. Mk. 10:6). In Christ, on the contrary, 'there is no "male and female".' Paul's statement was echoed later in those gnostic circles which held that, in the new age, man would no longer be separated into 'male and female' but would revert to a (supposedly) pristine androgynous state (cf. *Gos. Egy.*, quoted by Clem. Alex., *Strom*. 3.45, 63ff., 91, where Jesus is recorded as foretelling the day 'when the two become one and the male with the female neither male nor female'). W. A. Meeks, 'The Image of the Androgyne: Some Uses of a Symbol in Earliest Christianity', *History of Religions* 13 (1973–74), 165–208 (cited favourably by H. D. Betz, *Galatians*, 196 n. 122), thinks that Paul is here quoting a 'baptismal reunification formula' which envisaged the restoration of a pristine androgynous image. But Paul himself is not concerned with any such fantasy; he is concerned with practical church life in which men and women (like Jews and Gentiles, slaves and free persons) are here and now fellow-members. It is not their distinctiveness, but their inequality of religious role, that is abolished 'in Christ Jesus'.

Whereas Paul's ban on discrimination on racial or social grounds has been fairly widely accepted *au pied de la lettre*, there has been a tendency to restrict the degree to which 'there is no "male and female" '. Thus it has been argued that these words relate only to the common access of men and women to baptism, with its introduction to their new existence 'in Christ'. True, Paul may have had in mind that circumcision involved a form of discrimination between men and women which was removed when circumcision was demoted from its position as religious law, whereas baptism was open to both sexes indiscriminately. But the denial of discrimination which is sacramentally affirmed in baptism holds good for the new existence 'in Christ' in its entirety. No more restriction is implied in Paul's equalizing of the status of male and female in Christ than in his equalizing of the status of Jew and Gentile, or of slave and free person. If in ordinary life existence in Christ is manifested openly in church fellowship, then, if a Gentile may exercise spiritual leadership in church as freely as a Jew, or a slave as freely as a citizen, why not a woman as freely as a man?

In other spheres, indeed, the distinctions which ceased to be relevant in church fellowship might continue to be observed. In Roman law the distinction between slave and free person remained; in the family the cooperation of husband and wife, or father and mother, depended (as it still does) on the distinction between them. But superiority and inferiority of status or esteem could have no place in the society whose Founder laid it down that among his followers 'whoever would be first . . . must be slave of all' (Mk. 10:44).

How Paul allowed the principle of 'no "male and female" ' to operate in practice may be seen, for example, in his appreciation of the Philippian women who 'laboured side by side' with him in the gospel (Phil. 4:3) or his recognition of the right of women to pray and prophesy in church—the veil being the symbol of their authority (ἐξουσία) to do so (1 Cor. 11:10; cf. M. D. Hooker, 'Authority on her head: an examination of 1 Cor. xi.10', *NTS* 10 [1963–64], 410–416; A. Jaubert, 'La voile des femmes (1 Cor. xi.2–16)', *NTS* 18 [1971–72], 419–430). Paul states the basic principle here; if restrictions on it are found elsewhere in the Pauline corpus, as in 1 Cor. 14:34f. (on the text of which see G. Zuntz, *The Text of the Epistles* [London, 1953], 17) or 1 Tim. 2:11f., they are to be understood in relation to Gal. 3:28, and not *vice versa*. Attempts to find canon law in Paul, or to base canon law on Paul, should be forestalled by a consideration of Paul's probable reaction to the very idea of canon law.

See J. Leipoldt, *Die Frau in der antiken Welt und im Urchristentum* (Leipzig, ²1962); K. Stendahl, *The Bible and the Role of Women* (Philadelphia, 1966); P. K. Jewett, *Man as Male and Female* (Grand Rapids, 1975); S. B. Clark, *Man and Woman in Christ* (Ann Arbor, 1980); A. Cameron, ' "Neither Male nor Female" ', *Greece and Rome*, series 2, 27 (1980), 60–68.

πάντες γὰρ ὑμεῖς εἷς ἐστε ἐν Χριστῷ ᾽Ιησοῦ, 'you are all one by being in Christ Jesus' (M. J. Harris, *NIDNTT* 3, 1192). For ἐν Χριστῷ ᾽Ιησοῦ see note on v 26. Although Paul does not use 'body' language in Galatians, his present statement is practically equivalent to ἓν σῶμά ἐσμεν ἐν Χριστῷ (Rom. 12:5), ἓν σῶμα οἱ πολλοί ἐσμεν (1 Cor. 10:17). Here, however, there is special emphasis on Jews and Gentiles (not to speak of free persons and slaves, males and females) being one in Christ (cf. 1 Cor. 12:13; Eph. 2:15).

3:29 εἰ δὲ ὑμεῖς Χριστοῦ. Those who are ἐν Χριστῷ are also 'Christ's' (Χριστοῦ), not only in the sense that they belong to Christ or follow Christ (cf. 2 Cor. 10:7) but even more in the sense that they participate in him by the Spirit; cf. Rom. 8:9b (εἰ δέ τις πνεῦμα Χριστοῦ οὐκ ἔχει, οὗτος οὐκ ἔστιν αὐτοῦ); also Rom. 14:8 (τοῦ κυρίου ἐσμέν).

ἄρα τοῦ ᾽Αβραὰμ σπέρμα ἐστέ. If Christ is Abraham's offspring, according to the promise (cf. v 16), then those who are Christ's, participating in him by faith, whether Gentiles or Jews, are likewise Abraham's offspring (cf. v 7). If the agitators had insisted to the Galatians that it was desirable, and indeed necessary for salvation, to become sons of Abraham (by circumcision), Paul counters their arguments by insisting that union with Christ by faith is the only way of becoming Abraham's children in the sense that matters with God.

κατ' ἐπαγγελίαν κληρονόμοι. Because 'there is neither Jew nor Greek', Gentile as well as Jewish believers are Abraham's offspring in Christ, heirs with him of the blessing promised to Abraham. The idea of inheritance here is on all fours with that expressed later in Eph. 1:13f.; 3:6, where Gentiles are fellow-heirs (συγκληρονόμα) and have received the Spirit as the guarantee and initial instalment (ἀρραβών) of their inheritance, equally with Jewish believers (*pace* P. L. Hammer, 'A comparison of *klēronomia* in Paul and Ephesians', *JBL* 79 [1960], 267–272, who argues that the sense of κληρονομία in Ephesians is different from that in the Pauline *homologoumena*, since in the latter it is orientated to the past, but in Ephesians to the future). According to Rom. 8:18–25, believers enter upon their full heritage when they receive their public investiture as sons of God on the day of final redemption (see 4:6f. below, with notes). Cf. also J. D. Hester, *Paul's Conception of Inheritance* (Edinburgh, 1968).

The principles enunciated in this paragraph (vv 26–29) were revolutionary enough even within the fellowship of small local groups here and there throughout the Graeco-Roman world. But when these groups and their members multiplied until they formed a significant segment of society, there was a real possibility that such revolutionary principles would infect society at large, and the imperial authorities in the second and third centuries saw the spread of Christianity as a disintegrating ferment in the body politic. In historical fact, however, influences worked in two directions: if the church increasingly influenced pagan society, pagan society in some degree at least influenced the church.

(i) From slavery to sonship (4:1–7)

Let me put it this way: so long as the heir is an infant, he is no different from a slave, though he is owner of everything, but he is under guardians and stewards until the time fixed by his father. So it was with us: when we were infants, we were enslaved under the elemental forces of the world. But when the appointed time had fully come, God sent forth his Son, born of a woman, born under law, to redeem those who were under law, in order that we might receive our instatement as sons. Now, because you are sons, God has sent forth the Spirit of his Son into our hearts, crying 'Abba, Father!' So then, you are no longer a slave, but a son, and if a son, then also an heir through God.

TEXTUAL NOTES

v 3   ημεθα P⁴⁶ א D* G 33 *al* / ημεν *cett*
v 6   ο θεος *om* B 1739 lat' copˢᵃ Tert
      του υιου *om* P⁴⁶ Mcion Aug
      ημων / υμων D² K L Ψ *al* latᵛᵍ·ᶜᵒᵈᵈ syr copᵇᵒ
v 7   δια θεου P⁴⁶ א* A B C* lat copᵇᵒ Clem Ambst / δια Ιησου 431 / δια Χριστου 81 copˢᵃ Hier / θεου δια Χριστου א² D byz / θεου δια Ιησου 326 *al* syr / δια

θεον G *pc* / θεου eth arm / μεν θεου συνκληρονομος δε Χριστου Ψ *pc* (cf. Rom. 8:17)

4:1 Λέγω δέ, 'I mean', 'let me put it this way'. Paul takes up a different analogy from those used in 3:22–26 to set forth the contrast between the previous period of spiritual immaturity and the new life of full-grown freedom, bringing it up to date by including the theme of inheritance, introduced in 3:29. The law has been compared to a prison-warden and a slave-attendant; now its role is compared to that of the guardians and trustees appointed to take care of a minor and his property.

ἐφ' ὅσον χρόνον ὁ κληρονόμος νήπιός ἐστιν. The κληρονόμος is the son to whom the patrimony is to come in due course. While he is a νήπιος, an 'infant' in the legal sense—one who has not yet come of age—he is not given his freedom, he is hedged about with restrictions. He is 'no different from a slave' (οὐδὲν διαφέρει δούλου) in this sense, that he is not his own master. The patrimony is legally his, yet he has no power to dispose of it.

4:2 ἀλλὰ ὑπὸ ἐπιτρόπους ἐστὶν καὶ οἰκονόμους. Here it is ἐπίτροποι and οἰκονόμοι, guardians and stewards or trustees, who correspond to the παιδαγωγός in 3:24, and like the παιδαγωγός they represent the law.

In Roman law the heir, until he came of age at fourteen, was under the control of a *tutor*, nominated by the father in his will; then, until he reached the age of twenty-five, he was under a *curator*, appointed by the *praetor urbanus* (Justinian, *Inst*. 1.22, 23). In some parts of the empire at least, the father was permitted to appoint by will the *curator* as well as the *tutor*; thus the fifth-century Syro-Latin law-book (see note on 3:15) allows him to nominate both an ἐπίτροπος and a κουράτωρ (the Latin term transliterated) for his children who are under age (ed. K. G. Bruns and E. Sachau, 12). However, Paul's ἐπίτροποι and οἰκονόμοι need not be taken to correspond respectively to the *tutores* and *curatores* of Roman law in any strict sense; if there is any distinction between the two terms he uses, it might be suggested that the ἐπίτροπος is in personal charge of the minor while the οἰκονόμος looks after his property.

ἄχρι τῆς προθεσμίας τοῦ πατρός. In Roman law the time at which the son came of age and became a free agent (namely, at the completion of fourteen years) was fixed by statute. Yet some discretion was reserved to the father; cf. Justinian, *Inst*. 1.14.3: 'ad certum tempus, uel ex certo tempore, uel sub condicione, uel ante heredis institutionem, posse dari tutorem non dubitatur' ('Beyond question, a tutor may be appointed until a fixed time, or from a fixed time, or conditionally, or before the institution of an heir'). The *certum tempus* could be what Paul means by the προθεσμία τοῦ πατρός (so A. Halmel, *Über römisches Recht im Galaterbrief*, summarized by D. Walker, 'The Legal Terminology in the Epistle to the Galatians', 118–120).

Paul's expression in this kind of context is illustrated by *P. Oxy*. 491.8–10, in the will of one Eudaemon of Oxyrhynchus (AD 126), relating to two of his sons who were minors: 'If I die before the said Horus and Eudaemon have completed twenty years, their brother Thonis and their maternal grandfather Harpaësis, also called Horus, son of Thonis, shall be guardian (ἐπίτροπος) of each of them until he completes twenty years.' Here the twentieth birthday anniversary is the προθεσμία τοῦ πατρός.

The word προθεσμία is used from classical times onwards of a 'fixed term' in a variety of legal contexts, e.g. of the appointed day for the repayment of a loan, as in *P. Oxy*. 485.20, 27.

See E. D. Burton, *Galatians*, 212–215, for a detailed discussion.

4:3 οὕτως καὶ ἡμεῖς, ὅτε ἦμεν νήπιοι, ὑπὸ τὰ στοιχεῖα τοῦ κόσμου ἤμεθα δεδουλωμένοι. The juxtaposition of the two forms of the 1st plural imperfect of εἰμί—ἦμεν (classical) and ἤμεθα (Hellenistic)—is to be noted. While the textual evidence is divided, the natural tendency towards assimilation of the two forms speaks in favour of the UBS³ and Nestle-Aland²⁶ reading. The periphrastic construction of the pluperfect passive, ἤμεθα δεδουλωμένοι (cf. BDF 352), emphasizes the state in which 'we' were 'when we were infants' more than ἐδεδουλώμεθα would have done; in any case, many of the straight pluperfect forms were falling into disuse.

The question arises whether the emphatic ἡμεῖς is inclusive ('we Christians, whether Jews or Gentiles by birth') or exclusive, distinguishing Paul and his fellow-believers of Jewish birth from his Galatian converts of Gentile origin ('we Jews by birth as well as you Gentiles'). It is true, as v 9 indicates, that the latter also were enslaved to the στοιχεῖα, but probably Paul is making his point here with primary reference to the Jewish law; in v 8 he makes it with reference to the pagan worship of unreal gods.

He moves from the institution of guardians and stewards in ordinary life to the analogical situation in spiritual experience: when we were in our religious 'infancy', he says, we were enslaved under the στοιχεῖα of the world; they were our controllers or custodians. Whatever else may be said of these στοιχεῖα, they plainly include the law, in the sense of 3:23 (which refers to the same situation): 'Before faith came, we were guarded ὑπὸ νόμον.'

The word στοιχεῖα means primarily things placed side by side in a row; it is used of the letters of the alphabet, the ABCs, and then, because the learning of the ABCs is the first lesson in a literary education, it comes to mean 'rudiments', 'first principles' (as in Heb. 5:12). Again, since the letters of the alphabet were regarded as the 'elements' of which words and sentences are built up, στοιχεῖα comes to be used of the 'elements' which make up the material world (cf. 2 Pet. 3:10, 12). This would be the natural sense of τὰ στοιχεῖα τοῦ κόσμου unless the context dictated otherwise; the exact phrase is used in this sense by Philo (*Aet. Mund*. 109).

Elsewhere (*Vit. Cont*. 3) Philo speaks of the Greeks who revere the four elements (στοιχεῖα)—earth, water, air, fire—and give them the names of divinities (respectively Demeter, Poseidon, Hera, Hephaestus); in yet another place (*Decal*. 53) he says that 'some have deified the four elements (στοιχεῖα), earth, water, air and fire; others the sun and moon and the other planets and fixed stars; others again the heaven alone; others the whole world', and he mentions not only the names by which the elements are worshipped but those given to the luminaries and so forth. Cf. Wis. 13:2, where the various elements are mentioned as receiving worship from those who are ignorant of God, but are not called στοιχεῖα but rather πρυτάνεις κόσμου ('rulers of the world').

Ps.-Callisthenes (*Alexander Romance*, 1.1) says that the royal enchanter Nectanebo 'subjected to himself all the cosmic στοιχεῖα, including the ἀέρια πνεύματα καὶ οἱ καταχθόνιοι δαίμονες (the spirits of the air and the demons of the underworld)' and later (1.12) Nectanebo is said to observe τοὺς οὐρανίους δρόμους τῶν κοσμικῶν στοιχείων ('the heavenly courses of the cosmic elements').

If Paul had been referring only to the former paganism of the Galatians, the στοιχεῖα τοῦ κόσμου might have had the same kind of meaning as in those quotations from Philo and Ps.-Callisthenes, but in the immediate context existence ὑπὸ τὰ στοιχεῖα τοῦ κόσμου is equated with existence ὑπὸ νόμον (vv 4f.). He speaks of the time during which the people of God lived 'under law' as the time they spent in the infant class learning their ABCs—which for them amounted to 'the rudimentary notions of the world' (B. M. Metzger, *The New Oxford Annotated Bible* [New York, 1977], 1413). But this was not merely a time of elementary education; it was a time of bondage. Two further questions have to be asked about the στοιχεῖα, although the attempt to answer them is best postponed to the further occurrence of the word in v 9: (i) Why are they called the στοιχεῖα *of the world*? and (ii) In what sense could it be said that the Galatian Christians in their pagan days were under the same στοιχεῖα as had controlled Paul and his fellow-Jews? For the present stage of Paul's argument it suffices to observe that the law ranks as one of the στοιχεῖα.

In arguing that Paul's reasoning proceeds back from his conviction of the universal solution (salvation by grace) to the human plight, E. P. Sanders (*PPJ*, 474 with n. 2) points to the variety of expressions used by Paul to describe the human plight, of which universal enslavement to the *stoicheia* of the world is one—others being universal sin (Rom. 3:22) and universal death in Adam (Rom. 5:18; 1 Cor. 15:22).

4:4 ὅτε δὲ ἦλθεν τὸ πλήρωμα τοῦ χρόνου. The πλήρωμα τοῦ χρόνου in the divine act of adoption corresponds to the προθεσμία in the adoptive procedure envisaged in v 2. Here, it may be said, we have the προθεσμία of the heavenly Father—the time fixed 'for us to receive the υἱοθεσία'. The υἱοθεσία is the subject in the forefront of Paul's mind at this point in his argument: the sending of God's Son and his redemption of those who were 'under law', important as these are in their own right, are here means to an end, the end being the υἱοθεσία of believers.

That the sending of God's Son took place at the nodal point of salvation-history Paul both believed and affirmed. It is for this reason that the people of Christ are those 'upon whom the ends of the ages (τὰ τέλη τῶν αἰώνων) have met' (1 Cor. 10:11). Cf. Mk. 1:15, πεπλήρωται ὁ καιρός (see H. N. Ridderbos, *When the Time had Fully Come* [Grand Rapids, 1957], 48, 68f., *et passim*). But what is emphasized here is that the nodal point of salvation-history, marked by the coming of Christ (cf. 3:24, εἰς Χριστόν) or the coming of 'faith' (cf. 3:23, 25), constitutes the divinely ordained epoch for the people of God to enter into their inheritance as his mature and responsible sons and daughters. It is the coming of Christ that makes this particular epoch the πλήρωμα τοῦ χρόνου. Here it is the 'realized' aspect of Christian eschatology that Paul presents, the 'already' rather than the 'not yet'. The Galatians must understand that the period of tutelage is past; their spiritual majority has arrived. See G. Bornkamm, *Paul*, 196–200.

ἐξαπέστειλεν ὁ θεὸς τὸν υἱὸν αὐτοῦ. R. H. Fuller, 'The Conception/Birth of Jesus as a Christological Moment', *JSNT*, Issue 1 (1978), 37–52 (especially

40f.), developing a suggestion of E. Schweizer (*TDNT* VIII, 374–376, *s.v.* υἱός), discerns here the beginning of a pre-Pauline summary, perhaps of the kind described as a 'baptismal anamnesis' by N. A. Dahl ('Anamnesis: Mémoire et commémoration dans le christianisme primitif', *ST* 1 [1947], 69–95, especially 74f.), which Paul amplifies in vv 4–6. A tentative reconstruction of the summary, in six cola, would be:

> God sent forth his Son,
> born of a woman,
> that we might receive our instatement as sons.
> Now, because you are sons,
> God has sent forth the Spirit . . .
> crying 'Abba, Father!'

Here the first three cola speak of God's sending of his Son, the second three of his sending of the Spirit.

Does the 'sending' of the Son imply his pre-existence? If the Spirit was the Spirit before God sent him, the Son was presumably the Son before God sent *him*. Moreover, it seems clear that Paul believed in the pre-existence of Christ as the wisdom of God, his agent in the work of creation (1 Cor. 1:24, 30; 8:6b; cf. Col. 1:15–17), and as one who accompanied the people of Israel in the wilderness (1 Cor. 10:4, ἡ πέτρα δὲ ἦν ὁ Χριστός, an instance of the 'real presence' of Christ in the OT; cf. A. T. Hanson, *Jesus Christ in the OT* [London, 1965], 10ff.). If, then, Paul thought of Christ as in some sense pre-existent, this idea may well have been in his mind when he spoke of God as sending his Son, even if the Son's pre-existence would not be *necessarily* inferred from his present language (cf. Rom. 8:3, ὁ θεὸς τὸν ἑαυτοῦ υἱὸν πέμψας ἐν ὁμοιώματι σαρκὸς ἁμαρτίας κτλ, where pre-existence certainly seems to be in Paul's mind). But if we have to do with a pre-Pauline summary here, would pre-existence have been in the minds of those responsible for the summary? Probably it would, for the identification of Christ with the divine wisdom through which the worlds were made was not peculiar to Paul and does not appear to have originated with him (cf. Jn. 1:2f.; Heb. 1:2; Rev. 3:14). However, pre-existence is irrelevant to the present argument.

γενόμενον ἐκ γυναικός, 'born of a woman'; for this well-attested use of γίνομαι as a quasi-passive of γεννάω cf. 1 Esd. 4:16; Tob. 8:6; Wis. 7:3; Sir. 44:9; Jn. 8:58. The expression echoes Heb. yᵉlûḏ 'iššāh, 'born of a woman' (cf. Jb. 14:1; 15:14; 25:4; 1QH 13:14; 1QS 11:21). The plural ἐν γεννητοῖς γυναικῶν is found in Jesus' appraisal of John the Baptist in Mt. 11:11 // Lk. 7:28. Nothing can be made of Paul's use of γενόμενον rather than γεννητόν. In this kind of context they are synonyms (but see C. E. B. Cranfield, *Romans*, 59, on Rom. 1:3, τοῦ γενομένου ἐκ σπέρματος Δαυείδ). Paul's wording is applicable to any one of woman born; it throws no light on the question whether he knew of Jesus' virginal conception or not.

See J. G. Machen, *The Virgin Birth of Christ* (London, ²1932), 259f.; E. de Roover, 'La maternité virginale de Marie dans l'interprétation de Gal 4, 4', *Studiorum paulinorum congressus internationalis catholicus 1961* = *AnBib* 17–18 (Rome, 1963), 17–37; R. E. Brown, *The Birth of the Messiah* (Garden City, N.Y., 1977), 518f.; R. E. Brown etc. (ed.), *Mary in the NT* (London, 1978), 42–44.

The aorist participle γενόμενον is probably to be understood as 'simultaneous' or 'coincident' (see MHT I, 130–134); cf. Phil. 2:7, ἐν ὁμοιώματι ἀνθρώπων γενόμενος, where also γενόμενος seems to mean 'born': 'he emptied himself by taking the form of a slave, by being born in human likeness'. Here, then, God's sending his Son coincides with his birth from a woman. We may compare how in the OT the missions of the Servant of Yahweh and of Jeremiah are dated from their conception and birth (Is. 49:1, 5; Je. 1:5, 7); cf. also what Paul has said of himself in 1:15f.

γενόμενον ὑπὸ νόμον. If the context is taken over from a pre-Pauline summary, this could be Paul's contribution. By being born of a Jewish mother, Jesus was born a Jew and, as such, ὑπὸ νόμον. He entered into the prison-house where his people were held in bondage so as to set them free. It is implied that he himself was not enslaved to the bondage in which they were held, and while Paul does not say so here explicitly, the reason must be that he remained free from sin—while ὑπὸ νόμον, he was nevertheless not ὑπὸ ἁμαρτίαν (cf. 2 Cor. 5:21, τὸν μὴ γνόντα ἁμαρτίαν). He himself had no need of slave-attendant, guardian or steward, and he came to bring his people to the point where they too could dispense with their services.

Christ entered by birth into an inherited obligation to obey the law of God, but to him such obedience was no mere obligation but a spontaneous joy. Paul might have put on the lips of Christ the language of Ps. 40:8, 'I delight to do thy will, O my God; thy law is within my heart' (as the LXX version of the former clause [LXX 39:9a] is put on his lips in Heb. 10:7, 9); but when he speaks here of Christ having been born under law he bears in mind what he has already said about the *curse* of the law (3:10, 13). In Paul's thinking, for the Son of God to be born under that law which he rejoiced to fulfil involved his voluntarily taking on himself the curse which others, by their *failure* to fulfil it, had incurred. Only so could he accomplish the purpose of redeeming those who were 'under law' (v 5). 'He not only became *man*, bound to obedience . . .; but He became *curse* for us. He made our *doom* His own. He took on Him not only the calling of a man, but our responsibility as sinful men; it is in this that His work as our Redeemer lies, for it is in this that the measure, or rather the immensity, of His love is seen' (J. Denney, *The Death of Christ*, 156).

4:5 ἵνα τοὺς ὑπὸ νόμον ἐξαγοράσῃ, 'to redeem those who were under law', bound, guarded and enslaved (3:23f.; 4:1–3). To be redeemed from existence 'under law' is to be redeemed from 'the curse of the law' (3:13). This redemption, according to 3:13f., was effected by Christ's enduring the death on which a curse was pronounced; thus God's sending his Son (v 4) is immediately associated with the death of his Son. Similarly in Rom. 8:3 God's sending his Son 'in the likeness of sinful flesh' is immediately associated with the Son's self-offering περὶ ἁμαρτίας, by which God 'condemned sin in the flesh'.

Even if Paul begins this section (vv 3–7) by thinking in particular of Jewish Christians (καὶ ἡμεῖς), who had lived more directly ὑπὸ νόμον, it is plain now that the beneficiaries of Christ's redeeming work (as in 3:13f.) include Gentiles as well as Jews. The oscillation between 'we' (ἵνα . . . ἀπολάβωμεν, v 5; cf. εἰς τὰς καρδίας ἡμῶν, v 6), 'you' (ὅτι δέ ἐστε υἱοί, v 6) and 'thou' (οὐκέτι εἶ δοῦλος, v 7), attests the inclusive emphasis of Paul's wording and argument (as in 3:23–26).

The two ἵνα clauses in v 5 are formally parallel, like the two ἵνα clauses in 3:14, but this time the latter clause is materially dependent on the former, or at least carries on the thought to a point beyond that reached by the former. Those who have been redeemed by Christ from their former life 'under law' are the 'we' who through him receive their instatement as sons; indeed, it may be said that the purpose of Christ's redeeming them was that they—both Jews and (quite emphatically) Gentiles—should receive this instatement.

ἵνα τὴν υἱοθεσίαν ἀπολάβωμεν, 'that we might receive the adoption'— i.e. instatement as sons. υἱοθεσία (εἰσποίησις in Attic law) is the equivalent of Lat. adoptio.

It is frequently said that adoption was not a practice known to Hebrew law or custom. The nearest institution to it—the levirate marriage by which a dead man might receive by proxy a posthumous son who would perpetuate his name and inheritance in Israel—is nowhere referred to in terms of adoption. It may be that in the patriarchal age adoption was practised in a manner similar to that attested in the Nuzu documents—cf. Eliezer's potential relation to Abraham (Gn. 15:2f.) and Jacob's to Laban (Gn. 29:14ff.)—but there is no trace of it in post-settlement times. Neither υἱοθεσία nor the verb υἱοθετέω occurs in the LXX. Cf. R. de Vaux, *Ancient Israel*, ETr (London, ²1965), 21f., 37f., 42, 51f.

On the other hand, although the term is unknown in the OT, something very like adoption is implied in Yahweh's relation to Israel, his 'first-born son' (Ex. 4:22). Cf. Ho. 11:1, 'When Israel was a child, I loved him, and out of Egypt I called my son', with the comment by G. A. Smith: 'God's eyes, passing the princes of the world, fell upon this slave boy, and He loved him and gave him a career' (*The Book of the Twelve Prophets*, II [London, ²1928], 317). 'Paul's metaphor of adoption . . . might even have been derived from Israel's deliverance out of bondage in Egypt' (D. J. Theron, ' "Adoption" in the Pauline Corpus', *EQ* 28 [1956], 14). And this is rendered the more probable by Paul's own reference to 'Israelites, to whom belongs the υἱοθεσία' (Rom. 9:4).

But while the OT may have provided Paul with the theological background of his adoption terminology, contemporary practice is more likely to have provided him with some of his analogies (like the προθεσμία of v 1). By contrast with Jewish law, Greek and (especially) Roman law were well acquainted with the institution of adoption. In Paul's day it played an increasingly important part in Roman life; for example, from the late first century to the mid-second century AD and beyond successive Roman emperors adopted men not related to them by blood with the intention that they should succeed them in the principate.

If the son to be adopted was not yet of age, his original father conveyed him into the *potestas* of his adoptive father by a pretended sale. Once adopted into the new family, the son was in all legal respects on a level with those born into that family. If the son to be adopted was of age, he was adopted by his new father in the ceremony of *adrogatio*, in which the pontifex maximus and the augurs were involved. It was also possible, later, for a testator to adopt some one in his will.

The Roman process of adoption required the presence of seven witnesses. Their testimony was crucial if, after the adoptive father's death, his 'natural' heirs contested the validity of the adoption: the witnesses had to testify that a valid adoption had taken place in their presence. We may compare the twofold testimony confirming the divine adoption of believers in Rom. 8:15f.

Apart, then, from the theological background, there is justification for F. Lyall's statement that 'Roman law is the only source of reference for Paul' ('Roman Law in the Writings of Paul—Adoption', *JBL* 88 [1969], 459).

See also (in addition to literature cited in the preceding paragraphs) W. M. Calder, 'Adoption and Inheritance in Galatia', *JTS* 31 (1930), 372–374; W. H. Rossell, 'New Testament Adoption: Graeco-Roman or Semitic?' *JBL* 71 (1952), 233f.; J. I. Cook, 'The Concept of Adoption in the Theology of Paul', *Oudersluys FS*, 133–144.

M. D. Hooker finds here a further instance of the 'interchange' principle (see note on 3:14): 'It is because Christ is acknowledged as righteous, that believers are "justified"; because he is declared to be Son of God that we, too, receive sonship; because he is glorified that mankind is restored to glory' ('Interchange and Atonement', 479).

4:6 Ὅτι δέ ἐστε υἱοί. It is through faith that the Galatian Christians have become 'sons of God' in Christ Jesus (3:26), just as it is through faith that they have received the Spirit (3:2, 14) and through faith that they have been justified (2:16; 3:6–9, 11). Their instatement as sons and their receiving the Spirit would thus appear to be simultaneous. If, however, ὅτι be translated 'because' (and this is the most natural way to understand it), then it is implied that logically, if not chronologically, the receiving of the Spirit is the sequel to their instatement as sons. But Paul generally presents the Spirit as the ἀρραβών or initial downpayment of the ultimate inheritance, in which the υἱοθεσία (the final investiture as sons, in the sense of Rom. 8:19–23) is included. An attempt is made to accommodate the present statement to Paul's general presentation by such a rendering as that of the NEB: 'To prove that you are sons, God has sent . . .'— but this is a precariously free translation. One might suggest 'As for your being sons . . .' (cf. ὅτι δέ in Acts 13:34), but even this may not be necessary. 'The presence of the Spirit is . . . a witness of their sonship' (J. B. Lightfoot, *Galatians*, 169). 'The purpose of the Son's mission was to give the rights of sonship; the purpose of the Spirit's mission, to give the power of using them' (H. B. Swete, *The Holy Spirit in the NT* [London, 1909], 204). Cf. H. Schlier (*Galater*, 197): 'God bestows on us not only the status of sons [through the sending of his Son] but also the character and knowledge of sons [through the sending of the Spirit]. And he bestows on us the character and knowledge of sons because we are already in the status of sons'. H. D. Betz (*Galatians*, 209f.) wisely warns against trying to settle such questions of construction and interpretation by the importation of 'dogmatic and philosophical categories'. And statements in Galatians should not be assimilated to later Pauline statements on the same subject if this cannot be done without violating the natural sense of the language in Galatians.

ἐξαπέστειλεν ὁ θεὸς τὸ πνεῦμα τοῦ υἱοῦ αὐτοῦ εἰς τὰς καρδίας ἡμῶν. The 2nd person pronoun ὑμῶν would be expected after ἐστέ in the preceding clause (hence, no doubt, its wide attestation as a variant reading); ἡμῶν has patently the inclusive force: 'yours and ours'. The heart, as in the OT (e.g. Pr. 4:23), is the seat of the will; the Spirit therefore takes up residence there.

The Spirit is here called the Spirit of God's Son, 'crying "Abba, Father!" '

The fact that Christians call God 'Abba', using the same word as Jesus used, is a token that they are indwelt by the same Spirit as indwelt him; 'Abba', the *ipsissima vox Iesu* (on his own lips), is the voice of the Spirit of Jesus (on the lips of his people). In Rom. 8:14–17 this Spirit is called the Spirit of υἱοθεσία, the Spirit 'who imparts the assurance of sonship and enables believers to call God their Father' (F. Davidson and R. P. Martin, *NBCR*, 1031), so that they realize and express their new status as sons of God, anticipating their full manifestation as such at the parousia (Rom. 8:23). There, as here, the Spirit attests his presence by the invocation ἀββὰ ὁ πατήρ. 'When we cry "Abba! Father!" it is the Spirit himself bearing witness with our spirit that we are children of God' (Rom. 8:15f.).

Two sure signs of the indwelling Spirit, for Paul, are the spontaneous invocation of God as 'Abba' and the spontaneous acknowledgement of Jesus as κύριος, 'Lord' (1 Cor. 12:3).

κρᾶζον, 'Αββὰ ὁ πατήρ. In Aramaic and post-biblical Hebrew *'abbā* is freely used as a hypocoristic for 'father' (cf. *'immā*, 'mother'). Thus in the Palestinian Targums on Gn. 22:6, 10 Isaac addresses Abraham as *'abbā*. So far as can be ascertained, Jesus was unique in applying this designation to God— not the *'ăbînû* ('our Father') of synagogue prayers nor yet the more personal *'ăbî* ('my Father'), but the domestic term by which a father was called in the affectionate intimacy of the family circle. The one apparent exception to the avoidance of *'abbā* in reference to God comes in a prayer of Ḥanin ha-neḥba (late 1st century BC) who, in a time of drought, was mobbed by schoolchildren who cried, 'Abba, Abba, give us rain!' Thereupon he prayed, 'Lord of the universe, do it for the sake of these children, who cannot yet distinguish between an *'abbā* who can give rain and an *'abbā* who cannot give rain' (b. Ta'an. 23b). But *'abbā* is applied here to God ('the *'abbā* who can give rain') only because the children called Ḥanin 'Abba': Ḥanin's own preferred mode of address to God was evidently 'Lord of the universe' (*ribbônô šel 'ôlām*).

Jesus addressed God as Abba: in one place (Mk. 14:36) the term is taken over as a loanword in the Greek gospel narrative: ἀββὰ ὁ πατήρ (in Mt. 26:39 πάτερ μου correctly translates *'abbā*). It is reasonably certain that Abba lies behind the vocative Πάτερ with which the Lord's Prayer opens (Lk. 11:2; the fuller Πάτερ ἡμῶν ὁ ἐν τοῖς οὐρανοῖς of Mt. 6:9 seems to be an adaptation to liturgical usage). Jesus also spoke of God to others as Abba, thus expressing his sense of loving nearness to God and his implicit trust in him. In addition, he taught his disciples similarly to call God Abba and to look to him with the same trustful expectation as children show when they look to their fathers to provide them with food and clothes.

Abba was so distinctively a locution of Jesus and, after him, of his disciples that it passed without change into the vocabulary of Greek-speaking Christians— followed by the Greek rendering ὁ πατήρ which accompanies it in each of its three NT occurrences. Whether ἀββὰ ὁ πατήρ was current as an invocation in pre-Pauline Hellenistic churches is uncertain; what is certain is that Paul assumes its currency among the Gentile Christians of Rome, who were not converts of his (Rom. 8:15), as confidently as he knows it to be current among those of Galatia, who were his converts. Among these (and presumably other) Gentile Christians ἀββὰ ὁ πατήρ seems to have been used as a free-standing invocation;

when they said the Lord's Prayer, on the other hand, they evidently began with Gk. πάτερ (ἡμῶν).

See J. Jeremias, *Abba: Studien zur neutestamentlichen Theologie und Zeitgeschichte* (Göttingen, 1966), 15–67; 'The Lord's Prayer in Modern Research', *Exp Tim* 71 (1959–60), 141–146; *The Central Message of the NT* (London, 1965), 9–30; *The Prayers of Jesus* (London, 1967), 11–65; C. F. D. Moule, *The Phenomenon of the NT* (London, 1967), 47–55; G. Vermes, *Jesus the Jew* (London, 1973), 210–213 (he points out that Abba was used of God by charismatic Jews of later times).

It is noteworthy that both here and in Rom. 8:15 the verb used for the pronouncing of Abba is κράζω. E. Bammel compares Mk. 14:36, where Abba on Jesus' lips 'is there not as a simple matter of course, but a *cri de coeur*, which summons God, practically compels him—one is tempted to say—to be Father' ('The Jesus of History in the Theology of Adolf von Harnack', *Modern Churchman* n.s. 19 [1975–76], 100 with n. 25). He thinks particularly of the victim of persecution crying out loud: Rom. 8:12–39 in particular, he finds, expresses a martyr-theology. Persecution would certainly provide one occasion, but κράζον suggests the spontaneous ejaculation of 'Abba' in any situation not only of external compulsion but also of inward impulsion; it might, for instance, suggest a Spirit-inspired prophetic utterance (cf. Rom. 9:27, Ἡσαΐας δὲ κράζει . . .).

Whereas here it is the Spirit in 'our hearts' that cries 'Abba, Father!', in Rom. 8:15f. it is 'we' who by the Spirit cry 'Abba, Father!'—the same act is expressed either way.

4:7 ὥστε οὐκέτι εἶ δοῦλος ἀλλὰ υἱός. Instead of being imprisoned under law (or enslaved by the στοιχεῖα of the world), instead of being under the control of a slave-attendant or in care of guardians or stewards, believers are now full-grown sons and daughters of God; they have been given their freedom and the power to use it responsibly.

The transition from leading-strings to liberty is crucial for religious development, although there are some who never attain it but prefer to live indefinitely under spiritual direction. John Wesley, looking back in spiritual maturity on his Christian career before the crisis which is commonly called his conversion, said very aptly, 'I had even then the faith of a *servant*, though not that of a *son*' (*Journal* [London, 1872], I, 76n.).

'The soteriological significance of Christ's sonship with God . . . comes out in the fact that sonship of the believers is based on the sending of the "Son" and attested to them by his Spirit. He does not call them to be "Christs" and "Kyrioi", but "sons" and "heirs" ' (G. Bornkamm, *Paul*, 249).

εἰ δὲ υἱός, καὶ κληρονόμος (as in Roman law). See 3:29, with note on the κληρονομία. The wording is practically identical with Rom. 8:17, εἰ δὲ τέκνα, καὶ κληρονόμοι (there is no theological difference in Pauline usage between υἱοί and τέκνα). If Paul does not add συγκληρονόμοι δὲ Χριστοῦ here, as he does in Rom. 8:17 (from which the phrase is added here in Ψ), he implies it.

διὰ θεοῦ. The many variants indicate that this *lectio ardua* presented scribes and editors with a problem: the use of διά with the genitive might suggest that God was the agent through whom believers were made heirs; 'heirs of God', 'heirs through Christ', 'heirs of God through Christ' are felt to express the truth better. But an original διὰ θεοῦ will account satisfactorily for the variants, as none of them will account for διὰ θεοῦ. The preposition διά is implied before θεοῦ in 1:1, but there the preceding διὰ 'Ιησοῦ Χριστοῦ provides a sufficient explanation. Here the force appears to be 'through God who adopted you' (J. B. Lightfoot) or 'made so by God' (E. D. Burton).

(j) No turning back! (4:8–11)

Now at that time when you did not know God you were enslaved to those beings which by nature are no gods. But now that you have come to know God, or rather to be known by God, how can you turn back to the weak and beggarly elemental forces, to which you desire to be enslaved all over again? You are observing days and months and seasons and years! I am afraid for you, in case I have laboured over you in vain.

TEXTUAL NOTES

v 8 αλλα τοτε μεν ουκ ειδοτες θεον / ει μεν Tert Iren^{lat}
     φυσει *om* K lat^{ρd} Iren^{lat} M.Vict Ambst
v 9 δουλευειν / δουλευσαι ℵ B
v 10 παρατηρεισθε / παρατηρουντες P⁴⁶
v 11 κεκοπιακα / εκοπιασα P⁴⁶ 1739 1881

4:8 Ἀλλὰ τότε μὲν οὐκ εἰδότες θεόν. Here Paul addresses his Gentile converts more particularly. Like the Thessalonian Christians, it was only through Christ as proclaimed in the gospel that they had come to know and serve the 'living and true God' (1 Thes. 1:9; cf. the exhortation to the people of Lystra in Acts 14:15 to 'turn from these vain things [ἀπὸ τούτων τῶν ματαίων] to a living God'). οὐκ εἰδότες is a rare instance of the classical use of οὐ with the participle; in Hellenistic Greek there is a steady drift towards the use of μή, as in the following τοῖς φύσει μὴ οὖσιν θεοῖς (although there μή would be quite classical, since the sense is generic).

ἐδουλεύσατε τοῖς φύσει μὴ οὖσιν θεοῖς. The beings which they had served in their pagan days were at that time reckoned by them to be gods, but they were not really so. They were among the many 'so-called gods' of 1 Cor. 8:5. Cf. 1 Cor. 10:22, 'what pagans sacrifice they offer to demons and not to God' (from Dt. 32:17, ἔθυσαν δαιμονίοις καὶ οὐ θεῷ, θεοῖς οἷς οὐκ ᾔδεισαν). The deuteronomic Song of Moses provides further precedent for this kind of language, e.g. Dt. 32:21, according to which Israel in the wilderness provoked Yahweh to anger by worshipping a 'no-god' (ἐπ᾽ οὐ θεῷ); therefore he provoked them to anger by means of a 'no-people' (ἐπ᾽ οὐκ ἔθνει, cf. Rom. 10:19). This form of words appears to have become commonplace in Jewish polemic; cf. Is. 37:19; Je. 2:11; 5:7; 16:20; Bar. 6 (=Ep. Je.): 24, 28, 49–53, 64, 68, 71. The application of such language to Israel in Dt. 32:17, 21 warns us against assuming in advance that it could not embrace Jews as well as Gentiles here; however, Paul has dealt with Jews like himself in v 3 (καὶ ἡμεῖς), and for the moment he is now addressing former pagans. Here, then, we have a further description of the enslavement from which Christ has liberated his people: they were in bondage to counterfeit gods, 'dumb idols' (τὰ εἴδωλα τὰ ἄφωνα), as they are called in 1 Cor. 12:2.

In Paul's mind these so-called gods were thoroughly 'demythologized'; they were nonentities, as the 'men of knowledge' in the Corinthian church recognized (1 Cor. 8:4). But what those 'men of knowledge' did not sufficiently recognize was that, on people who still believed, or even half-believed, in them, these idols continued to exercise a sinister, indeed demonic, influence (1 Cor. 8:7).

4:9 νῦν δὲ γνόντες θεόν, 'but now, having come to know God' (the aorist participle is ingressive). This phrase is the antithesis to οὐκ εἰδότες θεόν (v 8); οἶδα and γινώσκω are thus used interchangeably (not that they are exact synonyms, but they share a considerable area of a wide semantic field).

Paul's swift correction, μᾶλλον δὲ γνωσθέντες ὑπὸ θεοῦ ('or rather having come to be known by God'), may be calculated not only to stress the divine initiative in this reciprocal knowledge, but also to exclude any gnostic inference from his words. Cf. 1 Cor. 8:3, 'if one loves God, he is known (ἔγνωσται) by him', where Paul overcomes the antithesis between γνῶσις and ἀγάπη which he has drawn in v 1b; also 1 Cor. 13:12b, where God's perfect knowledge of his people is expressed by the aorist (ἐπεγνώσθην), while their perfect knowledge of him is expressed by the future (ἐπιγνώσομαι). For μᾶλλον δέ introducing an epidiorthosis cf. Rom. 8:34, 'Christ Jesus who died, yes (μᾶλλον δέ), who was raised from the dead'.

A. D. Nock (*Essays*, 128) points out a verbal (though not material) parallel in *Corp. Herm*. 1.15, 21 where man, being 'subject to destiny' (ὑποκείμενος τῇ εἱμαρμένῃ), can be released from this subjection only by self-knowledge: ὁ ἔννους ἄνθρωπος ἀναγνωρισάτω ἑαυτόν. Yet even to Paul's epidiorthosis, he goes on to point out, there is a Hermetic parallel: 'God is not ignorant of man; he knows him thoroughly and would be known by him, for it is only knowledge of God (ἡ γνῶσις τοῦ θεοῦ) that brings salvation to man' (*Corp. Herm*. 10.15).

For Paul, there is no real distinction between being known by God and being chosen by him (Rom. 8:29).

πῶς ἐπιστρέφετε πάλιν ἐπὶ τὰ ἀσθενῆ καὶ πτωχὰ στοιχεῖα οἷς πάλιν ἄνωθεν δουλεύειν θέλετε; Those who behaved in the preposterous way contemplated by the Galatian Christians had manifestly no conception of the new order into which faith in Christ had brought them.

The στοιχεῖα (see on v 3), it is now made plain, not only regulated the Jewish way of life under law; they also regulated the pagan way of life in the service of gods that were no gods. To be enslaved to such counterfeit deities was to be enslaved to the στοιχεῖα, and the Galatians would be enslaved to the στοιχεῖα all over again if they 'reverted' not to their former paganism but to Jewish religious practices. That, as Paul saw it, his Gentile readers were tending to revert to a form of religion which they had practised before their conversion to Christianity is emphasized by his repeated πάλιν . . . πάλιν ἄνωθεν. For all the basic differences between Judaism and paganism, both involved subjection to the same elemental forces. This is an astonishing statement for a former

Pharisee to make; yet Paul makes it—not as an exaggeration in the heat of argument but as the deliberate expression of a carefully thought out position.

The στοιχεῖα to which the Galatians had been in bondage were the counterfeit gods of v 8; the bondage to which they were now disposed to turn back was that of the law. But in our discussion of 3:13f. and 4:4f. we concluded that Gentile as well as Jewish believers are reckoned to have been redeemed from existence 'under law'—not, so far as Gentiles are concerned, explicitly under the Mosaic law, in relation to which they were ἄνομοι (cf. 1 Cor. 9:21; Rom. 2:12ff.), but under legalism as a principle of life. 'The demonic forces of legalism, then, both Jewish and Gentile, can be called "principalities and powers" or "elemental spirits of the world" ' (G. B. Caird, *Principalities and Powers* [Oxford, 1956], 51).

Similarly B. Reicke, 'The Law and this World according to Paul: Some Thoughts concerning Gal 4:1–11', *JBL* 70 (1951), 259–276, recognizes that Gentiles and Jews alike were subject to the law and the στοιχεῖα. The Galatian Christians are, he finds, expected to know about the στοιχεῖα to which Paul refers; they did not know, however, that by submitting to the law they were reverting to the service of those στοιχεῖα by which they had formerly been enslaved, the entities of v 8 which received divine honours to which they were not entitled. Reicke further equates the στοιχεῖα with the 'angels' of 3:19 through whom the law was administered, considering that by that reference Paul has already prepared his readers for what he now says about the στοιχεῖα and that the Galatians probably thought already of angels as founders and guardians of the law. But Paul's reference to the angels in 3:19 is too incidental for us to be sure of this. The στοιχεῖα of Col. 2:8, 20 may well (as that context suggests) be identified with angels (possibly with the rulers of the planetary spheres), but only with caution may the argument of Colossians be allowed to influence the exegesis of Galatians. (Much greater caution is called for in admitting as evidence the teaching of Simon Magus, who justified his antinomianism, according to Iren. *Haer*. 1.16.2, by representing moral conventions as the arbitrary decrees of the angels who made the world and whose purpose was to bring people into bondage to them.)

Even if we distinguish, then, between Jewish converts, who had lived under lawful guardians and stewards, and Gentile converts, who had lived under beings that by nature were no gods, it could be said of both groups alike that they had lived in bondage to the elemental forces of the world until Christ released them from their bondage and disabled the elemental forces.

According to G. Howard, Paul looked on the Judaizers' religion as no better than paganism since it made Yahweh in effect the God of the Israelites only and not the God of the Gentiles also (cf. Rom. 3:29f.): 'For the Galatians to accept circumcision was for them to return to the concept of local deities and to be enslaved once again to the elemental spirits of the universe' (*Crisis*, 78).

D. E. H. Whiteley (*The Theology of St. Paul* [Oxford, 1964], 25) explains Paul's words on the ground that some Jews practised astrology. But the practice of astrology is not in view here; life under law is bondage, says Paul, and he equates bondage to the law with bondage to the στοιχεῖα.

A. J. Bandstra (*The Law and the Elements of the World* [Kampen, 1964]) identifies the στοιχεῖα with the law and the flesh. Law, in the sense of legalism, is certainly prominent among the στοιχεῖα, but the 'flesh' (human nature in its unregenerate weakness) is scarcely one of the στοιχεῖα, but is rather in bondage to them. Law, working on flesh, stimulates sin, and sin leads to death (cf. Rom. 7:7–11). It is because of the inadequacy of the flesh that to be 'under law' (3:23) is in practice to be 'under sin' (3:22), whereas to be dead to law (2:19) is in practice to be dead to sin (Rom. 6:2, 11). (Cf. further P. Benoit, 'La loi et la croix d'après Saint Paul', *RB* 47 [1938], 488–509, especially 502 n. 3.)

The στοιχεῖα were powerful enough to enslave those under their control; if now they are described as 'weak and beggarly', that is in relation to those who have been liberated from their control. Christ, the liberator of his people, is stronger than all elemental forces. Against those who enjoy 'the liberty of the glory of the children of God' (Rom. 8:21) the στοιχεῖα are powerless; they cannot reassert their authority over them unless these deliberately put themselves back under their power. That any should be so foolish as to do so Paul finds scarcely credible; yet this is what he feared some of his Galatian friends were actually in process of doing. This suggests that the στοιχεῖα are demonic forces which hold in thrall the minds of men and women who follow their dictates, but lose their potency as soon as those minds are emancipated, as they are by the grace of God and the power of his Spirit. If we think of modern counterparts to the στοιχεῖα, one of the most potent is the current climate of opinion (which, incidentally, might serve as a free paraphrase of 'the spirit that is now at work in the sons of disobedience' of Eph. 2:2). The description of the στοιχεῖα as ἀσθενῆ καὶ πτωχά is similar to the description of the 'rulers (ἄρχοντες) of this age' in 1 Cor. 2:6, 8 as 'on the way out' (καταργούμενοι).

Although no connective particle links v 10 with v 9, it is most probable that the Galatians' observance of the cultic calendar (v 10) is adduced as evidence of reversion to the service of the στοιχεῖα. The στοιχεῖα, therefore, include the forces by which the calendar is regulated, and since the calendrical divisions are for the most part controlled by the movements of the planets, the planets may well be included among the στοιχεῖα. Pagans had their sacred calendars, as the Jews had theirs, although they tended to ascribe divinity to the planets as the Jews did not. Paul is not thinking of any conscious reversion to planet-worship on the Galatians' part; he means that by treating the sacred calendar as a matter of religious obligation they are in effect putting themselves in bondage to the forces that control the calendar. It is not a valid argument against this interpretation that there is no example of the use of στοιχεῖον in the sense of 'star' or 'heavenly body' before the second century AD (Justin, *Apol.* II.5.2; *Dial.* 23.3) and no example of its use in the sense of 'spiritual power' before the fourth-century Testament of Solomon (G. Delling, *TDNT* VII, 681 n. 74, 683 n. 85, *s.v.* στοιχεῖον); the phrase στοιχεῖα τοῦ κόσμου seems to be Paul's own contribution to religious vocabulary (Delling, ibid., 685), and the sense which he put on it must be gathered from the context in which he used it. From the context it may be gathered that the στοιχεῖα τοῦ κόσμου 'cover all the things in which man places his trust apart from the living God; they become his gods, and he becomes their slave' (H. H. Esser, *NIDNTT* II, 453, *s.v.* 'Law').

See also J. B. Lightfoot, *Colossians*, 180, 202; E. D. Burton, *Galatians*, 510–518; E. Percy, *Die Probleme der Kolosser- und Epheserbriefe* (Lund, 1946), 156–167; H. N. Ridderbos, 'Vrijheid en Wet volgens Paulus' Brief aan de Galaten', *Grosheide FS*, 89–103;

E. Schweizer, 'Die Elemente der Welt Gal 4, 3.9; Col 2, 8.20', *Stählin FS*, 245–259, reprinted in *Beiträge zur Theologie des NT* (Zürich, 1970), 147–163; P. Vielhauer, 'Gesetzesdienst und Stoicheiadienst im Galaterbrief', *Käsemann FS*, 543–555.

4:10 ἡμέρας παρατηρεῖσθε κτλ. It is possible to treat this sentence as a question, but there seems to be no good reason for doing so. It would in any case not make much material difference: 'Are you actually observing . . . ?' is a more rhetorical way of saying, 'You are actually observing . . .'. P^{46}, by reading παρατηροῦντες instead of παρατηρεῖσθε, attaches the clause to the preceding question: 'how can you turn back to the weak and beggarly elemental forces, . . . by observing days . . . ?' H. D. Betz (*Galatians*, 217) thinks that Paul is not describing what the Galatians were actually doing, but rather 'the *typical* behavior of religiously scrupulous people', in which the Galatians would find themselves involved 'once they took up Torah and circumcision'. He cites for this view J. Eckert, *Die urchristliche Verkündigung im Streit zwischen Paulus und seinen Gegnern nach dem Galaterbrief* (Regensburg, 1971), 92f., 126ff. (where incidentally the sentence is construed as a question), followed by F. Mussner, *Galaterbrief*, 301f. But it is more likely that Paul is referring to news which he has just received, to the effect that the Galatians were actually adopting the Jewish calendar. The suggestion that they were making a point of observing special times and seasons characteristic of some strands of sectarian Judaism (so H. Schlier, *Galater*, 206f.) has little in the context to commend it; the same may be said of the attempt to find a parallel to their scrupulous observance in the practices mentioned in *Clem. Hom.* 19.22.2–9 (cf. H. Riesenfeld, *TDNT* VIII, 148, *s.v* παρατηρέω).

Perhaps the compound middle παρατηρέομαι is used not simply in the sense of observing special days and other seasons (in the sense of Rom. 14:6, ὁ φρονῶν τὴν ἡμέραν) but in the sense of watching for them, calculating their arrival (cf. the noun παρατήρησις in Lk. 17:20). A. Strobel, 'Die Passa-Erwartung als urchristliches Problem', *ZNW* 49 (1958), 163f., says that 'the verb παρατηρεῖν in Gal. 4:10 indicates the fixing of the calendar, obtained by observation of the sky . . . , and involving the thought of punctual observance as a religious obligation'.

Many Jewish Christians continued to observe the sacred occasions as a matter of course. Paul himself appears to have regarded some of them at least as convenient punctuation-marks in his apostolic schedule (cf. 1 Cor. 16:8; Acts 20:16). But for Gentile Christians to adopt them *de novo* as matters of legal obligation was quite another matter.

ἡμέρας . . . καὶ μῆνας καὶ καιροὺς καὶ ἐνιαυτούς. Cf. Gn. 1:14, where the heavenly luminaries are, among other things, to serve 'for signs and seasons and days and years' (εἰς σημεῖα καὶ εἰς καιροὺς καὶ εἰς ἡμέρας καὶ εἰς ἐνιαυτούς). (The omission of 'months' from the Genesis list, despite the mention of the moon as one of the two great luminaries in v 16, may have provided theological justification for the author of Jubilees and his school to delete the moon from the luminaries appointed 'for signs' on the fourth day [Jub. 4:9] and to ignore it in their divisions of time; in Jubilees the month, as well as the other divisions of time, is regulated by the sun.) The similarity between Paul's wording and that of Gn. 1:14 is too close for us to agree with W. Schmithals that Paul is simply 'employing a current familiar list which was not widespread in Jewish orthodoxy but frequently occurs above all in the apocryphal and Gnostic or gnosticizing literature' (*Paul and the Gnostics*, 44).

With the list here we may compare the later Col. 2:16, 'let no one sit in judgment on you . . . with respect to festival or new moon or sabbath' (ἑορτῆς ἢ νεομηνίας ἢ σαββάτων)—in which ἑορτή corresponds to καιροί here, νεομηνία to μήν, and σάββατα, perhaps, to ἡμέραι. In the Galatians list there is a progression from shorter to longer divisions of time: this is clearly so with the days, months and years, and 'seasons' are probably the OT festivals or κληταὶ ἅγιαι (cf. Lv. 23:2).

The observance of 'days'—i.e. specially sacred days—can scarcely exclude sabbath observance (cf. Col. 2:16); see, however, J. Murray, 'Romans 14:5 and the Weekly Sabbath', *Romans*, II, 257–259.

There is a relaxed attitude in Rom. 14:5f. ('Let every one be fully persuaded in his own mind. He who regards the day regards it "to the Lord" ') which presents a marked contrast to Gal. 4:10. Is this (like the contrast in tone between Gal. 1:8f. and Phil. 1:15–18) an indication of gradual mellowing on Paul's part? Or is a difference in principle involved? Paul sees 'a world of difference' between 'error in preaching (which, though harmful, might be committed in good faith)' and 'intended deception'—between 'theological error' and 'moral fault'. 'Where divergent opinion exists Paul is content to think and let think (Rom 14.5 . . .)', but elsewhere 'Paul is not content to disagree, but accuses his opponents of deceitfulness, not only of error but of moral perversity' (C. K. Barrett, 'ΨΕΥΔΑΠΟΣΤΟΛΟΙ [2 Cor. 11.13]', *Rigaux FS*, 383). Such opponents are the people whom he calls 'false apostles' or (as in Gal. 2:4) 'false brethren'. He is far from reckoning his Galatian converts among these opponents, but he does so reckon the men who were upsetting them, under whose influence they were being persuaded to accept circumcision and keep the sacred calendar: hence his peremptory tone here.

J. C. Kirby (*Ephesians: Baptism and Pentecost* [London, 1964], 79) thinks that the tolerant note in Rom. 14:5f. has to do with fast-days (*stationes*); in Gal. 4:10 (as in Col. 2:16), he suggests, Paul 'is not forbidding Christians to have any festivals whatever, but forbidding only those which have lost their meaning' and have become a mere 'shadow' (Col. 2:17). If so, the Galatians could be pardoned for failing to catch his meaning, as most commentators and other readers have failed to do. Agreed: he is not forbidding the Galatians to have any festivals whatever; he is deprecating their scrupulous παρατήρησις as something imposed by law.

The 'months', as has been said, are probably the new moons (cf. Nu. 28:11–15), and the 'seasons' may be equated with the religious festivals and holy convocations (cf. Lv. 23:1ff.). As for the 'years', it has been held (e.g. by J. Eckert, *Die urchristliche Verkündigung*, 92) that, in the short time since their evangelization, the Galatians could scarcely have got around to the observance of special years; but W. M. Ramsay, after his conversion to an earlier dating of the epistle than that which he had adopted in his *Historical Commentary*, made the attractive suggestion that a report had newly reached Paul that they were observing the sabbatical year AD 47/48 (*SPT*[14], xxxi).

The traditions of Judaism, when accepted as ritually binding, were in Paul's eyes fetters which impeded faith and excluded liberty (cf. Col. 2:20–23). Moreover, if former pagans accepted the Jewish calendar, old astral associations could easily reassert themselves.

4:11 φοβοῦμαι ὑμᾶς, 'I am afraid for you', not 'I am afraid of you'. Something like the οἶδά σε τίς εἶ construction is to be recognized here, except that it is not the *subject* of the subordinate clause, but another element in it, that has been attracted into the principal clause as object of the main verb. Winer-Moulton³ compares Sophocles, *O.T.* 767f.:

δέδοικ᾽ ἐμαυτόν, ὦ γύναι, μὴ πόλλ᾽ ἄγαν
εἰρημέν᾽ ᾖ μοι δι᾽ ἃ νιν εἰσιδεῖν θέλω
('I am afraid for myself, lady, lest too much may have been said by me; it is for this reason that I wish to see him'.)

μή πως εἰκῇ κεκοπίακα εἰς ὑμᾶς, a more specific expression of the cautionary μή πως εἰς κενὸν τρέχω ἢ ἔδραμον of 2:2. For similar language involving κόπος and κοπιάω cf. 1 Cor. 15:58; Phil. 2:16; 1 Thes. 3:5; the Servant's words in Is. 49:4, κενῶς ἐκοπίασα, may have influenced Paul's phraseology in all these passages. Paul would indeed have laboured over the Galatians in vain if they had really reverted to legalism, just as his Corinthian converts would show that they had received the grace of God εἰς κενόν (2 Cor. 6:1) if they lapsed either into legalism on the one hand or into libertinism on the other (see on 2:21).

(k) Personal appeal (4:12–20)

I beg you, my brothers, become as I am, because I am as you are. You have done me no wrong. You know that it was on account of a bodily infirmity that I first preached the gospel to you, and you did not despise me or reject me with abhorrence because of the trial that my bodily condition must have caused you. Instead, you received me as a messenger of God, as Christ Jesus (in person). (You counted yourselves happy then.) Where is that sense of happiness now? I bear you witness that, had it been possible, you would have plucked out your eyes and given them to me.

So then, have I become your enemy because I tell you the truth? It is from no honourable motive that they court your favour; they want to exclude you from other influences so that you may court theirs. It is always good to be courted from honourable motives (as you are by me), and not only when I am present with you, my children! (My children indeed)—I am enduring birth-pangs for you all over again, until Christ is formed in you. I could wish I were present with you right now, and change my tone of voice, because I do not know what to do about you.

TEXTUAL NOTES

v 14 υμων ℵ* A B C² D* Ψ G 33 1739 lat / μου P⁴⁶ C* D² Ψ byz syrʰᶜˡ copˢᵃ / om 69 al εν τη σαρκι μου praem τον ℵᶜ 81 1739 al
ουδε εξεπτυσατε om P⁴⁶

v 15 που / τις D byz latᵇʳ syrʰᶜˡ
ουν / add ην D G byz / add εστιν 103 latᵛᵍ

v 17 ζηλουτε / add ζηλουτε δε τα κρειττω χαρισματα D* G Ambst (cf. 1 Cor. 12:31)

v 18 ζηλοῦσθαι A *al* / το ζηλοῦσθαι D G byz / ζηλοῦσθε ℵ B *pc* lat^vg Orig
v 19 τεκνα ℵ* B D* G *pm* / τεκνια ℵ A C Ψ byz

4:12 Paul tries to make it plain that he is not speaking as he does out of a sense of personal resentment, as though he were offended by their giving up his teaching in favour of someone else's. He has already protested that even if he himself were to bring them a different gospel from that which he originally preached to them he would fall under the divine curse. Even in a situation where he appears to have been personally attacked in one of his churches, he is not the man to harbour a grudge: speaking as ὁ ἀδικηθείς he forgives the offence, εἴ τι κεχάρισμαι, 'if I have had anything to forgive' (2 Cor. 2:10; cf. 7:12). His concern is for his converts' well-being and ultimate salvation, not for his own reputation or esteem.

He is anxious that they should enjoy the same open feelings of friendship and confidence towards him as he cherishes for them. The plea γίνεσθε ὡς ἐγώ might in another context be taken as an instance of the *imitatio Pauli* theme (cf. 1 Cor. 11:1; Phil. 3:17, etc.; see W. P. De Boer, *The Imitation of Paul* [Kampen, 1962]), but here it must be understood in the light of the following ὅτι κἀγὼ ὡς ὑμεῖς (*sc.* γέγονα), 'I (have become) as you are', 'I have come to regard myself as one of you'—more particularly, I am your father and you are my children (cf. v 19). The situation is quite similar to that in 2 Cor. 6:11–13, where he appeals to his disaffected Corinthian converts as a father to his children: 'My heart is wide open to you; let yours be wide open to me.' He assures the Corinthians there that he has done none of them any wrong (2 Cor. 7:2), as he assures the Galatians here that they have done him no wrong: among friends there should be no suspicion of wrongdoing on either side.

4:13 He now reminds them of the circumstances in which he paid them his first missionary visit: it was, he says, 'on account of a bodily infirmity' (δι' ἀσθένειαν τῆς σαρκός). They knew exactly what he meant, so he had no need to go into details; his modern readers have not their advantage. It is natural to link this bodily infirmity with the 'splinter in the flesh' (σκόλοψ τῇ σαρκί) to which he refers in 2 Cor. 12:7–10, but we are too ill-informed to identify the two outright. Paul experienced the first attack of the 'splinter' about AD 43 (cf. the 'fourteen years' of 2 Cor. 12:2), and he was apparently still subject to its attacks when 2 Corinthians was written (*c*. AD 56). Whatever be the date of Galatians, it falls within these limits. (Both here and in 2 Cor. 12:7 σάρξ means 'body'; by contrast, διὰ τὴν ἀσθένειαν τῆς σαρκός in Rom. 6:19 apparently means mental incapacity.)

If, then, Paul's first visit to the cities of Galatia coincided with an attack of this ailment, it might be hoped that his present language about it would provide a clue to its nature. Unfortunately, quite different inferences have been drawn: no certainty is possible.

(i) W. M. Ramsay (*SPT*, 94–97), rightly taking δι' ἀσθένειαν to mean *'because of* an infirmity' (cf. MHT I, 172; BDF 223.3; E. Schweizer, *TDNT* VII, 125 n. 216, *s.v.* σάρξ), supposed that Paul contracted malaria in the low-lying territory of Pamphylia and made his way up to the high country around Pisidian Antioch, *c*. 3600 feet above sea-level, to recuperate.

(ii) The words οὐδὲ ἐξεπτύσατε (v 14) have been taken literally, 'you did not spit out', and related to the practice of spitting to avert the evil eye or to exorcize an evil spirit believed to be the cause of certain afflictions, including epilepsy. This has then been used to support other arguments identifying Paul's ailment with epilepsy: so W. Wrede, *Paul*, ETr (London, 1907), 22f.; J. Klausner, *From Jesus to Paul*, ETr (London, 1944), 325–330, etc.

(iii) The statement of v 15, 'if possible, you would have plucked out your eyes and given them to me', has been taken to show that Paul suffered from ophthalmia or some other affection of the eyes, as though he meant that, had eye transplants been a possibility, they would have given him their own healthy eyes to replace his diseased ones: so J. T. Brown, 'St. Paul's Thorn in the Flesh', in *Horae Subsecivae*, ed. J. Brown (Edinburgh, 1858).

The fact that such diverse ailments as malaria, epilepsy, ophthalmia (to mention no others) have been suggested on the basis of this passage indicates that there can be no certain diagnosis. The infirmity may have been one of these three, or it may have been something quite different; it may have been identical with the 'splinter' of 2 Cor. 12:7, or it may not.

If τὸ πρότερον in εὐηγγελισάμην ὑμῖν τὸ πρότερον is interpreted strictly to mean 'on the former occasion', Paul would have paid two visits to the cities where these Galatians lived. On the 'North Galatian' view these could be the visits of Acts 16:6 and 18:23 respectively; on the 'South Galatian' view there is the further possibility that they could be the eastward journey from Pisidian Antioch to Derbe (Acts 13:14–14:20), followed by the westward retracing of the same route (Acts 14:21). But it is not necessary to render τὸ πρότερον so strictly. In Hellenistic Greek 'πρότερος has surrendered the meaning "the first of two" to πρῶτος and now means only "earlier" ' (BDF 62); for τὸ πρότερον cf. Jn. 6:62; 7:50; 9:8; 1 Tim. 1:13.

E. H. Askwith, *The Epistle to the Galatians* (London, 1902), 73ff., has argued persuasively that τὸ πρότερον must be understood in relation to the implied 'now' of v 16: '*Formerly* (τὸ πρότερον) you congratulated yourselves on my coming to you; *now* you seem to regard me as your enemy.'

4:14 There seems to have been something repulsive in Paul's appearance at the time of his first visit to them: they might well have found it a trial (τὸν πειρασμὸν ὑμῶν means 'the trial which you experienced'; the variant τὸν πειρασμόν μου would mean 'the trial which I caused'). It might indeed have proved a πειρασμός to them in a fuller sense: they might have been tempted to treat both himself and his message with contempt and loathing. Like some of his critical converts in Corinth, they might have said, 'his bodily presence is weak, and his speech of no account' (2 Cor. 10:10). The verb ἐκπτύω might have its literal sense 'spit out' (see note on v 13), but it may simply express a feeling or reaction of disgust and disdain. In fact, the Galatians did the opposite of what they might well have been tempted to do: far from despising Paul (οὐκ ἐξουθενήσατε) because of his bodily condition, they welcomed him and his message with joy. They received him as a messenger of God (which indeed he was), as Christ himself (whom he represented).

When he says that they received him ὡς ἄγγελον θεοῦ he may, of course, mean that he was given a welcome worthy of an angel; cf. 2 Sa. (LXX 2 Ki.) 14:17 (καθὼς ἄγγελος θεοῦ οὕτως ὁ κύριός μου ὁ βασιλεύς); Ad. Est. 15:13

(LXX 5:2), εἶδόν σε, κύριε, ὡς ἄγγελον θεοῦ. But it is out of the question to relate this simile to the incident in Acts 14:11–13, where Barnabas and Paul were hailed at Lystra as gods who had 'come down . . . in the likeness of men'.

J. de Zwaan saw in this language the implication that the Galatians welcomed Paul as an angel whereas they might have been tempted to shun him as demon-possessed ('Gal 4,14 aus dem Neugriechischen erklärt', *ZNW* 10 [1909], 246–250).

Much less cogently W. Schmithals maintains that Paul's opponents accused him to the Galatians as being a man of the flesh (σάρκινος), not a 'spiritual' man (i.e. a gnostic), and that Paul replies ironically: 'You did not find any objection in my "flesh" when I first came to you, so it cannot be because I am said to be a "man of the flesh" that you object to me now and regard me as an enemy; it must be because I am telling you the truth' (*Paul and the Gnostics*, 50f.). Apart from the implausible transition from one meaning of σάρξ to another, there is no evidence in the letter that Paul's opponents accused him of being σάρκινος—it is an inference from Schmithals's assumption that the trouble-makers were themselves gnostics.

According to G. Howard (*Crisis*, 9–11), the judaizing visitors, hearing of the painful circumstances in which Paul had first preached to the Galatians, supposed that he had misgivings about his acceptance among them and had therefore refrained from saying anything about circumcision and other aspects of his message which he feared might be unacceptable to them. This is obviously untrue, says Paul; you remember that you were not at all put off by my repugnant presence but welcomed me as a messenger of God, and if I had wished to include circumcision in my message there was no reason why I should not. But this reading of Paul's words depends on the doubtful premise that his opponents believed that in his heart of hearts he still held to circumcision. (They charged him rather with having no firm convictions about it, so that he taught it or kept silent about it as he judged expedient; see 5:11.)

4:15 The Galatians rejoiced at Paul's arrival among them: they congratulated (μακαρίζω) themselves that this messenger of God had come with such good news. This was their μακαρισμός (a substantive derived from the verb μακαρίζω, 'congratulate', 'count happy'; cf. Acts 26:2, where ἥγημαι ἐμαυτὸν μακάριον, 'I count myself happy', might equally well have been expressed μακαρίζω ἐμαυτόν, 'I congratulate myself'). Where was that sense of congratulation now? Had it entirely evaporated?

μαρτυρῶ γὰρ ὑμῖν, 'I bear you witness', is in origin a forensic form of words ('I am ready to go into the witness-box and swear . . .'), amounting to a solemn declaration. It is not quite so emphatic as the expression in 1:20—no one is disputing Paul's narrative of events in the present passage.

εἰ δυνατὸν . . . ἐδώκατέ μοι is another unfulfilled condition (cf. 1:10; 3:21), this time without ἄν in the apodosis (its inclusion was no longer felt as obligatory). The ellipsis of ἦν with εἰ δυνατόν is comparable to Eng. 'if possible' for 'if it were possible'.

'You would have given me your most precious possessions; you would have given me the very eyes out of your heads', says Paul, emphasizing their readiness at that time to do anything at all for him. It is precarious to take the mention of 'eyes' too literally, especially to suppose that the language implies Paul's own eye trouble. The most that can be said is that, if it could be established otherwise that he suffered from some eye-affliction, there would be special force in his choice of words here.

What Paul's language does bring out is not only his own exceptional capacity for affection (cf. v 19) but also his capacity for inspiring a responsive affection in others. There is no sacrifice, it is implied, which one will not make for a friend. H. D. Betz, who sees the whole paragraph vv 12–20 as devoted to the *topos* of friendship, adduces at this point the story of the Scythian friends Dandamis and Amizoces in Lucian, *Toxaris* 40f.: Dandamis sacrificed his eyes to ransom Amizoces from captivity, and when Amizoces was then set free he blinded himself because he could not bear to see his friend's blindness (*Galatians*, 228).

4:16 It was natural that a certain uneasy reserve should begin to mark the Galatian Christians' attitude to Paul. They knew that the teaching to which they were now giving ear could not commend itself to him, and that he would disapprove of their accepting it. This reserve would be reinforced if they entertained suggestions tending to discredit him, or to diminish his standing in their eyes. When he heard of what was happening, he could be trusted to tell them they were wrong, and such plain speaking was bound to be unpalatable.

ὥστε is used here to introduce a rhetorical question.

It is hazardous to find in Paul's use of ἐχθρός here the source of his later designation among the Ebionites as ἐχθρὸς ἄνθρωπος (*Epistle of Peter to James*, 2; *Clem. Recog.* 1.70f.), as is done by H.-J. Schoeps, *Judenchristentum*, 120, 474; *Paul*, 82; a much more probable source is the ἐχθρὸς ἄνθρωπος of Mt. 13:28 (cf. Schoeps, *Judenchristentum*, 127).

ἀληθεύων ὑμῖν. In telling them the truth Paul is their friend. The truth he is now telling them is the same as what he told them when first he came among them, and on that occasion it won their friendship for him. For this 'truth' is nothing other than the good news of divine grace. If it is true, then the 'other gospel' brought by the trouble-makers is self-evidently false. It is reading an alien idea into the text to say with W. Schmithals, 'Precisely this argument of Paul shows that in truth people in Galatia were declaiming against Paul on account of the apostle's fleshly ["sarkic"] weakness' (*Paul and the Gnostics*, 50 n. 107).

The situation, in fact, is not unlike that in which Paul was later involved with the Corinthian church, when it was visited by interlopers who brought a 'different gospel' and tried to disparage Paul in his converts' eyes; Paul protests his unchanging love for his friends, even while he remonstrates vigorously with them: 'If I love you the more, am I to be loved the less?' (2 Cor. 12:15).

4:17 In that same context of 2 Corinthians, Paul expresses his 'divine jealousy' (ζηλῶ γὰρ ὑμᾶς θεοῦ ζήλῳ) over his converts (2 Cor. 11:2), and something of the same sense attaches to his use of the verb ζηλόω here. Even if some Zealot-like pressure lay behind the action of the trouble-makers in Galatia, ζηλόω in this context has nothing to do with that. It is used rather in the sense of paying court to someone. This may be done with honourable (καλῶς) or dishonourable intentions, and the intentions of the trouble-makers, says Paul, are dishonourable (ζηλοῦσιν ὑμᾶς οὐ καλῶς); they want to gain adherents for themselves and to shut them off (ἐκκλεῖσαι) from fellowship with Paul and, in effect, from fellowship with the Christ whose apostle Paul is. In Paul's eyes, to seek justification by legal works, as the Galatians were being urged to do by the trouble-makers, was to be 'severed from Christ' (5:4). Paul has no desire to gain adherents for himself—in the Galatian cities as at Corinth he would have repudiated the suggestion that any of his converts should say, 'I belong to Paul' (1 Cor. 1:12)—his ardent desire was to betroth his converts, so to speak, to Christ, to whom their undivided allegiance was to be given (cf. 2 Cor. 11:2).

ἵνα αὐτοὺς ζηλοῦτε (present subjunctive). The verb ζηλόω may be used not only of the quest for adherents but also of the adherents' attachment to their leaders or teachers, and such is the sense of ζηλοῦτε in this clause. J. B. Lightfoot (Galatians, 176f.) adduces a passage from Plutarch (De Virtute Morali 448E) where, after a reference to the mutual esteem between husband and wife (in an arranged marriage) developing into love, he goes on: 'so again, when young men happen upon cultivated teachers, they follow them and emulate (ζηλοῦσιν) them . . .'—but there ζηλόω is used of a less ardent attachment than that which develops when they become ἐρασταί of their teachers. Those people, says Paul to his converts, want you to count yourselves as exclusively their followers, enrolled members of their school.

4:18 It is always good, he goes on, to be courted with honourable intentions, as you were 'courted' by me when I was present with you; but as it is, no sooner has my back been turned than you let someone else come and 'court' you with *dis*honourable intentions!

4:19 τέκνα μου, οὓς πάλιν ὠδίνω. The masculine relative pronoun after the neuter antecedent is an instance of *constructio ad sensum*.

'Christ lives in me' (2:20) was true not only of Paul but (potentially at least) of all believers. Paul longs to see Christ visibly living in the Galatians—to see the likeness of Christ manifested in their lives. Cf. 2 Cor. 3:18 where believers in Christ are described as 'being changed into his likeness from one degree of glory to another' through the inward operation of 'the Lord who is the Spirit'. Here he expresses the same thought in terms of the embryo being formed in the mother's womb until it reaches maturity and is ready to be born. So Calvin *ad loc.*: *nascitur in nobis, ut vivamus eius vitam* ('he is born in us, that we may live his life'). This birth involves birth-pangs, but it is Paul himself who endures them on his converts' behalf. He is enduring them, in fact, for a second time (πάλιν); the first time was when he preached the gospel to them and they came to faith in Christ. Cf. 1 Cor. 4:15, where he is the father who has begotten his converts through the gospel, and 1 Thes. 2:7, where he cherishes them like a nurse (τροφός); here he plays a mother's part. The language vividly expresses the intensity of his love and concern for them.

H. Lietzmann (*An die Galater*, 28) renders the μέχρις οὗ clause as 'until Christ has become incarnate in you' (*bis Christus in euch Mensch geworden ist*). H. Schlier (*Galater*, 214 with n. 2) understands the language not of the formation of Christ in each individual among them but of the formation of the body of Christ in their community as a whole. But 'the community is born through the growth of Christ in individuals' (A. Wikenhauser, *Pauline Mysticism*, ETr [Edinburgh, 1960], 44).

Paul's thought here is not essentially different from his language about the daily renewal of the inner man (2 Cor. 4:16), about the putting on of the new man, who 'is being renewed in knowledge after the image of his creator' (Col. 3:10; cf. Eph. 4:23), or even about 'putting on the Lord Jesus Christ' (Rom. 13:14). But the thought is more vividly expressed here, and certainly the metaphor of birth is more effective than the catechetical formula of 'putting on'. (It is unlikely that any substantial analogy can be discerned between this passage and the description in 1QH 3.13 of the pangs preceding the birth of a 'wonder of a counsellor' [*pele' yô'ēş*] in the covenant community, even if the Messiah is meant (on this cf. H. Ringgren, *The Faith of Qumran*, ETr [Philadelphia, 1963], 191–194).

It is not that Paul sees two stages in Christian experience—being justified by faith and having Christ formed within one—it is rather that the one implies the other and reliance on law for salvation negates both. It should not have been necessary for him to endure birth-pangs all over again on their behalf, but if they put themselves under law, then they are not justified by faith in Christ and Christ is not 'in them': they have not yet been transferred from slavery to sonship (v 7) or from the old creation to the new (6:15). (Cf. E. P. Sanders, *PPJ*, 469.) The classic treatment of Christ's being formed within the believer is H. Scougal, *The Life of God in the Soul of Man*, published about 1672–73 (reprinted London, 1961), from which G. Whitefield learned 'that they who know anything of religion know it is a vital union with the Son of God—Christ formed in the heart' (Sermon preached in 1769, quoted in the foreword to the 1961 reprint of Scougal, *op. cit.*, 12; cf. G. Whitefield, *Journals* I [reprinted London, 1960], 46f.).

4:20 Paul's written words in his letters when he was absent from his friends were substitutes for his spoken words when he was in their company—and, in his view, inadequate substitutes. There are situations in which the tone of voice and even the look on the face convey nearly as much as the words that are said, but when one is writing from a distance only the words can be conveyed. True, when the writer is well known one can, with no great effort of imagination, hear him speaking and see his facial expression, but in matters of delicate personal relationship such imagination is insufficient. It is evident from 2 Cor. 10:10 that some of Paul's converts contrasted the power and severity of his letters with the unimpressive way he spoke when he was present with them. Paul may be afraid here that his Galatian friends will concentrate on the uncompromising severity of his language and overlook the underlying concern and affection: if only he could be with them he could adapt his tone of voice to his deep-seated emotions. He is at a loss to know how best to approach them: the arguments which he might expect to be most compelling could leave them cold, or even confirm them in the course which he so much deplored.

ἤθελον δὲ παρεῖναι πρὸς ὑμᾶς ἄρτι. J. Knox ('Galatians', *IDB* II, 343) infers from Paul's language that he would certainly have visited them, or at least promised (or threatened) a visit, had he not been prevented by *force majeure*, and thinks it possible that Paul may have been in prison at the time—in which case he argues further that Galatians was written *after* Romans. But we are too scantily informed about Paul's circumstances to know why he could not pay a personal visit to Galatia just then.

(l) A lesson from scripture (4:21–5:1)

Tell me, you who wish to be under law, do you not listen to the law? Scripture tells us that Abraham got two sons, one by the slavegirl and one by the freewoman. The son of the slavegirl was born according to the flesh, but the son of the freewoman was born through promise.

Now these are allegorical entities. These women represent two covenants— one deriving from Mount Sinai, bearing children for slavery: that is Hagar. Now Hagar is Mount Sinai in Arabia; she corresponds to the present Jerusalem, for she is in slavery with her children. But Jerusalem above is free: she is our *mother. Scripture says:*

> *'Rejoice, O barren one, you who bear no children,*
> *Break forth and shout, you who endure no birth-pangs,*
> *For the deserted woman has more children than she who has a husband.'*

Now you, my brothers, are children of promise, as Isaac was. But just as then the son that was born according to the flesh persecuted the son that was born according to the Spirit, so it is even now. But what does the scripture say? 'Drive out the slavegirl and her son, for the slavegirl's son shall not share the inheritance with the son of the freewoman.' So then, my brothers, we are children, not of the slavegirl but of the freewoman.

With freedom Christ has set us free: stand firm, therefore, and do not be encumbered again with a yoke of slavery.

TEXTUAL NOTES

v 21 αχουετε / αναγινωσκετε D G *pc* lat cop[sa bo (pt)] arm
v 23 μεν / om P[46] B lat[vg]
      δι' P[46] ℵ A *al* / δια της B D G byz
v 25 το δε Αγαρ A B D 69 *al* syr[hcl.mg] / το γαρ Αγαρ K L P byz lat[d e] syr[pesh hcl] /
      το δε P[46] lat[t] cop[sa] Ambst / το γαρ ℵ G lat Orig Epiph Aug
      Σινα om lat[d]
      εστιν om 1739 *pc* Orig
      συ(ν)στοιχει δε / η (om D*) συνστοιχουσα D* 1739 *pc* Orig G lat
v 26 ημων P[46] ℵ* B D G Ψ 1739 *pc* lat syr[pesh hcl.mg] / παντων ημων ℵ² A byz lat[t vg(3)]
      syr[hcl]
v 28 υμεις . . . εστε P[46] B D* G 1739 *al* cop[sa] Iren[lat] / ημεις . . . εσμεν ℵ A Ψ byz
      lat[r vg] syr cop[bo]
v 30 της ελευθερας / μου Ισαακ D* G lat[vet] Ambst
v 1 τη ελευθερια ημας Χριστος ελευθερωσεν· στηκετε ουν (om ουν D* 614 *pc*)
      ℵ A B P *al* / ῇ ελευθερια ημας Χριστος ηλευθερωσεν, στηκετε (add ουν G
      Orig) G lat Mcion Orig Ephr / τη ελευθερια (add ουν TR) ῇ Χριστος ημας
      ηλευθερωσεν, στηκετε K L byz

4:21 Paul now endeavours to reinforce his argument by means of an allegorical interpretation of the Genesis story of Hagar and Sarah, with their respective sons Ishmael and Isaac. Paul himself calls his interpretation 'allegorical' (v 24)—that is to say, the entities in the story stand for something other than their *prima facie* sense, whether that 'something other' was intended by the original author (as, say, in Bunyan's *Pilgrim's Progress*) or is the contribution of the interpreter (and even when it is the contribution of the interpreter, the interpreter frequently thinks that he is bringing out the intention of the original author).

Paul was not the first to allegorize the story of Abraham's two sons: Philo had done so already, although there is no relation between Philo's interpretation and Paul's. According to Philo, Abraham is the virtue-loving soul in its quest for the true God; Sarah is virtue and her son Isaac is the higher wisdom, whereas Hagar is the lower learning of the schools and her son Ishmael is sophistry, shooting his arguments as an archer (Gn. 21:20) shoots arrows from his bow (*Abr.* 68; *Fug.* 128, 209f.; *Mut.* 255, etc.). In other words, Philo finds set forth in the patriarchal narrative the philosophy which to his mind constituted ultimate truth; Paul finds set forth in it the gospel of free grace which he was commissioned to proclaim and which he had already seen to be summed up in the statement that Abraham's faith was counted to him for righteousness (cf. 3:6).

λέγετέ μοι, οἱ ὑπὸ νόμον θέλοντες εἶναι, τὸν νόμον οὐκ ἀκούετε; We note the transition in this sentence from νόμος in the strict sense of 'law'—'you who wish to be under law' (as in 3:23; 4:4f.)—to νόμος in the general sense of the Pentateuch. The patriarchal narrative does not belong to any of the law-codes of the Torah, but it is part of the Torah, and it is doubtful if Paul and his contemporaries made the explicit distinction in their minds between the narrower and wider senses of the term that modern students readily make. Similarly in Rom. 3:19, after a catena of quotations drawn mainly from the Psalter, Paul applies them particularly to Jews because 'whatever the law (ὁ νόμος) says, it says to those who are under the law (τοῖς ἐν τῷ νόμῳ)'—where ἐν τῷ νόμῳ has much the same sense as ὑπὸ νόμον here, whereas ὁ νόμος is used in its widest sense to include all the sacred scriptures.

Paul reminds his readers of a phase in the patriarchal narrative, which he treats in such a way as to emphasize the incompatibility of life under law and life under promise. If you insist on the priority in the inheritance of Abraham's descendants κατὰ σάρκα, he says in effect, remember this: Abraham indeed had a son κατὰ σάρκα, of whom it is expressly stated that he was *not* to share the inheritance.

4:22 γέγραπται, 'it is written', 'scripture tells us' (as in 3:10, 13).

'Αβραὰμ δύο υἱοὺς ἔσχεν, 'Abraham acquired (ἔσχεν, aorist) two sons'—Ishmael, the elder, and Isaac, his junior by fourteen years.

When Sarah, Abraham's wife, had given him no child, and had now reached an age at which she was unlikely ever to have one, she decided to give him one by proxy through Hagar, her Egyptian slave—a practice which appears to have been socially acceptable in their culture (cf. Gn. 30:3–13). Hagar became pregnant immediately, and did not conceal her sense of superiority over her mistress, who felt correspondingly humiliated. Relations between the two women were thenceforth strained. Hagar in due course gave birth to Ishmael, who was his aged father's pride and joy (Gn. 16:1–16; 17:18). But some years later Abraham and Sarah received the divine promise that Sarah herself would have a son, and the promise was fulfilled the following year in the birth of Isaac (*yiṣḥāq*)—so called because of the laughter (*ṣḥq*), first of incredulity and then of exultation, which attended his annunciation and birth (Gn. 17:17; 18:10–15; 21:1–7).

The status of Ishmael and his mother now suffered a radical change: the security they had enjoyed so long as Hagar was the mother of Abraham's one and only son was imperilled. Matters came to a head at the festivities which marked the weaning of Isaac: 'Sarah saw the son of Hagar the Egyptian, whom she had borne to Abraham, playing with her son Isaac. So she said to Abraham, "Cast out this slave woman with her son; for the son of this slave woman shall not be heir with my son Isaac" ' (Gn. 21:9f.).

Abraham's affection for Ishmael made him unwilling to do any such thing; he yielded only when God told him to do as his wife said and promised that Ishmael would become the ancestor of a great nation, 'because he is your off-spring' (Gn. 21:11–13; cf. v 18). (A parallel and expanded form of this promise, in Gn. 17:20, speaks of Ishmael as destined to become 'the father of twelve princes', who are doubtless to be identified with the twelve sons of Ishmael listed in Gn. 25:13–18, eponymous ancestors of the Arab tribes which occupied the territory 'from Havilah to Shur'—that is, in the Syrian desert, between the Euphrates and the Egyptian frontier.)

This narrative lends itself to interpretation at various levels, but most of these would be irrelevant to Paul's treatment. Source analysis of the narrative would be beside the point, for Paul's treatment views the narrative as a whole, within Genesis as a completed literary unit. Equally unhelpful here would be a study of the narrative in its dramatic setting, as compared with contemporary Near Eastern practice. According to the code of Hammurabi, for example, 'the children of the wife shall divide the property of the father's house equally with the sons of the bondmaid; the son and heir, the son of the wife, shall choose a share (first) and take it' (paragraph 170). As for the case of a childless wife (as Sarah was for long), it is stipulated in marriage contracts from Nuzu that if a wife proves to be childless she shall provide her husband with a slave wife and that the son of such a slave wife shall not be expelled (cf. E. A. Speiser, 'New Kirkuk Documents relating to Family Laws', *AASOR* 10 [1930], 1–73, especially 31–33). It may be that Sarah, in refusing to let Ishmael have a share of the inheritance and in insisting on his expulsion, was in breach of established usage; if so, Abraham would have been the more reluctant to accede to her demand, until he was divinely directed to do so.

The narrative was naturally of great religious and ethnic interest to Jews. They were the descendants of Isaac, the promised son; they were therefore the chosen people, the heirs of the promise, the true children of Abraham, to whom the divine oracle said, 'through Isaac shall your offspring be named' (Gn. 21:12). (It could not be denied that Isaac was the ancestor of the Edomites also, but the Edomites were not joint-heirs of the promise, for reasons which Paul points out in Rom. 9:10–13.) The Israelites were acquainted with their Ishmaelite neighbours who lived beyond the confines of the cultivated land, and they may have been familiar with some of their customs, such as the circumcision of boys at puberty, after the example of Ishmael himself (Gn. 17:25), and in contrast to their own custom of circumcision at eight days old, following the precedent of Isaac (Gn. 21:4). But as time went on, the Ishmaelites would readily rank as representatives of Gentiles in general, excluded from the special covenant which God made with Abraham and with his descendants through Isaac (and Jacob).

4:23 ἀλλ' ὁ μὲν ἐκ τῆς παιδίσκης κατὰ σάρκα γεγέννηται, ὁ δὲ ἐκ τῆς ἐλευθέρας δι’ ἐπαγγελίας. The perfect γεγέννηται may imply that the reference is not only to the historical event of Ishmael’s birth but also to the abiding truth that ‘what is born (τὸ γεγεννημένον) of the flesh is flesh’ (Jn. 3:6). Alternatively, the reference may be to the abiding record in scripture: γεγέννηται ‘approximately’ = γέγραπται ὅτι ἐγεννήθη (BDF 342 [5]).

κατὰ σάρκα means ‘in the ordinary course of nature’. No moral censure is implied: unlike Philo (*Sob.* 8), Paul does not call Ishmael illegitimate (νόθος). It is simply recognized that there was nothing exceptional about Ishmael’s birth. Nor is anything in the nature of a virgin birth implied for Isaac (so, e.g., Marius Victorinus *ad loc.*: ‘*non ex copulatione*’). Abraham’s real paternity of Isaac is implied in v 22, as it is, if anything, more clearly in Rom. 4:18–21. There is nothing here comparable to Philo’s allegorical statement that Isaac was born not as a human being but as ‘a most pure thought (νόημα καθαρώτατον), beautiful by nature rather than by practice’ (*Fug.* 167).

Yet the birth of Isaac was certainly contrary to the ordinary course of nature, in view of the advanced age of Abraham, and more particularly of Sarah, at the time of his conception: it took place by the enabling word of God, in direct fulfilment of his promise (cf. Gn. 17:19; 18:9–15).

4:24 ἅτινά ἐστιν ἀλληγορούμενα. The compound ἅτινα (cf. 5:19) has taken over the function of the simple neuter plural ἅ (so also ἥτις for ἥ in vv 24b, 26).

‘This is an allegory’, says Paul, or ‘these are allegorical entities’, each of them corresponding to a reality in the new situation (cf. NIV: ‘these things may be taken figuratively’). He is not thinking of allegory in the Philonic sense (allegory in the Philonic sense was introduced into Christian interpretation with Origen and his successors); he has in mind that form of allegory which is commonly called typology: a narrative from OT history is interpreted in terms of the new covenant, or (to put it the other way round) an aspect of the new covenant is presented in terms of an OT narrative. Typology presupposes that salvation-history displays a recurring pattern of divine action: thus the exilic prophets portrayed their people’s return from Babylon in terms of a second Exodus, and the NT writers portray the Christian redemption in terms both of the Exodus and of the return from Babylon. Paul supplies simple examples of such typology when he says that ‘Christ, our paschal lamb, has been sacrificed’ (1 Cor. 5:7) or shows how the people of Christ in this age experience their own counterparts of the Red Sea passage, the manna, the water from the rock and the vicissitudes of the wilderness wanderings (1 Cor. 10:1–11). The Exodus typology in partic-ular was widespread in the NT period (cf. Heb. 3:7–4:11; Jude 5).

The one rather clear instance of non-typological allegory in Paul is his treatment of the command not to muzzle an ox when it is treading out the grain (Dt. 25:4) as the authorization of those who preach the gospel to live by the gospel (1 Cor. 9:8–10).

See A. T. Hanson, *Studies in Paul’s Technique and Theology* (London, 1974); R. N. Longenecker, *Biblical Exegesis in the Apostolic Period* (Grand Rapids, 1975); F. P. Ramos, ‘Alegoria o tipologia en Gal 4, 21-31’, *Est Bíb* 34 (1975), 113–119, and *La Libertad en la Carta a los Galatas* (Madrid, 1977), 100–121; R. J. Kepple, ‘An Analysis of Antiochene Exegesis of Galatians 4:24–26’, *WTJ* 39 (1976–77), 239–249.

Paul presents a more elaborate example of biblical interpretation in 2 Cor. 3:7–4:6, in his midrash on Ex. 34:29–35. There the fading reflection of the divine glory on Moses' face is contrasted with the permanent glory in the face of Christ. But the argument is thoroughly typological in the sense that the distinctiveness of the new covenant is brought out by comparison and contrast with the old. The old covenant is the administration of law, meting out death to the transgressor, whereas the new covenant is the administration of the Spirit, imparting life to the believer. Since 'where the Spirit of the Lord is, there is freedom' (2 Cor. 3:17), the contrast between law and Spirit is identical with the contrast between legal bondage and spiritual freedom which Paul illustrates by his present 'allegory'.

In the present 'allegory', however, there is a forcible inversion of the analogy which is unparalleled elsewhere in Paul. Whereas in other typological passages the OT account is left intact, the argument here is up against the historical fact that Isaac was the ancestor of the Jews, whereas Ishmael's descendants were Gentiles. This unique clash between type and antitype demands an explanation, and a highly probable explanation has been put forward by C. K. Barrett ('The Allegory of Abraham, Sarah, and Hagar in the Argument of Galatians', *Käsemann FS*, 1–16)—namely, that the incident of the two sons of Abraham had been adduced by Paul's opponents in Galatia in support of *their* case, and that Paul felt obliged to refute their argument by inverting it and showing that the incident, properly understood, supported the gospel of free grace, with its antithesis between flesh and spirit.

αὗται γάρ εἰσιν δύο διαθῆκαι. The copula here means 'stand for' or 'signify'; cf. 2 Cor. 3:17, ὁ δὲ κύριος τὸ πνεῦμά ἐστιν, ' "the Lord" [in the particular context of Ex. 34:34 LXX] means "the Spirit" ', and for a typological parallel 1 Cor. 10:4, ἡ πέτρα δὲ ἦν ὁ Χριστός, 'and the rock was Christ' (see on v 4).

If the one διαθήκη is the Sinaitic covenant, as is here stated, the other is the covenant with Abraham (cf. 3:15–17), which was characterized by 'promise'. The initial fulfilment of the covenant-promise to Abraham was the birth of Isaac, who (with his mother) is presented by Paul as the embodiment or symbol of that promise.

A parallel to Paul's OT exegesis here has been recognized in CD 6.3–11 (J. D. G. Dunn, who mentions it in *Unity*, 396 n. 19, acknowledges indebtedness to G. I. Davies for drawing his attention to it): the Song of the Well (Nu. 21:18) is so interpreted that the 'well' is the law, the 'princes' who dig it are the members of the faithful community who left the land of Judah, the 'sceptre' or 'staff' with which it is dug is the 'expositor of the law', and the 'nobles of the people' are those who carry out his ordinances. But this exegesis, allegorical as it is, does not involve the reversal of historical actuality implicit in Paul's allegory; it probably has more in common with the treatment that Paul's opponents would have given to the story of Isaac and Ishmael.

If Paul, in the elementary class of his rabbinical school, had been set an exegetical exercise on the text, 'Abraham had two sons, one by a slave and one by a free woman', the outline of his exegesis would have been predictable: Isaac was the ancestor of the chosen people; the Ishmaelites are Gentiles. The Jews are the children of the free woman; the Gentiles are children of the slave woman.

The Jews have received the liberating knowledge of the law; the Gentiles are in bondage to ignorance and sin. The Jews are the people of the covenant; such blessings as the Gentiles enjoy (like the promise that Ishmael would become a great nation) are uncovenanted mercies.

If the trouble-makers in Galatia appealed to the story of Isaac and Ishmael, that is very much how they would have applied it. True, they would have conceded, the Gentiles of Galatia could not be sons of Abraham by natural descent, as Isaac was; yet there was hope for them: they could be adopted into Abraham's family by circumcision and so enjoy the covenant mercies promised to Abraham and his descendants. By accepting circumcision they would align themselves with the church of the circumcised in Jerusalem, the mother-church of the true followers of Christ.

Paul now inverts the exegesis which would have commended itself to him in earlier days. Now it is the people of the law who are the offspring of the slave woman; the children of the free woman are those who embrace the gospel of justification by faith, comprising a minority of Jews and a rapidly increasing preponderance of Gentiles. To Jews this exegesis must have seemed preposterous. It was crystal clear that they were Sarah's offspring, while Hagar's descendants were Gentiles. One could envisage a group like the Qumran community claiming that its members alone, because of their special devotion to the law, were sons of the promise, while the apostate majority of Israel deserved to be ranked with the Ishmaelites; but that bears no resemblance to Paul's argument. For Paul, law and promise are antithetical. His own experience had convinced him that the law brought men and women into bondage, while the gospel was a message of liberation. Therefore, he argues, the people of the law belong to Hagar's family, for she 'is from Mount Sinai, bearing children for slavery'; those who believe the gospel are the children of Sarah, the free woman. We cannot know how convincing Paul's Gentile readers found his argument; much would depend on the degree to which they had assimilated his principles of OT interpretation.

What Paul had learned from his personal experience corresponded with his reading of the history of God's dealings with mankind. The gospel is the fulfilment of the promise made to Abraham that in him and his offspring all nations would be blessed (cf. 3:8, 16). The law, which was given later, was a parenthetical dispensation introduced by God for a limited purpose; its validity continued only until the promise to Abraham was fulfilled in Christ, and even while it was valid it did not modify the terms of the promise (cf. 3:17–25).

4:25 τὸ δὲ Ἁγὰρ Σινᾶ ὄρος ἐστὶν ἐν τῇ Ἀραβίᾳ. This reading (the longer one) is preferable on intrinsic grounds; there would be little point in the shorter reading: 'For Sinai is a mountain in Arabia'. Of course it is, but why would Paul make such a bald statement of geographical fact? The copula once more means 'signifies' or 'represents': 'Hagar corresponds to Mount Sinai in Arabia' (from which the law was promulgated). It is probably irrelevant in this context that Hagar (Heb. *hāgār*) is similar (but not identical) to a Semitic word meaning 'rock' or 'crag' (Heb. *ḥāgār*, Aram. *ḥagrā'*, Arab. *ḥaǧar*): Paul certainly is not saying 'Hagar means "mountain" in Arabia' (*pace* W. Bousset, *Die Schriften des Neuen Testaments*, II [Göttingen, ³1917], 66). Nor is there much substance in the attempt of H. Gese ('τὸ δὲ Ἁγὰρ Σινᾶ ὄρος ἐστὶν ἐν τῇ 'Ἀραβίᾳ', *Rost FS*, 81–94 = *Vom Sinai zum Zion* [München, 1974], 49–62) to see a reference here to *el-Ḥeǧra* (Medain Salih, 200 miles north of Medina) on the basis of Gn. 16:7, Tg. Onq., where Hagar takes the way to *Ḥagrā*'; there, as elsewhere in Tg. Onq., *ḥagrā*' is the regular (updated) Aram. equivalent of Shur, on the way to Egypt (cf. G. I. Davies, 'Hagar, el-Heǧra, and the Location of Mount Sinai', *VT* 22 [1972], 152–163).

(The earliest witness to the traditional identification of Mount Sinai with Jebel Musa comes in Egeria's *Peregrinatio* [AD 383/4]; she was assured of the identification by local monks. The 'Hagrites' [Heb. *hagrîm*, *hagrî'îm*] are referred to as an Arab group in 1 Ch. 5:10, 19f.; 27:31; Ps. 83:6.)

The identification of Hagar with Sinai means simply that she and her descendants represent the law, which holds men and women in bondage. If she also corresponds to the present Jerusalem συστοιχεῖ δὲ τῇ νῦν 'Ιερουσαλήμ), it is not so much the literal city that is meant as the whole legal system of Judaism, which had its world-centre in Jerusalem. If Paul's opponents were trying to bring his Galatian converts into subjection to the church of Jerusalem and its leadership, that would add point to Paul's reference to 'the present Jerusalem'. The leaders of the Jerusalem church had reached an accommodation with Paul about the gospel which he preached and his commission to propagate it in the Gentile world (2:1–9); if they were now going back on that agreement, if they were a party to the attempt to impose the yoke of the law on the Gentile churches of Galatia (a charge against them to which Paul does not commit himself), then they would be making common cause with the community which is still 'in slavery with her children'.

In vv 25 and 26 Paul uses the form 'Ιερουσαλήμ (a fairly close transliteration of the Hebrew), whereas in 1:17f. and 2:1 he has used the hellenized plural 'Ιεροσόλυμα. In those earlier references he has the geographical site in view; here the emphasis is more on the religious significance of the city.

A. Harnack thought that 'we can without difficulty discern the rule which guides his use of the respective names: where Jerusalem has religious significance (Gal. iv.25, 26), and in passages of special solemnity where the Apostle thinks of the "saints" in Jerusalem (Rom. xv.25, 26, 31; here Jerusalem is everywhere combined with οἱ ἅγιοι) he writes 'Ιερουσαλήμ, *i.e.* he chooses the *Hebrew* name, elsewhere he writes 'Ιεροσόλυμα' (*The Acts of the Apostles*, ETr [London, 1909], 76). He notes that Rom. 15:19 and 1 Cor. 16:3 (in both of which 'Ιερουσαλήμ appears) seem to be exceptions to this rule, but considers that in the latter place Paul is *thinking* of the saints in Jerusalem, though he does not actually say οἱ ἅγιοι, and that in the former 'his feeling of reverent wonder at the grandeur of the work that had been accomplished through him may have led him to write the name 'Ιερουσαλήμ' (ibid., 77).

4:26 ἡ δὲ ἄνω 'Ιερουσαλήμ ἐλευθέρα ἐστίν. 'Jerusalem above' is the antithesis to 'the present Jerusalem'. No explicit antithesis to Mount Sinai is mentioned, but 'Jerusalem above' probably fills this role as well as that of antithesis to the present Jerusalem. The antithesis between Sinai and Jerusalem (or Zion) was early taken up and developed in a number of directions, as may be seen in Heb. 12:18–24 and later in the pseudo-Cyprianic anti-Jewish treatise *De montibus Sina et Sion* (*PL* IV.991–1000).

The idea of two Jerusalems, the lower and the upper, the earthly and the heavenly, is not peculiar to Paul. Two other NT writers make use of it (cf. Heb. 12:22, with 11:10, 16; Rev. 3:12; 21:2, 9ff.). Paul's use of the idea here is probably the earliest literary reference to it, although the way in which he introduces it suggests that it was no new idea to him nor, it seems, to the Galatians.

As the wilderness tabernacle was to be constructed according to the pattern shown to Moses on Sinai (Ex. 25:40), so the temple and city of Jerusalem were regarded as material copies of eternal and heavenly archetypes. In 1 Ch. 28:19 the plan of the temple which Solomon received from David is said to have been 'made clear by the writing from the hand of Yahweh concerning it'. More precisely, in Wis. 9:8 Solomon, in prayer to God, describes his temple as 'a copy of the holy tent which thou didst prepare from the beginning'—the 'holy tent' being God's heavenly dwelling-place. The existence of the heavenly Jerusalem was later inferred from Ps. 122:3 ('Jerusalem, built as a city which is bound firmly together'), rendered 'Jerusalem, built like the city which is its fellow' (with vocalization $ḥ^a\underline{b}ērāh$ for MT $ḥubb^erāh$; cf. Tg. and Midr. *Tehillim*, *ad loc*.). R. Me'ir (*c.* AD 140) said that, of the seven heavens, the fourth was called $z^e\underline{b}ûl$, 'in which are Jerusalem and the temple, and an altar is set up, at which Michael the great prince stands and offers sacrifice' (b. Ḥag. 12b). In the Apocalypse of Baruch, written shortly after the catastrophe of AD 70, Baruch is told that the earthly Jerusalem is not the true city of God: the true city was revealed to Adam before his fall, to Abraham when God made a covenant with him, and to Moses at the time when he was shown the plan of the tabernacle on Sinai (2 Bar. 4:2ff.).

In our present text, just as ἡ νῦν Ἰερουσαλήμ is not primarily the geographical site, so ἡ ἄνω Ἰερουσαλήμ is not spatially elevated but is the community of the new covenant.

ἥτις ἐστὶν μήτηρ ἡμῶν. Cf. Ps. 87 (LXX 86):5, μήτηρ Σιών, ἐρεῖ τις, ' "Zion is my mother", one will say' (i.e. 'I was born in Zion'); cf. C. Gore, *The Holy Spirit in the Church* (London, 1924), 150 = *The Reconstruction of Belief* (London, 1926), 770; C. F. D. Moule, *The Birth of the NT* (London, ³1981), 60. A later parallel is 2 Esd. 10:7, 'Zion, the mother of us all, is in deep grief . . .' (where again, as in Ps. 87, it is the earthly Jerusalem that is in view, after the disaster of AD 70). For the picture of Zion/Jerusalem as the mother of her citizens cf. also Is. 49:20f.; 54:1–13 (see quotation in v 27 below). For Paul it is the heavenly Jerusalem that is the counterpart of Sarah, the mother of the free-born people of God; cf. 'the city which has foundations, whose builder and maker is God', prepared by him for men and women of faith (Heb. 11:10, 16).

In Cyprian's *Testimonia* (1.20) the argument of Gal. 4:22ff. is summarized and then amplified with the inclusion of *Jacob's* two wives—the weak-eyed Leah representing the synagogue and Rachel, the mother of Joseph ('a type of Christ', he says), representing the church. He finds the same twofold analogy later in Elkanah's two wives, the church being represented by Hannah, the mother of Samuel (another 'type of Christ'). The motif of the sterile wife ultimately getting the better of her fertile rival is recurrent in the OT narrative, as a demonstration of the grace and power of God (cf. Ps. 113 [LXX 112]:9 and, for a NT parallel, Lk. 1:36f.).

4:27 The ultimate triumph of the formerly childless wife over the other is celebrated in Is. 54:1, quoted here by Paul not only because it is a *locus classicus* for this theme but also because the mother here congratulated is Zion/Jerusalem. The derelict (ἔρημος) city of Jerusalem, bereft of her children who have been carried into exile in Babylon, is destined to be restored and to be blessed with returning children more numerous than those whom she lost. The prophet is not contrasting two distinct 'women': he is rather contrasting the desolate Jerusalem, widowed and robbed of her children, with Jerusalem as she was in the days of her earlier prosperity and as she will be in days to come when she will be more abundantly compensated for her losses.

Moreover, Is. 54:1 is part of Is. 40–66, which in the NT is one of the most fertile fields of *testimonia*, from the 'voice' of Is. 40:3 (cf. Mk. 1:3 par.; Jn. 1:23) to the 'new heavens and new earth' of Is. 65:17 and 66:22 (cf. 2 Pet. 3:13; Rev. 21:1). By the NT writers, and especially by Paul, this whole corpus of prophecy is given a gospel interpretation. For such a fresh interpretation the early Christians (whether they were aware of it or not) had pre-Christian precedent, as has been shown by the Qumran texts. The 'voice' of Is. 40:3 ('In the wilderness prepare the way of the LORD; make straight in the desert a highway for our God') provided the Qumran sectaries with authority for their wilderness retreat (1QS 8.13f.); and in a fragmentary commentary on Isaiah from Cave 4 (4Q Is^d) parts of Is. 54 are referred to the elect community forming the nucleus of the restored Israel of the new age. The promise to the widowed city, 'I will lay your foundations in lapis lazuli' (Is. 54:11), is explained thus: 'Its interpretation is that they have founded the council of the community, the priests and the peo[ple, to be] a congregation of his elect, like a stone of lapis lazuli among the stones.'

So by Paul the promises of Is. 54 are understood as addressed to the church of the new age, Jerusalem above. But for Paul the contemporary church was a predominantly Gentile community. Formerly the Gentiles were spiritually sterile, producing no fruit for God, but now their response to the gospel has made them more fruitful than the synagogue: the new Jerusalem has more children than ever the old Jerusalem had. The two women of Is. 54:1 have now become two distinct entities.

This is not the only place where an OT situation within the bounds of the chosen family is applied in the NT on a more comprehensive scale, embracing Gentiles as well as Jews. More NT writers than one, for example, interpret Hosea's Lo-ammi and Lo-ruhamah (Ho. 1:6–9) not of temporarily apostate Israel but of the Gentiles who were formerly unrelated to God but have now been brought into his family (cf. Rom. 9:25f.; 1 Pet. 2:10). The principle of divine action is the same, but in the Gentile mission it is exhibited on a broader canvas.

The Christian application of Is. 54:1 was probably not peculiar to Paul; it may well have belonged to the common exegetical stock of the church. But, if it lay ready to Paul's hand, he found it specially appropriate to his handling of the patriarchal narrative. Sarah, who 'was barren (*^{a}qārāh*, στεῖρα, as in Is. 54:1) and had no child' (Gn. 11:30), certainly did exult when she gave birth to Isaac (Gn. 21:6f.). Even if Paul was moved to take up the Ishmael-Isaac analogy because of the use that was being made of it by his opponents in Galatia, he was able to turn it to his own purpose by tying it in with his insistence that

Abraham's true offspring comprises all believers and with the unquestioned fact that Isaac's birth fulfilled the divine promise, belief in which had procured Abraham's justification.

Philo (*Praem.* 158–160) treats Is. 54:1 (in conjunction with the words of Hannah in 1 Sa. [LXX 1 Ki.] 2:5) as an ethical allegory of the history of the soul—the children of the married woman being vices and those of the barren woman (the virgin impregnated by divine seed) virtues (cf. *Migr. Abr.* 224f.). But, however congenial to Philonism this allegorization is, it is an aberration from the main line of biblical interpretation.

4:28 κατὰ 'Ισαὰκ ἐπαγγελίας τέκνα ἐστέ. If the story of Abraham's two sons is to be allegorized at all in terms of the gospel order, it follows as the night the day that the analogy of Isaac, the son of promise, is maintained by those (Gentiles though they are) who in Christ Jesus have received 'the blessing of Abraham, . . . the promise of the Spirit through faith' (3:14).

4:29 ὁ κατὰ σάρκα γεννηθεὶς ἐδίωκεν τὸν κατὰ πνεῦμα. κατὰ πνεῦμα is the natural antithesis to κατὰ σάρκα, which in v 23 is set in opposition to δι' ἐπαγγελίας. We can distinguish two antithetic pairs: κατὰ σάρκα/κατὰ πνεῦμα and ὑπὸ νόμον/δι' ἐπαγγελίας. But in the present context the two pairs correspond so exactly that one element in one of them (κατὰ πνεῦμα) can be replaced by the corresponding element in the other (δι' ἐπαγγελίας), as in v 23. For the antithetic κατὰ σάρκα/κατὰ πνεῦμα cf. Rom. 1:3f., where the force of σάρξ is less 'theological' than it is here.

Biblical substantiation for the statement that Ishmael persecuted Isaac is not forthcoming, so far as the two individuals are concerned; there could be a reference to occasions when the descendants of Ishmael committed aggression against the Israelites, Isaac's descendants (cf. Jdg. 8:24; Ps. 83:6). But rabbinical tradition makes mention of rivalry between the two brothers, especially with regard to the inheritance. According to *Gen. Rab.* 55:4 (on Gn. 22:1), Ishmael claimed the inheritance because he had accepted circumcision willingly, at the age of thirteen (Gn. 17:25), whereas Isaac received it involuntarily when he was eight days old (Gn. 21:4).

More particularly, attention has been drawn to the statement that during the weaning festivities Sarah saw Hagar's son 'playing with her son Isaac' (Gn. 21:9). The words 'with her son Isaac' are absent from the MT, but as they appear in the LXX and in some Vg codices they may well have been present in the *Vorlage* of these versions. The MT as it stands says that Sarah saw Ishmael 'playing' or 'laughing' (*meṣaḥēq*). The 'laughing' motif is so prominent in the account of Isaac's conception and birth that it is hardly surprising that Ishmael should have joined in the universal laughter. Had not Sarah said, 'God has made laughter (*ṣeḥōq*) for me; every one who hears will laugh (*yiṣḥaq*) over me' (Gn. 21:6)? What was the nature of Ishmael's laughter? According to Jub. 17:4, 'Sarah saw Ishmael playing and dancing, and Abraham rejoicing with great joy, and she became jealous of Ishmael' and demanded his expulsion. But AV preserves a tradition that Ishmael's laughter was unfriendly: 'Sarah saw the son of Hagar the Egyptian . . . mocking.' But even 'mocking' is hardly tantamount to 'persecuting'.

Some rabbis suspected a more sinister implication beneath the innocent participle *meṣaḥēq* ('laughing', 'playing'), and adduced texts where the verb

denotes sinful or violent action (cf. *Gen. Rab.* 53:11 on Gn. 21:9). R. Ishmael
(*c*. AD 100) charged Ishmael with pagan worship, on the strength of Ex. 32:6,
where 'to play' (*l^eṣaḥēq*) is used in connexion with Israel's worship of the golden
calf: more specifically, he said that Ishmael caught locusts and offered them in
sacrifice (being a child, he could not catch larger animals). (Similarly *Tg. Neof.*
[*in loco*] says that Sarah saw Ishmael 'doing unseemly things', and an added
gloss explains these things as actions pertaining to a foreign cult.) R. Ishmael's
contemporary, R. Aqiba, identified Ishmael's conduct as sexual immorality, on
the strength of Gn. 39:17, where Potiphar's wife complains that Joseph came
'to insult me' (*lisḥōq bî*, literally 'to play with me'). But R. Azariah, in the name
of R. Levi, recalled the use of the same verb with a connotation of bloodshed
in 2 Sa. 2:14, 'Let the young men arise and play (*yiśḥ^aqû*) before us', and
expounded the situation thus: 'Ishmael said to Isaac, "Let us go and see our
portions in the field" [based perhaps on Cain's words to Abel in the original text
of Gn. 4:8]; then Ishmael would take a bow and arrows [cf. Gn. 21:20] and
shoot them in Isaac's direction, while pretending to be playing.' These observations are all later than Paul's day; whether there were earlier forms of any,
specially of the last, which he knew we cannot say.

οὕτως καὶ νῦν. For Jewish persecution of Christians (whether of Jewish
or Gentile stock) cf. 1 Thes. 2:14–16; on the genuineness of that passage see
K. G. Eckart, 'Der zweite echte Brief des Apostels Paulus an die Thessalo-
nicher', *ZTK* 58 (1961), 33f.; W. G. Kümmel, 'Das literarische und geschichtliche Problem des ersten Thessalonicherbriefes', *O. Cullmann FS* (1), 213–227;
B. A. Pearson, '1 Thessalonians 2:13–16: A Deutero-Pauline Interpolation',
HTR 64 (1971), 79–94; E. Best, *Thessalonians*, BNTC, 122f.; H. Boers, 'The
Form-Critical Study of Paul's Letters: I Thessalonians as a Case Study', *NTS* 22
(1975–76), 140–158 (especially 151f., 158). R. Jewett finds both in Galatians
(cf. also 3:4, τοσαῦτα ἐπάθετε, and 5:11, ἔτι διώκομαι) and in 1 Thessalonians
evidence for his view 'that Jewish Christians in Judea were stimulated by Zealotic
pressure into a nomistic campaign among their fellow Christians in the late
forties and early fifties' ('The Agitators and the Galatian Congregation', *NTS* 17
[1970–71], 205). This is probably true. But, if the Galatian churches in this
letter include those of Pisidian Antioch, Iconium and Lystra, then, according to
the record of Acts (13:50; 14:2–5, 19), the Christians of those cities had first-
hand experience of opposition stirred up by Phrygian Jews.

4:30 ἀλλὰ τί λέγει ἡ γραφή; For a similar question cf. Rom. 4:3; 11:2.
It is a rhetorical way of putting the point that 'the scripture says' (cf. Rom. 9:17;
10:11; 1 Tim. 5:18); but it is not a rhetorical question in the usual sense, for the
answer follows immediately, in the form of a text of scripture.

Ἔκβαλε τὴν παιδίσκην καὶ τὸν υἱὸν αὐτῆς. The original point of this
quotation (Gn. 21:10) was simple enough: the sight of Ishmael playing with her
baby son reminded Sarah that Isaac had this older brother who had been since
his birth the apple of his father's eye and she felt that Isaac's position was
insecure so long as Ishmael was around. There is no reason to look for a further
motive, as Josephus does when he credits her with the suspicion that, after
Abraham's death, Ishmael might do Isaac an injury (*Ant*. 1.215).

It is, however, noteworthy that Sarah's uncharitable demand, 'Drive out the
slavegirl and her son . . .', is treated here not simply as something which scrip-

ture records but as something which scripture *says* (cf. the use of ἡ γραφή as subject in 3:8). Whatever moral or legal issues might be raised by Sarah's demand in its historical setting, Paul treats it as the word of scripture—in effect, as the word of God. The reason for his doing so is not far to seek: apart from God's underwriting Sarah's demand (Gn. 21:12), the words οὐ γὰρ μὴ κληρονομήσει ὁ υἱὸς τῆς παιδίσκης μετὰ τοῦ υἱοῦ τῆς ἐλευθέρας (the end of the quotation is adapted to the present context by the substitution of τοῦ υἱοῦ τῆς ἐλευθέρας for τοῦ υἱοῦ μου Ἰσαάκ) enshrine the basic gospel truth: legal bondage and spiritual freedom cannot coexist. The inheritance promised to Abraham belongs to the children of the promise who, being believers themselves, are blessed with believing Abraham (3:9). It does not belong to those who, being 'under law', are still in bondage. If it was Paul's opponents who compelled him to take up the story of Ishmael and Isaac, they unintentionally provided him with a wonderful text to undergird the argument of this whole letter.

J. Bligh (*Galatians*, 390 *et passim*) regards Paul's appeal to the story of Ishmael and Isaac as the climax of his reply to Cephas at Antioch (which, he holds, runs, with occasional interruptions, from 2:14b to 5:13a)—as 'the final demonstration from Scripture that the law of Moses has no place in the Gentile churches and must be excluded from them'. So the demand 'Drive out the slavegirl . . .' requires as a practical measure to be enforced forthwith that those who continue to observe the law, Christians though they may be, must be banished from the Gentile churches. This, however, is contrary to Paul's policy elsewhere (cf. Rom. 11:13–21; 14:1–15:13) and is not a necessary inference from his language here. More convincingly C. K. Barrett argues that the quotation of v 30 is the 'next step' which logically follows when once it has been 'confirmed that the Jewish Christians are, theologically, Ishmaels, and the law-free Christians Isaacs'; it 'is not (*pace* Bligh) a call to the Gentile Christians in the Church of Antioch to rise up and expel their Jewish Christian brethren; it is rather the command of God to his (angelic) agents'—the singular imperative being presumably addressed to each of them individually—and 'expresses what the fate of each party [οἱ ἐξ ἔργων νόμου and οἱ ἐκ πίστεως] is to be' ('The Allegory of Abraham, Sarah, and Hagar . . .', 13).

4:31 διό. C. K. Barrett (ibid.) says that 'it is the fact of persecution that leads Paul' to the conclusion now stated. It was a matter of experience that Gentile Christians had not persecuted Jews or Jewish Christians (that was to come later); 'therefore' those who suffered persecution corresponded to Isaac and those who inflicted it to Ishmael.

οὐκ ἐσμὲν παιδίσκης τέκνα ἀλλὰ τῆς ἐλευθέρας. The summing up of the point of the 'allegory' repeats the sense of v 28 in slightly different words. Those who by faith belong to Christ 'are Abraham's offspring, heirs according to promise' (3:29), answering to the son of the free woman.

Paul's later, non-allegorical (but still in intention typological) reference to Abraham's sons in Rom. 9:7–9 comes to mind. There, emphasizing the sovereignty of the divine election, he insists that it is spiritual, not natural, descent that matters: 'Not all are children of Abraham because they are his descendants; but "Through Isaac shall your descendants be named" [Gn. 21:12]. This means that it is not the children of the flesh who are the children of God, but the children of the promise are reckoned as descendants'—the 'word of promise' being that spoken by God to Sarah in Gn. 17:21, confirming that she would give birth to a son.

5:1 τῇ ἐλευθερίᾳ ἡμᾶς Χριστὸς ἠλευθέρωσεν. In 5:1 Paul sums up and applies, in non-allegorical language, the lesson of the preceding allegory and indeed the lesson of all his preceding argument from 2:14 on.

The dative τῇ ἐλευθερίᾳ is best taken as instrumental. It is not simply intensive before ἠλευθέρωσεν (like Lk. 22:15, ἐπιθυμίᾳ ἐπεθύμησα, or Jas. 5:17, προσευχῇ προσηύξατο) because the article specifies a particular liberty—the liberty held out in the gospel. It is with this liberty that Christ has liberated his people. The dative is less likely to be a dative of design or destination (as though the sense were 'for liberty Christ has liberated us'). The dative τοῖς ἱμᾶσιν (Acts 22:25), sometimes adduced as an analogy for this usage, is more probably instrumental also (cf. RSV 'when they had tied him up with the thongs'). When, in v 13 below, Paul wishes to say 'for liberty', i.e. 'with a view to liberty', he says ἐπ᾽ ἐλευθερίᾳ. (It is a matter of interest that F. J.A. Hort [WH App., 122] conjectured, quite unnecessarily, that τῇ in 5:1 'is a primitive corruption of ἐπ᾽'.)

This freedom is enjoyed by the 'children of the free woman', the heirs of God's promise to Abraham. There is no hint that 'freedom' was a watchword of the trouble-makers. The context provides no warrant for the view which W. Schmithals thinks 'very probable', though not certain, that 'Paul consciously is referring to the expressions of the Galatian opponents' when he speaks of true freedom here (*Paul and the Gnostics*, 51). Here standing fast in their freedom will safeguard the Galatians against submission to legal bondage; in v 13 it will safeguard them against danger from the opposite direction.

στήκετε οὖν, 'stand fast therefore'. στήκω is a Hellenistic present formed from the classical perfect ἕστηκα, 'I stand'. Paul repeatedly urges his readers to stand fast—in the faith (1 Cor. 16:13), in one spirit (Phil. 1:27), in the Lord (Phil. 4:1; cf. 1 Thes. 3:8).

καὶ μὴ πάλιν ζυγῷ δουλείας ἐνέχεσθε, 'do not be subject again to a yoke of slavery'. The passive of ἐνέχω is well attested with the dative in the sense 'be involved in', 'be subject to'.

The word 'yoke' (ζυγός, Heb. 'ôl) was current in an honourable sense of the obligation to keep the law of Moses (cf. Nehunya b. Haqqanah in m. Ab. 3.5, kol hammᵉqabbēl 'ālāw 'ôl tôrāh, 'every one who takes on himself the yoke of the law'; Yohanan b. Zakkai in j. Qidd. 1.2 (59d), 'ôl malᵉkût šāmayim, 'the yoke of the kingdom of heaven'; Joshua b. Qarha in m. Ber. 2.2, kᵉdî šeyᵉqabbēl 'ālāw 'ôl malᵉkût šāmayim tehillāh wᵉ'ahar kak yᵉqabbēl 'ālāw 'ôl miṣwôt, 'in order that he may first take on himself the yoke of the kingdom of heaven [by reciting the Shema'] and then the yoke of the commandments [by obeying them]'). The words of Jesus in Mt. 11:29f. (ὁ γὰρ ζυγός μου χρηστός) are probably not related to this use of 'yoke' but to enrolment in the school of wisdom (cf. Sir. 51:26, τὸν τράχηλον ὑμῶν ὑπόθετε ὑπὸ ζυγόν). (It is to the words of Jesus that the paradox of 1 Clem. 16:17 is due: 'we who through him have come under the yoke of his grace', ὑπὸ τὸν ζυγὸν τῆς χάριτος αὐτοῦ.) But 'yoke' can also be used *in malam partem* of a disagreeable burden, unwillingly tolerated, like slavery (cf. πρὸς οἷα δουλείας ζυγὰ χωροῦμεν, Soph. *Aj*. 944f.; ὑπὸ ζυγὸν δοῦλοι, 1 Tim. 6:1). There is a hint of this in

Peter's description of the law in Acts 15:10 as 'a yoke . . . which neither our fathers nor we have been able to bear'; he criticizes the policy of imposing it on Gentile Christians as a tempting of God (cf. his use of similar language in Acts 5:9). By submitting to the legal obligation which was being pressed upon them, Paul warns the Galatians, they would be enslaving themselves to the στοιχεῖα all over again (cf. 4:9).

V
CHRISTIAN FREEDOM
(5:2–12)

Let them not think that the law's demands can be satisfied by a token compliance with this or that requirement (such as circumcision); the law's demands can be satisfied only by total performance.

Those who have misled them into the course which they are now disposed to follow will have much to answer for.

(a) The law demands total commitment (5:2–6)

See, this is myself, Paul, speaking to you: if you get yourselves circumcised, Christ will be of no use to you. Once again, I solemnly assure every man who gets himself circumcised that he is under an obligation to perform the whole law. Those of you who seek justification by the law have been estranged from Christ; you have fallen out of your state of grace. For we by the Spirit, on the ground of faith, wait expectantly for the hope of righteousness. For in Christ Jesus neither circumcision nor uncircumcision has any validity; what matters is faith, working through love.

TEXTUAL NOTES
v 3 παλιν *om* D* G 1739 *pc* lat$^{vg(2)}$ got arm
 οτι *om* ℵ* 062
 ποιησαι / πληρωσαι 436 *pc* syr^{hcl} Mcion (*ex* Mt. 5:17?)

5:2 To his exposition of gospel freedom as against legal bondage Paul adds further arguments, by no means unrelated to what he has already said: in particular, he emphasizes the hopelessness of their plight if they rely on law-keeping, and the blessedness of the life of the Spirit to which they are called.

Ἴδε ἐγὼ Παῦλος λέγω ὑμῖν. J. L. White (*The Body of the Greek Letter* [Missoula, Montana, 1972], 60–63) regards this personal note as a feature of what he calls the 'body-closing' (cf. R. W. Funk's 'apostolic *parousia*', *Knox FS*, 249–268); he compares Phm. 19 (ἐγὼ Παῦλος ἔγραψα) and Rom. 15:14f.

(καὶ αὐτὸς ἐγὼ ἔγραψα). He does not compare 1 Thes. 2:18 (ἐγὼ μὲν Παῦλος . . .), for that does not come in the 'body-closing' but in a passage where Paul distinguishes himself from his colleagues Silvanus and Timothy. But Phm. 19 is also a doubtful parallel, for there Paul incorporates a signed IOU into a personal letter. Both in Rom 15:14f. and here, however, Paul is projecting his presence as effectively as he can among those to whom his letter is sent.

Paul speaks with the authority of an apostle of Jesus Christ—*the* apostle of Jesus Christ, so far as his Galatian readers are concerned—but he does not expressly invoke his apostolic authority in giving them the serious warning which immediately follows. 'This is Paul speaking to you'—Paul whom you know, Paul your friend and father in Christ, not 'the brothers who are with me' (1:2) but I, Paul, myself. Others had apparently undertaken to say what Paul believed or practised in the matter of circumcision (cf. v 11); here is Paul's own account.

ὅτι ἐὰν περιτέμνησθε. The verb is probably to be taken in the middle voice: 'if you have yourselves circumcised' (cf. περιτεμνομένῳ, v 3). Paul applies directly to the Galatians the general principle stated above in 2:21: 'if righteousness [before God] is attained through law, then Christ died in vain'. For the Galatians to submit to circumcision as a legal obligation would be an acknowledgement that law-keeping (in this particular form) was necessary for the achievement of a righteous status in God's sight. Such an acknowledgement would be to nullify the grace of God (ἀθετεῖν τὴν χάριν τοῦ θεοῦ, 2:21).

Χριστὸς ὑμᾶς οὐδὲν ὠφελήσει. Christ will provide unlimited help to those who place their undivided trust in him, but no help at all to those who bypass his saving work and think to become acceptable to God by circumcision or other legal observances.

5:3 μαρτύρομαι δὲ πάλιν. This solemn asseveration repeats and reinforces the warning of v 2. That is the point of πάλιν here; it does not imply that he had already given them this warning when he was with them. When he was with them there was probably no occasion to mention circumcision. The occasion to mention it had only recently arisen.

παντὶ ἀνθρώπῳ περιτεμνομένῳ, 'to every one who has himself circumcised' (middle voice; cf. also 6:12, 13). One might be circumcised involuntarily—as, of course, every male Jewish infant was (although even that was reckoned to carry an obligation with it)—but for a Gentile Christian to accept circumcision by choice, as a matter of religious duty, implied the acceptance of the whole way of life to which circumcision was the initiatory rite.

ὀφειλέτης ἐστὶν . . . ποιῆσαι, a periphrasis for ὀφείλει ποιῆσαι, 'he is obliged to do. . . .' Cf. Soph. *Aj.* 589f.: οὐ κάτοισθ' ἐγὼ θεοῖς / ὡς οὐδὲν ἀρκεῖν εἴμ' ὀφειλέτης ἔτι; ('Do you know that I am under no obligation to satisfy the gods any longer?').

In vv 2 and 3 it is indicated explicitly for the first time that the Gentile Christians of Galatia were being urged to accept circumcision. This might have been inferred from earlier references to circumcision in the letter, and its Galatian recipients knew from the outset what Paul was getting at, but only now does he say so in so many words. The 'agitators' had not insisted on Gentile converts' submission to the Jewish law in its entirety; they strongly recommended circumcision as a token fulfilment of the law—together, possibly, with the observance of sacred days (4:10). It may be that they thought the Galatians could be more easily persuaded to take further steps in legal observance when once they had taken the primary step of circumcision; if, on the other hand, they themselves were acting under the pressure of militants in Judaea, circumcision was the one thing needful. If fraternizing with the uncircumcised was treasonable in the militants' eyes, then the 'agitators', by persuading Gentile Christians to be circumcised, would (they fondly imagined) be immune from the charge of treason (see further on 6:12 below).

Paul, for his part, emphasizes that the Galatians cannot hope to make the legal grade by a merely token fulfilment of the law. If the agitators represented cicumcision as the final (but necessary) stage in the initiatory process of which the earlier stages were faith, baptism, reception of the Spirit—completing in the flesh what had been begun in the Spirit, as Paul ironically puts it (3:3)—Paul argues that this is an impossible position to hold. Circumcision as a minor surgical operation is neither here nor there, but circumcision voluntarily undertaken as a legal obligation carries with it a further obligation—nothing less than the obligation to keep the whole law. He who submits to circumcision as a legal requirement, necessary for salvation, accepts thereby the principle of salvation by law-keeping, and salvation by law-keeping implies salvation by keeping the whole law.

Not all rabbis would have agreed with Paul on this point, but many would. Gamaliel II, for example, is said to have wept when he came to the end of the thirteen requirements of Ezk. 18:5–9, saying, 'Only he who keeps all these requirements will live, not he who keeps only one of them' (b. Sanh. 81a). A similar story is related of him in b. Makk. 24a, with reference to the 613 precepts of the law; but his colleagues held that he who kept but one was regarded as having kept them all (cf. *Midr. Tehillim* 15.7). R. Aqiba is credited with a specially liberal attitude in this regard, summed up in L. Finkelstein's statement that he sometimes 'asserted God's mercy to be such that a single meritorious act will win a man admission to the future world' (*Akiba* [New York, 1936], 186; cf. E. P. Sanders, *PPJ*, 125–147). The difference among rabbinical interpreters in this regard does not run along the line separating Shammaites from Hillelites. What concerns us here is Paul's position, which has already been set out in 3:10, where he interprets Dt. 27:26 in this sense. He may well have held the same position before his conversion: we cannot know for certain (see note on v 11).

ὅλον τὸν νόμον ποιῆσαι. Cf. ὁ πᾶς νόμος, v 14 (with note *ad loc*.).

There was ample precedent for Gentiles' acceptance of circumcision as a prelude to full incorporation into Jewish faith and life. In Jud. 14:10 Achior the Ammonite, impressed by the downfall of Holofernes, had himself circumcised (περιετέμετο τὴν σάρκα, middle voice) there and then and joined the house of Israel, with his family, 'unto this day'. The Idumaeans subdued by John Hyrcanus were allowed to retain their homeland 'provided they had themselves circumcised (εἰ περιτέμνοιντο τὰ αἰδοῖα, middle voice) and were willing to follow the Jewish laws' (Josephus, *Ant.* 13.257). It was not unknown, indeed, for a man to accept circumcision from self-regarding motives, with no serious intention of conforming to the Jews' religion; examples are Azizus of Emesa, for a short time husband of Drusilla (Josephus, *Ant.* 20.139), and Polemo of Cilicia, for a short time husband of her elder sister Berenice (*Ant.* 20.145f.). On the other hand, no amount of law-keeping or conformity to Jewish ways mattered in the eyes of stricter Jews unless circumcision had been accepted: only when King Izates of Adiabene had himself circumcised did the Galilaean Eleazar acknowledge him as a true proselyte (*Ant.* 20.44–48).

In warning the Galatians as he does here, does Paul mean, 'Circumcision carries with it the obligation to keep the whole law, and this you are quite unable to do'? If one of them were to say, in answer to his warning, 'In that case, we will keep the whole law', Paul could not have said, 'That is quite impossible', for he himself had kept it all (Phil. 3:6b). The Pauline reply to such a declaration of intent would have been rather, 'Even if you do keep it all, there is no salvation that way; I speak from personal experience.' Perhaps his choice of words, ὀφειλέτης ἐστίν, implies that the way of law-keeping is a way of bondage—no fit way for those whom Christ has liberated (v 1). Being obliged to keep the law, in part or in whole, is for such people a return to bondage under the στοιχεῖα (4:9), a return to the curse incurred by all who are ἐξ ἔργων νόμου (3:6). (When Paul uses similar language of himself, ὀφειλέτης εἰμί, in Rom. 1:14, he speaks of his Christian duty in terms of a personal debt, not in terms of a legal requirement; cf. Rom. 8:12; 15:27.)

5:4 κατηργήθητε ἀπὸ Χριστοῦ, proleptic aorist, 'you have become estranged from Christ'; 'your association with Christ has been nullified'. Cf. the same verb used in the opposite sense in Rom. 7:6, κατηργήθημεν ἀπὸ τοῦ νόμου, 'we have been released from the law'. Circumcision would be 'the sacrament of their excision from Christ' (E. Huxtable, *Galatians*, 239, quoted by G. G. Findlay, *Galatians*, 306).

οἵτινες ἐν νόμῳ δικαιοῦσθε, 'you who (the class of people who) seek to be justified by law'—conative present. They could seek justification through faith in Christ (and obtain it) or they could seek it through legal works (and miss it; cf. Rom. 10:3). To seek it through faith in Christ was to seek it on the ground of God's grace; to seek it through legal works was to seek it on the ground of their own merit. Whether this antithesis is supported by rabbinical teaching or not (see E. P. Sanders, *PPJ*, 297), it expresses Paul's understanding of the situation. Paul has already made it clear (3:10) that those who seek justification through legal works do not attain it (cf. Rom. 11:7) but rather incur the curse of the law; what he emphasizes here is the incompatibility of faith and works, of divine grace and human merit, where the justification of the sinner before God is in question.

τῆς χάριτος ἐξεπέσατε, 'you have fallen out of grace'—the reverse experience to that of Rom. 5:2, τὴν προσαγωγὴν ἐσχήκαμεν . . . εἰς τὴν χάριν ταύτην ἐν ᾗ ἑστήκαμεν, 'we have obtained access into this grace in which we stand'—'into our present state of grace'. God had called the Galatians ἐν χάριτι (1:6); to forsake his call for the way of law involved self-expulsion from his grace, because they no longer relied on it (see on 2:21).

5:5 ἡμεῖς γὰρ πνεύματι ἐκ πίστεως ἐλπίδα δικαιοσύνης ἀπεκδεχόμεθα. Perhaps because he is so concerned with the current situation in the Galatian churches, Paul in this letter makes minimal reference to the Christian hope. Here is such a reference, however: by contrast with the vain hope of righteousness by legal works, he says, we who believe in Christ are enabled by the Spirit, through faith, to wait confidently for the hope of righteousness. The law holds out no such sure hope as this. The 'hope of righteousness' is the hope of a favourable verdict in the last judgment (Rom. 2:5–16). For those who believe in Christ such a verdict is assured in advance by the present experience of justification by faith, with its concomitant rejoicing 'in hope of the glory of God' (Rom. 5:1f.; cf. 1 Thes. 5:8, 'the hope of salvation'). In their case the eschatological verdict of 'not guilty' is already realized. Their hope is not vague or uncertain; it is fostered and kept alive by the indwelling Spirit of God. The theme of the Spirit's ministry in giving actuality here and now to the heritage of glory which awaits the believer in the resurrection order is amplified elsewhere in the Pauline corpus (cf. Rom. 5:1–5; 8:10f.; 2 Cor. 5:5; Eph. 1:13f.); it is in fact the most distinctive feature in Paul's doctrine of the Spirit. Compare the present and future aspects of 'adoption' (Gal. 4:4–7; Rom. 8:15–25). (See F. D. Bruner, *A Theology of the Holy Spirit* [Grand Rapids, 1970], 273.)

Here and in v 6 it is faith and Spirit that Paul opposes to circumcision (cf. 3:1–5). It is noteworthy that here he does not make baptism (cf. 3:27) the Christian counterpart to Jewish circumcision (contrast Col. 2:11f.).

5:6 ἐν γὰρ Χριστῷ Ἰησοῦ οὔτε περιτομή τι ἰσχύει οὔτε ἀκροβυστία. The Christian fellowship embraced both circumcised and uncircumcised; it made no difference whatsoever to their new existence 'in Christ Jesus'. In the old order the distinction between circumcision and uncircumcision was of great impor-tance; in the new order it had lost all relevance (cf. 3:28a; also Col. 3:11, where in the new humanity οὐκ ἔνι . . . περιτομὴ καὶ ἀκροβυστία).

The statement that for Christians neither circumcision nor uncircumcision has any religious validity appears in two other places in Paul's writings: Gal. 6:15 (see below) and 1 Cor. 7:19. In each place a different positive statement is added to the negative statement. In 1 Cor. 7:19 the positive statement is: 'but (what matters is) the keeping of God's commandments.' This could be taken, in an appropriate context, as a rabbinical ruling comparable (say) to Yohanan b. Zakkai's comment on the water of purification: 'Neither does a dead body defile, nor does water purify; but the Holy One, blessed be he, says, "I have laid down a statute, I have issued a decree; you shall not transgress my decree" ' (*Num. Rab.* 19:8 on Nu. 19:2). So one might envisage another rabbi as saying, 'Neither circum-cision nor uncircumcision matters in itself, but God has given a commandment, and his commandments must be kept.' Paul's intention is quite different: being circumcised or uncircumcised, he means, is irrelevant to the doing of God's will. J. W. Drane, *Paul: Libertine or Legalist?* (London, 1975), 65, sees in the clause 'but the keeping of the commandments of God' (1 Cor. 7:19) an instance of Paul's more positive attitude to the principle of law (as a rule of life) in 1 Corinthians than in Galatians. Paul probably knew that the permissive Corin-thians required a different emphasis from the Galatians, with their leaning to legalism.

ἀλλὰ πίστις δι' ἀγάπης ἐνεργουμένη, 'but (what avails is) faith operating through love'. It is better to construe ἐνεργουμένη as middle voice than as passive, as though the meaning were 'faith energized (produced) by love'. In every NT occurrence of a form of ἐνεργέω which might be either middle or passive, a good case can be made out for taking it as middle (*pace* J. A. Rob-inson, *Ephesians*, 241–247). More importantly, in keeping with the general teaching of this and other Pauline letters, faith is viewed as the root, love as the fruit. See J. B. Lightfoot, *Galatians*, 204f.; E. D. Burton, *Galatians*, 281.

G. S. Duncan (*Galatians*, 157f.) inclines to the rendering 'faith . . . which is set in motion by love'; he refers to 2:20, where 'Paul declares that what brought him to rest exclusively on *faith* was the revelation of a Saviour who *loved* him'. But in the present context the 'love' is much more likely to be Christian love than the love of God in Christ; cf. v 13: 'through love serve one another'. J. B. Lightfoot observes that 'these words δι' ἀγάπης ἐνεργουμένη bridge over the gulf which seems to separate the language of St Paul and St James. Both assert a principle of practical energy, as opposed to a barren, inactive theory' (*Galatians*, 205).

Love, the primary fruit of the Spirit (v 22), is poured out through the Spirit into the hearts of those who are justified by faith (Rom. 5:5). It may be formally true that Paul does not make justification by faith the basis of his ethical teaching (cf. A. Schweitzer, *Mysticism*, 220–226, 294–297; E. P. Sanders, *PPJ*, 434–442), but the faith by which believers are justified is the faith which operates through love; it was by hearing with faith, the Galatians have already been reminded, that they received the Spirit (3:2). Justification by faith and life in the Spirit are like two sides of one coin; neither is present without the other. 'Works based on faith are wrought through love, but man is not justified by love' (M. Luther, *In epistulam Pauli ad Galatas*, 1535, WA 40/2, 35).

This reference to 'love', after the mention of 'faith' and 'hope' (v 5), completes the 'primitive Christian triad' of graces—faith, hope and love, 'the quintessence of the God-given life in Christ' (G. Bornkamm, *Paul*, 219). Cf. 1 Cor. 13:13; 1 Thes. 1:3; 5:8; Rom. 5:1–5 (see A. M. Hunter, *Paul and his Predecessors* [London, ²1961], 33–35). See p. 41.

(b) Stern words for the trouble-makers (5:7–12)

You were running well. Who put an obstacle in your way to prevent you from following the path of obedience to the truth? This persuasion does not come from him who calls you. 'A little leaven leavens the whole batch of dough.' I have confidence in the Lord with regard to you that you will not be otherwise minded; but the one who is causing you trouble will bear his judgment, whoever he may be. As for me, my brothers, if I am still preaching circumcision, why am I still being persecuted? In that case the cross has ceased to be a stumbling-block. I wish that those who are upsetting you would complete their cutting operation— on themselves!

TEXTUAL NOTES

v 7   τη *om* ℵ* A B
       μη πειθεσθαι *add* μηδενι πειθεσθε G lat*abvg(s)* Lucif Pelag
v 8   ουκ *om* D* *pc* lat*b* Lucif M.Vict
v 9   ζυμοι / δολοι D* lat Lucif
v 10   εν κυριω *om* B
v 11   ετι κηρυσσω / κηρυσσω D* G *pc* lat*abvg(3)* Ambst
v 12   οφελον / αρα P⁴⁶
       αποκοψονται / αποκοψωνται P⁴⁶ D G

5:7 Ἐτρέχετε καλῶς. Paul uses an athletic metaphor for their spiritual progress, as he had used it of his own apostolic service in 2:2, μή πως εἰς κενὸν τρέχω ἢ ἔδραμον (see note *ad loc.* and cf. 1 Cor. 9:26; 2 Tim. 4:7; Acts 20:24). When Paul last saw the Galatians, and when he last had news of them, up to the moment that he learned of the agitators' visit, the reports of their progress were encouraging. It was all the more astounding that they should have been side-tracked so quickly.

τίς ὑμᾶς ἐνέκοψεν; The verb was used in this kind of context originally of breaking up a road so as to prevent progress (προκόπτειν), but then came to mean 'hinder' or 'delay', originally with the dative of disadvantage (cf. Rom. 15:22; 1 Thes. 2:18 for other Pauline occurrences). C. E. DeVries takes ἐνκόπτω here to be an athletic term, 'cutting in' in front of a runner so as to trip him up ('Paul's "Cutting" Remarks about a Race: Galatians 5:1–12', *Tenney FS*, 115–120). His further suggestion that the reference might be to the particular form of 'cutting' involved in circumcising is far-fetched, despite the use of ἀποκόπτω in v 12 (the literal force of κόπτω in ἐνκόπτω is otiose, and Paul is not much given to etymologizing).

[τῇ] ἀληθείᾳ, the truth of the gospel mentioned above in 2:5, 14. Cf. R. Bultmann, *TDNT* I, 238–247 (*s.v.* ἀλήθεια); D. J. Theron, 'ΑΛΗΘΕΙΑ in the Pauline Corpus', *EQ* 26 (1954), 3–18; A. C. Thiselton, *NIDNTT* III, 874–901 (*s.v.* 'Truth').

μὴ πείθεσθαι. The phrase τῇ ἀληθείᾳ μὴ πείθεσθαι was imported from here in some texts into 3:1, to follow the question τίς ὑμᾶς ἐβάσκανεν; which is closely parallel to τίς ὑμᾶς ἐνέκοψεν; and manifestly requires the same answer. The Western addition μηδένι πείθεσθε makes the whole sentence run: 'Who has hindered you? Obey no one (in such a way as) not to obey the truth.' The addition may have been due to a desire to make πεισμονή (v 8) more immediately relevant to the preceding construction.

5:8 ἡ πεισμονὴ οὐκ ἐκ τοῦ καλοῦντος ὑμᾶς. With the Western addition at the end of v 7, this means: 'Obedience (to someone in such a way as not to obey the truth) does not come from him who calls you' (so BDF 488.1 *(a)*). If οὐκ be omitted in v 8, with a few Western witnesses, the meaning must be: 'Obedience (to the truth) comes from him who calls you.'

This is the only Pauline (and NT) instance of πεισμονή. It is, in fact, a rare word; apart from 'persuasion' it is used to mean 'confidence', 'reliability'. If we reject the Western addition (at the end of v 7), v 8 must mean: 'The persuasion (that draws you away from the truth) does not come from him who calls you'—'persuasion' in the sense of 'being persuaded'.

'He who calls you' is, of course, God: the present tense is used here because (as in Rom. 9:11; 1 Thes. 2:12 (?); 5:24) there is no emphasis on the time at which he called them, as there is in 1:6, where Paul expresses astonishment at their defecting so quickly from him who had (recently) called them, ἀπὸ τοῦ καλέσαντος ὑμᾶς.

If the persuasion does not come from him who called them, it is implied that it comes ultimately from his great adversary, whoever the human agents were who put obstacles in their path (cf. 1 Thes. 2:18, ἐνέκοψεν ἡμᾶς ὁ σατανᾶς).

5:9 μικρὰ ζύμη ὅλον τὸ φύραμα ζυμοῖ. A few Western witnesses have δολοῖ ('spoils', 'adulterates') in place of ζυμοῖ ('leavens'). This is plainly a proverbial saying, used by Paul also in 1 Cor. 5:6, where he introduces it with οὐκ οἴδατε . . .; and goes on in some detail to apply the figures of ζύμη and φύραμα ('lump,' 'batch of dough') to the alarming possibilities of the tolerance of πορνεία in the Corinthian church. (To much the same effect is the proverbial verse from Menander's *Thais* quoted in 1 Cor. 15:33, φθείρουσιν ἤθη χρῆσθ᾽ ὁμιλίαι κακαί.) Here he thinks primarily of the principle of legalism, which has no more right to invade the Christian community than leaven had any right to be present in a Jewish house on Passover Eve, although he could have used the same figure in relation to the quarrelsomeness against which he issues a warning in v 15 below and in relation to the general tendency to gratify 'the desires of the flesh' (v 16).

The use of leaven as a symbol of evil and corrupting influences goes back to the prohibition of leaven for seven days at Passovertide (Ex. 12:14–20; Dt. 16:3–8). Hence Paul urges the Corinthian church to sweep out the 'old leaven . . . of malice and evil' and celebrate their lifelong Christian festival 'with the unleavened bread of sincerity and truth' (1 Cor. 5:7f.). When Jesus reminded his hearers that great enterprises may spring from small beginnings (with special reference to the kingdom of heaven) and illustrated his point with the parable about the handful of leaven which could leaven three measures (σάτα τρία) of flour (Mt. 13:33), he drew his analogy from the normal use of leaven in bread-making; but there is no direct relation between this parable and the proverb twice quoted by Paul.

In a discussion of the defiling property of leaven in m. Orl., Gamaliel I (Paul's teacher) is quoted as saying that a quantity of leaven falling into dough 'can never render the dough forbidden unless it suffices of itself to leaven the dough' (2.12)—but that is a halakhic ruling, not a proverbial saying.

5:10 ἐγὼ πέποιθα εἰς ὑμᾶς ἐν κυρίῳ. The omission of ἐν κυρίῳ in B is probably accidental. The inclusion of the phrase adds weight to Paul's expression of confidence: his confidence arises from his trust in Christ and from his awareness that his Galatian friends and he are fellow-members of Christ: 'I have confidence regarding you in the Lord.' For similar phraseology cf. Rom. 14:14; Phil. 2:24; 2 Thes. 3:4 (πεποίθαμεν δὲ ἐν κυρίῳ ἐφ᾽ ὑμᾶς). He knows how the logic of the gospel works, and if they have really received the gospel (as he is convinced they have), they must accept the same logic and think no differently (οὐδὲν ἄλλο φρονήσετε) from himself. Cf. RSV: 'that you will take no other view than mine'. Something to the same effect comes to expression in Phil. 3:15 (ὅσοι οὖν τέλειοι, τοῦτο φρονῶμεν· καὶ εἴ τι ἑτέρως φρονεῖτε . . .).

ὁ δὲ ταράσσων ὑμᾶς βαστάσει τὸ κρίμα. Paul's converts may still have been wavering at the time his letter reached them; they may already have been persuaded by the agitators. But even so, there was hope—good hope, Paul persuaded himself—that his letter would make them change their minds and rely on free grace as they had done before. The agitators were no converts of his—more probably they were his settled opponents—and he could expect to make no impression on them by his arguments. Yet some of them might read his letter, or learn of its contents, and a word of warning for them would not come amiss.

This presupposes that the singular ὁ ταράσσων is generic, in view of the plural οἱ ταράσσοντες in 1:7 (cf. v 12 below, οἱ ἀναστατοῦντες ὑμᾶς). They could indeed have had an outstanding leader, or they may have invoked some impressive authority in Judaea. In any case, whoever troubled them by trying to impose circumcision on them would have to endure the judgment such conduct incurred. Similarly Paul says of the 'false apostles' who infiltrated the church of Corinth, 'Their end will be according to their works' (2 Cor. 11:15).

ὅστις ἐὰν ᾖ, an instance of the Hellenistic encroachment of ἐάν on ἄν after a relative (cf. Acts 3:23, ἥτις ἐὰν . . .); see also v 17; 6:7. The meaning may be that Paul is not quite sure of the identity of the agitators, or of the authority behind them. Or it may be that he suspects the identity of that authority, but prefers to name no names.

J. L. White (*The Body of the Greek Letter*, 61, 64f.) finds in the 'confidence formula' of this verse a further feature characteristic of the 'body-closing unit' of a letter; he compares Rom. 15:14f.; Phm. 21.

5:11 Ἐγὼ δέ, ἀδελφοί, εἰ περιτομὴν ἔτι κηρύσσω. This argument, not obviously related to anything in the immediate context either before or after, can be explained only as a reply to some allegation which was being made about Paul, and to which (he suspected) his converts might be disposed to pay heed. The allegation was apparently to the effect that Paul 'still' preached circumcision. (The mainly western omission of ἔτι before κηρύσσω is stylistically motivated; ἔτι was felt to be inelegant here so shortly before its occurrence in the apodosis.) 'If I *still* preach circumcision', he says—but when had he preached circumcision? Not, we may be sure, since he was commissioned to be an apostle of Jesus Christ: the logic of the law-free—and therefore circumcision-free—gospel was implicit in his Damascus-road experience. But if Paul had engaged in proselytization among Gentiles before his conversion, he would certainly have preached circumcision then: such a zealot for the traditions would not have viewed circumcision as optional, as something which might be neglected if expediency so directed (as the merchant Ananias advised King Izates of Adiabene, according to Josephus, *Ant.* 20.40–42). Paul's critics, if they knew of such earlier activity on his part, might have said, 'He used to preach circumcision, and (when expedient) he still preaches it' (cf. E. Barnikol, *Die vor- und frühchristliche Zeit des Paulus* [Kiel, 1929], 18ff., for Paul's pre-conversion mission to the Gentiles).

G. Howard (*Crisis*, 10, 39, 44) holds that those who represented Paul as still preaching circumcision honestly believed that he did so: it was only recently that he had disclosed the law-free character of his gospel to the 'pillars' in Jerusalem, and that at a private meeting (2:2), so that others were still unaware of it.

But did Paul, by word or action, lend any verisimilitude to this representation? From our perspective, it is easy to see how preposterous was the charge that he still preached circumcision; but his contemporaries may not always have seen the situation so clearly. Perhaps he was accused of being a trimmer: of recommending circumcision on some occasions and forbidding it on others. Such an accusation might spring from his essentially neutral attitude towards circumcision. Circumcision *per se*, he held, was neither here nor there (cf. v 6): a Jewish believer had no need to remove the mark of circumcision, any more than a Gentile believer needed to receive it (1 Cor. 7:18f.). Should Jewish believers circumcise their sons? According to Acts 21:21, 24, it was rumoured that Paul forbade the Jews of the dispersion to do so, but James the Just and his fellow-elders are sure that the rumour is false. The Paul of the epistles, who himself conformed to Jewish ways when living among Jews (1 Cor. 9:20), would not have forbidden other Jewish believers to follow his example in this. If they wished to circumcise their infant sons out of regard for an ancestral custom and not as though the rite retained any covenant significance or established any claim on God, it is difficult to see how, on his own principles, he could have objected to their doing so. His own circumcision of Timothy, which took place, according to Luke (Acts 16:3), after the decision reached at the Council of Jerusalem (Acts 15:28f.), was intended for sociological convenience, not religious validity. (If this epistle should be dated after Timothy's circumcision, the Galatian Christians—especially if they were South Galatians—would certainly have known of it. If, in accordance with the position preferred in this commentary, the epistle be dated earlier, and the recipients learned of Paul's circumcision of Timothy some time later, what must they have thought about it?)

True, even in the matter of Timothy's circumcision, Paul could not be said to *preach* circumcision; but his critics could have claimed some colourable ground for insisting that he was not always so totally opposed to circumcision as he appeared to be in his dealings with the Galatians. To claim this would be to overlook, whether inadvertently or deliberately, a fundamental distinction: the Galatians were Gentile believers for whom circumcision was not an ancestral custom, and they were being urged to accept it in order to secure the approval of God. The agitators who visited them may well have said, as the strict Jew Eleazar said to King Izates (in contrast to the earlier advice given him by the accommodating Ananias), 'In your ignorance . . . you are guilty of the greatest offence against the law and thereby against God. For you ought not only to *read* the laws but also, and even more, to *do* what they command. How long will you remain uncircumcised? If you have not yet read the law concerning this, read it now, that you may know the nature of your impiety' (Josephus, *Ant.* 20. 44f.).

τί ἔτι διώκομαι; 'Our former persecutor', as some Christians called him (1:23), now endured persecution himself. Elsewhere Paul speaks of his θλίψεις, 'tribulations' (neither θλῖψις nor the verb θλίβω occurs in this letter), frequently in close association with his διωγμοί, 'persecutions', and treats them as tokens of his participation in the sufferings of Christ (cf. 2 Cor. 1:5; Phil. 3:10; Col. 1:24). His afflictions came to him from a variety of quarters, but those which he has in mind here were due to his proclamation of a law-free gospel. He implies that, if he included some element of law (e.g. circumcision) in his preaching (cf. 1:10, εἰ ἔτι ἀνθρώποις ἤρεσκον), he would be exempt from persecution. He would indeed have been exempt from the kind of attack launched by the militants who insisted on circumcision; for him to have preached circumcision would have meant going along with them. That the agitators' own zeal was reinforced by a desire to avoid persecution is stated in 6:12 below (see note *ad loc.*).

ἄρα κατήργηται τὸ σκάνδαλον τοῦ σταυροῦ. The σκάνδαλον of the cross, for Jews (cf. 1 Cor. 1:23), lay in the curse which it involved for one who was hanged on it (cf. 3:13). That one who died such a death should be proclaimed as Lord and Christ was intolerable. In the eyes of Gentiles the idea that salvation depended on one who had neither the wit nor the power to save himself from so disreputable a death was the height of folly. But there is a more general σκάνδαλον attached to the cross, one of which Paul is probably thinking here: it cuts the ground from under every thought of personal achievement or merit where God's salvation is in view. To be shut up to receiving salvation from the crucified one, if it is to be received at all, is an affront to all notions of proper self-pride and self-help—and for many people this remains a major stumbling-block in the gospel of Christ crucified. If I myself can make some small contribution, something even so small as the acceptance of circumcision, then my self-esteem is uninjured.

But to nullify the scandal of the cross is to rob the cross of its saving potency, it is to nullify Christianity as such: 'the aim of the Epistle to the Galatians is to show that all Christianity is contained in the Cross; the Cross is the generative principle of everything Christian in the life of man' (J. Denney, *The Death of Christ*, 152).

5:12 Ὄφελον καὶ ἀποκόψονται οἱ ἀναστατοῦντες ὑμᾶς. Here the agitators are called οἱ ἀναστατοῦντες ὑμᾶς, a stronger expression than οἱ ταράσσοντες ὑμᾶς (1:7). The aorist participle of this verb is used in Acts 17:6 (οἱ τὴν οἰκουμένην ἀναστατώσαντες) of those (presumably Jewish militants) who had sown subversion in one city after another of the Roman Empire and in Acts 21:38 of the Egyptian who fomented a rising with 4,000 *sicarii* (ὁ . . . ἀναστατώσας . . . τοὺς τετρακισχιλίους ἄνδρας τῶν σικαρίων) in the neighbourhood of Jerusalem about AD 54. The most famous non-literary instance of the verb comes in P. Oxy. 119.10 (2/3 cent. AD), where the bad boy Theon, writing to his father, reports his mother as saying of him, ἀναστατοῖ με· ἆρρον αὐτόν ('he upsets me; away with him!'). Paul's point here is that the agitators are subverting the Galatians, undermining their faith.

Ὄφελον with the future indicative expresses an attainable wish: 'Would that they would . . .!' As for the middle of ἀποκόπτω, there is little doubt that Paul means 'they had better go the whole way and make eunuchs of themselves!' (NEB)—or rather 'have themselves made eunuchs'. A eunuch is called ἀποκεκομμένος in Dt. 23:1 (LXX), where he is debarred from the ἐκκλησία κυρίου. Several commentators since R. Bentley, *Critica Sacra*, ed. A. A. Ellis (Cambridge, 1862), 48, have noted the verbal parallel in Dio Cassius, *Hist.* 80 (79).11, where ἀποκόπτειν completes the process which begins with περιτέμνειν. Greek commentators regularly understood Paul's language thus; the Latins operated with a more ambiguous form of words, like Vg. *utinam et abscindantur qui vos conturbant* (cf. AV 'I would they were even cut off which trouble you'). Some more recent commentators (e.g. H. N. Ridderbos, *Galatians*, 194f.) have noted that Pessinus, in North Galatia, was the centre of the cult of Cybele, who was served by *galli*, emasculated priests; but there is no need to posit such an allusion here. Elsewhere Paul demotes literal circumcision to the status of mere mutilation, κατατομή (Phil. 3:2), reserving the sacral term περιτομή for those who 'worship by the Spirit of God' (Phil. 3:3).

VI
FLESH AND SPIRIT
(5:13-26)

The law of God is summed up in the commandment to love one another; but such love, with all its attendant graces, is fostered in those who live by the Spirit. The old order of the 'flesh' manifests itself in a very different set of attitudes and activities.

(a) The way of love (5:13-15)

For you, my brothers, were called for freedom. Only, do not treat your freedom as a springboard for the 'flesh', but serve one another through love. For the whole law is fulfilled in one commandment, namely this: 'You shall love your neighbour as yourself.' But if you bite and devour one another, take care that you do not exterminate one another.

TEXTUAL NOTES

v 13 δια της αγαπης / τη αγαπη του πνευματος D G 104 lat$^{vg(s,cl)}$ cop$^{sabo(codd)}$ Ambst (*ex* Rom. 15:30)

v 14 ενι λογω / υμιν Mcion Epiph / υμιν εν ενι λογω D* G lat^{ab} Ambst / ολιγω 2495 syr^{hcl}

πεπληρωται / πληρουται D G Ψ 0122 byz / ανακεφαλαιουται 365 *pc*

ως σεαυτον / ως ἑαυτον P^{46} G L N* P (The same variant appears in Rom. 13:9 G L P. The cause in both places may be haplography, but the reflexive pronoun of the 3rd person encroaches on the forms for the 1st and 2nd persons in Hellenistic Greek; cf. BDF 64(1).)

5:13 'The dogmatic part of the Epistle . . . passes naturally over to the practical part, inasmuch as the νόμος is one of the chief ideas of the dogmatic part. It was necessary to show that freedom from the law does not by any means do away with the obligations of moral conduct' (F. C. Baur, *Paul*, ETr I [London, 1875], 255). But henceforth the obligations of moral conduct are fostered not by the dictates of the law but by the operation of the free Spirit.

ὑμεῖς γὰρ ἐπ᾽ ἐλευθερίᾳ ἐκλήθητε, ἀδελφοί. ἐπί with the dative here expresses purpose ('you were called for freedom'); cf. 1 Thes. 4:7 (οὐ γὰρ ἐκάλεσεν ἡμᾶς ὁ θεὸς ἐπὶ ἀκαθαρσίᾳ); Eph. 2:10 (κτισθέντες . . . ἐπὶ ἔργοις ἀγαθοῖς). This is the purpose for which God originally called them (cf. 1:6)—ἐπ᾽ ἐλευθερίᾳ. If in v 1 Christian freedom is the bulwark against legal bondage, here it is the bulwark against libertinism: μόνον μὴ τὴν ἐλευθερίαν εἰς ἀφορμὴν τῇ σαρκί (note the ellipsis of the verb: some such imperative form as λαμβάνετε or ἔχετε is to be understood with τὴν ἐλευθερίαν as its object). If freedom can be misused as an ἀφορμή ('occasion') for undesirable ends, law is similarly misused in Rom. 7:8, where 'sin, taking occasion (ἀφορμὴν . . . λαβοῦσα) through the commandment [forbidding covetousness], wrought in me all kinds of covetousness'.

W. Schmithals (*Paul and the Gnostics*, 51–53) thinks that Paul here launches an attack on the libertinism of the gnostics. But not all libertines were (or are) gnostics, any more than all gnostics were (or are) libertines; and there is nothing in the present context to suggest that the libertinism against which Paul now warns his readers was gnostic in origin or character.

The 'flesh' (σάρξ) is used here not simply of weak human nature nor yet of life under bondage to the στοιχεῖα as opposed to life in the Spirit; it denotes (as in vv 16f., 19, 24; 6:8) that self-regarding element in human nature which has been corrupted at the source, with its appetites and propensities, and which if unchecked produces the 'works of the flesh' listed in vv 19f.

Many of Paul's friends would have assured him that the tendency to misuse the freedom of the Spirit as an excuse for enthusiastic licence could be checked only by a stiff dose of law. But Paul could not agree: the principle of law was so completely opposed to spiritual freedom that it could never be enlisted in defence of that freedom: nothing was more certainly calculated to kill true freedom. The freedom of the Spirit was the antidote alike to legal bondage and unrestrained licence.

The danger of unrestrained licence is touched on but briefly in the letter to the Galatians: it was danger from the opposite extreme that currently presented the greater threat to them. But how seriously Paul warned against the tendency to pervert gospel liberty into unrestrained licence may be seen in his Corinthian correspondence. The particular 'work of the flesh' to which the Galatians were chiefly prone at this time seems to have been quarrelsomeness (v 15).

According to R. Jewett ('The Agitators and the Galatian Congregation', 209–212), the Galatian Christians had been disposed to accept 'external' features of the law, such as circumcision and the sacred calendar, without appreciating its more ethical emphases; hence Paul's ethical admonition to them. But Paul's understanding of the gospel excluded the principle of law in any form: to be 'under law' was compatible with being under the dominion of sin, with living κατὰ σάρκα. The ethical emphases of the law could be effectively satisfied not through submission to the law but through 'walking by the Spirit' (v 16). The law belongs to existence in the flesh, and stimulates the very sins that it forbids (3:19).

ἀλλὰ διὰ τῆς ἀγάπης δουλεύετε ἀλλήλοις, resuming the theme of v 6b. The article preceding ἀγάπης may refer back to the ἀγάπη of v 6b. There is at least one form of δουλεία that is not incompatible with Christian freedom.

As Paul himself is the δοῦλος of Christ (1:10) and of his converts (2 Cor. 4:5), so his converts should be δοῦλοι one of another. But this is a completely different form of slavery from that against which he otherwise warns them. It is as though he said, 'If you must live in slavery, here is a form of slavery in which you may safely indulge—the slavery of practical love for one another.' One could similarly envisage him as saying, 'If you must live under law, live under the law of love—that is, the law of Christ' (cf. 6:2). This slavery, this law, are impelled by the Spirit within, not imposed by an external authority.

The call to freedom, then, is a call to oneness in Christ and to loving service within the believing community. The liberty of the gospel is not to be exercised in isolated independence. The Christian does not emulate the self-sufficiency of the Stoic, *in se ipso totus teres atque rotundus* (Horace, *Satire* 2.7.86); his sufficiency is in Christ, and he is involved in the interdependent and loving fellowship of the people of Christ.

5:14 ὁ γὰρ πᾶς νόμος ἐν ἑνὶ λόγῳ πεπλήρωται. In v 3 Paul has warned his readers that everyone who submits to circumcision (as a legal requirement) thereby undertakes the obligation to keep every other requirement of the law (ὅλον τὸν νόμον). Here he tells them how the whole law may be fulfilled—by loving one another. Whereas ὅλος ὁ νόμος in v 3 is the sum-total of the precepts of the law, ὁ πᾶς νόμος here is the law as a whole—the spirit and intention of the law. On the distinction see H. Hübner, 'Das ganze und das eine Gesetz', *KD* 21 (1975), 239–256; *Das Gesetz bei Paulus* (Göttingen, 1978), 37–39. In the phrase ἐν ἑνὶ λόγῳ we should probably understand λόγος in the sense of 'commandment' which, like Heb. *dābār*, it sometimes bears in the Pentateuch (cf. Ex. 34:28 and Dt. 10:4, καὶ ἔγραψεν . . . τοὺς δέκα λόγους). The commandment in which 'the whole law' is fulfilled (perfect πεπλήρωται, 'stands fulfilled') is Lv. 19:18b, Ἀγαπήσεις τὸν πλησίον σου ὡς σεαυτόν. In Rom. 13:9, after quoting some sample commandments from the second half of the decalogue which express one's duty to one's neighbour, Paul says that they are all summed up ἐν τῷ λόγῳ τούτῳ—'You shall love your neighbour as yourself'. He spells out the lesson of this: 'Owe no one anything, except to love one another; for he who loves his neighbour has fulfilled the law. . . . Love does no wrong to a neighbour, therefore love is the fulfilling of the law' (Rom. 13:8–10). By thus quoting Lv. 19:18b Paul 'has isolated a *kᵉlāl* (basic principle of the law), as was customary in rabbinic practice' (H.-J. Schoeps, *Paul*, 208). Aqiba called this text 'the great *kᵉlāl* of the Torah' (*Gen. Rab.* 24:7 on Gn. 5:1; cf. *Sipra, Qᵉdôšîm* 2.4).

Lv. 19:18b was quoted by Jesus as the 'second' commandment alongside the 'first' commandment of Dt. 6:4, enjoining perfect love to God (Mk. 12:28–31). In Lk. 10:27 a lawyer sums up the law in these two commandments, in response to Jesus' question; Jesus then tells him the story of the good Samaritan to explain what is meant by loving one's neighbour as oneself. Between them these two commandments, on which 'all the law and the prophets depend' (Mt. 22:40), comprehend the whole of one's duty to God and neighbour; therefore, said Jesus, 'there is no other commandment greater than these' (Mk. 12:31b).

If Aqiba summed up the law in terms of Lv. 19:18b, Hillel, four generations earlier, is said to have summed it up, and incidentally explained the meaning of

Lv. 19:18b, when he quoted the negative golden rule to a would-be proselyte: 'What is hateful to you, do not to your neighbour, that is the whole law (*kol hattôrāh* [cf. Paul's ὁ πᾶς νόμος]), everything else is commentary (*pērûšāh*); go and learn it' (b. Shab. 31a). (On the historicity of this Hillel tradition see J. Neusner, *The Rabbinic Traditions about the Pharisees before 70*, I [Leiden, 1971], 321–324.) Compare Jesus' positive formulation of the golden rule: 'whatever you wish that men would do to you, do so to them; for this is the law and the prophets' (Mt. 7:12).

For this reason loving behaviour is said to 'fulfil the law of Christ' (Gal. 6:2). 'Thus the true intention of the Law is fulfilled in the man who is set in love by Christ' (W. Gutbrod, *TDNT* IV, 1076, *s.v.* νόμος).

Here and elsewhere Paul's ethical teaching is based on the tradition of Jesus' teaching (cf. especially Rom. 12:9–13:14, and compare Rom. 14:14 with Mk. 7:19b); perhaps that is why he calls this tradition 'the law of Christ' (6:2). 'Paul is in complete accord with Jesus: the real demand of the law is love, in which all the other commandments are summed up' (R. Bultmann, 'Jesus and Paul' [1936], ETr in *Existence and Faith* [London, 1964], 224).

See J. Moffatt, *Love in the NT* (London, 1929); A. Nygren, *Agape and Eros*, ETr (London, 1932–39); C. S. Lewis, *The Four Loves* (London, 1960); H. W. Montefiore, 'Thou shalt love the neighbour as thyself', *NovT* 5 (1962), 157–170; C. Spicq, *Agape in the NT*, ETr, I–III (St. Louis, 1963–66); V. P. Furnish, *The Love Command in the NT* (Nashville, 1972).

5:15 εἰ δὲ ἀλλήλους δάκνετε καὶ κατεσθίετε, βλέπετε μὴ ὑπ' ἀλλήλων ἀναλωθῆτε. Paul's concern for the well-being of all his converts, weak and strong alike, comes out clearly from here to 6:10.

The introduction of the new teaching into the Galatian churches appears to have provoked controversy and quarrels: this was not the least of the troubles caused by the agitators. Internecine strife is the only 'work of the flesh' against which Paul specifically warns the Galatians. There is no allusion in this letter, for example, to the sexual irregularities against which he puts the Thessalonians on their guard (1 Thes. 4:3–8), apart from their inclusion in the comprehensive list of vices in vv 19–21 below.

But the vice against which he does warn the Galatians here is serious enough; if not checked, it could lead to the disintegration of their fellowship and the disappearance of the churches of Galatia. The language which Paul uses suggests a pack of wild animals preying on one another: 'if you keep on biting one another and tearing one another to pieces, take care lest you be annihilated by one another' (cf. BAG, *s.v.* κατεσθίω, ἀναλίσκω).

(b) Walking by the Spirit (5:16–18)

What I mean is this: walk by the Spirit, and you will not fulfil the desire of the flesh. For the desire of the flesh is opposed to the Spirit, and that of the Spirit is opposed to the flesh; these are contrary to each other, to prevent you from doing the things you wish. But if you are led by the Spirit, you are not under law.

TEXTUAL NOTES

v 17 ταυτα γαρ P⁴⁶(vid) א* B D* G 1739 lat / ταυτα δε א² A C D² Ψ byz syrʰᶜˡ

5:16 Λέγω δέ, 'What I am saying is this' (cf. 4:1, λέγω δέ).

πνεύματι περιπατεῖτε, 'walk by the Spirit'. For this ethical or religious sense of περιπατέω (the prefix is otiose) cf. Heb. *hālak*. Nouns meaning 'way' are found in many languages in the sense of the ethical or religious life (Gk. ὁδός as in 1 Cor. 4:17; Acts 9:2, etc.; Heb. *hᵃlākāh*, Syr. *'urhā*, Arab. *assabīl*, Sanskrit *pathin*, *mārga*, Chinese *tao*, etc.). The Galatian Christians have already been reminded that they received the Spirit when they believed the gospel and that his presence with them was attested by mighty works (3:2, 5); let his presence be attested also by their way of life. 'Walk by the Spirit' means 'let your conduct be directed by the Spirit'.

The way of the Spirit is the way of freedom; the way of the Spirit is the way of love. The law of love (v 14) has the same construction as the statutes of the decalogue and of the Torah in general, but it is a different kind of law. No external force or sanction can compel the loving of a neighbour as oneself; such love must be generated from within—by the Spirit.

καὶ ἐπιθυμίαν σαρκὸς οὐ μὴ τελέσητε, 'and you will by no means fulfil the desire of the flesh'—οὐ μή with the aorist subjunctive expresses a strong negative statement relating to the future. The RSV mistakenly translates the clause as a negative command: 'do not gratify the desires of the flesh'. The words rather express a promise, which will be realized in those who walk by the Spirit. One might substitute hypotaxis for parataxis and render: 'if you walk by the Spirit you will not fulfil the desires of the flesh' (cf. NEB). According to Philo (*Migr. Abr.* 92), circumcision was held to signify 'the excision of pleasure and all passions' (ἡδονῆς καὶ παθῶν πάντων ἐκτομήν). It was no doubt natural to suppose that the most effective prophylactic against gratifying the flesh was the law, but Paul denies this. His persecuting activity in earlier days he now recognized as a species of gratifying 'the desire of the flesh' (little as he thought so at the time), and the law did not guard him against it; it rather encouraged it. But the incapacity of the law (τὸ . . . ἀδύνατον τοῦ νόμου, Rom. 8:3) had now given way to the power of the Spirit.

The antithesis between πνεῦμα and σάρξ can be brought out in written English if both Spirit and Flesh are spelt with initial capitals: 'the Flesh' is 'the power that opposes God' (E. P. Sanders, *PPJ*, 553) and enslaves human beings (cf. Rom. 8:6ff., 12f.). According to R. Jewett, 'the flesh is Paul's term for everything aside from God in which one places his final trust' (*Paul's Anthropological Terms* [Leiden, 1971], 103). E. Käsemann makes some penetrating observations on the antithesis between πνεῦμα and σάρξ in *Perspectives on Paul* (London, 1971), 25–27; cf. his *Romans*, 218–227.

5:17 ἡ γὰρ σάρξ ἐπιθυμεῖ κατὰ τοῦ πνεύματος, τὸ δὲ πνεῦμα κατὰ τῆς σαρκός, ταῦτα γὰρ ἀλλήλοις ἀντίκειται, lit., 'for the flesh desires against the Spirit and the Spirit against the flesh, for these are opposed to each other.' There is a *formal* resemblance between this statement and Philo's μάχεται ὁ λόγος τῷ πάθει καὶ ἐν ταὐτῷ μένειν οὐ δύναται, 'Reason is at war with passion and cannot remain in the same place with it' (*Leg. All.* 3.116). The writer to Diognetus goes in another direction when he says (Ep. Diog. 6:5f.), 'The flesh hates the soul and wages war against it, . . . and the world hates the Christians, because they are opposed to its pleasures. The soul loves the flesh and limbs which hate it, and Christians love those that hate them' (this involves a confusion between the 'ethical' and 'physical' senses of σάρξ, and yields a meaning not unlike Eph. 5:29, οὐδεὶς γάρ ποτε τὴν ἑαυτοῦ σάρκα ἐμίσησεν, ἀλλὰ ἐκτρέφει καὶ θάλπει αὐτήν).

The antithesis between flesh and Spirit is treated later in Rom. 8:5–9, 12f., where it is emphasized that the flesh leads to death whereas the Spirit is the guarantee and, indeed, the very principle of resurrection life. The conflict between the two in human experience belongs to that 'eschatological' tension which, so long as believers remain in mortal body, is inseparable from their life in Christ (cf. 2 Cor. 4:16–5:5).

It is natural to compare the interior conflict between flesh and Spirit with the tension described in Rom. 7:7–25, and the resolution of that tension in v 16 above ('walk by the Spirit, and you will not fulfil the desire of the flesh') with the liberating experience of Rom. 8:2—'the law of the Spirit of life in Christ Jesus has set you free from the law of sin and death'. But (so far, at least, as Paul's language is concerned) the two forms of conflict are not identical. In Rom. 7:7–25 the power of indwelling sin prevents the person existing under law from fulfilling the divine law in which his inmost self delights: the 'law of sin' in his members wages war against the 'law of his mind' (Rom. 7:22f.), and at this stage no mention is made of the Spirit, whereas the conflict in the present text is that between flesh and Spirit. It might be said, indeed, that it is basically the same conflict that is described in different language in this passage and in that, but this would have to be established by exegetical argument: it could not be assumed.

Certainly v 16 expresses the gist of Rom. 8:5–9, 12f.; but it does not necessarily follow that v 17 expresses the gist of Rom. 7:7–25. Further light might be shed on the question by the final clause of v 17, ἵνα μὴ ἃ ἐὰν θέλητε ταῦτα ποιῆτε (lit. 'in order that you may not do whatsoever things you wish' or 'lest you do whatsoever things you wish'), if its precise force were certain. The construction (ἵνα with the subjunctive) normally expresses purpose, but sometimes in Hellenistic literature (e.g. 1 Thes. 5:4) it is used to express consequence (cf. BDF 391.5; C. F. D. Moule, *Idiom-Book*, 142f.), and if this were so here, the meaning would be: 'The result of this conflict is that you cannot do the things you wish'.

But to whom does the pronoun 'you' refer? Presumably to the Galatian Christians who are being addressed. They had received the Spirit (3:2); otherwise they would have no experience of the conflict between the Spirit and the flesh. Is the meaning then that the 'flesh' prevents them from doing what their mind approves and following the promptings of the Spirit? This is the view of those who relate v 17 closely to Rom. 7:7–25; so J. B. Lightfoot, *Galatians*, 210: 'The parallel passage, Rom. vii.15, 16, determines the meaning of θέλειν here. It denotes the promptings of the conscience; "video meliora proboque".' Or is it that 'the object of the striving of the Spirit in the believer is that he may be saved from yielding to the evil tendencies of his own nature' (preferred by C. F. Hogg and W. E. Vine, *Galatians*, 278f.)? The main difficulty with both of these views is that the inhibiting of 'you' from doing 'the things you wish' is ascribed either to the flesh or to the Spirit, to the exclusion of the other, whereas the text seems to ascribe it to both, or (unless ταῦτα γὰρ ἀλλήλοις ἀντίκειται is a parenthesis) to the conflict between them. E. D. Burton (*Galatians,* 302) takes the ἵνα clause to be a proper clause of purpose, the purpose being that 'of both flesh and Spirit, in the sense that the flesh opposes the Spirit that men may not do what they will in accordance with the mind of the Spirit, and the Spirit opposes the flesh that they may not do what they will after the flesh. Does the man choose evil, the Spirit opposes him; does he choose good, the flesh hinders him' (so, with variations of emphasis, F. Sieffert, *Galater,* 332f.; H. Schlier, *Galater,* 248–250; F. Mussner, *Galaterbrief,* 377f.). But the believer is not the helpless battleground of two opposing forces. If he yields to the flesh, he is enslaved by it, but if he obeys the prompting of the Spirit, he is liberated and can make a positive and willing response to the command 'Walk by the Spirit' and similar moral imperatives, 'doing the will of God from the heart' (as it is put in Eph. 6:6).

H. D. Betz (*Galatians,* 280) concludes (perhaps rightly) that v 17 presents a 'pre-Pauline' anthropology on the basis of which Paul works out his own more complex doctrine, which finds more developed expression in Rom. 7–8. What is said in Rom. 7–8, however, is not simply to be substituted for his statements here, as though these were insufficient and merely preliminary; they are appropriate to their present context.

5:18 εἰ δὲ πνεύματι ἄγεσθε, οὐκ ἐστὲ ὑπὸ νόμον. Here existence 'under law' is antithetic to being 'led by the Spirit'. It is existence 'under law', according to Rom. 7:15, that exposes one unprotected to the malignity of indwelling sin, and involves one in the frustrating situation: 'What I do is not what I want; it is rather the very thing I hate.' But there is no reason why those who were born under law should continue in this state any longer; even more emphatically there is no reason why those who have been delivered from spiritual bondage should gratuitously place themselves under law. With the coming of Christ and the completion of his redeeming work, the age of law has been superseded by the age of the Spirit. For the Galatians to retreat from grace to law would be to exchange the freedom of the Spirit for bondage to the *stoicheia*. When Paul in 2 Cor. 3:17 concludes his contrast between the death-denouncing letter and the life-giving Spirit with the affirmation that 'where the Spirit of the Lord is, there is liberty', he sums up in one epigram all that he has taught on this subject.

To be 'led by the Spirit' is to walk by the Spirit—to have the power to rebut the desire of the flesh, to be increasingly conformed to the likeness of Christ (2 Cor. 3:18), to cease to be under law. To be under law affords no protection against the desire of the flesh. 'Spirit' is equally opposed to 'law' as to 'flesh'. To be led by the Spirit brings simultaneous deliverance from the desire of the flesh, the bondage of the law, and the power of sin: 'sin will have no dominion over you, since you are not under law but under grace' (Rom. 6:14). To be 'under grace' is to be 'led by the Spirit'. 'The grace of God is the gift of God; but the greatest gift is the Holy Spirit himself, and therefore he is called grace' (Aug. *Sermon* 144.1). Cf. N. P. Williams, *The Grace of God* (London, 1930), for the thesis that the grace of God cannot be adequately conceived in impersonal terms—that it must be frankly equated with the person of the Holy Spirit, so that 'there *is* no "higher gift than grace"; grace *is* "God's presence and his very Self, and Essence all divine" ' (110, quoting J. H. Newman's hymn 'Praise to the Holiest' from *The Dream of Gerontius*). To experience grace of this order as a living reality is the effect of receiving 'the Spirit of sonship' (Rom. 8:15).

It is not surprising that, in the one other reference to the leading of the Spirit to be found in his letters, Paul says that 'all who are led by the Spirit of God are sons of God' (Rom. 8:14). So in Gal. 4:4f. the redemption effected by Christ for those previously 'under law' meant their receiving 'adoption as sons' (υἱοθεσία, as in Rom. 8:15). If to be 'under law' is to be a slave, to be led by the Spirit is to be a freeborn son or daughter, to enjoy 'the glorious liberty of the children of God' (Rom. 8:21)—the liberty for which, as Paul has just told the Galatians, they had been 'called' (v 13).

Bringing 'the Jewish nomism against which Paul fought' up to date, E. Käsemann affirms that 'it represents the community of "good" people which turns God's promises into their own privileges and God's commandments into the instruments of self-sanctification' (*Perspectives on Paul*, 72). Walking by the Spirit, the antidote to nomism of every kind, calls for resolution and staying power, as is made plain by Paul's frequent use of athletic metaphor for the Christian life. The struggle between flesh and Spirit is bound up with that 'eschatological tension'—arising from 'belief in Jesus' resurrection as an event of the past and the experience of the Spirit as already given'—with which Christians are compelled to live so long as they exist on earth in mortal bodies (see J. D. G. Dunn, *Unity*, 23).

(c) The works of the flesh (5:19–21)

Now the works of the flesh are well known; they are as follows: fornication, impurity, wantonness, idolatry, sorcery, enmity, quarrelsomeness, jealousy, outbursts of rage, selfish ambitions, dissensions, party-spirit, envy, drunkenness, revelry and the like. I warn you, as I have warned you before, that those who practise such things will not inherit the kingdom of God.

TEXTUAL NOTES

v 19 πορνεια / praem μοιχεια א² D (μοιχειαι G) Ψ 0122 byz syr^hcl Iren^lat Ambst

v 20 ερις / ερεις C G Ψ 0122 byz lat syr^hcl cop Mcion Clem.Alex Epiph Iren^lat

ζηλος / ζηλοι א C Ψ 0122 byz lat syr^hcl cop Mcion Clem.Alex Epiph Iren^lat Cypr

v 21 φθονοι P^46 א B pc cop^sa Mcion Clem.Alex Orig Iren^lat Aug / φθονοι φονοι A C D G Ψ 0122 byz lat cop^bo (for this 'Gorgiastic' assonance cf. Rom. 1:29, φθονου φονου, which may indeed have influenced the reading here).

5:19 φανερὰ δέ ἐστιν τὰ ἔργα τῆς σαρκός. 'Paul considers that what constitutes proper behaviour is self-evident' (E. P. Sanders, *PPJ*, 513)—even the pagans having an innate awareness of it (Rom. 1:18–21, 32; 2:14–16). Therefore violations of proper behaviour show themselves publicly for what they are.

Lists of vices and virtues, such as we have here in vv 19–23, are well attested in literature of this period.

Examples outside the NT are found in 1QS 4.2–14 and in the catechesis of the Two Ways (Did. 1:1–6:3; Barn. 18:1–21:9). As for the NT catalogues of vices, these are studied by E. Schweizer in 'Traditional ethical patterns in the Pauline and post-Pauline letters and their development', *Black FS* (2), 195–209; in addition to the present list, he examines those in 1 Thes. 4:3–6; 1 Cor. 5:9–13; 6:9–11; 2 Cor. 12:20f.; Rom. 13:13; 1:29–31; Col. 3:5–8; Eph. 4:17–19; 5:3–5. These lists 'emphasize sins against the common life in the brotherhood'; their function is not to 'distinguish an outstanding group of high moral standards from the abominable immorality of the world' but 'to show the church how much this world is still living in its midst' (207).

See A. Vögtle, *Die Tugend- und Lasterkataloge im NT* (Münster, 1936); S. Wibbing, *Die Tugend- und Lasterkataloge im NT und ihre Traditionsgeschichte* = BZNW 25 (Berlin, 1959); W. Barclay, *Flesh and Spirit* (London, 1962).

πορνεία, 'fornication', means primarily traffic with πόρναι ('harlots'); it is found also as a near-technical term (like Heb. $z^e n\hat{u}\underline{t}$) for sexual relations within prohibited degrees (as in Mt. 5:32; 19:9; Acts 15:20, 29; 21:25; 1 Cor. 5:1) and, more widely, of sexual irregularity in general. This wider sense is probably intended here. In some of his letters Paul warns his converts specifically against this vice: ἀπέχεσθαι ὑμᾶς ἀπὸ τῆς πορνείας, 1 Thes. 4:3; φεύγετε τὴν πορνείαν, 1 Cor. 6:18. It was so common in Graeco-Roman antiquity that, except when carried to excess, it was not regarded as specially reprehensible. Some of the Pauline churches had difficulty in abandoning their former pagan tolerance of it; there is no hint, however, that it was a major problem in the churches of Galatia.

ἀκαθαρσία, 'impurity', has a wider range of meaning than πορνεία. It includes the misuse of sex, but is applicable to various forms of moral evil: Demosthenes, for example, uses it of one who, pretending to be a man's friend, uses perjury to do him an injury (*Meid.* 119). In Pr. 6:16 LXX ἀκαθαρσία ψυχῆς is a paraphrase for *tô'ăḇaṯ napšô*, 'an abomination to his [God's] soul'. The word is used, naturally, of physical and ritual uncleanness, but it is its ethical sense that is relevant here, the tendency of vice to spread its corrupting influence.

ἀσέλγεια, 'wantonness', is vice that throws off all restraint and flaunts itself, 'unawed by shame or fear', vice paraded with blatant impudence and insolence, without regard for self-respect, for the rights and feelings of others, or for public decency.

5:20 εἰδωλολατρία, 'the worship of idols'—not only of graven images but of any substitute for the living and true God. In Col. 3:5 covetousness is described as a form of idolatry, because the thing coveted becomes an object of worship. In 1 Cor. 10:14 participation in a feast in a pagan temple is participation in idolatry.

φαρμακεία, 'sorcery', the use of φάρμακα, 'drugs', as in black magic, to do harm to others. In itself the word is as neutral as 'pharmacy', its English derivative, meaning the dispensing of drugs for medical purposes. But it acquired two pejorative senses: the use of drugs to poison people and (as here) the use of drugs in witchcraft. In Ex. 7:11 φαρμακοί is used of the 'sorcerers' (Heb. *m^eḵašš^epîm*) at Pharaoh's court. Apart from its present occurrence, the only occurrences of φαρμακεία in the NT are in Rev. 9:21; 18:23 (cf. φάρμακον, Rev. 9:21, and φαρμακός, Rev. 21:8; 22:15). Sorcery was a serious offence in Roman law: it was dealt with by a standing court, the *quaestio perpetua de sicariis et ueneficis* (in which no very sharp distinction was made between the *ueneficus* as sorcerer and as poisoner).

ἔχθραι, 'enmities', 'hostilities'—between individuals, or between communities, on political, racial or religious grounds. Not only hostile acts but the underlying hostile sentiments and intentions are in view. The ἐχθρός is the one who cherishes the hostile thought and performs the hostile act; the object of his hostility is not necessarily ἐχθρός towards him (the term is not inevitably correlative). Jesus told his disciples to love their ἐχθροί (Mt. 5:44; Lk. 6:27, 35), and in this sense Paul quotes Pr. 25:21, 'If your ἐχθρός is hungry, give him bread to eat' (Rom. 12:20). Plainly the disciple who takes this teaching to heart does not cherish a spirit of ἔχθρα towards his ἐχθρός. This particular 'work of the flesh' can be neutralized by ἀγάπη, the primary fruit of the Spirit (v 22).

ἔρις, 'strife' or 'quarrelsomeness', occurs frequently in lists of vices. 'Strife' was personified and deified in early Greek thought: in Homer and Hesiod Eris is the goddess whose malignant influence produces war and destruction. Paul is specially concerned to keep ἔρις out of his churches (cf. 1 Cor. 1:11; 3:3); it is the antithesis of the 'peace' which belongs to the fruit of the Spirit (v 22).

ζῆλος is not necessarily a vice (see note on ζηλωτής, 1:14). It was a word with an honourable heritage in the Greek Bible: Phinehas (Nu. 25:11), Elijah (1 Ki. 19:10, 14) and Mattathias (1 Macc. 2:24–26) had all shown zeal for God in times of apostasy, and it was from their precedent that the militant Zealots of the first century AD took their designation. Paul not only refers to the zeal which he showed in his persecuting days (Phil. 3:6) but speaks of his θεοῦ ζῆλος, a 'zeal' or concern like God's, for the fidelity of the Corinthian church (2 Cor. 11:2). In Rom. 10:2 he credits his Jewish brethren with ζῆλος θεοῦ, 'zeal for God' (here the genitive is objective, whereas in 2 Cor. 11:2 it is subjective), but it is an uninformed zeal, οὐ κατ᾽ ἐπίγνωσιν. It is only the context that can indicate whether ζῆλος is used in a good or bad sense; when, as here, it appears in a list of vices, it is plainly used in a bad sense, of selfish jealousy (cf. Rom. 13:13; 1 Cor. 3:3; 2 Cor. 12:20, in all of which places it is associated with ἔρις). Another's success may move a man to ζῆλος in the sense of noble emulation, which is a good thing, or it may stir him to ζῆλος in the sense of resentment that another has enjoyed success or distinction (thus far) denied to him, and that is a bad thing, a work of the flesh. But vigilance and grace are necessary to prevent the good ζῆλος from degenerating into the evil ζῆλος.

θυμοί, 'outbursts of rage', is the plural of θυμός, another word which (like ζῆλος) can be used in a nobler and a less noble sense. For Plato θυμός is the 'spirited' element in the human soul, which needs to be directed by the rational element, much as a sheep-dog requires to be controlled by the shepherd (*Rep.* 4.440D). Aristotle is specially aware of the menace of uncontrolled θυμός which, he says, 'does seem to hear the voice of reason, but to hear it wrongly, like those impetuous servants who rush off before hearing all that is said and then do not carry out their orders properly, or like dogs which start barking before waiting to see if one is a friend or not' (*Eth. Nic.* 7.1149a3). Paul uses θυμός of divine retribution against those who 'obey wickedness' in Rom. 2:8;

elsewhere (2 Cor. 12:20; Eph. 4:31; Col. 3:8) he uses it pejoratively, of something which Christians should renounce. The plural appears here and in 2 Cor. 12:20. The word has much in common with ὀργή. Τὸ θυμός as to ὀργή the injunction applies, 'Be angry (ὀργίζεσθε) without sinning' (Eph. 4:26, quoting Ps. 4:4 LXX)—a way to achieve this ideal being 'Do not let the sun go down on your anger' (ὀργή).

ἐριθεία in the NT is always something to be avoided as evil. The plural is found here and in 2 Cor. 12:20 (indeed, the sequence ἔρις, ζῆλος, θυμοί, ἐριθεῖαι occurs in both passages). It is derived from ἔριθος, 'hireling', 'one who works for pay'; thus, when Tobit became blind, his wife Anna ἠριθεύετο (as a dressmaker, evidently) to maintain the household (Tob. 2:11). But ἐριθεία came to denote a mercenary spirit, selfish ambition, and its similarity to ἔρις (with which it is not connected etymologically) probably suggested the rivalry and contention to which such a spirit gives rise. Cf. Rom. 2:8; Phil. 1:17; 2:3 (and Jas. 3:14, 16).

διχοστασίαι, 'dissensions', 'divisions'. The other NT occurrence of the word is in Rom. 16:17, where Paul puts his readers on their guard against those who cause 'dissensions' and stumbling blocks (σκάνδαλα), meaning probably those who introduce divisive teaching. Its one LXX occurrence is in 1 Macc. 3:29, which speaks of the διχοστασία caused by the Seleucid decrees abolishing the distinctive features of Judaism, the cleavage between those who adhered uncompromisingly to the old ways and those who were more pliable. The introduction of legalism was bound to cause divisions in the Galatian churches.

αἱρέσεις are not so different from διχοστασίαι. The noun is a derivative from αἱρέομαι, 'choose', and means basically 'choice'; it gives us our word 'heresy' and in the later NT documents, together with the associated αἱρετικός, has the sense of 'heresy' (2 Pet. 2:1) and 'heretic' (Tit. 3:10). (See M. Simon, 'From Greek Hairesis to Christian Heresy', Grant FS, 101–116.) In Acts it is used of parties within Judaism—the Sadducees (5:17), the Pharisees (15:5; 26:5), the Nazarenes (24:5, 14; 28:22). Its other Pauline occurrence is in 1 Cor. 11:19, of factions in the Corinthian church (it is not expressly used, though it might well have been used, of the partisan spirit deplored in 1 Cor. 1:11f.; 3:4; these undesirable manifestations are called ἔριδες). The formation of cliques, with the resultant exhibitions of party spirit, is in view both at Corinth and in Galatia.

5:21 φθόνοι are related to ζῆλος, but whereas ζῆλος can have a noble side to it, φθόνος is wholly evil. It is the grudging spirit that cannot bear to contemplate someone else's prosperity. 'The envious', said Socrates, 'are pained by their friends' successes' (Xen., Mem. 3.9.8). W. Barclay (Flesh and Spirit, 48) illustrates this vice by the story of the illiterate man who asked Aristides (not recognizing him) to record his vote for Aristides's ostracism 'because I am tired of hearing him called "the Just" ' (Plut., Aristides 7). Or we may think of the reply of the owner of the vineyard to the man who complained that the last-hired workmen had been over-generously paid: 'do you begrudge my generosity?' (lit. 'is your eye evil because I am good?') (Mt. 20:15).

μέθαι, 'drunkennesses', i.e. drunken orgies. As gluttony is excessive indulgence in food, so μέθη is excessive indulgence in wine (and strong drink): both forms of excess are vices, but drunkenness is the more perilous because it weakens people's rational and moral control over their words and actions. In 1 Cor. 5:11 and 6:10 it is closely associated with rapacity and verbal abuse (the μέθυσος is neighbour to the λοίδορος and the ἅρπαξ). In 1 Thes. 5:7 it weakens the vigilance which is necessary for safety in moments of crisis; it is an enemy to sobriety (νήφειν) and leads to dissipation (ἀσωτία, Eph. 5:18).

κῶμοι, 'revels', 'revelry', occurs three times in the NT, and always in close association with drunkenness (μέθαι here and in Rom. 13:13; πότοι in 1 Pet. 4:3). In classical Greek the word does not have such bad repute: it denoted, for example, the joyful procession and banquet held in honour of a citizen who had distinguished himself, as in a victory at the games (cf. Pindar, Pyth. 5.22, δέδεξαι τόνδε κῶμον ἀνέρων). The closing stages of such a celebration, however, might well be attended by insobriety that would invite moral censure. W. M. Ramsay (Galatians, 453) reminds us that among the Greeks 'Komos, the Revel, was made a god, and his rites were carried on quite systematically, and yet with all the ingenuity and inventiveness of the Greek mind, which lent perpetual novelty and variety to the revellings. The Komos was the most striking feature in Greek social life.'

Here, then, we have been given a list—not an exhaustive one—of 'the works of the flesh' or, as they are called in Eph. 5:11, 'the unfruitful works of darkness'. Some of them are perversions of qualities neutral or even good in themselves; others (like ἀσέλγεια and φθόνος) are by their very nature evil. It is not necessary to suppose that all of them, including fornication and impurity, 'reflect the actual behaviour of the Galatians' (R. Jewett, 'The Agitators and the Galatian Congregation', 211). The fact, however, that the list includes not only those vices which belong to the stock-in-trade of Jewish polemic against paganism but enmity, quarrelsomeness, jealousy, outbursts of rage, selfish ambitions, dissensions, party spirit and envy, suggests that it was in these forms that the 'flesh' manifested itself in the Galatian Christians (cf. v 26). For Paul, as R. Jewett wisely points out, flesh 'is not rooted in sensuality but rather in religious rebellion in the form of self-righteousness which was in his terms a "boasting in one's own flesh" ' (Paul's Anthropological Terms, 114).

ἃ προλέγω ὑμῖν, καθὼς προεῖπον. The relative ἃ has τὰ ὅμοια τούτοις as its antecedent but it also anticipates τὰ τοιαῦτα, the object of οἱ πράσσοντες in the following ὅτι clause. For the wording cf. 2 Cor. 13:2, προείρηκα καὶ προλέγω.

ὅτι οἱ τὰ τοιαῦτα πράσσοντες βασιλείαν θεοῦ οὐ κληρονομήσουσιν. τὰ τοιαῦτα means the various 'works of the flesh'. In 1 Cor. 15:50, 'flesh and blood (σὰρξ καὶ αἷμα) cannot inherit the kingdom of God', σὰρξ has a different sense from its present one: there, as the collocation with αἷμα makes plain, it denotes the mortal body as presently constituted. But a close parallel to the present passage is provided in 1 Cor. 6:9f., where (without using the word σάρξ) Paul gives a catalogue of eleven types of wrongdoer who 'will not inherit the kingdom of God' (cf. also Eph. 5:5). While good deeds in themselves do not admit one to the kingdom, evil deeds of the type mentioned certainly exclude one (cf. E. P. Sanders, PPJ, 517f.). In m. Sanh. 10.1–3 several categories of sinners are listed as having no 'portion in the world to come' (ḥēleq lā'ôlām habbā'); contrariwise, according to m. Ab. 5.22, 'the disciples of Abraham our father . . . inherit the world to come' (nôḥ^a îm hā'ôlām habbā').

The expression 'kingdom of God' has not appeared earlier in the letter, but Paul could evidently assume his readers' familiarity with it, no doubt because it had figured in his original preaching to them (προεῖπον may refer to oral instruction). (According to Acts 14:22, he and Barnabas warned their South Galatian converts that 'through many tribulations we must enter the kingdom of God'.) The kingdom of God for Paul lies in the future: it is the heritage of the people of God in the age to come, the resurrection age. The gift of the Spirit here and now is the first instalment (ἀπαρχή, Rom. 8:23) and guarantee (ἀρραβών, 2 Cor. 1:22) of that coming heritage.

In the later epistles there is more of a 'realized' emphasis than in the earlier ones; cf. Col. 1:13, where believers have already been transferred by God 'into the kingdom of his dear Son'—but there may be a distinction between the (present) kingdom of Christ (cf. 1 Cor. 15:25) and the (future) kingdom of God. (In Eph. 5:5 'the kingdom of Christ and of God' is one and the same kingdom.)

(d) The fruit of the Spirit (5:22–26)

But the fruit of the Spirit is love, joy, peace, patience, kindness, goodness, faith, gentleness, self-control: against such things as these law has nothing to say. And those who belong to Christ [Jesus] have crucified the flesh with its passions and desires.

If we live by the Spirit, let us also keep in line with the Spirit. Let us not become boastful, challenging one another, envying one another.

TEXTUAL NOTES
v 23   εγκρατεια / add αγνεια D* G lat^vet vg (s, cl) Iren^lat Cypr Ambst
v 24   Χριστου P^46 D G byz lat syr / Χριστου Ιησου ℵ A B C P Ψ 1739 pc cop

5:22 ὁ δὲ καρπὸς τοῦ πνεύματος. There may be some significance in the contrast between the 'works' of the flesh and the 'fruit' of the Spirit, but it is not because the figure of 'fruit' or 'harvest' is inappropriate to evil. In 6:8 below the process of sowing and reaping is applied equally to the flesh and to the Spirit. (Cf. the principle 'you will know them by their fruits' in Jesus' teaching in Mt. 7:16–20//Lk. 6:43–45.) Paul lists nine graces (again, not an exhaustive list) which make up the fruit of the Spirit—the lifestyle of those who are indwelt and energized by the Spirit. The first of these and, as he puts it in 1 Cor. 13:13, 'the greatest of these' is ἀγάπη.

It is not quite accurate to say, as R. C. Trench does, that 'ἀγάπη is a word born within the bosom of revealed religion' (*Synonyms of the NT* [London, ⁹1880, reprinted 1961], § xii, 41); it is true that (unlike the verb ἀγαπάω, which is attested as early as Homer) it is not found before the LXX, but the LXX translators used it because of its superficial similarity to Heb. 'aʰᵃbāh as much as for any other reason, and as a synonym for ἔρως as often as not (in the LXX there is none of the contrast between ἀγάπη and ἔρως suggested, e.g., in the title of A. Nygren's *Agape and Eros*; it is used of Amnon's passion for Tamar in 2 Sa. [LXX 2 Ki.] 13:15 and repeatedly of the mutual ardour of the lover and his beloved in Canticles). In the LXX and the NT it means divine love when this is the meaning indicated by the context (as, in the NT, it most usually is).

Paul has already spoken of love as the expression of faith (v 6) and of practical neighbourly love as the fulfilment of 'the whole law' (vv 13f.). As for its being the fruit of the Spirit, he enlarges on this in Rom. 5:5, where the love of God has been 'poured out' (ἐκκέχυται) into the hearts of believers by the Spirit. This is God's own love, as manifested in Christ (cf. Rom. 8:25, 38f.), which floods their lives and springs up in a responsive love to God and Christ and to one another, and overflows to all mankind (cf. 6:10, πρὸς πάντας). 'The love of Christ' is the motive force behind Paul's own apostolic ministry, as he beseeches men and women on Christ's behalf to be reconciled to God (2 Cor. 5:14f., 18–20). Paul's classic celebration of divine love is 1 Corinthians 13, where, as many expositors have said, his description of love could be a pen-portrait of the character of Jesus. 'Christian love springs to life when Christ is incarnated again in a man [or woman] who has given himself [or herself] absolutely to him' (W. Barclay, *Flesh and Spirit*, 76). (See the bibliography at the end of the note on v 14 above.)

χαρά, 'joy', is mentioned, like love, in Romans 5 among the blessings which accrue to believers. We 'rejoice in God through our Lord Jesus Christ', says Paul, 'through whom we have now received our reconciliation' (Rom. 5:11). This rejoicing includes rejoicing 'in hope of the glory of God' (Rom. 5:2)— paraphrased in the RSV as 'our hope of sharing the glory of God'—another aspect of 'the hope of righteousness' for which, according to Gal. 5:5, believers wait 'through the Spirit, by faith'. Hope (ἐλπίς) is not listed separately here as belonging to the fruit of the Spirit, but it is an important element in Christian joy. It is hope that enables believers to rejoice even in sufferings, and their endurance of sufferings in a Christian spirit strengthens their hope (Rom. 5:3–5). Paul prays that 'the God of hope' may fill the Roman Christians 'with all joy and peace in believing' (Rom. 15:13); the kingdom of God, he tells them, means 'righteousness and peace and joy in the Holy Spirit' (Rom. 14:17).

The juxtaposition of peace and joy in these two texts is not haphazard: 'since we are justified by faith, we have peace with God through our Lord Jesus Christ' (Rom. 5:1), and peace and joy are spiritual twins. To have peace with God (the indicative ἔχομεν in Rom. 5:1 is a preferable reading to the subjunctive ἔχωμεν) is to be reconciled to him, and it is those who have been reconciled through Christ that have greatest cause to rejoice in God (Rom. 5:11).

In Paul's usage εἰρήνη may have in it something of the sense of 'wellbeing' or 'wholeness' inherent in Heb. *šālôm*. Those who are at peace with God receive something of the 'peace of God' which, as Paul puts it elsewhere, garrisons their hearts and minds 'in Christ Jesus' (Phil. 4:7) and should act as arbiter within their community (Col. 3:15). God himself is 'the God of peace' (Rom. 15:33; 16:20a; 2 Cor. 13:11; Phil. 4:9; 1 Thes. 5:23; cf. Heb. 13:20); dissension and all that threatens peace come from a very different source (cf. v 20). In the OT wisdom literature the sowing of discord among brothers is hateful and abominable to God (Pr. 6:19). Peace is therefore one of the marks of the children of God—not only peace with God but peace with one another: in the home (1 Cor. 7:15), in the church (1 Cor. 14:33; Eph. 4:3), in the world (Rom. 12:18), between Jew and Gentile (Eph. 2:14–18). 'Let us then pursue what makes for peace (τὰ τῆς εἰρήνης) and for mutual upbuilding' (Rom. 14:19); this is the way to receive the blessing pronounced by Jesus on 'the peace-makers, for they shall be called sons of God' (Mt. 5:9).

One could well believe that love, joy and peace formed a triad in early Christian language, like faith, hope and love (see end of note on 5:6). In the upper-room discourse of the Fourth Gospel Jesus gives his disciples 'my peace' (Jn. 14:27), bids them abide in 'my love' (Jn. 15:9f.) and desires that they know 'my joy' (Jn. 15:11).

μακροθυμία, 'patience', is a positive virtue. It shares the same semantic field as ἀνοχή, ὑπομονή and καρτερία, but is specially close to the third of these. It embraces steadfastness and staying-power. If in English we had an adjective 'long-tempered' as a counterpart to 'short-tempered', then μακροθυμία could be called the quality of being 'long-tempered'. The Latin NT renders μακροθυμία by *longanimitas*, but the English derivative 'longanimity', used as its equivalent in the Douai-Rheims-Challoner NT, has not passed into common currency.

μακροθυμία is a quality of God: he is μακρόθυμος καὶ πολυέλεος (Ex. 34:6; Ps. 103 [LXX 102]:8, where μακρόθυμος renders Heb. *'erek 'appayim*, lit. 'long in nostrils' [from which anger is vented], RSV 'slow to anger'). The same quality is to be reproduced in men and women—perhaps it is included in the image of God—so that ἐλεήμων ἀνὴρ μακροθυμεῖ (Pr. 19:11), 'a merciful man is patient', i.e., he defers his anger, Heb. *he'erîk 'appô*).

In 1 Macc. 8:4 the Romans' advance to world dominion is ascribed to their μακροθυμία, 'that Roman persistency which would never make peace under defeat' (R. C. Trench, *Synonyms of the NT*, § liii, 184). In Test. Jos. 2:7 Joseph tells how he was steadfast (ἐμακροθύμησα) in all his temptations, and adds that 'μακροθυμία is a great medicine and ὑπομονή yields many good things'.

In the NT God shows patience (μακροθυμεῖ) over his elect (Lk. 18:7; NEB 'he listens patiently to them'); and towards the impenitent (Rom. 2:4; 9:22; in great μακροθυμία he postpones the day of retribution). ἡ ἀγάπη μακροθυμεῖ, says Paul (1 Cor. 13:4); he urges his Christian friends to display μακροθυμία to one another and to all (Eph. 4:2; Col. 1:11; 3:12; 1 Thes. 5:14).

χρηστότης, 'kindness', is also a quality of God. 'Taste and see that the Lord is kind' (ὅτι χρηστὸς ὁ κύριος), says the psalmist (Ps. 34:8 [LXX 33:9]), in words echoed in 1 Pet. 2:3, and again, 'O give thanks to the Lord, for he is kind' (ὅτι χρηστός, Ps. 136 [LXX 135]:1). God is 'kind (χρηστός) to the ungrateful and ungenerous', and those who imitate him in this 'will be sons of the Most High' (Lk. 6:35). His 'kindness and severity' (χρηστότης καὶ ἀποτομία) are displayed in his dealings with mankind (Rom. 11:22): his kindness to sinners is designed to lead them to repentance (Rom. 2:4) and his kindness to believers should encourage them to 'continue in his kindness' (Rom. 11:22). There is no better way to continue in his kindness than by showing others 'the kindness of God' (cf. 2 Sa. [LXX 2 Ki.] 9:3, although ἔλεος, not χρηστότης, is the LXX word there), treating them as God has treated us (Eph. 4:32). For love, according to 1 Cor. 13:4, is not only patient (μακροθυμεῖ) but kind (χρηστεύεται).

ἀγαθωσύνη, 'goodness', has a range of meaning as wide as the adjective ἀγαθός. But in the present setting it may well mean 'generosity'—it is the antithesis to φθόνος, which figures among the works of the flesh. The comment on φθόνος (v 21) referred to Mt. 20:15, 'is your eye evil (πονηρός) because I am good (ἀγαθός)?'—where 'generous' is precisely what ἀγαθός means.

πίστις may mean either the act or attitude of believing (πιστεύειν), i.e. faith, trust, which is its most frequent sense in Paul's letters, or the quality of being worthy of belief—faithfulness, trustworthiness, loyalty. The sense of 'faith' is probably to be attached to πίστις when it is listed as one among various 'gifts' of the Spirit (1 Cor. 12:9; cf. Rom. 12:3, 6)—not the exercise of justifying faith but the appropriate measure of faith necessary for accomplishing some work for God. But the decisive factor in the present instance is the context in which the word appears. Its eight companions denote ethical qualities, and one should expect πίστις to denote an ethical quality also, the quality of being πιστός. The adjective πιστός usually means 'faithful', 'dependable', in Paul, although occasionally, as in Gal. 3:9, it means 'believing' (cf. 2 Cor. 6:15). God is πιστός (1 Cor. 1:9; 10:13; 2 Cor. 1:18; 1 Thes. 5:24; 2 Thes. 3:3); in the one place where Paul speaks explicitly of God's πίστις (Rom. 3:3) it is his faithfulness that is plainly intended. Because God is faithful, because he can be relied upon, his people are to be faithful too, and the Spirit enables them to be so. The statement, 'it is required of stewards that they be found trustworthy' (1 Cor. 4:2), is made with primary reference to apostles and their colleagues, but every Christian is in some degree a steward (οἰκονόμος) and is expected to be trustworthy (πιστός) in the discharge of whatever the stewardship may be (cf. Lk. 12:42). This is the lesson of the parallel parables of the talents (Mt. 25:14–30) and the pounds (Lk. 19:11–27): 'he who is faithful in a very little is faithful also in much' (Lk. 16:10).

In the Apocalypse Jesus Christ is called 'the faithful witness' (Rev. 1:5) and each of his followers is called to be his 'faithful witness', even though, as with Antipas of Pergamum, this witness involves martyrdom (Rev. 2:13): 'here is the patience and faith (πίστις) of the saints' (Rev. 13:10).

5:23 πραΰτης, 'gentleness', is defined by Aristotle (*Eth. Nic.* 2.1108a) as the mean between excessive proneness to anger (ὀργιλότης) and incapacity for anger (ἀοργησία). Moses was πραΰς σφόδρα, 'very gentle' (Nu. 12:3), in the sense that, in face of undeserved criticism, he did not give way to rage but rather interceded with God for the offenders. Jesus was 'gentle (πραΰς) and lowly in heart' (Mt. 11:29) but was perfectly capable of indignation (Mk. 3:5). Paul entreats the Corinthians 'by the meekness (πραΰτης) and gentleness (ἐπιείκεια) of Christ' (2 Cor. 10:1), but if the words that follow that entreaty are an expression of meekness and gentleness, one wonders what he would have said had he been unrestrained by these qualities. (There, as here, Paul's affectionate concern for his converts is matched by his fierce denunciation of those who troubled them.) 'The meek (οἱ . . . πραεῖς) shall inherit the land' (or 'the earth'), according to Ps. 37 (LXX 36):11—a saying which is incorporated in one of the Matthaean beatitudes (Mt. 5:5)—the suggestion perhaps being that the hotheads will wipe one another out and leave the meek in possession. For an animal to be πραΰς is to be tame or tamed (the verb πραΰνω is used of taming wild animals), but as an ethical quality πραΰς implies self-control, the fruit of control by the Spirit of God. πραΰτης has much in common with μακροθυμία, with which it is conjoined in Eph. 4:2 and Col. 3:12. Christians should show 'all gentleness (πᾶσαν . . . πραΰτητα, RSV 'perfect courtesy') to all men' (Tit. 3:2).

ἐγκράτεια, 'self-control', has something in common with πραΰτης, but denotes control of more sensual passions than anger. According to Aristotle, who devotes the seventh book of his *Nicomachean Ethics* to a discussion of the difference between ἐγκράτεια and its opposite, ἀκρασία, the man who is ἐγκρατής has powerful passions, but keeps them under control; the ἀκρατής does not deliberately choose the wrong, but he has no strength to resist temptation (*Eth. Nic.* 7.1145bff.). As an ethical term, ἐγκράτεια was introduced by Socrates (Xen. *Mem.* 1.5.4). Plato sets it in opposition to over-indulgence in food and sex (*Rep.* 3.390B, C). Paul says that the athlete practises it (ἐγκρατεύεται) in all things, and applies the lesson to the spiritual athlete (1 Cor. 9:25). In 1 Cor. 7:9 he advises single or widowed persons who cannot exercise sexual restraint to marry (εἰ δὲ οὐκ ἐγκρατεύονται, γαμησάτωσαν). The word-group is more often used with a sexual connotation than otherwise; hence 'chastity' can usually be a suitable rendering. In the second century AD we meet a Christian sect called the Encratites (their best-known member being Tatian, the compiler of the *Diatessaron*); they were so called because of their insistence on ἐγκράτεια which, however, they interpreted as asceticism, including abstention from flesh, wine and marriage (Iren. *Haer.* 1.28.1; Euseb. *HE* 4.28f.). How far this lifestyle departed from the NT standard of ἐγκράτεια may be seen from 1 Tim. 4:1–5.

The punctuation of Nestle-Aland[26] (but not of UBS[3]) divides these nine virtues into three groups of three, which would make for ready memorization. They are not the preconditions of justification; they follow it spontaneously. They are naturally found together, unlike the *gifts* of the Spirit, which are variously apportioned, one to this person and another to that person (Rom. 12:6–8; 1 Cor. 12:8–11). Where love is present, the other virtues will not be far away; it is love that binds them all together in perfect harmony (cf. Col. 3:14).

If the works of the flesh as a whole be compared with the fruit of the Spirit as a whole, it will appear that the works of the flesh are disruptive of κοινωνία, whereas the fruit of the Spirit fosters it.

κατὰ τῶν τοιούτων οὐκ ἔστιν νόμος. Paul does not simply mean that the nine virtues which make up the fruit of the Spirit are not forbidden by law; he means that when these qualities are in view we are in a sphere with which law has nothing to do. Law may prescribe certain forms of conduct and prohibit others, but love, joy, peace and the rest cannot be legally enforced. 'A vine does not produce grapes by Act of Parliament; they are the fruit of the vine's own life; so the conduct which conforms to the standard of the Kingdom is not produced by any demand, not even God's, but it is the fruit of that divine nature which God gives as the result of what he has done in and by Christ' (S. H. Hooke, 'What is Christianity?' in *The Siege Perilous* [London, 1956], 264).

In Aristotle (*Pol.* 3.13, 1284a) the statement κατὰ δὲ τῶν τοιούτων οὐκ ἔστι νόμος is used of persons who surpass their fellows in virtue (ἀρετή) like gods among men. They do not need to have their actions regulated by laws; on the contrary, they themselves constitute a law (a standard) for others (αὐτοὶ γὰρ εἰσι νόμος). Paul probably does not quote directly or consciously from Aristotle: the saying may have passed into proverbial currency, like many phrases from Shakespeare or the AV which are frequently quoted without awareness of their source. Aristotle's statement shows some (rather remote) affinity with what Paul says here; it has more in common with the observation in 1 Tim. 1:9 that 'the law is not laid down for the just but for the lawless and disobedient'.

5:24 οἱ δὲ τοῦ Χριστοῦ ['Ιησοῦ], 'the people of Christ [Jesus]'. For the designation cf. 1 Cor. 15:23. It includes all believers, unlike the misuse of the name of Christ by those who claimed in a distinctive sense ἐγὼ δὲ Χριστοῦ (1 Cor. 1:12; cf. 2 Cor. 10:7).

τὴν σάρκα ἐσταύρωσαν. It is because they are Christ's in the sense of being members of Christ, incorporated ἐν Χριστῷ, that they have 'crucified the flesh'. The aorist probably indicates their participation in Christ's historical crucifixion. When Paul said earlier Χριστῷ συνεσταύρωμαι (2:19), he meant that the cross of Christ severed his relation to the law; here he says that the cross of Christ severs believers' relation to the 'flesh'. For Paul, as we have seen already, the law and the flesh belong to the same pre-Christian order. But the cross of Christ severed Paul's relation to the law only as he himself was 'crucified with Christ', thus becoming 'dead to the law' that he might live to God; so also the cross severs the relation of believers in general to the flesh only as they reckon themselves to have been crucified in the historical crucifixion of Christ. The crucifixion of the former self-centred ego, that it may be replaced by the new Christ-centred mind—'it is no longer *I* who live, but Christ lives in me' (2:20)—is not materially different from the crucifixion of the flesh, that it may be replaced by a Spirit-imparted life and a Spirit-directed conduct. Cf. Rom. 8:13, 'if by the Spirit you put to death the deeds of the body, you will live'.

Those who belong to Christ, then, those who acknowledge his lordship in no merely formal way (cf. Rom. 14:8, τοῦ κυρίου ἐσμέν), have made a clean break with what they formerly were (cf. Rom. 6:6, ὁ παλαιὸς ἡμῶν ἄνθρωπος συνεσταυρώθη, ἵνα καταργηθῇ τὸ σῶμα τῆς ἁμαρτίας); they have been delivered from the 'present evil age' (1:4) and have become members of the new creation (6:15). It is the cross of Christ that makes this clean break. As truly as law and flesh are bound up for Paul with the present evil age, so truly is the indwelling Spirit the witness that the age to come has already broken in through the Christ-event. 'Ideally, we must understand, this crucifixion of the flesh is involved in Christ's crucifixion; really, it is effected by it. Whoever sees into the secret of Calvary . . . is conscious that the doom of sin is in it; to take it as real, and to stand in any real relation to it, is death to the flesh with its passions and desires' (J. Denney, *The Death of Christ*, 162).

Alongside such a historical statement as this, in the indicative, stands the hortatory counterpart, in the imperative, as in Rom. 6:11 ('reckon yourselves to be dead to sin but alive to God in Christ Jesus'); Col. 3:5 ('put to death therefore your members that are on earth . . .'). What has been effected once for all by the cross of Christ must be worked out in practice.

σὺν τοῖς παθήμασιν καὶ ταῖς ἐπιθυμίαις. The ἐπιθυμίαι are the desires by which the παθήματα ('passions') are directed this way or that; if unchecked, they will express themselves in 'works of the flesh'. There can be no more decisive check upon them than their 'crucifixion'. Paul's own misdirected ζῆλος, which had found expression in the persecution of the church, was now recognized by him to have been a πάθημα or ἐπιθυμία τῆς σαρκός. As such, it had been decisively 'crucified'; as a quality of his character, it had been redirected along the path of God's will and Christ's service. See further on 6:14.

5:25 Εἰ ζῶμεν πνεύματι, πνεύματι καὶ στοιχῶμεν, 'If the Spirit is the source of our life, let the Spirit also direct our course' (NEB). That their new life in Christ was lived by the Spirit they knew; the moral corollary of this, Paul reminds them, is that their conduct should be governed by the Spirit: they should march in line (keep in step) with him. For this ethical sense of στοιχέω (denominative from στοῖχος, 'row') cf. 6:16; Rom. 4:12; Phil. 3:16; also Acts 21:24. On its significance here cf. A. Oepke, *Galater*, 145f.

Here too we have the characteristic Pauline interplay between indicative and imperative: we live by the Spirit (granted); therefore let us keep in step with the Spirit. He does not suggest that it is possible to do the former without also doing the latter. There is little material difference between πνεύματι στοιχεῖν (here), πνεύματι περιπατεῖν (v 16) and πνεύματι ἄγεσθαι (v 18). Walking by the Spirit is the outward manifestation, in action and speech, of living by the Spirit. Living by the Spirit is the root; walking by the Spirit is the fruit, and that fruit is nothing less than the practical reproduction of the character (and therefore the conduct) of Christ in the lives of his people. 'In his usual way, Paul draws an exhortation out of his doctrine. The death of the flesh is the life of the Spirit. If God's Spirit lives in us, let Him govern all our actions' (J. Calvin, *Galatians*, 106).

It is those whose conduct is directed by the Spirit who are, in Paul's estimation, the true πνευματικοί (cf. 6:1), in contrast to those who claimed to have reached a stage in spirituality where ethical considerations lost their relevance.

5:26 The ethical considerations which were in danger of losing their relevance in the Galatian churches were those affecting personal relationships. The positive exhortation 'let us keep in line with the Spirit' had, for their situation, the corollary: 'let us not become boastful, challenging one another, envying one another'. To be κενόδοξος is to boast where there is nothing to boast about: κενοδοξία (cf. Phil. 2:3) is empty pride or conceit, mere pretentiousness; it is synonymous with ἀλαζονεία (cf. 1 Jn. 2:16). The verb προκαλέομαι (here only in the NT) is used of mutual challenges to combat or athletic contest; it can be extended to other areas of life, as in Philo's story of Demosthenes who, when challenged to a slanging match (προκληθεὶς ἐπὶ λοιδορίας), declined because, as he said, the winner would come off worse than the loser (*Agric.* 110). The spirit which Paul here deprecates has a refined manifestation in challenge to theological debate; perhaps it was in this way that the Galatians were challenging one another. As for envy, Paul has already warned them against this in general terms by including φθόνοι among the works of the flesh (v 21); his specific warning against it here implies that it threatened the peace of the churches of Galatia. (The use of the dative of the person after φθονέω—ἀλλήλοις φθονοῦντες—is classical; P^{46} B and many other manuscripts have the unclassical accusative ἀλλήλους.) As has been indicated above (v 15), these were the evils against which the Galatians had to be put specially on their guard.

'Gnostic pneumatics', says W. Schmithals, 'are splendidly described by the characterization in Gal. 5:26' (*Paul and the Gnostics*, 49). The language might indeed be applicable to certain Gnostics, if Gnostics were known to be in view;

but any one acquainted with church life at local level knows that the tendencies against which Paul utters this warning—spiritual pride, mutual provocation and envy—can arise among the most ordinary Christians, who are quite innocent of gnosticism or ecstasy.

VII
MUTUAL HELP AND SERVICE
(6:1–10)

Mutual help is the hallmark of the community of faith. Gentleness, not arrogance, is the way of Christ. The teacher deserves the support of those whom he teaches. There is a rule of sowing and reaping in life; those who do good to others will reap a harvest of eternal life.

My brothers, even if some one be caught in some fault, you who are spiritual are to put the person in question right, in a spirit of gentleness. Have regard to yourself, lest you be tempted also. Bear one another's burdens; so you will fulfil the law of Christ. If any one thinks he is something when he is a mere nothing, he is hoodwinking himself. Let each one examine his own work; then he will keep his achievement to himself alone and not compare it with someone else's, for each person will carry his own load.

Let the person who receives instruction in the word give a share in all good things to the one who imparts it.

Do not be misled: God is not to be treated with contempt. Whatever a person sows, this is what he will reap. Whoever sows for the flesh will reap a harvest of corruption from the flesh; whoever sows for the Spirit will reap a harvest of eternal life from the Spirit. Let us not grow slack in doing good; at the proper time we shall reap a harvest if we do not give up. So then, as we have opportunity, let us do good to all, especially to fellow-members of the family of faith.

TEXTUAL NOTES
v 1 ανθρωπος / τις εξ υμων P syrᵖᵉˢʰ / ανθρωπος εξ υμων Ψ *pc* syrʰᶜˡ copˢᵃ
v 2 αναπληρωσετε B G lat syrᵖᵉˢʰ Mcion / αποπληρωσετε P⁴⁶ / αναπληρωσατε ℵ A C D Ψ byz Clem.Alex
v 4 εκαστος *om* P⁴⁶ B syrᵖᵉˢʰ copˢᵃ⁽ᶜᵒᵈᵈ⁾
v 7 μη *om* Mcion Tert
v 10 εχομεν / εχωμεν ℵ B* 33 *al*

6:1 Ἀδελφοί, ἐὰν καὶ προλημφθῇ ἄνθρωπος ἔν τινι παραπτώματι, ὑμεῖς οἱ πνευματικοὶ καταρτίζετε τὸν τοιοῦτον. The general teaching of

5:13–26 is now applied to some more specific situations. If mutual envy and provocation are to be renounced, mutual aid is to be fostered. One form of aid is that given to a member of one of the churches who may fall into some 'transgression' (παράπτωμα). The precise force of προλημφθῇ is uncertain: it may mean that he finds himself inadvertently involved in some wrongdoing, or that he is detected in it by someone else. The wrongdoing may fall under the heading of one of the 'works of the flesh' (5:19–21); it will certainly be inconsistent with the fruit of the Spirit. Whatever form it takes, the offender must be rehabilitated, and not made to feel like a pariah. It is likely that Paul is not thinking of behaviour which so flagrantly flouts accepted standards that it brings the community into public disrepute (cf. 1 Cor. 5:5) or which can best be dealt with by a temporary withholding of social fellowship (1 Cor. 5:11; Rom. 16:17). A παράπτωμα is not a settled course of action but an isolated action which may make the person who does it feel guilty. The rehabilitation must be undertaken by those who are truly πνευματικοί, whose life and conduct alike are controlled by the Spirit of Christ. Paul uses the same verb (καταρτίζω) in an ethical sense when he begs the Corinthian Christians to be joined (κατηρτισμένοι) in unity of mind (1 Cor. 1:10) and, more generally, to mend their ways (καταρτίζεσθε, 2 Cor. 13:11).

Since gentleness is included in the fruit of the Spirit (5:23), it follows that spiritual people will take this or any other kind of action 'in a spirit of gentleness' (ἐν πνεύματι πραΰτητος). It is easy for certain types of religious people to sit in judgment on one who has suddenly yielded to some moral temptation, to make their disapproval manifest, but this is not the way of Christ. If there were in the Galatian churches, as in the church of Corinth, some who regarded themselves as πνευματικοί in a superior sense (cf. 1 Cor. 2:15; 3:1; 14:37)—'whoever feels himself a *Pneumatiker*' (H. Lietzmann, *An die Galater*, 38)—Paul impresses on them that one test of true spirituality is a readiness to set those who stumble by the wayside on the right road again in a sympathetic and uncensorious spirit. Similarly in Rom. 15:1 Paul calls on the δυνατοί, those who are spiritually 'strong', to show their strength by consideration for those who are spiritually weak, to the point of restricting their own liberty on their behalf. There Paul includes himself with the 'strong' (ἡμεῖς οἱ δυνατοί), and here, though he says ὑμεῖς οἱ πνευματικοί, he no doubt reckons himself a πνευματικός (cf. 1 Cor. 7:40).

σκοπῶν σεαυτὸν μὴ καὶ σὺ πειρασθῇς. The realization of one's personal vulnerability to temptation should prevent self-righteousness in the treatment of those who have yielded to it. Cf. 1 Cor. 10:12, 'let any one who thinks that he stands take heed lest he fall'. This cautionary word is directed to each individual: 'consider yourself'.

6:2 Ἀλλήλων τὰ βάρη βαστάζετε. This more general injunction includes the precept of v 1. The obligation of burden-bearing is reciprocal, but a special responsibility lies on the πνευματικοί to bear the burdens of the weaker; cf. Rom. 15:1, 'we who are strong ought to bear with (βαστάζειν) the failings (ἀσθενήματα) of the weak'. Paul himself was foremost in doing this very thing (cf. 1 Cor. 8:13; 2 Cor. 11:28f.). To bear the burdens of others is a divine quality; cf. Ps. 55:22 (LXX 54:23), ἐπίριψον ἐπὶ Κύριον τὴν μέριμνάν σου, καὶ αὐτός σε διαθρέψει, echoed in 1 Pet. 5:7, πᾶσαν τὴν μέριμναν ὑμῶν ἐπιρίψαντες ἐπ᾽ αὐτόν, ὅτι αὐτῷ μέλει περὶ ὑμῶν. To obey this injunction therefore is to be God-like.

J. G. Strelan, 'Burden-Bearing and the Law of Christ: A Re-examination of Galatians 6:2', *JBL* 94 (1975), 266–276, argues that Paul is here enjoining the sharing by each member of a common financial burden (primarily the maintenance of missionaries and teachers, as in v 6, together possibly with their contribution to the Jerusalem relief fund). The 'law of Christ' which would be thus fulfilled is that referred to in 1 Cor. 9:14 'that those who proclaim the gospel should get their living by the gospel'. Financial burdens would not be excluded from the βάρη which are to be shared, but the case for seeing financial burdens as predominantly in view has not been made out.

καὶ οὕτως ἀναπληρώσετε τὸν νόμον τοῦ Χριστοῦ, 'by so doing you will fulfil the law of Christ'. The 'law of Christ' is not essentially different from the commandment of love to one's neighbour (quoted in 5:14), in which 'the whole law' is comprehended. Paul speaks of his commitment to this 'law' in 1 Cor. 9:20, where he describes himself as ἔννομος Χριστοῦ (cf. C. H. Dodd, '᾽Έννομος Χριστοῦ', *More NT Studies* [Manchester, 1968], 134–148). It may be that Paul speaks of the law of Christ here as a contrast to the law which his converts were being urged to accept: the law of Christ is a 'law' of quite a different kind, not enforceable by legal sanctions. 'The law of Christ is essentially concerned with the *quality* of the act and the *direction* in which it is moving' (C. H. Dodd, *Gospel and Law* [Cambridge, 1951], 77f.).

See E. Bammel, 'Νόμος Χριστοῦ', *SE* 3 = TU 88 (1964), 120–28; H. Schürmann, ' "Das Gesetz des Christus" (Gal 6, 2). Jesu Verhalten und Wort als letztgültige sittliche Norm nach Paulus', *Schnackenburg FS*, 282–300.

In fine, the 'law of Christ' is for Paul the whole tradition of Jesus' ethical teaching, confirmed by his character and conduct (cf. Rom. 13:14; 2 Cor. 10:1) and reproduced within his people by the power of the Spirit (cf. Rom. 8:2, ὁ . . . νόμος τοῦ πνεύματος τῆς ζωῆς ἐν Χριστῷ Ἰησοῦ). The existence of this tradition provided a criterion by which claims to be guided by the Spirit were to be tested. 'The Spirit of Christ must accord with "the law of Christ" ' (J. D. G. Dunn, *Unity*, 193).

'Galatians, which in attacking "Jewish" legalism proclaims the true freedom based on Christ, consequently contains more exhortation, admonition, and summons to obey the "law of Christ" . . . than any other letter, and to quite a remarkable degree—a third of the whole letter' (G. Bornkamm, *Paul*, 83).

6:3 εἰ γὰρ δοκεῖ τις εἶναί τι μηδὲν ὤν. Twice over in this clause a neuter pronoun (τι, μηδέν) is used in agreement with a masculine. For δοκεῖ τις εἶναί τι ('. . . to be someone special') cf. Gal. 2:6, οἱ δοκοῦντες εἶναί τι. With μηδὲν ὤν ('being a mere nothing, a mere cipher') cf. 1 Cor. 13:2; 2 Cor. 12:11, οὐδέν εἰμι, 'I am nothing' (for the distinction between the two negative pronouns cf. Eur. frag. 532, τὸ μηδὲν εἰς οὐδὲν ῥέπει, 'what is good-for-nothing tends to become absolutely nothing').

Like other gnomic sayings of which this section provides several examples, this one is not thrown out at random but is relevant to the situation in the Galatian churches: it is a warning against spiritual pride. The Galatians were not to think of themselves more highly than they ought to think (cf. Rom. 12:3). If they did, they would be inhibited from fulfilling 'the law of Christ' by bearing one another's burdens or restoring those who had been overcome by some sudden temptation (this is probably the significance of the connective γάρ in the present sentence).

The form of the saying is similar to that of 1 Cor. 8:2, where knowing nothing, not being nothing, is the subject: εἴ τις δοκεῖ ἐγνωκέναι τι, οὔπω ἔγνω καθὼς δεῖ γνῶναι (cf. 1 Cor. 3:18; also Plato, *Apol.* 21D, where Socrates contrasts the man who οἴεταί τι εἰδέναι οὐκ εἰδώς, 'thinks he knows something when he does not', with himself, ὅτι ἃ μὴ οἶδα οὐδὲ οἴομαι εἰδέναι, 'because what I do not know I do not even think I know').

φρεναπατᾷ ἑαυτόν, 'he deceives his own mind (φρήν)'. The verb (not attested earlier) is *hapax legomenon* in the NT; cf. the noun φρεναπάτης in Tit. 1:10, where members of the circumcision party are called ματαιολόγοι καὶ φρεναπάται, 'foolish speakers and deceivers'.

6:4 τὸ δὲ ἔργον ἑαυτοῦ δοκιμαζέτω ἕκαστος. The most practical principles of the gospel are apt to be debased. In his *Diocesan Letter* of February 1980 the Bishop of Peterborough (D. R. Feaver) remarks that at the General Synod of the Church of England there was 'a confusion in the minds of many which identified the apostolic precept, "bear ye one another's burdens", with minding other people's business'.

What Paul stresses here is personal responsibility. It is not for one Christian to assess or judge the ministry of another; each one is answerable to God for his own. Cf. 1 Cor. 4:3–5, where he takes little account of other people's estimate of his service: 'it is the Lord who judges me'. The duty of self-examination was inculcated in several contemporary schools; the Pythagoreans, for example, were required to interrogate themselves regularly: πῇ παρέβην; τί δ᾽ ἔρεξα; τί μοι δέον οὐκ ἐτελέσθη; 'Wherein have I transgressed? What have I done? What duty have I left unfulfilled?' (Diog. Laert., *Vit. Phil.* 8.22). The Christian's self-examination is conducted in the light of the law of Christ—especially the law or standard which is embodied in the person of Christ. (Cf. 1 Cor. 15:28 for self-examination before the Lord's Supper.)

καὶ τότε εἰς ἑαυτὸν μόνον τὸ καύχημα ἕξει καὶ οὐκ εἰς τὸν ἕτερον. The καύχημα is the ground of a person's boasting, his achievement. When in Rom. 15:17 Paul says that he has reason to boast (καύχησις) so far as his work for God is concerned, he goes on to say that he will not venture to speak about what Christ has not done through him and that he will avoid building on anyone else's foundation (vv 18, 20). Similarly in 2 Cor. 10:13–18 he refuses to boast εἰς τὰ ἄμετρα, beyond the limit of his apostolic sphere (which includes Corinth), in contrast to those who invade another's sphere and boast of their achievements there. As the interlopers in Corinth are in view in 2 Cor. 10:13–18, so the trouble-makers in Galatia are probably in view here. It is not comparison with another (εἰς τὸν ἕτερον) that provides a true standard of assessment; in 2 Cor. 10:12 Paul speaks of the folly of those who 'measure themselves by one another, and compare themselves with one another'. The Pharisee in the parable made the same kind of mistake when he thanked God that he was not 'like other men, . . . even like this tax collector' (Lk. 18:11).

6:5 ἕκαστος γὰρ τὸ ἴδιον φορτίον βαστάσει, 'for each person will carry his own load'. This is another common maxim, applicable to a wide variety of situations. Here the connective γάρ suggests that Paul applies it to the situation with which v 4 deals: one's responsibility before God. In the 'day of Christ' Paul would not be asked how his achievement compared with Peter's: his καύχημα would be the quality of those who had been won for Christ through his own ministry (Phil. 2:16). At that tribunal 'each of us will give an account of himself to God' (Rom. 14:12; cf. 2 Cor. 5:10). Cf. R. Jewett, 'The Agitators and the Galatian Congregation', 211.

The partial resemblance between this maxim and v 2a (ἀλλήλων τὰ βάρη βαστάζετε) is fortuitous; the φορτίον of v 5 is not one of the βάρη that can be borne for another (φορτίον, a classical word, occurs here only in Paul; of its other NT occurrences the best known is Mt. 11:30, 'my burden is light'— but the dominical φορτίον there [see note on 5:1] is quite different from the personal φορτίον here).

6:6 Κοινωνείτω δὲ ὁ κατηχούμενος τὸν λόγον τῷ κατηχοῦντι ἐν πᾶσιν ἀγαθοῖς. The relevance of this injunction in the present context is not immediately obvious, but it is an instance of the mutual help inculcated in v 2a. The teacher relieves the ignorance of the pupil; the pupil should relieve the teacher of concern for his subsistence. This is another way of stating the principle that 'the labourer deserves his wages' (Lk. 10:7; 1 Tim. 5:18; cf. Mt. 10:10) or, as Paul elsewhere paraphrases those words of Jesus, 'those who proclaim the gospel should get their living by the gospel' (1 Cor. 9:14). Whereas the emphasis in those other places is on the right of the preacher or teacher to claim his support, here it lies on the duty of those who are taught to make material provision for their teachers.

If Paul followed with his Galatian converts the policy which he adopted in Thessalonica (1 Thes. 2:9), Corinth (1 Cor. 9:15–18) and Ephesus (Acts 20:33–35), he could give them this instruction all the more freely because he refrained from claiming his own support from them. His unwillingness to accept material support from his converts may have as its background the rabbinic injunction not to derive worldly profit from the Torah (so Hillel, m. Ab. 1.13; 4.7; Zadok, Ab. 4.7); but he made it his personal policy both by way of example to his converts not to live at the expense of others (2 Thes. 3:6–13) and, where necessary, to stop the mouths of those who would have liked to ascribe mercenary motives to him (2 Cor. 11:7–12). Besides, he had a naturally independent spirit in this regard: it embarrasses him even to express gratitude for a gift of money from Philippi, while he deeply appreciates the loving thought which prompted it (Phil. 4:10–20).

It has been asked why, if 'the Lord *commanded* that those who proclaim the gospel should get their living by the gospel' (1 Cor. 9:14), Paul felt free to disregard a dominical command (cf. D. L. Dungan, *The Sayings of Jesus in the Churches of Paul* [Oxford, 1971], 1–39). The answer probably is that Paul interpreted the Lord's command not as a duty to be performed but as a right to be claimed—or not claimed, as might be most expedient. He was not free to choose whether to preach the gospel or not, but he was free to choose whether to preach it free of charge or not, and he chose to make it free of charge (1 Cor. 9:12b, 15–18).

Nevertheless, the claim which he chose to forgo for himself he asserted strongly for others, as he does here. The singular ὁ κατηχῶν is a generic reference to those who exercised a teaching ministry in the churches—certainly not to the intruding trouble-makers! Pagan priests received fees for their sacrificial services; 'one of the objects that Paul had most at heart was to train his converts in voluntary liberality, as distinguished from payments levied on ritual. He saw what a powerful, educative influence such liberality exerts on the individual, and what a strong unifying influence it might exert between the scattered parts of the Church' (W. M. Ramsay, *Galatians* 459).

The content of the κατήχησις would include predominantly the παραδόσεις which the apostle-founders had delivered to the churches. The verb κατηχέω ('instruct') is treated like διδάσκω, which takes two objects—the person taught and the subject taught—and so the passive can be accompanied by one of these objects (here τὸν λόγον, the content of the teaching). Cf. Acts 18:25 (κατηχημένος τὴν ὁδὸν τοῦ κυρίου); 1 Thes. 2:15 (τὰς παραδόσεις ἃς ἐδιδάχθητε). As for the verb κοινωνέω ('go shares with'), it may have as its subject the giver (as here; so also Rom. 12:13, ταῖς χρείαις τῶν ἁγίων κοινωνοῦντες) or the receiver (so Rom. 15:27, τοῖς πνευματικοῖς αὐτῶν ἐκοινώνησαν τὰ ἔθνη). The ἀγαθά are the 'good things' of life in general (cf. Lk. 1:53; 12:18f.; 16:25), not least τὰ σαρκικά of Rom. 15:27; 1 Cor. 9:11.

6:7 Μὴ πλανᾶσθε, 'make no mistake', 'do not be misled', a common phrase in such paraenetic passages (cf. 1 Cor. 6:9; 15:33; Jas. 1:16). Marcion and Tertullian (*Adv. Marc.* 5.4) knew a text which (accidentally) omitted the negative, so that πλανᾶσθε was construed as indicative: 'you are mistaken'. Possibly the middle voice should be recognized rather than the passive: 'do not mislead yourselves' (cf. 1 Cor. 3:18, Μηδεὶς ἑαυτὸν ἐξαπατάτω).

θεὸς οὐ μυκτηρίζεται. μυκτηρίζω, 'turn up the μυκτήρ' ('snout') in mockery or contempt, is found here only in the NT, but is common enough in the LXX (as is also the derivative noun μυκτηρισμός), not explicitly of the mocking of God, with the probable exception of Ezk. 8:17 (καὶ ἰδοὺ αὐτοὶ ὡς μυκτηρίζοντες). In 2 Ch. 36:16//1 Esd. 1:51 and Je. 20:7 the verb is used of mocking the prophets and other messengers of God. The mocking or despising of God lay in the behaviour of those who, 'consciously stressing the possession of the divine Pneuma, for this reason held themselves to be perfect Christians and openly boasted of their piety (Gal. 5:26; 6:3), but at the same time were sowing to the σάρξ and were doing that equally consciously and emphatically' (W. Schmithals, *Paul and the Gnostics*, 54). One may agree with this, without accepting Schmithals's view of the anti-gnostic thrust of the letter.

ὃ γὰρ ἐὰν σπείρῃ ἄνθρωπος, τοῦτο καὶ θερίσει. This is a common prudential maxim, applying a law of nature to human conduct (cf. Mt. 7:16–20//Lk. 6:43; Lk. 19:21; 1 Cor. 9:11; 2 Cor. 9:6, the last passage referring to the quantity, not the quality, of seed and crop). LXX instances are Ho. 8:7 ('sow the wind and reap the whirlwind'); Jb. 4:8; Pr. 22:8; Sir. 7:3. Cf. also Test. Levi 13:6 (καὶ σπείρετε ἐν ταῖς ψυχαῖς ὑμῶν ἀγαθά, . . . ἐὰν γὰρ σπείρητε κακά, πᾶσαν ταραχὴν καὶ θλῖψιν θερίσετε); Plato, *Phdr.* 260D (ποῖόν τινα οἴει . . . τὴν ῥητορικὴν καρπὸν ὧν ἔσπειρε θερίζειν;); Dem., *De Cor.* 159 (ὁ γὰρ τὸ σπέρμα παρασχών, οὗτος τῶν φύντων αἴτιος); Gorgias *ap.* Aristot. *Rhet.* 3.3.4, 1406b (αἰσχρῶς μὲν ἔσπειρας, κακῶς δὲ ἐθέρισας); Plut. *De Pythiae oraculis* 394E (σπείροντες λόγους καὶ θερίζοντες εὐθὺς μετὰ μάχης ὑπούλους καὶ πολεμικούς); Cicero, *De Or.*

2.65 (*'ut sementem feceris, ita metes'*). Things being what they are, the conse-
quences will be what they will be.

6:8 ὅτι ὁ σπείρων εἰς τὴν σάρκα ἑαυτοῦ ἐκ τῆς σαρκὸς θερίσει φθοράν.
The σάρξ here, as in 5:13, 16f., 19, is the unregenerate, 'uncrucified' self.
Sowing 'for the flesh' is the practising of such things as are included among 'the
works of the flesh' in 5:19–21; such sowing cannot produce the harvest of the
kingdom of God but the harvest of destruction (as in the parable of the weeds,
Mt. 13:24–30). Paul has more particularly in mind here such 'works of the
flesh' as quarrelsomeness and envy, to which the Galatian Christians appear to
have been specially prone (cf. 5:15, 26); indulgence in such things would have
disastrous results in their personal and corporate lives alike. To sow εἰς τὸ
πνεῦμα, on the other hand, is to cultivate the fruit of the Spirit and reap eternal
life. Cf. Rom. 6:20–23 ('the wages of sin is death, but the free gift of God is
eternal life through Christ Jesus our Lord'); 8:13 ('if you live according to the
flesh you will die, but if by the Spirit you put to death the deeds of the body
you will live') for the same idea expressed without the metaphor of sowing and
reaping. The eternal life is the resurrection life of Christ, mediated to believers
by 'the Spirit of him who raised Jesus from the dead' (Rom. 8:11); cf. G. Vos,
The Pauline Eschatology (Grand Rapids, 1952), 163f. But its future aspect, with
their appearance before the tribunal of Christ, to 'receive good or evil, according
to the deeds done in the body' (2 Cor. 5:10), is specially implied here. Any one
who did not seriously believe in such a coming assessment, or thought that the
law of sowing and reaping could safely be ignored, would indeed be treating
God with contempt.

6:9 τὸ δὲ καλὸν ποιοῦντες μὴ ἐγκακῶμεν. Cf. 2 Thes. 3:13, ὑμεῖς δέ,
ἀδελφοί, μὴ ἐγκακήσητε καλοποιοῦντες. Exhortations to perseverance are
common in Paul's writings: cf. 1 Cor. 15:50, 58; 16:13; Phil. 1:27f.; 2:15f.; 4:1;
1 Thes. 3:5, 13; 5:23. For the Hellenistic verb ἐγκακέω ('give up', 'slacken')
see also Lk. 18:1; 2 Cor. 4:1, 16; Eph. 3:13 (in all its NT occurrences it is
preceded by the negative). Christians have been justified by faith and cleansed
from guilt, they have received the Spirit, but they must persevere in holy living
and not rest on their oars. Paul knew the necessity of this in his own life (cf.
1 Cor. 9:26f.).

καιρῷ γὰρ ἰδίῳ θερίσομεν, μὴ ἐκλυόμενοι. To persevere in doing what
is good is to 'sow to the Spirit'; those who do so without growing faint (for this
classical sense of ἐκλύομαι cf. Mt. 15:32//Mk. 8:3; Heb. 12:3, 5 [quoting Pr.
3:11]) will reap the appropriate harvest in due course. With καιρῷ . . . ἰδίῳ
cf. καιροῖς ἰδίοις in 1 Tim. 2:6; 6:15; Tit. 1:3, where the proper time for the
fulfilment of God's promises is indicated, either at Christ's first advent or at the
parousia. Here the eschatological harvest may be in view. It is unlikely that the
Jerusalem relief fund is specifically referred to in τὸ . . . καλὸν ποιοῦντες,
even if Paul does speak of its completion as 'this fruit' or 'this harvest' (τὸν
καρπὸν τοῦτον, Rom. 15:28).

6:10 It has been pointed out, however, that Paul not only speaks of the
Jerusalem relief fund as 'this fruit' or 'this harvest' but uses the very figure of
sowing and reaping when writing about this matter in 2 Cor. 9:6–9. Contributions to the fund are there described as a form of sowing which will yield for
the donors a harvest of eternal blessing. To enforce this lesson Paul quotes Ps. 112

(LXX 111):9, 'he has scattered abroad, he has given to the poor; his righteous (or charitable) conduct remains for ever.' It is pointed out further that the present exhortations καλὸν ποιοῦντες μὴ ἐγκακῶμεν (v 9) and ἐργαζώμεθα τὸ ἀγαθὸν πρὸς πάντας (v 10) coincide in sense with the exhortation in 2 Cor. 9:8 to 'abound to every good work' (εἰς πᾶν ἔργον ἀγαθόν). (Note the synonymity of ἀγαθόν and καλόν in this sense.)

These affinities form part of the evidence on which it is argued that these verses (Gal. 6:6–10) 'are specific in intent, and form an exhortation to participate in the Jerusalem collection' (L. W. Hurtado, 'The Jerusalem Collection and the Book of Galatians', *JSNT*, Issue 5 [Oct. 1979], 53). If this is so, the allusiveness of the language makes it necessary to suppose that Paul had already communicated with the Galatians about the collection, so that they would understand the present allusion in the light of what they had already been told. Such a prior communication can be neither denied nor affirmed.

A connexion between Gal. 6:6–10 and the Jerusalem collection was earlier suggested by J. B. Lightfoot, *Galatians*, 55, and H. Lietzmann, *An die Galater*, 39f. K. F. Nickle notes the affinity between Gal. 6:6–10 and 2 Cor. 9:6–9, but finds in it only a reflection of 'the extent to which Paul's involvement in his collection project moulded the vocabulary he used to refer to sharing of sustenance for any purpose' (*The Collection* [London, 1966], 59 n. 55). Paul uses the same vocabulary in reference to his apostolic ministry in Corinth: 'if we have sown spiritual good among you, is it too much if we reap your material benefits?' (1 Cor. 9:11)—where he is not 'apparently' speaking as 'the agent of the movement of the Gospel from Jerusalem to the Gentiles' (so Hurtado, 'The Jerusalem Collection . . . ', 61 n. 27). See on 2:10, above.

ὡς καιρὸν ἔχομεν, 'as we have opportunity'; but ὡς is here used very much in the sense of ἕως, 'while'.

ἐργαζώμεθα τὸ ἀγαθὸν πρὸς πάντας. Cf. Barn. 19:8, κοινωνήσεις ἐν πᾶσιν τῷ πλησίον σου καὶ οὐκ ἐρεῖς ἴδια εἶναι· εἰ γὰρ ἐν τῷ ἀφθάρτῳ κοινωνοί ἐστε, πόσῳ μᾶλλον ἐν τοῖς φθαρτοῖς;

μάλιστα δὲ πρὸς τοὺς οἰκείους τῆς πίστεως. Cf. Eph. 2:19, where Gentile believers are called οἰκεῖοι τοῦ θεοῦ, 'members of God's household', fellow-members with believers of Jewish birth, who belonged to his οἶκος—the οἶκος of faith—before any Gentile did. Here the οἰκεῖοι τῆς πίστεως include Jews and Gentiles indiscriminately: there is no priority given to the Jerusalem church, although it naturally comes within the scope of the injunction. Fellow-Christians had a prior claim on the generosity of their brethren, not only in the same local church but in any or every church. This principle is illustrated in the Jerusalem relief fund, but it is outrunning the evidence to see a specific reference to that fund in this paragraph.

VIII
CONCLUDING COMMENTS
AND FINAL GREETING

(6:11–18)

Let others boast in their achievements or in the number of disciples they can notch up: Paul will boast in nothing but the cross of Christ. The scars which he will carry to the end of his days mark him out as the branded slave of Christ: let no one else interfere with him.

With a final benediction he concludes his letter.

(a) The true ground of boasting (6:11–16)

See in how large letters I write with my own hand!

Those who wish to make a fine show in external matters are the people who urge you to accept circumcision; they do so only to avoid being persecuted for the cross of Christ. For not even those of the circumcision party keep the law themselves; they want you to be circumcised so that they may have cause for boasting in your flesh. But far be it from me to boast except in the cross of our Lord Jesus Christ, by which the world has been 'crucified' to me and I to the world. Neither circumcision nor uncircumcision is anything in itself: there is now a new creation. As for all those who keep in line with this rule, peace and mercy be on them and on the Israel of God.

TEXTUAL NOTES
v 11 πηλικοις / ηλικοις P⁴⁶ B* 33 / ποικιλοις 642
v 12 Χριστου / *add* Ιησου P⁴⁶ B K Ψ *pc*
      διωκωνται / διωκονται P⁴⁶ A C G K L P *pm*
v 13 περιτεμνομενοι / περιτετμημενοι P⁴⁶ B F (G) L Ψ *al*
v 15 ουτε γαρ / εν γαρ Χριστω Ιησου ουτε ℵ A C D G byz lat syrʰᶜˡ ** copᵇᵒ arm
      (*ex* 5:6)
      εστιν / ισχυει ℵ² D² K L P Ψ byz latᵛᵍ (*ex* 5:6)
v 16 στοιχησουσιν / στοιχησωσιν P⁴⁶
      και ελεος *om* M.Vict

6:11 Ἴδετε πηλίκοις ὑμῖν γράμμασιν ἔγραψα τῇ ἐμῇ χειρί. ἔγραψα is best taken as epistolary aorist: Paul is writing at this very moment. It is just conceivable that he refers to the whole letter if (contrary to his custom) he wrote it all with his own hand (so Chrysostom *ad loc.*). In 1:20 he used the present γράφω but without emphasis on the act of writing and without the implication that he was dispensing with the services of an amanuensis: *qui facit (scribit) per alium facit (scribit) per se*. (For similar uses of γράφω cf. 1 Cor. 14:37; 2 Cor. 1:13; 13:10; 2 Thes. 3:17; for the epistolary ἔγραψα cf. Rom. 15:15(?); 1 Cor. 5:11; 9:15; Phm. 19, 21.) But it is much more probable that Paul, having dictated the letter up to this point, now takes the pen himself and writes the remaining sentences with his own hand. Whether the 'large letters' were due or not to the condition of his eyesight cannot be said. Still less probable is A. Deissmann's explanation that 'writing was not an easy thing to his workman's hand' (*Light from the Ancient East*, ETr [London, 1927], 166 n. 7). Most improbable of all is N. Turner's suggestion that he 'had actually been crucified at Perga in Pamphylia' and sustained permanent damage to his hand (*Grammatical Insights into the NT* [Edinburgh, 1965], 94; reference is made in this connexion to Gal. 2:19; 6:14, 17).

Elsewhere Paul penned the final greetings (cf. 1 Cor. 16:21; Col. 4:18; 2 Thes. 3:17f.); here he took the pen in order to write the concluding comments, and to write them in large letters for emphasis, as likely as not. Some of these comments recapitulate the main emphases of the letter. Plutarch (*Cato Maior* 20.348B) reports that Cato wrote a history of Rome for his son 'with his own hand and in large letters' (ἰδίᾳ χειρὶ καὶ μεγάλοις γράμμασιν), but that was to make it easier for the boy to read. Paul used unusually large letters here, said Theodore of Mopsuestia, 'to show that he himself was neither ashamed of what he was saying nor inclined to deny it' (ed. H. B. Swete, I, 107).

Paul evidently expected the original letter to be read by all the churches to which it was addressed; otherwise he could not assume that all of them would see the 'large letters' which he made. So far as this letter is concerned, then, he did not arrange for several copies to be made so that each church would receive a copy for itself. If one or more of the Galatian churches wished to have a copy for permanent reference, then a copy would have to be specially made before the original was sent to the next place. Cf. A. Lindemann, *Paulus im ältesten Christentum* (Tübingen, 1979), 29.

6:12 Ὅσοι θέλουσιν εὐπροσωπῆσαι ἐν σαρκί. The idea that this is a deliberate contrast to Paul's handwriting, which did not make a fine external show (H. Alford, *The Greek Testament*, III [London, ⁵1871], 64, endorsed by F. Field, *Notes on Translation of the NT* [Cambridge, 1899], 191), is far-fetched. Whereas Paul was concerned about the Spirit's inward work in his converts, so that Christ should be 'formed' in them (cf. 4:19), the Judaizers' concern was for an external mark, a mark produced in the 'flesh' of those whom they could win over to their side. The verb εὐπροσωπέω, 'make a good showing (πρόσωπον)', is found in P. Tebt. 19.12 (114 BC). While ἐν σαρκί may mean 'externally' (cf. Phil. 3:3f.), the literal sense of σάρξ cannot be excluded where circumcision is the subject.

οὗτοι ἀναγκάζουσιν ὑμᾶς περιτέμνεσθαι. The present has conative force here ('they try to compel you', 'they urge you'), as the imperfect has in

Acts 26:11, ἠνάγκαζον βλασφημεῖν ('I tried to make them blaspheme'). If the trouble-makers insisted that circumcision was necessary to salvation, this was a form of pressure approaching compulsion: ἀνάγκη ὑμᾶς περιτέμνεσθαι, they may have said. (Cf. 2:14, ἀναγκάζεις ἰουδαΐζειν.)

μόνον ἵνα τῷ σταυρῷ τοῦ Χριστοῦ μὴ διώκωνται. The dative τῷ σταυρῷ expresses cause ('because of the cross of Christ'); for such a use of the dative cf. Rom. 11:20, 30, 31; 2 Cor. 2:13 (τῷ μὴ εὑρεῖν με). See BDF 196.

If the trouble-makers could persuade the Gentile Christians to accept circumcision, that might preserve the Jerusalem church and its daughter-churches in Judaea from reprisals at the hands of Zealot-minded militants for being linked with uncircumcised Gentiles. To such militants the cross of Christ, as it was proclaimed by Paul and those who agreed with him, was a σκάνδαλον (cf. 5:11) because it excluded the principle of salvation by adherence to the law of Moses. Those who refused to require circumcision from Gentile converts (a refusal enshrined in the Jerusalem decree of Acts 15:28f.; 21:25) were liable to be persecuted—persecuted in fact, as Paul says, for the cross of Christ. Those who demanded that Gentile believers should be circumcised hoped to avoid such persecution. This clause of purpose provides a strong argument in support of R. Jewett's thesis 'that Jewish Christians in Judea were stimulated by Zealotic pressure into a nomistic campaign among their fellow Christians in the late forties and early fifties' ('The Agitators and the Galatian Congregation', *NTS* 17 [1970–71], 205).

6:13 οὐδὲ γὰρ οἱ περιτεμνόμενοι αὐτοὶ νόμον φυλάσσουσιν. In οἱ περιτεμνόμενοι we have a grammatical and an exegetical problem. Is the participle middle or passive, and if middle, what is the force of the middle? And who, in fact, are οἱ περιτεμνόμενοι? They are not the addressees; they are indicated by the third person, not the second. The two problems are interdependent: the exegetical problem will be treated first.

E. Hirsch, 'Zwei Fragen zu Gal 6', *ZNW* 29 (1930), 192–197, understood οἱ περιτεμνόμενοι ('those who receive circumcision') to be Gentiles who had yielded to the persuasion of the Judaizers: the task of keeping the whole law to which their circumcision had committed them was beyond their capacity, so they made up for their defective law-keeping by persuading other Gentile converts to be circumcised. A similar interpretation is maintained by J. Munck, *Paul*, 87–89; H.-J. Schoeps, *Paul*, 65; A. E. Harvey, *The New English Bible: Companion to the NT* (Oxford/Cambridge, 1970), 615f. It has the advantage of taking the present participle here in the same sense as in 5:3 (παντὶ ἀνθρώπῳ περιτεμνομένῳ).

E. D. Burton (*Galatians*, 352–354) takes οἱ περιτεμνόμενοι as referring 'in general to those who under the influence of the judaizers receive circumcision', not 'specifically to those who among the Galatians had been circumcised'. 'Other Gentile believers who get themselves circumcised do not in fact keep the law', Paul is understood as saying, 'and no more will you.' But Burton takes the subject of the following θέλουσιν ὑμᾶς περιτέμνεσθαι to be not οἱ περιτεμνόμενοι but the Judaizers—the people who, in v 12, ἀναγκάζουσιν ὑμᾶς περιτέμνεσθαι. He is right in recognizing the subject of θέλουσιν to be the Judaizers (θέλουσιν ὑμᾶς περιτέμνεσθαι and ἀναγκάζουσιν ὑμᾶς περιτέμνεσθαι mean almost the same thing), but the construction of v 13 demands that the subject of θέλουσιν and of οὐδὲ . . . φυλάσσουσιν be one and the same, i.e. οἱ περιτεμνόμενοι. The present participle περιτεμνόμενοι is best taken as middle voice with causative significance ('causing to be circumcised'); cf. W. W. Goodwin, *Greek Grammar* (London, 1887), 266; A. T. Robertson, *Grammar of the Greek NT* (New York, 1914), 808f.; E. V. N. Goetchius, *The Language of the NT* (New York, 1965), 104. (The variant περιτετμημένοι would denote people who are already in a state of circumcision.) That Judaizers are intended is confirmed by οὐδὲ . . . αὐτοί—they are the last persons who might be expected to be remiss in law-keeping. W. Schmithals (*Paul and the Gnostics*, 27f.) identifies οἱ περιτεμνόμενοι with the trouble-makers, but (in accordance with his thesis) he regards them as basically antinomian (which would make Paul's statement that not even they keep the law pointless). J. B. Lightfoot (*Galatians*, 222f.) renders οἱ περιτεμνόμενοι aptly enough as '*the circumcision party*, the advocates of circumcision', and quotes as a parallel the apocryphal *Acts of Peter and Paul*, 63 (ed. C. Tischendorf) = *Martyrdom of Peter and Paul*, 42 (ed. R. A. Lipsius and M. Bonnet), where Simon Magus refers to Peter and Paul as οὗτοι οἱ περιτεμνόμενοι (but Peter and Paul insist that the circumcision of which they speak is of the heart). Cf. J. Bligh, *Galatians in Greek* (Detroit, 1966), 218.

G. Howard (*Crisis*, 15) compares Paul's rebuke to Cephas who, while living like a Greek himself, 'compelled' Gentile Christians to live like Jews (2:14). The parallel is inexact: Cephas did not habitually compel Gentile Christians to judaize, although that could have been the effect of his temporary withdrawal from table-fellowship with them at Antioch. The persons referred to in 6:13 made it their policy to persuade Gentile Christians to submit to circumcision. Whether or not they taught that, after circumcision, it was necessary to go on and keep the rest of the law, Paul says that in practice they failed to keep it themselves. In his eyes, indeed, they were as guilty of ὑπόκρισις as were the 'play-actors' at Antioch: their concern, he implies, was not for the law as a matter of principle but for the sake of boasting about those who followed their teaching: ἵνα ἐν τῷ ὑμετέρῳ σαρκὶ καυχήσωνται. The more Gentiles they could notch up as having been circumcised at their instance, the weightier the evidence which they could adduce of their zeal for the law. This was mere scalp-hunting—or (*salva reverentia*) an apter description would be suggested by the bride-price which David paid for Michal (1 Sa. 18:25–27).

6:14 Ἐμοὶ δὲ μὴ γένοιτο καυχᾶσθαι εἰ μὴ ἐν τῷ σταυρῷ τοῦ κυρίου ἡμῶν Ἰησοῦ Χριστοῦ. Let others boast in things external: Paul makes his boast in something nobler. Boasting in one's own record belongs to the old order of law (cf. Rom. 2:23, ὃς ἐν νόμῳ καυχᾶσαι) and flesh (cf. Phil. 3:4, πεποιθέναι ἐν σαρκί); it is 'excluded' (ἐξεκλείσθη, Rom. 3:27) from the new order of faith.

μὴ γένοιτο elsewhere in Paul is used absolutely (cf. 2:17; 3:21); its integration here into a sentence is similar to the instances of γίνομαι with the infinitive found (e.g.) in Acts 20:16 (ὅπως μὴ γένηται αὐτῷ χρονοτριβῆσαι); 22:6 (ἐγένετο δέ μοι . . . περιαστράψαι φῶς).

In 2 Cor. 11:21f. and Phil. 3:4–6 Paul mentions some aspects of his heritage and personal achievement in which he would have naturally boasted before his conversion—the very things in which the trouble-makers in Galatia now make their boast. Such boasting 'refers to man's attitude of sinful self-reliance before God, and so is characteristic of life in the old dominion' (R. C. Tannehill, *Dying and Rising*, 62; cf. R. Bultmann, *Theology of the NT*, ETr, I [London, 1952], 242f.).

But the nobler object of Paul's present boasting was, by all ordinary standards of his day, the most ignoble of all objects—a matter of unrelieved shame, not of boasting. It is difficult, after sixteen centuries and more during which the cross has been a sacred symbol, to realize the unspeakable horror and loathing which the very mention or thought of the cross provoked in Paul's day. The word *crux* was unmentionable in polite Roman society (Cicero, *Pro Rabirio* 16); even when one was being condemned to death by crucifixion the sentence used an archaic formula which served as a sort of euphemism: *arbori infelici suspendito*, 'hang him on the unlucky tree' (Cicero, ibid. 13). In the eastern provinces of the empire the Greek word σταυρός must have inspired comparable dread and disgust to its Latin equivalent.

One could have understood it if the early Christians, knowing that the crucifixion of Jesus was an undeniable fact, had admitted it reluctantly when they were compelled to do so. But Paul, Roman citizen by birth and religious Jew by upbringing, not only dismisses as the merest refuse (σκύβαλα, Phil. 3:8) those things in which he had once taken a proper pride but embraces as the most worth-while goal in life the knowledge of the crucified Christ and boasts in his cross—a shocking paradox indeed. The 'utterly vile death of the cross' (*mors turpissima crucis*, as it is called in the Latin version of Origen's commentary on Mt. 27:22ff.) was so central to Paul's gospel that he called his message 'the word of the cross' (ὁ λόγος τοῦ σταυροῦ, 1 Cor. 1:18), nor was he surprised that such an offensive message should be a scandal to Jews and sheer absurdity to Greeks. How could a message like that win any acceptance in the Graeco-Roman world of Paul's day? That it did find acceptance was due, Paul declared, to its being the power and the wisdom of God; but only the 'demonstration (ἀπόδειξις) of the Spirit' (1 Cor. 2:4) could make this plain to believers. See M. Hengel, *Crucifixion*, ETr (London, 1977), with bibliography at end; also U. Wilckens, 'Das Kreuz Christi als die Tiefe der Weisheit Gottes zu 1. Kor 2, 1–16', in *Paolo a una Chiesa Divisa*, ed. L. de Lorenzi (Rome, 1980), 43–81, with discussion, 81–108.

δι' οὗ ἐμοὶ κόσμος ἐσταύρωται κἀγὼ κόσμῳ. The relative οὗ may have as its antecedent either Ἰησοῦ Χριστοῦ or σταυρῷ. The latter is more probable, with a play on the rather wide range of meaning of σταυρός and σταυρόω. Because Paul has been 'crucified with Christ' (2:19), the cross is a barrier by which the world is permanently 'fenced off' (ἐσταύρωται, perfect) from him and he from the world.

For one who makes the cross his supreme, indeed his solitary, ground of boasting all the accepted standards of social life are necessarily turned upside down: a total 'transvaluation of values' has taken place. Not only does he no longer know any one κατὰ σάρκα (by 'worldly standards'); he has made a radical reassessment of everything in the light of the cross. It is true that 'crucifixion to the old world of boasting means a lasting separation from that world' (R. C. Tannehill, *Dying and Rising*, 63); a lasting separation has also been effected from the whole *contemporary* world, with its climate of opinion and canons of honour and dishonour.

The crucifixion of the world does not here mean, as M. Werner supposed (*The Formation of Christian Dogma*, ETr [London, 1957], 73f., 95, 107), that because of its 'crucifixion' through the cross of Christ the world is now in process of passing away in the sense of 1 Cor. 7:31.

When κόσμος is used thus by Paul, it denotes a power opposed to God; cf. 4:3 (τὰ στοιχεῖα τοῦ κόσμου); 1 Cor. 2:12; 3:19, where the Spirit/wisdom of the world are contrasted with the Spirit/wisdom of God. In this κόσμος sin, death and the law are dominant forces, the sting of death being sin and the strength of sin being the law (1 Cor. 15:56). Elsewhere Paul uses αἰών in much the same sense (cf. 1:4, 'the present evil age'; 1 Cor. 1:20; 2:6; 2 Cor. 4:4); in Eph. 2:2 (κατὰ τὸν αἰῶνα τοῦ κόσμου τούτου) the two words are combined.

κἀγὼ κόσμῳ. Cf. 2:19; being 'crucified to the world' is part of what is involved in being 'crucified with Christ'. The cross here is the cross as it has been presented and interpreted throughout the epistle. 'With this interpretation it is the annihilative and the creative power in Christianity; the first command-ment of the new religion is that we shall have no God but Him who is fully and finally revealed there' (J. Denney, *The Death of Christ*, 163).

In response to the question, 'what difference does Christianity make—to you or to a society of Christians?' J. E. Powell quotes Gal. 6:14 in full and adds: 'The Christian is the individual to whom that is true, and to him the difference is nothing and everything: nothing that can be defined in terms of opinion or policy or judgement or decision; and yet everything, through thinking and judging and acting in the knowledge that men and human society, though not improvable, are redeemable, and that, in the way which only Christians know, their redemption has been performed and is available for ever' (*Wrestling with the Angel* [London, 1977], 64).

But let Isaac Watts have the last word:

When I survey the wondrous cross,
    Where the young Prince of glory died,
My richest gain I count but loss,
    And pour contempt on all my pride.

Forbid it, Lord, that I should boast
    Save in the death of Christ, my God;
All the vain things that charm me most,
    I sacrifice them to his blood.

See from his head, his hands, his feet,
    Sorrow and love flow mingled down;
Did e'er such love and sorrow meet,
    Or thorns compose so rich a crown?

His dying crimson, like a robe,
    Spreads o'er his body on the tree;
Then am I dead to all the globe,
    And all the globe is dead to me.

Were the whole realm of nature mine,
   That were a present far too small;
Love so amazing, so divine,
   Demands my soul, my life, my all.

6:15 οὔτε γὰρ περιτομή τί ἐστιν οὔτε ἀκροβυστία. In some strands of transmission the text of this verse has been largely contaminated by the text of 5:6, which in any case speaks to very much the same effect. It is striking that, for all the sternness of his warning against accepting circumcision as something required by God, Paul should twice in this letter emphasize that circumcision and uncircumcision *per se* matter nothing at all. In the old order of the law, where the distinction between Jew and Gentile was of fundamental importance, it mattered greatly whether a man was circumcised or not; now it is totally irrelevant.

ἀλλὰ καινὴ κτίσις. Cf. 2 Cor. 5:17, εἴ τις ἐν Χριστῷ, καινὴ κτίσις. To be ἐν Χριστῷ is what matters. In him the μεσότοιχον τοῦ φραγμοῦ which separated Jew and Gentile has been demolished (Eph. 2:14). In this new situation the issue of circumcision or of any other ancestral tradition (cf. 1:14) loses all religious significance. Paul, as a man in Christ, conformed or did not conform to these traditions indifferently, according to his current company and other circumstances. To insist on them as matters of obligation was wrong, completely inconsistent with membership in the 'new creation'—life in Christ.

The 'new creation' in its fulness belongs to the future, but to those in Christ it is already realized through the Spirit. Christ is head of the new creation; in him they have been transferred from their former existence 'in Adam', the head of the old creation, and await the final manifestation of the new creation on the day of resurrection when 'in Christ all shall be made alive' (1 Cor. 15:22).

B. D. Chilton ('Galatians 6[15]: A Call to Freedom before God', *Exp Tim* 89 [1977–78], 311–313) suggests that, after the analogy of *b^eriyyāh* in rabbinical Hebrew (cf. m. Ab. 1:12; 4:1; 6:1), κτίσις here may mean 'humanity': 'God has set aside the polarity of Jew and Gentile (cf. 3[28]) in favour of an altogether "new humanity". There is available for "anyone in Christ" (2 Co 5[17]) a status before God which frees him from the constraints which he once suffered.'

According to Georgius Syncellus (8th cent. AD), *Chron.*, ed. Dindorf (= CSHB 20), 1, p. 48, Gal. 6:15 is a quotation from the *Apocalypse of Moses*, an apocryphon not otherwise known. Syncellus may have derived this information from Euthalius (5th cent. AD). But in the absence of hard evidence the statement must be regarded with scepticism.

6:16 καὶ ὅσοι τῷ κανόνι τούτῳ στοιχήσουσιν, εἰρήνη ἐπ᾽ αὐτοὺς καὶ ἔλεος, καὶ ἐπὶ τὸν Ἰσραὴλ τοῦ θεοῦ. The classical construction of the opening clause would be ὅσοι ἄν with the subjunctive. The κανών is apparently the principle just laid down about the 'new creation': the reference then is to members of the new humanity who are guided by this principle, in contrast to those who maintain the continuing validity of circumcision and similar legal requirements. For στοιχέω cf. 5:25.

For the mention of Israel cf. Ps. 125 (LXX 124):5; 128 (LXX 127):6 (εἰρήνη ἐπὶ τὸν Ἰσραήλ); also the closing ascription of the Eighteen Benedictions: 'Blessed art thou, O Lord, who dost bless thy people Israel with peace' (*bārûḵ 'attāh Y'' hammᵉḇār'ᵉḵ 'eṭ 'ammô Yiśrā'ēl bᵉšālôm*).

The relation of 'the Israel of God' to 'all those who keep in line with this rule' is disputed. A common interpretation equates the two categories, the καί before ἐπὶ τὸν Ἰσραὴλ τοῦ θεοῦ being treated as epexegetic. 'They who pursue these things [the 'new things of grace']', says Chrysostom *ad loc.*, 'shall enjoy peace and amity, and may properly be called by the name of "Israel".' This is in agreement with the position which is taken up explicitly as early as Justin Martyr, that the Christian church is 'the true, spiritual Israel' (*Dial*. 11.5). This interpretation is defended by N. A. Dahl, 'Der Name Israel: Zur Auslegung von Gal 6, 16', *Judaica* 6 (1950), 161–170. There is a continuity between the older Israel and the church in that the church is a community of both Jews and Gentiles; thus U. Luz equates the Israel of God with the church of Jews and Gentiles (*Das Geschichtsverständnis bei Paulus* [München, 1968], 269). On this W. D. Davies remarks that if it were correct one would expect to find support for it in Rom. 9–11 'where Paul extensively deals with "Israel" ' ('Paul and the People of Israel', *NTS* 24 [1977–78], 10 n. 2)

Dahl's *Judaica* article is followed by G. Schrenk's 'Der Segenwunsch nach der Kampfepistel' (*Judaica* 6 [1950], 170–190), which takes the Israel of God to be a designation for Jewish Christians. (In an earlier article, 'Was bedeutet "Israel Gottes"?', *Judaica* 5 [1949], 81–94, Schrenk gives a survey of interpretations.) A similar position to Schrenk's is maintained by D. W. B. Robinson, 'Distinction between Jewish and Gentile Believers in Galatians', *ABR* 13 (1965), 29–48. But it is difficult to see how Paul, with his concern to treat as indifferent those distinctive features which divided Jews from Gentiles, could have continued to think or speak of Jewish Christians as a separate group within his churches.

W. D. Davies ('Paul and the People of Israel', 10) thinks that the Israel of God 'may refer to the Jewish people as a whole'. It may, provided we bear in mind Paul's observation that 'not all who are descended from Israel belong to Israel' (Rom. 9:6). If ὁ Ἰσραὴλ κατὰ σάρκα (1 Cor. 10:18) denotes the empirical Israel, ὁ Ἰσραὴλ τοῦ θεοῦ may denote the Israel seen by God as the true Israel. So Marius Victorinus, the earliest Latin commentator on Paul, comments on the phrase: 'not "on Israel" in the sense of any and every Jew, but "on the Lord's Israel"; for Israel is truly the Lord's if it follows the Lord, not expecting its salvation from any other source'.

E. D. Burton (*Galatians*, 357f.) construes the sentence so as to have 'peace' invoked on 'them' (i.e. 'those who keep in line with this rule') and 'mercy' on the Israel of God. The order 'peace and mercy', if the two are taken closely together, is illogical, he says, 'placing effect first and cause afterwards' (the logical order is 'mercy and peace' or 'grace and peace'). P. Richardson (*Israel in the Apostolic Church* [Cambridge, 1969], 81–84) follows Burton's construction, placing the comma after ἐπ' αὐτούς, not after καὶ ἔλεος. In Burton's opinion, καὶ ἔλεος is an afterthought, with καὶ ἐπὶ τὸν Ἰσραὴλ τοῦ θεοῦ a second afterthought.

But the reference to the Israel of God need not be an afterthought. If Paul knew the additional (19th) benediction to the Eighteen Benedictions, he would have been familiar with a prayer which asks God for 'peace . . . and mercy on us and on all Israel thy people' (šālôm . . . wᵉraḥᵃmîm 'ālênû wᵉ'al kol Yiśrāʾēl 'ammeḵā). If so, the words 'and on the Israel of God' would have come readily from his tongue.

F. Mussner (Galaterbrief, 417 n. 59) probably indicates the true sense when he identifies the Israel of God here with πᾶς 'Ισραήλ of Rom. 11:26. For all his demoting of the law and the customs, Paul held good hope of the ultimate blessing of Israel. They were not all keeping in line with 'this rule' yet, but the fact that some Israelites were doing so was in his eyes a pledge that this remnant would increase until, with the ingathering of the full tale (πλήρωμα) of Gentiles, 'all Israel will be saved'. The invocation of blessing on the Israel of God has probably an eschatological perspective.

(b) The marks of Jesus (6:17)

From now on let no one cause me any trouble: I carry in my body the marks of Jesus.

TEXTUAL NOTE

v 17 Ιησου P⁴⁶ A B C* 33 *al* lat^{ft} / Χριστου P Ψ 81 *pc* cop^{bo} / κυριου Ιησου K L byz lat^{vg} syr^{pesh} / κυριου Ιησου Χριστου ℵ lat^{dr} cop^{sa} / κυριου ημων Ιησου Χριστου D* G Ambst Pelag

6:17 Τοῦ λοιποῦ, a classical formula (cf. Eph. 6:10); the genitive may be regarded as a specimen of the 'genitive of time within which' construction: 'within the time that remains'. The accusative (τὸ) λοιπόν is commoner in the NT, especially (like τοῦ λοιποῦ here) in epistolary conclusions; cf. 2 Cor. 13:11; Phil. 3:1; 4:8.

Let no one interfere with me (κόπους μοι μηδεὶς παρεχέτω), says Paul, because I am the slave—the branded slave—of another. We may compare his words in Rom. 14:4 (not referring to himself): 'Who are you to pass judgment on the servant (οἰκέτης) of another? It is before his own master that he stands or falls.' Paul's opponents might criticize his presentation of the gospel and his missionary policy; but it was not to them that he was responsible. Nor was it for him to make decisions about the content of his gospel or the wisdom of making it equally available on the same terms to Jews and Gentiles: it was for him to obey the Lord who commissioned him to preach that gospel to the Gentiles (as others were commissioned to preach it to the Jews).

The 'marks of Jesus' which he carried in his body are accepted by him as the marks of branding or tattooing which certified that a slave (especially a recaptured runaway slave) was the property of this or that owner. The simple name 'Jesus' occurs, as W. Kramer has pointed out, in 'statements about participation by Christians in the death and resurrection of Christ', such as 2 Cor. 4:10f., 14b (*Christ, Lord, Son of God*, ETr [London, 1966], 200). One of these statements (2 Cor. 4:10) bears a specially close resemblance to this: Paul speaks of carrying around in his body 'the dying of Jesus' (πάντοτε τὴν νέκρωσιν τοῦ 'Ιησοῦ ἐν τῷ σώματι περιφέροντες) and explains his language by saying that 'while we live we are always being given up to death for Jesus' sake, so that the life of Jesus may be manifested in our mortal flesh' (2 Cor. 4:11).

In contrast to the now irrelevant mark of circumcision, Paul asserts that he has marks on his body which do mean something real—the στίγματα or scars which he has acquired as the direct consequence of his service for Jesus. These proclaim whose he is and whom he serves. Among them the most permanent were probably the marks left by his stoning at Lystra (Acts 14:19; cf. 2 Cor. 11:25), and if the church of Lystra was one of those to which this letter was addressed, some at least of his readers would have a vivid recollection of that occasion.

W. Klassen, 'Galatians 6:17', *Exp Tim* 81 (1969–70), 378, compares the incident in Josephus, *War* 1.197 where Antipater (Herod's father) strips off his clothes and exhibits his many scars (τραύματα) as witnesses to his loyalty to Caesar.

It has been pointed out that the term στίγματα was used of the tattoo-marks by which devotees of various religious cults were identified as worshippers of this or that divinity—a practice forbidden in Israel by Lv. 19:28, although in Is. 44:5 a faithful Jew will write 'Yahweh's' on his hand to indicate whose servant he is.

E. Dinkler thought that Paul's body was marked (probably at baptism) with X, the initial letter of the Greek form of 'Christ' ('Jesu Wort vom Kreuztragen', *Bultmann FS*, 125).

See F. J. Doelger, *Sphragis: Studien zur Geschichte und Kultur des Altertums*, V, 3–4 (Paderborn, 1911), 49f., 105 n. 3; U. Wilckens, 'Zu den syrischen Göttern', *Deissmann FS*, 1–19, especially 7–9.

Less probable explanations of the στίγματα have been offered—e.g. by E. Hirsch, 'Zwei Fragen zu Gal 6', *ZNW* 29 (1930), 196f., that Paul refers to the eye-trouble resulting from his exposure to the blinding light of the divine glory on the Damascus road (see reply by O. Holtzmann, 'Zu E. Hirsch, Zwei Fragen zu Gal 6', *ZNW* 30 [1931], 82f.).

While the genitive τοῦ 'Ιησοῦ denotes Jesus as Paul's κύριος, the one whose slave he is, the wording of 2 Cor. 4:10f. already quoted reminds us that when dealing with this subject Paul can use τοῦ 'Ιησοῦ to denote his partici-pation in the sufferings of Jesus (as also in his risen life); see O. Schmitz, *Die Christusgemeinschaft des Paulus im Lichte seines Genetivgebrauchs* (Gütersloh, 1924). It is plain in any case that Paul accepted the sufferings he endured in the course of his apostolic ministry as his participation in the sufferings of Christ (κοινωνία τῶν παθημάτων αὐτοῦ, Phil. 3:10); in fact, he was eager to absorb in his own person as great a share as possible of the sufferings of Christ in order that his fellow-Christians might have less of them to bear (cf. 2 Cor. 1:5–7; Col. 1:24). But this aspect of his thought is not to the fore in the present passage.

See also J. H. Moulton, 'The Marks of Jesus', *Exp Tim* 21 (1909–10), 283f.; O. Betz, *TDNT* VII, 663f. (*s.v.* στίγμα); E. Güttgemanns, *Der leidende Apostel und sein Herr* (Göttingen, 1966), 126–135; U. Borse, 'Die Wundmale und der Todesbescheid', *BZ* NF 14 (1970), 88–111.

(c) Final greeting (6:18)

The grace of our Lord Jesus Christ be with your spirit, my brothers. Amen.

TEXTUAL NOTE

v 18 ημων / *om* ℵ P 1739 *al*
Χριστου / *om* P *pc*

6:18 Ἡ χάρις τοῦ κυρίου ἡμῶν Ἰησοῦ Χριστοῦ μετὰ τοῦ πνεύματος ὑμῶν, ἀδελφοί. The 'grace' of the opening salutation (1:3) is caught up and repeated in this closing benediction. Apart from the added vocative ἀδελφοί, the benediction is identical, or nearly so, with that of Phm. 25 and Phil. 4:23 (where ὑμῶν is lacking). Cf. 2 Tim. 4:22a, ὁ κύριος μετὰ τοῦ πνεύματός σου).

μετὰ τοῦ πνεύματός ὑμῶν is a variant on the simpler μεθ᾽ ὑμῶν, as found in Rom. 16:20; 1 Cor. 16:23; Col. 4:18; 1 Thes. 5:28; 1 Tim. 6:21; 2 Tim. 4:22; cf. μετὰ πάντων ὑμῶν in 1 Cor. 16:23; 2 Cor. 13:14; 2 Thes. 3:18; Tit. 3:15. 'The grace of our (the) Lord Jesus (Christ)' appears in Rom. 16:20; 1 Cor. 16:23; Phil. 4:23; 1 Thes. 5:28; 2 Thes. 3:18; it is abridged to ἡ χάρις in Col. 4:18 (cf. Eph. 6:24, ἡ χάρις μετὰ πάντων τῶν ἀγαπώντων τὸν κύριον ἡμῶν Ἰησοῦν Χριστὸν ἐν ἀφθαρσίᾳ); 1 Tim. 6:21; 2 Tim. 4:22b; Tit. 3:15; Phm. 25; it is expanded to the triadic Ἡ χάρις τοῦ κυρίου Ἰησοῦ Χριστοῦ καὶ ἡ ἀγάπη τοῦ θεοῦ καὶ ἡ κοινωνία τοῦ ἁγίου πνεύματος μετὰ πάντων ὑμῶν in 2 Cor. 13:14.

ἀμήν, from Heb. *'āmēn*, 'steadfast', 'sure', a formula of confirmation (cf. 1:5). It would form the congregation's response to the reading of the letter; it would be pleasant to think that a well-meant and hearty 'Amen' was forthcoming in all the congregations to which this letter was sent.

* * * *

There is no means of knowing what effect Paul's letter had on the Galatian churches to which it was addressed. To be sure, circumcision soon ceased to be an issue in the lands of the Gentile mission. (If, as Col. 2:11 has suggested to some, it figured in the tendency against which Paul polemicizes in Colossians, it did so as part of a voluntary asceticism which was believed to lead its devotees on to a higher spiritual plane.) The disappearance of circumcision as an issue could have been due in part to Paul's letter, or it could have been due to the apostolic decree of Acts 15:28f., which circulated far beyond the Gentile Christians of Syria and Cilicia to whom it was primarily addressed. In any case, the judaizing movement received a setback from which it never recovered through the catastrophe of AD 70. The church of Jerusalem in exile made nothing like the impact on Gentile Christianity that was made by the first-generation church of Jerusalem.

This does not mean that the positive teaching of Galatians was embraced and maintained in its entirety. The religious mind is too prone to subject itself to regulations; the liberating gospel of sovereign grace is too 'dangerous' to be allowed unrestrained course. As Paul became less a figure of controversy, as his memory was venerated and his writings canonized, his teaching was overlaid with a new legalism. When, from time to time, someone appeared who understood and proclaimed the genuine message of Galatians, he was liable to be denounced as a subversive character—as, indeed, Paul was in his own day. But the letter to the Galatians, with its trumpet-call to Christian freedom, has time and again released the true gospel from the bonds in which well-meaning but misguided people have confined it so that it can once more exert its emancipating power in the life of mankind, empowering those who receive it to stand fast in the freedom with which Christ has set them free.

GENERAL INDEX

Galatic Lycaonia, 5f., 10, 12
Galatic Phrygia, 5, 10-14, 44
Galilee, 95f., 103
Gallio, 10
Gamaliel I, 41, 91, 159, 235
Gamaliel II, 230
Gaul, 3, 14
Gauls, 6-8
Genesis, book of, 136, 153, 171, 214, 216
Gentile church
    'barren one' of Isaiah, 35
    no place for Mosaic law, 225
Gentile converts
    and Abraham, 154, 168f., 172
    address God as *Abba*, 199
    and circumcision, 37, 52, 55, 111-13, 115-17,
        130, 154, 229f., 236f., 269f., 277
    fellowhip with Jewish Christians, 129, 131,
        142, 193
    former idolatry, 91
    and Jewish way of life, 133
    liberated, 203
    majority in church, 222
    members of God's household, 266
    nations of promise, 172
    and persecution, 150, 225, 269
    and Peter, 23, 124, 129, 270
    redeemed from law, 203
    released from elemental powers, 203
    and sacred calendar, 205
    and Spirit, 168
    and yoke of law, 83, 116, 142, 227
Gentile mission
    circumcision ceases to be issue, 277
    embraces all nations, 172
    and externals of religion, 40
    fellowship with Jerusalem church, 111, 134
    fulfils promise to Abraham, 45, 154, 157, 172
    and God's people, 222
    headquarters at Antioch, 115, 117, 123, 129,
        134
    intruders' aim, 112
    Paul's commission, 35, 110f., 119, 123
Gentiles
    admission to church, 38, 124, 219
    apostle to, 73, 88, 105f., 120f., 123, 125,
        154
    Barnabas' commission to, 22, 36f., 92, 107
    and blessing of Abraham, 28, 156f., 163, 172
    in bondage, 219
    children of Abraham in Christ, 34
    children of Abraham by faith, 24
    and circumcision, 111, 114
    fraternization with, 31, 110, 128f., 132
    God-fearers, 29, 32, 125
    gospel to, 109, 119f.
    and grace, 94, 108
    heirs of promise, 34, 154, 183, 226
    and Ishmaelites, 216

justified by faith, 57, 124, 135-47, 153, 183
law-free gospel for, 95
and law's requirements, 167, 182, 203
'living like Jews,' 90, 128
not natural sons of Abraham, 219
outside Jewish covenant, 137
paganism as slavery, 30
Paul's commission to, 22, 26, 36f., 87, 92f.,
    119, 124, 220, 275
Paul's preaching to, 26, 82, 87, 93, 95f., 109,
    119f., 220
Peter evangelizing, 119f.
Peter living like, 132f.
and promise of seed, 173
response to gospel, 222
and salvation-history, 154
'sinners of the,' 136f.
status in church, 37
subject to elemental powers, 203
terms for proselytes to Judaism, 29
not under law, 148, 166f., 182
under sin, 182
Gentleness, 42, 251, 254, 259f.
Gerizim, Mount, 158
gezerah shawah, rabbinic exegesis, 35, 165
Gift, irrevocable, 171
Glory, 41, 54, 77f., 93, 141, 182, 218, 232,
    276
Gnosticism, 25, 95, 140, 152, 187, 202, 206,
    210, 240, 257f.
God-fearers, 29, 32, 125
God of Israel, 77, 203
    unity of, 178f.
Gods, 202-04
Golden calf, 224
Golden rule, 242
Goliath, 179
Goodness, 42, 251, 253
Gordion (Juliopolis), 7
Gospel
    acceptance in ancient world, 271
    age of, 183
    for circumcised, 119
    of circumcision, 120f.
    circumcision-free, 109, 117, 124, 236
    cross central to, 271
    delivers from present age, 76
    equality of Jews and Gentiles, 188
    excludes religious distinctions, 187
    exposes elemental powers, 30
    extended worldwide, 172
    and faith, 105, 162, 181, 243
    false, 27, 82, 147
    fulfils promise to Abraham, 135, 172f., 219
    of God, 92
    of grace, 80, 112f., 120, 215, 218, 277
    interchange principle, 168
    and law, 125, 135, 149, 240
    law-free, 31, 85, 95, 110, 115, 141f., 146,

Seed, 172f.
Seleucids, 96, 249
Self-control, 42, 251, 254f.
Self-examination, 262
Self-giving, Christ's, 75, 77, 145f., 184, 196
Self-righteousness, 250, 260
Self-sufficiency, 241
Separation
   of Barnabas, 131-33
   of Cephas, 19, 129-33, 270
   between Jews and Gentiles, 142, 188, 273
Septuagintalism, 78
Servant of God, 37, 75, 92, 111, 146, 196, 207, 276
Service, Christian, 41, 58, 239, 241, 257, 276
Seth, 'another seed,' 173
Severity of God, 253
Severity of Paul's letters, 213
Sexual irregularities, 242, 247
Shammai, school of, 29, 159, 230
Shechem, 80
Shechemite dodecalogue, 158
Shema, reciting, 226
Signs, 151f., 205
Silas, Silvanus, 11, 55, 229
Simon, son of Judas the Galilaean, 130
Simon Magus, 86, 129, 203, 270
Simon the tanner, 129
Simon the Zealot, 91
Sin
   action of, 182
   agent of, 141
   and baptism, 34
   Christ made, 47
   and Christ's death, 33, 75, 77, 81, 144, 148, 166
   and cross, 256
   death to, 142-44, 186, 204, 256
   dominion of, 143, 181f., 240, 245, 272
   and expiation, 75
   and forgiveness, 75
   indwelling, 245
   as jailer, 180f.
   law of, 244
   and law, 82f., 135, 141-43, 175, 180-82, 204, 240, 244, 272
   leads to death, 180, 204, 272
   and old order, 144
   ownership of, 181
   power of, 143, 175, 182, 185, 244f.
   prison-house of, 175
   servant of, 141
   slavery to, 46
   under, 180-82, 204
   universal, 194
   wages of, 265
Sin-bearer, 144
Sin-offering, 160f.
Sinners of the Gentiles, 136f., 139f.
Sinai, 173f., 177, 179, 214, 219, 221

identified with Hagar, 214, 219f.
identified with Jebel Musa, 220
and Jerusalem above, 220
Sinaitic covenant, 218
Slave
   in Christ no distinction, 183, 190
   of Christ, 72, 86, 188, 241, 267, 275f.
   Christian, 188-90
   form of, 196
   minor treated as, 135, 191f.
   social inferiority in Judaism, 187f.
Slave-attendant, 135, 182f., 192, 196, 200
Slave-wife, 216
Slave-women, 218f.
Slavery
   children for, 214, 219
   to elemental powers, 77, 204
   forms of, 241
   to law, 30, 113, 246
   religious, 82
   to sin, 46
   and sonship, 57, 191-201, 213
   yoke of, 23, 28, 41, 214, 226
   (see also Bondage)
Solomon, 173, 221
Son of David, 35
Son of God, Christ as
   and believers, 183f., 198
   and divine love, 145f.
   and faith, 50, 136, 144, 168
   in gospel message, 35, 88
   and law, 191, 194, 196
   Messiah, 166
   Paul's preaching, 93, 96
   pre-existence, 195
   and redemption, 48, 194
   revelation to Paul, 87, 91
   soteriological significance, 200
   and Spirit, 198
   vindicated, 81, 168
   and virgin birth, 195
Song of the Well, 218
Sons, Hebrew idiom, 155
Sons of God, believers as, 39f., 46, 48, 183f., 191, 198-200, 246, 253
   (see also Children of God)
Sonship, 34, 48, 57, 197-99, 213
Sorcery, 246-48
Soteriology, Paul's, 51, 160
South Galatia, 5f., 43, 55, 73f., 86, 128, 132, 237, 251
South Galatian hypothesis, 7-18, 44, 171, 209
Sowing and reaping, 47, 251, 259, 264f.
Spirit
   administration of, 218
   age of, 54, 124, 245
   and baptism, 185f.
   and body of Christ, 184f.
   and conduct, 254, 257, 260
   divine gift, 35, 48, 115, 147, 149f., 152, 168,

INDEX OF MODERN AUTHORS